FIRST AND SECOND
THESSALONIANS

Sacra Pagina Series

Volume 11

First and Second Thessalonians

Earl J. Richard

Daniel J. Harrington, S.J.
Editor

A Michael Glazier Book
THE LITURGICAL PRESS
Collegeville, Minnesota

Cover design by Don Bruno.

A Michael Glazier Book published by The Liturgical Press.

1   2   3   4   5   6   7   8   9

Library of Congress Cataloging-in-Publication Data

Richard, Earl.
   First and Second Thessalonians / Earl J. Richard ; Daniel J.
Harrington, editor.
      p.   cm. — (Sacra pagina series ; v. 11)
   ''A Michael Glazier book.''
   Includes bibliographical references and indexes.
   ISBN 0-8146-5813-X
   1. Bible. N.T. Thessalonians—Commentaries. I. Harrington,
Daniel J. II. Title. III. Series: Sacra pagina series ; 11.
BS2725.3.R53   1995
227'.81077—dc20   95-18414
                                                            CIP

CONTENTS

EDITOR'S PREFACE

Sacra Pagina is a multi-volume commentary on the books of the New Testament. The expression *Sacra Pagina* ("Sacred Page") originally referred to the text of Scripture. In the Middle Ages it also described the study of Scripture to which the interpreter brought the tools of grammar, rhetoric, dialectic, and philosophy. Thus *Sacra Pagina* encompasses both the text to be studied and the activity of interpretation.

This series presents fresh translations and modern expositions of all the books of the New Testament. Written by an international team of Catholic biblical scholars, it is intended for biblical professionals, graduate students, theologians, clergy, and religious educators. The volumes present basic introductory information and close exposition. They self-consciously adopt specific methodological perspectives, but maintain a focus on the issues raised by the New Testament compositions themselves. The goal of *Sacra Pagina* is to provide sound critical analysis without any loss of sensitivity to religious meaning. This series is therefore catholic in two senses of the word: inclusive in its methods and perspectives, and shaped by the context of the Catholic tradition.

The Second Vatican Council described the study of "the sacred page" as the "very soul of sacred theology" (*Dei Verbum* 24). The volumes in this series illustrate how Catholic scholars contribute to the council's call to provide access to Sacred Scripture for all the Christian faithful. Rather than pretending to say the final word on any text, these volumes seek to open up the riches of the New Testament and to invite as many people as possible to study seriously the "sacred page."

DANIEL J. HARRINGTON, S.J.

PREFACE

Christian fascination for the work of Paul the Apostle dates back to NT times. Such interest, however, was both a blessing and a curse. On the one hand, the author of 2 Peter, in a polemic tone, is led to state: "There are some things in [Paul's letters] hard to understand, which the ignorant and unstable twist to their own destruction" (3:16). Thus, there was not only opposition to Pauline missionary activity and teaching but even reckless "twisting" of his thought (see 1 Cor 6:12f.; 16:9). On the other hand, that same author reverently refers to the Apostle as "our beloved brother Paul" (2 Pet 3:15) and other NT writers show their admiration and indebtedness by writing letters in his name to address the issues of their own communities.

The modern or extended reader of the Pauline corpus is confronted by an even more complex challenge. If the popular reading of Paul "as Scripture" leads to an undifferentiated grouping of the thirteen letters of the corpus as representing the Pauline voice in the NT, modern scholarship presents a considerably different picture of the NT period, of Paul and his thought, and of the thinking of his disciples. Thus, one routinely hears of Pauline and Paulinist letters, the latter being documents written in Paul's name by disciples. There are solid reasons, as demonstrated in this commentary, to view 1 Thessalonians as being Pauline and 2 Thessalonians as deriving from a Paulinist writer who employs the Apostle's authority and thought to confront apocalyptic fervor rampant at a later time. Such a conclusion is reached as a result of linguistic and rhetorical analysis; the author of 2 Thessalonians uses the language and themes of 1 Thessalonians to address a new ecclesial situation. Thus, 2 Thessalonians provides another window (see the Book of Revelation and Mark 13) on the popularity of apocalyptic speculation and a pastor's adept handling of the situation. The author sympathizes with the community's hardship but insists that "the end is not yet" and that the community should focus less on Jesus' future role as apocalyptic warrior and more on his present lordship. Such a reading of 2 Thessalonians requires a solid grasp of the original community's situation and a sophisticated discernment of both the author's strategy and thought, for considerable use is made of contemporary apocalyptic tradition, Pauline thought and rhetoric, and traditional Christian themes. The commentary attempts to provide modern or extended readers with the background and insight of and sympathy for the original readers to whom the letter was addressed. Only by grasping the situation of the original addressee can the extended reader be sympathetic to the author's strategy and thought.

At first blush, the reading of 1 Thessalonians seems straightforward in historical, rhetorical, and theological terms. Traditionally, the historical setting for its interpretation is derived from the Lukan account of Paul's travels and particularly the founding of the Thessalonian Church (Acts 17–20). Thus, a date of 51–52 is usually given for its composition. Careful comparison, however, between the Lukan and Pauline data tends to support modern scholarship in following the latter in determining Pauline chronology and in perceiving the circumstances of the Macedonian mission (e.g., earlier dating of mission and composition, Gentile character of community, and role played by Silvanus and Timothy). Additionally, in rhetorical terms one is confronted by dual thanksgivings (1 Thess 1:2; 2:13) and conclusions (3:11–4:2; 5:23-28) and by a marked difference in tone between the central part of the document and its introductory and concluding chapters. The document seems to presuppose two different situations and epistolary strategies. Finally, the theology of the document, while readily characterized as Pauline, is rarely featured in studies of Pauline thought, which usually focus on the major letters. In chronological, historical, and developmental terms there seems to be no room for the distinct themes and emphases of 1 Thessalonians in overviews of Pauline theology. Thus, in most discussions of Pauline thought, save those that provide some attention to the Corinthian correspondence, there is little thought given to the evolution of his theology, thereby providing room for his earlier correspondence.

A careful linguistic and rhetorical reading of 1 Thessalonians reveals two successive moments in Paul's correspondence with the community of Thessalonica: first, an exuberant letter of joy in response to Timothy's report that all is well with the new converts (2:13–4:2) and secondly, a lengthy letter of response to the concerns of the maturing community (1:1–2:12; 4:3–5:28). Thus, the document, understood in its complex historical and epistolary context, provides an interesting series of vignettes for the study of the evolution of an important, early Pauline foundation. One hears of the difficulty and challenge of public, street preaching (2:1-2), of the fierce competition and motivation of public speakers (2:2-7), of Paul's attempts at nurturing and forming community (2:7-12), and of the missionaries' pastoral care offered through embassy (3:1-6) and epistolary activity (4:9, 13; 5:1). In these early epistolary responses to community concerns about blameless behavior, Christian love, the death of fellow believers, the time of the end, and proper community dynamics, one encounters Pauline language and terminology which is both haltingly formulated and clearly a foretaste of later development. A major concern then of this study is the examination of early Pauline thought, as the Apostle struggles with Jewish and early Christian tradition and with Septuagint and other religious terminology to formulate his advice and encouragement to a maturing Macedonian community.

In methodological terms the principal concerns of this study relate to extended philological and rhetorical analysis. In the first case examination of the language of the documents proves most helpful in determining the special character of Paul's earliest correspondence. On the one hand, the constant comparison of the terminology of 1 Thessalonians with contemporary usage helps to situate Paul more firmly in his Hellenistic Jewish milieu and, on the other, the examination of this terminology in the later Pauline correspondence highlights the early character and focus of the Thessalonian correspondence and its remarkably rich theological language. This philological approach also provides assistance in determining the Paulinist writer's usage of Pauline language and thought in addressing a new situation and in providing a Paulinist alternative to the community's apocalyptic fervor.

The second major feature of this study is the use of rhetorical analysis to relate the specific author to the addressees' situation and the issues raised by the correspondence. The epistolary character of these documents, whether relating to the emotional state of the addressees or to their openness to new information and exhortation, has led to careful analysis of the authors' strategy in communicating with the readers and in dealing effectively with their specific situations. Attention therefore is given both to the language of the correspondence and to its particular epistolary context and function. The result of this analysis is a fascinating glimpse at the founding, building, and nurturing of an important Pauline community and at a later pastor's use of Pauline tradition to address the problems raised by apocalyptic fervor.

After treating a variety of introductory matters, this commentary provides a new translation of each section of the canonical text, explains in notes the pertinent textual and linguistic features of each, and then offers in a series of interpretive essays a literary, rhetorical, and thematic analysis of the biblical documents. The Notes for 2 Thessalonians underscore the differences between Paul and the Paulinist writer while those for 1 Thessalonians focus on the early character of the Pauline text and the peculiarities of the distinct situations presumed by the canonical document. The commentary proper provides a more synthetic view of the

Thessalonian documents, their community setting, and the author's message. The order of this study, as concerns 1 Thessalonians, follows that of the canonical text though the discussion of Pauline usage pays particular attention to the epistolary context involved. Nonetheless, the constant concern of this commentary is the assistance provided modern readers in discerning the relationship between the authors and their intended readers.

This study of the Thessalonian correspondence is not a solo performance since it owes much to past commentators, particularly B. Rigaux, E. Best, T. Holtz, and W. Trilling. Additionally, the extensive work of R. F. Collins has been most helpful as have been the studies of A. J. Malherbe, J. Plevnik, and R. Aus. Special thanks is owed Professor H. W. Kuhn for sharing prepublication copies of his work on the Qumran scrolls and their relation to the Thessalonian correspondence.

Finally, gratitude is owed a number of significant others: Michael Glazier for graciously and perceptively accepting a suggestion to create this NT series, Daniel J. Harrington for his gentle, firm, yet wise editing, The Liturgical Press personnel for its professional support, and Mary Ann (also Elizabeth, Marie-Anne, and Joseph) for encouragement, support, and a sympathetic ear.

ABBREVIATIONS

Biblical Books and Apocrypha

Gen	Nah	1-2-3-4 Kgdms	John
Exod	Hab	Add Esth	Acts
Lev	Zeph	Bar	Rom
Num	Hag	Bel	1-2 Cor
Deut	Zech	1-2 Esdr	Gal
Josh	Mal	4 Ezra	Eph
Judg	Ps (*pl.*: Pss)	Jdt	Phil
1-2 Sam	Job	Ep Jer	Col
1-2 Kgs	Prov	1-2-3-4 Macc	1-2 Thess
Isa	Ruth	Pr Azar	1-2 Tim
Jer	Cant	Pr Man	Titus
Ezek	Eccl (*or* Qoh)	Sir	Phlm
Hos	Lam	Sus	Heb
Joel	Esth	Tob	Jas
Amos	Dan	Wis	1-2 Pet
Obad	Ezra	Matt	1-2-3 John
Jonah	Neh	Mark	Jude
Mic	1-2 Chr	Luke	Rev

Other Ancient Texts

ApocZeph	Apocalypse of Zephaniah
B	Vaticanus
Bar	Baruch
BGU	*Berliner griechische Urkunden*
CIG	*Corpus Inscriptionum Graecarum*
En	Enoch
GTh	Coptic Gospel of Thomas

JA	Josephus' *Jewish Antiquities*
JosAs	Joseph and Aseneth
Jub	Jubilees
JW	Josephus' *Jewish Wars*
LXX	Septuagint
ms(s)	Manuscript(s)
NT	New Testament
OT	Old Testament
P	Papyrus
PssSol	Psalms of Solomon
1QH	Qumran: Thanksgiving Hymns
1QM	Qumran: War Scroll
1QS	Qumran: Manual of Discipline
S	Sinaiticus
SibOr	Sibylline Oracles
T	Testament

Periodicals, Reference Works, and Serials

BAGD	W. Bauer, W. F. Arndt, F. W. Gingrich, and F. W. Danker, *Greek-English Lexicon of the NT*
BDF	F. Blass, A. Debrunner, and R. W. Funk, *A Greek Grammar of the NT*
BG	M. Zerwick, *Biblical Greek*
Bib	*Biblica*
BTB	*Biblical Theology Bulletin*
CBQ	*Catholic Biblical Quarterly*
ETL	*Ephemerides Theologicae Lovanienses*
FN	*Filología Neotestamentaria*
GNTG	*Grammar of NT Greek*
HTR	*Harvard Theological Review*
IBNTG	C. F. D. Moule, *An Idiom Book of NT Greek*
IBS	*Irish Biblical Studies*
Int	*Interpretation*
JBL	*Journal of Biblical Literature*
JETS	*Journal of the Evangelical Theological Society*
JSNT	*Journal for the Study of the New Testament*
JTS	*Journal of Theological Studies*
LSJ	H. G. Liddell, R. Scott, and H. S. Jones, *A Greek-English Lexicon*
M-M	J. H. Moulton and G. Milligan, *The Vocabulary of the Greek Testament*
NJBC	*New Jerome Biblical Commentary*
NovT	*Novum Testamentum*
NRSV	*New Revised Standard Version*

NTS	*New Testament Studies*
PT	J. M. Bassler, ed. *Pauline Theology*, vol. 1
RB	*Revue biblique*
SBLSP	*Society of Biblical Literature Seminar Papers*
SFLT	R. F. Collins, *Studies on the First Letter to the Thessalonians*
SR	*Studies in Religion/Sciences religieuses*
ST	*Studia Theologica*
TC	R. F. Collins, ed., *The Thessalonian Correspondence*
TCGNT	B. M. Metzger, *A Textual Commentary on the Greek NT*
TDNT	*Theological Dictionary of the New Testament*
TZ	*Theologische Zeitschrift*
ZNW	*Zeitschrift für die neutestamentliche Wissenschaft*
ZTK	*Zeitschrift für Theologie und Kirche*

INTRODUCTION

The name of Paul looms large in the NT collection of books and in Christian history generally. Since his name is associated with thirteen canonical letters and since early in the Church's history he became known simply as "the Apostle," his writings and the ideas attributed to him have had a profound influence on later centuries. As scholarship has lent its attention to the work and thought of Paul, it has come to appreciate the profound intellectual contribution he has made and to distinguish more clearly between his achievements and those of contemporaries and later disciples. Thus, while his place in the annals of Christian thought is assured, his precise contribution continues to be the subject of debate as scholars attempt to rediscover Paul, his communities, and his thought. As he is taken seriously as pastor and letter writer, as his correspondence is subjected to focused analysis, and as he is increasingly liberated from confessional and historicist streams of interpretation, the variety, originality, and development of his thought emerge more clearly.

This volume focuses on 1 and 2 Thessalonians, two documents attributed to Paul over the course of centuries. While few question the authenticity of the first, increasingly the opposite is the case for the second. Additionally, it is readily held, correctly, that 1 Thessalonians represents Paul's earliest extant correspondence. It is at this point that various issues concerning these documents are raised.[1] This commentary, therefore, offers a brief introduction to the issues which affect their interpretation: the methodological consequences of following the Lukan or Pauline account of the mission, the literary character and analysis of the two works, and the pastoral and theological perspectives of each. The commentary itself presents a literal but rhetorical translation of the texts and a dialogue with their authors and intended readers. The focus of this reading then is on the epistolary texts to discover their context and their meaning in early Pauline and later Paulinist terms.

1. E. Richard, "Contemporary Research on 1 (& 2) Thessalonians," *BTB* 20 (1990) 107–15.

1. *Thessalonian Milieu of the Mission*

Early in his career Paul heads west after doing missionary work in Arabia and Asia Minor in the environs of Syria and Cilicia (Gal 1:17, 21). Crossing the Aegean Sea he connects with the Egnatian Way and works his way west, stopping at Philippi before arriving at Thessalonica, where he and his coworkers are given a warm reception (1 Thess 1:9; 2:2).

The new site of Paul's missionary activity was an important port city of the Roman province of Macedonia, situated at the head of the Thermaic Gulf. Thessalonica, a major commercial city with a long Greek history (founded by a general of Alexander in 315) and a favorable Roman status (declared a free city by Mark Antony in 42), was made capital of the Roman province and was a thriving cosmopolitan urban center, whose prosperity is archaeologically attested by its abundant coinage. Owing to its privileged position as a prominent station on the east-west Egnatian Way and due to its free, autonomous status politically, the city retained its Greek legal and social institutions which greatly influenced its treatment of political issues and its tolerance of religious practices. The last mentioned have left their imprint both on the Thessalonian correspondence and the Lukan account of the mission.[2]

On the one hand, the political status of the city during the early Roman period allowed a degree of autonomy that permitted the city to retain its Greek institutions of internal governance—the city was run by several politarchs, an institution which is attested in Acts 17:6, 8. Its close alliance to Rome, though having the status of non-colony, fostered the cults of the goddess Roma, of Roman benefactors, and of the emperor. While political in intent these cults had the effect of drawing a close relationship between imperial benefaction and loyalty to Roman political and religious interests (see discussion below of Luke's perception of Pauline preaching and its ramifications at Thessalonica). Indeed, Paul's correspondence with his Thessalonian readers shows his sensitivity to the converts' relation to outsiders both in a negative and a positive sense (3:3-4 and 4:12); they are to encounter ostracization in social and religious terms and yet are to live honorably among their non-Christian neighbors.

On the other hand, the city's religious milieu fostered the cultivation of mystery cults, particularly those of Dionysus, Sarapis, and the city cult of the Cabiri. While some scholars attempt to draw a connection between

---

2. C. Edson, "Cults of Thessalonica," *HTR* 41 (1948) 105–204; W. Elliger, *Paulus in Griechenland: Philippi, Thessaloniki, Athen, Korinth* (Stuttgart: Katholisches Bibelwerk, 1978), 78–114; H. L. Hendrix, *Thessalonicans Honor Romans*, Ph.D. dissertation (Harvard, 1984); K. P. Donfried, "The Cults of Thessalonica and the Thessalonian Correspondence," *NTS* 31 (1985) 326–56.

Paul's preaching and these cults, that of the Cabiri in particular,[3] one can at least point to the community's interest in eschatological matters as owing to its exposure to cultic interests. But it is Paul's insistence on religious as opposed to economic and political motivation for the mission (2:1-12) which demonstrates his acquaintance with the Thessalonian religious milieu. While Paul's comment that the community's turning away from idols to the living God (1:9) confronts, in a Jewish manner, the city's numerous religious cults, his insistence on the apostles being agents of the God who has approved them and whose message they preach (2:2, 4), emphasizes the religious rather than political or social motivation of the mission. Their gospel is not one of patronizing ideology, nor is it preached for financial gain or popular applause (2:3) but one which addresses behavior deemed proper by the God who calls them to a future kingdom (v. 12). Paul extricates himself from the religious and political competition of the Thessalonian milieu of cults and benefactions and defines his community's religious and social ideology as having an inward and outward dynamic which involves lives of holiness, love of fellow Christians, and a quiet life of communal sharing and concern (4:3f., 9f., 13f.); this holiness and behavior, nonetheless, also have those beyond the community in view (4:9-12). In this way, the non-Christian outsiders provide a context for the community's life of holiness and are beneficiaries of that community's loving behavior.

Thus, one should attribute Paul's concern in this correspondence for social issues and treatment of outsiders as owing to the Thessalonian milieu wherein a major politico-religious concern was the honoring of the deities and patrons who contributed to the city's well-being. The new converts were to do their share in social and economic terms and conduct themselves properly in the company of their neighbors.[4]

2. *Circumstances of Mission and Correspondence according to Acts*

The traditional chronological and social setting for the Thessalonian mission is taken from the Lukan account of the event. According to Acts, Paul and Silas, having preached in Philippi and been expelled by the city magistrates (16:39), pass through the cities of Amphipolis and Apollonia before arriving in Thessalonica. Their first order of business is to visit the local synagogue where they, according to their usual practice, discuss

3. Donfried, "Cults," 337–42 and R. Jewett, *The Thessalonian Correspondence: Pauline Rhetoric and Millenarian Piety* (Philadelphia: Fortress, 1986) 113–32, 168–78.

4. See Hendrix' stress on the motivation for public honors as being the city's political and social well-being, *Thessalonicans*, 291–92, 315–16.

the Christian message and its scriptural foundation on three successive Sabbaths. Luke's summation of the missionary effort ends by speaking of apostolic success within the Jewish community and among the Gentile population, especially God-fearers (17:1-4). Luke's narrative then speaks of the ending of Paul's stay in the city by describing a Jewish-inspired riot which results from the mission's success and which brings about the abrupt departure of the missionaries.

The sequel in Acts along with data from 1 Thessalonians are employed in descriptions of the occasion and place of the letter's composition. Having been sent off by night Paul and Silas arrive in Beroea and preach in its synagogue with success but are interrupted by their Thessalonian opposition which has followed them to their new missionary site. Again Paul is dispatched by the community, this time to Athens, where, after having summoned Silas and Timothy, he preaches at the Areopagus and departs for Corinth to be soon joined by Silas and Timothy (17:10–18:5). To these data scholars add Timothy's embassy from Athens to Thessalonica (1 Thess 3:1-5); his return is then made to correspond to the arrival of Silas and Timothy as recorded in Acts 18:5. Since Paul indicates that the latter brings back a positive report concerning the community (1 Thess 3:6), it is then assumed that 1 Thessalonians is both a reaction to this good news and an attempt on Paul's part to "supply what is lacking in [their] faith" (3:10). It is also assumed that the correspondence originated from Corinth and, following the chronology of Acts and statements of Paul (1 Thess 2:17), was composed in 50 or 51.[5]

One might assume that, in dealing with the Thessalonian mission and correspondence, the historian is fortunate in possessing two historical resources, an autobiographical account of the events and the report of a near-contemporary. While commentators frequently noted the difficulties involved in using these resources, recent scholarship is relentless in underscoring the problems presented by the Lukan text. Acts 17:1-9 is straightforward, short, and succinct; it is marked off, at the beginning and end, by notices of departure and, thematically and stylistically, falls into three interrelated units: the successful preaching of the good news by the missionaries (presentation—vv. 1-4), organized Jewish opposition to the mission (rejection—5-7), and civil resolution of the disturbance (affirmation of the gospel—8-9). First, Paul and Silas, arguing from the Scriptures, persuade many Jews, devout Greeks, and leading women, that Jesus is the Christ. Then, the Jews who are not persuaded foment an uproar out of jealousy and bring accusations before the city authorities. Finally, the politarchs, though disturbed by the allegations, free the

---

5. True of most commentaries; see, for example, R. F. Collins, "The First Letter to the Thessalonians," *NJBC*, 772-73.

accused group after collecting bail, thereby affirming the nonseditious character of the apostolic preaching. Careful analysis of the Lukan passage and of 1 Thessalonians shows on the one hand that the former is thoroughly Lukan in theme, pattern, and concern and on the other that these features conflict with Paul's composition.

(1) The short, self-contained Lukan account of the mission presents familiar patterns and themes. Synagogue preaching, a motif underscored by the term "custom," is a constant in Acts for the Pauline mission (chapters 9–19), constituting Luke's version of the adage: to the Jews first and then to the Gentiles. Also Lukan are Jewish opposition to the ever-widening and successful Pauline mission (beginning in 9:29), jealousy as motive for antagonism (also 5:17; 13:45), "arguing in the synagogue with the Jews" (chapters 17, 18, 19, 24), a divided response to the apostolic message among Jews and Gentiles (see Luke 2:34), and organized opposition by some in the audience (also Acts 13 and 14). Additionally, riots, civic disturbances, and forced appearances before magistrates are stock Lukan features accompanying the preaching of the good news. Also Lukan are the following: (a) "arguing from the Scriptures" as to the necessity of the Messiah's suffering and rising, (b) the conversion of many Jews, devout Greeks, and leading women, (c) expert management of rioting crowds, (d) a liking for politically motivated, but nonetheless "customary accusation," and (e) the civil or judicial resolution of an issue by having Roman officials either insist on proper procedures or refuse to intervene in religious squabbles (e.g., chapters 18 and 19 respectively).

(2) If one were to compare the Lukan account of the mission with Paul's, one would have to agree with Ernest Best that the former presents problems in at least the following areas: (a) the length of the missionaries' stay in the city, (b) the Jewish character of the new community, (c) the nature of Paul's preaching in Thessalonica, (d) the absence of Timothy during the mission, and (e) the nature of the "security" taken from Jason and Paul's expected return.[6] In fact, Paul's statements in 1 Thessalonians require (a) that he be in the city for more than three weeks, (b) that the community not be primarily Jewish in background, (c) that the content of his preaching was different from what Luke mentions in Acts 17, (d) that Timothy played an active role in the mission, and (e) that the community expected and wanted Paul to return. Each of these could be discussed in detail; three however are crucial. Scholars generally agree that the Lukan time schema (a) is incorrect for Paul in Phil 4:16 mentions receiving help "more than once" from Philippi, speaks of imitation, making demands, and working extensively, and discusses the community's maturing problems. Such issues imply more time than three

6. *The First and Second Epistles to the Thessalonians* (New York: Harper, 1972) 5–6.

weekends of preaching in the synagogue. Luke's description of the mission as being addressed primarily to Jews (b) is simply not borne out by Paul's text, where one learns instead that the converts were Gentile in origin (1:9: "turned to God from idols"). Such a difference is crucial for analyzing 1 Thessalonians and calls into question Luke's knowledge of the facts (see also discussion of 2:14-16). Even more troublesome is Timothy's noninvolvement in the Lukan version of the mission (d), since according to Paul he along with Silvanus is cosender of the letter, apparently a fellow worker during the mission, and the envoy sent from Athens by Paul and others to the city (3:1-6).

From the above one must conclude that the Acts account of the mission owes more to Luke's project and remote acquaintance with the Apostle's role than to first-hand data. Scholars are thus correct in favoring the Pauline account both in terms of chronology and treatment of the mission and correspondence. Also, it should be noted that recent attempts to bolster Luke's historical reliability in regard to the mission fail to convince, whether use of the term "politarch" for city authorities indicates solid historical tradition, whether "the decrees of Caesar" and the political accusations against the missionaries point to an original millenarian conflict, or whether reference to Jason argues for Luke's use of reliable tradition.[7] In the first case, use of politarch in Acts 17 does not indicate reliable sources but supports Luke's well-known Hellenistic culture, which would include acquaintance with Thessalonian political tradition. In the second case, the religious and political terminology and accusations of Acts 17:4, 7 owe not to original tradition but to Lukan formulation of alternating religious and political accusations (see Luke 22:67 and 23:2; also Acts 16-17 and 18-19). In the third case, identification of the Jason mentioned in Rom 16:21 with that of Acts 17 is conjectural at best and relies too readily on the traditions of Romans 16 and 1 Thess 2:14-16 as proving the Jewish background of Jason and suggesting an intimate relation with Paul and the Thessalonian mission. Instead, Jason's appearance in Acts 17 as a key figure owes little to Pauline tradition available to us but conforms to Luke's less than accurate use of details from the Pauline tradition to construct ever-widening patterns of conversion and opposition among the Jewish and Gentile populations of the Hellenistic world.

Lastly, no information can be gleaned from Acts for a discussion of the occasion, date, or place of composition of 2 Thessalonians. Instead, discussion of this document focuses on a comparison of it to 1 Thessalo-

---

7. Donfried, "Cults," 342–43; Jewett, *Correspondence*, 113–32; and F. Morgan-Gillman, "Jason of Thessalonica (Acts 17:5-9)," *TC*, 39–49, respectively.

nians, on its relation chronologically and thematically to it, on its authenticity, and on its particular purpose and setting.

3. *New Views on the Pauline Mission and 1 Thessalonians*

a. *Arrival at Thessalonica: Chronology*

Scholars insist more frequently now that Paul's correspondence, not Acts, should determine Pauline chronology.[8] Indeed, once the temporal and local references of his letters are liberated from a Lukan framework, a different picture emerges. The chronological framework of Paul's career must be drawn from Galatians 1–2 rather than from the Lukan journeys, particularly the series of Corinthian episodes in Acts 18, which is a compilation by Luke of available Corinthian traditions.[9] Without attempting here to establish an overall temporal framework for Paul's career and correspondence,[10] it is possible to situate the Thessalonian mission within the time span between the two Jerusalem visits mentioned in Gal 1:18 and 2:1, that is, the fourteen years between his arrival in the areas of Syria and Cilicia and his return to Jerusalem for the apostolic conference. While the journey of 1:18-21 may have ended in southern Asia Minor, his activity, as suggested by temporal and local references, was wider in scope. We may presume that Gal 4:13 indicates a western journey when Paul fell sick and, during the course of his recuperation, missionized the local inhabitants with success. We conclude that he resumed his journey west to the coast of Asia Minor and eventually across the Aegean Sea to the northeastern coast of the Greek mainland where he picked up the Egnatian Way. Also, it should be noted that Phil 4:15, to the effect that no other Church assisted him save that of Philippi, suggests that he engaged in missionary work in Asia Minor before he crossed the Aegean Sea and arrived in Philippi.[11]

In relative terms the mission in Thessalonica could have been conducted any time during the fourteen years in question, allowing for a stay in his homeland, for his accidental detention in Galatia, travel (and

---

8. R. Jewett, *A Chronology of Paul's Life* (Philadelphia: Fortress, 1979); G. Lüdemann, *Paul, Apostle to the Gentiles: Studies in Chronology* (Philadelphia: Fortress, 1984); and J. Murphy-O'Connor, "Pauline Missions before the Jerusalem Conference," *RB* 89 (1982) 71–91.

9. E. Richard, *Jesus: One and Many. The Christological Concept of New Testament Authors* (Wilmington: Glazier, 1988) 242–44, 276; see also Lüdemann, *Paul,* 174–80 and Murphy-O'Connor, "Missions," 87.

10. See broader discussion of Pauline chronology in Richard, *Jesus,* 239–48, 274–81.

11. See discussion of Murphy-O'Connor, "Missions," 80–82.

preaching?) in western Asia Minor, and mission in Philippi. We might therefore attempt to narrow this time span for the Thessalonian mission. We must date the beginning of this period, i.e., his departure from the Damascus area and first trip to Jerusalem, to ca. 37–39 when the Nabatean king Aretas was in control of the city and forced his ignominious escape (2 Cor 11:32-33).[12] From Paul's writings we know that the itinerary led him from Philippi along the Egnatian Way to Thessalonica (1 Thess 2:2; Phil 4:16) and eventually to Athens (1 Thess 3:1); Acts 17:10-11 adds an intermediate stop in Beroea. Nonetheless, a stop subsequent to that at Thessalonica was Corinth.[13] This we deduce from the list of persons in 1 Thess 1:1 and 2 Cor 1:19, namely, that the senders of the Thessalonian missive are the same that directed the Corinthian mission (see further indications of this in 2 Cor 11:9 and Phil 4:15-16). This list of names also suggests that the Thessalonian correspondence originated from Athens and Corinth. The Corinthian mission itself, however, can be dated with some confidence to the mid-forties,[14] ca. 45, i.e., after Corinth became the capital of the province of Achaea and therefore served as the major base for an Achaean Pauline mission.[15] We would therefore date the Thessalonian mission to the early 40s and the correspondence to the early and mid-40s from Athens and Corinth.

b. *The Thessalonian Mission*

Paul's arrival in the city followed a mission in neighboring Philippi to the east. He mentions the rude treatment endured by the missionaries in that city and then underscores their courage in the face of their new challenge. Rather than follow the scenario offered in Acts 17 consisting of successful synagogue preaching and subsequent Jewish opposition and civil turmoil, some propose a Hellenistic approach to the missionary task and so view Paul as an artisan (tentmaker as noted in Acts 18:3) who employs the workshop to evangelize the artisan classes, as an itinerant preacher who focuses on household preaching as a means of reaching

12. Murphy-O'Connor, "Missions," 74–78 and Jewett, *Chronology*, 30–33.

13. Paul directed a mission in Corinth prior to his trip to Athens (1 Thess 3:2), contrary to the Lukan schema in Acts 16; see Paul's reference in 1 Cor 16:15 to the Corinthian household of Stephanas as his first converts in Achaia and his statement in 1 Thess 2:18 that he attempted repeatedly to visit Thessalonica prior to his Athenian visit.

14. One could argue with Lüdemann, *Paul*, 164–70 and Murphy-O'Connor, "Missions," 84–86 and *St. Paul's Corinth: Texts and Archaeology* (Wilmington: Glazier, 1983) 130–40, that Paul's arrival in Corinth follows shortly after the Claudian edict (as noted by Luke in Acts 18:2), which is plausibly dated to 41 rather than 49.

15. Richard, *Jesus*, 276.

the general populace or to create a network of house churches, or as a preacher in the mold of contemporary philosophers (e.g., Dio Chrysostom) who employs various modes of public speaking and exhortation and pastoral methods in dealing with urban audiences.[16] From such considerations one can discern an approach to Paul which embraces the entire missionary endeavor from arrival, to preaching while supporting oneself, reception, community formation and instruction, to nurturing, and pastoral care at a distance.

Paul's approach to mission can be discerned from his numerous references to coworkers, cosenders (of letters), travel notices, and various indications of community formation and pastoral care. One should envision Paul and companions ("cowriters") as the key figures of a missionary band who direct the work of a larger group. Once established in major cities, the senior missionaries send out their junior associates to neighboring areas for given periods of time for preaching, founding communities, instructing their converts, and setting up structures before moving on to new missionary fields. Presumably, the sites chosen for the mission's center were either major cities on principal Roman highways or centrally located and politically significant sites, Corinth for the latter and Philippi and Thessalonica for the former.

The missionaries' activity at Philippi and arrival at Thessalonica are starkly described in 1 Thess 2:2 as Paul speaks of the challenge and public scoffing experienced at Philippi and the resulting rededication of the apostles to do the same at Thessalonica. Their initial work involves public presentation of the gospel in a way similar to that of contemporary moral philosophers though not in the name of a rational, virtuous life but as honest, approved agents of a God who desires a people which lives worthily of its call to a future kingdom of glory (2:2-4, 12). The arrival and appeal of the missionaries are described at length in terms of their motivation, authority, and goal, while their reception is expressed in the glowing words of the inhabitants of the Greek mainland (1:9).

Paul and coworkers establish themselves as artisans within the area, possibly in view of their missionary strategy, but certainly to support their pastoral endeavors (2:9). No doubt, the apostles provide for their livelihood since it is Paul's objective to avoid any hint of avariciousness (2:3, 5) and certainly not to place burdens on the gospel's recipients (v. 9) nor

16. R. F. Hock, *The Social Context of Paul's Ministry: Tentmaking and Apostleship* (Philadelphia: Fortress, 1980) 37–42; S. K. Stowers, "Social Status, Public Speaking and Private Teaching: The Circumstances of Paul's Preaching Activity," *NovT* 26 (1984) 59–82; W. A. Meeks, *The First Urban Christians: The Social World of the Apostle Paul* (New Haven: Yale, 1983) 74–110; A. J. Malherbe, *Paul and the Thessalonians: The Philosophic Tradition of Pastoral Care* (Philadelphia: Fortress, 1987).

on its preachers, save that of sharing gospel and self with the new converts (v. 8).

The preachers spend much time in Thessalonica as they are wont to. do in each major location; such is true of Corinth and Ephesus. The time spent there was longer than the three weeks mentioned in Acts 17:1, enough time for trips of assistance from Philippi (Phil 4:16), for difficult labor and toil, and for mutual affection and commitment to develop.

Paul's missionary work must be seen in a comprehensive way as involving the founding, shaping, and nurturing of community.[17] Such an extensive task required public preaching, focus on receptive households, work contexts, and lecture settings where the good news could be targeted to potential converts who were challenged to turn away from idols ''to serve the living and true God'' (1 Thess 1:9), thereby accepting a new social and religious identity and community. It is precisely this change in status and its consequent alienation which is discussed by Paul when he speaks of the converts receiving the word of God in the midst of difficulties (1:6) or of warning his Thessalonian audience beforehand concerning their present difficulties as being their ''appointed lot'' (3:3-4). On the negative side, conversion meant a social, religious separation of believers from their Roman neighbors, a situation which caused tension and hostility on the part of some in the general population. The converts in effect adopted a new value system which radically changed their social, cultic, and religious affiliations and loyalties. But disruption of their social world also led, on the positive side, to the creation of a new world and the establishing of new familial and social relations. Fellow converts became brothers and sisters, thereby replacing and redefining familial ties. Paul and his co-missionaries speak of their mission in Thessalonica in parental terms for they compare their roles and methods of operation to the activity of a nurse or a father with their own children (2:7, 11). One also understands Paul's use of ''Father'' for God and of ''Lord'' for Jesus as he redefines the converts' social world and their relationship to the principal figures of their religious ideology. Thus, conversion implied both the turning away from and the turning to a way of life with its whole range of relationships, community, and goals.

Finally, while this correspondence gives the reader valuable clues concerning conversion and community formation, it provides abundant information regarding Paul's advice to and exhortation of a cherished Macedonian community. Paul and his fellow workers are concerned with the community's ability to survive and with its mature, spiritual health or nurture. While this correspondence speaks incidently of the founding and shaping of the community, it is devoted to its nurturing.

17. Malherbe, *Paul*, chapters 1-3.

c. *The Thessalonian Correspondence*

(1) *Composite Character*. It is readily admitted that the structure of 1 Thessalonians presents a number of anomalies, not the least of which is its having two thanksgiving sections. Thus, one finds in 1:2-10 a fully developed thanksgiving whose structure bears similarities to Phil 1:3-8 and Phlm 4-6 and a shorter but fully structured thanksgiving period in 2:13 with affinities to Rom 1:8-9 and 1 Cor 1:4-7. While unconvincing attempts have been made to characterize chapters 1-3 as extended thanksgiving (see also 3:9 for use of *eucharistia*),[18] one is led to agree with Murphy-O'Connor's caustic comment regarding "the absurdity of a thanksgiving running from 1:2 to 3:13."[19] It should be noted that only 1 Thessalonians and the Paulinist 2 Thessalonians possess such a feature.

Other anomalies involve the un-Pauline, interpolated 2:14-16 (see discussion below), the conclusion-like structure and tone of 3:11-4:2, and the temporal tension and difference in content between chapters 1-2, 4-5 on the one hand and 2:17-3:13 on the other. In 2:17 Paul writes after a short absence from Thessalonica, while in 1:6f. he presumes a lapse of time following the mission. The end of chapter 2 and all of 3 focus on the apostles' fear, prior to Timothy's embassy, that the community has not survived and, following his return, express their desire to assist them and be among them. The final two chapters treat at length community issues which also presume a lapse of time. Other points of interest concern double conclusions in 3:11f. and 5:23f. and distinct differences of tone in 2:13f. (where Paul had feared he had "labored in vain" and expresses joy, relief, and warmth) and in 1:2f. and 4:3f. (where he knows that the preaching has not been "in vain" and treats in a more circumspect way the problems experienced and the issues raised by a maturing community). Lastly, the expression of affection in 2:1-12, as opposed to that found in 2:13f., concerns the original missionary visitation and acts as introduction to the letter's paraenesis in chapters 4 and 5.

In light of these considerations,[20] I am led to accept the composite character of 1 Thessalonians, whereby a short earlier missive (2:13-4:2)

---

18. Most recently see J. Lambrecht, "Thanksgivings in 1 Thessalonians 1-3," *TC*, 183-205 and P. T. O'Brien, *Introductory Thanksgivings in the Letters of Paul* (Leiden: Brill, 1977) 164-65.

19. Review of R. Jewett's *Correspondence* in *RB* 95 (1988) 311.

20. The integrity of the document is defended by the majority of scholars; see discussions of W. G. Kümmel, "Das literarische und geschichtliche Problem des ersten Thessalonicherbriefes," in W. C. van Unnik, ed., *Neotestamentica et Patristica: Eine Freundesgabe O. Cullmann* (Leiden: Brill, 1962) 213-27; R. F. Collins, "Apropos the Integrity of 1 Thess," *SFLT*, 96-135; and Jewett, *Correspondence*, 31-46.

was inserted into a later Thessalonian letter (1:1–2:12 + 4:3–5:28). Some scholars have been reluctant to accept such a conclusion, thinking that a refutation of debatable points in W. Schmithals's reconstruction of the mission and correspondence thereby disproves his literary observations concerning the division of 1 Thessalonians into two Pauline letters.[21] On the basis of the above data, along with comparison of 1 Thessalonians with other Pauline letters, and with due consideration given to the temporal and content tensions between the two resulting documents, I am led to accept such a division of the text as best fitting what is known from Paul himself about the missionary and epistolary context. It should be stressed that the presumption of integrity is an assumption unless it explains satisfactorily serious structural and temporal anomalies.

(2) *Early Missive—2:13–4:2.* 2:13–4:2 represents a virtually complete missive from Paul to Thessalonica, one written shortly after the apostles' departure (2:17). How soon after is hard to determine since Paul states that repeated attempts were made to return during the Corinthian mission, prior to an Athenian journey. The body of the letter is fully preserved; but its opening was omitted during editing because it was identical to the other opening, and its conclusion was combined with the other because of their similarity (see discussions of 1:1 and 5:23-28). The short missive was written subsequently to Timothy's return from a visit with the community and so the thanksgiving reflects the heartening news that the community still exists, that it is thriving, and that its members are eager for the missionaries' return (3:6). Thus Paul thanks God for the faith of his beloved converts.

Paul turns in 2:17 to a discussion of the missionaries' anxiety regarding the community, anxiety which had reached an unbearable level prior to Timothy's embassy (3:1-5). Apparently the missionaries grew fond of this early community and perceived a high degree of vulnerability. They had responded favorably to the divine message (2:13) but such a sincere response had not spared them accompanying difficulties (3:3-4), which might cause them to have second thoughts about their new commitment. Thus, though they had warned them beforehand about this, the missionaries had misgivings about the strength of their converts' faith and so feared they might be enticed by their former polytheistic loyalties (3:3, 5). Paul then is concerned about the converts' survival, for the community itself is the only fruit of his missionary labor in the eyes of the returning Lord (2:19).

---

21. *Paul and the Gnostics* (Nashville: Abingdon, 1972) 126–35; 212–14; see critiques of Schmithals in recent commentaries. In agreement with the present analysis see Murphy-O'Connor, "Missions," 82.

Being unable, despite several attempts, to visit Thessalonica (Satan is said to be the obstacle; see 2 Cor 12:7), Paul and others, while visiting Athens, decided to dispatch Timothy to inquire about the community's survival and, in the event of favorable news, to strengthen and encourage the converts in their faith. Following this show of concern and affection, Paul recounts Timothy's return with good news regarding the community's faith commitment and the enactment of its faith in acts of love toward others. Timothy's report also speaks of reciprocal affection and the desire of the community for a return visit. Paul reiterates his joy that all is well (v. 8), speaks of his intention to return to supply them with further instruction (10), and prays that their intra-and-extra love may increase in view of their presentation before the returning Lord (12-13). He draws the letter to a close with a brief exhortation (for a similar short, final exhortation introduced by the verb *parakaleō*, see Rom 15:30-32) that the community continue to act according to the apostolic instruction it received in Jesus' name (4:1-2).

Paul's "first" letter to the Thessalonians therefore is a brief message of concern whose contours can be delineated from the point of view of epistolary structure and content:

1. Epistolary Opening
   [identical or nearly so to that of 1:1]
2. Thanksgiving: 2:13
   [The Jews and Divine Retribution: 2:14-16—interpolation]
3. Reason for Concern and Frustration: 2:17-20   (Body-Opening)
4. Timothy's Mission to Thessalonica: 3:1-5   (Body-Middle)
5. Timothy's Return and Report: 3:6-8
6. Paul's Joy and Prayer: 3:9-13   (Body-Closing)
7. Final Exhortation—4:1-2
8. Epistolary Closing
   [edited and partially preserved in 5:25-28]

Paul's first extant writing then is a short missive in the style of popular papyrus letters, from a missionary who experiences concern at being separated from a recently founded, struggling community. In terms of content, the missive offers a fully developed thanksgiving (2:13), reiterates the concern of the community's founders (2:17f.), recounts their efforts at redressing the problems the converts face (3:1f.), expresses their joy and thanks (3:11f.), and finally encourages them to continued efforts in their conduct toward one another and all in view of the state of holiness to which they are called (4:1-2).

In terms of structure, however, the letter, owing to its brevity and purpose, corresponds closely, along with Philemon, to popular Hellenistic letters,[22] whose principal section consists of a short, unified body. 2:17-20 offers a distinct body-opening which is delineated by direct address, a focus on the reason for writing in lieu of a disclosure formula (failed attempts to visit), and expressions of reassurance. 3:1-8, the body-middle, speaks of the decision to send Timothy as ambassador and gives a report of the visit. The section is marked off by an inferential conjunction ("therefore"), by a focus again on the frustration resulting from the apostles' inability to visit, and a discussion of the cause for concern and the reassurance resulting from the visit. Finally, 3:9-12, the body-closing, "finaliz(es) the principal motive for writing" and "form(s) a bridge to further communication." Indeed, the apostles thank God again for the splendid news brought by Timothy, reiterate their desire to visit, and encourage the community to greater effort. This last section introduces a final exhortation on the part of the missionaries (4:1-2).[23]

Finally, the document's focus is on apostolic presence: the desire to be there, the pain at being separated in trying circumstances, and the sending of an emissary and letter because of the missionaries' absence. The reader encounters a letter of concern and affection from a young missionary whose energies are devoted to the Christian mission and whose work can be measured only by the communities he has founded, communities that are his "hope, joy, and crown of pride . . . in the presence of [the] Lord Jesus at his coming" (2:19).

(3) *Later Missive—1:1-2:12 + 4:3-5:28.* The remainder of the document (chapters 1, most of 2, and 4-5) constitutes another letter written by Paul to the same community. It seems to be complete and to have lost none of its text during the editing process. This second missive is a more fully developed letter, much in the style and form of Paul's later correspondence. During the course of the editorial process the document was used as a frame for the short missive discussed above. This collation was facilitated by the similarity in themes between 2:9-12 and 3:10-4:2. This document presupposes a greater lapse of time than does the earlier one, for by now the community's faith commitment, activities, and missionary assistance are well known to the other communities of the Greek mainland and beyond (1:6-9). After a standard opening with customary tripartite formula identifying writer and addressees and expressing a salutation, one finds another, more extensive thanksgiving period (1:2-10) where Paul

---

22. Such comparison calls into question recent attempts to impose upon 1 Thessalonians the artificial structures of sophisticated rhetoricians, whereby the letter consists of exordium, narratio, probatio, and peroratio; see C. A. Wanamaker, *Commentary on 1 & 2 Thessalonians* (Grand Rapids: Eerdmans, 1990) and Jewett, *Correspondence.*

23. The above epistolary analysis owes its inspiration to J. L. White, *The Body of the Greek Letter* (Missoula: Scholars, 1972) 1-41; the citations are from p. 25.

speaks of the community's growth, its wholehearted response to its divine election, and its reputation as a premier Christian foundation in the region of Macedonia and Achaia.

This thanksgiving period provides clues to understand the entire letter and further support for viewing this missive as resulting from questions received from the community. [1] In the first place, the faith, love, and hope of 1:3 prepare for the moving paraenesis of 5:8 and its military imagery. Further, the concept of the "echo" of faith is employed to describe the community's ever-growing influence (1:8), while "love" and "hope" figure prominently in its pastoral debates, whether about "love of brother and sister" and of community leaders (4:9f.; 5:13) or of proper eschatological vision as solidly founded hope (4:13). The notions of divine election and sanctifying Spirit (1:4-6) point to the general paraenesis on God's will as defined by holiness and reception of the Spirit (4:3-8). On the one hand, Paul's insistence on the missionaries' demeanor and motivation (1:5) prepares for the treatment in 2:1-12 of these issues as appeal and behavior (vv. 3, 10). On the other hand, Paul's reference in 1:9 to the apostolic visit as successful leads in 2:1f. to a lengthy discussion of the founding visitation.

[2] While it is the threefold formula "now concerning the . . ." in 4:9, 13 and 5:1 (introducing successive topics) which provides the clearest evidence for maintaining that Paul's letter is in large measure a response to questions received from the community, additional data for this conclusion are forthcoming from an examination of the remainder of the letter, particularly the thanksgiving period. It is significant that in 1:5, as an explanation of the community's influence and missionary activity, Paul dwells on how the good news arrived in Thessalonica, on the sort of persons the missionaries were, and on why they preached in the first place. He returns to these issues in 2:1-12, because an emissary has brought an oral report, along with the community's letter, concerning the founding mission and the continued role of the missionaries in offering encouragement, consolation, and exhortation (2:12). Also, Paul insists in 1:8 that while the Lord's word, vis-à-vis the community's missionary endeavors, originated "among" the Thessalonians, it nonetheless came from the apostolic preachers (v. 5). Following this, he introduces the subject of the visit. After discussing the circumstances and motivation of the original appeal, the apostles' approval and commissioning by God, and their arduous, loving, and blameless behavior, he justifies both the request of some in the community for advice (imitation motif of 1:6) and the manner and tone of his paraenesis as being that of "a father for his own children" (2:11).

Further, 2:1-12 and 4:3-8 are called forth, much as is the case in 1 Corinthians 1-6, by oral reports from the community concerning the missionaries' past and current roles vis-à-vis the community. Scholars are right in pointing out that there is no evidence for attacks from opponents and in noting the similarities between Paul's language and that of current moral philosophers (see 2:1-12). But it is equally important to note that the focus of the discussion is on the divine origin of the gospel and human agency of the preaching as the basis for the apostles' role then and now. They were and continue to be parental figures. Paul insists that his readers not misread the apostles' refusal to stand on their importance as apostles of Christ (2:7) during the original mission as a sign of a termination of their role, but rather notes that they acted then and now as loving parents (2:7 and v. 11), but as parents all the same (see Paul's later insistence in 1 Cor 3:5-9 on the rightful division of missionary labor). Also, Paul in 4:6 insists that the missionaries have already instructed the community in the matter of holiness and in verse 8 that this paraenesis finds its origin in God's will. Finally, his parting words in 5:27 that the letter be read to all in the community points to the document's character as pastoral care at a distance.

Paul's second missive, therefore, represents a later stage in the community's development and in Paul's relation to its members. This Church's history is paradigmatic for understanding other Pauline foundations, for while this dynamic and thriving community itself had become the source and perhaps center of missionary activity and exemplary hospitality (1:6-9), it nonetheless sought a continued relationship with its apostolic founders or parents in the guise of well-reasoned advice and paraenesis. The overall structure of Paul's "second missive" may be delineated as follows:

1. Epistolary Opening: 1:1
2. Thanksgiving: 1:2-10
3. Missionary Behavior as   (Body-Opening relating
   Paraenetic Model: 2:1-12   to an oral report)
4. Initial Exhortation on Holiness: 4:3-8   (Body-Middle relating
                                         1) to oral reports
5. On Love of Others: 4:9-12   2) to written queries)
6. On the Faithful Departed and the Parousia: 4:13-18
7. On Being Ready for the Lord's Return: 5:1-11
8. Final Exhortation on Community   (Body-Closing as
   Life: 5:12-22   final exhortation)
9. A Final Prayer and Epistolary Closing: 5:23-28

In structural terms this second missive recalls the framework of 1 Corinthians as it relates to oral and written queries received from the community and consists of apostolic responses to the issues raised.[24] Further,

24. See Richard, *Jesus*, 282-84.

the letter is clarified by the categories noted when discussing the body of the earlier missive. 2:1-12 consists of a body-opening relating to an oral report received from Thessalonica. The section is clearly delineated by a disclosure formula ("you yourselves know"), direct address, and a lengthy discussion of the mission as a basis for advice given as answers and concluding exhortation. 4:3-5:11, consisting of the body-middle, relates first to the report brought from the community and secondly to the repeated use of a standard formula (*peri* with the genitive) for responding to written queries (see 4:9, 13; 5:1). Finally, 5:12f., in the guise of a concluding exhortation, reiterates what was stressed and implied throughout the body of the letter.[25] Paul's letter then is a pastoral response to issues raised by one of his communities and offers an excellent example of how he keeps in touch with his earlier foundations as he moves farther west in his missionary campaigns.

(4) *2:14-16 as Interpolation.* Despite the tendency of some to treat verses 13 and 14-16 as a unit, whether in defending Pauline authorship they insist that the latter verses provide a new reason for giving thanks or in denying authorship they eliminate the problematic second thanksgiving and the highly polemical verses, my intention here is to examine only the character and origin of verses 14-16. Anomalies which draw the attention of scholars involve the polemical tone of the passage, a large number of non-Pauline terms and expressions, the unusual statement about imitation of the Judaean churches, a series of un-Pauline accusations, and a conclusion about Israel's future which contradicts what is said in Rom 11:26.

While it is precarious to deny authorship on the basis of vocabulary which recurs infrequently or not at all in other Pauline letters, it is less conjectural to focus on the content of the verses and the relation of their themes to other Pauline passages, all the while being conscious of the "occasional" character of these themes and statements. Several minor problems should be mentioned at the outset: the Jews are said to have "killed the Lord Jesus" (a historically questionable and non-Pauline statement); the term "imitation" in verse 14 is not properly used and does not parallel Pauline occurrences (the Thessalonians do not imitate but rather "become like" the Judaean churches; besides, Paul speaks not of ecclesial but apostolic imitation); the concept of "suffering" in verse 14 is more Lukan than Pauline; and, finally, the term translated "persecute" (*ekdiōkō*) should be rendered "drive out or expel."

More important for the analysis of verses 14-16 is whether one should assume that the community of Thessalonica is Jewish Christian. From

---

25. See note 23 above.

Paul's text (excluding 2:14-16) there is no hint of a Jewish element in the community—this is true of both missives. In fact, 1:9-10 indicates that the community is Gentile in origin; only 2:14-16 speaks of Jewish opposition. Reading of the Lukan account in Acts 17:1-9 leads some to speak of a Judaeo-Christian community which undergoes Jewish opposition. The evidence is external and relies principally on verses 14-16.

Thus, scholars are obliged to defend Paul's uncharacteristic use of the term "the Jews" in verse 14 as the source of severe accusations. These recriminations concern [1] the Judaean participants in the trial and death of Jesus, those who allegedly persecuted the early Judaean churches, and the Jews of the past who according to legend "killed the prophets" and [2] the Jewish people for banishing Jewish Christians from the synagogue (2:15) and for making a profession of displeasing God and despising the rest of humanity. Some explain this polemic as Jewish self-critique, i.e., Paul the Judaeo-Christian criticizing other Jews, much as Matthew or John do against the contemporary synagogue as perhaps a Deuteronomic reflection on Israel's current situation. However, verses 14-16 sound more like the anti-Judaic condemnations of later generations. It is especially the accusation of "hostility against the rest of humanity" which indicates non-Pauline authorship, for this is said to justify Jewish opposition to the Gentile mission. Finally, the author's polemic reaches its extreme when the text insists that the Jews are approaching the limits of divine tolerance and so are getting what they deserve.

Having looked carefully at the above factors, I conclude that 2:14-16 constitutes an interpolation, originally composed as a scribal, marginal comment and later admitted into the body of the composite letter. The theology of these verses is un-Pauline in tone, content, and overall treatment of Israel and represents a later generation's misreading of polemical NT texts, particularly from Matthew and Luke-Acts, in the context of a Hellenistic anti-Jewish perspective. The difficulties of the early Church are laid at the feet of the dispersed nation of Israel. Verses 15-16 indeed constitute an unrelenting condemnation of all Jews, an attitude with which the Church will do battle throughout the centuries.

Finally, I should note a methodological dilemma which confronts the scholar, a dilemma usually stated in a one-sided fashion: the scholar's responsibility lay in making sense of a text "as it now stands." In the world of antiquity with its methods of composition, editing, and scribal transmission, it is odd to insist that a text, especially with the special characteristics of 2:14-16, should be presumed authentic. At best presumption either way is open to debate. True, Paul probably did change his mind on certain subjects from the time he composed his Thessalonian missives to the period he sent his massive epistle to the Romans, but one must admit that it is only 2:14-16 which contains such anti-Jewish polemic. The remainder of 1 Thessalonians is patently different in tone and content and surprisingly silent concerning Judaeo-Christian issues.

4. *Paulinist Character and Occasion of 2 Thessalonians*

a. *A Pseudonymous Letter*

While there is a tendency among recent scholars to opt for pseudonymity in regard to 2 Thessalonians, its Pauline authenticity continues to be defended. In the view of the latter this letter is part of Paul's correspondence to a favorite Macedonian community early in his writing career. It is asserted that it was written shortly after the first to pursue its principal concerns. From the outset scholars have recognized serious difficulties posed, among other issues, by the eschatology of 1 Thess 4:13–5:11 which presumes the Lord's imminent return and 2 Thess 2:1-12 which attempts to dispel such a notion. Also few fail to note the structural, stylistic, and rhetorical similarities between these.

Faced with these issues champions of Pauline authorship choose various lines of defense. Some appeal to the flexibility of apocalyptic language to explain the differences between these, e.g., a sudden coming as opposed to a parousia preceded by signs. Paul, it is maintained, is beginning his writing career and is experimenting with language and idiom. Also, it is pointed out, "both conceptions—the End is coming suddenly, and it has historical antecedents—occur together in the apocalyptic of Judaism and early Christianity, and lie within the same perspective."[26]

A few attempt to resolve these difficulties in differing apocalyptic perspectives by proposing different audiences within the community for the two documents, or by insisting that the more explicitly apocalyptic 2 Thessalonians was written first. In defense of the latter it is also pointed out that the community's affliction is going on at the time of writing (present tenses in 1:3-5), while in 1 Thess 1:6; 3:4-5 (though note 3:3) the distress is in the past. Still others advance partition theories to account for the ideology of 2 Thessalonians and for its peculiar literary composition. Among the last mentioned one recognizes the proposal of Schmithals,[27] whose acceptance of Pauline authorship of the entire but allegedly fragmented Thessalonian correspondence is invariably employed against the defense of pseudonymity.

There are serious objections to these proposals and increasingly scholars either choose to accept only the simplist of these, namely, that Paul

---

26. W. G. Kümmel, *Introduction to the New Testament* (Nashville: Abingdon, 1975) 266.
27. *Paul and the Gnostics*, 191–95, 212–14; also see note 21 above.

wrote the second Thessalonian letter shortly after the first, while its contents were still fresh or else they opt for pseudonymity. For the latter, the literary, theological, and sociological problems raised by this letter can only be resolved by subscribing to a theory of pseudonymity. Thus, it is proposed that someone in the Pauline churches wrote a letter in Paul's name to counter the dubious proposals made by apocalypticists in the community. It is concluded that the differences and similarities between the two owe to a later writer's appropriation of Pauline vocabulary and tradition to counter apocalypticist solutions to the community's unhappy predicament, i.e., its attempt to escape what it perceives to be persecutions and afflictions (1:4) by appealing to the imminent return of the Lord who will inflict punishment on the ungodly (1:8) and even in idly failing to do good while waiting for the Lord (3:13).

The author employs traditional apocalyptic lore to show the reader that (to quote Mark 13:7) "the end is not yet." Their present tribulations are no cause for being "shaken in mind or disturbed" (2:2) for these are not yet an indication of the evil one's reign, but a foretaste of "lawlessness" (2:7). Indeed, the mysterious "restrainer" (2:6, 7) is keeping the evil one at bay and believers must roll up their sleeves and get back to work, "never growing tired of doing what is right" (3:13). Those who persecute believers will get their just desserts, but the latter must strive to be worthy of God's call, in view of the Lord's return. For this purpose the new author chose as model a letter which the apostle had written early in his career to the Thessalonians.

b. *Use of 1 Thessalonians as Model*

The relationship of the two documents to one another is close, closer it might be added than any others in the Pauline corpus, save Colossians and Ephesians. The choice of 1 Thessalonians as model, a document known to both sides of the apocalyptic controversy, explains the letter's peculiar character, un-Pauline on the one hand and closely related to 1 Thessalonians on the others. These similarities and differences are examined under three headings.

(1) *Structural and Source Considerations.* Several features of 2 Thessalonians are striking even to the cursory reader. This letter, unlike other Pauline letters, has two thanksgivings as does 1 Thessalonians. Its epistolary opening is nearly verbatim in agreement with that of its model, a situation which occurs nowhere else in Paul, not even in the two Corinthian letter openings. Likewise there are parallel, double prayers and conclusions. The following overall structural parallels (with formulaic indicators) are easily discernible:

2 Thess	1 Thess
letter opening	
1:1 Paul, Silvanus, Timothy	1:1 idem
to church . . .	idem
in God . . .	idem
2 grace to you and peace	idem
+ from God . . .	- - -
thanksgiving 1	
1:3 we ought to give thanks	1:2 we give thanks
to God . . .	to God . . .
faith	3 dynamism of faith
love	dedication of love
endurance *(hypomonē)*	constancy of hope *(hypomonē)*
	4 brothers and sisters
	beloved by God
formulaic intro.	
2:1 we urge you, brothers and	
sisters, concerning . . .	
(erōtōmen, adelphoi, hyper tēs)	
thanksgiving 2	
2:13 we ought to give thanks	2:13 we give thanks
to God . . .	to God . . .
brothers and sisters	
beloved by the Lord	
formal prayer 1	
2:16 now may our Lord Jesus	3:11 now may God our Father
Christ himself and God	himself and our Lord
our Father (with optative	Jesus (with optative
singular verbs)	singular verb)
formulaic intro.	
3:1 finally, brothers and sisters	4:1 finally then, brothers and sisters,
(to loipon, adelphoi)	we urge
	(loipon, adelphoi, erōtōmen)
paraenetic intro.	
3:6 we command you, brothers	4:1 we exhort you
and sisters, in the name of	in the Lord Jesus
our Lord Jesus Christ	
formulaic intro.	
	4:9 now concerning . . . *(peri tēs)*
	also 4:13; 5:1
formal prayer 2	
3:16 now may the Lord of peace	5:23 now may the God of peace
himself (with optative)	himself (with optative)
letter closing	
3:17 "I" statement	5:27 "I" statement
18 blessing: the grace of . . .	28 blessing: idem

It is striking that the author follows so many of the structural and formulaic pecularities of 1 Thessalonians. Thus, these parallels include double thanksgivings, with similar content in one case, and twofold prayers whose unusual features consist of stark double subjects with singular optative verbs. Even formulaic expressions are borrowed and strategically situated to provide maximum structural similarity.

Thus, in structural terms 2 Thessalonians recalls the overall framework of its composite prototype. Between similar opening and closing one finds several blocks of material which perform similar functions: 1:3-12—a thanksgiving that corresponds with that of 1 Thess 1:2-10; 2:1-12—a long treatment of the Lord's day that parallels Paul's discussion of the foundation visit in 1 Thess 2:1-12; 2:13-3:5—a second thanksgiving and prayer section that reproduce some of the structural features and themes of 1 Thess 2:13-4:2; and 3:6-16—a paraenetic section which focuses on issues raised in the discussion of the Lord's day and so recalls Paul's own paraenesis in 4:3-5:25 relating to the mission.

Another source-critical area needs attention, namely, the entire letter's relation to the thanksgiving section of 1 Thessalonians. Apart from 2 Thessalonians' epistolary introduction (1:1-2) and conclusion (3:17-18), both of which relate closely to 1 Thessalonians, one might divide the new letter into four blocks of material, each of which relates directly in thematic terms to 1 Thessalonians 1. The first block (2 Thess 1:3-12) begins by developing themes from 1 Thess 1:2-3 (faith, love, and endurance in the context of the community's situation of persecution and affliction); the second block (2:1-12) focuses on eschatology, the theme of 1 Thess 1:9-10 (namely, waiting for and return of the Son, and divine wrath); the third block (2:13-3:5) reproduces the model's second thanksgiving (1 Thess 2:13) and joins this to a treatment of 1 Thess 1:4-5a (beloved and chosen by God, our gospel); and the fourth block (3:6-16) treats the topics of 1 Thess 1:5b-7 (imitation, example, presence). Only 1 Thess 1:8 concerning the spreading of the Lord's word seems neglected, though see 2 Thess 3:1: "the word . . . may speed on and triumph."

(2) *Vocabulary and Style*. One also discerns the author's craft in the area of terminology and usage. Phrases and terms are repeated from 1 Thessalonians but usually the new usage has an un-Pauline character, e.g., Paul often speaks of hope and comfort (*paraklēsis*) but never, as in 2:16, "give eternal comfort and good hope." Idioms like "give comfort," "eternal comfort," or "good hope" are never found in Paul nor elsewhere in the NT.

While Paul often speaks of "the gospel of Christ," 2 Thessalonians offers only one parallel expression: "the gospel of our Lord Jesus" (1:8). The author's favorite Christological titles are Pauline: "Lord Jesus Christ,"

"Lord Jesus," and even "Christ" (3:5) but the characteristic usage "Christ Jesus" is missing. Also un-Pauline in usage are a host of idioms, idioms not usually found in the rest of the NT: "inflicting punishment on," "to be shaken in mind," "love of truth," "believe the truth" (1:8; 2:2, 10, 12) and "comfort the heart." The last mentioned is never found in Paul though it is used once in 2 Thess 2:17, twice in Colossians and once in Ephesians. Despite the value of such lists of rare terms, it is nonetheless more important to note their particular epistolary usage, context, and nuance, a constant goal of the following notes and commentary.

Also un-Pauline is a host of stylistic peculiarities. (a) The author makes extensive use of parallelism. An impressive list has been made of such consecutive phrases as offering complementary, antithetical, and synonymous parallels.[28] For example, the author speaks in complementary fashion, "your faith is growing abundantly and the love of each . . . is increasing" (1:3), and then in an antithetical way, "to repay with affliction those who afflict you and to you who are afflicted to grant rest" (1:6-7). (b) There is an absence of typically Pauline vocabulary and themes. Instead of stressing the Christ-event, 2 Thessalonians casts a glance on future reality and focuses on eschatology, with far less regard for past realities, apart from the concepts of "choice, call, and grace." The author, owing to the community's situation, has focused on divine retribution as "comfort for believers" (1:9) rather than on Paul's fundamental concern for the Cross and resurrection. Beyond this particular focus on the future, however, there is a concern for the community's present existence (see discussion of methodological issues). (c) The author chooses an authoritative rather than an argumentative approach to issues. Authority is a major issue for 2 Thessalonians; there is a polemical use of terms such as letter, hand, listen to. (d) Many stylistic features and emphases are more easily discerned by examining the author's redaction of Pauline passages, appropriation of Pauline themes, and peculiar repetitive style.

(3) *Tone and Strategy.* These concerns are evident throughout the letter but more easily discerned in 2:1-3a. The issue is the Lord's return and so the author's strategy in combating the notion that the Lord's day has arrived or that the end-time scenario is unraveling is an appeal to Pauline authority. Thus, the disavowal of misguided interpretations of the apostle in the teaching and writing of some opponent (2:2-3) amounts to a defense of the author's point of view (2:5, 15) and composition (3:14, 17). The appeal to authority to reestablish order and the stress on authenticity

---

28. W. Trilling, *Untersuchungen zum zweiten Thessalonicherbrief* (Leipzig: St. Benno-Verlag, 1972) 52–53.

to gain the allegiance of the readers further underscore the pseudonymity of 2 Thessalonians. Finally, the tone of the document is strongly authoritative. While retaining occasional pleas ("we urge you" in 2:1 or "we exhort" in 3:12) the author's preference is for command (3:4, 6, 10, 12) and authoritative teaching (1:8; 2:5, 12; 3:14). Tone and strategy go together in making this document a resolutely focused one.

c. *Literary Analysis: Structure and Content*

The structure of 2 Thessalonians may be delineated as follows:

1. Epistolary Opening 1:1-2
2. First Thanksgiving 1:3-12
3. Concerning the Lord's Day 2:1-12
4. Second Thanksgiving 2:13-17
5. Mutual Prayer 3:1-5
6. Command and Exhortation 3:6-16
7. Epistolary Closing 3:17-18.

An important feature of the letter's structural organization is its relationship to 1 Thessalonians. Like its prototype it offers the unusual features of having two thanksgiving periods, the second of which is followed by an equally distinctive prayer (2:16), a similarly phrased closing statement (3:1), paraenetic reference to the *ataktoi* (3:6f.), and a concluding prayer addressed to the "Lord of peace" as opposed to the "God of peace" (3:16). These imitative features, however, are incorporated into a unified work whose parts are delineated by content and function.

The opening and closing sections of the letter follow standard epistolary practice and so are easily identified. The former employs the usual tripartite structure of sender, addressee, and salutation; the latter consists of a complicated greeting and blessing. The five middle divisions given above are each delineated by a statement of direct address (*adelphoi*: 1:3; 2:1, 13; 3:1, 6). Also, four of these middle sections end with a prayer (1:11-12; 2:16; 3:5, 16), while the fifth passage concludes with a distinct statement of God's purpose ("therefore": 2:11-12). Additionally, two other statements of direct address (2:15; 3:13) are employed, both preceding unusual prayers in the optative (2:16-17; 3:16).

Each of the five middle sections of the letter contributes to the author's treatment of the major issues. The first of these (1:3-12) presents the community's afflictions in a sympathetic way and appeals to divine vengeance as the resolution of such ungodly activity. The passage ends by focusing on present realities ("being made worthy of God's call"). The next division (2:1-12) discourses at length on the hearers' apocalyptic fervor and proceeds to argue, employing a standard end-time scenario, that the actual process has not yet begun to unfold. Again, the author shifts from an exclusive consideration of eschatology to that of present evil ("those on the road to ruin"). The second thanksgiving (2:13-17) presents further reasons (adherence to traditional teaching) for concluding that "the end is not yet." The section is concerned about proper Christian thinking and practice. A further division concerning mutual prayer (3:1-5) resituates the community in the present; it should be concerned about mission, daily life and work, and righteous behavior. Finally, a section of stern exhortation (3:6-16) focuses on flagrantly irresponsible behavior within the community: the failure of some to discharge their duties and earn their keep, while indulging in the disruptive chatter of busybodies. They are called back to a state of peace (3:16).

d. *Reading 2 Thessalonians: A Question of Methodology*

The reading of 2 Thessalonians presents a challenge to modern audiences. Does it make a difference in one's interpretation if one accepts or denies Pauline authorship? Is it possible or laudable to attempt to bracket this question? A recent experiment in approaching this text in three different ways (presuming non-Pauline or Pauline authorship and avoiding an assumption either way) proves instructive to the method followed in this commentary, which treats 2 Thessalonians as a document written to apocalypticist Christians by a writer who is intent on sympathetically treating the community's concerns but also in dispelling its exaggerated notions of a realized eschatology.

(1) By means of a consistent analysis of the document's apocalyptic terms, themes, and perspective, E. Krentz offers a pseudonymous reading of 2 Thessalonians which highlights a writer in the Pauline tradition who employs the traditional topics of divine election, judgment, and eschatological lordship to offer a message of future salvation "directed to the life of waiting under pressure." For him the document is written to a community under persecution by an author who is undergoing the same difficulties. The author's main concern therefore is the judgment of the oppressors by the returning Lord Jesus who is to manifest God's just judgment. In the meantime the community is to remain faithful to its commitment as it awaits the Lord's return. The major theme is "faithful endurance under persecution" and the writer's "goal is to rouse his readers to steadfast waiting as the apocalyptic calendar unrolls." Composed in the apocalyptic tradition, the letter then is a moral treatise written by and for apocalypticists who are undergoing persecution.[29]

---

29. E. Krentz, "Through a Lens: Theology and Fidelity in 2 Thessalonians," *PT*, 52–62; the citations are from pp. 61 and 61–62.

(2) From a different perspective, R. Jewett offers a Pauline reading of the letter which acknowledges its future-oriented perspective but which maintains that the community's "false sense of 'already' needed to be countered by the 'not yet,' stated in thoroughly apocalyptic terms." He maintains that the future dimension of salvation as preached by Paul had been misunderstood by millenarian believers who thought the Lord's day had arrived. Paul's goal is to show them that the parousia has not yet come (future signs are noted in chapter 2) and that grace "provides the basis both of the current experience of faith, love, and patient endurance and of the anticipation of future participation in the kingdom of God." The letter is a Pauline response to Thessalonian misunderstandings about the Lord's day and a firm reminder that it is grace which provides support for the community in the midst of its affliction.[30]

(3) In a rebuttal of the above, J. M. Bassler proposes to refrain from authorship considerations and to analyze the letter from a strictly literary perspective. She takes as clue to her analysis the *inclusio* formed by references to "grace and peace" at the beginning and ending of the letter. Her focus is on the theme of peace which she demonstrates as being the author's primary goal in each section of the letter, whether rest for the persecuted as opposed to affliction for the persecutor (1:3-12), calm and steadfastness as contrasted with apocalyptic chaos (2:1–3:5), or a state of quietude as opposed to the disorderliness of some within the community. Peace is the author's goal though grace provides "the matrix for the letter's arguments" and "apocalyptic eschatology . . . the primary theological resource out of which they are constructed."[31]

Something important can be learned from each, whether the document's relentless apocalyptic concerns as noted by Krentz, the obvious tension which exists between futuristic and present themes as shown by Jewett, or the insight of Bassler that the author has as a consistent goal the theme of community peace. Each however presents methodological problems which limit, in my opinion, the analysis of the text, its occasion, and its message. In the case of Krentz the apocalyptic reading is too monolithic for it ignores not only the epistolary opening and closing but also fails to distinguish between the points of view of the author and audience and between the situation of the community and that of the apocalyptic chaos of the end-days. In the case of Jewett one must appreciate the focus on nonapocalyptic themes but lament the reading of terms in a Pauline way when the context of 2 Thessalonians either does not

30. R. Jewett, "A Matrix of Grace: The Theology of 2 Thessalonians as a Pauline Letter," *PT*, 63–70; see pp. 66 and 65 for citations.

31. J. M. Bassler, "Peace in All Ways: Theology in the Thessalonian Letters: A Response to R. Jewett, E. Krentz, and E. Richard," *PT*, 71–85; citations are from p. 81.

suggest such or even points in a different direction. Finally, Bassler's method while shedding light on an important goal of the document fails to consider what the text allows the reader to discern concerning the author and audience, the views of each, the situation which brought about the composition, and the contrast between the author's strategy and thought. Bracketing the question of authorship can lead to a serious consideration of the letter's structures and rhetorical goals but in the long run can only lead to a limited view of the document and its purpose. Approaching the letter from a Pauline or a Paulinist perspective is in the final analysis a necessity since the questions of authorship, audience, and epistolary occasion are too basic to be ignored or slighted. Ultimately, the light shed on 2 Thessalonians determines the viability of the perspective employed.

e. *Discovering Author and Strategy*

(1) *The Issues.* The above assists us in sorting out the data for such a task. In defense of non-Pauline authorship scholars too readily conclude that 2 Thessalonians is exclusively focused on future, apocalyptic issues. Indeed, the author deals repeatedly and at length with the community's eschatological concerns, particularly in chapters 1 concerning affliction and divine vengeance and 2 about the end-time scenario. To this one must add chapter 3 regarding idleness and busy chatter while awaiting the Lord's return. While these scholars point to differences between this author and Paul in Christological and theological issues, one should not see these differences as indicating a noninterest of the author in present realities whether the Christ-event, tradition, or peace and calm. It is possible to distinguish between the community's apocalyptic stance, the author's attempt to dissuade it from such a perspective, and the author's own traditional approach to Christian thinking and behavior.

An important conclusion that emerges from an analysis of 2 Thessalonians is that despite the document's interest in and development of apocalyptic themes, there are many clues of an anti-apocalyptic perspective. The author considers the community's apocalyptic beliefs sympathetically, at least the sufferings which have led it to the conclusion that the messianic woes have begun. In chapter 1 the community's endurance in adversity is greatly praised. Also, the author dwells at length on the eschatological punishment of the community's oppressors. Toward the end of the chapter, however, there is a change in tone and topic. The author in 1:11-12 speaks of "being worthy of God's call" and of Christian living. What one discerns, after an apocalyptic discussion of issues of concern to the community, is a focus, for the audience's benefit and instruction, on the present. One distinguishes here, and in the other major

divisions of the letter, a better glimpse of the author's thinking as opposed to the letter's strategy. The author's concern for eschatology derives from the audience's situation and leads to intense development of
the issues that are important to the addressees. Repeatedly, however,
one encounters nonapocalyptic themes and the disavowal of exaggerated
eschatological ideas. Methodologically, one must approach 2 Thessalonians, not as an apocalyptic tract or moral treatise, but as a letter written
by a given writer to a community whose situation and beliefs are addressed in concrete terms.

(2) *Occasion and Purpose of the Letter.* 2 Thessalonians provides suffi-
cient clues for a solid understanding of the occasion which gave rise to
its composition. It is possible from a reading of the document to delineate between what the writer thinks and what, through that writer's
presentation, the audience believes and is doing. From the outset one
learns that the community is undergoing hard times at the hands of people
who will undergo divine punishment (1:4-10). These afflictions are interpreted as signs of the end-time and have led to further apocalyptic agitation within its ranks. In fact, the author speaks of doomsday preachers
who are active within the community via ecstatic pronouncements, extended preaching, and use of a letter allegedly by Paul. These have
brought about a radical change in members' perspectives, from a firm
adherence to the community's venerable traditions (2:15) to a full-blown
apocalypticism (2:2). They are spending their time and energy discussing these issues, trying to influence their neighbors, and are neglecting
their personal, community, and spiritual duties (3:6-12).

The letter is composed to combat this apocalyptic fervor and its multi-
faceted effects. The author adopts an anti-apocalyptic strategy, whether
in sympathizing with the members' afflictions, suggesting that divine
judgment awaits such ungodly people, or especially in pointing out, by
using the audience's knowledge of the standard end-time scenario, that
the important final stages of the process have not yet begun to unfold.
The author further suggests that the community's problems are a sign
not of the end-time but of the mysterious power of evil in the present.
Additionally, the author suggests that satanic arrival of the evil person
of the end-days is being restrained for the present; thus, the Lord's day
has not arrived, contrary to their apocalyptic teachers' conclusions.

Finally, one detects at the end of chapter 1 and throughout this letter
a preference for traditional Christian teaching with its focus not on Jesus'
eschatological role but his present lordship. Thus, the term *kyrios* is the
author's preferred title for Jesus both because of the community's apocalyptic situation and the author's strategy of focusing on Jesus as present Lord (see 1:12; 3:16, 18). Additionally, the author appeals often to

the community's tradition to counteract the new, false claims of the apocalypticists within the community and severely reprimands in the final exhortation these people's irresponsible behavior whether in ignoring the community's tradition, neglecting its mutual duties, or bringing the fellowship into disrepute in the eyes of outsiders (3:6-12). Finally, the author fights fire with fire by counteracting the Pauline claims of the apocalypticists through appropriating Paul's authority whether by carefully imitating 1 Thessalonians, by appealing repeatedly to apostolic tradition, or by insisting that the greeting is in Paul's own handwriting (3:17).

5. *Reading the Thessalonian Correspondence*

In light of the previous discussion regarding the complexity of 1 Thessalonians and the Paulinist character of 2 Thessalonians, how then should one read the correspondence? While the reading of an ancient text is a perennial challenge for modern readers, a reasonable grasp of the background of these documents is crucial for understanding their theological perspective and message. The approach taken is that one must do justice to the variety of contexts out of which these emerged, whether the early missionary career of Paul the Apostle in the Greek mainland or that of a later disciple who wrote in his name to address apocalyptic issues. Each letter was composed for a specific situation and its message must be viewed first from the perspective of its intended readers and then from that of its modern, extended readership.

The overall perspective of this commentary derives from the conclusions reached earlier that 1 Thessalonians, itself a composite of two early missives, offers a complex record of early Pauline activity and consists of an interesting repository of his developing thought. In effect, this first Pauline document presupposes two distinct periods in his missionary career. The first of these looks back to a time shortly after the missionaries' departure from Thessalonica, probably while they are on an Athenian mission (1 Thess 3:1). The second presupposes a length of time has lapsed since Paul first wrote them following Timothy's hurried journey. The tone and content of the two missives are considerably different and, we conclude, address different situations in Paul's missionary work vis-à-vis the Thessalonian community.[32]

A further, basic conclusion also reached after considerable analysis is the pseudonymous, Paulinist character of 2 Thessalonians. This document bears many similarities to the Pauline letter which it has employed

---

32. E. Richard, "Early Pauline Thought: An Analysis of 1 Thessalonians," *PT*, 39–51; see also I. H. Marshall, "Pauline Theology in the Thessalonian Correspondence" in M. D. Hooker and S. G. Wilson, eds., *Paul and Paulinism: Essays in Honour of C. K. Barrett* (London: SPCK, 1982) 173–83.

as model in structural, thematic, and strategic terms. The author addresses, in the name of Paul, the problem of apocalyptic fervor which has clouded the community's vision of Christian living. In a careful reading of this document the modern reader is able to discern both the community's situation and the author's strategy and thought.

What then can modern readers obtain from this series of documents which are addressed to the ancient Church of Thessalonica? If Paul and a later Paulinist writer were responding to a series of complex religious and social issues of concern to early converts (first missive), to involved believers (second missive), and to overly agitated apocalypticists (Paulinist letter), then what theological insights might modern readers derive from these historical documents? Hopefully, the extended readers for whom this commentary is written will profit in two important, related ways. In gaining a better grasp of what the original addressees understood when reading these documents, modern readers are in a better position to judge the ideas proposed and strategies adopted by these early Christian writers and the value these have in the present. Therefore, the following observations are made about each document as they relate to their original purpose and the extended reader's benefit.

a. *An Early Missive by a Young Missionary (1 Thess 2:13–4:2)*

Paul's first letter to the young community of Thessalonica is a study in contrast. He and colleagues have recently departed and are worried about the new converts. After having tried repeatedly to make a return trip they agree to remain in Athens while Timothy, their colleague, becomes their emissary to the Macedonian city to inquire about the converts and to bring them help and comfort. The return of Timothy with the splendid news of the community's survival, success, and affection leads Paul, in a state of joy and thanksgiving, to write the community a letter of acknowledgment, which ends by promising a future visit.

On the one hand, this short narrative presentation of the document's context highlights the emotional, human character of the early Pauline mission and its subsequent pastoral care. One senses the strong affection that exists between the missionaries and their converts, yet one also notes from the start the care that is discerned in distinguishing between the divine message and its human agents (2:13). Additionally, this short missive is about the challenge converts encountered as they turned from their pagan lifestyle to a life of faith in the one God and the love of others. At the same time one cannot fail to see the importance Paul placed on the missionaries' achievements, for they are coworkers with the God who will assess their accomplishments. On the other hand, modern readers will appreciate the concern and affection which coworkers in Christ should have for one another and will perhaps be more cautious of religious preaching which exhibits little joy and no love. Paul's short missive of concern and joy can only enhance what believers have been taught is the ideal of Christian fellowship in action and pastoral care.

b. *Pastoral Care and Epistolary Activity (1 Thess 1:1–2:12 + 4:3–5:28)*

At a later date the missionaries are requested by letter to provide advice and answers to a series of questions which are of concern to the community. These questions are brought to the missionaries by a messenger or Christian traveler who also provides news in the form of an oral report. The second missive then takes shape as Paul responds to the news initially and then to the queries sent from Thessalonica.

Paul's letter then serves as a means of pastoral care given at a distance and it is to this purpose that the themes of the document are dedicated. After a thanksgiving which praises the community for its dynamic growth in faith and love and for its laudatory imitation of the missionaries, Paul sets about his paraenetic task. Seizing upon the missionaries' behavior and motivation during the foundation visit, Paul describes ideal missionary work: on the one hand, dedication to God's gospel and presentation of its message as frank speech and, on the other, pastoral care comparable to the dedication of parents for their children. This description of the first visit is presented, in light of the community's own missionary endeavor, as preparation for the tone and content of the exhortation regarding holiness, the issues formulated by some of the addressees, and finally community life.

Paul's letter of response provides insights which modern readers will find challenging and applicable. While the discussion of the foundation visit provides welcome information on the Pauline missionary method, it also offers a model of Christian work in terms of self-concept, motivation, and approach. Paul, like a loving mother and a challenging father, provides advice, answers questions, and exhorts the community, ''encouraging, consoling, and imploring [them] to conduct [them]selves worthily of the God who calls [them] to his own kingdom and glory'' (2:12). Paul counsels a love that reaches out beyond the fellowship and a life and work that are proper in the eyes of outsiders. He consoles those who are grieving and admonishes those too concerned about the time of the parousia by reminding them of the community's eschatological teaching. Finally, he addresses community issues of concord, patience toward all, and the activity of the Spirit. What the modern reader finds in this pastoral letter is a sampling of Paul's insights into Christian living and community building. The issues addressed are those of an ancient community which he and his missionary band founded and which he continues to nurture as he moves farther on his missionary campaigns. Paul's insights into issues have a way of shedding light on those issues confronted by modern Christians as they in their turn confront the challenges of daily life in a non-Christian world and within a community of diverse believers who are also called "to a state of holiness" (4:7).

c. *Paulinist Response to Apocalyptic Fervor (2 Thessalonians)*

Among the problems encountered by the early Church was the harsh treatment of its members who were liable to interpret this as the work of the satanic forces of the end-time. To counter such apocalyptic fervor, an unknown author, following current practice, employs Paul's authority by composing a shrewd letter in his name. One detects sympathy toward the misguided sufferers, diplomatic confrontation of the popular apocalyptic agitators, and strategic use of apocalyptic lore, general tradition, and Pauline authority to oppose false expectations and their disastrous consequences for Christian thinking and living.

Since apocalypticism is a perennial problem, this NT document merits study for the light it sheds on this phenomenon. Not only does understanding of its context and strategy raise one's estimation of the author, but study of its approach to these problems proves interesting to modern readers as well. One needs to learn from the document's sympathy for those suffering abuse, its concern for them as brothers and sisters, its appeal to the Church's broader tradition, as well as the author's balanced sense of eschatology and righteous behavior.

Modern readers encounter a challenge in picking up the Thessalonian correspondence since these complex documents were composed as responses to specific, historically conditioned issues. But the goal of scholarship, particularly of this commentary, is to assist modern readers, in their role as extended readers, to perceive the original intent and insights of these early Christian writers as they address their original hearers.

6. *General Bibliography*

Commentaries:

Adinolfi, M. *La prima lettera ai Tessalonicensi nel mondo greco-romano.* Rome: Antonianum, 1990.

Aus, R. D. "II Thessalonians." *I-II Timothy, Titus, II Thessalonians.* A. J. Hultgren and R. Aus. Minneapolis: Augsburg, 1984, 191–223.

Best, E. *A Commentary on the First and Second Epistles to the Thessalonians.* New York: Harper, 1972.

Bruce, F. F. *1 & 2 Thessalonians.* Waco: Word Books, 1982.

Collins, R. F. "The First Letter to the Thessalonians." *NJBC*, 772–79.

Dibelius, M. *An die Thessalonicher I-II. An die Philipper.* Tübingen: Mohr, 1937, 1–58.

Ellingworth, P. and Nida, E. A. *A Translator's Handbook on Paul's Letters to the Thessalonians.* Stuttgart: United Bible Societies, 1975.

Frame, J. E. *A Critical and Exegetical Commentary on the Epistles of St. Paul to the Thessalonians.* Edinburgh: T. & T. Clark, 1912.

Friedrich, G. "Der erste Brief an die Thessalonicher" and "Der zweite Brief an die Thessalonicher." *Die Briefe an die Galater, Epheser, Philipper, Kolosser, Thessalonicher und Philemon.* J. Becker, et al. Göttingen: Vandenhoeck & Ruprecht, 1981, 201–76.

Giblin, C. H. "The Second Letter to the Thessalonians." *NJBC*, 871–75.

Holtz, T. *Der erste Brief an die Thessalonicher.* Zürich: Benzinger, 1986.

Marshall, I. H. *1 and 2 Thessalonians.* Grand Rapids: Eerdmans, 1983.

Marxsen, W. *Der erste Brief an die Thessalonicher.* Zürich: Theologischer Verlag, 1979.

_____. *Der zweite Thessalonicherbrief.* Zürich: Theologischer Verlag, 1982.

Masson, C. *Les deux épîtres de saint Paul aux Thessaloniciens.* Neuchâtel: Delachaux et Niestlé, 1957.

Menken, M. J. J. *2 Thessalonians: Facing the End with Sobriety.* New York: Routledge, 1994.

Milligan, G. *St. Paul's Epistles to the Thessalonians: The Greek Text with Introduction and Notes.* London: Macmillan, 1908.

Morris, L. *The First and Second Epistles to the Thessalonians.* Grand Rapids: Eerdmans, 1959.

Reese, J. M. *1 and 2 Thessalonians.* Wilmington: Glazier, 1979.

Trilling, W. *Der zweite Brief an die Thessalonicherbrief.* Zürich: Benzinger, 1980.

von Dobschütz, E. *Die Thessalonicherbrief.* Göttingen: Vandenhoeck & Ruprecht, 1909.

Wanamaker, C. A. *The Epistles to the Thessalonians: A Commentary on the Greek Text.* Grand Rapids: Eerdmans, 1990.

Whiteley, D. E. H. *Thessalonians in the Revised Standard Version.* Oxford: Clarendon, 1969.

Studies:

Bailey, J. A. "Who Wrote II Thessalonians?" *NTS* 25 (1978–79) 131–45.

Barclay, J. M. G. "Conflict in Thessalonica." *CBQ* 55 (1993) 512–30.

Bassler, J. M., ed. *Pauline Theology.* Vol 1: *Thessalonians, Philippians, Galatians, Philemon.* Minneapolis: Fortress, 1991.

Bjerkelund, C. J. *Parakalō: Form, Funktion und Sinn der Parakalō-Sätze in den paulinischen Briefen.* Oslo: Universitetsforlaget, 1967.

Boers, H. "The Form Critical Study of Paul's Letters. 1 Thess as a Case Study." *NTS* 22 (1975–76) 140–58.

Collins, R. F. *Studies on the First Letter to the Thessalonians.* Leuven: Leuven University, 1984.

_____. "The Second Epistle to the Thessalonians." *Letters That Paul Did Not Write: The Epistle to the Hebrews and the Pauline Pseudepigrapha.* Wilmington: Glazier, 1988.

_____., ed. *The Thessalonian Correspondence.* Leuven: Leuven University, 1990.

_____. *The Birth of the New Testament: The Origin and Development of the First Christian Generation.* New York: Crossroad, 1993.

Donfried, K. P. "The Theology of 1 Thessalonians" and "The Theology of 2 Thessalonians." *The Theology of the Shorter Pauline Letters.* K. P. Donfried and I. H. Marshall. Cambridge: Cambridge University, 1993, 3–113.

Fee, G. D. "On Text and Commentary on 1 and 2 Thessalonians." *SBLSP* (1992) 165–83.

Fitzmyer, J. A. *Paul and His Theology: A Brief Sketch.* Englewood Cliffs: Prentice Hall, 1989.

Giblin, C. H. *The Threat to Faith: An Exegetical and Theological Re-examination of 2 Thessalonians 2.* Rome: Biblical Institute Press, 1967.

Hartman, L. "The Eschatology of 2 Thessalonians as Included in a Communication." *TC*, 470–85.

Havener, I. "The Pre-Pauline Christological Credal Formulae of 1 Thessalonians." *SBLSP* (1981), 105–28.

Henneken, B. *Verkündigung und Prophetie im 1. Thessalonicherbrief.* Stuttgart: Katholisches Bibelwerk, 1969.

Hock, R. F. "The Workshop as a Social Setting for Paul's Missionary Preaching." *CBQ* 41 (1979) 438–50.

_____. *The Social Context of Paul's Ministry: Tentmaking and Apostleship.* Philadelphia: Fortress, 1980.

Holland, G. S. *The Tradition that You Received from Us: 2 Thessalonians in the Pauline Tradition.* Tübingen: Mohr-Siebeck, 1988.

Holmberg, B. *Paul and Power: The Structure of Authority in the Primitive Church as Reflected in the Pauline Epistles.* Philadelphia: Fortress, 1978.

Holtz, T. "Traditionen im 1. Thessalonicherbrief." *Die Mitte des Neuen Testaments: Einheit und Vielfalt neutestamentlicher Theologie. Festschrift für Eduard Schweizer.* Eds. U. Luz and H. Weder. Göttingen: Vandenhoeck & Ruprecht, 1983, 55–78.

Hughes, F. W. *Early Christian Rhetoric and 2 Thessalonians.* Sheffield: JSOT, 1989.

Jewett, R. *Paul's Anthropological Terms: A Study of Their Use in Conflict Settings.* Leiden: Brill, 1971.

_____. *A Chronology of Paul's Life.* Philadelphia: Fortress, 1979.

_____. *The Thessalonian Correspondence: Pauline Rhetoric and Millenarian Piety.* Philadelphia: Fortress, 1986.

_____. "A Matrix of Grace: The Theology of 2 Thessalonians as a Pauline Letter." *PT*, 63–70.

Johanson, B. C. *To All the Brethren: A Text-Linguistic and Rhetorical Approach to 1 Thessalonians.* Stockholm: Almqvist & Wiksell International, 1987.

Kaye, B. N. "Eschatology and Ethics in 1 and 2 Thessalonians." *NovT* 17 (1975) 47–57.

Kemmler, D. W. *Faith and Human Reason: A Study of Paul's Method of Preaching as Illustrated by 1-2 Thessalonians and Acts 17, 2-4.* Leiden: Brill, 1975.

Koester, H. "1 Thessalonians—Experiment in Christian Writing." *Continuity and Discontinuity in Church History: Essays Presented to George Huntston Williams.* Eds. F. F. Church and G. George. Leiden: Brill, 1979, 33–44.

_____. "Apostel und Gemeinde in den Briefen an die Thessalonicher." *Kirche: Festschrift für Günther Bornkamm.* Eds. D. Lührmann and G. Strecker. Tübingen: Mohr—Siebeck, 1980, 287-98.

Krentz, E. "Through a Lens: Theology and Fidelity in 2 Thessalonians." *PT,* 52-62.

Krodel, G. "2 Thessalonians." *The Deutero-Pauline Letters: Ephesians, Colossians, 2 Thessalonians, 1-2 Timothy, Titus.* G. Krodel et al. Minneapolis: Fortress, 1993, 39-58.

Kuhn, H. W. "Die Bedeutung der Qumrantexte für das Verständnis des Ersten Thessalonicherbriefes. Vorstellung des Münchener Projets: Qumran und das Neue Testament—The Impact of the Qumran Scrolls on the Understanding of Paul's First Letter to the Thessalonians. Presentation of the Munich Project on Qumran and the New Testament." *The Madrid Qumran Congress, Proceedings of the International Congress on the Dead Sea Scrolls, Madrid 18-21 March, 1991.* Eds. J. Trebolle Barrea and L. Vegas Montaner. Leiden: Brill, 1992, 1:339-53.

Kümmel, W. G. "Das literarische und geschichtliche Problem des ersten Thessalonicherbriefes." *Neotestamentica et Patristica.* Ed. W. C. von Unnik. Leiden: Brill, 1962, 213-27.

Langevin, P.-E. *Jésus Seigneur et l'eschatologie. Exégèse de textes prépauliniens.* Bruges: Declée de Brouwer, 1967.

Laub, F. *Eschatologische Verkündigung und Lebensgestaltung nach Paulus. Eine Untersuchung zum Wirken des Apostles beim Aufbau der Gemeinde in Thessalonike.* Regensburg: Pustet, 1973.

_____. "Paulinische Autorität in nachpaulinischer Zeit (2 Thes)." *TC,* 403-17.

Lindemann, A. "Zum Abfassungszweck des Zweiten Thessalonicherbriefes." *ZNW* 68 (1977) 35-47.

Lüdemann, G. *Paul Apostle to the Gentiles: Studies in Chronology.* Philadelphia: Fortress, 1984.

Lyons, G. *Pauline Autobiography: Toward a New Understanding.* Atlanta: Scholars, 1985.

Malherbe, A. J. "Exhortation in First Thessalonians." *NovT* 25 (1983) 238-56.

_____. *Paul and the Thessalonians: The Philosophic Tradition of Pastoral Care.* Philadelphia: Fortress, 1987.

_____. "Did the Thessalonians Write to Paul?" *The Conversation Continues: Studies in Paul and John in Honor of J. Louis Martyn.* Eds. R. T. Fortna and B. P. Gaventa. Nashville: Abingdon, 1990.

Marshall, I. H. "Pauline Theology in the Thessalonian Correspondence." *Paul and Paulinism: Essays in Honour of C. K. Barrett.* Eds. M. D. Hooker and S. G. Wilson. London: SPCK, 1982, 173-83.

Mearns, C. L. "Early Eschatological Development in Paul: The Evidence of I and II Thessalonians." *NTS* 27 (1981) 137-57.

Meeks, W. A. *The First Urban Christians: The Social World of the Apostle Paul.* New Haven: Yale University, 1983.

_____. *The Moral World of the First Christians.* Philadelphia: Westminster, 1986.

Neyrey, J. H. "Eschatology in 1 Thessalonians: The Theological Factor in 1, 9-10; 2, 4-5; 3, 11-13; 4, 6 and 4, 13-18." *SBLSP* (1980), 219-31.

Ollrog, W. -H. *Paulus und seine Mitarbeiter: Untersuchungen zu Theorie und Praxis der paulinischen Mission.* Neukirchen: Erziehungsverein, 1979.

Reumann, J. "The Theologies of 1 Thessalonians and Philippians: Concerns, Comparison and Composite." *SBLSP* (1987), 521–36.

Richard, E. "The Letters of Paul" and "The Paulinist Letters." *Jesus: One and Many. The Christological Concept of New Testament Authors.* Wilmington: Glazier, 1988, 235–332 and 333–61, respectively.

_____. "Contemporary Research on 1 (& 2) Thessalonians." *BTB* 20 (1990) 107–15.

_____. "Early Pauline Thought: An Analysis of 1 Thessalonians." *PT*, 39–51.

Schade, H.-H. *Apokalyptische Christologie bei Paulus: Studien zum Zusammenhang von Christologie und Eschatologie in den Paulusbriefen.* Göttingen: Vandenhoeck & Ruprecht, 1981.

Schmidt, D. "The Authenticity of 2 Thessalonians: Linguistic Arguments." *SBLSP* (1983), 289–96.

_____. "The Syntactical Style of 2 Thessalonians: How Pauline Is It?" *TC*, 383–93.

Schmithals, W. "The Historical Situation of the Thessalonian Epistles." *Paul and the Gnostics.* Nashville: Abingdon, 1972, 123–218.

Schnelle, U. "Der erste Thessalonicherbrief und die Entstehung der paulinischen Anthropologie." *NTS* 32 (1986) 207–24.

Schütz, J. H. *Paul and the Anatomy of Apostolic Authority.* Cambridge: Cambridge University, 1975.

Snyder, G. F. "Apocalyptic and Didactic Elements in 1 Thessalonians." *SBLSP* (1972), 233–44.

Steele, E. S. "The Use of Jewish Scriptures in 1 Thessalonians." *BTB* 14 (1984) 12–17.

Stowers, S. K. "Social Status, Public Speaking and Private Teaching: The Circumstances of Paul's Preaching Activity." *NovT* 26 (1984) 59–82.

Trilling, W. *Untersuchungen zum zweiten Thessalonicherbrief.* Leipzig: St. Benno, 1972.

_____. "Literarische Paulusimitation in 2 Thessalonicherbrief." *Paulus in den neutestamentlichen Spätschriften: Zur Paulusrezeption im Neuen Testament.* Ed. K. Kertelge. Freiburg: Herder, 1981, 146–56.

Tuckett, C. M. "Synoptic Tradition in 1 Thessalonians?" *TC*, 160–82.

White, J. L. "Saint Paul and the Apostolic Letter Tradition." *CBQ* 45 (1983) 433–44.

Wiles, G. P. *Paul's Intercessory Prayers: The Significance of the Intercessory Prayer Passages in the Letters of St. Paul.* Cambridge: Cambridge University, 1974.

TRANSLATION, NOTES, INTERPRETATION

FIRST THESSALONIANS

I. LATER MISSIVE, PART 1—1:1–2:12

1. *Epistolary Opening* (1:1)

1. Paul, also Silvanus and Timothy; to the community of Thessalonians assembled by God the Father and the Lord Jesus Christ; grace to you and peace.

NOTES

1. *Paul, also Silvanus and Timothy:* Paul's letter begins by listing three names as senders. The first *Paulos* is assumed to be the writer (see discussion below of polysyndeton or the repeated use of *kai* as justifying the translation: "Paul, also Silvanus and Timothy"). The name occurs 158 times in the NT, 19 in the seven uncontested Pauline documents and 128 in Acts. The name is Roman and is associated, in Acts 7–13, with a Jewish name Saul. The use of two names by Luke derives from Jewish usage whereby individuals bore Jewish as well as Greek or Latin names (e.g., John Mark and Simon Peter in the NT). Paul employs only the Roman form of his own name and that of the second letter sender. This second name of the series, *Silouanos* (see 1 Pet 5:12), seems to refer to the same historical person called Silas in Acts, who, among other things, was Paul's early colleague in the Greek mission. He appears elsewhere in Paul only in 2 Cor 1:19 where he is called a companion of Paul and Timothy in the Corinthian ministry and is listed in the same position relative to the other two. He was Paul's associate in founding the communities of Thessalonica and Corinth. He disappears from the Pauline correspondence and is replaced by Timothy (*Timotheos*), the third member of the group, whose name continues to appear in the openings of Paul's letters: Phil 1:1; Phlm

1; and 2 Cor 1:1. In all likelihood, Timothy was, initially, a younger missionary attached to the Pauline group, who frequently functioned as envoy for
the group and for Paul individually (1 Thess 3:1-6; Phil 2:19-24). As is true
for Paul and Silvanus, additional but questionable biographical data are forthcoming from Acts and, in this case for Timothy, from the Paulinists. It should
be stressed that priority must be given to the Pauline accounts of the Greek
mission in discerning the roles played by these apostolic figures. In each letter
opening, save the present one, Paul refers to himself as "servant, prisoner,
or apostle"; also in each case, save Romans, he associates his name with that
of other missionaries. Thus, it is clear that in his early correspondence he
more readily and simply associates his name with that of colleagues when
writing (1 Thess 1:1; Phil 1:1; and Phlm 1) than he does later on when he
is compelled to dwell upon his status within and vis-à-vis the community.

to the community of Thessalonians: The addressees are designated by the term
ekklēsia ("church, assembly, community"), a word which, along with *syn-
agōgē*, represented the Jewish assembly either as a liturgical body or, in more
theological terms, as God's people. Its frequent use in the LXX for both concepts made it a natural choice for designating the new Christian assemblies,
particularly since the alternative "synagogue" was commonly used by the
Jewish community (though see Jas 2:2). Additionally, its use in the Greek
world to designate a political assembly or philosophical school made the term
attractive to denote both a local assembly and the general movement. In the
present case it is employed in the former sense. The term translated "of Thessalonians" (*Thessalonikeōn*) is of interest. Paul usually employs the names of
countries or cities to characterize his addressees but here uses a gentilic noun
and so refers to the people rather than the city (see Phil 4:16 for the name
of the city). Translators resolve this idiosyncrasy either by substituting the
name of the city ("Church in Thessalonica") or by adding an article ("Church
of the Thessalonians"). The latter gives the impression that the genitive indicates possession ("belonging to"), whereas it probably constitutes a partitive genitive ("the community made up of Thessalonians").

assembled by God the Father and the Lord Jesus Christ: Interpretation of this
complex prepositional phrase (*en theō patri kai kyriō Jēsou Christō*) is rendered
difficult owing to grammatical and lexical considerations. The absence of an
article before the *en* phrase to connect it unambiguously to "the community"
allows the possibility, grammatically, that it modifies the initial list of senders,
the addressees, or the following salutation. Additionally, use of the "maid-
of-all-work" preposition *en* complicates matters. The above translation anticipates discussion below of Pauline usage of the preposition and the epistolary context of that usage. From the start Paul insists on the theological and
Christological character of the community's being called together, namely,
the community's monotheistic and loving relationship to the deity (see discussion of "God as Father" at 3:11) and its commitment to God's messianic
agent (on the full expression "Lord Jesus Christ" see below).

grace to you and peace: The opening of Paul's letter ends with a customary
blessing, a blessing, however, which differs from the traditional epistolary

form, "greetings" *(chairein)*. The origin of the Pauline formula is variously explained. (1) Paul modified the Hellenistic salutation by substituting the related, theological *charis* and added the traditional Jewish salutation "peace" *(shalom)*. (2) Paul employs a liturgical Jewish formula, traces of which appear in 5:23, 28 (also Gal 6:16), in place of the customary greeting. (3) The Pauline formula relates to a less well-known tradition which employs "mercy and peace" (2 Bar 78:2; Tob 7:12 in Codex Sinaiticus; Gal 6:16) or "greeting/grace and peace" (2 Macc 1:1; 1 Thess 5:23, 28), a tradition more germane to his apostolic mode of discourse. The last mentioned provides a plausible explanation, since it offers a literary precedent and combines elements from the other two. This expression is standard in Paul's letters though all, except this one, are modified by a theological-Christological formula similar to the one noted above.

INTERPRETATION

The missive opens with the traditional three-part epistolary formula of Hellenistic letters: writer, to addressees, greetings. This epistolary opening is closest in simplicity to that of the popular letter; indeed, Paul's letter openings become increasingly more complex though the basic tripartite structure is retained. In the present instance the reader is confronted by several interesting features: the listing of several writers or senders, the initial designation of the Christian group as an *ekklēsia* "assembled by God the Father and the Lord Jesus Christ," and the formulaic introduction of the themes of grace and peace.

Paul and Cosenders. Paul begins his letter by naming three people: Paul, Silvanus, and Timothy. It is presumed that the three were responsible for the conversion of the Thessalonian population during the foundation visit (see 2:1-12). It is clear from the text, whether the first or second missive, that the sentiments of all three are being expressed, especially when the first person plural is used. But who in effect wrote the letter and why are all three listed at the beginning of this missive?

Despite earlier suggestions that Silvanus and Timothy composed the Thessalonian letters or perhaps served Paul as scribes, it is generally admitted that several factors point to Paul as sole writer. (1) While the repeated use of the plural pronoun "we" in 1 Thessalonians indicates neither an epistolary plural or a plural of majesty but rather some role for all three apostolic figures, the use occasionally of the first person singular points to Paul as writer, though there are indications that he occasionally employed a scribe (see 1 Cor 16:21; Gal 6:11; and Rom 16:22; see also discussion below of 5:27 where Paul shifts at the end from "we" to "I"). Consideration of the minutiae of style, word order, vocabulary, and thought compares favorably with the other authentic Pauline letters and so points to common authorship. (2) If all of Paul's letters mention some cosender, except Romans, one is not compelled in these cases to imagine cosenders as being responsible for the letters in question, particularly the extreme case of Gal 1:1-2 where Paul's cosenders are simply referred to as "all the brothers and sisters who are with me."

If Paul then is the actual writer of the letter, why does he mention his associates, here or in his other letters? Clearly, they are cosenders. Paul speaks in the name of all three, since his use of "we" throughout the document shows that greetings as well as content and sentiment are from all three. This is further reinforced by his use of "I" in the first missive to express his deep concern (2:18; 3:5) or in the second to reinforce his exhortation for all members of the community (5:27). That he speaks for his cosenders probably accounts for his use in the letter opening of the popular, Hellenistic polysyndeton or repeated use of *kai* ("and") rhetorically to emphasize (BDF 460.3) that the work at Thessalonica as well as the sentiments expressed and advice given derive from all three— see 2 Cor 1:19 where Paul insists that "by us" includes "Paul *as well as* Silvanus and Timothy." Rather than indicating cowriters, polysyndeton and the repeated use of "we" underscore both the intimacy which existed between the missionaries and their converts (2:7) and Paul's reluctance to make overt use of apostolic authority (2:6).

The Thessalonian Community's Character as Assembly. Paul's choice of *ekklēsia*, a common LXX term to designate the chosen people or its assembly, owes more to early Christian usage than to other factors. Nonetheless, this term, though frequently employed by Paul, particularly in the Corinthian correspondence, does not appear often in his early letters—only here in 1 Thessalonians. In 1 Thess 1:1 it designates the local assembly of relatively recent converts in the city of Thessalonica. Interestingly, its first use by Paul exhibits its Greek, local sense rather than its more developed universal usage. Such an observation leads us to examine in greater detail both the modifying double prepositional phrase and the term's contextual usage.

Contextually the *en* phrase ("in God the Father . . .") is related to all three elements of the epistolary opening. Connecting the prepositional phrase to the list of senders and claiming that Paul writes "by the authority" or "in the name of God" would demand too much of a reader and would not conform to Pauline epistolary practice. Relating the phrase to the following salutation would be less difficult for a reader and would bring the anomalous salutation of 1 Thessalonians closer to that of the other letters which offer a similar prepositional phrase immediately after the salutation, though with the preposition *apo* and genitive rather than *en* with the dative. The main difficulty is in seeing a parallel between the functions of these phrases. By the use of *apo* in his other letters Paul indicates the origin of peace and grace. Here by the use of *en* something else is intended. Most scholars opt to connect the phrase with its immediately preceding context.

How then does the preposition *en* function as a modifier of "the community"? Within the range of usage attested for this preposition, two are regularly discussed in this context. The first represents a spatial use of *en* to express close personal relationship, usually involving the formula *en Christō*. This "mystical" use is variously interpreted as "spiritual incorporation," i.e., "being in" or "belonging to." The first, though popularly defended, is unlikely since the parallel construction ("in God" and "in Christ") implies that the believer is incorporated in both "in the spatial sense," a non-Pauline usage as regards God (for the usage "in God," see 1 Thess 2:2). The second, though both more likely and less often proposed, is conceptually Pauline since believers belong, in varying ways, both to God (see 1 Thess 3:11 and Phil 2:15) and to Christ (Gal 3:29). There are difficulties, however. Communities are often enough said to be God's, 7 occurrences, all of which are expressed as genitives of possession, but rarely are they identified as Christ's. For the latter, two passages merit consideration. The first is the enigmatic: "not known by sight to the communities of Judaea which are in Christ" (Gal 1:22) and the second, a formulaic passage, from the problematic final chapter of Romans: "all the communities of Christ greet you" (16:16). Even if one were to agree that the former means "the communities of Christ in Judaea," one would be left with the tenuous situation that all of these cases, whether referring to God or Christ, save once in case of the latter, Paul employed genitives of possession, not *en* with the dative.

A more promising avenue is the instrumental use of *en*, a usage interpreted as "community brought into being by," "which lives through," or, as translated here, "assembled by." In each case some activity is attributed to the agents, God and Christ. Moreover, since each of these activities can be defended as Pauline, the last is proposed because it pays closer attention to context, namely, Paul's use of *ekklēsia*. It is suggested that, in its initial usage within the community, the word retained, for its Gentile, Greek readers as well as for Paul, the Hellenistic Jew, its verbal sense of being "assembled." Thus, it was "brought into being" or, better still, "assembled by God the Father and the Lord Jesus Christ." Even its prepositional prefix (*ek-klēsia*) is not lost on the attentive reader since the group of believers was "called out of" and consisted "of Thessalonian residents," residents who continued to live among their former co-religionists. The translation given above, "the community of Thessalonians assembled by," attempts to do justice to Paul's vocabulary and peculiar use of syntactic forms: *ekklēsia* (with verbal force), partitive genitive of gentilic term, and instrumental *en*. The community then is a group of people "called out" from among the Gentiles of Thessalonica, "assembled by God and the Lord Jesus," and finally "consisting of" those who "turned to God from idols . . . and await his Son from heaven" (1:9-10).

The Community's Theological and Christological Character. Paul insists on the two characteristics which render the community different from other Thessalonian associations. Its monotheistic focus, described in Jewish terms as the rejection of the Thessalonian gods (1:9), is characterized by reference to God as Father: *theos patēr* (see 3:11 for discussion of this theme). In this expression both nouns are anarthrous; as regards the first, the article is often omitted after prepositions; as regards the second, the expression is often a name for God. Thus, the idiom is formulaic, is found in liturgical fragments (Phil 2:11) and epistolary salutations (Gal 1:1; 1 Thess 1:1), and resembles other Pauline expressions in form and usage: "from God our Father" and "(our) God and Father" (1 Thess 1:3). "God the Father," it should be noted, chooses (1:4), calls (2:12), gives the Spirit (4:8), wills the believer's sanctification (4:3), and will, at the end, make each "perfectly holy" (5:23). From the outset Paul wishes the community to be fully aware that it has been "assembled by" this loving Parent who gives grace and peace to all who serve the living and true God.

The second characteristic of the community is its relation to "the Lord Jesus Christ." These titles and a personal name appear together for the first time in the Pauline writings. The personal name Jesus (*Iēsous*), the shortened Greek form of the Hebrew *Yehoshua* ("Yah will save"), is common in Paul's letters though rarely without the titles of "Lord" or "Christ," as is true in the present case. The latter, *Christos*, is Paul's preferred appellation and, while even in his letters it regularly functions as a personal name, it nonetheless retains its titular force, particularly in conjunction with the name of Jesus. The former, *kyrios*, also frequently used by Paul, was borrowed by him from early Judaeo-Christian tradition as a confessional title, a process facilitated by the term's broad usage: from early references to the gods of the classical world as *kyrioi* to the more personalized concepts of the Hellenistic world, both pagan and Jewish. For Paul's pagan contemporaries, the term *kyrios* expressed a close relationship between a deity and its devotee, a relationship indicated by the terms "lord" and "servant" (*TDNT* 3:1052). The term was also used increasingly in Roman contexts to refer to the emperor's supreme power and religious dignity, in the LXX to translate the divine name, and in NT usage to describe God's lordship over creation, humanity, and history (Matt 9:37-38; Acts 17:24-27; also Rom 1:19-21).

Paul's early use of the three terms, "Lord Jesus Christ," along with other variations inherited from the early Judaeo-Christian community as confessional acclamations, is of particular interest in our understanding of the roots of his thinking as well as for its usage in 1 Thess 1:1. His use of the name "Jesus" lays stress on the death; that of the title "Christ" emphasizes the resurrection; and that of the term "Lord" expresses the believer's profession of faith in God's agent. Increasingly Paul employs such formulas to express the full extent of the Christ-event: the death, resurrection, and profession of these by the believer. Paul's focus in this particular instance is the reality of the Christian community at Thessalonica, a community which owes its existence to God's parental love and to God's agent, the one whose death and resurrection has constituted him Lord of faith "to the glory of God the Father" (Phil 2:11). "The Lord Jesus Christ" has died and been raised for their sake (1:10; 4:14; 5:10), has been determined by God as their means of salvation and holiness (5:9, 18), delivers from divine wrath and gives grace (1:10; 5:28), and is their source of hope as they await his return from heaven (1:3, 10; 4:15; 5:23) in lieu of the resurrection and eternal life with him (4:14, 17; 5:10). Jesus' role in the community's being called together and constituted into a fellowship addresses past, present, and future, whether it is continuous belief in his death and resurrection, acknowledgment and submission to his lordship as a community, or constancy of hope in his return and their active participation in the end-time scenario.

Further, Paul's spontaneous joining of God and Christ as actors in the drama of human salvation points not to a high Christology but to their unity of purpose and action which has brought about a community of faith and love. The audience to which Paul writes, then, consists of Thessalonian residents whom God has called out of love to submit to Jesus' lordship and thereby to constitute a Christian fellowship.

Election and Well-being as Early, Major Themes. Paul's almost casual introduction of the themes of "grace and peace" in the salutation of the letter as well as the subsequent formulaic use of these terms in Christian letters and liturgy often lead commentators to underestimate their function and importance in Paul's early correspondence. Both terms are frequently used by him, beyond epistolary salutations, and represent major themes in his later correspondence. In fact, their use at the beginning and ending of the second missive (1:1 and 5:23, 28), in what appear to be liturgical formulations, both confirms Paul's great debt to early community tradition and reveals some of his principal theological concepts. These two concepts are basic to Pauline thinking. Grace is related to God's being and acting which form the basis for Christian existence, while peace is the result of God's salvific activity in Christ. From the start, it is Paul's wish, and that of his colleagues, that the converts appreciate ever more fully the gift of God's grace and choice (1:4) and that they continue in that state of well-being or reconciliation to God (1:9) which has made them examples to other believers (1:7-8).

The themes, however, extend beyond the initial greeting. That of election is a key Pauline idea for it typifies God's graciousness toward humanity. In 1:4 Paul will call the audience, "brothers and sisters beloved by God" and will speak of their "election" by God. For this theme Paul will employ a variety of terms and idioms, a choice which will increasingly involve the term *charis* (see comments on 1:4). The notion of God's calling of Israel will expand in Paul to include also the Gentiles in Christ. The graciousness of God is said to include the giving of the Holy Spirit (4:8); the believer is seen as being God-taught (4:9) and destined by God for attaining salvation (5:9). In actuality God calls believers to a state of holiness (4:7), a state in which they have been placed at baptism through their acceptance of the grace of Christ and in which they will be confirmed and perfected at Jesus' return (5:23). Their conversion (evidenced by power and the coming of the Spirit), says Paul, confirms the graciousness of their election (1:5-6). Also, the apostles, acting as "agents of God" (2:2) have shown God's graciousness (1:4) as they have and are treating their converts with the love, affection, and care of a mother and a father for their own children (2:7, 11). A loving God not only calls to holiness but also gives the sanctifying Spirit to assist the beloved in their quest for holiness and the attainment of salvation. To those who are worried about their faithful departed, Paul gives the assurance that "God will fetch with Jesus those who will have fallen asleep believing in him" (4:14). The ultimate gift to believers will be perfection in holiness (5:23) and eternal bliss with the Lord (4:17; 5:10).

The theme of peace likewise will be developed at great length as Paul speaks not only of the eschatological peace given as reconciliation with the Lord of creation (1:1f.; Rom 5:1) and the God of peace (5:23) but also the wish of peace and concord (5:13b) which a community of beloved should manifest toward and for the good of one another and all (5:15). The well-being of believers, whether in their relationship to God or in their communal relations, becomes ever more focused a concern for Paul as he looks toward and encourages the upbuilding of the community (5:11) and acknowledgment of God's lordship (1:9; 2:12; 4:8).

Paul's seemingly casual salutation at the beginning of his letter, "grace to you and peace," points to some of his major ideas and concerns. These two themes sum up the good news of God; the former is the loving gift of God through Christ which initiates and makes possible the human response, while the latter is a present and future reality from the God of peace who alone is able to bring to perfection the holiness of believers (5:23).

FOR REFERENCE AND FURTHER STUDY

Collins, R. F. "The First Letter to the Thessalonians" in *NJBC*, 772–79.

Doty, W. G. *Letters in Primitive Christianity.* Philadelphia: Fortress, 1973.

Fitzmyer, J. A. "Introduction to the New Testament Epistles" and "Paul" in *NJBC*, 768–71 and 1329–37, respectively.

Stowers, S. K. *Letter Writing in Greco-Roman Antiquity.* Philadelphia: Westminster, 1986.

White, J. L. *Light from Ancient Letters.* Philadelphia: Fortress, 1986.

_____. "Saint Paul and the Apostolic Letter Tradition." *CBQ* 45 (1983) 433–44.

2. *Thanksgiving* (1:2-10)

2. We give thanks to God always for all of you as we mention you continually in our prayers, 3. for we call to mind the dynamism of your faith, the dedication of your love, and the constancy of your hope in our Lord Jesus Christ, in the very presence of God our Father, 4. for we, brothers and sisters beloved by God, are sure of your election, 5. since our gospel came to you not only in word, but also in power, both with the Holy Spirit and with full conviction—as indeed you know what sort of persons we were among you for your sake; 6. and since you, for your part, became imitators of us and of the Lord, in the way you accepted the word—despite all its attendant difficulty—with joy inspired by the Holy Spirit, 7. so that you became an example for all the believers in Macedonia and in Achaia. 8. For starting from among you, not only has the word of the Lord sounded forth in Macedonia and in Achaia, but the news of your faith in God has gone forth everywhere else, so that we have no need to say anything. 9. For they themselves report concerning us what sort of visit we had among you and how you turned to God from idols to serve the living and true God 10. and to await his Son from heaven, whom he raised from the dead, Jesus who delivers us from the coming wrath.

NOTES

2. *We give thanks to God always for all of you:* The thanksgiving period of the second missive begins in typical Pauline fashion with the verb *eucharisteō* (without personal pronoun), arthrous *theos* in the dative, and a temporal adverb. On the background of Paul's epistolary use of "giving thanks to God," see notes on 2:13, the thanksgiving of the first missive. As in that passage, his use of the first person plural expresses the sentiments of his cosenders for

whom thanksgiving to God is a fundamental attitude ("always") to be fostered in all who believe (5:17). Also, Paul's use of "for all of you," along with "always" (see also Rom 1:8; 1 Cor 1:4; Phil 1:3-4), is formulaic rather than polemic; that is, Paul is not counteracting community division but employing comprehensive language to underscore the divine initiative in the lives of all who believe.

as we mention you continually in our prayers: It is possible to render the phrase *mneian poieō*, according to its root meaning, as "remember" but classical and epistolary usage requires the sense "mention"; also the NT and papyri often employ the idiom "of mentioning in prayer" (BAGD 524.2—see 3:6 for discussion of a related idiom). The latter is further indicated since the related verb *mnēmoneuō* appears in the following verse. The adverb *adialeiptōs* ("continually") appears in three Pauline thanksgivings (1 Thess 1:2; 2:13; and Rom 1:9), in the first and last in combination with "always." Though Pauline usage of this term is limited and its position in the present text has caused debate (whether it modifies the preceding or succeeding participle), it is convincingly pointed out that the rhythmic structure of the following clauses, each with participle in initial position, favors the former. On the expression "in our prayers," see Interpretation below.

3. *for we call to mind:* A second participial construction expresses the immediate as opposed to ultimate ground (see v. 4) for Paul's gratitude (see Phlm 5 for a similar series of participial constructions). By employing the verb *mnēmoneuō* in the context of thanksgiving and mentioning in formal prayers (v. 2), Paul probably intends more than "remembering." The concept of "calling to *another's* mind or mentioning" (LSJ 1139.II; also BAGD 523.1a) is probably intended, i.e., "calling to mind . . . in God's presence." Paul's prayer then included a recitation of the community's activity as believers, a topic developed at several points in the thanksgiving pericope; see 2:9 for a different use of the verb.

the dynamism of your faith, the dedication of your love, and the constancy of your hope in our Lord Jesus Christ: The verbal expression "call to mind" has as object (in the standard genitive) a threefold statement concerning the community's faith, love, and hope. In stylistic terms, the lengthy object begins with a possessive pronoun ("your"), is followed by three pairs of nouns in genitival relationship, the last part of which is modified by a Christological phrase (also in the genitive), and terminates with a prepositional, theological phrase. While there is debate concerning the relationship of these various items to one another, whether of the Christological and theological phrases or of the triad of virtues and their accompanying nouns, the above translation presupposes the discussion below of the function these virtues play in Paul's prayerful recitation of the community's activity. The possessive pronoun *hymōn* in Paul can either precede or follow an arthrous substantive (3:10; 2:17) or substantive series (1:3; 3:6—see BDF 284). In the present case opinion is divided as to whether the pronoun modifies the first or second of the threefold pairs of nouns. In light of discussion in the "interpretation" below, it is my conclusion (1) that emphasis falls on the second term of each pair ("faith, love, and hope"), (2) that the initial term in each case designates a specific quality or characteristic of the second (whether "dynamism," "dedication," or "constancy"), (3) that the Christological phrase relates to hope rather than to all three pairs, and (4) that the theological phrase modifies the entire participial construction (see following Note).

in the very presence of God our Father: The verse ends with a lengthy, solemn prepositional phrase, whose relation to the rest of the verse is problematic. Owing to its position, distance from the initial participle and following the triple pairs of nouns, it is assumed either that it modifies the immediately preceding statement on hope or the triad of Christian activities. The first enhances the eschatological character of Christian motivation; the second insists on God's presence in the midst of human activity (for discussion of Paul's use of the unusual preposition *emprosthen*, see 2:19 and 3:9). Both themes are Pauline; nonetheless, both choices make for awkward translations and obscure the overall thanksgiving context and structural character of the passage. It is preferable to connect this phrase with the participle "call to mind," since verse 3 continues the theme of prayer, as addressed to God, introduced in the preceding verse and constitutes a parallel to it, and since stylistically "your" and "in the presence of" set clearly the boundaries of the list of items to be mentioned in prayer. In the present translation I have opted not to move the prepositional phrase in question to connect it directly to the participle as do most translators. While such a strategy clarifies the relation of the two grammatical components, it nonetheless weakens the reader's ability to sense the logical progression of Paul's thought as he moves in verse 4 to the community's election. It is the mention of "God our Father" (see 3:11 for discussion of this expression and theme) at the end of the verse which brings to mind in the following the theme of God's parental choice of the audience as beloved children.

4. *for we, brothers and sisters beloved by God, are sure of your election:* A final participial clause expresses the ultimate reason for giving thanks to God. The verb *oida* in the perfect is employed to stress certitude or knowledge already acquired ("we are sure") rather than *ginōskō* (see its only use in 3:5). The reason for Paul's certitude will be given by a double *hoti* clause in verses 5 and 6-7. Paul provides added stress to this clause by addressing his readers as "brothers and sisters beloved by God." His use of *adelphoi* (for discussion of inclusive translation, see comments on 2:17) to describe fellow believers is frequent in all his letters and, in the Thessalonian correspondence, highlights his affection for the young community. His addition, however, of the idiom *ēgapēmenoi hypo tou theou* focuses attention less on attachment than on divine benefaction and the theme of election, introduced immediately following. In place of the more usual adjective *agapētos* ("beloved") which Paul uses to express attachment (1 Thess 2:8; Phil 3:1; and often), one finds the unique (see also 2 Thess 2:13 and Col 3:12), biblically inspired "beloved by God" (Sir 45:1; Bar 3:37; etc.), i.e., the perfect participial form of *agapaō*, to indicate God's eternal and presently effective devotion and to underscore the divine character of their election.

5. *since our gospel came to you not only in word:* The conjunction *hoti* ("since") introduces a first reason for Paul's certitude that the community has been called by God. Verse 5 focuses in pastoral terms on the evidence for God's work among the missionaries and their Macedonian audience. Use of "our" in the expression "our gospel" and of a series of *en* phrases later in the clause indicates that *euangelion* (see 3:2) here stresses the apostolic missionary activity or proclamation of the good news rather than the content of the message. Of further interest is Paul's usage of the impersonal expression "came to you" (a Hellenistic aorist for a middle form; see *BG*, 230), to indicate the missionaries' work at Thessalonica. By use of such a phrase Paul contrasts the intermediary role of the missionaries, already expressed by "our gospel," with that of God, whose activity claims the attention of the remainder of the verse. But having recourse to an often-used contrast formula ("not only but also") Paul stresses first human agency and then its divine power.

but also in power, both with the Holy Spirit and with full conviction: The translation given here presupposes discussion below of the meaning and relationship of the terms: "power," "Holy Spirit," and "full force or conviction" (*dynamis, pneuma hagion,* and *plērophoria,* respectively). Since all three are introduced by *en,* are interconnected by *kai,* and form a contrast with the preceding *en* phrase ("in word") the following conclusions are reached and incorporated above: (1) the three terms in question are not synonymous expressions, (2) the major contrast in the verse is between "word" and "power," and (3) the last two terms stand in apposition to power and describe two of its aspects: its divine source ("the Holy Spirit") and its effect on the apostolic ministry ("full conviction"). For further discussion of the Spirit, see 4:8.

—as indeed you know what sort of persons we were among you for your sake: Shift from the activity of the Spirit among the addressees to the effects of divine power on the preachers ("full conviction") leads to a brief discussion of apostolic behavior, a topic developed at length in the following chapter. The statement is introduced by "as you know" (also 2:2, 5; 3:4), a phrase described as a "recall device," for it along with other uses of *oida* (2:1, 11; 3:3; 4:2; 5:2), other constructs with *kathōs* ("as"—4:1, 6, 11), and a variety of "remembrance" terminology (2:9, 10; 4:9, 13; 5:1) appeal to knowledge and experience writer and readers have in common or to advice given the latter by the former. Such a phrase functions as a paraenetic commonplace since it reminds the readers of what they already know; the Thessalonians have witnessed the missionaries' pastoral activity and are simply reminded of this in terms of power ("what sort of persons we were") and focus ("for your sake"). Paul's appeal is to what the addressees themselves have experienced during the foundation visit. It is this shift in Paul's train of thought which leads him to speak of the community's reaction in terms of apostolic imitation.

6. *and since you, for your part, became imitators of us and of the Lord:* Paul turns again with emphasis to the readers' reaction to the good news, "and *you* for *your* part" (use of *hymeis*) and presents this fact as a second proof for his certitude that God chose the addressees for salvation ("since" is added to clarify the clause's relationship to verses 4-5). The members of the community

are called "imitators of us and of the Lord" (*mimētai hēmōn . . . kai tou kyriou*). The theme of imitation occurs explicitly in four Pauline passages (also Phil 3:17; 1 Cor 4:16; 11:1) and is often hinted at in his correspondence (e.g., 3:3-4). Thus, whether employing imitation terminology or more general expressions (see Phil 4:9), Paul on many occasions speaks of his readers emulating him. (1) Context therefore becomes important in interpreting this theme and understanding Pauline usage, particularly in its Thessalonian context, and (2) the added phrase "of the Lord" presents further difficulty. For the latter 1 Cor 11:1 provides the clue for understanding this particular Pauline usage (see Interpretation below).

in the way you accepted the word—despite all its attendant difficulty—with joy inspired by the Holy Spirit: The imitation passage is followed by a long, complex participial construction which ostensibly provides the needed context and so is often given a causal connection with what precedes. This connection, however, seems best characterized by the expression "in the way you," since what follows is meant to explain the imitation clause. The participial expression translated "you accepted the word" occurs also in the other thanksgiving section (2:13). In the case of the latter it expresses the community's ability to distinguish between message and messenger; in the former, between the dynamism and results of the original mission. Additionally, the two following prepositional phrases, while variously related to the theme of imitation, are here understood, the first ("despite all its attendant difficulty") as expressing the circumstances of the activity and the second ("accepted the word . . . with joy") as providing the participle with an adverbial complement. On the themes of "difficulty" and "joy" (*thlipsis* and *chara*) see below, and for further discussion of the Spirit, see comments on 4:8.

7. *so that you became an example for all believers in Macedonia and in Achaia:* The dependent clause of verse 7 expresses the far-reaching result (*hōste* + infinitive) of the Thessalonians' conversion, for the dynamism of the community's response, expressed as "Spirit-empowered joy," naturally manifested itself in a ripple effect, whereby the imitators themselves became an example (*typos*) to other believers regarding Christian behavior and activity. The singular term is to be preferred (*TCGNT*, 629) and indicates a focus on the community as a whole rather than on its members. But Paul's use of the term "example" (see also Phil 3:17), of the expression "all believers," and of a geographical phrase referring to the whole of the Greek mainland ("in Macedonia and in Achaia"—introduction of the two provinces by parallel prepositions and articles indicates independent, equal areas of concern) leads scholars and, presumably, his readers to wonder concerning his meaning. He attempts in the following verse to clarify this ambiguity. On the expression "believers" see 2:13; for information on the Roman provinces, see Introduction.

8. *For starting from among you:* The overall structure of the verse, its relation to verse 7, and its meaning will be discussed below; but the translation of the verse indicates the options taken in explaining this awkward construction and the function it plays in Paul's thanksgiving. Verse 8 is connected to what

precedes by the postpositive conjunction *gar* ("for") and therefore explains the term "example" of verse 7. The Thessalonian community has become a model to be imitated and from the start Paul sets out to explain the nature of this concept. The point of origin or source of this influence is precisely his audience, "starting from among you"; the expression introduces the two following clauses.

not only has the word of the Lord sounded forth both in Macedonia and in Achaia: After the transitional prepositional phrase there follow two parallel clauses and geographical phrases. While some contrast one or the other, it seems best to mark a contrast not only between the geographical terms ("in Macedonia and in Achaia" and "everywhere else," later in the verse) but also between the two striking clauses of verse 8 (use of "not only . . . but"). In this first clause two unique Pauline expressions are used. (1) The verb *exēcheō*, occurs only here in the NT, although the root is used by Paul in 1 Cor 13:1 in a similar, though negative, context. Since this rare word group is used to portray a variety of sounds, both in classical authors and the LXX, it seems best to seek no further specificity than that of a sound emanating in all directions from a source (BAGD 276 and 349). Such a conclusion explains Paul's use of the rarer compound since he wishes to underscore the origin and wide diffusion of the sound ("*from* you has sounded *forth*"; note also the second compound verb, *exerchomai*). (2) The second idiom, "the word of the Lord," a common OT expression, occurs only here in Paul (see later comments on 4:15), though it is employed in 2 Thess 3:1. Several questions arise concerning the use, meaning, and overall significance of this expression, questions which are addressed below. At this point we observe that Paul's preference for this unique expression, early in his career, relates to his prophetic self-concept and that its meaning is to be seen in Paul's missionary concerns. Lastly, the translation "both in Macedonia and in Achaia" reflects the longer reading of the majority of MSS; a shorter text, without preposition and article (*en tē*) before Achaia, is offered by MSS B 69 *al*. One could follow the shorter text and argue for assimilation with the identical phrase in verse 7 but probably should reject such weak textual evidence especially since the strongest part of that evidence, Vaticanus (B), is well known for omitting such textual data (see Notes on 2 Thess 1:2). Either choice, however, is defensible on internal grounds since Paul seemingly intends to contrast one geographical area (the whole of Greece) to another (everywhere else).

but the news of your faith in God has gone forth everywhere else: The second clause focuses on a broader phenomenon, the fame of the Thessalonian community. A similar expression is used in Rom 1:8, where Paul, also in hyperbolic fashion, says, "your faith is proclaimed throughout the world" (see also Rom 16:19). It is clear from such usage that the intended meaning is that the report of their faith has spread everywhere, beyond the area of Macedonia and Achaia. Again, the prepositional prefix *ex* is used (and rendered "forth") to underscore the source of the news and the perfect tense is employed to indicate that the addressees' good example has spread and is still echoing far and wide. Paul's unusual formulation "your faith in God" (*hē pistis hymōn hē pros ton theon)*, by its use of *pros* with the term *pistis* (as attested in Philo, *De Abrahamo* 262–69 and as a parallel to verse 9 where the Thessalonians are said to "turn to *[pros]* God") points to conversion as the theme of this clause. Thus, the first clause of verse 8 refers to missionary activity while the second alludes to the community's turning or conversion to God.

so that we have no need to say anything: In artistic terms Paul's boast reaches its rhetorical climax in his insistence that the missionaries can add nothing ("we have no need"—see 4:9 for discussion of this idiom) to the community's reputation (note the use of *laleō* to stress the act of speaking rather than *legō* to dwell on its content). It is unnecessary to wonder why Paul changes his mind and later boasts about the community (2 Cor 8:1-5) or to explain the statement of 2 Thess 1:4 about Paul's boasting as evidence that Paul wrote this letter prior to 1 Thessalonians. The exaggerated language, whether geographical ("everywhere"), inclusive ("all believers"), or disengaging ("need say no more"), adds to the rhetorical effectiveness of the letter's thanksgiving period; the community's reputation speaks for itself.

9. *For they themselves report concerning us:* Further evidence, indicated by *gar* ("for"), that the missionaries need not speak up concerning the converts' accomplishments is Paul's claim that the community's renown has taken a life of its own. Not only are they and their deeds known to fellow believers beyond Thessalonica (simply referred to as "they") but believers who found them exemplary have in their turn ("themselves"—*autoi*) contributed to their fame. To express the concept of growing repute, Paul employs the present tense of the verb *apangellō* ("report, speak about, bring news"), a term commonly used for this purpose (LSJ 173). Thus, it is probably not advisable to view this term as meaning "proclaim" (by association with other *angellō* words) and to insist that the report concerning the addressees' reception of the gospel formed part of the missionaries' message. Additionally, to add specificity to the report, the verb introduces double, parallel clauses, focusing on different aspects of the report. Finally, the reading "concerning you" (B *al* d) in place of "concerning us" is a scribal attempt to correct the Pauline text which seems like a report about the converts rather than about the missionaries. Nonetheless, choice of the latter supports the parallelism between verses 9-10 and 5-6 whereby there is a focus first on the missionaries ("our gospel came to you" and "what sort of visit we had among you") and then on the converts ("the way you accepted" and "how you turned").

what sort of visit we had among you: In the first clause of the report Paul alludes briefly to the apostolic visit before turning his attention to the conversion story itself. The term *eisodos* is used, a noun which occurs in Paul only here and at 2:1. The word means "place of entrance," "entering," and, in relation to the latter, "visit" (BAGD 233; LSJ 496). Its meaning in 2:1 and consequently in 1:9 suggests the coming or visit of the apostolic missionaries. The translation "welcome" is less advisable since it makes too explicit and overemphasizes what Paul suggests in passing by the term "what sort of." Paul has a highly successful visitation in mind, but, by the use of allusive terminology, is able to deemphasize the theme at this point (see 2:1-12) and to amplify the report's suggestive quality. Besides, Paul has already described the missionaries' activity (v. 5), the community's response (v. 6), and its consequences (7-8).

and how you turned to God from idols: There follows the second part of the report, a lengthy adverbial clause which itself extends into parallel infinitive phrases. The first two terms, "and how," link what follows to the first element of the report and express both the result of the successful visit and the quality of commitment. The result therefore of the visit was the conversion of some inhabitants of the city, a fact which is expressed by an un-Pauline expression: "you turned to God from idols." The verb *epistrephō* became a technical Jewish term for "conversion" and is so used in the NT (Acts 15:19; 26:18) but rarely in Paul (see discussion in Excursus below). The usage here resembles most that of Acts 14:15 where the Lycaonians are said to "turn from *(apo)* these worthless things to the living God." The turning "from idols" underscores the LXX usage whereby the term "idol" is used both for false gods and their images, and suggests that these are as false as their images, a concept which is suggested by the following infinitive phrase (*TDNT* 2:375-78).

to serve the living and true God: After contrasting the two religious domains involved in the "turning from and to," Paul directs his attention in parallel infinitive phrases to the latter, to describe what it means to turn or commit oneself to God. The phrases express first a theological motive, and then a Christological one for the converts' new commitment. In the first case Paul invokes service to God as the converts' basic response. The term *douleuō* ("serve") describes wholehearted commitment to and service of God in the LXX (*TDNT* 2:367). The term also reinforces Paul's insistence in the thanksgiving and later in the body of the letter that commitment to God calls for righteous lives. The portrayal of God as "living and true" contrasts sharply with the community's previous adherence to false gods and underscores divine transcendence and holiness (Deut 5:26). This particular terminology illustrates the strong monotheistic tone of the passage and the reason for Paul's use of the text.

10. *and to await his Son from heaven:* A second infinitive phrase introduces the Christological component of the report. The hapax *anamenō* ("await") is employed for the more common Pauline term *apekdechomai* (Rom 8:23; Phil 3:20) and expresses the Christian hope of Jesus' coming in the end-time (1:3). He is called God's Son rather than Lord Jesus, as usually in the Thessalonian correspondence and, in apocalyptic fashion, is said to reside in heaven (use of the plural: *ek tōn ouranōn*).

whom he raised from the dead: One next encounters a relative clause which contains an early Christological formula, a clause which provides further information concerning God's Son. The formula itself is well defined: God as subject (implied here), aorist form of the verb *egeirō*, a relative pronoun replacing an original "Jesus" or "Lord Jesus" as object, and the prepositional phrase "from the dead."

Jesus who delivers us from the coming wrath: By means of the name "Jesus" (see 1:1 for comments on the name) Paul resumes the train of thought interrupted by the resurrection formula. The returning Lord's role is that of delivering (*rhyomai* in place of the Pauline *sōzō*) from the divine wrath which is still to come. One should note that the participial form could be translated as a present "who delivers us" or interpreted as an obsolescent future "who will deliver us" (*BG*, 372).

Excursus

on Pauline and Non-Pauline Usage in 1:9b-10

There are an unusual number of non-Pauline terms and idioms clustered in verses 9-10 (see also comments on verse 8). The passage is a complex, rhythmic unit about which scholarly debate persists. Attention focuses on the unusual vocabulary and formulas employed in these verses. Some propose that verses 9b-10 are a pre-Pauline fragment consisting of a summary of Jewish-Christian preaching to Gentiles, whether that of Paul or of other Hellenistic missionaries. Also describing verses 9-10 as a pre-Pauline unit, but less convinced of its missionary provenance, others look to the liturgy for Paul's source and classify the verses as a baptismal hymn used by the community to welcome newly baptized converts. More generally, it is suggested that Paul employs traditional formulas used in Hellenistic-Jewish missionary discourses; one is thus able to reject fragment theses and opt for a Pauline composition that freely employs such phraseology. Still others, in reaction to such hypotheses, either insist on the Pauline character of verse 9 and Paul's editorial use of a catechetical formula in verse 10 or argue for the nonformulaic nature of verses 9-10 and postulate the Pauline composition of the entire passage in view of the epistolary situation. Thus the goal of this discussion is to examine the linguistic and religious background of this uncharacteristic vocabulary before offering some overall observations concerning the form, meaning, and function of these verses in Paul's thanksgiving period.

(1) *and how you turned to God from idols:* The verb employed here, *epistrephō*, under the Semitizing influence of the LXX, soon acquired the technical, though not exclusive, meaning of "turning about" in a religious or moral sense (*TDNT* 7:723-29). During the intertestamental period Jewish usage took on two clearly identifiable directions, either the repentance ("returning to the Lord") of a Jewish character who had strayed from the right path, or the conversion of a Gentile to Judaism. It is the latter which is of interest, particularly as expressed in the story of Aseneth's conversion and marriage to Joseph. There is a contrast between Joseph who "blesses the living God" and Aseneth who, before her conversion, "blesses dead and mute idols" (JosAs 8:5; also 11:8; 12:5; 13:11). In her moment of truth, Aseneth acknowledges: "I have heard many say the God of the Hebrews is a true God (*theos alēthinos*), and a living God (*theos zōn*), and a merciful God . . .; from now on, miserable as I am, I will be bold and turn to him (*epistrepsō pros auton)*" (11:10-11). The Jewish

language of Gentile conversion certainly matches Paul's expressions in 1 Thess 1:9. NT usage, apart from Paul, is found in Acts whose author, under LXX influence, favors this terminology to describe Gentile conversion as "turning to *(epistrephō epi)* the Lord" (9:35; 11:21) or "God" (15:19; 26:18, 20; see also 14:15 where Luke speaks of the Lycaonians "turning from *(apo)* these worthless things to the living God."

Pauline usage, however, is not easily categorized. While the term is uncharacteristic of Paul who favors the expressions "believe" or "accept the word" to describe this religious change, it nonetheless occurs in two other conversion contexts, Gal 4:9 and 2 Cor 3:16. In the first case the Galatians are warned about reconverting to idolatrous slavery, i.e., returning once again to their pagan ways. In the latter Paul intentionally borrows an OT idiom for conversion to modify his citation of Exod 34:34; in this way he is able to insist that Israel's hope for salvation lies in its "turning to the Lord [Jesus]" and not Moses. On the basis of such analysis one could defend the Pauline composition of 1 Thess 1:9 as owing to early Pauline usage which finds few echoes later in his letters; however, other factors make Pauline borrowing more credible.

Thus, the prepositional phrases, "to God from idols," along with the verb of motion ("turn"), underscore, on the one hand, the basic parting from pagan beliefs and customs and, on the other, an exclusive commitment to the one God. As the contrast between God and idols was basic to Jewish monotheism, so was some sort of separation between the socioreligious cultures they represented. The statement about idols, for Paul and his audience, would have underscored the great difference which the Christian message made in the lives of its adherents, for they no longer belonged to mainstream religious and social institutions of their cities. As Gentiles converting to the God of Israel or of Christian preaching, they were much like Aseneth, who, in her first conversion monologue, laments being abandoned or orphaned by her family and friends because she had turned her back on their gods and no longer shared from their sacrificial tables (JosAs 11:3-4, 9). Thus, in verse 9 Paul reminds the converts of the difficult situation in which they found themselves as they turned away from mainstream Greco-Roman culture to begin an existence which called for new cultural, social, and religious relationships and institutions. This issue was a central concern of the first missive (see 3:3) and again plays an important part in Paul's description of the community's conversion. As he had praised them in verse 6 for the way in which they had "accepted the word . . . despite all its attendant difficulty" so now, through the words of other believers, he compliments them on the way they turned their backs on, what Aseneth called, "dead and mute idols" to lead lives worthy of the living God who both chose them and repeatedly calls them "into his own kingdom and glory" (1:4; 2:12).

(2) *to serve the living and true God:* While the Greeks were reluctant to employ the *doulos* word group to express "service," especially service to the gods, as antithetical to their anthropological focus on freedom (though see Plato regarding Socrates, *Apology* 30 and Epictetus concerning the Cynic's relation

to Zeus, *Discourse* 3:22), the situation was quite different in the Semitic world, for the verb *douleuō*, as in the LXX, becomes a common term for total commitment to God (*TDNT* 2:261-68). On the one hand, apostasy is described as sinning against God, making a covenant with other gods, and serving them (Exod 23:32-33), while returning wholeheartedly to the Lord requires the abandoning of other gods, preparing one's heart, and serving God alone, who is able to grant deliverance (1 Sam 7:3). In a touching passage the Israelites are described as turning their backs on God for gods of their own choosing who are unable to save (*sōzō*) them from their affliction (*thlipsis*: Judg 10:6-16). Thus, the context of this usage is that of choice between the gods of the nations or the one God. On the other hand, a second important usage is discernible in texts where Israel's exemplary figures are called "servants" (*douloi*; e.g., Josh 24:27; Pss 88:3; 104:42) or the righteous are described as "serving the Lord" (Job 21:15; Ps 2:11), i.e., keeping the Lord's ordinances and walking as suppliants before the Lord (Mal 3:14; Ps 99:2).

Pauline usage of *doulos* terminology, however, is Christological rather than theological. Paul speaks of serving Christ as Lord rather than the Law, sin, or the demonic powers (Rom 6:16-20; 7:6, 25; Gal 4:3, 8). Indeed, Paul speaks of humans without Christ as being subject to the domains of sin, the world, death, and the Law, but as a result of the Christ-event as adopted children and "servants of Christ" (Rom 6:6f.; 8:15). Thus, *doulos* and *douleuō* are related to Christology in Paul and imply a master/servant relationship (Paul does employ *douloō* in this sense once: Rom 6:22: "freed from sin and enslaved to God"; *TDNT* 2:274-79). In light of the above analysis of Pauline and Jewish LXX usage, the following conclusions should be drawn. The expression, "serving . . . God" in 1:9 (1) derives from non-Pauline usage, namely that of Jewish communities on the Greek mainland which are impressed by the Thessalonian converts and (2) requires a different interpretation from other Pauline uses of the term. On the one hand, the context of the expression is that of choosing between gods described as idols and the one God, a context which suggests several links with Paul's thanksgiving period (choice by God, abandoning of false gods, a turning to God, and a looking for deliverance). On the other hand, divine service, described in OT passages as consisting of righteous lives, is a unifying theme of Paul's thanksgiving, whether the community's achievements (3), imitation of missionaries and the Lord (6), acceptance of the word, and exemplary role throughout the Greek mainland (7-8). Serving God, evident in the discussion of the apostolic mission (2:1f.), is also said to be the goal of Christian life as the community is urged to "lead a life worthy of God" (2:12), to seek sanctification through pure lives (4:3f.) and loving service of others (4:9f.). *Douleuō* then, as used in 1:9, especially as expressing divine service, emanates from non-Pauline, Jewish thinking, a usage nonetheless with which Paul would have been sympathetic and which further served his epistolary purpose.

The portrayal of God (omission of the article before *theos* underscores the text's descriptive character) as "living and true" is uncharacteristic of Paul, consonant with the usage of *Joseph and Aseneth*, and fitting in the present context. Both the expressions, "the living God" and "the true God," are frequently encountered in Jewish texts, whether to express God's transcendence, power over life, and holiness (Deut 5:26; Ps 42:2; JosAs 8:5) or to underscore divine trustworthiness and exclusivity (Exod 34:6; 3 Macc 6:18). In Paul the latter is limited to the present text while the former occurs in two additional passages, which have in common a close connection to LXX usage. Rom 9:26 is indeed a citation of Hos 1:10 and 2 Cor 3:3 is a reworking of Exod 31:18, wherein "written by the finger of God" becomes "written . . . by the spirit of the living God"; note that 2 Cor 6:16 is part of an interpolated unit. These observations would confirm the suggestion that 1 Thess 1:9 approximates the idiom of Jewish Christian Hellenists regarding the Thessalonian community. Additionally, the combined expression, as attested in JosAs 11:10 and in Jer 10:10 (though missing in the LXX), would derive from intertestamental Jewish idiom and find its context in missionary discussions of conversion and idolatry. Implied in the reference to idols is the Jewish and Christian insistence that they are "wood and stone" (Deut 28:64), the antithesis of the "living God" of Israel, a God also who gives life by raising Jesus from the dead. Also inferred in the contrast drawn between God and idols is the exclusive claim of monotheists that their God is the only true God, a God who is also truthful, trustworthy, and faithful (1:10; 5:23-24).

(3) *and to await his Son from heaven:* The text offers several challenges. While the verb "to await" *(anamenō)* occurs nowhere else in the NT, its appearance in the LXX in eschatological contexts is instructive, particularly Isa 59:11 which states: "we waited for judgment and there is no salvation" and Jdt 8:17 which exclaims: "let us wait for salvation from him." The idea of eschatological waiting is not lacking in Paul; however, he favors other verbs for expressing this concept (1 Cor 1:7; Phil 3:20; Gal 5:5; Rom 8:23). So again, Paul is not only agreeing with the ideas of other believers but is also citing their formulation of these concepts.

Also intriguing in this context is the identifying of the returning Messiah as "Son" (of God) rather than as "Lord Jesus (Christ)" or simply as "Lord" (2:19; 3:13; 5:23; 4:15). Indeed, just prior to this statement Paul speaks of belief in Jesus' return (1:3). Why then the unusual association of "Son" with parousia? In light of Synoptic tradition, as represented by Mark, which associates the parousia with the Son of Man (13:26; 14:62) and in view of the usage of the Q-Document (Matthew and Luke's additional source) which also focuses on the eschatological role of the Son of Man (Matt 10:32-33 = Luke 12:8-9), two solutions are suggested for this unusual association of themes. It is proposed either that the "Son from heaven" expression is a fusion of the Son of Man and Son of God traditions or that an original Son of Man title is replaced by Son (of God) to accommodate missionary preaching to Gentiles. While one could defend the first by appealing to the Q community's use of the two titles in eschatological contexts, it is preferable to envision the language of verse 10 as requiring a Son of Man title, particularly its portrait of a deliverer descending from heaven, much in the fashion of Dan 7:13f. The modification from Son of Man to Son (of God) owes probably to Paul rather than to other Jewish-Christian missionaries or pre-Pauline tradition.

The phrase "from heaven" (*ek tōn ouranōn:* lit.: "from the heavens") is non-Pauline in its formulation, for Paul favors the singular to the plural form, i.e., Greek to Semitic usage, and usually omits the article. Further, on the two other occasions where he employs the expression "from heaven" (with the preposition *ek*) he uses the singular noun with article (1 Cor 15:47 and Gal 1:8).

(4) *whom he raised from the dead:* In discussing the provenance, function, and meaning of this resurrection formula, it is necessary to examine several factors. Scholars readily note the peculiar use of the article in the phrase "from the dead." Indeed, Paul regularly omits the definite article in such a case (Gal 1:1; Rom 4:24; etc). One could opt to omit the article on admittedly weaker textual grounds, appeal to Paul's use of an attested (Col 1:18; Eph 5:14) but uncommon tradition, explain the phenomenon as owing to Paul's use, more generally, of an early Jewish Christian missionary statement, or posit an intentional parallelism to the preceding "in the heavens."

Additionally, some scholars have pointed to the disruption of thought between the phrase "to await his son from heaven" and what follows the resurrection clause, "the one who delivers us. . . ." In effect, the passage flows better if the relative clause, bearing the resurrection theme, is omitted. Thus, one could consider the relative clause as a Christological addition to a Jewish missionary formula, as a Pauline "afterthought" intent on correlating the coming Son with the risen Jesus, or as the Pauline addition of a resurrection formula to a pre-Pauline Jewish-Christian "catechetical formula" in order to ground in God's raising activity the believers' hope in future deliverance. Since what precedes and follows the relative clause is characterized by non-Pauline language and since the resurrection formula is frequently employed by Paul elsewhere, it seems preferable to envision the addition of the resurrection clause to a non-Pauline passage as owing to Paul himself. We will return below to the function and meaning of this formula.

(5) *Jesus who delivers us from the coming wrath:* The concluding section of verse 10 further underscores the disruption of thought from the beginning to the end of the verse and Paul's attempt to correlate grammatically the various themes he is bringing together. Thus, the name "Jesus" plays a resumptive role syntactically, joining the "awaited Son" to the statement of his eschatological function. Paul's choice of the name "Jesus" in this instance probably owes both to its frequent association with resurrection formulas, whether alone (Rom 8:11) or in more developed contexts (Gal 1:1; 2 Cor 4:14; Rom 4:24; 10:9) and to Paul's desire to interconnect as clearly as possible the "awaited Son" and "Jesus" the historical figure in whom believers have placed all their trust.

Verse 10 ends on a stark eschatological note, namely, deliverance and coming wrath. Use of the verb *rhyomai* to express the concept of eschatological deliverance as a function of the returning Jesus is non-Pauline, for he prefers the verb *sōzō* for this purpose. In fact, the two verbs are interchangeable in intertestamental literature when calling upon God for both present and eschatological deliverance. While Paul's use of *rhyomai* in Rom 11:26 ("out of

Zion will come the Deliverer'') is a parallel to the present case (though not Christological in function), its OT provenance (citation of Isa 59:20) suggests both that Paul understands this usage and prefers the more common term *sōzō* (see 5:9 and Rom 5:9).

The final phrase of verse 10, "from the coming wrath," adds further to the list of uncommon Pauline themes, for "wrath" is not a frequent Pauline concern until he writes Romans, where the term occurs eleven times. In the latter Paul develops at length the nature and consequences of God's love and mercy, carefully noting its counterbalance in the notion of wrath which is already being revealed in the lives of evil doers (Rom 1:18) but which is to be consummated on the Lord's day (1 Thess 5:2). In the present passage the focus is on "deliverance *from*" rather than "salvation *to*" as in 5:9. Finally, the wrath is described as approaching or coming; that is, it is placed in emphatic position (after the noun with repeated article—*tēs orgēs tēs erchomenēs*) to add a note of eschatological urgency.

INTERPRETATION

In typical epistolary fashion Paul begins by thanking God for the active community life of the converts, recounting and praising in prayer the vibrancy of their commitment, the dedication of their devotion to others, and the sustaining power of their hope, and concludes by praising their response to the gospel as a result of the foundation visit. The description of their original response, the praise of their missionary activity, and the thanks offered to God for their dedication point to the multiple purpose this part of Paul's letter serves in his correspondence with his beloved Macedonian community.

Form, Function, and Content of the Thanksgiving Period. Paul introduces his letter with a lengthy thanksgiving where he expresses gratitude to God for the faith of the Thessalonian community. He begins then by employing a form which becomes standard for his later epistles. While the thanksgiving of the earlier missive, 2:13, belongs to a type which immediately introduces the cause for thanks by means of a *hoti* clause and concludes with a dependent consecutive clause (also true of Rom 1:8-9 and 1 Cor 1:4-7), that of the second, 1:2-7, follows the initial thanksgiving clause with a series of first-person participles which introduce final clauses (see also Phil 1:3-6 and Phlm 4–6).

Indeed, Paul begins with a general statement of gratitude ("we give thanks to God always for all of you") and continues with three participial clauses, literally: "mentioning" (2b), "calling to mind" (3), and "knowing or being sure" (4). These three clauses are grammatically parallel and artistically more developed in terms of length and detail. Their meaning and function, however, do not correspond to their parallel structure. Instead, each has a different relation to the initial verb of thanksgiving. Thus, Paul begins by expressing his gratitude to God for the gift of faith, a gift bestowed upon the addressees by divine choice and power (1:4-5), but especially a gift that had profound, tangible results in the lives of the converts (vv. 3, 6, 9-10) and widespread consequences for neighboring communities and the Greek mission (7-8). Each of the participial constructions has its own role to play in Paul's statement of thanksgiving.

(1) ''As we mention you continually in our prayers'' (v. 2b). This participial clause has been described as a virtual repetition of the thanksgiving statement, which serves as an explanation or example of ''thanking God always.'' Thus, the translation, ''as we mention,'' attempts to define the complementary relationship between it and the main verb (see Phlm 4 for a similar construction). Thanksgiving to God then is the equivalent of devotional presence, that is, the believers' appearance before God as the object of the missionaries' prayer. On the concept and content of Paul's prayer, see discussion below.

(2) ''For we call to mind'' (3). The clause represents the second participial construction and expresses the immediate reason for thanksgiving, for upon recalling what has transpired in Thessalonica Paul is inspired to address God in gratitude. In fact, his particular use of the verb *mnēmoneuō*, after ''we mention,'' confirms its meaning here as ''calling to mind . . . in God's presence.'' What follows in the remainder of the verse, as object of the participle, is a recitation of the community's activity, namely, the results of its faith, love, and hope. This topic too will be discussed in relation to the content of Paul's prayer.

(3) ''For we . . . are sure of your election'' (4). The final participial clause expresses the ultimate reason for Paul's thanksgiving, the community's divine election. He insists that he is certain of this (use of *oida*) and proceeds in verses 5 and 6-7 to provide proof by means of a double *hoti* (''since'') clause. To further underscore this theme Paul calls them ''brothers and sisters beloved by God.''

The remainder of the thanksgiving pericope then provides evidence of divine election, namely, God's power at work among the converts through the missionaries (v. 5) and the reaction of the Thessalonian residents to the apostolic preaching (vv. 6-7). Mention in verses 6 and 7 of the concepts of ''imitation'' and ''example for all believers'' leads in verse 8 to further praise both of the community's mission work and of its reputation as devoted Christians. Again, led by something said at the end of verse 8 (''we have no need to say anything''), Paul has recourse to the report of other Christians (v. 9) to bring his laudatory introduction to a close. It is from this report that we inherit, via Pauline editing, one of Christianity's earliest credal formulas (vv. 9b-10).

The thanksgiving pericope then plays a crucial role, as do Pauline thanksgivings generally, in preparing the readers for the content and advice which follow. In the first place the community's situation is addressed at several points when Paul in complimentary terms speaks of its exemplary activity within the community and beyond (vv. 3, 7, 8). Paul comments on its praiseworthy reception of the gospel despite the difficulties which such a socioreligious change might create (v. 6). The comments about the community's situation and experiences give hints about the letter's subject matter. Mention of love and hope in verse 3 calls to mind the discussion about *philadelphia* in 4:9-12 and eschatological subjects in 4:13–5:11. Also, the themes of divine power and Spirit (1:5) prepare for advice regarding the Spirit and prophecy (5:19-22) and again hint at the members' situation and communal life. Further, the emphasis placed on mission, example, and imitation in verses 6-8 point to the extended treatment of the foundation visit as exemplary behavior and so paraenetic in character (2:1-12), to Paul's insistence on love for all throughout the Greek mainland (1:8; 4:10), and to his concern for those who labor in, for, and in the name of the community (5:12-13). Finally, Paul's remarks on service of God in the present while awaiting the Son's return from heaven (1:9-10) prepare the readers for the subsequent advice on the subjects of holiness, vigilance, and mutual exhortation (4:3f.; 5:1f., 14f.).

Prayer: Concept and Content. Paul's thanksgiving in verse 2 becomes a profound statement on prayer and its content: "we mention you continually in our prayers." In this case "prayer" is in the plural and refers not to intercessory or petitionary prayer but to prayer more generally as vow, worship, or praise addressed to God. This theme has already appeared in the first missive, 3:10, where Paul "earnestly prays or begs" for the opportunity to return to Thessalonica. In this missive the theme of prayer, use of both noun and verb, takes on a more central role and is more theologically significant. Indeed, Paul's prayer in this missive might be characterized by four qualities: universality, frequency, concreteness, and mutuality. His prayer of thanksgiving involves all his converts (1:2), who are urgently exhorted to "continual prayer" (5:17). His prayer presumably was manifested in frequent, concrete acts of prayer (use of the plural) to and in praise of God for the gift of faith (1:4) and the joy of new life (5:16-17). Finally, his concept of prayer involved mutual prayer, for he ends his missive with this address: "brothers and sisters pray also for us" (5:25). As Paul mentioned their names in thanksgiving before God so he requests that they do the same for him and his colleagues in mission.

Paul's prayer in the thanksgiving pericope is further characterized by the following, complementary participial clause: "for we call to mind . . . in the very presence of God our Father" (3). Not only does Paul mention the members' names and intentions in his prayers but, as the verb suggests, recites before God the community's acts of service to God and neighbor. The recitation itself focuses on the threefold virtues of faith, love, and hope, whose content and function as part of the prayer deserve some attention, since each is judiciously qualified by an accompanying noun and, in the case of the last, by a subsequent prepositional phrase.

The first pair, *tou ergou tēs pisteōs* (lit.: "the work of faith"), consists of two frequently used and key Pauline terms. The noun "work" is often used by Paul in a negative sense, in the plural however, to contrast faith and works. In the singular, as is the case here, it has a positive sense. Indeed, Paul can speak of "the work of God" or "of the Lord" (Rom 14:20; 1 Cor 15:58), even "of a good work or deed" (Rom 2:7; 13:3), or simply of work as human achievement (1 Cor 3:13). Its use in 1:3, with the modifying genitive "of faith," has generated two different interpretations. In the first instance, it is claimed that faith as total commitment or state of belief (see comments on 3:2) is the source of work or human activity or conversely that work is the fruit of faith (*TDNT* 2:649). Gal 5:6 ("faith working through love") is invariably cited as support. One suspects, however, that such an interpretation presumes a plural, "works or deeds," rather than the singular and lays stress on the first rather than on the second noun—an un-Pauline usage. The second approach underscores the second noun either by claiming that "of faith" is an epexegetical genitive and refers to active faith rather than the activity of faith or insisting that *ergon* in this instance means "manifestation" or "practical proof" (BAGD 308b) and that the phrase focuses on "faith in action," and could be translated adjectivally as "active or efficacious faith" or, substantively (following the structure of the Pauline text) as "the dynamism of your faith" (see also BDF 163). Paul then is thankful not for acts of faith but for the community's vibrant faith.

The second pair, *tou kopou tēs agapēs* (lit.: "the labor of love") also introduces two frequently used Pauline terms. The first is similar in meaning to *ergon* but stresses the difficulty or toil in a given activity. In Paul the term is usually used in relation to missionary activity, whether referring to the product of the mission (3:5) or the exertion of the activity (2:9; 1 Cor 4:12; *TDNT* 3:828-29). It is joined to a second term, *agapē* (see discussion at 3:6) and forms a contrast to and parallel with the other two pairs. Here as in other passages of 1 Thessalonians, "love" refers to a concern for mutual support and extends to relations with outsiders. In its present context it describes concern which is never weary and which is dedicated and constant in the face of daily challenge in a new way of life. The above translation attempts to focus on love and its enduring, dedicated, and hard-working character as the community faces the demands of those inside and outside the community.

The third pair, *tēs hypomonēs tēs elpidos,* also combines well-known Pauline terms. The first of these implies "sustaining power, constancy, perseverance, or patience" (BAGD 846); the second, "hope," suggests three interrelated concepts: waiting for the future, confidence, or patience (see discussion of 2:19). The combination by Paul of this term with *hypomonē* seems to focus on the second concept, namely, the confidence or constancy which hope inspires in the present in terms of belief and action. This constancy, it should be noted, is firmly based on the notion that Jesus will return in the future (see 1:10). Paul then is alluding here to steadfastness or constancy in the face of the challenges of daily Christian living, not to endurance or patience in the midst of persecution (see the earlier discussion of "difficulties at Thessalonica" in relation to 3:3). In this case, Paul does not mean that "suffering produces endurance" (Rom 5:3) in the sense of Greek *andreia* ("courage") as though "hope" were the promise of what might happen. Instead, he modifies the phrase by adding another genitive to establish the basis of Christian hope; that is, it is "hope in our Lord Jesus Christ." While it would be possible to link the last phrase to all three pairs, it seems best, in stylistic and Pauline terms, to view it as modifying "hope." Thus, hope for Paul is the promise of what is already guaranteed by belief in the Christ-event.

Thus, Paul's choice and combination of these three traditional virtues, as representing the essential qualities of Christian life, are important in discerning his theological, Christological, and ecclesiological perception of the Christian reality; see also 5:8. If faith lends attention to the Christ-event and its acceptance as a past, objective happening, if love points to Christian life as the present ecclesial manifestation in a human context of what a right relationship with God means, and if hope defines Christian motivation as teleologically focused on a future event, in Paul's hands each concept receives an added dimension. By prefixing the noun *ergon* to *pistis* Paul acknowledges that the community's faith is also an active, present force in its life at Thessalonica. Having turned to God and having accepted Jesus as their Lord, the converts have received a dynamic force which now energizes their lives as Christians. By combining *agapē* with *kopos* Paul notes not only that the community members provide "loving service" to one another but also that this love which is God-taught (4:9), must know no limits and so must be dedicated, without weariness, even to outsiders (4:12; 5:15; see also 3:12). Love then is characterized proverbially by the challenge that it presents to those who would be imitators of the "labors" of the missionaries and of the Lord (1:6). Lastly, by adding *hypomonē* to the concept of *elpis* or "hope in the Lord Jesus Christ" Paul prepares for the eschatological discussion of chapters 4 and 5. Indeed, it is the "constancy of hope" (*their* hope in a future reality) which should redress their grief and give them comfort and encouragement in their present distress and perplexity (4:13, 18; 5:11). Christian existence then is conditioned by its theological origin (v. 4) and direction, is grounded, in both past and future terms, in its relation to the Christ-event, and is focused on "aspiring to what is good both for one another and for all" (5:15). Paul's prayer then rehearses before God the dynamic quality of the believers' lives, their dedication to one another and to others, and their persevering outlook as they focus on becoming imitators also of the Lord (1:6).

Divine Election as Ground for Thanksgiving. While verses 2b-3 express the content of Paul's thanksgiving prayer in the form of a recitation, verse 4 focuses on the principal reason for giving thanks to God, namely, divine election, a theme which is fundamental to his thinking. Surprisingly, however, the term used is *eklogē*, a noun which occurs only five times in Paul, the four others in Romans 9–11, where they concern God's choice of Israel. Only in the present verse does this rare term (note its non-occurrence also in the LXX) address God's choice of believers in Christ. The theme of election, however, is not limited to Paul's use of this term for elsewhere he speaks also of being "called" and favors the nouns *klēsis* and *klētos* ("call"), expressions involving *charis* (e.g., "sharers in grace," "call in grace," "receive grace"), or more simply "to call" *(kaleō).* The last mentioned occurs in 1 Thess 2:12; 4:7; and 5:24. From these, one detects an early presupposition of Pauline thought that the initiative for salvation comes from God, as it does always in the Hebrew scriptures, for as Paul states toward the end of his letter: "God did not destine us for wrath but for the attainment of salvation through our Lord Jesus Christ, who died for us" (5:9-10). Election and call in the thought of Paul, particularly here in 1 Thessalonians, is not one of predestination but of goal and actualization. Out of perduring love God has chosen the community and has called it to a godly life now and to the divine kingdom in the future (2:12; 4:7). Thus, proof for Paul that this is so comes from the community's exemplary behavior (v. 3) and from its reception of the good news (v. 5-7).

One may detect in the use of *eklogē* an early attempt on Paul's part to express the underlying theme of faith as gift or divine call. In later letters, beginning with Phil 1:7 ("sharers in grace"), *charis* will appear increasingly, beyond the formulaic opening and closing greetings, to express the theme of divine choice. Paul, the Jewish Christian, can be seen expanding a cherished Hebrew idea of God's choice of a people to that of a people that includes Jews and Gentiles in Christ.

The basic reason for Paul's thanksgiving is the certitude of the community's election. By means of a double clause he introduces the proof for his conviction that God has chosen the community and destined it for salvation. The whole of verse 5 then serves as a first pastoral testimony that God was at work both among the missionaries and their Macedonian audience. God was at work in word and power within the community. This activity for Paul serves as proof of God's choice. There follows in verses 6-7 a second reason for Paul's certitude and that is the community's reaction to the gospel. Interestingly, Paul describes them as imitators of the missionaries and of the Lord precisely in their relationship to the word. We turn therefore to the two reasons Paul gives for his certitude.

Gospel in Word and Power as Proof of Election (v. 5). By means of a *hoti* ("since") clause Paul in verse 5 introduces the first of two proofs for his conviction of divine choice. The verse serves as pastoral testimony of God's work among the missionaries and their Macedonian audience. By means of a well-known "not only . . . but also" construction, Paul underscores the dynamism of the gospel beyond the rhetoric of the proclaimers—the contrast has much in common with that made earlier by Paul in the thanksgiving of the first missive (see comments on 2:13). By use of this construction it is not Paul's wish to denigrate the "human word," as may be implied in 1 Cor 1:17f. since such was required by the situation, but to insist first that God employs human intermediaries and their "words," and secondly that divine power is thereby released. The reader is not to choose between word or power but to understand that God's power comes through the human word (also Rom 10:14-15).

The second part of the construction continues the contrast by presenting three striking terms (*dynamis, pneuma,* and *plērophoria*) in three successive *en* phrases. What is the relationship of the three terms to the preceding "not only in words"? Are all to be interpreted objectively as parallel or synonymous terms? Also, do these refer entirely or partly to the missionaries or to their hearers? The questions and their responses are clearly interrelated. (1) Most translators opt, for stylistic reasons, for three parallel phrases as contrasted to a preceding negative statement: "not in word only, but also in power and in the Holy Spirit and with full conviction." Such a translation, though frequent, avoids a decision concerning these matters and seems unnatural. Others, in attempting to overcome the difficulty of interrelating the first two terms appeal to NT evidence, particularly Rom 15:13, and translate: "in the power of the Holy Spirit." Such does not seem to be what Paul intends since the three terms are interconnected by *kai . . . kai* and so would exclude such a complementary relationship. Even the suggestion that *dynamis* refers to miraculous power does not convince since it is here used in the singular and does not really clarify the relationship between the two terms.

(2) It has been argued that all three terms should be interpreted in an objective way, i.e., describing the coming of the good news rather than,

in the third member, focusing on the subjective state of those involved and so represent three parallel or synonymous expressions. Part of the difficulty lies in interpreting the rare term *plērophoria* which can designate "fullness" but which, along with its verb, also refers to "full assurance or conviction." The context, particularly the remainder of verse 5, seems to require just such a change.

(3) It has been suggested that by use of the third term, Paul refers to the converts' inward conviction about the trustworthiness of the word preached to them. Again, the context seems to support the contrary since both the preceding and succeeding discussion focuses on the missionaries' preaching and only in verse 6 does Paul attend to the audience's reaction.

I suggest that Paul's contrast is between "word" and "power" and that the two following terms are appositional descriptions of this force, first the source of divine power and secondly the effect of that power in the apostolic ministry. Thus, we propose the following translation: "our gospel came to you not only in word, but also in power, both with the Holy Spirit and with full conviction." Such an interpretation is supported by the only instance of a Pauline parallel between Spirit and power, 1 Cor 2:4, where a similar contrast is found between the Spirit as power and apostolic proclamation. Both themes will receive further elaboration as the Spirit reappears in 1:6; 4:8; 5:19 and 23 and as the missionaries' manner of preaching occupies Paul in 2:1f.

What then does Paul mean by "not only in word but also in power"? Rhetorically, one would expect Paul to contrast his words and deeds or his speech and achievements to underscore his trustworthiness, particularly in view of his references in verses 5-6 to behavior and imitation. Instead, he focuses on the manner in which the good news reaches the addressees as the basis of his certitude concerning their election. He is convinced of this because of the divine power which characterized the coming of the gospel in their midst. Indeed, in Paul the term *dynamis* most often characterizes God's power whether manifested in creation, Jesus as Son, the Spirit, or the dynamism of the good news (Rom 1:16, 20; 15:13, 19; 1 Cor 1:24). In the present case, the activity of the Holy Spirit is the manifestation par excellence of divine power. The pneumatological phenomena, which are described later in the letter (see 4:8), are clear proof for Paul of divine election and love. But divine power manifests itself also in the missionaries' pastoral activity, characterized as "conviction" (1:5) and "courage" (2:2), because it is divinely entrusted to them (2:4).

Imitation also as Proof of Election (vv. 6-7). Paul offers a second reason for insisting on divine election, a reason which focuses not on divine power but on the audience's reaction to the missionary preaching, described in terms of apostolic and Christological imitation ("imitators of us and of the Lord"). Whether employing imitation terminology *(mimētēs)* or more general expressions, Paul, on several occasions, speaks of his readers emulating him. It is debated, however, whether this theme refers to exemplary behavior according to his manner of living (his "ways in Christ Jesus"—1 Cor 4:16-17), to obedience to apostolic authority and teaching ("doing the things that you have learned and received and heard and seen in me"—Phil 4:9), or, more basically, to the sharing of Christian existence or life in Christ ("be imitators of me as I am of Christ"—1 Cor 11:1). Additionally, it is debated whether Paul's meaning is to be derived by focusing on his *mimētēs* passages, on the context provided by 1 Thess 1:6b, or, more generally, on Paul's developing thought. Finally, the curious formulation, "imitators of us and of the Lord," offers further difficulty.

(1) "Imitation" in Paul. Some argue, based on an analysis of Paul's four *mimētēs* passages (1 Cor 4:16; 11:1; Phil 3:17; 1 Thess 1:6), that the theme of imitation, while applicable to specific contexts, nonetheless, addresses the issue of Paul's right to teach and direct his churches despite conflicts. Thus the focus of imitation in Paul is the defense of his apostleship, and more particularly the imitation terminology of 1 Thess 1:6 defends his position as founder and pastor of his converts. Others prefer to focus on the Thessalonian context ("receiving the word" or "receiving the word in great affliction") for a clue to Paul's meaning. Imitation then would consist either in the obedience of faith or in the sharing of persecution or tribulation in an eschatological sense. Either option fails to convince. In the first case, by limiting oneself to *mimētēs* passages one fails to consider the full range of pertinent data. In the second instance, if imitation were determined by the expression "accept the word," then it is hard to imagine what that would mean in terms of imitation "of the Lord." Thus, it is necessary to examine both the full range of Pauline usage and the particular context of 1 Thess 1:6.

The focus of Paul's meaning can be illuminated by two crucial Pauline passages. The first is Gal 4:12 where Paul, without using *mimētēs* terminology, speaks of mutual imitation: "Friends, I beg you, become as I am, for I also have become as you are." While the Galatian context surely suggests that Paul has in view his own missionary approach of becoming like his converts (for their sake), it is clear that the topos for interpreting his imitation theme is that of friendship. Paul is here appealing to the mutuality of true friendship. His ideal relationship to his converts is that of mutuality whether at Galatia or Thessalonica, since they share both joys and difficulties in their new mode of existence. Missionary and convert have become brothers and sisters in Christ and so can exhort one another to excel in Christ-like action and behavior.

The second text, 1 Cor 11:1 ("Be imitators of me, as I am of Christ"), provides the background and probably constitutes an expanded form of our passage (so "you for your part became imitators of us [as we] also [are] of the Lord"), for imitation of Paul is in fact imitation of the Lord. Since for Paul Christ is the norm of authentic human existence, he insists that, just as he in imitation of Christ is a person for others among his readers, so must they act with the interests of others in mind. Christ's example is mediated by the missionary's activity among the community's members who are then exhorted to pattern their own treatment of others according to Paul's Christ-like behavior. In the present instance Paul presumes a similar context and meaning, i.e., the emulation of the missionaries who have patterned their lives on that of the master with the goal being that the new converts, by casting an eye to the interests of the inhabitants of the Greek provinces, have become for them an example and a means to faith (vv. 7-8). Mutual imitation then is based on the model offered by the Lord and is defined by its concern for others. Such an interpretation is supported by Paul's statement in 5c ("you know what sort of persons we were among you for your sake") and by what follows.

(2) Imitation in a Thessalonian Context. Paul's imitation text has led to several interpretations, since his initial statement concerning acceptance of the word is modified by two prepositional phrases. Thus, one could either focus on the participle and insist on conversion as being the content of imitation ("accepting the word") or, more commonly, noting its proximity to the participle, conclude that the following noun "difficulty or persecution" provides the key to Paul's imitation theme. A third, and better option, is to insist that the first prepositional phrase *(en thlipsei pollę)* expresses attendant circumstance and provides a contrast for Paul's basic statement ("despite all the attendant difficulty"), while the second *(meta charas pneumatos hagiou)* serves as an adverbial complement to the participle (the community "accepted the word . . . with joy inspired by the Holy Spirit"). Also, one might be tempted to translate *dechomai* not as "receive" but as "welcome" since that is surely Paul's meaning; however, by having separated the participle from its complementary adverbial phrase, Paul wished further to stress the notion of joy. Thus, the word order of the clause demands such an interpretation; the focus of Paul's thought is not on the "difficulties" nor even on the "acceptance of the word" but rather on the note of "joy" which has resulted in the Thessalonians becoming "an example" to others.

This brings us therefore to a second reason for choosing this third option, a reason provided by the rhetorical context of the statement. While verses 7-8 explain how the community became the source of fellow missionaries to the Greek provinces, it should be noted that Paul, in 1:3f., already insisted on the new community's noteworthy achievements.

There he underscores its "dynamism, dedication, and constancy," all terms which suggest characteristics of the audience which make them very much like the apostolic missionaries. The Thessalonians became imitators of Paul and colleagues in the way they responded to the word they heard and to the extent they dedicated their lives to the Lord's gospel.

Additionally, it should be noted that Paul speaks twice in 1 Thessalonians of the community "accepting the word," an idiom which appears nowhere else in Paul and so is limited to his early writing career (see also 2 Cor 11:4). Further, the difference in usage should be underscored. Both occur in thanksgiving periods: 1:6 and 2:13. The expression is used by Paul in 2:13 to compliment the Thessalonians on their ability to distinguish between messenger and message. They were able to see in the words of the apostolic preachers the very word of God, a fact which contributed to their survival as a community. In 1:6 Paul focuses on the growth of the apostolic mission in Thessalonica. While he mentions the social challenge presented by the audience's conversion, in this case he dwells on the dynamism of the mission, both in its initial display of power in the apostles' foundation visit (1:5) and in its far-reaching success (1:7-8). Indication of Paul's focus in this later contact with the community is his characterization of its members in glowing terms as productive members (1:3) as well as his claim that they are like the missionaries in their joy-filled commitment to the word.

The double prepositional phrases concerning "difficulty" and "joy" require further attention both in terms of meaning and function. The first term, *thlipsis*, occurs only here in the second missive, but it along with the verb is used three times in the first letter: 3:3, 4, 7. Here also it seems to indicate "troubles or difficulties" of a socioreligious nature rather than systematic or unofficial "persecution" (see earlier discussion). The second principal term, *chara*, also occurs only in this particular passage of the second letter (though see 5:16 where the verb is used), but several times in the first missive: 2:19, 20; 3:9. Whereas in the first missive the term relates to the missionaries and only secondarily to the community as being their joy or giving them joy, in the second it is used of the community's reception of the word. While some scholars wish to see *thlipsis* as the Satanic persecution of the end-days, but counterbalanced by divinely inspired joy among the righteous, it is best to consider the statement's overall function in Paul's thanksgiving period.

Beginning with verse 4 Paul proceeds to marshal evidence for his conviction concerning the community's maturity (v. 3) and presents a series of parallel statements, first concerning the apostolic mission during the foundation visit (4-5) and then concerning the mission's success among the new converts (6-7).

(a)	4 certainty of election	6 imitators of Paul & Lord
(b)	5 gospel not in words only	word accepted amid difficulty
(c)	in power: Spirit & conviction	with joy of the Spirit
(d)	missionaries as models	7 Thessalonians as example.

As regards the first parallel (a), one observes a note of certainty or confidence in both elements: one expressed in verse 4 by Paul's use of *oida* ("we . . . are sure of your election") and the other by his use of the aorist ("you . . . became imitators").

The next two elements of the parallel (b and c) require more explanation. In verse 5 the contrast is between word and power, not as exclusive elements but as one working through the other. Divine power operates through human intermediaries and manifests itself, at the gospel's service, as dynamic conviction. Paul's concern is divine communication of the gospel. In verse 6 again there is discussion of the word being transmitted to the Thessalonian audience but in this case the focus is on the context of the hearers and the contrast is between the human situation and the audience's divinely inspired reaction. This human situation is not so much an interior conflict of converts who abandon their former cultural and religious heritage for a new one as it is the resulting socio-religious conflict and ostracization which the converts experienced as they lived among pagan neighbors in a polytheistic society. The focus then in verse 5 is on effective power and in verse 6 on joy as the divine sign of effective commitment and productive behavior.

The final parallel (d) dwells, on the one hand, on the role played by the missionaries and, on the other, on the consequent role played by the new converts. Thus, in light of these rhetorical parallels, we conclude that it is not the joy of resisting "persecution," whether eschatological in nature or historical in character (based on the alleged situation as reflected in Acts 17 and 1 Thess 2:14-16), which is Paul's concern but rather the divinely given joy which makes the new converts imitators of the missionaries and of the Lord and so "an example for all believers" (1:7), both signs of the new age (see further discussion of the Spirit at 4:8). Finally, it should be noted that in verses 5 and 6 the expression "the Holy Spirit" occurs without the article, a good indication that Paul intends to stress the element of divine power operative in the preaching of the good news (vv. 4-5) and in its reception in faith (6-7).

Example in Faith and Mission. Paul's statement in verse 7 that the converts of Thessalonica "became an example for all the believers in Macedonia and in Achaia" has generated discussion concerning the author's meaning, especially as related to the enigmatic claims of verse 8. Besides, much has been said regarding the disjointedness of verses 7-8, particularly the formulation of verse 8. While the majority of scholars opt for the traditional punctuation given below, others opt to join the double geographical references to either of the two dependent clauses—either the expression "not only in Macedonia and in Achaia but everywhere else" is connected to the following statement about faith or added to the preceding clause concerning the word of the Lord. This is done seemingly because the two geographical statements, linked by "not only . . . but also" would have neither the same subject nor the same verb.

However one explains the awkwardness of verse 8, whether as owing to Paul's impulsive style or a lapse in grammatical finesse, it is still possible, from his text, to discern clues both to its formulation and interpretation. One key to Paul's meaning, undoubtedly, is his use of the contrastive construction: "not only but" (*ou monon . . . alla*). Additionally, the omission of the usual *kai* after *alla* seems intentional, for Paul wishes to insist that "the second member [of the contrast] includes the first" (BDF 448.1). While most interpreters take this to mean that "everywhere else" includes "Macedonia and Achaia," such a construction may be used, as here, also to contrast clauses and sentences (LSJ 67). The following literal rendering of verse 8, in light of the above observations, attempts to demonstrate Paul's logic and will guide our interpretation of its meaning:

> for from you,
>> has sounded forth   a
>> the word of the Lord   b
>> not only in Macedonia and in Achaia,   c
>> but everywhere else   c'
>> your faith in God   b'
>> has gone forth,   a'
> so that we have no need to say anything.

In structural terms the sentence begins by indicating the source from which ("from you") the subjects of the two clauses have emanated. There then follows in parallel, chiastic word order the elements of the two clauses. From these observations and from a comparison of the two verses we propose (1) that verse 8 attempts to explain what Paul meant by the ambiguous terminology of becoming "an example to all the believers" (v. 7) and (2) that verse 8 combines two elements of the explanation into one sentence and attempts to contrast these two related themes. Paul therefore claims that the Thessalonian community was an example or model in missionary terms to others on the Greek mainland (first clause of verse 8) and that they also became model Christians in the eyes of believers there and far beyond (second clause).

We turn our attention therefore to the first clause of verse 8. From Thessalonica there has sounded forth (see Note on verb *exēcheō*) "the word of the Lord." It is clear from usage already in the Thessalonian correspondence that Paul employs "word" or "gospel," with a variety of qualifiers, as virtual synonyms to describe his message concerning the Christ-event; but the former he employs (also in his later correspondence) either absolutely (1:5) or with *tou theou* (2:13). So why the peculiarity of the present verse: its singular usage here and nonappearance in later Pauline texts? Further, in this expression does *kyrios* refer to Christ or to God? While most scholars either pass over the issue in silence or insist simply that for Paul Jesus is the *kyrios,* others give the following complementary reasons for such a conclusion: [1] the expression "word of the Lord" in 1:8 functions as a parallel to "our gospel" in 1:5 and [2] "of the Lord" is an objective genitive thereby pointing to the message about Jesus. These reasons, in light of Pauline usage, are less than compelling, since not only "our gospel" but also "the word of God" (2:13), "the gospel of God" (2:2, 8, 9) or "of Christ" (3:2) are virtual synonyms for Paul's message. Additionally, to insist that "of the Lord" must function as objective genitive and therefore describe the content of the message is to overlook the parallel phrase, "the word of God" whose content must undoubtedly be the same (about the Christ-event) and whose genitive phrase must of necessity function as a subjective genitive (God as source of message).

The key to understanding Paul's usage and meaning in verse 8 is the phrase "the word of the Lord," an idiom which is commonly used in the historical and prophetic books, almost invariably in prophetic contexts. Of particular interest is the expression, "the word of the Lord came to" *(ginomai pros);* see especially 1 Kgs 12:22; 2 Kgs 24:2; 1 Chr 17:3 and often in the Prophets. Interestingly, Paul speaks of "our gospel having come to" the Thessalonians *(ginomai eis)* to describe the apostolic mission there (1:5) and ostensibly refers to the Thessalonian missionary activity on the Greek mainland by employing still further prophetic terminology, "the word of the Lord" (1:8). In keeping with OT usage Paul, by employing this terminology, emphasized God's message of salvation which came first to the Thessalonians through him and his colleagues ("our gospel") and then from that dynamic community rang out loudly to all parts of Greece. Paul employs OT terms to underscore what some scholars have described as his prophetic self-concept and its missionary goal.

Two further points require attention in this regard, whether "the word of the Lord" is to be understood as referring to God or Christ and whether the clause underscores missionary activity or, as a parallel to the second clause, focuses on the community's conversion and Christian behavior.

In the first case, it is correct to insist that for Paul and colleagues "Lord" usually refers to Christ. However, in this instance we might make a distinction between what Paul suggests, in his use of prophetic terminology and what the Christian community might understand, not only from its religious tradition, but also from this epistolary experience. It is very possible that Paul intended this ΟΤ phrase, "the word of the Lord," to function much as "the word of God" does in the first thanksgiving period (2:13) and it is just as probable that the Gentile community in hearing Paul speak of "the Lord" would have understood this to mean "Christ" since its previous uses in the second missive (1:1, 3 and 6) clearly have "Christ" as reference. In this way one can explain both Paul's later avoidance of such an ambiguous expression and his insistence in the following clause upon the believers' "faith in God."

In the second case, while most favor a missionary sense for the first clause, some prefer instead to see it, as well as the following, as bearing echoes of what happened at Thessalonica. The main objections are (a) the community's activity could not possibly have been as widespread as this passage suggests and (b) the first clause is really a rephrase of what the second clause states. The first objection relates to the time which allegedly lapsed between the foundation visit and the writing of the passage in question. The objection relies more on the statement of Acts 17:1 concerning a three-Sabbath Pauline ministry than on Paul's own version of the matter. Beyond this one must reckon with the temporal contrast between 1:7f. and 2:13f. (see Introduction). The second objection fails to examine the differences between the clauses (particularly between "word" and "faith"), pays too little attention to Paul's "not only . . . but" contrast in verse 8, and does not explain sufficiently Paul's earlier statement that the Thessalonians "became an example for all believers."

The second clause of verse 8 in its turn also states that from Thessalonica there has gone forth "the news of your faith in God." The subject of the clause requires some attention owing to its unusual formulation, for while Paul employs a variety of prepositions with the noun *pistis* ("faith or trust"—see 3:2), only in Phlm 5 and here does he use *pros* with the noun. That Paul intends more than stylistic variation in this instance is borne out by two considerations. [1] There is contemporary evidence to support Pauline usage and to assist interpretation. In Philo, *De Abrahamo*, one encounters an extended contrast (262f.) between "faith or trusting in" created things or God (*pisteuō* + dative). The latter he expresses later as "faith directed toward God" (*hē pros theon pistis*—268) and, in a passage reminiscent of Paul, insists on the twofold direction of faith: disbelief in one and belief in the other (269; see also 271, 173 and 3 Macc 15:24; 16:22). [2] Scholars readily note the context of 1 Thess 1:8 and insist on its relation to verse 9: "turning to *(pros)* God away from idols," particularly its use of *pros* to emphasize the turning "toward God" in conversion. The focal point of verse 8b then is the community's conversion, a theme which Paul describes at greater length in verses 9-10.

Verses 7-8, therefore, are to be seen in their epistolary context as forming part of Paul's thanksgiving pericope. In his continued effort to curry favor with his audience, in verse 7 Paul lavishes praise on them by underscoring their special relation to the wider Christian community but employs what might be considered ambiguous terminology: "an example for all the believers." Sensing that this could be read in a variety of ways, Paul, in verse 8, addresses the dual themes of example and imitation in mission and faith to clarify his meaning. Both themes receive his attention later as he describes the missionaries' behavior (2:1-12) and the community's turning to God (1:9-10) and life of holiness (4:3f.).

Jewish-Christian Report about the Thessalonians. In completing his statement about the community's well-known and deserved reputation Paul makes a concluding comment which immediately leads to the topic of verses 9-10. He insists at the end of verse 8: "we have no need to say anything" and follows this by what other Christians say instead. Their report mentions two things: the foundation visit and the community's conversion. It is the latter, extending from verses 9b to 10, which has received the greatest attention and which requires some discussion.

In light of the extended discussion in the Excursus above, what therefore can we conclude concerning verses 9b-10? Since the whole passage contains so much non-Pauline language and rare or uncommonly expressed themes, one is led to postulate Pauline borrowing for these verses. Such is commonly held by scholars who envision usage by Paul of a carefully structured missionary summary or liturgical hymn. However, the somewhat clumsy use, in stylistic and thematic terms, of a resurrection formula in verse 10 suggests Pauline editorial activity and allows less confidence in the notion that Paul borrowed all of verses 9b-10 from a given source. Even the proposal that Paul edits a catechetical statement or uses Jewish missionary terminology in these verses leaves unexplained the reason for this phenomenon. In the case of the latter, why would Paul cite the views of other missionaries, either their texts or their language, when these differ from his own? This is puzzling since it was he who preached to this community in the first place. As to the former, one must concede that the problem of non-Pauline language and context extends to the whole of verses 9-10. Also, some scholars have rightly insisted that proper understanding of the passage should take into consideration the letter's Thessalonian context. This has been pursued especially in attempts to see a close connection between verses 9-10 and the rest of the letter.

Nonetheless, it is necessary to return to the epistolary context to understand the unusual character of these verses and their anticipatory use in the thanksgiving section. It is important to note that the beginning of verse 9 is not about missionary work but about widespread reports regarding the community. The reason verses 9-10 contain so much non-Pauline language and so little typically Pauline thought is that Paul is verbalizing what he and his colleagues have heard either from other Greek communities during their travels or, preferably, from other Jewish-Christian missionaries. The issue is not whether the theme of conversion formed part of the good news announced throughout the Greek mainland but that Paul is appealing to the witness of Christians far and wide to attest to the maturity of the community (1:3; 2:1) as *captatio benevolentiae* and to prepare for some of the letter's major components. In opting to employ the thoughts and words of other missionaries (note the Jewish missionary terminology) Paul chose ideas that suited his epistolary goal but ideas that needed, from his standpoint, Christological editing.

(1) Verses 9-10, as part of Paul's thanksgiving period, contribute to the success of his epistolary strategy. As the thanksgiving begins by underscoring the community's commitment and choice (3-4) and insists on the missionaries' work and behavior (5), so it dwells at greatest length on the community's reaction ("you for your part") to the apostolic preaching (6-10). In three successive, complex statements Paul discusses various aspects of the addressees' conversion. Verses 6-7 develop the themes of imitation and resulting example, while verse 8 focuses on the two ways the new converts became an example to other believers and verses 9-10 return to the theme of conversion. The last two verses, strategically situated by Paul at the end of the thanksgiving section, offer important clues for understanding the structure and purpose of the second missive.

An oral or written report (v. 9—use of *apangellō*) reaches Paul and is used to introduce his letter of example (2:1f.), advice (4:3f.), and consolation (4:13f.). As the report begins by referring to the missionaries' successful visit, so the body of Paul's letter opens with a statement about the visit's effectiveness (2:1). Just as the believers of the Greek mainland describe the community's conversion as a turning to God away from idols and what they represent, so Paul, in discussing the apostles' calling, motivation, and purpose, insists that the apostolic preachers, in contrast to current moral philosophers, are entrusted by God to preach a divine message that the audience might lead lives pleasing to God (2:2f.). Next, the report states that the community's conversion resulted in its "service" of God and, in 4:3-12, Paul defines this commitment as a life of holiness and quiet love among Christian and pagan neighbors. Finally, verse 10 underscores an eschatological theme and prepares for the discussions first about believers who have died before the Lord's return (4:13-18) and then about the time of the end (5:1-11). The report of 1:9-10 then announces the various parts of the body of the letter and from such an analysis one understands Paul's choice of such a handy report to introduce his advice to a maturing community.

(2) Choice of someone else's statement, however, has led to some editing. Obviously, use of this report necessitated several changes in person. What was originally said to or about the missionaries is now expressed in the first person plural ("concerning us" and "visit we had"). Also, the second person plural replaces an original third person plural (from "they turned" to "you turned"; also "among you"). Modifications suggested earlier are the change of an original "Son of Man" to "his Son" and the insertion of a resurrection formula in verse 10 to render more Pauline a statement concerning Jesus' role as eschatological deliverer.

Thus, labeling verses 9-10 pre-Pauline is probably misleading. Instead, they represent the thinking of Jewish-Christian missionaries, contemporary with Paul, whom some modern scholars have associated with the Q community or thinking of the Q-Source, a text which Paul brought more into line with his own Christology by insisting on Jesus' resurrection from the dead as the basis for eschatological hope. By adding such a reference to the resurrection, Paul is able to delineate more clearly the period of Jesus' absence in heaven, a period which will come to an end at the time of his return from heaven—in anticipation in 1:10 and in reality in 4:16.

Lastly, the composition of the passage requires attention. In arguing for Pauline use of a baptismal hymn, some have proposed a two-strophe structure of three lines each:

> you turned to God from idols
>> to serve the living and true God
>>> and to await his Son from heaven,
> whom he raised from the dead,
>> Jesus who delivers us
>>> from the coming wrath.

Additionally, the first strophe centers on God and the second on Jesus, and successive lines of the strophes address past, present, and future. While this suggestion has been criticized for positing a poetic structure for the whole or for assuming that the entire passage is non-Pauline, its basic understanding of the overall schema is defensible. In effect, the careful temporal delineation of the effects of the Christ-event as representing past, present, and future realities is the result of Pauline editing and consonant with his way of thinking. The conversion of the Thessalonians as well as Jesus' death and resurrection are past events with present effects, namely, service and deliverance. At the same time, believers look forward, in the present, to the future realities of the Christevent: Jesus' return as eschatological deliverer. While the infinitives "to serve" and "to await" are in the present, their literary and thematic contexts require that one see the service of God as a present reality and the waiting, also in the present, as focusing on a future reality. Likewise, the participles, "one who delivers" and "coming," are in the present tense. While one assumes that a Q-like reading would insist on deliverance as an eschatological fact, a Pauline reading, in light of the resurrection theme, would suggest a present soteriological function for Jesus.

Thus, analysis of Paul's choice, use, and editing of the ideas of fellow missionaries indicates both the variety of and tolerance for early Christological views and Paul's own creativity as he helped one of his earliest communities face the problems and challenges of being Christians in a non-Christian world.

For Reference and Further Study

Castelli, E. A. *Imitating Paul: A Discourse of Power.* Louisville: Westminster-Knox, 1991.

Collins, R. F. "Paul's Early Christology," in *SFLT*, 253–84.

Elias, J. W. " 'Jesus Who Delivers Us from the Wrath to Come' (1 Thess 1:10): Apocalyptic and Peace in the Thessalonian Correspondence." *SBLSP* (1992), 121–32.

Friedrich, G. "Ein Tauflied hellenistischer Judenchristen, 1 Thess 1, 9f." *TZ* 21 (1965) 502–16.

Havener, I. "The Pre-Pauline Christological Credal Formulae of 1 Thessalonians." *SBLSP* (1981), 105–28.

Holtz, T. " 'Euer Glaube an Gott.' Zu Form und Inhalt von 1 Thess 1, 9f." *Die Kirche des Anfangs: Festschrift für Heinz Schürmann.* Eds. R. Schackenburg, et al. Freiburg: Herder, 1978, 459–88.

Langevin, P.-E. *Jésus Seigneur et l'eschatologie: exégèse de textes prépauliniens.* Brussels: Desclée de Brouwer, 1967.

Munck, J. "1 Thess i.9-10 and the Missionary Preaching of Paul. Textual Exegesis and Hermeneutic Reflexions." *NTS* 9 (1962–63) 95–110.

O'Brien, P. T. *Introductory Thanksgivings in the Letters of Paul.* Leiden: Brill, 1977.

Reinhartz, A. "On the Meaning of the Pauline Exhortation: 'mimētai mou ginesthe—Become Imitators of Me.' " *SR* 16 (1987) 393–403.

Schubert, P. *Form and Function of the Pauline Thanksgivings.* Berlin: Töpelmann, 1939.

Stanley, D. M. " 'Become Imitators of Me.' The Pauline Conception of Apostolic Tradition." *Bib* 40 (1959) 859–77.

3. *Missionary Behavior as Paraenetic Model* (2:1-12)

1. For you yourselves know, brothers and sisters, about our visit among you, that it was not ineffective; 2. yet, after having struggled on its account and been scoffed at, as you know, at Philippi, we spoke openly as the agents of our God so as to declare to you also the gospel of God in a strenuous public contest. 3. For our appeal did not originate from delusion or impure motive, nor was it made through deception; 4. but, just as we have been examined and approved by God to be entrusted with the gospel, so we speak not to please mortals but God, the one who examines our hearts. 5. Neither, indeed, did we ever come using flattering speech, as you know, nor acting for an avaricious reason— God is witness; 6. neither were we seeking renown from mortals, whether from you or from others, 7. though we might have insisted on our importance as apostles of Christ. Instead, we came into your midst with gentleness, like a nurse caring fondly for her own children. 8. Having such affection for you, we gladly decided not only to impart to you the gospel of God but also to share our very selves because you had become so dear to us. 9. For you will recall, brothers and sisters, our labor and toil: how we worked night and day so as not to burden any of you, while we proclaimed to you the gospel of God. 10. You are witnesses, and so is God, how devoutly and uprightly, and thus blamelessly we behaved while among you believers; 11. how, as you also know, we treat each one of you like a father his own children, 12. encouraging, consoling, and imploring you to conduct yourselves worthily of the God who calls you to his own kingdom and glory.

NOTES

1. *For you yourselves know, brothers and sisters:* The connection between chapters 1 and 2, made explicit by the conjunction *gar* ("for"), is further stressed by appeal to the audience's own experience ("you . . . know"). Such a recall device was employed in 1:5 (see discussion there) in a context similar to the present one. Author and audience, by this formula, are called upon to relive the experience of the foundation visit as the basis of their epistolary exchange. Verse 1 introduces the reader to the body of the letter; there is a shift in topic and focus which is underscored both by a change in subject ("you yourselves"—*autoi*) and by a renewed address of the audience (*adelphoi*; see 1 Cor 1:10; 2 Cor 1:8; Phil 1:12).

   about our visit among you, that it was not ineffective: The term "visit" is repeated from 1:9 and recalls the earlier, unqualified praise given the audience regarding its reception of the missionaries. A further clue to the continued emphasis given this praise is Paul's double use of the article to introduce the noun and its adjectival phrase *(tēn eisodon hēmōn tēn pros hymas)*, thereby emphasizing the modifier. In this way, Paul focuses on the missionaries' activity within the community (see verse 7 and the following contrast with the Philippian mission). The expression "that it was not ineffective" *(hoti ou kenē gegonen)* contrasts with a similar statement in 3:5. In the first missive Paul states that the missionaries were concerned, prior to Timothy's trip, lest their activity had been nullified by the community's fall. Timothy's report set those worries to rest. In the second missive, after showing in the thanksgiving how successful the mission has been, Paul appeals to the community's knowledge of the facts. He further underscores its success by employing the perfect of the verb *ginomai:* "it was and continues to be" so.

2. *yet, after having struggled on its account and been scoffed at, as you know, at Philippi:* At first glance the conjunction *alla* might seem an awkward transition from verse 1; in place of an adversive statement one expects a justification of the claim just made. But the conjunction indicates a change of subject with a contrastive sense (rendered "yet"—BAGD 38.2), for Paul refers back to the events prior to his arrival in the city and is thereby able to contrast the difficulty of the task with an effective ministry made possible by God's assistance. He alludes to the visit at Philippi and, in a long participial clause, describes their treatment there with the verbs *propaschō* and *hybrizō.* The translation of these two terms as "having struggled . . . and been scoffed at" rather than the usual "having suffered and been maltreated" presupposes discussion below of a missionary rhetorical context rather than relying on the Lukan account of the episode in Acts 16:19-40. The recall device ("as you know"—also verse 5) in this case is employed to involve the audience directly in the author's story of the mission, first at Philippi and then at Thessalonica.

we spoke openly as the agents of our God: Paul turns to the apostolic arrival in the city. The preaching activity is described by the verb *parrhēsiazomai* ("speak openly or freely") and the prepositional phrase *en tō theō hēmōn* (lit.: "in our God"). Their meaning in this context has been variously understood especially as it relates to the following prepositional phrase and infinitive complement. The rhetorical context leads me to render the expression not as "having courage in our God to . . ." but rather as "speaking openly as the agents of our God so as to . . ." (see discussion below). Paul's use of the rare phrase "our God" (see 3:9) further stresses the contrast between the manner and message of the Christian missionaries and of other contemporary preachers. Also here as in 3:9, one senses the intense bond which exists between the missionaries and their converts as they share gospel and lives (2:8).

so as to declare to you also the gospel of God: The expression "so as to declare to you," interpreted as an infinitive of purpose, is unusual since this is the only case in Paul of *pros* with *laleō* or of this verb with "gospel," a fact which suggests that Paul is responding to issues raised at Thessalonica (see use of *laleō* in verse 4). Interestingly, the expression, "the gospel of God," used only three other times by Paul (Rom 1:1; 15:16; 2 Cor 11:7), occurs three times in 1 Thessalonians, all within 2:2-12. The focus here on divine message (subjective genitive, i.e., God as subject), the earlier mention of "turning to God," as well as the frequent occurrence of *theos* in this pericope (9x) point to a peculiarly Thessalonian issue. There is a need to underscore the fact that the apostles were divinely approved messengers bearing a divine message, a message presented in a surprisingly open, gentle, and generous manner to bring the hearers "to lead lives worthy of God" (2:12). The term "also" has been added to the translation to capture the nuance intended, namely, that the reception at Philippi is paradigmatic of the missionaries' experience as they move on to the public contest about which the addressees are well informed.

in a strenuous public contest: Paul terminates his Philippian-Thessalonian comparison with a striking phrase, *en pollǭ agōni,* whose interpretation is much discussed. His use of athletic imagery is interpreted as referring to physical, mental, or moral struggle, each rendering related to a presumed epistolary context. Contemporary usage, however, by moral philosophers and the term's rhetorical nuance suggest a Pauline reference to the presentation of the gospel by the missionaries as a public contest vying for the attention and allegiance of urban crowds (see discussion below of the public presentation of God's gospel).

3. *For our appeal did not originate:* With verse 3 one encounters the first of a series of contrasts, which are introduced by the connective *gar* ("for") and which explicate the rhetorical nature of the public contest. To introduce his subject Paul employs the noun *paraklēsis,* a term which has a range of meaning: from "consolation," to "exhortation," to "appeal" (BAGD 618), each of which is proposed for verse 3. Defense of the term as meaning "consolation" stems from the claim that in 2:1-6 Paul employs ᴏᴛ language (Isa 49:10) to present himself as a messianic prophet with a message of consolation. This meaning, however, is rhetorically inappropriate here and is more consistent with Pauline usage of the verb in 4:18 and 5:11. More frequent is the claim that the term designates "exhortation," a common meaning for verb and noun. Thus Paul is seen as presenting prophetic, paraenetic, or homiletic exhortation. The major objection, and the strongest argument for opting for the meaning "appeal," is that the text refers to the original visit and the proclamation of the gospel. Also, the epistolary context of public address suggests the rhetorical sense of inviting or appealing to the audience's commitment to the message being proclaimed. At the same time, the term refers back to *laleō* ("speak") of verse 2 and forward to the same term in verse 4. Thus, the emphasis lies on the activity of preaching and the manner in which the appeal is made. Additionally, since a verb is lacking in Greek and the literal meaning of the clause ("was not out of") is somewhat awkward, the above translation supplies the interpretive expression "did not originate from." Finally, while it is possible to view the action of verse 3, in light of the present tense of verse 4, as occurring in the present, it is preferable to consider verses 3f. as referring to the Thessalonian mission and to view verse 4 as a parenthetical comment about Paul's usual missionary practice.

from delusion or impure motive, nor was it made through deception: There follow three statements which define the apostolic preaching in negative terms. The first two are introduced by the repeated preposition *ek* and thus suggest source, while the third is preceded by *en* and so implies manner of speaking or acting. All three terms (*planē, akatharsia,* and *dolos,* rendered "delusion," "impure motive," and "deception," respectively) have provoked discussion concerning their background, meaning, and function within the Pauline text. After discussion of each it is concluded below that the three terms (a) have a rhetorical, moral origin, (b) focus on God or error, self-interest, and servile behavior, and (c) serve as antithesis to the motivation of the apostolic mission.

4. *but, just as we have been examined and approved by God to be entrusted with the gospel:* This verse provides the second, positive part of the contrast begun in verse 3. Before addressing the point of comparison later in the verse, Paul introduces a *kathōs . . . houtōs* statement ("just as . . . so") to reinforce the immediately preceding denial that the preaching might have been based on some delusion or other. Paul and colleagues are not demented fools dedicated to empty words or lifeless idols but the agents of the one true God who has approved and appointed them for this task. To express this concept Paul employs the verb *dokimazō* in the passive (rendered "examined and approved") and the standard complementary infinitive of the verb *pisteuō* ("to be entrusted") to underscore investiture by God. Such language is taken from the Hellenistic chancery and used to describe the missionaries' authority and responsibility, as well as the source of their message. Finally, Paul uses the term "gospel" without modifier presumably to avoid the repetitiveness which characterizes verse 2.

so we speak, not to please mortals but God: Paul presents himself and his co-missionaries as ideal agents of the God who commissioned them, their manner of speaking ("so we speak") being determined by a divine standard and not the negative, all-too-common characteristics listed previously. While some translators render the construction as "trying to please," it seems that the use of the unusual negative *ou* rather than *mē* with the participle, as attested in the papyri, requires an absolute statement: "not to please mortals." By the use of another antithetical construction Paul contrasts competing spheres of interest: mortals and God. The theme of "pleasing mortals" especially through flattery and deceitful behavior was common in both Greek and Jewish literature but that of "pleasing God" as a motive for missionary rhetoric and behavior is due to Pauline creativity.

the one who examines our hearts: The verb *dokimazō* is repeated from the beginning of the verse in a stereotyped phrase which derives from OT usage (Jer 11:20; 12:3; Pss 16:3; 25:2), much as does the variant expression of Rom 8:27 ("the one who searches hearts") and the earlier phraseology "pleasing God or mortals." With this expression Paul not only claims that the missionaries have been sent or delegated by God for their evangelical task but, in anthropological terms, lays before God his innermost being and the integrity of his motives. God, he insists, knows and continually examines (use of a present participle) the human heart, the source and center of affection, will, and thought.

5. *neither, indeed, did we ever come using flattering speech:* After addressing the issue of delusion ("pleasing God") in verse 4b, Paul in verse 5 focuses on the two other negative motives mentioned in verse 3, but in reverse order,

a change which owes probably to his anticipation, in the previous verse, of the theme of deception under the guise of "pleasing mortals." Having mentioned in negative contrast that his preaching was motivated by divine service, not human approval, Paul returns emphatically ("neither indeed did we ever") to the latter in terms of deceptive speech. Use, however, of the amorphous verb *ginomai,* much favored in this early letter (four and five times in chapters one and two respectively), presents difficulties to translators who variously render it as "we never used . . ." or "we never came with." In fact, Paul employs the verb in 1:5 and 2:7 with the meaning "come" to refer to the foundation visit (the gospel or missionaries' coming). Also, his usage in the former with the addition of the identical *en logǭ* phrase suggests the translation adopted here, a translation which stresses two important Pauline themes: the mission at Thessalonica and the manner of its execution. The phrase "flattering speech," a Hebraism with the literal meaning "with a word of flattery," like much of the language of this pericope has a rich rhetorical and moral history in the Hellenistic world (see discussion below).

as you know, nor acting for an avaricious reason: Once again Paul appeals to the audience's personal experience ("as you know") to defend his claim that the divine message, not rhetorical devices, was the focus of the missionaries' appeal. Paul's repeated reference to shared experience concerning the preachers' behavior prepare for verses 10-12 where, after alluding once again to past behavior as justification, he claims that his forthcoming paraenesis is given with the authority and in the spirit of what he has said in 2:1f. As a parallel ("neither . . . nor") to his denial that he used "flattering speech" and as a commentary on his protest that his appeal did not originate from an "impure motive" (v. 3), Paul now focuses on "avarice" as the customary reason given for the use of flattery by speakers (see also Rom 1:29 where *pleonexia* appears in a vice list). Paul's expression of this theme will require further attention below.

God is witness: After speaking of outward behavior and its assessment by the Thessalonian community ("as you know"), Paul addresses the interior motive which only God can know and judge ("God, the one who examines our hearts"—verse 4). Thus, Paul, in a Hellenistic manner, calls on God as the only witness to the missionaries' interior motives (also Rom 1:9; 2 Cor 1:23; Phil 1:8; *TDNT* 4:491). Thus, God is the ultimate judge of their motivation and witness that they are speaking truthfully. The appeals to God are noteworthy as Paul tells the story of the Thessalonian mission (vv. 2, 4, 5, 8, 10, 12), for it is the story of God's approval and sending of servants who have acquitted themselves worthily of their divine task.

6. *neither were we seeking renown from mortals:* Use of the term *oute* ("neither") serves in this case as a contrast to the previous two occurrences of the term in verse 5, which introduced separate but related denials. In this third denial one finds an alternate motive to that of monetary gain, but also one whose attainment is made possible by flattery or ingratiating language. To express this alternate motive Paul introduces a participial construction with the verb *zēteō* ("seeking"—translating the term as "demanding" seems unnecessarily

to anticipate what is said later in verse 7) and employs the term *doxa* with the meaning "renown or popularity" (see 2:19-20).

whether from you or from others: The statement concerning "renown from mortals" is qualified by parallel prepositional phrases. Thus, renown of all types, whether the seeking of disciples ("from you") or applause for rhetorical reputation ("from others"), is rejected as motive for the apostolic mission.

7. *though we might have insisted on our importance as apostles of Christ:* How one interprets the beginning of verse 7 and relates it to its context hinge on the meaning attached to the expression *en barei einai.* Since the noun *baros* means either "burden" in a more literal sense or "weight" with its derived meaning of authority or dignity, there have arisen two ways of reading the passage. In the first case, it is suggested that, in accordance with Pauline and papyrus usage as well as context, there is a reference to financial support (*doxa* in the previous verse would allude to money). Most scholars, however, find the arguments unconvincing and suggest that the term refers to authority or influence, so "insist on one's influence" (BAGD 133.2) or "importance as." Such an interpretation corresponds better to the context, particularly of the previous reference to "renown from mortals" and of the succeeding contrast concerning "gentle" behavior. On the expression "as apostles of Christ" see discussion below.

Instead, we came into your midst with gentleness: Verse 7b stands in stark contrast to verses 5-7a. As the preceding verses had introduced a series of negative statements (introduced by *oute*) to characterize the missionary visit and had insisted "we never came" thus (*pote . . . egenēthēmen*), so the whole assertion is counteracted by a positive, affective statement, whose contrastive force is underscored by a strong adversive conjunction and repetition of the verb from verse 5: "instead, we came" (*alla egenēthēmen*). The clause presents a serious textual problem since the majority of MSS read *nēpioi* ("infant": P65 S B D G *al* lat) and a far smaller number have *ēpioi* ("gentle": A K 33 *pm* sy sa). Further, either reading could be explained as the result of scribal error: duplicating a preceding *n* or omitting the second of a series. It is preferable, however, to follow the majority of scholars in arguing from internal evidence that *ēpioi* fits the context better: the missionaries are parental figures, not children (2:7b, 11); their gentle manner contrasts with the negative attributes presented in the pericope; and the familiar Pauline "infant" (never as a vocative) would have replaced the rare term "gentle" (see *TCGNT,* 629-30).

like a nurse caring fondly for her own children: The image of the nurse (*trophos*), owing to its uniqueness, context, and etymology continues to generate discussion. It has been suggested, since the verb *trephō* means "to feed or nurse," since the clause implies the "nursing of one's own children," since there exists classical justification of such usage (BAGD 827), and since the image of the mother is frequent as opposed to that of the nurse, that the word really means "mother" or "nursing mother." However, the term commonly means "nurse" and the image makes sense in the context. More important, and decisive for its interpretation, is the ending of the clause: *ta heautēs tekna* ("her own children"). While one could insist that the reflexive pronoun has lost its emphatic meaning (see also verse 8), it seems to mean precisely that Paul and colleagues act more like a nurse towards her own children, than a nanny toward those under her charge. Additionally, to describe the activity of the mother, who happens to be a nurse, Paul has recourse to the rare verb *thalpō*, literally "to warm or brood" (Deut 22:6 of a bird and its young) or figuratively "to cherish, comfort or foster" (BAGD 350; also LSJ 783). Its precise nuance is difficult to gauge, whether it is that of care or fostering, of warmth or affection, or even of nurture. In the case of the last mentioned, appeal is made to the etymology of the word "nurse" either to interpret the subject as "nursing mother" or to provide the verb with some nuance of "feeding." While many opt for the more neutral sense of "care," some, probably more correctly, add a hint of affection, as in the above translation.

8. *Having such affection for you:* The participle *homeiromenoi* presents a lexical problem since its etymology and meaning are uncertain and since there exist few data on which to base a firm conclusion. Despite a recent attempt to relate the verb to *meiromai*, meaning "to separate," it is best to retain the traditional interpretation, "long for or have affection for" (BAGD 565; LSJ 1221), for the following reasons (see M-M, 447; *TDNT* 5:176). (1) Survey of the context of the word's rare occurrences confirm such a reading (Job 3:21 in the LXX, Ps 62:2 in Symmachus' translation; and CIG 3.4000.7, a fourth-century A.D. sepulchral epigram), (2) as do the marked tendency in the ms tradition to substitute the better known verb *himeiromai* ("to long for," whether in the LXX for Job 3:21 or the NT for 1 Thess 2:8), and (3) the concurrence of early interpreters (whether Hesychius who equates the term with *epithymeō* or the Vulgate with *desidero*). The verb therefore resumes what was said at the end of the previous verse through nursing imagery concerning the missionaries' behavior and strategy and prepares for a striking description of the affection which resulted (*houtōs*—"such") from the Thessalonian visit.

we gladly decided: The emotional, affective tone of the passage suggests, as in 3:1 where the same term is employed, that the verb *eudokeō* be rendered etymologically as "gladly decide" rather than simply "decide or be ready or determined." Since the context of the principal verb is the author's progression from gentle treatment to loving care to deep affection, it seems that the last mentioned implies great willingness rather than simple duty. The verb, though seemingly present in form, should be read as an imperfect, since temporal augments of *eu*-words are often missing in the NT period (BDF 67.1). Thus, the entire verse refers to the Thessalonian mission, as does most of 2:1-12. Use of the imperfect stresses continuous action and so alludes to the work of imparting the gospel and to their affectionate relation to the new converts.

not only to impart to you the gospel of God but also to share our very selves: The object of the missionaries' desire is expressed by a customary Pauline complementary infinitive phrase, itself governing a double object. On the one hand, a complementary (not an exclusive) contrast is intended between these objects which are introduced by a trademark of Pauline style (see 2:5, 8) "not only . . . but also." On the other hand, the two objects are not on the same footing, being neither of the same order nor shared in the same way. Since the verb *metadidōmi* means both "give" and "give a part" and owing to the difference between the two objects, the translation should read: "to impart the gospel of God" (see 2:2) and "to share our very selves." Thus, in the first case the missionaries give something ("share" is inappropriate; see Rom 1:11) and in the second they share what they are, i.e., "their very selves." The second object is to be interpreted not as the "giving up of life" but as the "sharing of one's very self," a saying wherein *psychē* designates the total person and that person's behavior.

because you had become so dear to us: The reason for such dedication and generosity, Paul concludes, was the friendship which had developed. As a result of the gentle and loving care of the missionaries, the addressees became believers in the true God and beloved friends; thus, they are "beloved" both of God (1:4) and of the apostles (*agapētoi*—"so dear").

9. *For you will recall, brothers and sisters, our toil and hardship:* The connection between verses 8 and 9 is indicated by *gar* ("for"), for the latter provides an example of apostolic sharing. Again, Paul makes explicit use of a recall device to situate his audience more concretely in the context of the foundation visit. In a way similar to 2:1 he repeats his wish that they think back to the time of the initial proclamation and again employs direct address to focus more exclusively on the missionaries' conduct. He asks his readers to remember the missionaries' "toil and hardship," an expression which sets the tone and gives the context for what follows. The two nouns, *kopos* and *mochthos*, have similar ranges of meaning, though the first might point to the fatigue of manual labor and the latter to the hardship involved (LSJ 978, 1149). While one could focus on the first as often describing missionary activity (see 3:5), several considerations point to the terms being a formula for the fatigue and hardship of labor.

how we worked night and day: After the set formula regarding fatiguing work, Paul employs another set phrase to address the temporal character of that labor. The expression "night and day" is identical in form and function to its usage in 3:10, namely in the genitive to express "time within which" and, hyperbolically, stressing the endless, exhausting hours devoted to one's task.

so as not to burden any of you: The construction *pros to mē* with infinitive introduces the reason for the long hours of labor, while the rare verb *epibareō* (only here and in the citation of 2 Thess 3:8), related to the generic term *baros* also meaning "burden or weight," implies not only financial independence on the part of the missionaries but a desire, in the giving of their labor as a sharing of their lives (v. 8), to present the gospel without ulterior motive or apostolic pressure.

while we proclaimed to you the gospel of God: Paul employs the verb *kēryssō* ("announce or proclaim") for the first time. Its use in the present context (only once in the Thessalonian correspondence) as a synonym for "declaring or speaking the gospel" (2:2, 3; also "imparting" of 2:8) suggests a general meaning for the term as describing the apostolic mission or work of preaching (see Rom 10:14-15; 1 Cor 15:11). Its choice in this context probably is due to Paul's desire to reiterate what he has underscored in verse 2 concerning the apostles as agents or heralds of the God who commissioned them. Further, the rare expression "to proclaim the gospel of God" (see also Gal 2:2) is identical to Mark's introduction of Jesus and his message (1:14). Such contact with the early Jesus tradition, as well as the passage's focus on the theological character of the message, confirm the tentative nature of Paul's language in this correspondence as he formulates his developing thought.

10. *You are witnesses, and so is God:* In a manner reminiscent of verse 5 Paul calls on God and the audience to testify to the truth of what he is saying. On the one hand, the addressees to whom the preceding verses are addressed, can attest to the fact that Paul and colleagues fearlessly preached the gospel and generously shared their time, effort, and being with their converts; they are witnesses both to what Paul has already said and is about to express. On the other hand, Paul, as in verse 5, calls on God the only one who can judge the missionaries' motives. This procedure is reminiscent of a passage in Josephus where a woman begs Antipater: "Listen to me, O king, and may God hear me too, a witness to the truth of my words who cannot be deceived" (*JW* 1:595; see also Acts 5:32). Both in the usage of Josephus and that of Paul the addition of a divine oath, beyond the direct appeal to the audience, points to a serious rhetorical maneuver, a move to prepare for the following paraenetic section (4:3f.).

how devoutly and uprightly, and thus blamelessly we behaved while among you believers: A first *hōs* ("how") statement describes the apostolic mission by the use of three unusual adverbs: *hosiōs* ("devoutly"), *dikaiōs* ("uprightly"), and *amemptōs* ("blamelessly"). The first occurs only here in Paul; the second, in its adverbial form, appears one other time in his letters (1 Cor 15:3); and the third is slightly more frequent in his writings (adverb: 1 Thess 2:10; 5:23 and adjective: 1 Thess 3:13; Phil 2:15; 3:6). The first two are interpreted as referring to behavior (use of adverbs to characterize conduct rather than adjectives to describe character) which relates to divine and human statutes, respectively. The third serves as a summarizing statement concerning the apostles' conduct vis-à-vis God and the Thessalonians (see discussion below). Further, the expression translated "we behaved while among you believers" represents the ubiquitous verb *ginomai* preceded by an anomolous dative construction *(hymin tois pisteuousin)*, the whole of which is variously interpreted. The verb which is understood in verses 5 and 7 as indicating the "coming" of the apostles in mission is here similarly understood but translated so as to stress the apostles' behavior while at Thessalonica. Additionally, the dative phrase, usually interpreted as behaving "toward you," is viewed locally as referring to the foundation visit and thus expressing past time: "while among you." On the expression "believers" and its developing, technical meaning, see 1:7 and discussion of 2:13.

11. *How, as you also know, we treat each one of you:* A second *hōs* construction is introduced by a familiar recall device (1:5), which draws a connection between the audience's knowledge of the missionaries' past activity and methods and

what follows in the paraenetic statements of verses 11-12 and the second half of the letter. In this way Paul addresses a new phase of the missionaries' activity. The remainder of the passage is problematic since it has no explicitly stated verb. While some scholars presume that the clause must be read as a parallel to verse 10, "we behaved" (the verb would do double duty—the accusative case of verse 11, however, seems to rule this out), others supply a verb, as done above. But contrary to the preference of many and following various clues in the text we interpret the passage as referring to present exhortation (see below).

like a father his own children: Paul's manner of treatment is that of a parent, a father in this case, with its own offspring (*heautou*—see Notes on verse 7). There is an obvious appeal to affective parental imagery in verses 7 and 11 and a contrast between the role of a mother in the birth process (foundation visit) and that of a father in the fostering of growth and discipline (see Interpretation for further development).

12. *encouraging, consoling, and imploring you:* Paul's activity as a father is expressed as a series of present participles whose meanings are hortatory in character and cover a range of paraenetic concerns. In light of discussion below of Pauline usage, I conclude (1) that the terms, *parakaleō, paramytheomai,* and *martyromai* should be rendered "encourage," "console," and "implore," respectively, (2) that cumulatively they prepare for the paraenetic section that follows (4:3f.), and (3) that each points to a specific part of Paul's discussion in the second part of the letter.

to conduct yourselves worthily of the God: Paul expresses the purpose of his exhortation by a familiar *eis to* with infinitive: "that you might." The Greek for the expression "conduct yourselves worthily" translates the Jewish and Hellenistic idiom "to walk worthily" which Paul already employed in the first missive (see 4:1). His focus is on behavior and its motivation; and the goal of this counsel is the audience's proper conduct vis-à-vis God whom it has accepted to serve (1:9).

who calls you to his own kingdom and glory: The theme of divine service leads Paul to recall that of choice or call (*kaleō*). In the present context, as well as in 5:24 and Gal 5:8, the verb is employed in the present tense as a virtual name for God—God is the "one who calls" (see also 4:8). This call is specified by two important themes: kingdom and glory. While both point to a future, eschatological reality, each has its own focus: the first concerns divine lordship; the second, the state of divine glory. In both cases, however, it is implied that the future reality has a bearing on the present and teleologically conditions Christian thinking and conduct.

INTERPRETATION

Following the thanksgiving period one encounters a lengthy description of the foundation visit. After a brief description of a less-than-glorious visit to Philippi, Paul discusses the apostles' motivation for undertaking the visit and dwells at length on the preachers' divine motivation and gentle approach. Paul employs both maternal and paternal imagery (vv. 7 and 11) to describe the group's missionary strategy and personal commitment to the God-given task (4). This complex passage requires attention to discern more readily its content and function in Paul's second missive to the Thessalonians.

Background, Form, and Function of 2:1-12. Paul's discussion of the Thessalonian visit in 2:1-12 has occasioned debate concerning its background and function. Some scholars seek the interpretive key in the source of the passage's language. While some identify this background as owing to philosophical influence, particularly of the Cynic tradition, others look to the OT, especially the prophetic tradition. Others, however, maintain that Paul carefully combines these two traditions. Even more crucial for reading 2:1-12 is the position taken by interpreters regarding its function, either by examining its Thessalonian situation or by focusing on Paul's intention. In the first case scholars maintain that Paul is responding to the accusations of Gnostics, is countering the opposition of non-Christians, is distancing himself from the practices of traveling charlatans, is countering charges of false prophecy, or is engaged in the religious and specifically millenarian situation of the community. In the second case others focus on Paul's intention or the text's function. They maintain that Paul is establishing his role as eschatological prophet to the Gentiles, is employing Cynic hortatory tradition to present himself as agent bearing a divine message, is offering himself in his autobiographical remarks as a model for the community's imitation, or offers a statement of his mission and self-understanding.

This passage presents unusual terminology, striking rhetorical contrasts, and memorable Pauline themes. The notes and the following discussion focus more especially on the peculiarities of the language used by Paul to determine with more specificity their rhetorical and epistolary function. At this point we are able to address briefly and in a general way the background, form, and function of these verses. (1) While earlier studies of the background of this pericope were preoccupied with its presumed apologetic function (usually as a defense against a variety of accusations), recent study has focused on the language and epistolary context of the passage. Two important avenues of study have emerged: Paul either patterns his missionary persona on OT prototypes and thus borrows from prophetic terminology or else he is employing the language and ideals of contemporary moral preachers to describe the work, methods, and motivation of the apostolic group during its foundation visit. In the case of the former it is the language of verses 3-6 which has attracted the most attention. While one might not accept the interpretation of Paul's disclaimers in verses 3 and 5 as countering eschatological opposition or answering accusations of false prophecy (see discussion below), one can hardly deny the importance of ΟΤ usage for the interpretation of verse 4. In the case of the latter, one is more convinced by the similarity of the themes and terms used by Paul in describing the missionary work of the foundation visit to those employed by Dio Chrysostom in rebuking Cynic philosophers. What Dio accuses contemporary moral preachers of doing, Paul insists that he and colleagues have not done. He further maintains that the motivation of the mission was not gain nor fame (5-6) but the gentle treatment of the hearers whose divine vocation was always in view (v. 12). The vocabulary, themes, and concerns of 2:1-12 then reflect those of the moral preachers of the day and study of these contributes to our analysis of the passage's meaning and epistolary function.

(2) Despite attempts to extend the thanksgiving period to 3:13, it is best to view 2:1f. as the transition from the letter's thanksgiving to its body or central section. The new section thus functions as body-opening, a fact which is borne out by the emphatic use of "for you yourselves" and "brothers and sisters." The first, while underscoring continuity with the previously mentioned visit (1:9), indicates the focus of the new section, namely the missionaries' work during the foundation visit (*"our* visit to you"). The second, as often in Paul (see discussion of 2:17-20 as body-opening), introduces the central section of the letter with a direct form of address. Analysis shows that the lengthy paragraph bears a distinct form and function. Paul begins by pointing to the challenge of the mission (1-2), then in successive "not . . . but" constructions contrasts his work and that of his colleagues with the appeal of the moral preaching of contemporary charlatans, first by insisting that the mission did not originate from delusion, impure motive, or deception but from a divine motive (3-4) and secondly by reiterating that their method was not one of flattery for gain or renown but one of gentle care (5-7). From the parental imagery of verse 7 (a nurse with her own children) Paul is led to discuss both the affection which resulted from their care (8) and the extent of their efforts during the mission (9). The paragraph draws to a close by dwelling on the nature of the apostles' past behavior (devout, upright, and blameless lives) and current exhortation (a father with his own children—10-12).

(3) What function then does the pericope serve or what is Paul's intention? One is probably right in insisting that there is no polemic or apologetic motive at work here. Instead, Paul's use of contemporary themes and terminology to describe the mission points to a hortatory goal, namely, the presentation of the apostles as models for the community's

believers and even missionaries to follow. On the one hand, Paul dwells repeatedly on the missionary task, its motivation and method. Thus, his discussion would resonate with the community and its missionary concerns (1:8). On the other hand, his insistence that the apostolic group's behavior was exemplary and that their relationship with the converts was one of affection and concern underscore Paul's pastoral interests and goals. Thus, in this pericope Paul develops the motivation and recalls the manner of the group's work to strengthen his claim that he now treats them as a father would his children (v. 11) and to prepare for the message of his letter (v. 12): encouragement (4:3f.), consolation (4:13f.), and advice (5:12f.). Additionally, he reinforces his earlier statement that the community's members have become imitators of the missionaries and of the Lord. Their Christian lives have made them an example to all believers, lives which were patterned on the apostolic example which they witnessed during the foundation visit and which they now hear in Paul's words. Interestingly, Paul calls on the audience's past experience in verse 1 to bolster the discussion of his earlier missionary activity and returns in verse 11 to the same formula to appeal to their experiential knowledge to underscore the fatherly nature of his epistolary instruction. In rhetorical terms then the entire passage is placed under the rubric of shared experience, a theme which is repeatedly underscored (vv. 2, 5, 9, 10, and 11) and utilized for effective communication. Also, this theme assists Paul in developing the theme of imitation and prepares for his exhortation.

An Effective Foundation Visit. Paul draws a connection with the ending of the previous chapter as he picks up the term "visit" from 1:9. As he hinted earlier, in the words of others, that the missionary endeavor successfully resulted in conversions, so Paul, in rhetorical fashion, stresses what the community itself experienced. Further, as there was a hint in 1:9 concerning the type of visit the missionaries had enjoyed at Thessalonica, so there is in 2:1f. an attempt to develop further, not so much the results of the visit as its manner. From the start, he insists on its continued success, a fact which is underscored by the perfect tense of the verb, that is, the mission was and continues to be successful.

Paul's use of *ou kenē* in 2:1, however, calls for some attention. While it is customarily assumed that the word bears the same meaning as it does in 3:5 ("without effect or result"), corresponds to Pauline usage elsewhere (Phil 2:16; Gal 2:2), and fits into the context of a successful Thessalonian mission, it should be noted that the expression could also be interpreted as meaning "empty," that is, "without power or content" (BAGD 427). In the first case it might refer to divine power or miracles and relate to 1:5 or in the second it might describe the rhetorical effectiveness of the missionaries. The latter fits more directly into the discussion which begins in chapter 2 concerning the character or manner of the apostles' visit as opposed to its results. Thus, the translation ("you . . . know about our visit among you, that it was not ineffective") attempts to capture the text's rhetorical nuance while still hinting at the concept of "result or effect." This interpretation is further supported by Pauline style in this verse, both the classical repetition of the article and the explanatory function of the dependent clause. Since the audience is well acquainted with the apostolic visit, Paul wishes to focus in the *hoti* clause on one of its characteristics, its "effectiveness." Verse 1 then, by its reference to the previously mentioned visit (1:9), draws a close connection between Paul's thanksgiving and what follows and, by its appeal to the community's experience, sets the stage for Paul's extended discussion of the motivation and manner of the mission.

Finally, the reference in verse 2 to the apostolic visit to Philippi requires attention. Presumably, the Thessalonian audience will have heard (owing to geographic proximity) or been told by the missionaries (as part of their strategy) concerning the vicissitudes of the Christian preachers. But more important (anticipating the following discussion on public proclamation) they would have been aware, probably from personal experience, of the treatment that was commonly reserved for wandering philosophers and preachers. They too, prior to their conversion, will have sent or seen others send charlatans packing. Additionally, one must be careful not to misconstrue Paul's description of the apostolic mission at Philippi or even at Thessalonica either by misinterpreting verse 2a as underscoring a disastrous visit in the former or relying too simply on Acts 17 as describing a troublesome, abortive, and largely unsuccessful mission in the latter. Verse 2a and, indeed, much of 2:1-12 deal not with the narrative detail known from Acts 16-17 but describe in socioreligious terms the context within which Paul and colleagues announced the good news to the populations of the Greek mainland. Their reception by the general population is described in 2:2a as a rhetorical struggle or contest (see below) which often resulted in verbal insult and ridicule. This was part of the apostolic endeavor, an effort however which both in Philippi (Phil 1:5-6) and Thessalonica (1:5, 7, 9; 2:13) resulted in the conversion of those who formed the nucleus of the two Macedonian communities. Paul's reason for alluding to the Philippian mission in 2:2a is not that of comparing a pleasant to a negative visit but rather to contrast the endeavor of human agents with the source of their effectiveness.

Public Proclamation of God's Gospel. Verse 2 offers an intriguing picture of missionary activity. First Paul speaks of the apostles' less-than-welcome treatment at Philippi and then states that, despite similar circumstances, the missionaries preached the gospel at Thessalonica as well. Several crucial terms require focused attention. (1) In a long participial clause Paul describes the missionaries' treatment at Philippi by means of two terms, which are usually translated "having suffered earlier and been maltreated" and interpreted, in light of the Philippian episode as recounted in Acts 16, as physical and legal treatment, respectively. The first term, *propaschō*, whose prefix renders it a NT hapax legomenon, means "to experience or be treated," usually in a negative sense. While scholars usually presume that the simple root means "suffer," especially in persecution or at the hands of enemies, the verb can have an active sense in Paul and mean "to fight or struggle." This is clearest in Phil 1:27-30 where athletic imagery abounds and Christians are said "to suffer or battle for" Christ in a common struggle or conflict (see *agōn* below). This seems to be the sense in Acts 9:16 and here in 1 Thess 2:2, in light of the *agōn* motif (*TDNT* 5:920). Thus, the translation "struggled on its account" captures the active meaning of the verb and its implied goal "on account of" the gospel of God.

(2) The second verb *hybrizō* can refer to physical and verbal abuse; and though scholars wish to see official punishment of the missionaries as Paul's intended meaning (*TDNT* 8:305), such an interpretation relies more on Acts 16 than on the Pauline text. While many opt for a generic verbal or etymological meaning ("insult, mistreat, or insolently treat"), a closer examination of the epistolary context allows for more precision. Seemingly, Paul is referring to the harsh treatment or scoffing of the disapproving crowd which was often the fate of public speakers. In fact, Dio Chrysostom, in rhetorical terms, describes the speaker's misgivings before a city crowd: "was I not to fear your noise, laughter, fury, hissing, mocking jokes, means by which you scare everyone and always take advantage of everyone everywhere?" (*Oration*, 32.22). Rather than employ this experience as justification for bold, accusing speech, Paul points to God as the source of the missionaries' message and gentle speech.

(3) A third term, with its prepositional complement, describes the missionaries' activity in light of their experience at Philippi. Paul employs the key term *parrhēsiazomai* with an enigmatic phrase *en tǭ theǭ hēmōn*, an idiom which reads literally "we spoke openly or freely in our God." The concept of *parrhēsia*, which originally comes from Greek political philosophy to express frank and truthful speech and later is associated with the moral philosopher's use of free speech to cure human ills, seems to have been limited to the sphere of human relations in the Greek world but to have taken on a religious sense in Jewish writings. While for the Hellenistic moral philosophers *parrhēsia* is both something attained and applied like a harsh medicine to the human condition, in Jewish and NT writings it usually concerns human relations to God and the consequences

of that relationship. Paul's use of the term in 2:2 does not refer to "receiving courage from God," a meaning proposed to avoid a seeming tautology with the following infinitive (BAGD 631.2; BDF 392.3) or to fit a context of bold preaching in spite of persecution. Instead, the term, idiomatically and contextually (public preaching) refers to "open or free speech" in view of announcing the gospel.

Additionally, the prepositional phrase "in our God" must be examined not as the source of the missionaries' courage but in relation to frank speech. One should view this "speaking openly in God" as analogous to "speaking in Christ before God," i.e., as "belonging to Christ," either as Christians or, more specifically in view of 1 Thess 2:4 ("approved by God to be entrusted with the gospel"), as agents. Thus, Paul's meaning here has both a Hellenistic and a Jewish nuance. Paul appeals to the openness or truthfulness with which the missionaries presented their message, that is, without subterfuge (2:3) or false frankness (v. 5). But in place of the Cynic appeal to harsh words and a philosophical ideal, we see Paul describe the method and motivation of his ministry as being divinely directed. From the outset the missionaries present themselves as God's emissaries, with no ulterior motives of gain or trickery. Their openness is grounded not in a moral freedom acquired through suffering and harsh treatment as the Cynics might have claimed but in their empowerment by the God who entrusted them with the gospel (2:4). By presenting themselves unabashedly as ambassadors of "the living and true God" the missionaries are able both to forgo the false *parrhēsia* of contemporary charlatans and to act "devoutly, uprightly, and blamelessly" as the agents of a God who calls the listeners "to his own kingdom and glory" (2:10, 12).

(4) The final term occurs in a striking athletic phrase *en pollǭ agōni*, whose meaning is variously interpreted as referring to anxiety, widespread opposition, or strenuous effort. The word *agōn*, originally a technical term for the struggle of athletic contests, came to signify conflict of any sort, as well as the moral struggle of life (*TDNT* 1:135). Thus, the phrase is often interpreted as internal struggle or anxiety in a presumed context of receiving courage (see interpretation above of *parrhēsia*) or in light of Acts 17 (and 1 Thess 2:14-16) as fitting in a context of Jewish opposition to the Christian mission. The third option ("strenuous effort") is preferable. Closer look at the epistolary context suggests that there is a conscious use here by Paul of the agon motif, not in the sense that his apostolic mission is a struggle against opposition and suffering but that the missionary proclamation was situated in a competitive rhetorical context. While it has been pointed out that true Cynic philosophers were concerned about engaging in the great struggle of life, it does not seem that Paul is concerned about the apostolic mission as the proclamation of the gospel in the midst of life's struggle. Instead, he is describing the

actual preaching of the good news. In rhetorical terms what Paul has in mind is a public debate or contest (public speaking as contest rather than demonstration) in which the missionaries made their case before the crowds of the city (for the meaning of *agōn* as debate and public or legal speaking, see LSJ 18-19; *TDNT* 1:135). Thus, the suggestion by some that Paul was trying to distance himself from the wandering preachers of his day is instructive for understanding the situation of the original visit (as participation in such a rhetorical contest) and the function of 2:1-12 in the Pauline letter (as germane to the Thessalonian mission).

In light of the above, we can conclude that verse 2 offers the reader a vivid portrait, agreeing in large measure with what Dio Chrysostom and others present as current practice, of the apostles' initial contact with and preaching to the crowds of Philippi and Thessalonica. The picture of wandering Cynics and other street preachers would have been familiar to the Pauline addressees who had experienced such public appeal on many occasions. Also familiar to them would have been the treatment reserved for these wandering moralists by the boisterous crowds. The apostle's meaning is that in spite of the scoffing crowds the missionaries offered their message unabashedly as God's gospel when they addressed their audience and competed rhetorically in the forum for their attention, intelligence, and commitment (for further observations on the apostolic mission, see comments below on "toil and hardship").

Not from Delusion, Impure Motive, or Deception: Rhetorical Background. Verse 3 reintroduces the theme of Pauline preaching by employing the term "appeal" to stress its public, rhetorical character; the apostle's preaching is a public "appeal" to the crowds of the city. There then follow three negative statements to contrast the missionaries' divine motivation. The background of the principal terms is crucial in understanding Paul's meaning and the threefold statement's function in his discussion. First, Paul insists that the source of his message was not "delusion or error" but, as he insists in verse 4, God who approves and entrusts him with the task of announcing the gospel. What this error consists of is hard to say in the present case. On the one hand, it has been proposed that Paul's insistence on conversion "to the living and true God" in 1:9 suggests the meaning of idolatrous delusion (or false concept of God) for *planē*. Indeed, the missionaries present themselves as agents of the one true God, whose message they preach and to whom their audience turned in expectant service. On the other hand, apart from 1:9 where the audience is said to turn to God from idols, there is no attempt to focus on idolatry (though see 4:5). Instead, Paul like Dio Chrysostom wishes to distance himself from the charlatans of the period who induce their hearers to error, error which consisted of "seeking the praise of mortals"

(2:4, 6) by the basest of means. Thus, the context for understanding this term is not that the missionaries announce the one God as opposed to wandering preachers who promote pagan gods but rather that Paul and fellow travelers claim to be divinely approved to preach a divine message; they do not create empty shows of sophistry designed to flatter fickle crowds or to pad tricksters' pockets. The one does not necessarily exclude the other; but Paul's focus in this and the following verses favors the latter, more general sense of "delusion."

Secondly, Paul denies that the apostolic message was conceived from "an impure motive." The term *akatharsia* refers in a general way to "immorality" or "impurity." While many propose a sexual sense for the term and defend this meaning as being typically Pauline (reference is made to 4:7; Rom 1:24; Gal 5:19—see discussion of the first below) or suggest that it refers to idolatrous behavior here and sexual immorality in 4:1-8, others argue, more convincingly, that the term has the general sense of "impurity." Appealing to Hellenistic usage (Demosthenes, *Oration* 21.119; BGU 393.16), the latter propose that it is used with the sense of "impure motive" (BAGD 28.2). Further, such an interpretation agrees with Cynic usage, which describes the true philosopher as speaking with pure mind or motive. To this topic Paul returns with more specificity in verses 5-7, where he denies acting out of greed, popularity, or ambition (i.e., satisfaction, applause, and profit), and later insists that he did not seek recompense (9) but instead lovingly shared gospel and self with them.

Thirdly, Paul focuses on the manner of the apostolic address: "it was not made through deception" *(dolos)*. The methods employed by the missionaries were not the facile tricks of charlatans for whom all means were justifiable in the quest for adherents but frank acknowledgment of their message and its source (vv. 2 and 4). What these undesirable means were, we can only guess, though we might point to what Paul says concerning flattering speech (5) or harsh rebuke (vs. gentleness—7) or to what was often said about contemporary charlatans who "play upon the credulity of lads and sailors and crowds of that sort, stringing together rough jokes and much tittle-tattle and that low badinage that smacks of the market place" (Dio, *Oration* 33.9). Paul's approach to preaching at Thessalonica will not have focused on human eloquence, especially not underhanded trickery, but, as he tells the Corinthians, "on a demonstration of the Spirit and of power" (1 Cor 2:4; see 1 Thess 1:5-6).

What can one conclude regarding the terms, *planē, akatharsia,* and *dolos?* On the one hand, these have served, unconvincingly, as the keys to several interpretations which should at least be mentioned in passing. Focusing on the issue of the collection, one theory sees in each term some relation to monetary matters, whether deception, lack of integrity, or deceitful avarice. Another relates these to the theme of false prophecy within the Christian community or as addressing an apocalyptic situation. Still another associates these terms to concerns about Gentile idolatry. On the other hand, it is here proposed that the terms concern three important spheres of interest: God, self, and other humans (see comments on *areskō* in 2:4 and 4:1), i.e., God or error, self-interest, and servile behavior. Each of these is addressed further as Paul focuses in verse 4 on God as source of his mission and on his desire to please God rather than mortals, and in verses 5-6 as he speaks of possible motives and praise from mortals. As Paul insists in the following verse, the missionaries' speech was dominated by the one, true God and not their own gain or the tastes of the crowds.

Apostolic Motivation: Pleasing the God Who Commissions Them. Interestingly, both verses 3 and 4 dwell on the missionaries' activity as one of preaching whether by use of the term "appeal" in the former to insist on what was not their motivating principles or of "speaking the gospel" in the latter to insist on their divine message. Further, in typical Pauline fashion one encounters in these two verses an *ouk/alla* ("not . . . but") construction by which the negative and positive elements are starkly contrasted; Paul and colleagues undertook their mission, despite the challenge of public appeal to "please the living and true God." However, Paul rarely expresses things in so simple a fashion. Not only does he mention the ultimate motive as "pleasing God" but, by means of another *ouk/alla* construction, contrasts this motive to "pleasing mortals." Additionally, on the one hand, he insists that the mission was pursued according to divine standards and by divine commission and, on the other, reminds the readers that this same God who reviews the deepest reaches of human motivation provides the guarantee of their trustworthiness.

(1) The theme of pleasing God and not mortals is in striking contrast to what one presumes was the common fare of public speakers in the city squares as described in verse 3. Indeed, the theme of "pleasing mortals" was especially popular in the Hellenistic world, where the art of rhetoric often became either the cultivation of strategies to please or sway audiences by providing hearers what was pleasing to them or else disintegrated into the ribald art of flattery (see discussion of v. 5). The theme was also current in the Jewish world: Ps 52:5; PssSol 4:7-8; interesting is the latter which expressly asks God to expose the deeds of "men-pleasers" or those who thrive on deceitfully impressing the crowds. By contrast the theme of "pleasing God" occurs with some frequency in biblical literature (Gen 5:22; Ps 69:31; Wis 4:10) in contexts of prayer and righteous living rather than in rhetorical situations. The contrast of competing spheres of interest as related to the rhetorical situation of announcing the gospel then is due to Pauline creativity.

Public speakers could direct their words to please or serve their listeners either by satisfying their whims and entertaining them with ribald
humor or by elevated rhetoric. Also they could, as genuine philosophers,
address their philanthropic, divine message to the situation of their
hearers. In Paul's case, it was not the pleasure of the fickle crowd that
he sought through this service but that of God whose plan for humanity
was defined by the gospel entrusted to him and his colleagues. In the
final analysis, it was not for the crowd's pleasure that he preached but
for its conversion or turning to God; it was for this purpose, after all,
that he and his colleagues had been tested and approved by God.

(2) The pleasing of God and not mortals, according to Paul, stems from
the fact that the task is both divine and divinely imposed. To express this
concept he employs the verb *dokimazō* twice in verse 4 to insist emphatically that God is the agent who has commissioned the apostles for this
task. While this verb originally meant "to test or examine" in the Hellenistic period, as attested both in contemporary literature and inscriptions,
it also conveyed the sense of a successfully passed test and, in its technical usage, described the one fit for public office (M-M 167). Paul would
be using the language of the chancery to focus on apostolic authority,
activity, and the reliability of the gospel message. But what range does
he wish to give to the verb; what exactly does God do? This question
is asked in view of the term's basic meaning of testing or examining, on
the one hand, and, in light of what is surely a hallmark of Pauline thought,
on the other, his insistence that God's choice of him and others was
gratuitous and not dependent on qualifications (1 Cor 1:27).

Both Paul's use of political, judicial terminology and the epistolary
context argue for a comprehensive sense of the imagery. Having examined the apostolic missionaries, much as potential political candidates were
scrutinized and then approved, God declared them qualified or approved
to be ministers of the gospel. The imagery implies both qualification and
approval and so is translated in its first occurrence as "examined and
approved." In epistolary terms Paul implies that he and colleagues are
not only approved and appointed by God but possess the qualifications
demanded by God: a divine message (not falsehood), a God and other-
centered motivation (not an ulterior motive), and frank speech and a
gentle manner (not deception).

How then does qualification correspond to free choice? Just as Paul
believed in God's election or rejection of individuals as related to human
decision, so does he see the divine choice of missionaries as related to
fitness for the divine task. Thus, for Paul these are two sides to the one
coin, God's free choice of willing and able agents. Also, we might point
out that the theme of grace or choice becomes progressively important
in his writing career (on *charis*, see 1:1) and that the Thessalonian situa-

tion called for a discussion of the source of the missionaries' authority and manner of preaching as models for the converts and as a prelude for the advice which Paul communicates to them in writing.

While one could maintain that the divine commissioning in verse 4 refers to Paul's consciousness of being sent by God to minister to the Gentiles (Gal 2:7) and further to relate this past event (past tense) to his conversion (Gal 1:15-16), his use of the plural and his reference in 2:7 to his colleagues as "apostles" warns us against seeking too quickly in 1 Thessalonians a sense of Paul's self-consciousness which emerges later in his correspondence. The commissioning then is not particularly that of Paul but that of the group that evangelized the Thessalonian community. They were given as task the guardianship of the gospel (see Rom 3:2; 1 Cor 9:17; Gal 2:7) and their speech is determined by their commission.

Finally, the apostolic preachers have as motive the pleasing of the God who is described as "the one who examines our hearts." The God to be pleased and preached is the one who knows and tests human motives (second use of *dokimazō*). By this statement Paul wishes to underscore the divine approval of the apostolic message and the trustworthiness of its messengers. Thus, the judgment motif of verse 4 serves to authenticate the missionaries and their message. Additionally, one senses a paraenetic thrust to this general statement as he prepares to discuss and encourage proper behavior.

Not with Flattery for Gain or Renown: Profitability of Public Discourse. Paul employs three important terms to suggest what was usually the motivation of popular, public discourse and to deny firmly what an outsider might have presumed to be the missionaries' ulterior motives. Clearly, contemporary preachers had a vested interest in the reaction of the crowds and in their own level of success. It is to these topics that Paul in another contrastive construction turns his attention in describing the apostles' radically different motivation.

In the first case he insists that the apostolic preachers did not address their task by means of flattery or literally, "with a word of flattery." The term *kolakeia* suggests the tortuous means by which people attempt to manipulate others for their own ends (M-M 352), usually, according to Aristotle (*Nicomachean Ethics* 4.6.9), "for money and monetary equivalence." In moral terms, the theme often appears in vice lists and is characterized as insidious, the antithesis of friendship, indeed "diseased friendship" (Philo, *Allegorical Laws* 182; see also *Migration of Abraham* 111-12; Plutarch, *Moralia* 50CE; see discussion of friendship at 1:6). In rhetorical terms, the theme becomes a literary topos to describe "the dishonorable and profitable discourse" (Theophrastus, *Characters* 2) which was common in the public preaching and speaking of "flatterers, charlatans, and sophists" (Dio, *Orations* 32.11; 51.4). In the present case Paul connects "flattery" with speech and so directs his attention to the manner of the apostolic preaching. The missionaries, he insists, did not employ deceptive language, empty praise, or false promises to trick the hearers in accepting their message. What Paul has in mind is not self-serving speech to ingratiate himself to the crowds but, in light of the preceding and succeeding phrases ("to please mortals" and seeking the "praise of mortals," verses 4 and 6) and in view of the full idiom "with flattering speech," we are to see a more general reference to the base methods employed by popular Hellenistic rhetoricians.

In the second case he employs an idiom *(en prophasei pleonexias)*, which has traditionally been interpreted as "cloak" or "pretext for *(satisfying)* greed" (BAGD 722.2). Such an interpretation is based on the assumption that *prophasis* always bears a negative meaning in the NT and that the context of verse 5 points to deception in the service of greed rather than to its motive. Since *prophasis* also means "motive or reason" and since the genitive construction parallels that of "flattering speech," it is best translated as "acting for an avaricious reason" or "with a motive of greed." Thus, it constitutes a parallel to and explicitation of 2:3.

The third term, *doxa*, focuses on still another motive commonly ascribed to popular speakers. Paul continues the series of denials begun in verse 5. While the first two simply state that the preachers have not acted in a similar manner and for the same motive as charlatans of the day, the third introduces and denies that the former acted for still another popular motive, that of reputation or renown. Indeed, Dio Chrysostom describes philosopher-rhetoricians who deliver orations for "their own profit and renown" and not for the hearers' betterment as opposed to true philosophers who do so "out of good will and concern" (*Oration* 32.10-11). In both passages he employs the word *doxa* as does Paul.

From the above discussion it is clear first that Paul presupposes, as background for his discussion, the themes of gain and renown in a popular context and, secondly, that the reader obtains from this discussion a better grasp of these themes as they relate to the Pauline context. (1) As is obvious from Dio Chrysostom's statements, the perennial method of charlatans of the period was that of flattery or deceptive speech whose goal was profitability, whether greed or popularity. Public speaking in such a context easily became a sideshow for hucksters seeking a fast buck or entertainers intent on winning the adulation of the crowds. In either case the objective was not the moral betterment of the crowds but the self-aggrandizement or profitability of the speaker. Like true philosophers who neither spoke for the adulation of the crowds nor sought to enhance their reputations through rhetorical prowess or deceptive, sophistic language, Paul insists that he and his colleagues acted for reasons other than gaining disciples or greater popularity.

(2) In Pauline terms gain and renown are rejected as motives for apostolic preaching. In other words, Paul rejects both monetary and rhetorical profitability as motives for missionary activity. What, however, is his attitude toward these two realities since he receives assistance from his communities while at Thessalonica (Phil 4:16) and revels in the Macedonian repute of that community (1:7-9)? Additionally, by denying "renown from mortals" Paul seems to suggest a contrast with valid renown that comes from God (see 2:19-20). Since Paul returns to the theme of work and subsistence in 2:9, I reserve discussion of the theme of gain for later and direct my attention to the latter.

Not only does Paul deny renown from a human source but adds "whether from you or from others." What is the significance of such an addition? The "you" clearly refers to the Thessalonian addressees; the identity of the "others" is unclear. Does the latter refer to Christians or the general populace? In the first case Paul could be referring to the believers in Macedonia and in Achaia and beyond (1:7-8) or in the second to his statement about "renown from mortals." It is also possible that we have here an early hint of Paul's desire to establish the independence of his mission (see Gal 1 and 2 Cor 10-13). Further, how does one reconcile Paul's rejection of "human renown" in 2:6 with what he tells the community in 2:20: "you yourselves are already our renown and joy"? There is a contrast between seeking and receiving honor from others. In other words, Paul rejects renown as a motive for his missionary endeavor; he is not seeking followers or setting up a school of disciples (see 1 Cor 1:10-17), like the popular sophists who, in peacock-like fashion, "are lifted up as though on wings by renown and disciples" (Dio, *Oration* 12.5). Nonetheless, he knows that, in the present, the existence and vibrant success of the community is the basis of the apostles' reputation (2:20) and that, in the Lord Jesus' presence at the end-time, the community "will be [their] hope and joy and crown of pride" (2:19). Finally, Paul is aware of the difference between renown as self-aggrandizement and missionary success (resulting in glorious reports—1:9) as the outcome of divine choice and power (1:5). Thus, the gift of faith and the concomitant success of the mission form the subject of Paul's thanksgiving.

Missionary Method: Gentle Persuasion, Care, and Affection. Before broaching the subject of gentle persuasion in 2:7b, Paul ends the previous sentence by stating that the apostles chose not to insist on their authority or "importance as apostles." In effect the ending of the sentence consists of a concessive participial construction, depends on the verb "seek," and should be rendered "we were not seeking renown . . . though we might have. . . ." Evidently Paul wishes to underscore what the missionaries did not do by insisting that they forfeited honors to which they were entitled by virtue of their divine approval. Just as we have Paul insisting that "pleasing God" rather than "seeking human renown" was the motivation of the mission, so we now see him shifting the discussion to the missionaries' behavior and stressing that their approach to the mission was one of "gentle" persuasion rather than authoritarian demand. We therefore encounter a first example of Paul's preference for free discourse and persuasion rather than the ready use of authority.

Paul's strategy at Thessalonica then was one of frank or bold speech (v. 2) and gentle action, a description of which follows in his appeal to the image of the nurse. Paul claims that he and his colleagues approached their mission in a manner similar to that of certain Cynics, who employed gentle persuasion and admonition to present their demanding message. Instead of relying on their status as delegates of the living God or of asserting their apostolic authority, they lived among their converts not as misanthropic judges of human foibles but as agents of a loving God (1:3-4) who entrusted them with a gospel which engenders love of others (4:9-12). We are to see not the special affection of the missionaries for one Macedonian community but a basic mission strategy, characterized by the imagery of nurse and father, which underscores a philanthropic anthropology, whose perspective is that human beings are to be lovingly assisted in "leading lives worthy of the God who calls" (2:12).

Paul pursues the theme of missionary method by employing the image of a nurse, imagery which is striking in its present rhetorical and paraenetic context. Just as Hellenistic philosophers often made use of this affective image to describe the challenge of persuading crowds to opt for their own welfare and betterment, so Paul employs it to describe apostolic behavior during the foundation visit and prepare for the advice that is to follow. Use of the image with the reflexive phrase "her own children" further underscores the affective nature of the apostolic care. The image is not simply that of a nurse, a strong image in its own right, but of a nurse acting with even deeper affection as a mother. Paul and colleagues go beyond the demands of duty toward their charges; indeed, they treat them like their own children. Such an interpretation is borne out by what follows ("sharing of themselves" and fatherhood imagery—2:11; also 1 Cor 4:14-15; Phlm 10) and by a later use of motherhood imagery in Gal 4:19. Further supporting this line of interpretation is Paul's use of the verb *thalpō* (see Notes) to underscore the affective nature of the care, an interpretation supported by the etymology of the word ("to heat or brood") and by the epistolary context: concern of the nurse as a mother and the following expression of affection.

Thus the theme of parent and child, mother and children in verse 7 and father and children in 11, is a frequent concern of Paul in describing his own relationship to his communities, whether as father (1 Cor 4:14-15), parent (2 Cor 12:14; also 6:13), or mother (Gal 4:19), and to individual converts, always as father: Timothy (Phil 2:22; 1 Cor 4:17) and Onesimus (Phlm 10). His use of this imagery in the present context is not motivated by protective concern for the converts but by his desire to describe the caring manner of the apostolic preaching, a manner dictated by wise rhetorical strategy, commissioning of a loving God, and Christian behavior.

Verse 8 intensifies the emotional tone of the discussion by use of such expressions as "having such affection" and "we gladly decided." The former resumes what was said in the previous verse concerning parental imagery and the latter, while introducing an element of resolve, further underscores the natural desire, more that of a parent than of a nanny, that motivates the missionaries in giving in missionary and personal terms.

Having communicated the gospel to their new audience and witnessed a favorable response to God's word (1:6; 2:13), the preachers seem to have developed intimate bonds with their new converts. Paul sees himself and his colleagues as meeting the demands of duty as they pursue their mission and going beyond these in giving of themselves. This self-giving can hardly mean that the apostles did more for these converts than to others. Instead, it seems to underscore a special, deep relationship that developed between them, that of friendship and fellowship, variously involving services, sharing, unity, and imitation (*TDNT* 9:151-53; see also 1:6). The missionaries, while exercising their divine commission with gentleness, shared the community's fortunes, gave of themselves, and worked at their side. There developed such mutuality that Paul will later say concerning the churches of Macedonia that "they gave themselves first to the Lord and then, by the will of God, to us" (2 Cor 8:5).

An interesting comparison can be drawn between Paul's use of nursing imagery in verse 7 and the intent of his statement in verse 8. Just as the nurse does her job competently by caring for the children in her charge, so do the missionaries in accomplishing their task by announcing God's gospel and ministering among their converts. In both cases, however, Paul by slight rhetorical touches intensifies the affective tone of the statements. In verse 7, after stressing the gentle strategy of the mission by comparing it to a nurse's care, Paul strengthens his statement by noting that the missionary process resembled more the love of the nurse as a mother of her own children than her competence as a guardian of children. Similarly, after describing the mission in verse 7 as the object of loving care and in verse 8a, after noting the affection with which the gospel was communicated, Paul intensifies his statement by noting that the missionary process was done with pleasure, accompanied by self-giving.

Toil and Hardship as Sharing Activity and Time. The much-discussed topics of apostolic labor and support are introduced in verse 9 and receive their context from their relationship to the issues discussed in the preceding verse. Verse 9 and its statements concerning long hours of work and the desire not to burden the new converts provide an important example of how the missionaries shared more fully their activity and time with the Thessalonian audience. (1) Paul opens the discussion with a formulaic or proverbial expression, "toil and hardship," whose function and meaning are conceptualized by the further use of the term "to work" immediately following. Such usage suggests that this passage functions as a general statement about hard labor and demanding circumstances, a statement which then receives more specific treatment. Such a conclusion is supported by the other instance where Paul employs this combination of nouns, 2 Cor 11:27: "in toil and hardship, through many a sleepless night, hungry and thirsty, often without food, cold and naked." In this context the phrase acts as a heading for what follows, namely, the difficulties associated with an artisan's life. So in 1 Thess 2:9, after a general statement about exertion and distress, Paul describes in more specific terms what the missionaries did at Thessalonica.

There follows immediately in verse 9 another set phrase to address the temporal character of this labor, "working night and day." This expression is meant to underscore the long, demanding hours and tedious labor of the artisan and can hardly be taken so literally as to mean Paul and colleagues were at work from sunrise to sunset and on the basis of this to conclude that Paul made use of the workshop for missionary purposes. Paul therefore means that the missionaries worked continuously throughout the time they were at Thessalonica. Paul then turns first to the reason for the long hours of work and then connects this to the proclamation of the gospel. In effect, Paul insists that, in taking pains not to give the appearance of "acting for an avaricious reason" (2:5), they devoted a great deal of their time and effort (the set phrases have a clear rhetorical effect) to supporting themselves rather than being a financial burden on any of the new converts. Verse 9 then becomes an extension of Paul's claim in verse 8 that he and his fellow missionaries "not only imparted . . . the gospel of God" to them but, out of affection, "also shared [their] very selves." It is in such precise circumstances that we discern the gradual development of Paul's attitude toward apostolic support, a topic to which we now turn.

(2) Thus, we are brought to inquire regarding the nature and purpose of Paul's work, its relationship to the proclamation of the gospel, and

the more general issue of Paul's attitude toward apostolic support. In view of what Paul says, at a later date, concerning his "toil and hardship" (2 Cor 11:27) and manual labor (1 Cor 4:11-12) and their accompanying burdens, one is led to agree with recent opinion that Paul and fellow missionaries were likely of the artisan class, a common phenomenon among Cynic and Stoic philosophers of the period. Also, it is claimed that the artisan's workshop, on the one hand, furnished them a means of support and, on the other, provided their principal forum for evangelization. But it is also suggested that the private home was the likely locus of apostolic preaching since Paul and colleagues lacked the status for most forms of public speaking and so welcomed the invitations of well-to-do converts to join their households, while supporting themselves through manual labor.

In the first case the tandem construction of 2:9 regarding working and preaching is interpreted as suggesting that one see Paul as preaching while working. However, careful examination of the verse does not support nor imply such a conclusion. The participle "working" is modified by a following articular infinitive, which gives the reason for the long hours of work, and is temporally, not causally, linked with the subsequent statement about preaching. Thus, we translate: "we worked night and day so as not to burden any of you, while we proclaimed to you the gospel of God." While not excluding the probability that Paul employed the artisan's workshop as a locus for evangelization, I am more inclined to insist that 2:9 is intent on presenting the apostle's manner of labor and conduct as a model for the new converts to emulate, a model based on a philosophical ideal of the day.

In the second case, while the suggestion that the apostles made extensive use of the household as the focus of their preaching may be correct (though this is based on Lukan, not on Pauline, evidence), the further claim that evidence is lacking for postulating public preaching on Paul's part is contradicted by data from 1 Thess 2:1-12. Indeed, 2:2, with its insistence on being scoffed at by the crowds, on public and open speech, and on oratorical or public contest, points to a public forum, at least for the initial contact which the missionaries had with the prospective converts. Perhaps a more comprehensive view of the apostles' activity at Thessalonica would make more sense of the wide range of data available. The acceptance of invitations from householders interested in the gospel does not preclude preaching in the city forum, no more than working and even teaching while in the artisan's workshop exclude the likelihood that the private house and other social groupings offered greater opportunity for the formation of communities.

Finally, a word should be said concerning Paul's attitude toward apostolic support. It is clear from later statements that he maintained the right of missionaries to ecclesial assistance (1 Cor 9:3-7) and received such from converts, even while at Thessalonica (Phil 4:15-16). What is at issue is Paul's concern that no one "put an obstacle in the way of the gospel of Christ" (1 Cor 9:12). He wished to avoid the impression that the missionaries acted for financial gain (2:5) or that the appeal for financial support should hinder the freedom of potential converts. What developed as Pauline policy was the refusal to collect money or receive support from audiences. Once he left, however, he was willing to receive and even demand support from churches he had founded. Thus, the missionaries' appeal was made with pure motive and their manner was one of gentleness that focused on the frank communication of God's gospel and the generous sharing of what they had and were.

Past Missionary Behavior and Current Paraenesis. Interpretation of verses 10-12 must deal with the cumbersome character of the text. Though many render Paul's thought into two or three relatively independent sentences, it should be noted that the passage consists of one lengthy period whose complex structure is governed by the opening oath formula. Thus, "you are witnesses, and so is God" introduces contrasting statements, each introduced by "how" (see also Rom 1:9 and Phil 1:8). Further analysis shows that the first statement addresses the missionaries' Thessalonian behavior (v. 10b) and the second, the gentle pastoral advice given in the letter (11-12).

(1) First Paul gives his attention to past missionary behavior. To describe this he employs three rare adverbs whose meanings are clearly related to apostolic conduct. Since the first two, "devoutly and uprightly" commonly occur in tandem in contemporary literature, as here, we are led to conclude that the Pauline phrase is idiomatic and that together they represent the two spheres of divine and human statutes (see *TDNT* 5:490 on "fac et jus"), that is, the first describes the apostles' fidelity to their divine mission and the second their just behavior toward the people of Thessalonica. Thus, Paul refers back directly to the two witnesses just cited: God toward whom they are fully devoted and the audience whose every need was their concern. Thus, together these terms refer to the whole range of human and divine relations.

The third term, "blamelessly," requires attention on several counts. Though relatively rare in Paul, the term, as employed in 1 Thess 3:13, clearly expresses divine judgment or evaluation of human conduct. Its meaning in 2:10 seems to bear such an interpretation for both the apostles' task and their conduct are divinely appointed and examined (2:4). What then is the term's relationship to the preceding two adverbs? Since this third term refers equally to behavior conditioned by divine and human law, it seems best to view its role as that of summarizing statement:

"devoutly and uprightly, and thus blamelessly." Since their behavior at Thessalonica was in accordance both with their divine vocation and respected social and cultural mores, Paul can claim that they were irreproachable in the treatment of their converts.

Finally, the dative pronoun *hymin*, though often interpreted as behavior "toward you," is here seen as referring locally to the missionaries' visit "among" the Thessalonians. It thus provides a further indication that the whole of verse 10 refers to the original Macedonian mission and past apostolic behavior.

(2) In a second construction also marked by the conjunction "how," Paul turns to a second phase of the missionaries' activity, namely, their extended pastoral care. His use of "as you also know" directs attention to this new pastoral phase, which continues into the present as epistolary paraenesis and compares this present activity to the apostles' exemplary behavior in Thessalonica. While scholars usually render verses 11-12 as referring to past missionary activity, several considerations suggest otherwise. It is presumed, owing to the parallel structure of the two "how" clauses, that the second should, like the first, refer to the apostles' visit at Thessalonica. The situation is more complex still, since this second *hōs* clause has no verb. One assumes that the close parallel between the two clauses has led Paul to omit the second verb. Either one assumes that *egenēthēmen* of the first clause does double duty (grammatically this is unlikely), that Paul's readers must supply a verb such as "counsel, treat, or bring up," or that Paul has produced an incomplete sentence (the last mentioned leads some to render the three participles of verse 12 as finite verbs). In each case, nonetheless, scholars assume that the verbal solution for verse 11 alludes to past missionary activity. This is only partly true. Instead, Paul is stating a general principle concerning pastoral care and not simply past behavior. The recall formula and the appeal to the audience and God as witnesses further confirm this fact. Paul is interested in establishing in the consciousness of his readers not only the blameless conduct of his missionary band but also its usual method of pastoral care. The missionaries can be expected to offer trustworthy encouragement, consolation, and advice in the present missive for they have done so in the past in person and through messages, a fact which is well known to the audience. Thus, the second *hōs* clause is expressed in the present tense of timeless statements; Paul treated his converts in a caring manner in the past and assures them that his paraenesis (4:3f.) is composed in the same spirit.

Finally, the pastoral treatment is directed to "each one of you." From this phrase (see Acts 20:31) some conclude that the apostles preach to individuals as they perform their daily work, particularly in the artisan's workshop. On the one hand, it is clear that Paul wishes by the use of these terms to stress the individual character of Christian commitment which was involved in community founding and nurturing. On the other hand, from the context of the present passage it does not seem that Paul is speaking of the initial preaching of the foundation visit but of later pastoral activity, activity which is described in the following verse. "Each one of you" does not have a bearing on the nature or locale of the apostolic preaching but on the focus and particularity of the apostles' oral and written paraenesis addressed to the converts in the long process of shaping and nurturing the community (see "each one" in 5:11). Verses 10-11 therefore address past behavior and current exhortation and prepare for the latter by referring to the exemplary character of the former.

Method, Content, and Purpose of Paul's Exhortation. After introducing the topic of exhortation and in preparation for his treatment of the community's questions and problems, Paul addresses the method, content, and purpose of his exhortation. (1) Paul describes his paraenetic method by employing the image of a father's treatment of his own offspring. The image of the missionaries as fathers immediately calls to mind the equally striking image of the apostles as nurses acting in the role of mothers (2:7). While the first image, as suggested by its context of "gentleness," refers to the original preaching and the resulting conversion or birthing process, the second, situated in the specific context of instruction and exhortation, implies a different function for the father image. In the present context, Paul presumes an affective relationship between father and children much like that of mother and child. Like the mother in 2:7, the father reacts toward his charges as he would his own children. As a result of the comparison between past behavior and present paraenesis, there is even a hint of the theme of the "gentle father" as known from Homeric tradition (*Odyssey* 2.47; *Iliad* 24.770). Nonetheless, Paul's focus here is on moral discipline and instruction, the domain more properly of the father. It is true that paternal imagery in Paul can focus on spiritual birth (1 Cor 4:15; Phlm 10) but it can also be employed to describe the relationship that exists between the two and thus treat explicitly of the authority one has over the other (1 Cor 4:14; Phil 2:22; see *TDNT* 5:1005). Thus, by use of father-child imagery Paul continues the resocializing process begun during the foundation visit by addressing the demands of their new socioreligious context, a task he accomplishes by establishing the source of his authority for addressing the community's problems and concerns in the following chapters. He does this, however, by appealing once more to affective imagery which rhetorically lessens his overt use of authority.

(2) To describe the content of his exhortation or what the apostles do in the manner of a father's treatment of his own children, Paul employs

three problematic participles. All three are often employed in paraenetic contexts and reveal a range of meaning. The first verb, *parakaleō*, is a frequent Pauline term, appears three times in the earlier missive (3:2, 7; 4:1), and recurs here and in the following paraenetic section five times (2:12; 4:10, 18; 5:11, 14). The term though employed with a variety of nuances seems to demand the meaning of "encouragement" or "exhortation to greater effort" as it does in 3:2, rather than "exhortation or entreaty" as in 4:1 and 5:14 (in both cases with the verb *erōtaō*). Also, its appearance in the conclusions of Paul's successive paragraphs of advice (4:10, 18; 5:11), particularly the first and last, suggests encouragement to greater effort and diligence. The second term, *paramytheomai*, is infrequent in Paul, appearing only two times in 1 Thessalonians and bearing the meaning of "encouragement" with particular focus on "consolation" regarding tragedy or death or "cheering up" in the context of depression (BAGD 620). In the present case we opt for "consolation" but more generally for "encouraging" in its occurrence at 5:14. The third verb, *martyromai*, which occurs in Paul only here and once in Galatians (5:34), offers the range of meaning from "bear witness," to "affirm" or "implore."

In their present context, the three terms are clearly paraenetic in use and their various nuances seem related to the texts they introduce. As noted earlier, verses 11-12 address the apostles' habitual treatment of the community and point to the advice which the community had sought by letter. Thus, *parakaleō* points to Paul's discussion, advice, and encouragement to greater effort in regards to the community's sanctification, love of others, and proper behavior (4:3-12). Such a meaning is suggested by more general usage in both Thessalonian missives and by the repeated suggestion that the readers "do so more and more" (4:10; also 5:11). The particular nuance of the second verb, *paramytheomai*, as conveying "consolation" (see also 1 Cor 14:3 and Phil 2:1 for similar usage of the first two verbs), is suggested by the content of 4:13–5:11 which is dominated by the subjects of death, grief, and uncertainty regarding the end-time (see also 5:14). The final verb, *martyromai*, then would suggest Paul's final, insistent list of commands or instructions. Such an interpretation is suggested by the insistent tone, the vocabulary, and content of 5:12-22, to which the final verb points. Paul then uses three paraenetic terms to qualify, in general terms, the content and tone of the message of the remainder of the letter.

Such a conclusion regarding the interpretation of 2:12 gives added reason for seeing 2:13–4:2 as an editorial addition to a complete, later Thessalonian missive. The conclusion to verse 12, regarding the divine calling, will have facilitated the editorial process, for verse 13 launches into thanksgiving both for the divine call and for the community's discerning reception of God's word as expressed in human speech.

(3) Paul proceeds to express the purpose of his exhortation as "conducting oneself or walking worthily of God." This ethical walk or behavior has as goal the pleasing of God. In effect the expression "worthily of God" is borrowed from Hellenistic religion and was often used to describe the behavior expected of a god's devotees (M-M 51), a pattern of behavior which was determined by the character or demands of the god in question. For Paul, the devoted monotheist, and for his new converts, Christian conduct was a call to a life of holiness (see Lev 11:45), a theme to which Paul returns in 4:3-8. In the present context, as he insists on God's prior call, Paul focuses on Christian behavior as receiving its motivating power from a prior turning to God from idols and a consequent serving that is patterned on the living and true God's nature.

This ethical walk is further qualified by three themes: call, kingdom, and glory. Interestingly, as Paul's attention is directed to the converts' service of the Holy One of Israel, he is quick to return to the notion of choice or call in describing the God toward whom all Christian activity and service are to be directed. This is the God of gift or of choice, the one of whom they are beloved (1:4). Without doubt, the concept of election is fundamental to Pauline thought (see 1:4) and frequently appears in discussions of conversion. Thus, Paul's use of the present tense in 2:12 focuses on the character of God as the one who chooses a people and prepares them for the coming kingdom. It is a God who takes the initiative and who has destined humans to live in holiness in the present (4:3f.) and to share in "his own kingdom and glory." The Christian convert, as devotee of such a God, is exhorted to live a life worthy of this call.

Christian conduct is further qualified by the prospect of belonging to or entering God's kingdom. The term *basileia*, traditionally rendered "kingdom" or more dynamically "reign," though a favorite theme of the Jesus tradition, is not frequent in Paul (eight times—see 1 Cor 15:23-28 where it plays a key role in his lordship Christology). Paul focuses more readily on the future reality of the concept (as in the present case—emphasized by use of "his own") than on its present or proleptic reality (see Rom 14:17; 1 Cor 4:20). The kingdom is a reality to be inherited (Gal 5:21), a place or state of destiny. Paul focuses in this passage, and generally, on the kingdom as an eschatological reality, one which is yet to come but one which impinges on present conduct.

The above conclusion is further confirmed by the accompanying term *doxa* ("glory") which also qualifies the type of behavior which is worthy of God. This term which appears rather frequently in all NT traditions has two basic meanings: renown or fame (see 2:6, 20), and glory or splendor. It is the latter which concerns us here and which offers an extensive OT background. Basically, it describes the divine mode of being or God's visible splendor, either as revealed in heaven or as shared with human creatures (Rom 5:2; 8:18). While one might be tempted to view the combination "his own kingdom and glory" as constituting a hendiadys, i.e., "his glorious kingdom," it is preferable to view this rare Pauline construction in light of other *doxa* passages. Paul here presumes the biblical story of Adam's creation and humanity's loss of God's shared glory (Rom 3:23). It is a glory, nonetheless, in which believers are called to share now as reflected in the risen Jesus (2 Cor 3:18) but more fully in resurrection (1 Cor 15:4). In 1 Thess 2:12 Paul insists that the Christian vocation is no less than submitting fully to God's reign and reclaiming that state of glory, which was in the first analysis a sharing in God's "own glory" (see 5:9-10 where this glorious state is described as "salvation" through Jesus and life with him). Service of God is teleologically and eschatologically conditioned by the demands of God's sovereignty and the promise of shared glory.

A Final Note on "Apostles of Christ." Paul's statement in 2:7, that the apostles could make demands "as apostles of Christ," has generated debate and varying solutions to the problems raised. Of concern in this passage is Paul's inclusion of Silvanus and Timothy within the apostolic group (use of the plural). This, it is presumed, conflicts with the traditional, technical meaning of the term "apostle" and with later Pauline usage which grounded apostleship in the commissioning of the risen Lord. In the latter case, Paul's companions would not seem to qualify as apostles. (1) It is occasionally proposed that Paul is employing a "non-real" first person and so is referring only to himself. (2) Another solution is to view the plural as including Paul and Silvanus but not Timothy, on the assumption that Silvanus was from Jerusalem and so commissioned by the risen Lord and that Timothy, the convert from paganism, was not. And (3), it is frequently proposed that Paul uses *apostolos* here in an early, less formulated sense to mean missionary or agent.

Objections have been raised against all three. While the issue of authorial plural concerns the authorship of the letters generally, i.e., whether the first person plural stands for Paul alone or for Paul and associates, we must insist, contrary to the first solution offered above, that in 2:1-12 Paul the author speaks without exception in the name and about the experience of his cosenders. Seemingly, the only thing which makes some scholars hesitate is presumed Pauline usage concerning the term *apostolos*. In the second case, the same presumption leads others to overestimate available data: the possible apostolic status of Silvanus (based on data from Acts concerning Silas) and the unlikelihood of such status in Timothy's case (based on Paul's failure ever to call Timothy an apostle). In effect, Paul seems to call both apostles in 2:7; so what needs to be clarified is the meaning of *apostolos* in the present case.

The third solution is more likely and requires more attention. One can detect in Pauline usage two basic meanings for the term, either that of emissary or accredited agent (patterned on the Jewish institution of the *shaliah*) or of missionary (individuals participating in the apostolate). Indeed, there are clear cases where Paul assumes that churches have messengers whom he calls "apostles" (Phil 2:25; 2 Cor 8:23). Nonetheless, Paul seems to employ the term most frequently to designate people involved in the missionary endeavor, as he does in 1 Thess 2:7, usually groups that exceed what one presumes to have been Jesus' immediate followers (1 Cor 4:9; 9:5; 15:7 and even 2 Cor 11:5, 13; 12:11), individuals who clearly were not part of this group and whose status was simply that of missionary (Rom 16:7; 2 Cor 12:12), and, of course, himself as missionary (Rom 1:1; 11:13; 1 Cor 9:1-2; Gal 1:1). Further, one sees in the Pauline data evidence of ecclesial structural evolution: use of the term to designate the highest of many ministries (1 Cor 12:28-29) and implicit association of the term with ecclesial (Jerusalem) authorities (Gal 1:17), though in the latter case one should note that Paul says they "were already apostles before me." Additionally, there seems clear evidence to support an evolution in Paul's sense of the special nature and prophetic meaning of his calling and that one of the major contributing factors of this evolution was the repeated challenge of his apostolic status (*TDNT* 1:441). Paul's later insistence that he was commissioned by the risen Lord (1 Cor 9:1; see also Gal 1:16) then is understandable in light of his evolving relations with his communities and should not be imposed either on his earlier statements or on the totality of his remarks concerning apostles.

Thus, Paul considers his cosenders apostles; and on this basis they are on the same footing, whatever their standing in terms of seniority. They are missionaries, examined and commissioned by God (2:4) to be entrusted with the gospel. Interestingly, it is the theological rather than Christological motif which predominates in the present context. So in 2:7 Paul insists that, though they could have relied upon their position as divine envoys to operate within the community, they chose instead to act with gentle persuasion and much affection.

FOR REFERENCE AND FURTHER STUDY

Collins, R. F. "Paul, as seen through his own eyes," *SFLT*, 175–208.
Denis, A.-M. "L'Apôtre Paul, prophète 'messianique' des Gentils. Etude thématique de 1 Thess, 11, 1-6." *ETL* 33 (1957) 245–318.
Gaventa, B. R. "Apostles as Babes and Nurses in 1 Thessalonians 2:7," in *Faith and History: Essays in Honor of Paul W. Meyer.* eds. J. T. Carroll, et al. Atlanta: Scholars, 1991, 193–207.

Gillman, J. "Paul's *Eisodos:* The Proclaimed and the Proclaimer (1 Thess 2, 8),"
TC, 62–70.

Henneken, B. *Verkündigung und Prophetie im Ersten Thessalonicherbrief: Ein Beitrag zur Theologie des Wortes Gottes.* Stuttgart: Katholisches Bibelwerk, 1969.

Hock, R. F. "The Workshop as a Social Setting for Paul's Missionary Preaching."
CBQ 41 (1979) 438–50.

Horbury, W. "1 Thessalonians ii.3 as Rebutting the Charge of False Prophecy."
JTS 33 (1982) 492–508.

Lyons, G. *Pauline Autobiography. Toward a New Understanding.* Atlanta: Scholars, 1985.

Malherbe, A. J. " 'Gentle as a Nurse': The Stoic Background of 1 Thess. ii." *NovT* 12 (1970) 203–17.

Meeks, W. A. *The First Urban Christians. The Social World of the Apostle Paul.* New Haven: Yale University, 1983.

Schmithals, W. *Paul and the Gnostics.* Nashville: Abingdon, 1972.

Stowers, S. K. "Social Status, Public Speaking and Private Teaching: The Circumstances of Paul's Preaching Activity." *NovT* 26 (1984) 59–82.

White, J. L. *The Body of the Greek Letter.* Missoula: Scholars, 1972.

II. EARLY MISSIVE—2:13–4:2

For a discussion of 2:13–4:2 as constituting Paul's earliest letter and first missive written to the Thessalonians, see Introduction, pp. 11–14.

4. *Thanksgiving* (2:13)

13. So for the following reason also, we give thanks to God continually because, having received the word of God as heard from us, you accepted it not as the word of mortals but, as what it really is, the word of God, who indeed is also at work in you who believe.

NOTES

13. *So for the following reason also:* This initial phrase *(kai dia touto kai hēmeis)*, which occurs nowhere else in Paul (see 2 Thess 2:11 for use of the first three terms), has been variously understood: as pointing back to the preceding paragraph with the reason for renewed thanksgiving, as looking forward to what follows

and so culminating the thanksgiving section begun in 1:2, or as an unnecessary transitional phrase. In reading the canonical, edited text, a forward-directing meaning is preferable, since 2:13 offers not a summary of what precedes (renewed thanks) but new content (thanks for an added reason—such is further indicated by the following "because" clause). Also, this non-Pauline phrase serves to join the two letters, focusing particularly on verse 13 as an added reason for thanksgiving. Even the use of the pronominal subject ("we") is due to the editor for Paul nowhere begins a thanksgiving period with such a pronoun.

we give thanks to God continually because: With this clause one encounters the beginning of a complete, independent thanksgiving. The expression translated "we give thanks" represents the verb *eucharisteō*, whose word-family, owing to Hellenistic Jewish and secular usage, became increasingly popular in early Christian literature in epistolary (24 occurrences in Paul), liturgical, and more general theological contexts (*TDNT* 9:407-15). Paul here follows the conventional thanksgiving to the gods to begin his letter to his community. His choice of this convention rather than the more usual wish for good health reveals his conviction that faith is a gift whose human response (itself a sign of the audience's well-being) must be one of gratitude to God. Paul refers no fewer than 9 times to God in the first missive and 25 times in the second. It is his preferred usage (25 of 34 occurrences) to employ the article before *theos*, which for him is virtually a proper name. The term "continually" stresses that Paul intends not a time or place of prayer but a state of mind.

having received . . . you accepted: While in lexical terms the two Greek verbs are synonyms (e.g., the Vulgate and Syriac translators employ one verb for both expressions), contextually they suggest a contrast. The first *(paralambanō)* is regularly used by Paul for the reception of a "spiritual heritage," though occasionally with a focus on approval, as in 1 Cor 15:1, but the second *(dechomai)* offers a wider range of meaning, from receiving someone or something to acceptance in the sense of approval. In the present case then the first verb emphasizes the hearing or reception of the message as preached by Paul and colleagues, while the second underscores discernment on the part of the hearers.

the word of God, as heard from us: The idiom, "the word of God," a relatively rare Pauline expression (7x), is employed twice in this thanksgiving section. It is an early synonym for gospel, a term which appears later in the letter (3:2; in his later missive Paul prefers "gospel of God": 2:2, 9) and which is chosen from his scriptural repertoire to underscore the divine character and origin of the message. The entire, compact construction, *logon akoēs par' hēmōn tou theou*, conforms to classical usage. Thus, Paul, by sandwiching the modifier ("heard from us") between the noun and adnominal genitive ("word" and "of God"), lays stress on the modifier. The focus of the participial construction is not the Thessalonians' reception of the gospel but rather its having been "heard from" the senders of the letter—the emphasis is on the message rather than the act of hearing, as in Rom 10:16. The participial construction lays the ground for the *hoti*-clause which states the object of the thanksgiving. On *logos akoēs* as the passing on of information, see Sir 41:26; cf. also Heb 4:2 for a similar contrast between hearing and accepting.

accepted it not as the word of mortals: The terms "it" and "as" are added to the translation, following the Vulgate and Syriac, a practice sometimes cited as a translation error. The "as" is crucial to Paul's meaning, is furnished later in the sentence ("as what it really is"), and thus does double duty. Further, Paul clearly insists that on both levels, that of "receiving" and of "accepting," the object is "the word of God." The difference lies in perception, the same words seen "as" or "from the perspective of" (see a similarly expressed argument in Phlm 15-16). One should translate *logon anthrōpōn* as a "human word" (not "word of men") in contrast to a "divine word" even if the plural secondarily refers to Paul and companions, all three being males, as preachers. It should be noted, however, that Paul customarily employs the plural of *anthrōpos* when contrasting the human and divine spheres (see 2:4 and 4:8).

but, as what it really is, the word of God: The expression "the word of God" represents Paul's first omission of the article before *theos* and is striking since the same phrase, with article, appears earlier in the verse. Presumably, the omission, as a parallel to the anarthrous "word of mortals," shifts the emphasis from the noun to its modifiers. While earlier Paul speaks of "the word of God as heard *from us*," thereby emphasizing its human mediation by placing the qualifying phrase between the noun and the articular modifier, so now he compresses the two phrases by omitting the articles to underscore their modifiers: "word *of mortals*" and "word *of God*."

who indeed is also at work: This translation presupposes the conclusions drawn in a discussion below that the verb *energeō* be read as middle rather than passive (thereby favoring the antecedent "God" over "word") and that preverbal *kai* ("also") has syntactic and contextual significance. Thus, Paul insists that God works through the missionaries ("the word of mortals") and in the lives of believers (use of postpositive *kai*) and stresses that the reason for the mission's success against all odds was God's active part in the enterprise (use of the middle voice of *energeō*).

in you who believe: "You" of the passage contrasts with the emphatic "we" of verse 17, while use of the present participle of *pisteuō* underscores the continuous, vital life and commitment of those who have placed their trust in God as a result of the message preached by Paul and companions.

EXCURSUS
God . . . who indeed is also at work (2:13)

The Greek text offers several possibilities: (1) the relative pronoun can refer either to "word" or "God," (2) the verb (*energeō*) can be taken as middle or passive, and (3) the term *kai*, in postposition, could give added force to the verbal expression. The choices are interconnected. Most scholars opt for "word" as antecedent of the clause because they view this term as expressing the dominant theme of the verse (term used 3x) and either because it is the only possible subject of the passive verb or because they see Paul employing the active verb when God is subject but the middle when using an impersonal subject. Others see little difference between the middle and passive since, in one case, the subject would be "the word of God" and, in the other, God "the virtual subject" of the passive expression. Much depends on how one marshalls the evidence. The verb *energeō* occurs 12x in Paul, 7x in the active (with God as subject in all but one case where the Spirit is subject—1 Cor 12:11) and 5x in the middle/passive. It is the latter that concerns us. This form occurs 9x in the NT and is not frequent in Hellenistic Greek. Beyond the Pauline letters it occurs three times in the Paulinists (2 Thess 2:7; Col 1:29; and Eph 3:20) and in Jas 5:16. While some in the past defended a passive meaning for all these, recent linguists, with some hesitation, opt for the middle. Further, the situation is not clarified when recent commentators treat the two occurrences of this form in 2 Corinthians both as a middle (1:6) and as a passive (4:12).

The above translation reflects the following choices: (1) "God" is the antecedent of the relative clause, (2) the verb is to be read as a middle, though not as a "middle instead of active" (BDF 316), and (3) the preverbal *kai* is of special significance syntactically and contextually. It is my goal then to make a credible defense of these options. (1) Admittedly, while the *logos* theme is important in this verse, that of *theos* is even more central, for not only does the term likewise occur three times in 2:13 but this theme is the focus of Paul's thought. He gives thanks to God not because the Thessalonians received the word of human missionaries but because they have received *God's* word. Also, the term "God" is the more plausible subject for several reasons. Nowhere in the Pauline letters is "the word" or "the word of God" said to be active or at work—the only NT parallel would be Heb 4:12 ("the word of God is living and active," *energēs*). On the contrary, God is regularly the subject of *energeō* in Paul. Also this word-family in the NT almost invariably relates to the activity of supernatural, whether divine or demonic, beings. The major issue seems to revolve around the middle/passive usage of *energeō* with alleged impersonal subject. Of the nine occurrences of the middle/passive form in the NT five are participial adjectives (2 Cor 1:6; Gal 5:6; Col 1:29; Eph 3:20; Jas 5:16) and four are finite verbs with explicit subjects—three of these are in Paul and one in 2 Thess 2:7. A case can be made that, in terms of Hellenistic cosmology, each Pauline and Paulinist usage concerns a supernatural power. In Rom 7:5 "the sinful passions, aroused by the law" are energies of the flesh in rebellion against God and so are "personal" agents active within the human sphere. The same is true of "death and life" in 2 Cor 4:12 (see Rom 5:12; 7:5; 8:38). Equally, "the mystery of lawlessness" (2 Thess 2:7) is readily seen as Satan's "personal" agent at work in the present age. Thus, to claim that the middle/passive form is limited to impersonal subjects in NT usage is less than correct in cosmological terms. *Theos* then rather than *logos* is the subject.

(2) But why should Paul employ the middle rather than the active voice? An answer to this question is more speculative and must rely on the exegetical sense such a choice would make. Again we focus on the finite uses of

the middle. In Rom 7:5 a reflexive nuance makes sense since the "passions" have a vested interest in "bearing fruit for death," their alter ego. In 2 Cor 4:12 the middle voice adds a degree of emphasis (further underscored by the word order: the *en*-phrase precedes *energeō* rather than follows it as in Rom 7:5; 1 Cor 12:6; Phil 2:13; and 1 Thess 2:13) to the contrast: "death is at work *especially* in us, but life in you" (on 2 Thess 2:7 see below). (3) This brings us finally to 1 Thess 2:13 and its use both of the middle voice and of the adverbial conjunction *kai*. Paul employs the middle form to emphasize his ultimate conviction, after Timothy's return (3:6), that God "*indeed* is also at work" in his converts. By means of the postpositive *kai* Paul stresses God's double activity: kerygmatic work through missionaries ("the word of mortals," see also Gal 2:8) and salvific ferment or divine action in the believers (see 1 Cor 12:6; Phil 2:13; Gal 5:6). By means of the middle voice he expresses his conviction and thanks that he has not labored in vain among them against satanic odds (2:18f.) because God especially had a hand in this outcome.

INTERPRETATION

It has been argued in the Introduction that Paul's first missive to Thessalonica consists of 2:13–4:2. Since the letter would have contained an opening prior to its thanksgiving section, it is advisable to begin our discussion with this topic.

Opening of the First Missive. The joining of two Pauline letters would have led to the elimination of obvious doublets either by the omission of one of the openings and closings or by the fusion of these. While it is possible that the present opening of the document, 1 Thess 1:1, be the salutation of either the first or second missive, it is argued that the latter is more likely. (1) It is suggested that the process which led to the preservation of Paul's occasional correspondence consisted in this case, as in that of the Philippian correspondence, in the insertion of a short, pared-down missive into a complete, longer letter at a convenient and logical point. Thus, after the simple elimination of the brief salutation and conclusion of the short document, the remainder (2:13–4:2) was inserted at a point which the editor considered appropriate for the preservation and meaningful reading of the Pauline texts by a later generation. (2) It is also proposed that the opening of the missives would have been nearly identical, thereby facilitating the editorial process. While it is possible that the first opening was identical to 1 Thess 1:1 and mentioned the same cosenders, it seems more likely that it bore only the names of Paul and Silvanus, since the letter focuses on two matters: the role of Timothy in obtaining "splendid news" from Thessalonica and the deep-felt concern and joyful thanksgiving of those who sent him. Thus, the first-person pronoun of the letter refers to "those who gladly agreed to remain alone in Athens'' (3:1). It is they who receive and are ecstatic about the news brought by Timothy (3:6); and it is they who have not yet been to Thessalonica and yearn for that to happen (vv. 6, 10, 11). From this we might surmise that Timothy begins as a junior colleague, who also serves as envoy (first Thessalonian missive), eventually becomes a more established co-missionary and colleague (second missive; Phil 1:1; Phlm 1; 2 Cor 1:1— see also 2 Cor 1:19), and later, around the time of the Jerusalem meeting, is both replaced at Paul's side by Titus (Gal 2:1-32) and seems to tread a more independent missionary course. (3) Finally, the salutation of the second letter, with the added name of Timothy, would have seemed appropriate as introduction to the new, composite document.

The remainder of the salutation would have been nearly identical and there seems little evidence to argue otherwise, save that the Christological title might have been ''Lord Jesus,'' as always in the first missive (see comments on 2:19) rather than ''Lord Jesus Christ,'' a title which, if the above is correct, would appear for the first time in the second Thessalonian missive (1:1, 3; 5:9, 23, 28). Thus, the opening of the first Thessalonian missive would have been as follows:

> Paul and Silvanus,
> to the community of Thessalonians
>   assembled by God the Father and the Lord Jesus,
> grace to you and peace.

For discussion of its content, see comments on 1:1 above.

Form and Function of the Thanksgiving (2:13). Verse 13 begins with a transitional phrase, ''so for the following reason also,'' a non-Pauline idiom which was added to facilitate the addition of a new thanksgiving. In effect, verse 13 offers not renewed thanks but a complete, standard thanksgiving, which employs the traditional Pauline expressions ''give thanks to God'' and ''continually'' or ''always.'' Further, each Pauline thanksgiving is complemented by one of two constructions, either by an immediately following *hoti*-clause and a dependent consecutive clause (Rom 1:8-9; 1 Cor 1:4-7; 1 Thess 2:13) or by a complex of first-person participles which introduce final clauses (Phil 1:3-8; 1 Thess 1:2-5; Phlm 4-6). Only Galatians and 2 Corinthians are anomolous, since the former intentionally omits the thanksgiving and the latter replaces it with a paragraph of blessing. In the case of 1 Thessalonians it should be noted that one finds two fully developed thanksgiving sections with requisite terminology and structure and that these belong to separate types. This suggests further that they derive from different Pauline letters.

The thanksgiving becomes a distinct section of the Pauline missive to express gratitude for the community's faith, to reveal a clear relation to the addressees' situation, to offer hints regarding the letter's subject matter, and to renew the rapport which exists between writer and reader. Though relatively brief the thanksgiving of 2:13 sets the tone for the short missive that it introduces. The principal reason for Paul's thanksgiving is the community's commitment, a degree of commitment which brought about their survival as a community. Its members have accepted God's word and thereby have allowed the divine power of salvation (see Rom 1:16) to work also in them. The letter is about the community's survival as a result of the divine energy that was released in their midst through the preaching of the gospel. While they recognize the human agency of this activity and are deeply attached to their parents in the faith, they nonetheless remain firm in their commitment to the Lord (3:8). Indeed, having received God's word during the apostles' extended mission, they allowed God's power to work among them to withstand the difficulties accompanying and resulting from their conversion. In stating that the Thessalonians accepted the good news as preached by the apostles, Paul prepares for his later statement that "we often warned you" about the difficulties the converts would encounter (3:3-4). Thus, the proof that "God is also at work" in the lives of the addressees is the welcomed news brought back by Timothy of the community's "faith and love" (3:6). This section, therefore, assures the audience from the outset that the apostolic mission has not been ineffective (3:5) for God is at work in the activity of the missionaries and in the lives of their converts. Also, by noting that God is also at work in the lives of his Thessalonian converts, Paul acknowledges the community's well-being (as do Hellenistic letters) and hints at greater expectations and achievements from the recipients of the letter (see 4:1).

Content of Paul's Thanksgiving. Paul's first missive begins with what will become a standard and eloquent feature of his letters as he thanks God for the commitment of his converts. For Paul thanksgiving is a theological concept whose fundamental goal is that of increasing God's glory (*TDNT* 9:413), whose context is daily living (3:9; 5:18; also Rom 1:21), whether worship, prayer, or the activity of "the spirit, soul, and body" (5:23), and whose opportune time is always. This prayer is directed to God who took the initiative by sending missionaries to preach "the word" and who continues to operate within the lives of those who receive this word and strive to live blamelessly in view of Jesus' return (3:13).

When Paul composes the letter, after Timothy's return (3:6), he is convinced that God is active among his converts in word and deed and thus is thankful that they, from the beginning, while impressed by human words, had given assent to a divine message. He is thankful because the audience transcended the messengers and accepted the message; i.e., they discerned in the preaching of Paul and companions the very word of God. Paul's style in this instance serves to underscore the point being made when he employs contrasting verbs in parallel phrases:

having *received* the word of God	a
as heard from us	b
you *accepted* it not as the word of mortals	b'
but . . . God's word.	a'

In this way he is able both to insist upon the human mediation of the message (and its importance in the apostles' life work—2:19-20) and to underscore its divine origin and significance ("what it really is").

Thus, Paul's reason for giving thanks is the community's discernment of the apostolic message as being "God's word" and of that community's understanding of the concept of faith. It is for this reason that at the end of verse 13 he does not say simply "who is also at work in *you*" but "in you *who believe*." The latter represents Paul's first use of faith language, a language which involves the adjective *pistos*, the verb *pisteuō*, and the noun *pistis*. His use of these terms is concentrated in Romans, Galatians, and surprisingly 1 Thessalonians (in the last mentioned these appear 1, 5, and 8 times respectively). In 1 Thess 2:13 the present participle in the plural is employed substantively to refer to the addressees and to underscore the verbal force of the expression (same usage in 1:7 and 2:10). The converts of Thessalonica accepted God's word and so receive the name of "believers," thereby expressing Paul's conviction that his audience's commitment to the gospel was genuine since it is evidenced by the release of divine power in their lives. Thus, in verse 13 we have a clear statement of the twofold nature of God's activity, first the preaching and hearing of the divine message and secondly its realization in lives of faith that allow free reign to God's salvific activity.

For Reference and Further Study

Boers, H. "The Form Critical Study of Paul's Letters. 1 Thess as a Case Study." *NTS* 22 (1975–76) 140–58.

Lambrecht, J. "Thanksgivings in 1 Thessalonians 1-3," in *TC*, 183–205.

O'Brien, P. T. *Introductory Thanksgivings in the Letters of Paul.* Leiden: Brill, 1977.

Schubert, P. *Form and Function of the Pauline Thanksgivings.* Berlin: Töpelmann, 1939.

White, J. L. "Saint Paul and the Apostolic Letter Tradition." *CBQ* 45 (1983) 433–44.

5. *The Jews and Divine Retribution* (2:14-16)—An Interpolation

14. For you yourselves have become, brothers and sisters, like the Churches of God which, through Christ Jesus, exist in Judaea, since you yourselves also suffered the same things from your own compatriots as they from the Jews, 15. who also have killed the Lord, that is, Jesus as well as the prophets, and have driven us out, and so do not please God, and, being hostile to the rest of humanity, 16. hinder us from speaking to the Gentiles, that they may be saved—in this way they are constantly filling up the measure of their sins. But divine retribution has caught up with them at last.

NOTES

14. *For you yourselves have become:* This verse is connected to what precedes by the conjunction *gar* and leads the reader to expect a close connection between the verses. In effect the new reason for thanksgiving has already been stated in verse 13b and what follows in verse 14 reveals no obvious link. The remainder of the text, "you yourselves have become like" (lit.: "imitators"— *mimētai*), is a restatement of 1:6, but its meaning, in light of what follows, is not that of imitation or emulation but rather of the two being alike in what they have experienced.

brothers and sisters, like the Churches of God: While some form of direct address usually marks the ending of the thanksgiving period or the transition to the body of the letter (1:4; see comments on 2:17; Phil 1:12; 1 Cor 1:10), in the present case *adelphoi* is strangely sandwiched in a non-Pauline way between the noun *mimētai* and its genitive modifier "of the Churches of God." Also, while Paul prefers the singular "Church of God" (Gal 1:13; 1 Cor 1:2; 10:16), he does employ the plural (1 Cor 11:16; see also Rom 16:16); nonetheless, it is un-Pauline to speak of "imitation of Churches" for Paul refers to apostolic imitation (see 1:6).

which, through Christ Jesus, exist in Judaea: The expression *tōn ousōn en tę̄ Ioudaią* has parallels in several Pauline prescripts, the closest of which is 1 Cor 1:2: "the Church of God which exists in Corinth" (see also 2 Cor 1:1; Rom 1:7; and Phil 1:1). The *en Christǫ Iēsou* phrase and the word order, however, are problematic. The text does not support, in Pauline terms, a translation such as "the churches of God in Christ Jesus" (for word order see Phil 1:1) but rather, in non-Pauline usage, to suggest a way of referring to the Judaeo-Christian communities of the Jerusalem area. The text gives the impression of being an imitation of Pauline idiom in its use of *en Christǫ* terminology, its formulation of local phraseology, and its use of the title "Christ Jesus." The reference to the Judaean churches either as models or a topic of concern is also un-Pauline.

since you yourselves also suffered the same things from your own compatriots: The conjunction *hoti* ("since") sets up a parallel between the common suffering of the Judaean and Thessalonian communities. Several terms require attention. a. Use of the verb *paschō* ("suffer") leads some to view the affliction as the result of "persecution" and to subscribe to the scenario in Acts of Jewish opposition. Paul does not employ this term to describe the Thessalonians' hardships; he uses *thlipsis* (see Notes on 3:3-4). b. The expression "the same things" suggests not only sharing in affliction but parallel suffering or persecution of the same kind and from a similar source—an impression reinforced by the emphasis "you yourselves also." c. The above conclusion is confirmed by use of a NT hapax "compatriot." While the term refers to fellow Thessalonians, its use in verses 14-16 as a parallel to the following "Jews" implies that, following again the scenario of Acts 17, the Judaeo-Christian community of Thessalonica is suffering at the hands of the non-Christian Jews of the city—a point underscored by the use of *idiōn* ("own"). The Jewish character of the Thessalonian community is not confirmed by the Pauline text.

as they from the Jews: Use of the term "the Jews" in the negative context of verses 14-16 has generated debate concerning historical issues (persecution of early Christians by Jews) and authorship. As regards the latter, scholars are hard put to defend such usage by Paul, the author of Romans 9–11, since the term in verses 14-16 already has the polemic meaning found in John's Gospel. This usage goes beyond inner-Jewish debate of Judaeo-Christians with Jewish opponents (Matthew 23). Instead one is reminded of Gentile-Christian attitudes toward and language describing Jews and even Jewish-Christians of later generations and centuries (already of concern in Romans 9–11). Thus, in verse 14 the author presents the first of a list of accusations laid at the feet of "the Jews"; they have inflicted suffering on or, more probably, have persecuted the Judaean community (the aorist points to events that are long past). It is to this suffering that the text compares the hardships to which the Thessalonians have been subjected. Furthermore, the expression "the Jews" in this context cannot refer only to Judaean Jews (vv. 14-15a) but also to the Jews of the Greco-Roman world who oppose the Christian mission (16a).

15. *who also have killed the Lord, that is, Jesus as well as the prophets:* Verse 15 begins a series of participial clauses (only the first is introduced by an article), which modify "the Jews," a construction best translated as a series of relative clauses. One might be tempted to translate the awkwardly worded phrase as follows "who killed both the Lord Jesus and the prophets" *(tōn kai ton kyrion apokteinantōn Iēsoun kai tous prophētas).* However, the strange separation of the terms "Lord" and "Jesus" by the verb and the nonhistorical order of "Jesus" followed by "prophets" suggest that the clauses are complementary in nature, i.e., the Jews added to their list of iniquities (including the slaughter of prophets) that of killing the Lord, whom all Christians identify as Jesus. The suggestion, as in Acts 7:52, is that past murderous activity against the prophets has continued recently in similar actions against the Messiah and the churches of God in Judaea and in Thessalonica. The author knows the widespread Jewish tradition, also cited by NT writers (Rom 11:3; Matt 23:29-37; Luke 13:34; Acts 7:52), that the chosen people were to blame for the maltreatment and

deaths of God's prophets (1 Kgs 19:10 [cited in Rom 11:3]; Jer 2:30; Martyrdom of Isaiah 5:1-14). The claim, baldly stated, that the Jews were responsible for Jesus' slaying, a statement which is historically inaccurate but sometimes hinted at in the NT tradition (John 5:18f.; Acts 3:15; 5:30), is not Pauline. Finally, choice of the term "kill" *(apokteinō)* rather than "crucify" may owe to the influence either of 1 Kgs 19:10 or the author's use of Jesus tradition such as Matt 23:29-39.

and have driven us out: This participial clause raises questions of interpretation. Are the "persecutions" a thing of the past, even those alluded to in Acts, since one must presume they continue in the present? One could argue for grammatical attraction, i.e., the tense of the previous participle exerted power over the present verbal form; however, the present tense of the following participle could have done the same. Some combine "the prophets and us" as objects of the participle in question; however, the temporal problem concerning the activity being inflicted remains. While some rely on the standard translation of *ekdiōkō* as "persecute" (BAGD 239), such a rendition relies on late materials for corroboration. Instead one should render the term according to its usual meaning, "drive out or banish" (LSJ 504) and view its interpretation as referring to the Judaeo-Christian expulsion from Jerusalem as stated in Acts 8:1 or to the excommunication of Christian Jews from the synagogue.

and so do not please God: This expression is Pauline (see 4:1) and, following its classical usage, means "to conform to someone's ways" (LSJ 238). For Paul, speaking to fellow Christians, the idiom means "to walk in newness of life" (Rom 6:4) and to exhibit behavior that has God's approval. In the present case, the only instance where the term applies to Jewish behavior, it is hard to envision what "displeasing God" might entail apart from the Christian reproach, similar to that of Acts 7:51-52, and deduced from the present context, that "the Jews" of this generation imitated their murderous ancestors (who killed the prophets and the Lord Jesus, persecuted early Christians, and expelled them from the synagogue) in now vitiating the Gentile mission. Not pleasing God must refer to Jewish opposition to what the author sees as God's plan for human salvation (see v. 16) and to what is characterized as "opposition to humanity."

and, being hostile to the rest of humanity: The concluding part of verse 15 presents a grammatical problem. While one could provide a copula to the adjectival phrase to bring it into line with the list of participial clauses ("who are hostile to . . ."), it is preferable to see this non-Pauline phrase *(enantiōn* with genitive of the person is a NT hapax) as complementing the following clause, which itself bears no coordinating conjunction. This phrase reflects the traditional Gentile anti-Judaism voiced by the Roman historian Tacitus (*Histories* 5.5: "they feel only hostility and hatred toward others") and others (Philostratus, *Life of Apollonius of Tyana* 5.33 and Juvenal, *Satires* 14.103.4). To defend Paul against such a statement some point to his other discussions of Judaism and note that the text in question is explained and limited by verse 16a, a text which would defuse the statement of its racial connotations by focusing on the issue of the Gentile mission. On the contrary, the text implies that it is because of Jewish opposition and hostility to Gentiles that they obstruct the world mission. This anti-Judaism is uncharacteristic of Paul and more likely the product of a later Gentile-Christian hand.

16. *hinder us from speaking to the Gentiles that they may be saved:* The author employs a rare Pauline term *kōlyō* (Rom 1:13; also 1 Cor 14:39) to express Jewish initiative in thwarting the mission that has as its purpose the evangelizing of the rest of humanity that they might gain salvation. The author employs a strange turn of phrase to describe the preaching of the gospel, namely, ''to speak to . . .,'' an expression which is probably a shortened form of the Pauline phrase ''to speak the gospel to . . .'' (see 2:2; also v. 4). The verb ''to save'' appears only here in the document, though the noun *sōtēria* occurs in 5:8-9.

—in this way they are constantly filling up the measure of their sins: The list of actions results (use of *eis to*) in a constant tabulating of Israel's rebellious activity as it reaches the measure or extreme limit required by God for judgment (*TDNT* 6:288). For this purpose the author borrows a traditional OT phrase, the closest in linguistic terms being Gen 15:16 (''the sins . . . are not yet filled up''; see also Dan 8:23 and 2 Macc 6:14) since only it employs the rare NT verb *anaplēroō*. A similar idea is found (using the term ''measure'') in Matt 23:32 but employing the unaugmented verb. This concept of a divinely fixed measure of human activity is also widely attested in late Judaism (1 QS 5.9-10; 11.2-7; 1 QH 4.26-29; Pseudo-Philo, *Biblical Antiquities* 26.13; also *Shepherd of Hermas,* Vision 2.2.2). The term *hamartia* (''sin'') appears only here in 1 Thessalonians but in the plural, a usage which is rare for Paul, though its appearance in what might be classified a formulaic OT expression would conform to Pauline passages such as Rom 4:7 or 1 Cor 15:3. The final term *pantote* (''constantly'' or ''completely'') hints at the imminence of the filling up process and underscores the vehemence of the polemic.

but divine retribution has caught up with them at last: This final statement presents problems concerning the meaning and tense of the verb and the interpretation of the final phrase. (1) The preceding list of actions ends with a succinct statement of retributive reassurance. The verb *phthanō* occurs in 4:15 where it means ''one group will not precede another.'' In the present case, modified by a prepositional phrase rather than an object, the verb must mean ''overtake or catch up with.'' Also, its use in the aorist must mean that ''wrath'' has already taken place (as in T.Levi 6:11). Various attempts are made to explain this anomaly: ''arrival at but with participation,'' ''beginning to come upon,'' ''proleptic participation,'' ''in the process of or already occurring,'' or ''about to occur.'' In addition, others are interested in discerning an event in Paul's time which might serve as a sign of divine retribution (the Claudian expulsion of Jews from Rome) or an occurrence such as the fall of Jerusalem which might indicate a writer later than Paul. (2) The phrase *eis telos* is given a variety of interpretations, each with its own historical, temporal, or eschatological presuppositions: ''at last,'' ''completely,'' or ''forever.'' Finally, the concept of *orgē* (''wrath'' or ''retribution''), a common OT and NT term, is introduced to explain the rectification of the situation which now exists between Christians who are pursuing God's salvific will and the Jews who are forever thwarting that plan in diverse ways.

INTERPRETATION

This part of 1 Thessalonians attracts attention from scholars, who wonder how these verses fit into Paul's approach to Judaism and method of composition or doubt whether they are in fact compatible with historical data or Paul's theological perspective.

Literary and Theological Analysis. If past analyses of 1 Thess 2:14-16 were invariably linked with compilation theories involving verses 13-16 and broader questions concerning the Thessalonian letters, recent studies focus on verses 14-16 and their alleged Pauline character. Before starting this analysis, however, it is necessary to consider the problem of verse 13, since verses 13-16 are sometimes viewed as a unit. This verse presents a problem since it contains a second thanksgiving, a structural feature which is clearly un-Pauline. Some assume that its elimination along with the non-Pauline sounding verses 14-16 resolves this problem. It should be emphasized that two, distinct issues are involved. Verse 13 indeed presents a structural problem and, in my estimation, offers a clue to editorial compilation. Verses 13 and 14-16, however, have little in common; the former is Pauline (and not a reworking of 1:2-5); the latter is not.

Whether one grants that verse 13 introduces a new Pauline thanksgiving period and also constitutes the introduction of a separate letter, one must admit that it is verses 14-16 that fit the least in their present context—scholars routinely speak of a parenthesis, tangent, or violent outburst. Paul's affectionate exhortation in 2:9f. is interrupted by a thanksgiving and by an uncharacteristic identification of "the Jews" as the source of the community's suffering (nothing is said of this in 3:1-5). There follows a bitter, strange condemnation not only of alleged Jewish antagonists in Thessalonica but of the Jews throughout history. The text ends with a chilling claim that the Jews are receiving a merited, divine condemnation.

Verses 14-16 present five accusations against the Jews; they have (1) caused the Judaean (and Thessalonian) Churches to suffer (v. 14), (2) have killed not only the prophets but also the Lord Jesus (v. 15), (3) have driven out (or expelled) us (the Jewish Christians), (4) do not please God, and (5) out of general hostility, hinder the Gentile mission (v. 16). While some attempt to exonerate Paul by placing these statements in his overall treatment of Judaism or by attributing them to an early apocalypticist

Paul, it is hard to see how a concrete event (persecution of the community and its missionaries—following Acts 17) should be taken up by Paul and transformed, in a fit of passion presumably, to condemn all Jews as actively conspiring, out of hatred for all non-Jews, against the God-directed mission for the salvation of Gentiles. Further, these five accusations are followed by two powerful conclusions. The first underscores the "extreme limit" of Jewish wickedness and the second, the universal, vengeful relief that they are finally getting what they deserve.

It is difficult, therefore, to explain the tone of the entire passage in Pauline terms. To insist that verse 16 provides the key to its interpretation and therefore is of Pauline authorship, that is, that the Jews are seen as a principal obstacle to Christian preaching, is to misread the end of verse 15 (the accusation that it is hostility to non-Jews which brings opposition to the Gentile mission) and other passages where Paul speaks of obstacles to his mission (see 2:18; 3:7). At the same time to overplay the passage's apocalyptic character is to overlook some of Paul's statements in 1 Thessalonians and to propose a questionable interpretation of verses 14-16. To insist that in 1 Thessalonians generally, Paul calls for the salvation only of those in the community, for disengagement of believers from the evil of the world outside, and so for condemnation of non-Christian Jews and Gentiles is to read the entire document in a strange way. Only in 2:14-16 does one encounter Jewish opponents; further passages such as 3:12 ("your love for one another and for all"), 2:9 (work in the marketplace), and especially 4:11-12 (the quiet life and "proper conduct in the company of outsiders") argue not for an apocalypticist condemnation of and separation from the outside world but rather the giving of advice to the community about being productive members of the society in which they live. Therefore, it is not particularly the thought and tone of Romans 9–11 which leads to the conclusion that 1 Thess 2:14-16 presents neither the tone nor the thought of Paul but the reading and contrasting of all statements in 1 Thessalonians with those of the passage under discussion.

In structural terms verses 14-16 constitute two related parts. Verse 14 consists of a marginal, scribal commentary on the situation of 1 Thessalonians. The community is said by Paul to have undergone "much suffering or hardship" (1:6; 3:3, 7). It is this "suffering" at Thessalonica which leads a later reader, in light of the Lukan treatment of the history of the mission (Acts 17), to identify the source of the suffering as Jewish. Thus, the writer speaks not only of the Thessalonian but also of the Judaean Churches (Acts 6:8f.) as having "suffered" at the hands of the Jews (the "compatriots" would be the Lukan mob of Acts 17:5). Verse 14 establishes a connection between the Pauline text, via Lukan history, and Jewish responsibility for the situation and so is the starting point for the author's polemic. Verses 15-16 consist of an anaphoric construction (a list of five participial clauses) with a conclusion, followed by a final condemning statement. Once the situation and its key term "the Jews" are stated in verse 14, the remainder of the intrusive text focuses on condemnation of Israel and a listing of its sins as manifesting hostility toward God and non-Jewish humanity and as deserving divine retribution.

An Interpolator's Perspective. We return to verse 13, especially as it might relate to our analysis of verses 14-16. It is defended, along with verses 14-16, as Pauline owing to linguistic and thematic parallels with 1:2f. or rejected as non-Pauline by insisting upon these same parallels for verse 13. There is no doubt that these two thanksgiving periods bear thematic similarity; in effect most of Paul's thanksgivings would fare well in such comparisons. A structural and content analysis of the two passages is instructive. In terms of content little in verse 13 can be called non-Pauline. In structural terms the two thanksgivings belong to different types. On the one hand, 1:2-5, in employing an *eucharisteō* clause complemented by a complex of first-person participles which introduce final clauses, relates to Phil 1:3-8 and Phlm 4-6. On the other, 2:13 belongs to the same category as Rom 1:8-10 and 1 Cor 1:4-7, since like them it uses an *eucharisteō* clause which is immediately followed by a *hoti*-clause and a dependent consecutive clause (see discussion of 2:13). Verse 13 therefore should be defended as Pauline but its structural features and relation to other Pauline thanksgiving periods point to the compilation of separate Pauline letters. One should note briefly that this editorial activity has left traces in 2 Thessalonians (two thanksgivings; see 1:3 and 2:13) while 2:14-16 and its anti-Judaism have not.

It is in 2:14-16 that one finds a fair number of non-Pauline or not-frequently-employed terms and expressions, such as "compatriots," "to kill," "drive out," or "being hostile to someone." The expression "the Jews" is non-Pauline in its negative usage. The idiom *ginomai mimētai* may seem Pauline in form (see 1:6) but is not in usage, since one cannot say that the Thessalonians are consciously imitating the Churches of Judaea but that they have "become like" these Churches owing to similar suffering. Also, Paul employs the term *thlipsis* and not *paschō* to describe the difficulties involved (see discussion of 3:3). Lastly, Paul does not use the idiom "to speak to" but rather "to speak the gospel to" (see 2:2).

Further the polemical tone and content to which scholars draw attention are also limited to verses 14-16. Use of the expression "the Jews" in such a negative context is stark, for Paul employs the term *Ioudaios* to contrast Jew and Gentile. Nonetheless, only Jewish Christians and Gentiles would employ such terminology in polemical contexts. Also, if one insists that the text refers in a limited fashion to the Jews of Judaea or Palestine as one would gather from the first and second accusations concerning the troubles of Judaea and the execution of Jesus, the remaining complaints and the reproach that "they have murdered the prophets" point to a global condemnation of Israel as a nation.

It is particularly the fifth accusation which confirms our conclusion that the passage is both non-Pauline and a later Gentile-Christian interpolation. While one can defend as Jewish self-critique the accusation that Israel often does not act in a way pleasing to God and even that the objection to Gentile repentance might find a precedent in Jonah's refusal to preach to the Ninevites, one can hardly accept the accusation as Pauline that the Jews' objection to the Gentile mission is motivated by a deep-seated "hatred for the human race." One is hard put, whether in 1 Thessalonians or in Paul's later letters, to envision a situation where the proud Jewish-Christian Paul would accuse his own kin of "being hostile to the rest of humanity." So sensitive was he to the issue of the Jesus movement's relation to Judaism that he was quick to point out that Gentile Christians were a "wild shoot" grafted to share the riches of the original olive tree (Rom 11:17). Whether Paul would have thought that Israel merited the fiercest of divine punishment for its opposition to God and the preaching of the gospel and then changed his mind by the time he wrote his last letter is questionable. Instead, what we have in 2:14-16 is a later development in the trajectory already witnessed in the community of Rome (see Romans 9–11), first that Jewish Christians were related to unfaithful ancestors and secondly that, as communities became more Gentile and as Christianity disassociated itself from contemporary Jewish groups, some within the Christian communities refined the anti-Jewish prejudices and employed the anti-Semitic slogans of the Greco-Roman world to explain their movement's situation within contemporary society. Also important was the movement's understanding of its foundational texts as it made its way more resolutely in the Gentile world of the eastern Mediterranean. Additionally, it was the rereading of Judaeo-Christian and polemically conditioned texts by later generations, which no longer appreciated the original contexts and intentions of their writers, that led them to reinterpret passages, such as Matt 23:31-36 and Acts 6:8f.; 17:1-15, in a decidedly anti-Jewish way and, in this case, to annotate their reading of the Apostle Paul much as Marcion did in his reading of the Pauline corpus.

Gentile-Christian Anti-Judaism. Whatever the sources of Christian anti-Judaism, or anti-Semitism more generally, might have been, it is clear that this passage presents problems to the modern reader. Either it was a forerunner of "the historical-theological anti-Judaism" of the NT period (done in a Deuteronomic vein) or, more likely, a statement of a later generation when such views became all too widespread within the early Church's popular literature. The text has little to recommend it because, contrary to the texts of Paul, Matthew, or Luke which foster hope for a repentant Israel, insist on its continued role as God's people, or leave open the door for a Jewish mission or more mysteriously for God's salvific activity, it loses not only the historical-theological perspective of its Jewish origins and blames Israel for Christian woes and non-success but also interprets what it perceives to be Israel's woes as the just punishment of its rebellious career as God's people and later as persecutor of God's new people.

The author is post-Pauline and is writing from a Gentile-Christian perspective which one should characterize as anti-Jewish. The plight of the Jew, following the destruction of Jerusalem and later dispersal from Palestine, is seen as the result of divine retribution finally being meted out for centuries of hostility toward God and the whole of humanity.

FOR REFERENCE AND FURTHER STUDY

Collins, R. F. "Apropos the Integrity of 1 Thess" in *SFLT*, 96–135.

Donfried, K. P. "Paul and Judaism. 1 Thessalonians 2:13-16 as a Test Case." *Int* 38 (1984) 242–53.

Hurd, J. C. "Paul Ahead of His Time: 1 Thess. 2:13-16" in *Anti-Judaism in Early Christianity*, vol. 1: *Paul and the Gospels*. eds. P. Richardson and D. Granskou. Waterloo: Wilfred Laurier, 1986, 21–36.

Okeke, G. E. "1 Thessalonians 2.13-16: The Fate of the Unbelieving Jews." *NTS* 29 (1980) 127–36.

Pearson, B. "1 Thessalonians 2:13-16: A Deutero-Pauline Interpolation." *HTR* 64 (1971) 79–91.

Penna, R. "L'évolution de l'attitude de Paul envers les Juifs" in *L'Apôtre Paul: personnalité, style et conception du ministère*. ed. A. Vanhoye. Leuven: Leuven University, 1986, 390–421.

Schmidt, D. "1 Thess 2:13-16: Linguistic Evidence for an Interpolation." *JBL* 102 (1983) 269–79.

Scott, J. M. "Paul's Use of Deuteronomic Tradition." *JBL* 112 (1993) 645–65.

6. *Reasons for Concern and Frustration* (2:17-20)

17. We for our part, brothers and sisters, though made childless by separation from you for just a short time, in person but not in heart, made every possible effort to see you in person, so great was our desire. 18. For while we had resolved to come to you—I, Paul for my part, tried more than once—Satan hindered us. 19. After all, who will be our hope or joy or crown of pride—does that not include you?—in the presence of our Lord Jesus at his coming? 20. To be sure, you yourselves are already our renown and joy.

NOTES

17. *We for our part, brothers and sisters: Hēmeis de* in Paul and in the NT generally, indicates a contrast between groups (1 Thess 5:8; 1 Cor 1:23) and often signals a change of focus from the first to the second, thereby introducing a contrasting development or application (e.g., 1 Cor 2:12; 2 Cor 10:13; Gal 4:28; and Acts 20:13). The shift here is from the believers of verse 13 to the missionaries and their anxiety in verses 17f. Zenon P. 59021 is instructive in this regard; following a short wish of good health in the second person singular, Apollonius begins the body of the letter with: "as for me" or "I for my part" *(kai egō de)*, much as Paul does here in 1 Thess 2:13 and 17. Thus, the translation, "we for our part," underscores the temporal and subject shift: time prior to Timothy's return and change from "you" to "us." Paul follows the common designation for fellow Christians when he refers to them as *adelphoi*, a plural masculine form translated "brothers and sisters" since it includes men and women. The usage comes from contemporary Jewish idiom and conforms with current Greek custom as well, since members of religious societies were often called *adelphoi* (*TDNT* 1:144-46). Paul regularly refers to Christians (also fellow Jews: Rom 9:3) as "brothers and sisters" (ca. 130x) and favors that designation for direct address, usually in the plural—in 1 Thessalonians no fewer than thirteen times. While the frequency of this term in 1 Thessalonians may owe to Paul's affection for his converts, it is probable that the editorial joining of two short missives contributes to the term's recurrent use.

though made childless by separation from you: This translation represents a choice among difficult options. The Greek expression *aporphanizō apo* is a hapax legomenon in the NT and etymologically means "to make someone an orphan." The *orphanos* word group is used primarily of children who have lost their parents (e.g., Sophocles, *Trachiniae* 942); but there exists an extended usage as well as a metaphorical meaning for this word group. In the first case the term may apply to a childless parent (e.g., Sophocles, *Antigone* 425) and in the second the word group acquires the general sense of "deprived of or separated from." Thus, recent translations represent a variety of options, from the literal "orphaned by separation from" to the metaphorical "separated from.'' Also to be noted are the metaphorical, yet interpretative ''bereft of'' (with an eye to the term's etymology) and ''torn away from'' (presumably reading the text in light of Acts 17:10 which speaks of the expulsion of the missionaries). In the present context, Paul calls himself a child deprived of its parents (one could claim a rapid switch of metaphor) or more logically a parent that is childless. The latter seems required by the logic of the situation (the missionaries are authority figures to the converts) and permitted by Greek usage. While Paul and cosenders could refer to themselves as childless parents and expect the Hellenistic readers to understand this idiomatic usage, modern English readers would not. Thus, the term ''childless'' better reflects Pauline usage and preserves the emotional tone of the original. Taking my cue from BAGD 98 (''made orphans by separation from you'') I offer the above translation—the idea of separation being underscored by the double use of *apo* rather than the simple genitive.

for just a short time: The rare expression *pros kairon hōras*, not used in the LXX and found only here in the NT, seems to be related to two Pauline phrases, *pros kairon* and *pros hōran*, both of which imply ''a moment or brief period of time,'' and seems to reflect a usage similar to a parallel contemporary Latin phrase *horae momento* (''in a moment of time'' or ''in a flash,'' Horace, *Satires* 1.1.7-8). Its meaning therefore would be ''for a short or limited time.'' Its function in the present context, however, calls for discussion. To what does the ''short time'' refer, since Paul has not yet returned but nonetheless employs an aorist or single-action participle? It has been suggested that he is referring to an earlier, short period of acute pain or that he is presuming the period will be short and so is promising a visit in the near future. Not only are these suggestions unsatisfactory renderings of the Greek but uneasily interpret the relationship of the phrase, as either causal or temporal, to the rest of the sentence. Instead, Paul's choice of the aorist for the participle and the meaning of *perissoterōs* later in the sentence are more satisfactorily explained by relating these along with the shortness of time to the period prior to Paul's efforts to return to Thessalonica—they missed them so much that after ''just a short time'' they initiated efforts to return.

in person but not in heart: The words ''person'' and ''heart'' (*prosōpon* and *kardia*), while often playing a crucial role in anthropological discussions, here bear the simple contrasting sense of physical presence versus inner person (see 2 Cor 5:12). Paul may be absent in person to them but they are united to the core of his being. This Hebraic terminology contrasts with the Hellenistic, but similar statement of 1 Cor 5:13, where Paul speaks of being absent in body but present in spirit (*sōma* and *pneuma*).

made every possible effort: Translation of the clause, *perissoterōs espoudasamen*, varies depending on whether one opts for the verb's emotive, precipitous, or active sense and whether one interprets the accompanying adverb as comparative or superlative in meaning. In light of its contemporary usage (BAGD 763.2) and in the context of verse 18, the third option (''make every effort'') seems most satisfying. Further, since the comparative adjective and adverb often replace the superlative in late Greek, the ''elative'' or superlative sense is adopted, "making every *possible* effort" (BAGD 651.2). A final reason for translating the text in this way is the later note that this was done "out of great desire."

to see you in person: The expression *to prosōpon hymōn idein* (lit.: "to see your face") is rare in the NT (5x; twice in 1 Thess: 2:17; 3:10). It is an obvious example of a secondary Hebraism, that is, an idiom derived from Hebrew via a literal LXX rendering (e.g., Gen 43:3, 5). The Pauline text could be rendered "to see you" or more literally "to see you face to face." The present translation favors the second option since the second use of *prosōpon* in this verse underscores a Pauline nuance. If Paul earlier claims that his converts are temporarily lost to him in a physical sense (first use), he nonetheless insists that intense desire is satisfied only by complete union, including the physical (second use).

so great was our desire: Literally, the Greek for this phrase reads: "with great desire" *(en pollēi epithymiā)*. While the term "desire" is most frequently employed in a negative sense in the NT, it is sometimes used, as in the present case and Phil 1:23, in its positive original meaning of "direction of one's yearning," a desire which relates to the heart's activity. Also, translation of the expression is a challenge owing to its adverbial use and position at the end of the clause. One could conflate the verb and adverbial expression, create a double verbal rendition of the entire construction, or treat this adverbial construct as related to the entire clause. I have chosen the last option, so that the phrase in question is seen as an adverbial modifier of the preceding clause and understood as follows: "so great was our [heart's] desire." It is that same heart, the center of Paul's being, to which the converts remain united during physical absence and which generates such intense desire for physical reunion.

18. *For while we had resolved to come to you:* On the connection between verses 17-18 ("for while . . ."), see below. The verb *thelō,* which reappears at 4:13, could be rendered "we wished or intended" but owing to its context (what follows in v. 18) and peculiar usage in Paul ("it always implies resolute will," *TDNT* 3:48), we opt for the meaning "decided purpose or resolve" (BAGD 355.2). The phrase, "to come to you" and its context resembles Paul's concerns in Rom 1:10-13 and 15:22f.

—I, Paul, for my part, tried more than once—: The switch from first person plural to first singular (also 5:27) is made more emphatic by the use of *men* without a contrasting *de* and insertion of the writer's name *(egō men Paulos)* to emphasize the speaker's emotional state (BAGD 503.2a). The phrase *kai hapax kai dis,* common in late Greek, including the LXX, is used only by Paul in the NT (also Phil 4:16), and stresses not number ("frequently or repeatedly") but determined effort ("more than once"). Also, the verb "tried" is added to underscore the active character of the expression, i.e., actions rather than intense desire to return.

Satan hindered us: Paul accepts the current scenario concerning Satan's activity in the end-time (*TDNT* 7:151-63). He insists that God has called and appointed him apostle (Gal 1:1, 15) but readily concedes that there is a supernatural adversary, named Satan (Paul never uses the term "devil"), who attempts to thwart God's plans. To describe Satan's activity Paul employs the verb *egkoptō*, a term which could be rendered "delay or detain" as is the case for Acts 24:4. This meaning could explain the situation prior to Timothy's successful embassy, but is not consistent with Paul's usage of *kōlyō* in Rom 1:13 and 15:22 to speak of his being "prevented" from going to Rome. The context then is not that of temporary obstacles but an eschatological sense of Satan's opposition to God's design.

19. *After all, who will be our hope or joy or crown of pride:* Three topics are of concern: the transition between verses 18 and 19, the present or future sense of the clause, and the specific Pauline usage of hope, joy, and crown. (1) Verse 19 is introduced by the transitional particle *gar* which usually has a causal but can also bear an inferential sense. In the present context the latter ("after all") allows for a better transition between verses 18 and 19, where, after a brief statement concerning Satan's activity, the writer returns to the theme of the pericope, the apostles' yearning to revisit the community. (2) Since verse 19 presents an interrogative subject and three nouns without a verb, there is debate whether one should supply a present or a future copula: "is" or "will be." Even though many favor the former and insist either that the hope and joy about which Paul speaks is a present reality or point to verse 20 where the thought is repeated and the present tense used, the more obvious sense is the future since Paul, in verse 19, addresses not the nature of hope, joy, or crown, but the identity of his witness in Jesus' presence when he returns. Verse 19 addresses the time of the parousia; 20, that of the present. (3) The expressions translated "hope, joy, and crown of pride" are striking images whose background and context are crucial for a proper understanding of Paul's trend of thought. The translation presumes a treatment of these in an Excursus, for each term refers to the community as evidence of the missionaries' successful work.

—*does that not include you?:* The Greek clause, *ē ouchi kai hymeis*, offers difficulties owing to formulation and placement, since it interrupts the flow of Paul's question. Translators resolve these difficulties in a variety of ways: by rendering the phrase as a rhetorical question placed after the main question, by transforming the question and additional phrase into one declarative statement, by retaining the two as one rhetorical question within another, or by using the phrase as a response to the main question. Also, some interpret the question as the equivalent of *ei mē hymeis* ("if not you"). Thus, a standard view of verses 19-20 sees Paul as employing "a lively style which adopts the rhetorical question as an answer into the question and then repeats the answer directly with an affirmative *gar*" (*TDNT* 7:630). Such an option, I suspect, is unwise since it takes into consideration neither the initial *ē* nor the particle *kai*. The former functions as a disjunctive conjunction joining two questions (BAGD 342.1d). The above translation reflects this exegetical analysis ("that" for *ē* and "including" for *kai*) and is important for interpreting the pericope. A good parallel to verse 19 is Rom 3:29 where one also encounters two rhetorical questions (the second with an identical *ouchi kai*) and a concluding affirmative response. In sum, Paul begins verse 19 by stating a general principle in the form of a question, "after all, who will be our hope or joy or crown of pride" (the communities of the apostolic mission) and then, before finishing his sentence, interjects a parallel, complementary question, "does that not include you?" (the thriving community of Thessalonica).

in the presence of our Lord Jesus at his coming: (1) The term *emprosthen* occurs seven times in Paul (four in 1 Thessalonians) and has the meaning "before" in the sense of being "in someone's presence," either in a judicial context (1 Thess 2:19; 3:13; also 2 Cor 5:10) or as related to prayer (1 Thess 1:3; 3:9). In the present context the returning Lord is portrayed as a judge before whom Paul, with his converts, will appear. (2) Paul's use of the title "Lord Jesus" (for discussion of *kyrios* and *Iēsous,* see 1:1), is of particular interest. While it is the preferred Christological title of the first missive (2:13–4:2), appearing five times (2:19; 3:11, 13; 4:1, 2), it is increasingly replaced by "Lord Jesus Christ" or some variation thereof. Its later usage by Paul (11 times) involves final blessings (1 Cor 16:23; Rom 16:20), explicit uses of the Jesus tradition (e.g., 1 Cor 11:23; 2 Cor 4:14; Rom 14:14), and an apocalyptic context (2 Cor 1:14) similar to that of 1 Thess 2:19 and 3:13. Thus, Paul's choice of this title, at this early stage, clearly underscores the lordship of the risen Jesus and continuity between his pre- and post-resurrection activities. (3) One encounters here the first mention of the *parousia* or Jesus' coming in Paul's letters. The term has a nontechnical (1 Cor 16:19; 2 Cor 10:10; Phil 1:26) and a technical background. It is the latter which is related to Paul's use of the term for Jesus' coming at the end-time as judge (1 Thess 2:19; 3:13; 4:15; 5:23; and elsewhere only 1 Cor 15:23—note that it occurs also in 2 Thess 2:1, 8, 9). It is usually assumed that the term found its way into Christian literature via Paul who was responsible for modifying the traditional "day of the Lord" motif (see 1 Thess 5:2). While it is hard to see how he could have influenced such a wide variety of Christian texts (Matt 24:3, 27, 39; Jas 5:7, 8; 2 Pet 1:16; 3:4, 12; and 1 John 2:28 employ the term for Jesus' return), it is also difficult to discern earlier usage to account for its appearance in Paul. Undoubtedly, the term's Christian usage is Hellenistic in origin (note that Josephus, *JA* 3.80, 203; 9.55, employs the term for God's activity vis-à-vis Israel) though the conceptual background is OT and early Christian messianism. The latter expected the Son of Man to come on the clouds (Mark 13:26; 14:62) or Jesus as Son to descend from heaven (1 Thess 1:10). Early Christians envisioned this return as that of the enthroned Lord who visits his devotees.

20. *To be sure, you yourselves are already our renown and joy:* The initial *gar* furnishes an affirmative answer to the preceding question (BDF 452.2). Additionally, the emphatic pronoun *(hymeis),* along with the present tense, focuses attention on the Thessalonian's present role in this matter; they already are the source of the apostles' joy and reputation (use of *doxa).*

EXCURSUS

Who will be our hope or joy or crown of pride (2:19)

The text of Paul is read in various ways. The debate centers on whether verse 19 is read as a present or future and, in relation to this, on the meaning of "hope, joy, and crown of pride" in Paul's argument. Not only does the future tense make more sense in this context, but Pauline use of the terms in question lends credence to such an interpretation. The first, *elpis* or "hope," appears frequently in his letters in a variety of usages (see 1:3). In 1 Thessalonians it occurs four times, once only in the first missive, where it has a peculiar meaning. Following classical usage (the term is applied to persons: LSJ 537; BAGD 253.3), Paul describes his converts as "our hope" at the time of Jesus' return, thus emphasizing the future aspect of the concept. Further, the context provides a legal nuance; the Pauline communities will be "evidence" of the missionaries' stewardship and thus the word points forward to the returning Lord's judgment. As Paul later calls the Corinthians his handiwork and the seal of his apostleship (1 Cor 9:1), so he characterizes them, as his letter of recommendation (2 Cor 3:2). In a similar manner, the community of believers will be the proof that Paul will present before the returning Lord as the ground of his expectations, for they will be the basis of his confidence before the Lord. Thus, of the three elements that characterize the Pauline concept of hope (waiting for the future, confidence, and patience), the second is the focal point of this Pauline usage.

The second term, *chara* or "joy," is also frequently employed by Paul and is related to his apostolic work (*TDNT* 9:369). If Pauline usage reveals a range of contexts for the concept (see 1:6), its meaning in 2:19, as an unmodified noun, must be sought in relation to the apocalyptic scene of the Lord's return. It does not refer to Paul's present happiness that all is well at Thessalonica but to his various communities as the source of the joy he will experience in the Lord's presence at the parousia. This term, like "hope," refers to the results of the mission as personified in the community of believers. Before the returning Jesus the missionaries will have an unassailable confidence, transformed into happiness, because they will not have worked in vain. Thus, the community will be the evidence of successful missionary work and the missionaries' joy or source of joy.

A third expression, "crown of pride" (*stephanos kauchēseōs*, lit.: "crown of boasting"), is used to describe the believing communities of the Pauline mission. It appears only here in the NT and is a secondary Semitism, for it represents the Hebrew idiom, *'ateret tipe'eret*, meaning "crown of beauty or glory," a phrase which is variously translated in the LXX. The rendering of the second term, whether in relation to "crown" or alone, has alternated between *kauchēma/kauchēsis* ("boasting": Ezek 16:12; Prov 16:31) and *doxa* ("glory": Jer 13:11; Prov 20:29). Beyond its traditional OT usage, ranging lexically from beauty to glory to honor, the expression and its first component have received an eschatological nuance in intertestamental and NT literature. "Crown of glory" (*stephanos doxēs*) is thus used in T.Benjamin 4:1; 1 Pet 5:4; (also 1QS 4:7; 2 Bar 15:8); and "crown" more generally as "crown of life" in Jas 1:12; Rev 2:10; as "crown of righteousness" in T.Levi 8:2 and 2 Tim 4:8; or as an athletic "crown or wreath" in 1 Cor 9:25 and 4 Macc 17:15 (*TDNT* 7:624-33). What then in all of this determines Pauline usage? Paul employs the term *stephanos* three times in his letters: 1 Cor 9:25; Phil 4:1; and 1 Thess 2:19. If his use of "crown" in the first case is correctly interpreted

as "crown or wreath of victory," reflecting use of the *agōn* or contest motif,
it is doubtful that a similar meaning can be attributed to the other two passages. Especially in the last case, Paul is not speaking of a prize to be gained
at the end of his ministry but of the communities as his crowning achievement. One must not read the two terms as separate Pauline themes but relate the expression to its LXX background and consider what the meaning of
the phrase as a whole would have for a Hellenistic writer and audience. Paul
employs *stephanos kauchēseōs* with its LXX meaning, whereby the first term
designates the culminating sign of his achievement (a community of believers)
and the second underscores his justifiable pride in the Lord's presence. Also,
he seems to have avoided *stephanos doxēs* which, at that time, meant "eternal
reward" as in 1 Pet 5:4; nonetheless he employs *doxa* alone in verse 20 in
a context where a Hellenistic audience would understand the term as referring to "reputation or renown." Thus, the third idiom of the series is translated as "crown of pride" and refers to the community as the culminating
product of the apostolic ministry, an achievement from which they will gain
great satisfaction on the day of the Lord's coming.

INTERPRETATION

After a well-developed thanksgiving period, Paul introduces the body
of the letter where he discourses on the occasion for writing. The reader
is introduced to the missionaries' concern about the recent converts and
their frustration about being unable to make a return visit. From the outset the reader is confronted by questions concerning the pericope's structure, function, themes, and role in Paul's epistolary schema.

2:17-20 as Body-Opening. By means of the contrastive phrase "we for
our part," Paul moves from the thanksgiving and focus on the audience
to the body of the letter and its concerns. There is a shift in person from
"you" to "us" and also temporally from the time following Timothy's
return and report (when the letter is being written) to that of the earlier
period of concern and frustration. Also, in accordance with epistolary
procedure, Paul introduces the body of the letter with a direct form of
address, "brothers and sisters," a convention he regularly follows (1 Cor
1:10; 2 Cor 1:8; Gal 1:11; Phil 1:12; 1 Thess 2:1; 2:17; also Rom 1:13 and
Phlm 7).

Since the body-opening usually focuses on the occasion for writing
and thereby provides the basis for the epistolary conversation between
author and audience, one is not surprised to discover in 2:17-20 information concerning this purpose. Immediately, the author contrasts the situation of the addressees whose perseverance is now well known from
Timothy's report (3:6) with that of the departed missionaries. It was precisely that situation and the subsequent events which formed the occa-

sion of the letter. The apostles' great concern about the new converts and their inability to visit set in motion a calculated visit by one of the missionaries. From the start Paul offers the audience the information needed for it to understand the purpose of the embassy. The body-opening introduces several points which make the letter more intelligible to its recipients. It is stated that immediately after the apostles' departure, attempts were made to return. It is also stressed that their best resolve did not measure up to the task and that the sending of Timothy was in lieu of a forthcoming visit. Likewise, Paul states that the desire to return was great because the parties had established mutual affection (3:6c) and because the community, if it remained faithful to its commitment to Christ, would be the apostles' evidence before the returning Lord that their missionary work was not ineffective (3:5; also 2:1). There also is in this opening the writer's reassurance, hinted at in the thanksgiving, that all is well at Thessalonica (though see 3:10) since the community not only will be but already is the missionaries' "renown and joy" (2:20).

Absence and Relationship. Among the issues of importance in these verses are mutual affection and its pervasive affective terminology. While it is the imagery of the second missive which usually receives attention (see 2:7, 11), it is the language of this pericope which sets the tone for the short missive of concern and thanksgiving. Paul employs emotive imagery to describe the concern of the apostles. While they have moved on to new fields of opportunity, they have become "childless" by force of circumstance. One sees here the work of young preachers whose attachment to their converts is seen in the language used. The separation is painful, particularly in view of what the apostles see as a potentially negative situation. While there is no question of their attachment, the physical separation is the principal concern of the missionaries as they make every possible effort to return. Those efforts are motivated by "intense desire" to be reunited with their children in the Lord.

The remainder of the letter draws upon this pathos to underscore the full extent of the embassy. Unable to be present among the converts the missionaries deprive themselves of the presence of a beloved brother by agreeing to be left alone in Athens and sending him in their name (3:1-2). The envoy becomes a substitute for the absent preachers, an envoy who inquires about them, encourages them, and renews the affective bonds developed during the founding mission. The relationship is affected by the pain of separation and the missionaries' inability to assist the new converts who are experiencing serious difficulties (3:2-4). The tone of the letter is set by the language of verse 17 whether it be that of "brothers and sisters," of parents separated from their children, of spontaneous affection, or of tireless effort to be reunited with the community. The tone is heightened by the pain of separation and frustration at not being able to render assistance to the struggling converts and by the realization that successful missionary work can only be measured by the existence of thriving communities of believers (2:19-20).

Satan and Ministry of the End-days. Verse 18 introduces the reader to two interesting issues. On the one hand, the missionaries, after stating that they "made every possible effort" to revisit Thessalonica, tell the community that their goal is "to come to you." On the other hand, they admit, despite their resolve, that they were thwarted by Satan's activity from doing so. The context of these themes is Paul's conception of the ministry of the end-days. The end is coming and the apostles, following early Christian tradition (Mark 13:10; Matt 24:14), must busy themselves with announcing the good news before the Lord returns. They paid the readers an extended visit devoted to preaching and community formation and then turned to other missionary areas. How then do the missionaries' proposed visit and Satan's opposition fit into Paul's perspective?

Between verses 17 and 18 one finds a causal connection which translators often omit, opting instead to begin a new sentence at this point. The rare, classical *dioti* expresses a weak connection between the two verbs (BDF 456.1), i.e., between Paul's efforts and resolve. At the same time the two verbs of verse 18 ("resolved" and "hindered") are joined by a simple *kai* and not an adversive conjunction. Our translation therefore attempts to lessen the tension between Paul's efforts and Satan's activity by stating the simultaneity of the two actions (both aorists): the apostles' determination and Satan's opposition. In the first case Paul employs the phrase "to come to you," a phrase he often uses in contexts similar to the present one. Of particular interest are Rom 1:10-13 and 15:22f., where several themes parallel those of 1 Thess 2:17-18: longing to come, to see you, often intending to come, and being prevented from going. From first to last letter Paul considers his missionary plans as being out of his immediate control and under the influence of the great eschatological struggle of the end-time. Satan may prevent (1 Thess 2:18) or God may allow (Rom 1:10) given activities.

Paul considers Satan, the supernatural adversary as a crafty deceiver (2 Cor 11:14), who is out to destroy believers (1 Cor 5:5; 2 Cor 2:11) by tempting them away from their allegiance, by thwarting the divine plan, and by harassing God's ministers (1 Cor 7:5; 2 Cor 12:7; 1 Thess 2:18; 3:5). In the end, however, its power will be crushed (Rom 16:20). In the present case Paul speaks of unspecified obstacles that have hindered the mission, obstacles attributed to Satan's activity. A variety of explanations are posited as the occasion or means of this harassment: Paul's illness as noted in 2 Cor 12:7, a city embargo on the missionaries' return (reference to Acts 17:9), the missionaries' inability to collect "the crown of victory" in absentia, or some unknown occasion prompted by a deep sense of Satan's opposition to God's design for the end-days. The last mentioned is the most satisfactory, in part since all the missionaries are involved and since the text focuses not on historical details but on the divine plan's eschatological rival. That Satan is perceived as responsible for hindering the mission by keeping the preachers away says little about the means and much about the seriousness of the community's situation —Paul in 3:5 will return to the theme of Satan's activity. He and other missionaries then saw their work in relation to God's plans for the end-time, part of which involved conflicts with the satanic powers.

Paul before the Divine Throne. Verses 19-20 offer a fascinating glimpse of Paul's early conception of the ministry. After insisting on the apostles' resolve and his own repeated attempts to return to Thessalonica, he proceeds in verse 19 to give the basic reason for the effort expended. The missionaries will appear before the tribunal of the returning Lord where they will be judged on the basis of the communities they have founded. This is the interpretation to which detailed analysis of verse 19 leads.

As noted earlier, verse 19 presents three noun phrases with an interrogative pronoun and no verb. Since the entire verse addresses the future coming of the Lord Jesus, it is assumed that the nonexpressed copula has a future sense. Additionally, the three nouns address essentially future concepts. The community as "hope" before the Lord Jesus suggests a legal sense whereby the believers are the proof or evidence of the missionaries' stewardship. In the present they are the basis of the apostles' confidence and will be presented as proof at the Lord's future coming. As "joy" the community will be evidence of the missionaries' successful work and the source of their pride and happiness; as "crown of pride" believers will stand before the Lord as the culminating product or achievement of a lifetime of missionary activity. Similar concepts are presented in Phil 2:16 and 2 Cor 1:14—note the mutual character of the evidence in the latter.

Further evidence for viewing verse 19 as a judgment scene is Paul's use of the phrase "in the presence of our Lord Jesus at his coming." The preposition *emprosthen* suggests being present before the returning Lord as judge before whom the missionaries will appear. We are probably justified in appealing to 2 Cor 5:10 for assistance in interpreting this passage, for there the risen Christ appears on a judgment seat and bestows good or evil on all. Admittedly, the latter addresses the judgment of all believers, while the former is concerned with the assessment of missionaries by the Lord, a theme which will gain prominence later in Paul's career (Phil 2:16; 1 Cor 4:5). Paul here presupposes the traditional apocalyptic scenario of the Lord's presence and activity as judge and posits an adjudicating scene for his apostolic ministry as the motivation of the missionaries' intense desire to return to Thessalonica.

Also important in this regard is Paul's first mention of the *parousia* or Jesus' "coming." While this term has a technical and a nontechnical background, it is the first which is of interest, its use either as a religious expression for the manifestation of a hidden deity to its devotees through acts of power or to an individual for the purpose of healing or as a political term for the official visit of a high-ranking person, even kings or emperors, visiting cities and provinces, involving elaborate public ceremonials and displays (BAGD 630.2b; *TDNT* 5:859-60). Paul employs this term for Jesus' coming at the end-time four times in 1 Thess: 2:19; 3:13; 4:15; and 5:23. Its use in each instance draws attention to the topic under discussion. In the case of 2:19 the theme of *parousia* is important to Paul's train of thought less as a consideration of the end-time as for the purpose of establishing a judgment scene wherein his apostolic activity in the Lord's presence will be evaluated. Early Christians probably envisioned the coming of their Lord much in the fashion of the pomp and circumstance accompanying official or imperial visits of the Roman period. It is probably in such a context that Paul postulates a judgment scene for the Lord's ministers who in apocalyptic fashion will be required to produce evidence of their righteous activity (see also 4:16-17). Thus, Paul offers a heavenly judgment as the basic motive for the earnest preaching of the gospel and for the missionaries' desire to return.

Community as Present Renown and Joy. Verse 20 follows emphatically the question of the preceding text by insisting that the Thessalonians not only will be the missionaries' proof of achievement at the final judgment but are already living proof of their missionary commitment and success. Interestingly, Paul switches from the terms "hope and crown of pride" to a new noun *doxa*. Use of this expression in the present context indicates not eschatological glory of the end-time but the missionaries' prestige or renown (LSJ 444). A Hellenistic reader would have readily understood Paul's claim that his good reputation derived from the fruits of his labor. In a slightly different vein Paul will later insist that the community of Corinth itself is a public witness to his work and reputation (2 Cor 2:1-3).

Paul's shift to the present, away from the eschatological emphasis of verse 19, gives added stress to the letter's occasion: the missionaries' reputation and joy. Indeed, the letter is being written because of Paul's heightened pleasure at Timothy's good news (3:6, 9) and reassurance that his work and that of his fellow missionaries was not "in vain." Verse 19 then, by its use of future concepts in an eschatological context, establishes the motive for the missionaries' great desire to visit Thessalonica, while verse 20, by shifting to present concepts and tense, expresses their ecstatic reaction to the report of the returning embassy. The community, in its life of faith and love (3:6), is testimony to the apostles' work and success. Thus, the community by its very existence and lived commitment is a constant source of the missionaries' exalted reputation.

FOR REFERENCE AND FURTHER STUDY

Cranfield, C. E. B. "A Study of 1 Thessalonians 2." *IBS* 1 (1979) 215–26.
Jewett, R. *Paul's Anthropological Terms: A Study of Their Use in Conflict Settings.* Leiden: Brill, 1971.
Malherbe, A. J. *Paul and the Thessalonians: The Philosophic Tradition of Pastoral Care.* Philadelphia: Fortress, 1987.
Pfitzner, V. C. *Paul and the Agon Motif.* Leiden: Brill, 1967.
White, J. L. *The Body of the Greek Letter.* Missoula: Scholars, 1972.

7. Timothy's Mission (3:1-5)

1. Therefore, able to bear this no longer, we gladly agreed to remain alone in Athens 2. and sent Timothy, our brother and God's coworker in the service of the gospel of Christ, so as to strengthen and encourage you regarding your faith, 3. so that no one be dissuaded by the present difficulties. Certainly, you yourselves know that such is our appointed lot. 4. And besides, when we were with you, we often warned you that we would certainly experience difficulties, just as it has turned out and as you now know. 5. Therefore, I for my part, able to bear it no longer, sent to inquire about your faith, for fear the tempter had successfully tempted you and that our work would be without effect.

NOTES

1. *Therefore, able to bear this no longer:* The conjunction *dio,* having lost its subordinating force, retains its function as an inferential conjunction ("therefore"— BDF 45.5) and is used thus by Paul to connect larger units of thought (1 Thess 3:1; also Phlm 8; Rom 2:1) or concluding statements (1 Thess 5:11; see Phil 2:9; Gal 4:31); for a similar tandem use of *dio* and *dia touto,* both as inferential conjunctions, see Rom 1:24 and 26. The idiom "able to bear this no longer" represents Hellenistic usage. On the one hand, use of the negative particle

mēketi rather than *ouketi* represents the Hellenistic norm whereby *mē* is regularly employed with participles and simply means "no longer" (BDF 430; *IBNTG*, 105). On the other, the verb *stegō*, which occurs four times in the NT, exclusively in Paul: 1 Cor 9:12; 13:7; 1 Thess 3:1, 5, is used with the metaphorical sense of "bear or endure" in all but the second case and is well attested in classical and Hellenistic literature (see e.g., P.Oxyrhynchus 1775.10: "my father caused me great harm and I endured it until you came"). Invariably translators render the participle as "able to bear no longer," a meaning which is derived *ad sensum* and is related to the causal force of the participle ("since we no longer endured" becomes "able to endure no longer").

we gladly agreed to remain alone in Athens: While some render *ēudokēsamen* as "we decided," it is preferable to retain its etymological sense and translate "we gladly agreed" since this fits the emotional tone of the passage. Further, the complementary infinitive phrase "to be left or remain alone" *(kataleiphthēnai . . . monoi)* is a common LXX expression employed to contrast a group with others who have either departed or died. Though the infinitive is passive in form, it is usually read with an active sense "to remain" (BAGD 413.1a), because the statement is being made from the point of view not of the envoy but of the letter writer.

2. *and sent Timothy: Pempō* is a common, nontechnical verb which Paul uses, along with other such terms, to describe the dispatch of various individuals: Timothy (1 Thess 3:2; Phil 2:19, 23; 1 Cor 4:17), Epaphroditus (Phil 2:25, 28), and others: "those accredited" (1 Cor 16:3), "brethren" (2 Cor 9:3), two "brothers" along with Titus: one a famous preacher and the other a brother who was "tested and found earnest" (Apollos and Timothy, respectively: 2 Cor 8:18, 22—use of *synpempō*), "those whom I sent" (2 Cor 12:17—use of *apostellō*), and "the brother" who accompanied Titus (2 Cor 12:18—use of *synapostellō*). Virtually all uses of *pempō* (and other "sending" verbs) involve mission contexts; the status of the individuals sent, in this case Timothy, remains to be clarified. Paul's colleague is mentioned no fewer than 23 times in the NT, 6 of these in Acts 16–20, 6 in the Paulinist writers, and the remaining 11 in Paul's letters.

our brother and God's coworker: Paul employs the term *adelphos* not only to describe fellow Christians and converts (2:17) but also missionaries, whether in epistolary prescripts (Phlm 1; Gal 1:2; 1 Cor 1:1; 2 Cor 1:6) or in descriptive contexts (1 Thess 3:2; 1 Cor 16:11-12; 2 Cor 2:13). The phrase "God's coworker" is troublesome for textual and theological reasons. Nonetheless, the reading followed here (1) is the most difficult of the several variants, (2) explains best the others, and (3) can be defended as Pauline, even if it is not well attested in the manuscript tradition. The basic text seems to have been *synergon tou theou* (read by D* 33 *d e* Ambrosiaster Pelagius Ps-Jerome), a text which scribes would have found bold or objectionable, thereby omitting *tou theou* (B 1962), substituting *diakonon* for *synergon* (S A P 81 629*, etc.) or creating various conflations, the most common of which reads: "God's servant and our fellow worker" (the majority of witnesses, most of which are of late date). The above text is chosen because it explains best the origin of the other readings (*TCGNT*, 240-42); the theological reasons for this choice are given below.

in the service of the gospel of Christ: The translation "in the service of," representing the preposition *en*, is proposed in view of parallel passages in Paul, the idiomatic usage of *synergos*, and the contextual reading of its present use. The phrase "gospel of Christ" is of importance on several counts. The noun *euangelion*, though employed widely in the NT, occurs principally in Paul (48 times in a variety of usages). If the term's background, origin, and meaning are debated, it is safe to say that its NT, and particularly Pauline, meaning is that of "the preaching, message, or working out of God's salvation," not that of later centuries when it refers to a narrative account about Jesus of Nazareth. Its background is to be sought in the OT (particularly the LXX verbal rendering of the Hebrew term *bāsār*, meaning "bring good tidings"), in contemporary Jewish usage, and in Hellenistic emperor cult (*TDNT* 2:707-37). It is generally admitted that the concept, especially expressed as a noun, does not have a firm basis in the Jesus tradition but rather is due to the early Church. So, his frequent use (22x) of the noun without modifiers indicates a usage common to Paul and his audience. Also, the frequent use of the absolute form in his early correspondence and the extended and developed usage of the noun in 1 Thessalonians (6x) argues for a pre-Pauline, community development. If I am correct in my delineation of 2:13–4:2 as Paul's earliest extant missive, then the occurrence of "gospel" in 1 Thess 3:2 is the first by Paul and thus its usage is important for determining the meaning of other occurrences of the phrase "gospel of Christ" in Paul (7x) as well as his use of the term "gospel" more generally; for a discussion of the title *Christos*, see 1:1.

so as to strengthen and encourage you regarding your faith: To express purpose (i.e., the goal of Timothy's mission) Paul employs a favorite (double) articular infinitive construction introduced by *eis to* (35 cases in Paul, 7 in 1 Thessalonians alone). The first verb, *stērizō*, has the basic meaning of "establishing or strengthening" but since it is clear from the context that Timothy is to work with an already existing reality, the second meaning ("to strengthen or make more firm") is to be preferred. The second verb, *parakaleō*, a frequent Pauline term with a range of meaning, here suggests "encouragement or exhortation to greater effort." Timothy is to address the community's faith. This use of the noun *pistis* (on use of the verb see 2:13) represents the first of eight occurrences of the term in 1 Thessalonians, five of which are found in the first missive (3:2, 5, 6, 7, 10), all qualified as "your faith." Paul is not speaking in general terms of the Christian faith nor even of the human response to God's gift but of the state of belief as it exists among the Thessalonians.

3. *so that no one be dissuaded:* The translation presupposes that *to mēdena* with infinitive represents a final clause introduced by an articular infinitive, though without a preposition (*IBNTG*, 140). The verb *sainomai* presents some difficulty since it is a NT hapax and since its meaning is deduced from context rather than current usage. Originally it was used by Homer of a dog "wagging its tail" and so in the classical period came to mean "fawn, cringe, or

pay court to" and in the passive "beguile or deceive" (LSJ 1580). The meaning favored by moderns is the one preferred by ancient versions and patristic commentators: "to move, disturb, agitate" (BAGD 740). There is, however, no contemporary evidence of such usage; also, textual emendations to alleviate the problem are mere conjectures. Even the 1941 papyrus discovery of the dialogue between Origen and Bishop Heraclitus, where the term occurs, does not strengthen the case, since it is probable that Origen is influenced by the patristic exegetical tradition noted earlier. I return to the first option and suggest that Paul is referring to believers being talked out of their faith. Converts, when confronted by the challenge of the new way of life and the alienation from neighbors and friends which resulted, might easily be enticed by their old customs and wandering preachers and thus dissuaded from their new commitment. The verb *sainomai* then can be read in an idiomatic way and makes good sense in the present context according to this interpretation.

by the present difficulties: The translation assumes extended discussion of the term *thlipsis* and of the presumed context of persecution as the setting for the Thessalonian correspondence. The term is taken to have the general meaning of "trouble or difficulty" and its context is sought in Paul's other statements in the letter (see below). Also, the term translated "present" *(tautais)* refers not to what "immediately preceded" (the persecution of 2:14-16) but to the "here and now" (BAGD 596.1a).

Certainly you yourselves know: Paul draws a twofold inference, both introduced by postpositive *gar* ("for") to explain why no one in the community should be taken by surprise. To introduce the first he employs a familiar expression, "you know that," to introduce a generally accepted, well-known fact (BAGD 556.1e). The first inference is drawn from common knowledge; the second, from the missionaries' teaching. Thus, the first is underscored by the addition of "you yourselves" and the second, by the clause "when we were with you." The double use of postpositive *gar* is frequent in biblical literature "to introduce several arguments for the same assertion," "to have one clause confirm the other," or "to have various assertions of one and the same sentence confirmed one after the other" (BAGD 152.1c). While most opt for the second possibility, i.e., they make the first assertion dependent on the second, usually by omitting the first *gar*, it is preferable to read parallel assertions, since, unlike the examples given in BAGD, the two occurrences of *gar* in this case are joined by a coordinating *kai* ("and"). The first (v. 3b) is translated "certainly" since the context highlights its proverbial character and the second (v. 4) is rendered "besides" to stress the supplementary function of the second assertion (see also 4:9-10). Additionally, both inferential statements are expressed in *hoti* clauses: "you know that" and "we often warned you that." Such expressions are called either "recall devices" (see comments on 1:5) or disclosure formulas in epistolary contexts.

that such is our appointed lot: This translation follows the traditional interpretation of the clause *eis touto keimetha*, lit., "we are set or destined for this." If the basic sense is clearly that of destiny, the "thing destined" is more presumed than stated, for *eis touto* (rendered "such") refers back to *tais thlipse-sin tautais*. While most presume a context of persecution and interpret the "difficulties" as "tests" for entry into the kingdom (following Lukan rather than Pauline thought—see Acts 14:22), the above rendering reflects instead the more general sense of the assertion, namely, that "the present difficul-ties" form part of the divinely appointed human condition—the "we" in-cludes the missionaries as well.

4. *And besides, when we were with you:* A new assertion, introduced by "and be-sides," underscores the missionary context of the community's knowledge. The clause refers back to the time when the apostles were in the city for the foundation visit, part of their task being to forewarn the converts about their new loyalties and challenges. Interestingly, the visit is described in terms of "presence," terminology which would not be lost on the addressees who know how much the missionaries miss their presence (3:6).

   we often warned you that we would certainly experience difficulties: The main verb, *prolegō*, is in the imperfect and so indicates repeated or frequent past action. Its meaning is "tell beforehand" and its context implies "forewarning," a nuance expressed by the futuristic "would" of the following clause. The *hoti* clause, consisting of the verb *mellō* followed by the present infinitive of *thlibō*, is used to express both the future and certain character of the "difficulties." It is unnecessary to interpret the text as though presupposing a "divine de-cree" (BAGD 501—see Acts 14:22); simply it expresses the apostles' convic-tion that conversion would bring about profound changes in the believers' lives.

   just as it has turned out and as you now know: Structurally, the Greek text is relatively simple, consisting of *kathōs* followed by double *kai*, each introduc-ing a verb. A similar construction occurs at 4:6 where some translators feel the need to transform the two verbs into a simpler verbal-adverbial construc-tion: "as we solemnly forewarned." One could follow the same pattern here: "and so it turned out, as you know." In both cases, the two verbs seem to have distinct functions (for 4:6, see below). In the present case, the first verb, "it happened or turned out," refers back to the prior warning; the second, "as you know," is related not to the addressees' verification of what hap-pened but to their understanding of the second assertion. Interestingly, as the first assertion (3b) begins with a self-evident claim ("you yourselves know"), so the second, though initially stated as wisdom drawn from the missionaries' experience and preaching, ends up being the experiential knowl-edge of the converts ("as you now know"). The "you know" formula of 3:3 and 4 constitute recall devices not of past advice but common knowledge and experience (see also 1:5).

5. *Therefore, I for my part, able to bear it no longer:* While this verse is a virtual rewriting of verses 3:1-3a, its new features and emphasis draw the reader's attention; for *dia touto* ("therefore") see comments on 3:1. The first differ-ence is the switch from first-person plural to first singular; see also 2:18. There is a contrast intended between verses 1f. and 5. The former expresses the

group's motivation, the second focuses on Paul's reason. While he may have similar concerns ("able to bear it no longer") he nonetheless contrasts his own motive for agreeing to the embassy.

sent to inquire about your faith: While similar to verse 2, the present passage does not contain an object. It seems ill-advised, as do some scholars, to supply one. Indeed, in verse 2 the stress is on the embassy: the name "Timothy" is given as object of the verb "send" and there is emphasis on his credentials and on the object of the mission. The thought of verse 2 might be paraphrased thus: "we sent Timothy . . . that he might do such and such." In verse 5, the emphasis is on purpose and should be translated as "I sent to inquire." Paul employs the verb *ginōskō* ("come to know or inquire about") rather than *oida* ("understand"; see 1:4); the verbal object is "your faith," i.e., "state of belief" (see 3:2). In verse 5 then we hear specifically about Paul's fear that the community might not have survived, a point which is confirmed by its similarity to 2:18-19, where Paul also emphasizes his personal concerns.

for fear the tempter had successfully tempted you: "For fear" represents the conjunction *mē pōs*, as though implying a verb of apprehension (BAGD 519) and introduces a double clause, the first employing an aorist indicative and the second, an aorist subjunctive. Thus, the first clause refers to something viewed as already having occurred and the second to something seen as a possible result (BAGD 519; BDF 370). The translation then, with the addition of "successfully" and use of the pluperfect "had . . . tempted," captures Paul's fear that at the time of writing already the tempter had succeeded in destroying their faith. Further, Paul emphasizes the notion of "seduction or enticement to sin" by employing the verb *peirazō* twice in this statement. Only here and in the Matthean temptation story (4:3) is the participial form *(ho peirazōn)* personified. It is clear that Paul is referring to Satan who is named in 2:18. Elsewhere he will speak of Satan tempting believers (1 Cor 7:5) or of believers being tempted, presumably by Satan (Gal 6:1; 1 Cor 10:13).

that our work would be: The second clause by employing an aorist subjunctive expresses a future, possible result concerning the missionaries' work *(kopos)*. This term may have the nuance of "toil or tedious labor" or more generally may express the idea of profession or occupation. In the first case one might focus on the wearisome toil of Paul the tentmaker who spent himself physically to support his missionary activity. In the second instance one would view the term as referring to missionary activity within and for the community *(TDNT* 3:829). In fact Paul employs both meanings, a range which is documented in 1 Thessalonians. In 2:9 wearisome toil is meant (see earlier notes on "labor and toil"). The other occurrences of *kopos*, however, demand the more general sense of "Christian activity or work" (as in Phil 2:16; Gal 4:11; 1 Cor 16:16; Rom 16:6, 12), whether the missionary work of Paul and colleagues (1 Thess 3:5), the pastoral intracommunity labor of some community members (5:12), or more generally the audience's participation in the Church's inner life and activity (1:3). It is doubtful that *kopos* in 3:5 refers to the missionaries' manual labor, done in supporting themselves while preaching, since that labor in effect would not be lost; it refers rather to the basic missionary task.

without effect: This expression, often rendered "in vain," translates the Greek phrase *eis kenon,* a phrase which appears often in the LXX and in Hellenistic texts but found only in Paul in the NT (see 2:1). Its use in this context strongly underscores the Apostle's fear that the community no longer exists, having returned to its pre-Christian ways, and that, as a result, their preaching in the end will have been "without result."

INTERPRETATION

These verses continue Paul's narrative concerning the apostles' desire to visit and their frustration at not being able to do so. Paul describes the apostolic decision to send Timothy in the name of the missionary band since its leaders are unable to make the trip themselves.

Further Development of the Body of the Letter. 3:1-5 introduces a further, discrete unit of the body of the letter, namely, the first part of the body-middle, the second part being 3:6-8. The unit is introduced by the inferential conjunction *dio* ("therefore") and so draws a close connection between the strong emotion of 2:17-20 and Paul's subsequent discussion. At the same time, the unit is marked off by a second inferential conjunction *dia touto* which rounds out the paragraph by introducing a similar, parallel construction and discussion (v. 5).

Additionally, 3:1-5 employs several traditional epistolary formulas and treats customary topics. Among these one encounters a well-stated disclosure formula: "you yourselves know," statements of reassurance ("we often warned you that we would certainly"), of grief ("able to bear this no longer"—vv. 1 and 5), and of responsibility ("such is our appointed lot"). These various statements relate to the problems confronted by the community and its understanding of the situation. Furthermore, in place of the stereotyped reference in Hellenistic letters to the author having written, we find an interesting reference to the foundation visit as a source of the converts' knowledge of what is happening (3-4).

A last issue, concerning the relation between 2:17-20 and 3:1-5, needs attention here, namely, the presumed object of the verb; what are the missionaries unable to bear? While translators readily supply an indefinite "it" after the verb, there is room for ambiguity. Proper interpretation depends on whether one reads the beginning of 3:1 as looking forward or backward. One might insist that Paul is referring forward to the lack of news regarding events or the inability of the missionaries to continue needed pastoral care. However, the force of the consecutive conjunction ("therefore") demands a backward look to 2:17f. where Paul speaks of unbearable separation and previous, unsuccessful attempts to return. Thus, the term "this" (referring back to the preceding verses) has been introduced into the translation (3:1) to underscore the unexpressed but logical object of concern and the continuing theme of the new pericope, the missionaries' separation from their converts. 3:1-5 develops further the pathos of the bereaved parents.

The Embassy to Thessalonica. Whatever the obstacles were to the missionary group's return, these did not seem to obstruct the sending of one of its members. Who exactly is that member, who decides to send him, and for what purpose?

(1) Concerning the envoy one can say he is an early Pauline colleague, for he appears as such in and is cosender of 1 Thessalonians, Philippians, and Philemon. In the first two he also acts as envoy, first as one sent by a group (1 Thess 3:2: "we sent") and then as one sent by Paul (3:5; Phil 2:19). In the present context he is called a "brother," a term which often designates coworkers, which does not seem to have acquired a titular sense, and which seems to underscore special affection or regard for the individual so described. Further, Timothy is also called "a coworker of God in the service of the gospel of Christ." While putting off until later the discussion of this important phrase, it can be noted here that Paul applies to Timothy an expression which describes the essence and full scope of missionary work. Thus, in this early part of Paul's career one should view Timothy as a junior associate forming part of the Pauline apostolic band, a missionary on equal footing with others though junior in authoritative terms. One can only surmise why it is he who is sent by the senior members to visit the distant Christian community of Thessalonica. But it would seem [1] that he was intimately involved in preaching to the Thessalonian converts who are experiencing problems and [2] that he was, at the time of Paul's visit to Athens, conducting a mission in that city. While senior members are unable to make the trip to Macedonia, they nonetheless agree to replace ("remain in Athens") Timothy while he makes a hurried exploratory and ministerial trip to Thessalonica in their name.

(2) The decision to send Timothy. On two occasions there is mention of sending Timothy to Thessalonica; in the first case it is stated that more than one person is responsible for the decision and in the second it obviously is due to Paul (3:2, 5 respectively). In the first case the plural is used throughout for the participle ("able to bear"), for the main verbs ("gladly agreed" and "sent"), and for the adjective ("alone"), and thus involves more people than Paul alone (*contra* Acts 17–18). The decision to send was that of the leadership, whose sense of separation was so great that they willingly agreed to a lesser hardship to gain access, via a messenger or junior colleague, to the Thessalonian community. They "gladly agreed to remain alone in Athens" in Timothy's place while he took a

hurried trip north. One must avoid an overly dramatic and even romantic view of Paul tragically languishing alone in Athens. Instead, Paul insists, as he does throughout this correspondence, that the relationship between missionaries and converts is genuine and mutual and that the decision to send a member of the apostolic team was a responsible and painful one for the leadership of the mission. It was responsible because it did not interfere with the progress of the Achaian mission and it was painful both in sparing a fellow worker for a while and in prolonging the anguish of not knowing what was happening in Macedonia. So in the first instance Paul expresses the collective motivation and decision of the apostolic group, including Silvanus and Paul. In the second case he expresses his own motivation. He does not say that he in his turn sent Timothy but that he had a special reason for insisting on the need for an embassy.

(3) The purpose for the mission requires more discussion. Not only does Paul insist that the missionary group arrived at a common decision to send an embassy to Thessalonica and also that he himself had further concerns, but he also offers two sets of reasons for this decision (use of *eis to* to express purpose in both cases). In the first instance the reason is stated: "so as to strengthen and encourage you regarding your faith" (3:2b). The missionaries apparently are concerned that the already established community needs assistance and exhortation to greater efforts. In view of the acute difficulties faced by the new converts, it is the leaders' hope that Timothy's visit and further ministrations will assist its members in facing their new religious loyalties and challenge with firm conviction. The danger is that the converts be "dissuaded" from their commitment to Christ (v. 3). Timothy is to continue his ministerial work which it is assumed involves further teaching and exhortation (v. 2). The special and combined use of these two verbal roots (1 Thess 3:2; Rom 1:11-12; 2 Thess 2:17; Acts 14:22; 15:32; 1 Pet 5:10) has led some to view these as early paraenetic or missionary terminology employed by Paul to describe the extent of pastoral care. In the second instance (3:5) Paul, in expressing his own view, states in an alarming vein his fears concerning his converts. He wishes to find out about their situation for he fears that "the tempter" has already lured them away from their commitment. Thus, in the second case, the object of the embassy seems to be that of fact-finding (does the community still exist or did the mission have any effect?), while in the first, the goal of the trip seems to be more preventive (assistance and encouragement in view of difficult times). The missionaries' hope then is that Timothy's embassy and persuasive powers will provide the Thessalonians new vigor for the challenge and counteract the allure of their former pagan ways and will at the same time reassure Paul concerning the converts' religious situation.

The Difficulties at Thessalonica. Chapter 3 provides interesting but ambiguous data concerning the community's situation and the apostles' fear concerning the well being of the converts. It is particularly Paul's use of the term *thlipsis* to describe the situation which causes debate. Nonetheless, the theme of persecution by Jews is often borrowed from Acts 17 to interpret Paul's contextual references and to confirm the authenticity and to explicate the anti-Judaic character of 1 Thess 2:14-16. A focused discussion therefore of Pauline usage in 1 Thess 3:1-5 is necessary to discern what he means when he speaks of *thlipsis* at Thessalonica.

The term *thlipsis* which occurs 45 times in the NT, is employed 20 times by Paul in a figurative sense, i.e., no longer meaning "pressing" but "oppression, suffering, affliction, trouble." The Pauline occurrences of the term reveal a range of usage, from the role it plays in character-building (Rom 5:3), to the trials and difficulties experienced by missionaries (2 Cor 1:8), to Paul's deep anguish and reluctant writing (2 Cor 2:4), and to the sufferings of the end-time (Rom 2:9). Symptomatic of recent philological study, however, is the tendency to read in a unified way all occurrences of the word as designating a technical Pauline term for the trials of Christians in the end-time. More fundamentally, it is regularly maintained that *thlipsis* in the NT, particularly in Paul, is characterized by three things: "it is inseparable from Christian life in this world," "it is the suffering of Christ, who is afflicted in his members," and it "is eschatological tribulation" (*TDNT* 3:144). All three elements merit consideration but it is doubtful, and even far-fetched, to maintain that most occurrences of the term involve all these characteristics. Suffering and pain are certainly constituents of the human condition but it is ludicrous to maintain, on the basis of a text such as 1 Thess 3:3, that persecution is either normal for or the destiny of Christians. Also it is clear that Paul often exhorts his audience to see its sufferings and misfortunes in light of Jesus' death, but this is more central to his paraenesis and soteriology than to his anthropology. Lastly, the occasional use by Paul of this term in apocalyptic contexts should not lead scholars to view all occurrences as eschatological in nature; even some occurrences which might have eschatological overtones (such as the activity of Satan or other nefarious opposition) need not suggest apocalyptic warfare or persecution.

A further element which complicates our task in interpreting Paul's statement in 1 Thess 3:3-4 is their customary contextual reading. Again Schlier's treatment of the issue can be cited as representative: "among the concrete afflictions generally signified by *thlipsis*, the reference is to persecution in 1 Th. 1:6; 3:3f. (= 2:14f.)" (*TDNT* 3:147). The key to this interpretation is provided by the severe statements of 2:14-16 and the seeming corroboration of Acts 17:1-9. Thus, the problem at Thessalonica would have been rampant persecution by the Jewish population. If one leaves out consideration of the doubtful evidence of 2:14-16 and Acts 17, then the situation appears quite different. Since *thlipsis*, as noted earlier, has a range of meaning, from concrete suffering to more general difficulty or trouble, then its meaning in 1 Thess 3:3 should be sought in relation to Paul's other statements in the Thessalonian correspondence. Paul clearly states that the community received the gospel "in the midst of great difficulty" (1:6) and though he does not elaborate, his terminology elsewhere points to a social, religious separation of believers from their non-Christian neighbors that caused problems for them. Thus, by the phrase "the present difficulties" (3:3) Paul refers to the alienation caused by the converts' adoption of a new value system which radically changed their social, cultic, and religious affiliations and loyalties.

Such an interpretation is confirmed by Paul's comments in 3:3b-4 and further supported by the "seduction" terminology of verse 5. He draws two interesting inferences to explain why his audience should not be surprised either in being discouraged by new difficulties or lured away from their commitment by the thought of their former lives as non-Christians. The interrelated inferences, drawn from common knowledge ("our common lot"—3:3) or from missionary preaching ("we often warned you"— v. 4), underscore not the unlucky persecution by jealous Jewish residents of Thessalonica (Acts 17) but the difficult transition and alienation resulting from the converts' new religious ideology and commitments. In sociological terms the missionaries and converts were fully aware of the consequences of their decision to follow the prophet from Nazareth. It was their lot to be a visible minority in an often inimical pagan context. Thus, the missionaries during their foundation visit often cautioned their converts about the difficulties that would arise from their new commitment. In fact, the use of the plural "we" in the *hoti* clauses of both inferences indicates that the two assertions are drawn from experiential knowledge, both on the human and Christian levels. In the first case, the Thessalonians should know that they and the missionaries have their appointed share of difficulties; the ones they are presently experiencing are no different when seen from God's point of view. In the second case, the apostles through their missionary experience have come to realize that Christian commitment modifies social relations and often dwelt on that topic in the course of their preaching. The warning was not "prophecy" but shared experience; by becoming Christians, old converts and new (missionaries and Thessalonians) necessarily experience disruption in their social world. This change is here expressed negatively because Paul's text deals with the difficulties, not the benefits which result from conversion.

In verse 5 Paul expresses his fear that the community no longer exists because it had succumbed to the seduction of Satan. His double use of the verb *peirazō* to describe this activity points not to fear of persecution and therefore abandonment of faith but to the enticement away from one's commitment back to the domination of sin and its satanic master. For Paul, Satan is responsible, at least in part, for putting up obstacles (some of which need not be demonic in origin; see Rom 1:13 and 15:22f.) and for luring away believers from their commitment to God, whether through daily, socioreligious events or the allurement of wandering philosophers and preachers. Thus, the notion of enticement in verse 5 strengthens our desire to see a similar nuance in Paul's use of *sainomai* ("dissuade") in the parallel text of 3a and supports our interpretation of *thlipsis* as referring to socioreligious alienation rather than religious persecution.

God's Coworker in the Service of the Gospel of Christ. While some early readers may have found such a text difficult theologically and have modified the reading (see Notes for a discussion of scribal activity), it can be defended as Pauline since it has a striking verbal parallel in 1 Cor 3:9 ("we are God's coworkers"—use of *synergoi*) and states in a stark way what Paul will express elsewhere, namely, that God makes generous use of human mediators or helpers (1 Thess 2:13; 1:5; also 2 Cor 5:20–6:2; Rom 10:14-17). Such passages lead me to interpret the phrase (also 1 Cor 3:9) as "God's coworker" rather than "coworkers in the service of God." To express the latter Paul would employ a prepositional construction (see *synergos eis* of 2 Cor 8:23). Such a conclusion is supported by his regular use of a genitive construction following *synergos*. Since this construction means "coworker with me or us," by analogy *synergos tou theou* signifies "coworker with God." Thus, while the majority of Pauline occurrences of the term "coworkers" serves to describe his missionary associates (nine of eleven times), on two occasions the noun (1 Thess 3:2; 1 Cor 3:9; see also 2 Cor 6:1 for the verb) draws an interesting picture of the missionaries as God's helpers. Such an idea is also well known in Greek literature where the gods are often called upon to be helpers (e.g., Euripides, *Medea* 396; *Hippolytus* 525, 676; and Aristophanes, *Equites* 588).

Further, this interpretation fits well into our reading of the letter. As Paul had been anxious in 2:13 to underscore God's part in the human endeavor of preaching, so here also he is eager to stress that same factor in the unfolding of the mission. Delays and difficulties may owe to Satan's influence (2:18; 3:5) but God is also at work and has coworkers for that purpose. The Thessalonians are to understand that both the apostles' effort among them and Timothy's work of strengthening and encouraging them (3:2) are the work of God while the danger of Christians being lured away from their faith is the work of the tempter (3:5).

More precisely, the apostles (Timothy in this case) are coworkers *en tǭ euangeliǭ*. For this Greek phrase one could propose a literal translation, "in the gospel," or opt for a more interpretive rendering: "in preaching the gospel'' or ''in the service of the gospel.'' In such a discussion, however, one must consider three other Pauline passages: Phil 4:3 which speaks of others who ''have fought at my side *en tǭ euangeliǭ* along with Clement and the rest of my coworkers,'' 1 Cor 15:1 which describes Paul's message as ''the gospel . . . in which *(en hǭ)* you stand,'' and Rom 1:9 which presents God as the one ''whom I serve with my inmost being *en tǭ euangeliǭ* of his Son.'' The first, literal rendering, ''in the gospel,'' is too vague and unintelligible in English unless one explains the usage as ''working in a domain or sphere.'' In defense of such an interpretation one could appeal to Phil 4:3 and 1 Cor 15:1 where ''gospel'' could be understood in a spatial sense (see BAGD 787). More appealing, and not unrelated to the above, is to view ''gospel'' as a task to be accomplished or a domain in which one works with God. With this would agree the idiomatic Greek use of *synergos* as ''helping someone in or in accomplishing something.'' While grammatically one would expect a dative of the person and a genitive of the thing following *synergos*, one sometimes, as in 1 Thess 3:2, finds a genitive with the person and with the thing a series of phrases introduced by the prepositions *eis*, *pros*, and *en* (examples given in LSJ 1711). Also the term *synergos* is invariably employed in the context of ''accomplishing some task or participating in some endeavor.'' Thus, the translations listed above as interpretive are of interest since they focus on ''activity.'' However, since 1 Thess 3:2, as well as the three Pauline passages cited above, seem to demand a meaning for ''gospel'' wider than ''preaching,'' the translation ''in preaching the gospel'' is probably too limiting. ''In spreading the gospel'' is more general and may properly fit some contexts, but in 1 Thess 3:2 it is restrictive, for immediately following, Timothy does more than ''preach or spread the gospel.'' So I opt for the meaning ''God's coworker in the service of the gospel of Christ''—such a rendering makes sense for Phil 4:3 (''fighting in the service of the gospel'') and Rom 1:9 (''God whom I serve in behalf of'').

Thus, the phrase ''in the service of the gospel of Christ'' in 1 Thess 3:2 refers less to the preaching activity of the apostles, though Timothy was indeed a member of that apostolic group (at Corinth as well—see 2 Cor 1:19), than to the full establishment of the Christian message (see Rom 15:19), a message which both presupposes and actualizes the Christ-event. Being ''at the service of the gospel of Christ'' (from the point of view of the missionary) is to be attentive to the entire reality, i.e., proclamation of the message as well as its firm acceptance by the converts (1 Thess 3:2b-5) and its implementation in a life of love and holiness (3:12-13). Also, it should be stressed that ''of Christ'' in this case is an objective genitive, i.e., it is the salvific message about Christ though a message that has God as author.

Not only does the phrase ''God's coworker in the service of the gospel of Christ'' express Paul's sense of the missionary's active cooperation in all phases of the salvific work, but in its present use it serves a function in Paul's epistolary task. In 3:2 he insists that since Timothy has been a full partner in the divinely sanctioned missionary activity, he has been chosen and sent to accomplish still another phase of that work, namely, to strengthen and encourage them in their commitment to Christ. Thus, Timothy not only represents the absent apostles but continues, as God's coworker, the missionary task begun during the foundation visit.

Paul or Acts 17. It is not my intention to discuss here the relation of the correspondence to the Lukan account of Paul's mission in Thessalonica (see Introduction). Instead, it is my desire to examine two issues raised by this pericope. The first concerns Paul's visit to Athens. In Acts 17:14f. it is clearly stated that neither Silas nor Timothy accompany Paul to Athens. Instead, unnamed believers conduct him to Athens where he is left, preaches, and eventually departs—in each case he is alone. It is only later in Corinth that his two associates join him. All of this is clearly in contradiction to Paul's text which states not only that he is not alone in Athens (there is clear contrast of plural and singular first persons in 3:1-5) but that he and others send Timothy precisely from their Athenian base to make his Thessalonian trip. To view Paul and his activity from Luke's perspective is to misconstrue his missionary strategy and practice.

Secondly, one should be concerned about local indicators, which are relatively rare in Paul. Usually they involve address to or discussion with specific Churches and occasionally appear in narrative contexts (e.g., the autobiographical section of Galatians 1–2). Only in 1 Thess 3:1 does the reader indirectly learn about the place of origin of a specific letter— seemingly, Paul is writing from Athens after Timothy's return. Strangely, some scholars conclude that Paul is no longer in Athens but rather in Corinth. One can only guess at the reason for such an inference, namely, dependence on the Lukan narrative of Acts 18:1, 5. By collating the text of Paul, which presupposes the presence of Silvanus and Timothy at the time of writing, with that of Acts, which brings the three together in Corinth after Paul's departure from Athens, one is led to conclude that Paul has indeed left Athens before writing to the Thessalonians and that the local and temporal references of 1 Thess 2:13f. relate to the time and situation prior to Timothy's mission. Only the data from Acts demand this conclusion. In fact, the text of 1 Thess 2:3–4:2 presupposes only two locales, that of Paul and companions (Athens) and that of the receivers of the letter and embassy (Thessalonica). In other words, Timothy leaves from Athens (''we sent''—3:2) and returns there (''to us from you''— 3:6). Thus, perceiving a change of locale between 1 Thess 3:5 and 6 is possible but conjectural at best and not motivated by exegesis of the Pauline text.

For Reference and Further Study

Barclay, J. M. G. "Conflict in Thessalonica." *CBQ* 55 (1993) 512–30.
Baumert, N. " 'Wir lassen uns nicht beirren.' Semantische Fragen in 1 Thess 3, 2f." *FN* 5 (1992) 45–60.
Chadwick, H. "1 Thess. 3.3, *sainesthai*." *JTS* 1 (1950) 156–58.
Cranfield, C. E. B. "Changes of Person and Number in Paul's Epistles," in *Paul and Paulinism: Essays in Honour of C. K. Barrett*. Eds. M. E. Hooker and S. G. Wilson. London: SPCK, 1982, 280–89.
Donfried, K. P. "The Theology of 1 Thessalonians as a Reflection of Its Purpose" in *To Touch the Text: Biblical and Related Studies in Honor of Joseph A. Fitzmyer, S.J.* Eds. M. P. Horgan and P. J. Kobelski. New York: Crossroad, 1989, 243–60.
_____. "The Setting of 1 Thessalonians," in *The Theology of the Shorter Pauline Letters*. Eds. K. P. Donfried and I. H. Marshall. Cambridge: Cambridge University, 1993, 3–27.
Jewett, R. *The Thessalonian Correspondence: Pauline Rhetoric and Millenarian Piety.* Philadelphia: Fortress, 1986.
Manus, C. U. "Luke's Account of Paul in Thessalonica (Acts 17, 1-9)," in *TC*, 27–38.

8. *Timothy's Return and Report* (3:6-8)

6. But since Timothy has just come to us from you and has brought us the splendid news of your faith and love and the report that you always think kindly of us, indeed that you long to see us as much as we do you—7. for this reason, brothers and sisters, we have been encouraged about you, in our every distress and difficulty, on account of this faith of yours, 8. because we now live again if you really stand firm in the Lord.

Notes

6. *But since Timothy has just come to us from you:* This new section begins with the transitional, postpositive *de* ("but") and expresses a contrast between what has preceded and what is now being discussed: great concern prior to Timothy's mission as opposed to great relief and joy following it. The paragraph is introduced by the term *arti* which can be interpreted as referring

to the immediate past ("just") or more generally to the present time ("now"). While good reasons can be adduced for choosing each option, the former is judged more appropriate for reasons provided below. Paul opens his narrative with a double genitive absolute, the equivalent of a dependent, adverbial clause. Though this construction may be considered temporal in function, the fact that it is resumed in verse 7 by the prepositional phrase *dia touto* ("for this reason") indicates that it also has a causal sense in this context: "since Timothy has come." For the expression "to us from you," see discussion below.

and brought us the splendid news of your faith and love: This passage represents the second part of a double genitive absolute construction and involves the use of a term, *euangelizomai*, which, in all other NT occurrences, has a technical Christian sense (see noun in 3:1). In this instance the verb has the meaning one finds in the LXX, "bring good tidings." Some attempt to explain its use as reflecting technical Christian usage, but it seems more plausible that Paul employs it here in its idiomatic sense at a time when the verb had not yet become limited to its technical missionary usage. Also, the verb is used only here in 1 Thessalonians (it is not found in Philippians or Philemon) and the noun appears once in 1 Thess 2:13–4:2, that is, at 3:2 in a formulaic expression, "gospel of Christ." Two items of "splendid news" follow, the first expressed as the object of the verb, the second introduced by a *hoti* clause (see below). Thus, the first item of news concerns "the faith and love" of the community. The term "faith" appears already in 3:2, 5 and bears the same meaning ("state of belief"); it is used again in verses 7 and 10. "Love" appears for the first time in this missive (see also 3:12) and its nuance must be sought in relation to the accompanying noun and the epistolary context. It focuses on the community's commitment to others which results from its new state of belief in God's saving activity.

and the report that you always think kindly of us: Grammatically, the *hoti* clause depends on the verb *euangelizomai* (see also Acts 13:32-33) and introduces the second part of Timothy's message. Despite attempts to defend Pauline style, one must admit that a double construction consisting of a double accusative ("your faith and love") and a *hoti* clause does not make for good style and further complicates a poorly constructed passage. The expression "the report that" is supplied to facilitate the translation and to clarify the clause's relation to the preceding verb. The idiom *echō mneian* (lit.: "to have a memory of"), modified by the adjective *agathos*, provides the meaning: "kind or affectionate remembrance." Further, the adverb "always," which, in Pauline usage, can either precede or follow the verb, seems to modify the preceding verb rather than the following participle (see also Rom 1:10; 1 Cor 1:4; Phil 1:4; 1 Thess 1:2; and Phlm 4). The adverb with the present tense then stresses continuous action and should be translated "that you always think kindly of" (BAGD 524.1).

indeed that you long to see us as much as we do you—: This clause represents a simple participial phrase introduced by the verb *epipotheō* ("desire or longing"). It is debated whether the prefix *epi* adds a degree of emphasis to the basic verb. Though Hellenistic writers prefer composite expressions and Paul does not employ the simple term, it is argued that Pauline usage of this term (Rom 1:11; 2 Cor 5:2; 9:14; Phil 1:8; 2:26, including noun and adjective: Rom 15:23; Phil 4:1) usually implies an intensive meaning, a sense which fits well in the present, emotional context, i.e., "long for" rather than "wish." The phrase "to see us" repeats the expression used earlier by Paul in 2:17 to describe the missionaries' effort to make a "personal visit," an expression which is again employed in 3:10 (see also Rom 1:11; 1 Cor 16:7; Phil 1:27). Finally, the reciprocal desire for the visitation is expressed by the comparative, elliptical use of *kathaper kai* ("as also or as much as," BAGD 387; see also 3:12). In this way the missive reaches an emotive climax and a stylistic quandary.

7. *for this reason, brothers and sisters, we have been encouraged about you:* The translation attempts to convey the disjointed character of Paul's text and the complexity of his ideas and emotions. He begins verse 6 by stating, in a dependent construction, Timothy's welcome twofold report, but is sidetracked by the emotional consequences of the news. So, the dependent construction begins to lose its focus and he is led to redirect his train of thought by means of a resumptive *dia touto* ("for this reason") and by addressing the readers directly. Paul then speaks of the effects of this great news; he and his colleagues "are encouraged" *(pareklēthēmen)*, not "comforted or consoled" (see 3:2) on account of what they have found out about the Thessalonian community ("about you"). This interpretation presupposes a particular reading of the three prepositional phrases (*epi . . . epi . . . dia . . .*—here rendered: "about . . . in . . . on account of") that follow the verb, that is, their relation to *parakaleō*. Translations show much variety of interpretation either by conflating the first and third prepositional phrases (these are seen as tautalogous) or by shifting the first or second phrases to underscore the role played by the "distress and difficulty" (see following Note and Interpretation below for futher discussion).

in our every distress and difficulty, on account of this faith of yours: Following the first *epi* phrase ("about you") are two others whose interpretation are crucial to Paul's meaning. The above translation preserves the word order of the text and treats the second prepositional phrase as a temporal (BDF 235.5), parenthetical remark, "in our every distress and difficulty." The apostles' "distress and difficulties" (that is, the vagaries of missionary work) are not caused by but are made more bearable by the splendid news from Thessalonica. The second phrase with its unusual word order (*dia tēs hymōn pisteōs*—the possessive pronoun is situated between the article and noun and so rendered "on account of this faith of yours") and the emphatic use of "you" in verse 8 lay stress on the community's faith as the key to Paul's joy and relief.

8. *because we now live again if you really stand firm in the Lord:* Verse 8 explains why the missionaries are overjoyed at receiving Timothy's message. The consequences of this good news are described by two interesting idioms. The first "we now live" *(nyn zōmen)* should be interpreted not in a theological sense ("eternal life") but in a metaphorical way ("removal of anxiety"—BAGD 336.1c). The second focuses on the theme of "steadfastness" *(stēkete en kyriǭ—*

"you stand firm in the Lord"), an idiom which is often employed by Paul (Rom 11:20; 2 Cor 1:24; Gal 5:1; Phil 1:27; 1 Cor 16:13; Phil 4:1) to convey a range of meaning (use either of *histēmi* or its Hellenistic biform *stēkō*). In the present case, introduced by the colloquial *ean* (for *ei*) with the indicative (BDF 372.1; *BG*, 330), the idiom stresses that the present joy of the missionaries is a reality only in view of the community's continued loyalty to its Lord.

INTERPRETATION

After discussing the apostolic decision to send Timothy to make inquiries and to assist the community members, Paul recounts in a highly emotive tone and in a somewhat disjointed way the results of the envoy's mission. The passage speaks of relief, joy, and mutual affection. Its focus is on the community's faith, survival, and well-being. The new pericope then is about Timothy's report.

Grammar, Structure, and Epistolary Context. 3:6-8 is introduced by a contrastive, postpositive *de* ("but") and underscores the time before and after Timothy's mission. Paul launches on a lengthy, emotive description of and reaction to the report he has received from his envoy. Thus, the passage contrasts the concern prior to the trip with the relief and joy following it. The style and grammar of verses 6-7, however, present problems to the translator and interpreter. For some verse 6 is a broken sentence and consists of a complex, temporal clause (a double genitive absolute), which Paul either abandoned at the start of verse 7 by starting a new sentence or transformed into a causal statement to give the reason for his having received comfort from the community. Additionally, it is pointed out that *dia touto* and *adelphoi* of verse 7 ("for this reason, brothers and sisters") usually indicate a new sentence or section in Pauline texts.

Since the double genitive absolute construction of verse 6 functions in a temporal and causal way in its capacity as dependent, adverbial clause, it is advisable to interpret verse 7 also as causal in light of the resumptive *dia touto* at the beginning of the verse. Thus, verse 7 reiterates what precedes and introduces the cause for the encouragement as stated later. The disjointedness of the sentence then derives from the complexity of structure and content of verse 6 and the author's attempt, by employing a resumptive technique and direct address, to focus on the main issue of the section, the missionaries' great relief on receiving Timothy's message.

The second part of the body-middle of the letter therefore consists of a refreshing statement of Paul's reaction to the returning envoy. The vocabulary and idioms chosen underscore the writer's emotional state and level of confidence. The passage opens with the splendid news about Christian commitment and practice (faith and love—v. 6) and closes on the note of steadfastness (standing firm—v. 8). Also, the pericope notes the mutual affection between the parties in verse 6 and ends in verse 8 by stressing great relief which this knowledge about the addressees has on the letter senders ("we live again"). Additionally, Paul heightens the letter's communicative potential by his use of terms such as "splendid news," "you always think kindly of us," "you long to see us as much as we do you," as well as by his stress on the "encouragement" and relief supplied by knowledge of the community's faith. The senders' daily problems are said to be bearable precisely because their work during the foundation visit was fruitful since it produced lives of faith and love and beyond that created a bond of friendship between missionaries and converts.

The Thessalonian Mission. From the previous passage we learn that Timothy was sent on a mission to Thessalonica in the name of the missionary band, since its leading members were unsuccessful in their previous attempts to visit. Paul's description of this trip and its report bears careful analysis for the light it sheds on the community's situation and the relationship that existed between the parties.

Strangely Paul begins his description by stating that Timothy has come both "to us" and "from you." This double prepositional phrase has been described in the past as an unnecessary rhetorical flourish on Paul's part and so translators often eliminate one or both phrases. While refusing to accept either phrase as unnecessary, some point to the frequent occurrence of "we, our, us" and "you, your" in verses 6-10 as rhetorically stressing the highly personal and emotional relationship between converts and missionaries. Nonetheless, one might wonder why both phrases, expressing points of departure and arrival of Timothy's latest travel, were deemed necessary by the writer, since these as they relate to the overall embassy are unambiguously stated in 3:1-6. The use of these prepositional phrases then seems calculated to underscore some aspect of Timothy's return trip. Indeed, in 3:6f. his journey is presented not simply as a return trip from the apostolic mission but as an embassy from the Thessalonians themselves to Paul and colleagues. The remainder of verse 6 reads like a message from the community. In this way, a parallel is drawn between the situation of the missionaries from their point of view (3:1-5) and that of the Thessalonians from theirs (3:6-8). Also, the emotional tone of the letter is heightened by the contrast between the "us, you" at the beginning of verse 6 and the "(you), us, us, you" at the end of the verse. Thus, the parallel between the missionaries who are agitated and uncertain about the community's survival and the actors in that drama is drawn out: not only is agitation and uncertainty unnecessary (the converts have responded) but the situation is one of splendid news designed to encourage sagging spirits and renew mutual affection. Another reason for the addition of "to us from you" concerns Timothy's role and that of other colleagues in the Pauline mission. In this case we get a glimpse of his role as he serves in the capacity of envoy for the missionary group (3:1-2, 5) and becomes the envoy and spokesperson of the Thessalonian Church.

Another important feature of the mission and its relation to the first missive concerns the interpretation of *arti*, the initial term of verse 6. The word is rendered either as pointing to the immediate past ("just") or more generally as referring to the present time ("now"). The latter is defended by many as being a common usage of the Hellenistic period, including the NT. It is pointed out that Josephus can alternate *nyn* and *arti* (*JA* 1.125—BAGD 110.3) and that Paul employs the term in this sense. The former then is the preference of commentators. But it should be noted that Pauline usage is limited (seven cases of *arti* used alone) and regularly involves an explicit (1 Cor 13:12bis; Gal 1:9) or contextual contrast (Gal 1:10; 4:20) where the term clearly means "now." But the situation is different in 1 Thess 3:6 since the grammatical and logical context suggests the former usage. The contrast is between the apostles' agitation in 3:1-5 and their encouragement in 3:7-8 (not Timothy's return as stated in v. 6); *arti* modifies the statement about Timothy's return, not verse 7. The most telling argument for insisting that *arti* does not mean "now" is the fact that *nyn* appears in verse 8 where a contrast is drawn between 3:1-5 and 3:6-10. *Arti* in verse 6, then, stresses the recent nature of the news and explains more logically the emotional tone of what follows and the occasion for the letter's composition. In other words, it is Timothy's recent return and the accompanying splendid news which has motivated the composition of this brief, joyful missive.

The report itself consists of two elements. The first of these addresses "the splendid news of [their] faith and love." Paul already speaks of "faith" in 3:2 and now introduces the concept of love which in its relation to faith addresses the community's unfailing commitment to others which flows from its members' new state of belief. The two nouns and the interrelated realities they represent sum up, on the objective level, what Timothy has found out during his visit. There exists in Thessalonica a believing community whose love for others is active and, by implication, exemplary. In this context then we have an early hint of the Galatian statement that "faith works itself out through love" (5:6). For Paul, already at this stage, faith and love are not two separate or principal virtues but dynamic, interrelated concepts that describe the vibrant life of the new communities. Interestingly, when led to contrast a dreaded disaster (abandonment of commitment) to its opposite, the author chooses the terms "faith and love." Already in 3:2 and 5 Paul speaks of the Thessalonians' faith and his fear in that regard; in 3:6 he returns without hesitation to the notion of faith but adds to it that of love of others. Faith in this context has a vertical and love a horizontal orientation. This love is directed not to God (Paul rarely speaks of human love for God) nor only to fellow Christians but also to other humans (see 3:12). In negative terms, "the present difficulties" have not dissuaded them; the tempter has not lured them away; and the missionary work has not been fruitless. In positive terms, the recent report sent by the Thessalonians celebrates not only the community's existence, and what this presupposes, but also underscores the working out of God's plan toward all through the loving treatment of others. Already at the end of the thanksgiving section Paul had told them: "indeed God is also at work in you who believe."

The second element of the report concerns the relationship between the missionaries and their converts. Strangely introduced by a *hoti* clause rather than as a parallel accusative construction, the report employs striking terms of endearment and responds in kind to the missionaries' desire to make a personal visit (2:18; 3:7). The desire of one is equal to that of the other; so strong in fact is this desire that it is equal to that of the missionaries, whose separation earlier was said to be "unbearable" (5:1, 5). Though the apostles may miss them as parents whose children are absent physically (2:17), they themselves "always think kindly of" their parents (3:6). Thus, the passage underscores the genuineness of the Thessalonians' attachment to the missionaries—not only do they have pleasant memories of the apostolic visit but they desire a return visit.

Effect of the Mission on Paul and Companions. While expressing Timothy's welcome twofold report, Paul is momentarily and stylistically distracted. At the mention of the community's deep attachment to the missionaries, he, instead of expressing the consequences of the news (v. 7), feels compelled, in highly emotive terms, to underscore the reciprocal character of the desired visit. In this way the missive reaches an emotional high point and a stylistic impasse. Thus, in verse 7 Paul refocuses his train of thought by means of a resumptive *dia touto*, addresses the community directly, and deals with the consequences of this news, i.e., the effect the mission and its report have on himself and his colleagues.

The result or effect of Timothy's news is introduced in verse 7 by the important Pauline verb *parakaleō*, a term which occurs nine times in 1 Thessalonians (once as a noun) with a range of meaning: "comfort, console, encourage, or reassure." The passage is variously interpreted depending especially on how one construes the syntactic relationship between the verb and its three modifying prepositional phrases.

(1) The first phrase, *eph' hymin,* could be translated "because of" or "about you." In defense of the first, scholars point to the community's faith as a source of consolation for the apostles in their general distress. In syntactic terms, the meaning of the verb and the function of the other phrases would be governed by the second phrase (*TDNT* 5:797). This interpretation is usually underscored by the elimination of the first (seen as repetitive in relation to the third) or by placing the first phrase at the beginning of the clause. The second option ("about you") is preferable, since the particular meaning of the verb would depend on the immediately following or first *epi* phrase and not on the more distant or second *epi* construction (thereby necessitating the conflation of the *epi* and *dia* prepositional phrases). So, the missionaries are "encouraged or reassured" about the Thessalonians whose faith or perseverance in the faith, in their minds, was in doubt prior to Timothy's visit.

(2) The second prepositional phrase, *epi pasē tē anagkē kai thlipsei hēmōn,* is treated not as the syntactic key to the interpretation of the passage (as above) but as a contemporaneous, parenthetical remark and translated "in our every distress and difficulty" (one could insist on a contrast between the troubles experienced by both and translate; "despite our . . ."). While the terms translated "distress and difficulty" were at an earlier stage distinguished as "physical privation" and "persecution," in recent times scholars have stressed their synonymous, eschatological meaning in Paul, though opting, under the influence of the Lukan account, to interpret these as the persecution and struggle of the end-days (*TDNT* 1:346). Pauline and LXX usage lead us in a different direction. Paul's use of *anagkē* in "lists of apostolic hardships" (2 Cor 6:4; 12:10) and his qualification of these as "present distress" and "worldly troubles" in 1 Cor 7:26, 28, respectively, point to a more generic and proverbial meaning for the passage under discussion. The word pair is also found in the LXX to express the distress and hardship of daily life (Pss 24:17; 118:143), the reward of the ungodly (Job 15:24), or the terrible character of the Lord's day (Zeph 1:15). Thus, Paul employs a generic expression to describe the multiplicity of apostolic difficulties. Only secondarily does the idiom have eschatological force, since Paul sees his entire missionary activity as a participation in the activities of the end-time. Further, the intensive use of "every" (*pasē tē;* see also 2 Cor 1:4; 7:4) underscores the generic (not the individual) character of the difficulties (BDF 275.3). Paul and fellow missionaries undergo the vagaries of apostolic work and, presumably, find these more bearable because of the news from Thessalonica.

(3) By means of the third prepositional phrase Paul proceeds to state the reason for *(dia)* his reassurance, the community's faith. The word order

here deserves attention. In 1 Thessalonians the possessive pronoun regularly follows "faith" (1:8; 3:2, 5, 6, 10—see discussion of 1:3), but in this instance the pronoun is placed between the article and noun *(tēs hymōn pisteōs)* to lay stress on that term, a point which is lost in translation and ignored by commentators. The term's emphatic position and the equally revealing addition of a subject pronoun in verse 8 ("on account of this faith of *yours* . . . if *you* really stand firm") show that the stress is clearly on the Thessalonian community's perseverance under adverse conditions. What Paul seems to have in mind by this change in word order is a contrast with what precedes immediately, namely, the missionaries' extreme distress and ample difficulty, for the subject of the letter often has been the *Thessalonians'* faith and the *missionaries'* inability to resolve their uncertainty regarding the community's faith.

While Paul speaks of Timothy's report as bringing encouragement to the toiling missionaries as they undergo the hardships of their travels and public debate while preaching the gospel of Christ (see 2:2), he also concludes that the consequence of this news is that the missionaries "now live again." This expression has been interpreted in opposed ways, either in a literal but theological sense ("eternal life") or with a metaphorical meaning ("removal of anxiety"). Some, appealing to passages from 2 Corinthians (4:2; 7:3), insist that Paul speaks here of Christian existence that is communicated between members at the horizontal level thereby implying a life of renewed vigor and spiritual power. Or more weakly, some would insist that Paul's spiritual life was greatly renewed despite the hardships he was experiencing. Nonetheless, most insist that Paul is speaking emphatically of the quality of life, i.e., Timothy's message allows the missionaries a fuller, less anxious life (see vv. 9-10). The translation given here points to the second option. The missionaries could now breathe freely or recover from their anxiety. The expression is idiomatic for "removal of anxiety" and fits into the epistolary context. The missionaries, who could no longer stand the uncertainty of not knowing about the community's fate, could now breathe a sigh of relief.

Standing Firm in the Lord. The notion of "steadfastness" (for *hypomonē* see 1:3 above) is important for Paul, particularly, as concerns the idiom "stand fast or firm." He employs the expression "stand fast in the faith" on two occasions (Rom 11:20; 2 Cor 1:24) but mainly he uses the verb absolutely (Gal 5:1) or with *en* phrases: "in one spirit" (Phil 1:27), "in the faith" (1 Cor 16:13), and "in the Lord" (Phil 4:1; 1 Thess 3:8). Pauline usage of this idiom offers a range of meaning, from resisting heresy, to safeguarding the unity of fellowship, to encountering the difficulties and sufferings of daily Christian life—in each case perseverance and its opposite ("falling away") are in view. Of assistance in discerning Paul's meaning in 1 Thess 3:8 is Phil 4:1, which is a verbal parallel to our text and offers an instructive context for its reading. In Phil 3:20, Paul, in opposition to the Judaizing preachers' emphasis on the present nature of salvation, stresses the eschatological nature and goal of the Christ-event, while looking forward to the Lord's return as Savior. He then expresses his love and longing for the community, calls them his "joy and crown," and exhorts them to "stand firm in the Lord" (4:1). This passage has much in common with our letter, for in 2:19 Paul focuses on the future return of the Lord and the community as the missionaries' future "hope or joy or crown of pride." He then insists that the Thessalonians are already the missionaries' "renown and joy" (v. 20). In the case of Phil 4:1 Paul insists that they "continue to stand firm in the Lord" (lit.: that they "stand firm thus in the Lord," *houtōs*). The term "thus" refers back to his having called them his "joy and crown," a designation which is true only proleptically in view of their perseverance. 1 Thess 3:8 provides an analogous context. The missionaries have a new lease on life (8a) only if the converts "really stand firm in the Lord" (8b). The present status of the missionaries depends on the continued steadfastness of the new converts. In Phil 4:1 the future quality of "stand firm" is conveyed by *houtōs* and in 1 Thess 3:8 by a conditional clause. The use here of a conditional construction relates not to possible doubt concerning their faith nor even to an implicit warning but rather to the nature of hope itself. Indeed, the present joy of the missionaries is a reality only in view of the community's continued loyalty (expressed as a conditional clause) to the Lord.

What however does standing firm "in the Lord" mean in this context, especially as opposed to the other Pauline usage "in the faith"? In the first case stress is given to the object of faith, "the Lord," rather than on faith itself as in 1 Cor 16:13. While one could insist that the phrase "in the Lord" here implies Christian existence as determined by the Christ-event (see also discussion of 1:1), it is best to see the phrase as relating to the verb and thereby stressing "the Lord" as the source of the community's strength and fidelity, the very object of Timothy's message and the reason for the missionaries' ecstatic reaction (see 3:9f.).

FOR REFERENCE AND FURTHER STUDY

Ellis, E. E. "Paul and His Co-Workers." *NTS* 17 (1970–71) 437–52.

Malherbe, A. J. "Did the Thessalonians Write to Paul?" *The Conversation Continues: Studies in Paul and John in Honor of J. Louis Martyn.* Eds. R. T. Fortna and B. R. Gaventa. Nashville: Abingdon, 1990, 246–57.

Ollrog, W.-H. *Paulus und seine Mitarbeiter: Untersuchungen zu Theorie und Praxis der paulinischen Mission.* Neukirchen: Erziehungsverein, 1979.

9. *Paul's Joy and Prayer* (3:9-13)

9. What thanks then can we give to God for you in return for all the joy we feel because of you in the presence of our God, 10. night and day begging as earnestly as possible to see you in person and to supply what is still lacking in your faith? 11. Now may God our Father himself, as also our Lord Jesus, direct our path to you. 12. But as regards you, may the Lord bring about an increase and abundance in your love for one another and for all, as much as we abound in love for you, 13. so as to establish your hearts as blameless in the sphere of holiness, that is, in the presence of God our Father at the coming of our Lord Jesus with all his holy ones.

NOTES

9. *What thanks then can we give to God:* The new pericope introduces a rhetorical question (vv. 9-10) followed by a solemn prayer (11-13). The text is closely connected to what precedes, a connection which is stressed by the inferential conjunction *gar* (''for or then''). The expression *eucharistian . . . antapodounai* is a NT hapax legomenon (though see Rev 4:9 for use of the simple verb *didōmi*) and does not occur in the LXX. It seems to be a paraphrase for the Pauline verbal usage ''we give thanks to God'' (1 Thess 1:2; 2:13). Since there is discussion whether the prepositional augment *anti* adds specificity to the verb and since neither form, whether *apodidōmi* or *antapodidōmi*, is frequently employed by Paul (4 times besides 1 Thess 5:15 for the former and twice in OT contexts in Romans besides 1 Thess 3:9 for the latter), it is appropriate to suggest that Paul's statement is reminiscent, in terms of structure and meaning, of Ps 115:3: ''what shall I give back to the Lord for all he has given me as reward'' *(ti antapodōsō tō kyriō peri pantōn hōn antapedōken moi)?* The parallel underscores the verb's reciprocal meaning.

for you in return for all the joy we feel because of you: The grammatical construction *peri* with genitive followed by *epi* with the dative occurs in Paul only here and in 1 Cor 1:4. In the latter it is clear that the first preposition introduces the object of the thanksgiving while the second gives the reason. ''In return'' renders the prepositional augment of the preceding verb, for the focus is less on the thanksgiving than on the returning of thanks. Such an interpretation is confirmed by the force of the rhetorical question and by the OT parallel noted above. The idiom translated ''all the joy we feel'' *(pasē tē charā hē chairomen)* involves a Semitism, whose most frequent form is ''rejoice with great joy.'' On the concept of joy, see 1:3 and Excursus on 2:19. The expression ''because of you'' further emphasizes the purpose of the thanksgiving in view of Paul's claim in 2:20 that the converts are already his ''renown and joy.''

in the presence of our God: The expression *emprosthen tou theou hēmōn* can only be translated ''before or in the presence of our God'' and seems to relate in a local sense to joy felt in God's presence, i.e., access to God through prayer and anticipation of eschatological realities (on Paul's use of *emprosthen* see 2:19 and below). Also, the designation "our God" is rare in Paul, for it occurs three times only: 1 Thess 2:2; 3:9; and 1 Cor 6:11; note also the related appellations: "our God and Father" and "God our Father," the first in 1 Thess 1:3; 3:11, 13; Phil 4:20; and Gal 1:4; the second in Phil 1:2; Phlm 3; 1 Cor 1:2; and Rom 1:7. The use of "our" in this case suggests intensity of common experience, expressed as courage in adversity (3:7-8) and joy in success (3:9) before the God they both serve.

10. *night and day begging as earnestly as possible:* The Pauline word order for the idiom "night and day" (also 2:9) does not derive from the Jewish method of viewing nightfall as the inception of day since such was also normal Greek usage, though the opposite order occurs in the LXX and elsewhere in the NT (BAGD 546). This hyperbolic idiom functions as do other rhetorical expressions used by Paul to stress continuous action in prayer or memorial contexts (e.g., "continuously" and "always," 2:13 and 3:6). The missionaries' request or prayer (*deomai*) is couched in terms and tone reminiscent of Paul's desire that he be allowed to visit the Christians in Rome (Rom 1:9-10—see discussion of visit requests below). This request is further qualified by the adverb *hyperekperissou*, whose prefix (*hyper*) gives the comparative term the superlative meaning of "as earnest as possible" (BAGD 840); see also 5:13 and the related expressions in Rom 5:20 and 2 Cor 7:4. Use of this forceful phrase is in keeping with the tone of the missive for earlier (2:17) it was said that the missionaries "had made every effort" (*perissoterōs*) to visit, "so great was their desire" for news. The missionaries' prayer then is both continuous in time and limitless in intensity.

to see you in person: This verbal phrase represents the frequent Pauline use of *eis* with the articular infinitive to express purpose (3:2, 5, 13), which purpose is already stated in 2:17, "to see you in person." The word order in 3:10, however, has been reversed (*to idein hymōn to prosōpon*). In the first passage the stress is on personal contact in contrast to presence ("in person but not in heart"), while in this text the emphasis is on seeing the community, not just hearing about its survival and success.

and to supply what is still lacking in your faith: Eis introduces a second articular infinitive to present another reason for the proposed apostolic visit. The verb *katartizō* appears five times in Paul and can variously be translated "restore, complete or supply, and make." The second term *hysterēma*, used seven times by Paul, also has a range of meaning, from "need" as opposed to abundance to "lack" implying imperfection or moral shortcoming (BAGD 417-18 and 849). While interpretation of this verbal construction is complex, owing to the terms' range of meaning and to the modern reader's perception of the historical context, we here conclude (and argue below) that Paul is referring to the complexity of the missionizing effort, namely, that the Thessalonian converts require further and repeated instruction. Paul's statement and later missive point to this complexity of missionary work beyond foundation visits.

11. *Now may God our Father himself, as also our Lord Jesus:* Verse 11 is introduced by the reflexive pronoun "himself" and the conjunction *de*. The latter, while

suggesting a slight contrast between the "we" of verses 9-10 and the "himself" of verse 11, acts as a transitional particle ("now" rather than "but": BAGD 171.2) between two movements of the writer's thought: thanksgiving (9-10) and prayer (11-13). Also, this is how he introduces the final prayer of the second missive (5:23; see also Rom 15:5, 13). The text of the prayer begins with the rare phrase *autos de ho theos* (elsewhere in Paul only in 1 Thess 5:23; see also the related passages of 2 Thess 2:16 and 3:16). Also, the text shares with other NT passages (though without *autos*) the use of a rare, older optative construction to express wish or prayer (BDF 65.2; 384). Only it combines God the Father and the Lord Jesus as subject and, strangely, employs a singular verb with this double subject. The above translation presupposes the discussion below of these issues and suggests (1) that an original prayer to God as Father of believers and of the Lord Jesus ("may God himself, who is our Father and that of our Lord Jesus") was modified later into one to Father and Son and (2) that the canonical text be read as addressing God primarily but also including the Lord Jesus (see translation). Lastly, the phrase, *ho theos kai patēr hēmōn*, is usually translated "our God and Father" since the possessive pronoun is assumed to modify both nouns. Since, however, *kai* is epexegetical or explanatory, the whole should be translated as "God who is our Father" or more simply "God our Father."

direct our path to you: The optative predicate expresses an attainable wish. The verb *kateuthynō* could be interpreted in two ways, as asking for guidance ("direct our path") or for the removal of obstacles ("make our path straight or smooth"). The latter represents the original meaning of the verb, the more common usage of the LXX (Ps 36:23; Prov 20:24), and the frequent choice of scholars. Nonetheless, the context favors the former, for the issue is a request on the missionaries' part that God lead them or allow them to reach Thessalonica, not that their journey there be hastened or made more direct. Why, however, should the expression be employed for physical rather than its more usual moral direction and why the aorist tense? See discussion below of Paul's two visit requests.

12. *But as regards you:* Postpositive *de* and the emphatic position of the pronoun *hymas* indicate a contrast between what precedes and what is stated in verse 12. In fact, verses 9-10, by repeated use of the first person plural ("can we give . . . we feel . . . our God"), focus on the apostles' concerns; verse 11, with its postpositive *de* and emphatic positioning of *autos*, stresses the Father's role in granting the travelers' request, and, finally, verses 12-13, by employing a similar construction, point the readers' attention to themselves. Indeed, the authors' prayer directly concerns them and their welfare, a nuance indicated by the phrase "but as regards you."

may the Lord bring an increase and abundance in your love for one another and for all: The author's prayer continues, again employs the optative of "attainable wish," and focuses on the recipients of the action. The actor in this case is no longer the Father in an eschatological role but the Lord Jesus, that is the risen Christ in a soteriological role, who is asked to increase (*pleonazō*) and make abundant (*perisseuō*) the community's love. The first, used only here in 1 Thessalonians, and the second, employed again at 4:1 and 10, are virtual synonyms for Paul to express superabundance (see 2 Cor 4:15; Rom 5:20; *TDNT* 6:264-65). As the first part of the prayer concerns a request that God allow the missionaries to reach Thessalonica to attend to the strengthening of their faith, so the second part turns to the needs of the community to request the Lord to bring its concern for others to even greater heights. Already the missionaries have been told about their faith and love, so again, in closing Paul addresses his prayer to those central concerns. On the concepts of mutual and universal love, see discussion below.

as much as we abound in love for you: The elliptical phrase, "as we also for you," refers not to the effect the missionaries' love has upon the community but rather to the abundance of their love for the community. Thus, the verb immediately preceding *(perisseuō)* does double duty.

13. *so as to establish your hearts as blameless in the sphere of holiness:* By means of *eis* with the infinitive to express finality (see 3:2), Paul intends a direct link between the Lord's action in verse 12 and the result expressed in verse 13. The combination of *stērizō* with *kardia* which occurs only here in Paul is a Semitism found frequently in the LXX though with a range of meaning. Additionally, the grammatical situation is somewhat complex since the verb is followed by a double accusative, *tas kardias* and *amemptous*, the second of which is further modified by a prepositional phrase, *en hagiōsynē* (lit.: "blameless in holiness"). The standard interpretation presumes that, since *stērizō* usually means "strengthen" and since the term "holiness" has an ethical sense, the whole of verse 13 is seen as a new petition for strength in living a morally blameless and holy life so as to be found such at the time of Jesus' return. The above translation, instead, presumes a different interpretation, argued below, which concludes that at the end-time believers will be established as blameless and presented to the heavenly sphere of holiness, that is, "in God's presence" (as the following expression suggests). Again, "heart," used in place of "you," stands for the inner being or center of volition and director of human activity (see 2:17).

that is, in the presence of God our Father: Mention of the source of holiness (God's very presence) leads Paul to describe the final cosmic scene, appearance before the divine throne. He appealed to this imagery in 2:19 to describe the vindication of the missionaries and their work and now turns to the evaluation of the Thessalonian believers. For discussion of the phrases "in the presence of God" and "God our Father," see 3:9 and 11. It should be noted that believers appear before God not just as judge but also as parent, since it is not the concept of judgment which is at the fore but that of the Lord's assistance (increasing love and rendering blameless) to the believers who aspire to be in the Father's presence.

at the coming of our Lord Jesus with all his holy ones: A second reference is made to the Lord's return (see 2:19). Once again it is not the end-time as such which is Paul's focus but the goal, in temporal terms, of human life, that is, a blessed union or meeting with God the Father. Interestingly, this arrival at the divine throne is associated, without explanation, with Jesus' return, an association of themes and an apocalyptic scenario which were clearly the subject of the missionaries' earlier preaching. This traditional end-time scenario involves the Lord's return in the presence of angelic helpers or "with all his holy ones" (see below). Again, as in 2:19, it is the title "our Lord Jesus" and not "Christ" which is used in relation to the *parousia*, presumably because it is Paul's preferred usage earlier in his career, a usage which tended to emphasize the continuity between Jesus' pre- and post-resurrection activity and the urgency of the missionary task in light of the imminent return of the risen Lord.

EXCURSUS

Now may God our Father himself, as also our Lord Jesus, direct . . . (3:11)

The Greek text presents several anomalies which need discussion. Verse 11 introduces the first of two prayers and begins with the rare phrase *autos de ho theos* (see 5:23). Besides sharing with a limited number of NT passages (though without the striking pronoun *autos:* Rom 15:5, 13; 2 Thess 3:5; 2 Tim 1:16, 18; Heb 13:20-21) the use of the optative for a prayer wish, the passage is also grammatically unusual, for a double subject, "God and the Lord Jesus," is followed by a singular verb. This phenomenon is variously explained. (1) Some propose that the initial *autos*, replacing an original "*you* in the vocative of oral prayer," is provided by Paul with a double apposition or results in the addition of the phrase "and our Lord Jesus" as an afterthought to an essentially theological formula. (2) With some hesitation, others, whether agreeing with the above explanation or not, insist that the usage seems intentional on Paul's part (owing to the combined use of *autos*, the singular verb, and the corroborating evidence of 2 Thess 2:16) to indicate intimate association between Father and Son, whether in action or prayer.

Such explanations are unconvincing on both linguistic and theological grounds. As regards the first, two differing solutions, rarely citing Pauline examples, are offered for the numerical nonagreement of subject and verb. The first argues that in the case of a double subject the verb agrees with the closer of the two; while the second insists that a singular verb may be used where two subjects are considered as a unit. Virtually all examples given concern word-pair subjects, such as "heaven and earth" (Matt 5:18; 24:35), "moth and rust" (Matt 6:19), or "flesh and blood" (1 Cor 15:50). Examples of such cognate pairs governing a verb in the singular hardly support the surprising conclusion that the Jewish-Christian Paul would consider the Father and the Son so closely united, whether in being or in action, as to feel justified in employing a verb in the singular to describe their "perfect unity of operation."

This brings us to more theological considerations. No doubt, one can concede, for Paul, both that God the Father and the Lord Jesus act in concert (for example, in conferring grace and peace; Rom 1:7 and parallels) and that the latter may be addressed in prayer (as in 1 Thess 3:12) but it seems preferable to see the prayer of verse 11 as addressed to God and that of verse 12 as involving more properly the Lord Jesus (see discussion below).

In light of the above considerations I propose that verse 11 has been clumsily modified by a later scribe to extend this eschatological function also to the credit of the Lord Jesus. The original text, *autos de ho theos kai patēr hēmōn kai [tou kyriou hēmōn Iēsou] kateuthynai . . .* (see Notes above), would have been transformed simply by modifying the genitival construction (in brackets) to the nominative, *ho kyrios hēmōn Iēsous,* i.e., "now may God our Father himself, as also our Lord Jesus, direct. . . ." In this way the canonical text, by the less-than-felicitous addition of a second subject, would suggest an associative function for God's agent, while still insisting on theological primacy. Such a modification would have been facilitated by the fact that "the Lord [Jesus]" appears again as subject in verse 12; apparently, the author of this modification saw no major problem in retaining the singular verb. Originally, then, Paul would have insisted that the God who was to grant the missionaries' "attainable wish," was precisely the Father of both the Lord Jesus and of believers. The above proposal makes sense in view of Thessalonian usage wherein God is called "our God" (2:2; 3:9) and "God our Father" (1:3; 3:11, 13) and also wherein Jesus is explicitly identified as God's Son (1:10; see also Rom 15:6: "the God and Father of our Lord Jesus Christ;" also 2 Cor 1:3; 11:31).

INTERPRETATION

These verses continue Paul's reaction to Timothy's report that the community has survived; in fact it is thriving and awaits a further visit from the founding missionaries. After having expressed the apostles' relief and joy at the news and having been apprised of the depth of the community's affection, Paul speaks of gratitude and launches into an extended, concluding prayer regarding a future visit and an increase in love for all. The pericope's structure and content offer insight into the missionary's early approach and attitude toward mission work and exhortation, and his initial conception of Christian life and holiness.

3:9-13 as Body-Closing. It is advisable to postulate here a new movement in the letter's development, first an emotional rhetorical question (vv. 9-10) and secondly an extended prayer for the addressees (vv. 11-13). Interestingly, both sections express the missionaries' prayer that they might find their way to Thessalonica (vv. 10 and 11) and thus draw attention to the occasion for the writing of the letter. The passage reiterates in the form of a rhetorical question the apostles' inexpressible joy and underscores, as the reason for writing, their renewed confidence in their converts and their earnest desire to return there to assist them in their growth in faith (3:2). The pericope then accomplishes what a body-closing is meant to do: focus or finalize for the reader the reason for writing and open or facilitate the lines for further communication (either a future visit, letter, or reminder of past instruction—see 4:1-2).

Instead of viewing verses 9-10 as expressing a sense of inadequacy on Paul's part ("what thanks . . . can we give") or proposing the theme of *ratio infusa,* it is best to interpret the long sentence as a rhetorical question. Here as in 2:19 ("after all, who will be . . . ?") Paul has recourse to a rhetorical question to redirect the train of his thought. In both cases the inferential conjunction *gar* is employed as a transitional and is here translated "then." In effect, verse 9 explains the stark language of verse 8, namely, that Timothy's report allows the missionaries to "live again." Knowledge of the community's survival and success leads Paul to express not the inadequacy of his thanksgiving but to suggest that no thanksgiving can match the joy the news has brought them. "Joy in God's presence" then is a synonym for "live again." If various hints of the missionaries' delight have already been expressed in the letter, it is in verses 8 and 9-10 that it finds its starkest description: full life and overflowing joy.

The second movement of the passage follows closely that of verses 9-10 which ended by expressing the missionaries' desire to return "to supply what is lacking" in the community's faith. As attention was directed in verses 9-10 to the missionaries themselves (constant use of the first person plural), so now the attention is focused on God in verse 11 (initial position of "himself") and on the Thessalonians in verses 12-13 (also initial position of "you"). The rhetorical question of verses 9-10 gives way to the prayer of verses 11-13, first a prayer which repeats the missionaries' desire to return and secondly a supplication that, through an increase in the community's love, God might prepare it for the final judgment. The first and second movements of the pericope then function as body-closing by underscoring the occasion and purpose for writing and by advancing further the author's paraenetic communication with his new converts, whether by promising a future visit, reminding them of past instruction (see 4:1-2), or by underscoring the eschatological motivation for a life of love toward all.

Joy in God's Presence. These terms express tersely the tone and theme of Paul's first missive to the community. He has already stressed the importance of the theme of joy in 2:19-20 where he noted that the converts would be the missionaries' "hope, joy, and crown of pride" in God's presence at the parousia and indeed that they were already their source of "renown and joy." The missive has rightly been described as the joyful letter of a missionary who is relieved that the community has survived and pleased that it is doing so well. Thus the entire missive relates to the anxiety of the missionaries and its euphoric resolution.

By means of a rhetorical question Paul compares the pleasure he and his cosenders feel to that of inexpressible thanks or rather that the joy they feel far surpasses their ability to render thanks in return. Indeed, now that Timothy has returned and has reported on the situation they, in spite of the "distress and difficulty" they experience daily, can "live again." They have full life and overflowing joy. As if to emphasize his point Paul insists both that the missionaries' gratitude to God concerns the Thessalonian converts and that they are the source of the apostles' joy. Finally, the parallel between 3:7 "in our every distress and difficulty" (*epi pasę tę anagkę kai thlipsei hēmōn*) and verse 9 "for all the joy we feel" (*epi pasę tę charą hę chairomen*) can only imply an intentional balancing of the missionaries' intense but paradoxical life in the mission field.

Interestingly the missionaries' joy is said to be "joy . . . in God's presence," for verse 9 ends with a phrase which can only be translated "before or in the presence of our God." Since the various occurrences of the term *emprosthen* were noted earlier (see 2:19), we need only discuss its particular meaning in 3:9. Some note that the phrase could relate to the first verb, "giving thanks" (1 Thess 1:3 is given as a parallel), but this is rightly rejected as implausible owing to that verb's modifier: "giving thanks to God." Thus, scholars readily relate the prepositional phrase to the immediately preceding "joy we feel . . . in the presence of our God." Discerning Paul's meaning, however, is more difficult. One could insist that Paul wishes to underscore the divine origin and character of the joy the missionaries feel. In defense of such an interpretation one can appeal to the structurally similar passage of 1 Cor 1:4 to underscore the theme of divine gift and insist that Paul adds the phrase in question to make a similar point. The prepositional phrase, however, seems to require a more concretely local sense. One should appeal more directly to a "divine sphere" wherein believers' lives are as present to God (1:3; 3:9) as they will be when Jesus returns (2:19; 3:13). The merit of this interpretation is that it unites the four uses of *emprosthen* in 1 Thessalonians. To the latter interpretation, I would add that two uses of *emprosthen* focus on future eschatology and judgment and two, in the context of prayer to God, anticipate, in the present, the judgment and reward of the end-time. In 1:3 Paul speaks of remembering in prayer the community's "achievements" in God's presence. In 3:9 he speaks of the joy which he and his fellow missionaries already enjoy in God's presence. What we find here is access to God through prayer and anticipation of eschatological realities.

It has been suggested that the expression "our God" in 1 Thess 2:2 and 3:9 ("joy . . . in the presence of our God") reflects, on the one hand, the apostles' intense experience of courage in adversity and joy in success and expresses, on the other, the Christian bond of brothers and sisters who acknowledge the same God. I am inclined to agree with both suggestions since these passages involve prayer, missionary activity, and the intense experience of conversion (see 1 Cor 6:11) and since the predominance of this usage in Paul's earlier correspondence points to his keen awareness (see 3:9) that missionaries and converts share belief and commitment to the "living and true God" (1:9). The use here in 3:9 of "our" further emphasizes the reciprocity one finds throughout this short missive.

What Is Still Lacking and Two Visit Requests. After expressing the missionaries' desire to return to Thessalonica, Paul states the reason as "supplying what is still lacking in your faith." It is doubtful that this verbal phrase concerns defective faith, whether moral deficiency on the part of the recipients or some type of failure on the part of the apostles, since Timothy's message is about the community's "faith and love" (3:6). Thus, translations which stress shortcomings in the community's faith seem inadvisable. Since Paul speaks in 3:12, of the community's "love for one another and for all," as a love which can increase, he seems to envision here a lived faith, but, nonetheless, one that can increase, whether in instruction or in degree of commitment (also 2 Cor 10:15). For this reason I adopt the translation "to supply what is still lacking in your faith." The community is a young community whose formation and development are not yet sufficiently advanced, that is, a community whose faith must continue to increase intellectually and experientially.

Many postulate an abrupt ending to the mission, based on the narrative of Acts 17, to account for a lack in instruction; and further propose that the missionaries' advice in chapters 4 and 5 serves to supplement what was left undone. What follows verse 10, however, is not a preparation for the advice found in chapters 4–5 but seemingly the conclusion of a letter wherein Paul prays even more earnestly that the missionaries might be allowed to return, that the the Lord might increase their love and strengthen their resolve, and, finally, that the community might remember the instruction it received from the missionaries (3:11–4:2). It was not an alleged shortness of time but the complexity of the missionizing effort (described in the second letter, especially 2:1-12) as well as of the cultural, religious context of the converts, which brought about the Thessalonian situation, a "state of belief" (see 3:2) which Paul describes as requiring further and repeated instruction.

This first request for a visit is couched in terminology reminiscent of Paul's prayer in Rom 1:9-10 that he be allowed to visit the Christians in Rome. In both instances, circumstances beyond the writer's control have prevented a much-desired visit. In both also the request is made with restrained confidence that the trip will somehow promote the apostolic mission. In 1 Thess 3:10 Paul stresses a personal and in 3:6 a mutual desire for a visitation. So great had been the missionaries' desire to visit that they "had made every possible effort" to return (2:17); so now they "beg as earnestly as possible" still to be able to visit. Timothy's embassy brings much needed relief, though they are no less desirous of making the trip to Thessalonica.

But why a second request for a visit in 3:11? As noted earlier the expression translated "direct our path to you" represents the relatively rare Hellenistic use of the optative "to denote an attainable wish." While there is discussion concerning the obstacles that hindered the apostles' journey, the text focuses on a request from God that they be allowed to reach Thessalonica. Paul's use of an aorist optative emphasizes the once-and-for-all character of the action, namely, that the missionaries be allowed a necessary visit to complete their work among their converts. The second request then concerns the missionaries' desire to complete their own task among the converts. It is a prayer addressed to God and concerns the outcome of the divine plan for the mission. Such a conclusion is reinforced by the beginning words of verse 12: "but as regards you." The second request of verse 11 concerns the apostles' task; verse 12 addresses the community's activity.

Several Important Themes. (1) Prayer to God the Father and the Lord Jesus. Discussion of 3:11, particularly its unusual address of the Father and the Lord Jesus and the use of a singular verb, has led us to view verse 11 as a prayer addressed to God and having an eschatological sense and that of verse 12, also placed in an eschatological context, as involving the Lord Jesus and having a soteriological and moral sense. Since verse 11 addresses the apostles' eschatological wish (note the Satanic opposition mentioned in 2:18; 3:5) that they finally be allowed to return to Thessalonica, we would not be wrong in suggesting that "neither the angels in heaven nor the Son, but only the Father knows when this might be" (Mark 13:32) and be able to grant such a request. The latter is implied in 1 Thess 5:9 where Paul will define domains of activity: eschatology for God and soteriology for "our Lord Jesus Christ." The prayer of verses 12-13, however, is addressed to Jesus as "Lord" of the community and concerns its members' lives and conduct, namely, their treatment of others and their holiness. We should stress, therefore, that the prayers of Paul are addressed first to God concerning the missionaries' eschatological request and secondly to the Lord concerning the community's moral well-being.

Additionally, this first occurrence of the theme of God's fatherhood in Paul's correspondence calls for some discussion. This parental theme, expressed in male terminology, is traditional both in general religious and in specifically Christian terms. The designation of the divine as Father is etymologically established in the name "Juppiter" (Greek: *Zeus Patēr*) and was made popular by Homer's famous epithet of Zeus as "father

of both humans and gods'' (*Odyssey* 1:28; 11:544). Furthermore, this concept was also in use in the Hebrew world of the OT where it designated
divine creative and providential power as well as God's love for Israel
(Deut 32:6; 2 Sam 7:14), for God is both Master and Father (Mal 1:6; also
Philo, *On the Cherubim* 27). This designation of God as Father, especially
in prayer, became increasingly popular among Jews of the intertestamental
period and, as attested in a broad range of the Jesus tradition, became
a distinctive feature of Christian usage (*TDNT* 5:945-1022), a usage which
owed its popularity to Jesus' preaching on God's fatherhood, use of the
''Our Father'' in the Church's liturgy, and early Christian belief. Thus
Paul inherited a well-developed theological concept, one which he employs no fewer than twenty-two times in his entire correspondence. Most
Pauline uses of *patēr* for God, often with a parallel designation of Jesus
as *kyrios,* can best be characterized not as Paul's attempt to define their
mutual relationship but rather to describe first God's relation to humanity in parental terms and that of Jesus in terms of lordship. Several Pauline passages, however, dwell precisely on the relationship between God
and Jesus by designating God as ''Father of (our) Lord Jesus'' (Rom 15:6;
2 Cor 1:3; 11:31). Invariably the latter (contextually: see 2 Cor 1:3) as well
as most of the former (by use of the possessive ''our God'' and by direct
appeal to the themes of resurrection and prayerful address of God as
''abba'') address the theme of offspring both in the case of Jesus and that
of Christian believers. Again, it is likely that, originally, in 1 Thess 3:11
Paul was addressing God as Father of believers and of the Lord Jesus.

(2) Love for one another and for all. Just as the missionaries have been
reassured by Timothy's message that the Thessalonians are still commited
to Christ, a commitment that involves a concern for others (v. 6: ''splendid news of your faith and love''), so in prayer they implore God to allow
them to return to address the issue of faith (v. 10: ''what is still lacking in
your faith'') and, in lieu of this return, beseech the Lord Jesus to provide
the community with a superabundance of love. Paul's use of double verbs
in 3:12 focuses on the community's activity, the inner and outer thrust
of its love; he asks that their faith be increased without bounds and calls
on the one who preached, lived, and commanded love of neighbor, and
thus received the title of *kyrios* (Phil 2:9-11), to bring about limitless growth
in what he will later characterize as ''the most excellent way'' (1 Cor
12:31b). From Timothy's report the missionaries know the community
is a vibrant one (3:6); so their prayer is that their daily lives be even more
concerned with the welfare of community members (''love for one another'') and of those beyond the Christian fellowship (''love for all'').
Mutual love is a common NT theme, one to be expected from communities whose very existence depended on mutual support and common action. But besides being a social and ideological necessity, mutual concern

was a basic feature of Jesus' preaching, as attested in the various strands of NT tradition. Such a theme supplements Paul's focus on community interaction and loving regard for fellow believers as a deciding factor in determining moral activity (see especially Paul's "edification" language; 1 Thess 5:11). Thus, "love for one another" expresses for Paul that profound ecclesiological reality, the Christian fellowship, which will become a major preoccupation in all of his subsequent correspondence. Indeed, in a later epistle Paul will advise his community concerning the goal of love: "through love be servants of one another" (Gal 5:13).

Consideration for outsiders, however, varied from one NT community to another; the communities that read the Fourth Gospel or the Book of Revelation focused on mutual support while Paul and the author of 1 Peter stressed openness to outsiders. The latter directed their attention to the wider, more sympathetic context of Christian living. It is particularly in this letter that Paul shows how aware he is of the difficulties early Christians encountered as they accepted the gospel and its demands (see 3:3). Thus, it is of interest that he insists on the wider perimeter of love, namely, that it encompass those outside the "Church of the Thessalonians," even extending, as did Jesus' teaching (e.g., Matt 5:43-47), to one's enemies. The community's relation to outsiders is a burning issue, for Paul has been made aware of the vicissitudes encountered by the converts as they distinguished themselves from their former coreligionists by their increasingly different religious mores. Nonetheless, Paul reminds them in 3:3 that such is their lot as commited Christians and further insists in 3:12 that their lives of faith not be a ghetto existence but a life of commitment that encompasses both insiders and outsiders (note Paul's double use of *eis:* "*for* one another and *for* all"). This concern for outsiders will be a frequent theme for Paul as he insists that Christians live in the world and extend their beneficence to those beyond the confines of the fellowship (1 Thess 4:9-12; 5:15; Rom 12:16-18; 13:8-10; Gal 6:10).

(3) Theme of Imitation. Following his prayer that "the Lord bring about an increase and abundance in" their love, Paul adds: "as we also for you" (12b), a phrase which is identical to the concluding words of 3:6 and needs some clarification, owing to its elliptical character. In 3:6 it is clear that the verb of the preceding clause must be supplied: "you long to see us as much as we [long to see] you." In the present case, despite the identical structure, the grammatical elements do not perform the same functions— indeed, the subjects are no longer parallel elements. This leads some to restructure the sentence and to focus on the theme of love: "as our love does for you." It is preferable to retain the structure of the original and to borrow the second verb of the preceding clause with its dative complement: "as much as we abound in love for you." In this way, we are better able to understand the thrust of Paul's statement, which focuses

on a comparison between the missionaries' love for the converts and their hoped for abundance which only the Lord can provide. We have here then the first expression of the frequent Pauline theme of imitation, namely, an invitation and an exhortation to the Thessalonians to allow the Lord to provide abundance and themselves to strive for an intensity of love which compares to that of the missionaries. This particular use of the theme presumes and underscores the deep relationship which exists between the Pauline missionary entourage and this particular Christian community. Thus, the mutual affection and longing for a visit are emphasized even further by Paul's assumption that the missionaries' love for the Thessalonian community is so great that it can serve as an adequate analogy for the Lord's bountiful gift.

(4) Eschatological Worthiness. The prayer to the Lord, while calling for an "increase and abundance in love" has as its goal a debated infinitive clause. The expression rendered "to establish your hearts" occurs in the LXX and NT with a range of usage, from bodily sustenance (Judg 19:5), to sapiential assistance (Sir 6:37), to firmness of resolve or character (Ps 112:6). Paul employs the verb *stērizō* in two other cases, Rom 1:11 and 1 Thess 3:2, both with the accusative pronoun "you" (Rom 16:25 is assumed to be non-Pauline). In both cases the context suggests that the meaning of the verb is "to strengthen" since in the first Paul wishes "to impart a spiritual gift" for the readers' benefit and in the second Timothy is dispatched to the Thessalonian community to assist them. Establishing Pauline usage in the present case is more complex because Paul chooses "heart" as object (only here) rather than "you" (see 2 Thess 2:17) and because of the grammatical construction associated with the verb.

Crucial to the interpretation of this passage is a proper evaluation of its grammatical construction. Some scholars speak of a stylistic "shortcut" which presupposes an expression such as "so as to be" or "so that they will be" following "your hearts" and so interpret verse 13, either as a new petition or as a statement of the purpose of growth in love. A closer examination of the grammatical construction, of the meaning of the verb, and of the epistolary context yield a different interpretation. The primary meaning of *stērizō* is "to set, fix, or establish" (LSJ 1644). Further, its use by Apollonides with a double accusative, a noun and an adjective as here ("for whom the sea has fixed *the wave to a calm*" (*Greek Anthology* 9:271), suggests a similar construction by Paul. Thus, the increase in love has as its goal the establishing of believers as blameless entities in God's presence at the parousia. Verse 13 then would present not a new petition of request for a strengthening of the heart but a statement concerning the outcome of the Lord's increased gift of love and its actualization in the lives of the new converts. Verse 13 focuses on eschatological finality; verse 12 dwells on the needs of the present.

Additionally, the term "blameless" is part of a double-accusative construction, and so modifies "hearts." It is used in the LXX, especially in the book of Job (13x; see 11:4), to express divine judgment or evaluation of human conduct. For Paul too it refers to God's eschatological judgment, a judgment which focuses on the parousia (3:13), which affects present missionary behavior (2:10), and which influences the interim period and wholeness of the believer vis-à-vis the Lord's return (5:23). Thus, Paul prays that the believer will be established or made "blameless" in God's presence, but in this case a qualifying term is used, namely, *hagiōsynē*, literally: "blameless in holiness." This last expression, part of the widely used *hagios* word family, is nonexistent in classical Greek, and is rare in the LXX (5x) and NT (3x). Its meaning and usage are difficult to determine. Presumably, it is given the generic meaning "holiness," owing to its etymological relation to *hagiotēs* or *hagiasmos,* and is considered either a state of being or a quality. So the term's usage in 1 Thess 3:13 is seen as possessing "an ethical character" whereby believers are said to achieve holiness through virtuous conduct, a conduct which is presumed by the earlier references to love in verse 12 and is described in 4:3f. (*TDNT* 1:114).

LXX and Pauline usage, however, call for circumspection. Of the five LXX occurrences of the term, four refer to a divine attribute, suggesting divine presence (Pss 29:5; 95:6; 96:12; and 144:5), while the fifth speaks, by extension, of the temple's holiness, thus also implying God's presence (2 Macc 3:12). None of these suggest human conduct. Further, discussion of Pauline usage is limited to three texts: Rom 1:4; 2 Cor 7:1; and 1 Thess 3:13. In the first, the pre-Pauline expression "appointed son of God in power according to the Spirit of Holiness" clearly refers to a divine attribute. Only the second is an unambiguous allusion to human activity, i.e., "making holiness perfect in the fear of God." The major obstacle to using this occurrence in determining the meaning of the latter is that the passage in question (2 Cor 6:14–7:1) is readily considered an interpolation, whose theology and idioms are markedly non-Pauline.

Thus, in determining Pauline usage in 1 Thess 3:13, we are left with unequivocal LXX usage, Pauline use of an early formula in Rom 1:4, the context of the Thessalonian passage, and the usage of third- and fourth-century Christian writers. In the first and second instances the reference is to a divine attribute or power, not to a human quality, whether attained or given. The Pauline meaning of Rom 1:4 is further specified by usage of the extended phrase "spirit of holiness" which in an intertestamental work (T. Levi 18:12) means "God's spirit." Thus, one could appeal to the third-century *Acts of Thomas* (58, 85, 86, 97, etc.) or to John Chrysostom's understanding of 1 Thess 3:13 (*Homilies on 1 Thess* 4:3) to interpret *hagiōsynē* as a virtue "obtained through struggle" or "simplicity of life" and insist that Paul employs the term as a synonym for *hagiasmos* (see 1 Thess 4:3, 4, 7). More probable, and based on available evidence and the important parallel of Rom 1:4, it is preferable to view *en hagiōsynē* as referring to the divine presence described in the Psalms as "holiness." For Paul, at the end-time believers will be confirmed as blameless and presented to the heavenly sphere of holiness, that is, "in the presence of God." Thus *en hagiōsynē* ("in the sphere of holiness") and *emprosthen tou theou* ("in God's presence") stand in apposition.

(5) Apocalyptic Scenario. Mention of the Lord's return already occurs at 2:19 as Paul establishes a judgment scene during which the apostles' evangelical activities are to be judged in the Lord's presence. Even such a judgment scene presumed Jesus' coming with pomp and circumstance much as did Roman officials during imperial visits. It is in this context that one must examine the much discussed phrase "with all his holy ones." Should the term *hagioi* be interpreted "the saints" or "angels"? The strongest argument in favor of the first option is that the frequently used term *hagioi* invariably designates believers in Paul; 2 Thess 1:10 and a number of post-NT texts are usually cited as corroborative (see below).

Most scholars opt for the second option for a number of reasons. [1] It is admitted that in OT and intertestamental literature (especially of an apocalyptic type) *hagioi* is regularly employed to designate angels and that these, whether called "holy ones" or "angels" (usually "holy angels"), are often associated with judgment in texts from both Testaments (e.g., Dan 7:10, 18f.; 1 En 1:9 [=Jud 14]; Mark 8:38; 13:27; Matt 13:41; 25:31; 2 Thess 1:7). Thus, one would presume that the term, used in an apocalyptic context (the only such case in Paul), would refer to angels. [2] It is also generally conceded that in 1 Thess 3:13 Paul is recalling Zech 14:5, "And the Lord my God shall come, and with him all the holy ones," where "the holy ones" are understood as "angels." This OT passage is reflected and, in some cases, literally cited in a number of Christian texts. In Matt 25:31 "holy ones" has been changed to "angels." In other texts, *Ascension of Isaiah* 4:14-16; *Apostolic Constitutions* 7:32; and *Apocalypse of Peter* 1, one encounters not citations of Zech 14:5 but late collages of gospel and Pauline texts (Mark 13:26-27 par; Matt 16:27; 25:31; 1 Thess 4:14f.) which portray the Lord as being accompanied both by angels and saints. Only the *Didache*, among early Christian texts, clearly applies Zech 14:5 to the resurrected saints (16:7). Again, one presumes that in the early Christian period this OT passage was understood as referring to angels. [3] Only by understanding 1 Thess 3:13 as referring to heavenly beings is one able to reconcile with it what Paul will say in 4:14-17. Had Paul taught and written that the faithful departed would accompany the returning Lord (3:13), the discussion of 4:13-18 would make little sense, for even then he does not state that "all" believers will accompany the Lord but rather that they will be "raised and ascend to meet the descending Christ."

The meaning of Paul, then, is that the returning Lord will be accompanied, following the standard apocalyptic scenario, by angelic helpers. It is his wish that at that time believers be confirmed as worthy to be in God's presence. The problem concerning the death of believers will not have been addressed until a later date, as the result of new developments within the community. Paul's two references (2:19; 3:13) to the parousia in this first missive, then, underscore the relationship that exists between the present (whether the missionaries' or the community's endeavors) and the future (though imminent appearance of the Lord Jesus among his own). In this instance Paul is less interested in describing the eschatological judgment scene than in motivating his converts to cause their increased gift of love to work itself out among fellow believers and to reach out to their apprehensive non-Christian neighbors.

FOR REFERENCE AND FURTHER STUDY

Lambrecht, J. "Thanksgivings in 1 Thessalonians 1-3." *TC*, 183–205.

Reinhartz, A. "On the Meaning of the Pauline Exhortation: '*mimētai mou ginesthe*— Become Imitators of Me'." *SR* 16 (1987) 393–403.

Schade, H.-H. *Apokalyptische Christologie bei Paulus: Studien zum Zusammenhang von Christologie und Eschatologie in den Paulusbriefen.* Göttingen: Vandenhoeck & Ruprecht, 1981.

Stanley, D. M. "Imitation in Paul's Letters: Its Significance for His Relationship to Jesus and to His Own Christian Foundations." *From Jesus to Paul: Studies in Honour of Francis Wright Beare.* Waterloo: Wilfred Laurier University, 1984, 127–41.

Wiles, G. P. *Paul's Intercessory Prayers: The Significance of the Intercessory Prayer Passages in the Letters of St. Paul.* Cambridge: Cambridge University, 1974.

10. *Closing Exhortation* (4:1-2)

1. Finally then, brothers and sisters, we urge and exhort you in the Lord Jesus that you act as you have learned from us, that is, how you must conduct yourselves and so please God—as you are indeed doing—and that you abound even more. 2. For you know what directives we gave you in the name of the Lord Jesus.

NOTES

1. *Finally then, brothers and sisters:* The unique NT expression *loipon oun* causes problems since its literal meaning "finally then or therefore" does not seem appropriate at this point in the letter. Despite attempts to resolve this issue either by conflating the two particles into "now" or "therefore" or by interpreting *loipon* to mean "in addition or lastly," it is best to view it as indicating the ending of a letter as is true of 2 Cor 13:11; Phil 3:1; 4:8; also Gal 6:10 (see discussion below). 4:1 then introduces the ending of the first missive much as a similar expression ("finally, brothers and sisters, farewell") brings 2 Cor 10-13 to an end (13:11). While the inferential conjunction *oun* ("then") marks the close connection which Paul wishes to draw between the community's present situation and his brief paraenetic conclusion, the formula of direct address brings the early missive to an end in the way that it begins in 2:17 by addressing the community and expressing the missionary group's concerns.

we urge and exhort you in the Lord Jesus: The verb "urge or ask" (*erōtaō*) appears only three times in Paul and always in close association with the second verb *parakaleō*: 4:1; 5:12-14; and Phil 4:2-3 (see 2 Thess 2:1 where it occurs alone). The second verb is more frequently used by Paul (38x) and, though it has a range of meaning (see 3:2), is translated "exhort" (BAGD 617.2). It is probably inadvisable to seek nuances for each verb since their combined use corresponds to current epistolary usage (BGU 1141.10; POxyrhynchus 7ff.6; 294.28-29) where they tend to replace *deomai* (a practice condemned by the rhetoricians), function as synonyms, and seem to underscore the urgency of the request made (M-M 484). Use of the prepositional phrase "in the Lord Jesus," employing *en* following the verbs of exhortation, must be seen in relation to what has been identified as a *parakaleō* formula and Paul's use in the following verse of a similar prepositional phrase also referring to the Lord Jesus but introduced by the preposition *dia* (see below).

that you act as you have learned from us: Following the double verbs of exhortation one finds two *hina* clauses and a double use of verbal expressions introduced by *kathōs*. These features lead scholars to adopt various solutions in attempting to recapture Paul's train of thought. The option taken here (and discussed below) is that a clause ("you act or behave") must be supplied from the epistolary context. The verb translated "you have learned" (lit.: "you received," *paralambanō*; see also 2:13) was a technical term in Judaism and in the early Jesus movement for the transmission of tradition (1 Cor 11:23; 15:1-3; Gal 1:9,12). Usually the term was employed for doctrinal matters and so its use here for moral exhortation (see also Phil 4:9) indicates a close connection for Paul between moral and doctrinal instruction. Further, the phrase "learned from us" indicates that the original apostolic preaching consisted of doctrinal and ethical content and also that what is now being said is not new, but rather corresponds (*kathōs*) to what had already been taught. Finally, Paul repeats from 2:13 the important phrase "from us," for the good news and its ethical demands reached the community through the missionary work of Paul and his entourage.

that is, how you must conduct yourselves and so please God: The entire construction constitutes the appositional object of the preceding clause "as you have learned from us" and is introduced by a unique case in Paul of a classical substantivized clause to introduce an indirect question (*to pōs dei hymas—*BDF 267.2). The translation clarifies the grammatical relationship of the clause to the preceding statement by adding "that is." The missionaries' paraenetic instruction then had as its focus the content of this indirect question, but its particular formulation in this verse lay stress not on *dei* ("that you must") but on *pōs* ("how"). Scholars, who defend the literary unity of 1 Thessalonians, point to what follows in chapters 4 and 5, as illustration of the apostolic paraenesis. The content of the indirect question is dominated by its two important verbs. The first derives from Judaism and its tradition of the "religious and ethical walk," a concept expressed by the Hebrew word *hālak* and increasingly rendered in late Jewish literature by the Greek term *peripateō* (lit.: "to walk," metaphorically "to conduct oneself"; *TDNT* 5:942). It is used frequently by Paul (18x) and always in its metaphorical sense. This would be his first use of the term to refer to the practical demands of Christian living. The second verb, *areskō* ("to please"), followed by anarthous *theos* (always in Paul: Rom 8:8; 1 Thess 2:4; though with arthous *kyrios* in 1 Cor 7:32), is also a relatively frequent Pauline term (12x) used to distinguish the various, competing spheres of interest, whether of the self, other humans, or God (Rom 15:1-3; 1 Thess 2:4—*TDNT* 1:455). In the present case, related to the previous verb by a "consecutive *kai*" and translated "and so" (BDF 442.2), it refers in a teleological way to the purpose and goal of Christian behavior.

as you are indeed doing: This short commendatory clause is in keeping with the character and tone of the missive and adds a phatic element or personal touch to foster reception of his advice. With this clause (use again of the verb *peripateō* in the present tense) Paul softens his stark request for behavior consonant with apostolic instruction, by insisting that what he is requesting is new neither in knowledge nor action. They are already doing (*kathōs kai;* also 4:13) what he asks. Thus, he prepares the readers for an intensification of his request in the following clause.

and that you abound even more: Verse 1 expresses two exhortations, both introduced by *hina* clauses, the first urging that the community manifest conduct compatible with apostolic instruction and the second, in the form of a polite request but implying a command, encouraging even more intensive progress. To express the latter Paul again employs the verb *perisseuō* (see 3:12) to describe this wished-for superabundance.

2. *For you know what directives we gave you in the name of the Lord Jesus:* The verse is connected with the preceding exhortation by the conjunction *gar* ("for") to underscore the connection between the final advice and the earlier apostolic instruction. Paul again employs a recall device ("you know") to stress continuity between past and present advice (see 1:5) and to soften the sense of command which the noun *parangelia* might convey. Indeed, the noun is used

only here in Paul, though the verb is found twice in 1 Corinthians (7:10; 11:17) and in the second Thessalonian missive (4:11). The term bears a military or authoritative sense of "orders or directives given by a superior" (the terms "instruction" and "advice" do not do justice to the Greek). There is a shift in meaning and emphasis from "as you learned from us" in verse 1 to "directives we gave you" in verse 2. In contrast to verse 1, Paul employs an unambiguous *dia* phrase, here translated "in the name of" (*IBNTG* 570).

INTERPRETATION

Paul ends his first missive to the Thessalonians with an expression of thanksgiving (3:9-10), prayers both to God the Father and the Lord Jesus (vv. 11-13), and finally offers a few words of diplomatic (4:1), yet firm (v. 2) exhortation. The last mentioned, though brief and succinct, corresponds to Pauline usage and thought.

Conclusion of First Missive. 4:1-2 presents several challenging features: Paul's use of *loipon oun*, the formulaic verb *parakaleō* to introduce paraenesis, and the train of thought of the two verses. (1) Interpretation of the first two terms relates to general structural analysis and the conclusion one draws concerning the unity and integrity of 1 Thessalonians. There is surely a malaise among scholars who, when faced with the analysis of this passage, admit that the adverb *loipon*, which usually means "finally," comes too early in the letter and observe that it probably introduces the last major section of the letter. In support, they point to its alleged use in Hellenistic Greek as a transitional particle with the meaning "therefore." It is admitted that *loipon* and variations thereof often come at the end of Pauline letters (2 Cor 13:11; Phil 3:1 and 4:8; and 1 Thess 4:1), but since the term does not appear at the end of the document, it is presumed that "finally" or a generic expression such as "for the rest," with or without "then" *(oun)*, suffices to indicate that Paul is approaching the last, if long, section of his letter.

The following considerations are offered for the proper analysis of the phrase in question. [1] While many ignore the particle *oun*, presumably because it does not fit in with a softened translation of *loipon*, we are led to agree with those who object to the observation that the term bears the meaning "therefore" in Hellenistic Greek, since it is here followed by *oun*, which itself means "therefore or then." One must assume that both terms had some function in the original text. Interestingly, some manuscripts and ancient versions omit *oun*, thereby agreeing with the tendency in late Greek where "*loipon* has displaced *oun*" (*IBNTG* 162). [2] The idiom *loipon oun*, a hapax in the NT, is attested in two contemporary papyrus letters: BGU 4:1078.6 and 1079.6 (A.D. 39 and 41, respectively). Both underscore the inferential sense of *oun* and the second merits citation to illustrate the meaning of our passage: "I sent you two other letters, one by Nedymus, another by Cronius the sword-bearer. Finally then, I received your letter from the Arab." *Oun* in our passage serves likewise to link inferentially the closing exhortation of 4:1-2 with the previous section dealing with prayer on the addressees' behalf (see 3:9). [3] Lastly, what is Pauline usage relating to *loipon*? Scholars agree that the term usually comes near the end of Paul's letters where its meaning is undisputed, but regularly list three possible exceptions: Phil 3:1; 1 Thess 4:1; and 2 Thess 3:1. Since the first points to the editorial joining of two letters, we presume that a similar situation occurs in 1 Thess 4:1—the last noted is best explained as a Paulinist imitation of the composite letter. The expression "finally then" makes sense as Paul approaches the end of his letter and concludes with an exhortation to more-sublime conduct.

(2) Pauline usage in introducing exhortation is clarified by form-critical study of the verb *parakaleō* in Hellenistic epistolary literature, particularly the detection of a standard, extended formula consisting of this verb (or a synonym) followed by a reference to the audience (usually direct address), an optional prepositional phrase, and a request expressed in a *hina* clause or infinitive construction. A dozen or so of these have been isolated, four of which are found in 1 Thessalonians: 4:1, 10b-12; 5:12, 14 (also 5:27). Some scholars appeal to such analysis to support their contention that Paul's use of this formula in 4:1 serves to indicate the beginning of his exhortation or paraenetic section. To maintain, however, that this formula tends to introduce the paraenetic sections of Paul's letters is to claim too much. The two occurrences of this formula in Romans are instructive in this regard. In 12:1-2 it is clear that Paul brings one part of his letter to an end and introduces a long paraenetic section. In 15:30-32, however, he brings the letter to a close by briefly exhorting the Roman community to pray for his deliverance. In the same fashion in 1 Thess 4:1-2 Paul brings his short letter to a close by using the *parakaleō* formula to offer a short exhortation to the community; see further discussion below of the ending paragraph of Romans in relation to the conclusion of the first Thessalonian missive.

The prepositional phrase "in the Lord Jesus" following the verbs of exhortation forms part of the formula noted above and its function and meaning should be sought in relation to that epistolary convention, one feature of which was an optional prepositional phrase modifying the verb of exhortation. Of the dozen or so cases noted in Paul only five have such a phrase, four introduced by *dia* (Rom 12:1-2; 15:30-32; 1 Cor 1:10; 2 Cor 10:1-2) and one by *en* (1 Thess 4:1). The first four, by their use of *dia*, stress the source of Paul's authority and its diplomatic exercise and so agree with general analysis that the *parakaleō* construction is used principally for its diplomatic and rhetorical effectiveness. Recent scholars then presume that "in the Lord Jesus" of 1 Thess 4:1 must be read in an analogous way. This last case, however, is more problematic and must be seen in light of the parallel between 4:1 and 2 where the *en* phrase ("in the Lord Jesus") with its behavioral context ("conduct yourselves") forms an interesting contrast with the *dia* phrase ("in the name of our Lord Jesus") with its focus on "directives." Since verse 2 undoubtedly stresses apostolic authority, one might question whether the *en* phrase of verse 1 accomplishes that goal. Further, the seeming infelicities of verse 1 along with the evident scribal activity in the manuscript tradition to correct these, lead us to reexamine this passage.

It is clear that 4:1 offers several features which render it an untypical *parakaleō* construction. Not only does it begin with the anomalous "finally then," which displaces the usually initial verb, but it also transforms the regular verb of exhortation into the epistolary formula "we urge and exhort you." Next Paul employs an *en*-prepositional phrase rather than his customary *dia* phrase, a phrase which could be understood as modifying either the object ("you"—so fellowship in Christ) or the verbs (thus, the missionaries' authority). I presume that it is this ambiguity which led Paul to attempt a clarification. Seemingly, verse 1 was to deal with the community's life in Christ, a fact indicated by his choice of prepositional phrase (see also 5:12). The construction itself, however, being suited to the appeal to authority, leads Paul directly, in a first *hina* clause, to recall former instruction when discussing the community's behavior in a complex statement of exhortation. Once he extricates himself from his involved exposition by a second *hina* clause (see below), he focuses in verse 2 on the source of the apostolic exhortation: "instruction given in the Lord Jesus' name" (use of an unambiguous *dia* phrase).

(3) The final point concerns Paul's train of thought in 4:1. Introduced by the verbs of exhortation, "we urge and exhort you," the remainder of verse 1 presents the reader with difficult choices, especially the repetition of *hina* and *kathōs* and the logical progression of the sentence. Many insist that, with the first *hina*, Paul begins to express the object of the verbs but gets sidetracked and leaves *hina* hanging as he reminds the readers of past instruction and speaks of their ethical conduct before resuming his train of thought with a second *hina*—this time followed by a clause. Thus, translators either omit one of the conjunctions (some MSS omit the first *hina*) or soften the awkward resumption of a poorly conceived subordinate clause by translating "even as . . . so" or by radically restructuring the sentence. Regardless, such an explanation presumes more than clumsy resumption since Paul would have anticipated the topic of the exhortation ("community conduct") in his parenthetical statement. On the contrary, the second *hina* does not resume

Paul's original exhortation; in fact, it presumes what is said previously and adds to it. Another way of viewing the structure of verse 1, particularly the interpretation of the first *hina* (see translation) is to assume that an implied clause is contextually derived, a construction which is attested in the papyri and in the NT (POxyrhynchus 1299.9; Mark 15:8; Gal 3:6; see BAGD 391.1). Thus, Paul's exhortation would be for the community "to act" as the missionaries had instructed them. A second, paratactic *hina* clause then supplements the writer's exhortation (Phil 1:9-10; see also Rom 7:13; 1 Cor 1:27; 9:20).

What conclusions then can one draw concerning the ending of the first missive? In such a paraenetic context the appearance of *loipon* is significant as it parallels several Pauline endings: 2 Cor 13:11; Phil 3:1 and 4:8 (also Gal 6:17) and argues for similar usage in 1 Thess 4:1. Also, Paul's use in Rom 15:30 of a *parakaleō* structure to bring his letter to a close is a good parallel to the presumed ending of this first missive. All the elements of the *parakaleō* formula are present in the Romans passage: the verb of exhortation, address *(adelphoi)*, double prepositional phrase, and the exhortation expressed by an infinitive construction and multiple *hina* clauses. Additionally, reference is made to prayer addressed to God, to the theme of service to the saints, and to a hoped-for visit with the community. Paul then brings the letter in verse 33 to a close with a brief, simple blessing. "The God of peace be with you all. Amen." In light, therefore, of this parallel, I suggest that the first missive, after a brief exhortation, ended with the blessing found in 1 Thess 5:28 or one similar: "The grace of our Lord Jesus Christ be with you." Perhaps the title would have been "Lord Jesus," as always in the first missive rather than "Lord Jesus Christ" (see 2:13, 19). Finally, the similarity or near identity of blessings for the two missives would have facilitated compilation.

Final Exhortation. Paul's letter from beginning to end reflects a sense of personal concern, particularly as seen in his use of "brothers and sisters." As the letter begins with direct address in 2:17 to explain the missionaries' anxiety regarding the community and their inability to visit, so the writer addresses the audience again in 3:7 to describe the group's ecstatic response on hearing Timothy's report and finally in 4:1 to bring the letter to a close with renewed encouragement and a reminder about previous instruction. With this last movement of the composition one sees Paul's pastoral concern emerge once more as he exhorts them to greater efforts. We direct our attention then to Paul's exhortation and apostolic instruction, to the author's sense of communication with his audience, and finally to the content of the exhortation.

(1) Employing current epistolary convention Paul ends his letter by "urging and exhorting" the converts to live according to their calling.

By employing a *parakaleō* construction Paul diplomatically calls his hearers to act in accordance with what they learned from the apostolic group (v. 1) and to recall the directives they were given in this regard (v. 2). Thus, his paraenesis relates to instruction given during the foundation visit, instruction which concerned doctrinal and moral matters. His exhortation then is not about new issues and concerns but corresponds to what the missionaries taught their converts—whether God's word (2:13) or Christian behavior in a challenging setting (3:3-4, 12). Also, there is a shift in meaning as Paul moves from "as you learned from us" in 4:1 to "directives we gave you" in verse 2. In the first case the converts are reminded of the role of their human teachers who exhort them as fellow Christians ("in the Lord Jesus"); in the second, they are reminded of the apostolic preaching and directives, but the emphasis is on its validating authority. Thus, Paul ends his exhortation and letter by reiterating what both parties know to be the source of apostolic authority, namely, the "Lord Jesus." Paraenesis and apostolic instruction go hand in hand but these are conveyed to the audience in an interesting manner, both by stressing diplomacy and by insisting on the apostolic origin and authority of the moral directives.

(2) The concluding paraenesis bears an obvious phatic character, for Paul is interested in keeping open the channels of communication. The expression, "as you are indeed doing," expresses his acknowledgment that the community is doing well and also verbalizes the confidence he has in them. This tendency to compliment his readers is obvious throughout the missive, for he claims that they have truly "accepted" the missionaries' preaching as God's word (2:13), suggests that the community is "already [their] renown and joy" (2:19-20), and on several occasions implies that, while the doctrinal and moral foundation is solid, an increase and strengthening are necessary (3:2, 4, 6, 9-10, 12). By stressing in 4:1 that the community is already doing what he asks, he can adroitly add that he wishes greater efforts. As a result of Timothy's message the missionary group is relieved and convinced that the converts are faithful to their commitment to God and sensitive to the needs of their neighbors. Such conviction is reflected in Paul's language as he admits that the converts are on the right track but also urges renewed effort, after having sought renewed assistance (3:11-13). Paul's language, then, is both diplomatic, as he encourages renewed commitment to a God-inspired life, and sincere, as he expresses joy for the splendid news received from Thessalonica and renews pastoral encouragement to recent, beloved converts.

(3) The content of Paul's exhortation is expressed by means of two key verbs: *peripateō* and *areskō*. The first expresses life in a metaphorical way as "walking," i.e., conducting oneself in a given way. Its content is not made explicit in this particular case though its context does lend

more specificity. The converts are both to draw the logical inferences from their new commitment to the risen Lord (2:13; 3:3, 6, 12) and to remember and follow the apostolic directives. This neutral term, however, is qualified by the second crucial verb "to please," a term which gives proper conduct a theological focus, for God rather than some human or moral ideal is the believer's perspective, i.e., Christian morality is theologically conditioned. Ultimately, "pleasing God," for Paul, is "walking (before God) in newness of life" (Rom 6:4), a life made possible by the Christ-event and affecting all behavior, whose goal is divine pleasure and approval.

FOR REFERENCE AND FURTHER STUDY

Bjerkelund, C. J. *Parakalō: Form, Funktion and Sinn der Parakalō-Sätze in den paulinischen Briefen.* Oslo: Universitetsforlaget, 1967.

Hollaway, J. O. *"Peripateō" as a Thematic Marker for Pauline Ethics.* San Francisco: Mellen Research University, 1992.

Malherbe, A. J. *Moral Exhortation: A Greco-Roman Sourcebook.* Philadelphia: Westminster, 1986.

Meeks, W. A. *The Moral World of the First Christians.* Philadelphia: Westminster, 1986.

III. LATER MISSIVE, PART 2—4:3–5:28

For a discussion of 4:3f. as continuing Paul's second missive, begun in 1:1–2:12, see Introduction.

11. *Initial Exhortation on Holiness* (4:3-8)

3. The above, then, is God's will, namely, your holiness: that you refrain from immorality, 4. that is, that each of you learn to master the vessel provided you in a holy and honorable way, 5. not in covetous passion as do the pagans who do not know God, 6. also that none transgress against or defraud their brother or sister in their activity, because the Lord is an executor of justice in all these things, just as we told you beforehand and as we emphatically declared. 7. Indeed, God did not call us to impurity but to a state of holiness. 8. Thus, anyone who acts wickedly breaks faith not with a human being but with the God who gives you his Holy Spirit.

NOTES

3. *The above, then, is God's will, namely, your holiness:* This translation rests on several grammatical conclusions. The first is that *touto* ("this" or "the above") functions as subject and anarthrous *thelēma tou theou* ("God's will") serves as predicate (see also 5:18). Also, it is proposed that *touto* refers not to what follows (see *BG* 213) but, following classical usage, to what precedes immediately, i.e., "conduct yourselves worthily of God" (2:12, or similarly in the edited document: "how you must conduct yourselves and so please God," 4:1). Thus, in the translation, "the above" refers back to proper conduct (*peripateō* of 2:12) and becomes the focus of God's intention or will. Paul has moved logically ("then") from a discussion of proper conduct before God (4:3 picks up where 2:12 leaves off) to his paraenesis, dwelling further on the theme of behavior. The focus then becomes "holiness," a term he places in apposition to *touto*. On the expressions "God's will" and "holiness," see discussion below.

that you refrain from immorality: Employing a list of infinitival constructions, Paul begins his description of the state of purity which God intends for the believer. His first precept is that the community "refrain from immorality." The verbal expression, *apechō apo*, is commonly used in the middle voice (elsewhere in Paul only in 1 Thess 5:22) to express abstinence whether from nonkosher foods (1 Tim 4:3) or unacceptable behavior (Paul; 1 Pet 2:11). In verse 3 the word *porneia* is used, a term whose meaning ranges from "prostitution," to "fornication," to "sexual misconduct or immorality," and, in Jewish literature, "idolatry," and whose cognates invariably bear sexual nuances. Debate continues among scholars who opt either for a restricted meaning ("fornication or incest") or a more general sense ("sexual immorality" or "unchastity"). The latter is the preferred choice, since it fits more clearly in Paul's trend of thought, namely, a general prohibition against sexual immorality (including fornication), a subject which is then discussed in verses 4-5.

4. *that is, that each of you learn to master the vessel provided you:* This verse, introduced by a simple infinitive, is usually viewed as providing a new, though related precept regarding a more specific sexual issue. Two stylistic features lead me instead to view the verse epexegetically as explaining what *porneia* means to each member of the community. (1) The precept of verse 3b is addressed to the community as a whole ("you"), but verse 4, by its use of "each of you," draws attention to the duty of each community member vis-à-vis the subject being discussed. In this way Paul develops his notion of *porneia* as the antithesis of a pure life and underscores the responsibility of every believer in this matter. (2) The infinitive construction of verse 6, being both negative and articular in form, suggests a new topic (see below) and a contrast between it and the positively stated prohibition of verse 3b. Thus, the new infinitive is understood as explicating what was said and is translated: "that is, that each of you learn. . . ." The remainder of the text is more problematic. While the first verb of the construction (*oida*) is readily seen as

introducting a second infinitive and meaning "learn or know how to" (BAGD 556), the meaning of the second, along with its object, is debated. For a discussion of the expression "to master the vessel provided you," see below.

in a holy and honorable way, 5. *not in covetous passion:* Verse 4 ends and verse 5 begins with an extended contrasting statement which describes the manner (the preposition *en* is used adverbially—*IBNTG* 78) in which believers are to master every aspect of their physical existence. Though Paul favors *ouk/alla* ("not . . . but") contrasts in all his letters, in the present case the reverse occurs, for a positive *en* statement precedes a contrasting negative *mē* phrase, a construction which he uses occasionally elsewhere (e.g., Gal 4:18; 2 Cor 5:12; 9:5). The first, "in a holy and honorable way," represents the literal phrase: "in holiness and honor." The term for holiness has been used in and is discussed in relation to verse 3, while that for honor represents the noun *timē* and designates the dignity which other humans deserve or receive (see Rom 13:7 and 1 Cor 12:23-24). The positive part of the contrast then focuses on the believer reflecting, in a life of holiness, the purity of God and treating others with the respect they deserve. The negative part of the contrast, literally, "not in (the) passion of desire," is almost without exception rendered, following the lead of BAGD (603), as "lustful passion," thereby reading an overly sexual interpretation of verses 3-4 into the Pauline phrase. Presuming discussion in an Excursus below on "Covetous Passion," I conclude that the first term *pathos* means not "erotic passion" but "passion" simply and that the second, *epithymia*, refers to "desire" which dominates the human creatures and leads them to covet the lordship of the Creator. Thus, the expression is rendered "covetous passion" to describe the opposite of holiness as rebellion against God; i.e., the phrase refers to the sway which human passions may have over human behavior.

as do the pagans who do not know God: Paul's converts are to be distinguished from the pagan world, a reality which he interestingly describes in monotheistic, i.e., theological rather than Christological, terms. Borrowing a stereotype formula from Jewish literature (the wording is from the LXX version of Jer 10:25; see also Job 18:21; Ps 78:6) Paul labels them precisely as "people that do not know God" (see also Gal 4:8; 1 Cor 1:21; and the Paulinist 2 Thess 1:8).

6. *also that none transgress against or defraud their brother or sister in their activity:* The interpretation of this compound infinitive construction involves the assessment of several stylistic, lexical, and contextual issues examined below. In overall terms, however, I would note that the unusual articular construction *to mē* which introduces the clause signals a change of subject from what precedes (from sexual to social morality) and that the verbs *hyperbainō* and *pleonekteō* ("transgress against" and "defraud") as well as the phrase *en tō pragmati* ("in their activity") point to issues of justice rather than sexuality. Also, it should be noted that the phrase *ton adelphon autou* is rendered "their brother or sister" in accordance with Pauline usage whereby *adelphos* regularly describes a fellow Christian. Paul is here concerned with community behavior, especially behavior that marks the community off from nonbelievers, and directs his attention to Christian relations to outsiders in verses 11-12.

because the Lord is an executor of justice in all these things: The complex sentence begun in verse 3 to describe the believer's state of holiness ends in verse 6 by stating an element of motivation ("because") and then by recalling earlier apostolic admonition. While it is often presumed that "the Lord" as judge here refers to Christ it is argued below, after consideration of OT and Pauline usage as well as Thessalonian context, that the referent is God. Also, the translation "executor of justice" underscores the immediate context of the phrase as referring to fraud and also preserves the root and extended meaning of *ekdikos* as referring both to matters of justice and judgment.

just as we told you beforehand and as we emphatically declared: The construction "just as . . . and as" occurs also in 3:4. Here as there I opt not to view the double verbal expression as a rhetorical means of stressing the solemnity of the teaching (e.g., "we told you before with all emphasis") but insist that the two verbs serve distinct functions. The first, *prolegō* (see Gal 1:9), refers directly to the missionary activity of the preachers. Paul's use of this verb in the aorist underscores the fact that the paraenesis is a repetition of earlier teaching and highlights his rhetorical strategy in nurturing his community by constantly reminding it of its conversion, commitment, and pastoral formation (see discussion of "recall devices" at 1:5). The second verb, *diamartyromai*, used only here in Paul (though see its cognate in 2:12), has a range of meaning from "declare with appeal to witnesses" to "declare emphatically." While some opt for the meaning "warn" or "forewarn," it is preferable to follow the second ("declare emphatically"—*TDNT* 4:511-12) as insisting that the original teaching on eschatological judgment continues to apply in the believers' lives.

7. *Indeed, God did not call us to impurity but to a state of holiness:* Paul begins his new sentence with the postpositive connective *gar* to indicate a causal connection not only with the preceding judgment clause (v. 6) but with the entire paraenetic period. The translation ("indeed") indicates the verse's relation to the overall discussion of holiness, thereby underscoring a return to the initial topic of purity (for a discussion of the term *akatharsia* or "impurity" and further comment on *hagiasmos* or "holiness," see below). Paul appeals once again to the theme of divine election (use of *kaleō*), a dominant theme in all his letters and already in the Thessalonian correspondence (see 1:4: "your election"). In typical Pauline fashion one encounters a "not . . . but" construction to contrast the negative (most of vv. 3-7) to the positive (the theme of holiness).

8. *Thus, anyone who acts wickedly breaks faith not with a human being:* Paul then draws a firm conclusion (use of intensive conjunction *toigaroun*, "thus") from what he has just said; if God is the one who calls to a life of purity, then living in any way which is less than pure and honorable (4) is a rejection of God's will and empowerment. The final verse of the section, however, poses an intriguing question about interpreting the double use of the verb *atheteō*. While the initial participle is usually supplied with an object and the whole translated (in view of the Synoptic tradition about rejection of Jesus and his disciples—see Luke 10:16) as "whoever rejects this rejects . . . God," it is

preferable to treat the first term as an absolute use of the verb bearing the meaning "acts wickedly" and the second, transitive use of the verb as offerring the legal meaning of "break faith" (see below). Thus, the reference is not to Paul's ethical teaching in verses 3-7 but to a breaking of faith with the God who calls believers to a state and consequent life of holiness. Further, the contrast between the human and divine spheres is expressed with the usual Pauline *ouk/alla* construction but untypically employs the singular rather than plural of *anthrōpos* (see 2:4, 13; also Gal 1:10; 1 Cor 1:25; 2:54; 14:2; Rom 2:29). If Paul wished to contrast primarily human and divine agents or human instruction as opposed to divine directives (or even human paraenesis viewed as divine in origin) he would have employed the plural as he does in 2:4 and regularly.

but with the God who gives you his Holy Spirit: The Greek text presents textual and stylistic anomalies. The least controversial of the textual issues is whether the verse should end with the pronoun *hēmas* or *hymas* ("us or you") since the latter is favored by the weight of the textual evidence (major and most MSS) and scholarly opinion. A second case, whether the participle should be in the aorist or present (*donta* or *didonta*), is also relatively clear owing to the state of textual (S* B D F *al*, i.e., major MSS and scribal activity in the case of S) and internal, stylistic evidence. Since Paul in three other passages (Rom 5:5; 2 Cor 1:22; 5:5) speaks of the Spirit as being given in the past (aorist participles) and since 1 Thess 4:8 seems to parallel the statement in verse 7 that "God called us" (aorist of *kaleō*; note also the pronoun *hēmas*), one must attribute the use of the aorist to scribal activity and the present to Paul himself. A final textual issue, whether the participle should be preceded by the particle *kai*, is more tenuous owing to the weight of textual evidence, whether for the longer reading (most MSS) or for omission (B A D¹ I *al* itsyᴾ). In favor of the former is the fact that the scribe of B often omits "unimportant" particles and pronouns (see notes on 2 Thess 1:2), or in favor of the latter is the fact that *kai* is added before "give" in a similar construction in 2 Cor 5:5 by scribes of S and D. In the final analysis, one should probably follow an important rule of textual criticism and opt for the shorter text, especially since the textual range of MSS for omission is relatively wide. Stylistically, the Greek text also presents several anomalies, anomalies which bear looking at since they offer insights into the development of early Pauline pneumatology (see discussion below).

EXCURSUS
on *Covetous Passion* (4:5)

The Greek expression *en pathei epithymias* ("in the passion of desire") is rendered in a variety of ways but generally reflecting sexual connotations ("lustful passion") and set in an overall sexual interpretation for verses 3-4. Its meaning and contextual interpretation, however, merit some attention. The first term *pathos* is rare in the NT, appearing in the present text, Rom 1:26, and the Paulinist Col 3:5. In the last mentioned it is part of a vice list whose components range from the sensual to the avaricious, while in the Pauline uses it is qualified. In Rom 1:26 disobedient creatures are said to be given over to "passions that dishonor" others (*pathē atimias;* see discussion of *timē* in v. 4 above). Interestingly, in a parallel statement in verse 24 Paul states concerning these that God "gave them up in the desires (*epithymiais*) of their hearts to impurity (*akatharsian;* see 1 Thess 4:7) that they might dishonor (*atimazesthai*) their own bodies." While the *pathos* of verse 26 points to sexual aberrations, the parallel *epithymia* of verse 24 speaks of idolatry or "worshipping and serving the creature." Also, the third reference to God punishing disobedient creatures (vv. 28f.) introduces a comprehensive list of vices said to be the products of "a debased mind." From this analysis two conclusions can be drawn. (1) *Pathos* in this context reflects the usual meaning of the term in Greek: "passion" and not "erotic passion" as so often claimed (by relying too readily on Col 3:5; see *TDNT* 5:928). (2) One detects here a slight influence of Stoicism on the thought of Paul especially his contrasting of "mind" and *pathos/epithymia.*

The second occurrence of *pathos* in Paul is again modified, this time by the term *epithymia,* which, along with its cognates, is employed at least fifteen times in Paul's authentic letters. Its basic meaning is "to desire or want something," a meaning which is attested in Paul (see 2:17; also Phil 1:23). In the other occurrences, however, one detects a less positive sense for the term. Thus, one finds expressions such as "desires of the heart" (Rom 1:24), "of the mortal body" (Rom 6:12), and "of the flesh" (Rom 13:14; Gal 5:16, 24). Additionally, one learns that the flesh desires something different than does the Spirit (Gal 5:17), that sin produces "all kinds of desire" (Rom 7:8), and that even believers might "desire evil" as did their Jewish ancestors (1 Cor 10:6). Thus, from the above, one could conclude simply that the term in the NT is most often used of evil desires or, in light of Paul's allusions to the Torah in 1 Cor 10:6 and Rom 7:7; 13:9 (Num 11:4, 34 and Exod 20:17, respectively), insist that desire is evil owing to the disobedience of divine commands (*TDNT* 3:171).

Another, and preferable, solution is suggested by Paul's use of *epithymia* in Rom 7:7, where he cites the final command of the Decalogue in abbreviated form: "I would not have known desire (or covetousness) if the law had not said, 'you shall not desire (covet)' " (Exod 20:17; Deut 5:21). Desire here refers to human exaltation or pride. It is not covetousness of itself which is evil but the creature's subservience to this desire. Desire becomes the means to self-assertion or self-seeking at the expense of God and, ultimately, also of other creatures. The human creature rather than God becomes the master. *Epithymia* is the means by which passion, the heart, the mortal body, and (in more typical Pauline terminology) the flesh gain dominance over the human being, a domination which defines the nature of sin. The meaning, therefore, of *pathos epithymias* (its use in T.Joseph 7:8 reveals the Stoic sense of domination by desire rather than the mind) as a motive of action is that unbelievers (those "who do not know God") act out of passion which is dominated by the creature's desire to replace the Creator or to covet lordship itself. *Epithymia* has more to do with rebellion against God than with lust or sexual aberrations (the latter are, according to Paul, visible signs of rebellion in the Gentile world; see Rom 1:18f.). I conclude, therefore that the phrase "in covetous passion" is an early formulation of the technical Pauline concept of *sarx* or "flesh" to describe pagan activity in the old aeon, wherein action is motivated by the flesh's wish to gratify its own desires. Even the concept of holiness or *hagiasmos* is an early substitute for the realm of the Spirit.

INTERPRETATION

After a discussion of the foundation visit and the character of that mission, Paul focuses on the theme which brought the discussion to a close. As in 2:11-12 he insists on the similarity between the apostles' treatment of the audience during the mission and in extended pastoral care (vv. 7 and 11) as a justification for the advice he wished to impart concerning behavior worthy of God, so now he turns his attention to what that behavior entails. The new section therefore focuses on a life of holiness as constituting proper Christian behavior modeled on missionary praxis (2:1-12) and demanded by apostolic teaching (4:6) as well as required by God's will and call (4:3, 7-8). Verses 4:3f. therefore constitute more properly the second missive's paraenetic section.

Structural and Thematic Observations. Some scholars argue for the paraenetic unity of 4:1-12 owing to the repetition of the verb "to walk or conduct oneself" (*peripateō*) in verses 1 and 12; one could also note the repeated phrase "to abound even more" (*perisseuō mallon*) in verses 1 and 10. Thus, verses 1-2 would act as a general introduction to two successive, tightly composed paraenetic sections, possibly consisting of multiple precepts for daily life. Closer structural analysis, however, shows that this unity is more apparent than real.

(1) The verb *peripateō* occurs not only in verses 4:1 and 12 but also in 2:12, the verse immediately preceding the document's second thanksgiving period. Thus, the threefold occurrence of this verb provides added evidence for editorial activity. Indeed, comparison of 2:8-12 and 3:9-4:2 provides interesting parallels, which confirm such a conclusion:

	2:9	affection		3:9	affection
		day and night		10	day and night
	10	appeal to God		11	appeal to God & Lord Jesus
		devout, upright,		12	abundance of love
		blameless behavior		13	hearts blameless
					in holiness before God
					coming of Lord Jesus

12	encourage, console,	4:1	urge & exhort
	implore		walk/conduct self
	walk/conduct self		please God
	worthily of God	2	directives
	who calls you		
	to kingdom & glory		

These similarities would have facilitated the joining of the two Thessalonian missives since the original link between the body proper of the letter (2:1-12) and the paraenesis (4:3f.) would in effect be reiterated at the conclusion of the added missive (paraenetic language, *peripateō*, pleasing God in 4:1). Additionally, 4:2 in its new context would seem, by its use of the term "directives" *(parangelia)*, to point to the ethical instructions that follow (4:3f.). Finally, it should be noted that, in the original missive, the themes of 2:12 prepare for and recur in the succeeding paraenetic discussion: "walk/conduct self" prepares for 4:12; divine "call" is developed in 4:7; and "kingdom and glory" as "waiting for, being with, and living with the Lord" is further developed in 4:15, 17; 5:10.

(2) The claim that 4:1-12 forms a tightly redacted unit is less compelling than the proposal that these verses contain several discrete units with varied functions. 4:1-2, as argued above, functions as the ending of the earlier missive, following as it does the solemn prayer of 3:11-13. There Paul addresses his audience a final time and reminds them, in closing, of "proper conduct" and apostolic instruction. 4:3-8, the focus of our attention, is rightly described as a complete unit whose concern is "holiness" (vv. 3, 4, 7). 4:9-12, however, does not form a close unity with what precedes but instead begins a series of three passages introduced by *peri* with genitive: 4:9-12; 4:13-18; and 5:1-11. As is argued below these passages, much as happens in 1 Corinthians 7-16, introduce Paul's responses to questions received from the community.

(3) The structural and thematic unity of 4:3-8 is much discussed. The focus of such analysis is verses 3-6 which consist of a single sentence in Greek. After discussions of the passage's peculiar vocabulary (*porneia*, *skeuos*, and *pragma* in vv. 3, 4, and 6) and structural components (five consecutive infinitives, the last two introduced by *to mē*), many conclude that Paul's text focuses on sexual morality by presenting a series of moral precepts. Either the text speaks successively about sin in general (3a), sexual immorality (3b), lack of sexual self-control (4-5), and adultery (6) or else Paul, in three progressively specific moral statements, provides the community with advice about general sexual morality (3), chastity within marriage (4), and warning against violating the marriage of other believers—even incestuous marriages have been considered a possibility (6). The position taken in this commentary and defended below, varies on two crucial points. [1] In structural terms I conclude that verses 3-6

present not three injunctions but two, namely, that the infinitive construction of verse 4 is epexegetical and explains the injunction of verse
3 (*skeuos* means "the body as vessel" rather than "wife"). [2] In thematic
terms I find more convincing the position that verse 6 introduces a second theme, that of social justice (*pragma* refers to "activity, trade, or business"). Thus, the "holiness" to which Paul refers in verses 3 and 7 is
to be characterized by lives in which personal, bodily activity and social
interaction are judged as pure (not *akatharsia*) before God.

Call to Holiness. The whole of 4:3-8 deals with the theme of holiness
and employs terms from the *hagios* ("holy") word family in verses 3, 4,
7, and 8. Further, verses 3-6, which constitutes a single complex sentence
in Greek, describes what this holiness consists of by focusing on two
crucial injunctions introduced in verses 3b and 6. Lastly, Paul reiterates
in verse 7 that God calls believers to a state of holiness.

(1) Holiness as God's Will (v. 3). Paul begins his paraenesis by introducing two important expressions. [1] The first phrase "the will of
God" appears in Paul for the first time, here and in 5:18, both in ethical
contexts (for the soteriological nuances see discussion below). The theme
of the divine will, however, has a broader scope in Pauline thought (*TDNT*
3:56-59), where it encompasses God's salvific purpose in Christ (Gal 1:4),
God's choice of ministers (1 Cor 1:1; 2 Cor 1:1), and God's ultimate control over the direction and scope of the apostolic mission (Rom 1:10; 15:32;
1 Cor 16:12). At the same time, Paul associates the divine will with human
behavior, whether of the Jew as instructed in the Law regarding what
is right (Rom 2:18; see 2:14-15 on the Gentile) or of believers and their
new life. It is the last mentioned which concerns us, what God expects
of believers. Rom 12:2 might be considered the *textus classicus* concerning the divine will and ethical responsibility, for there Paul pleads with
his Roman readers, "do not be conformed to this world, but be transformed by the renewing of your minds," that they might understand
God's will or intention, which is interestingly described as knowing and
doing "what is good and acceptable and perfect." While Paul admits in
Rom 1:19-21 and 2:14-16 that humans have moral guidelines and concrete responsibilities, he insists in 12:3-8 that there is a greater responsibility and potential for the believer to do even better. What Paul describes,
in concrete terms in Rom 12:3f., as "good, acceptable, and perfect," in
1 Thess 4:3, he puts under the rubric of "holiness," not in the sense of
concrete sexual modes of behavior, but as avoiding "impurity" and living in "a state of holiness" (4:7) which encompasses personal and inter-
personal activity. The ethical and spiritual activity of the believer is dictated
by God's will (see 5:17).

[2] The major theme of the section, introduced by the term "holiness"
(*hagiasmos*; see discussion of 3:13), requires attention owing to the peculi-

arities of Pauline usage and to the term's implications for understanding Paul's ethics. This noun is not used in secular Greek, is rare in the LXX, and infrequently used in Paul (6x, 3 of which occur in 4:3-8). Thus, its background must be sought in Jewish sources where the term and its cognates relate to the cult: the people must be holy, because God is holy (*hagios*—Lev 11:44f.) and so separation and dedication become characteristic marks of a people thus chosen, of its temple, cultic personnel, and objects (Judg 17:3; Amos 2:1). Equally prominent and presumably flowing from the former is a second usage for the word family and the term *hagiasmos*, namely, ethical purity. Of particular importance for our passage is Jer 6:16: "Stand *in the ways*, and look, and ask for the ancient paths *of the Lord*, and *what is the good way*, and walk in it, and *you will find holiness* for your souls" (the italicized text indicates LXX differences from the Hebrew; note especially the change from "rest" to "holiness *[hagnismos]* for your souls"). Like Paul, the LXX translator of Jeremiah sees a close connection between behavior expressed as walking on the Lord's way and purity of life (see also T.Benjamin 10:11).

Thus, does the noun in Paul focus on the process of sanctification or its achievement; is it to be taken passively (sanctification by God) or reflexively (self-sanctification); is it soteriological or ethical in connotation? Since *hagiasmos* occurs three times in 4:3-8 in different contexts, prior discussion of the other Pauline occurrences of this and related terms will be helpful. In 1 Cor 1:30, Paul insists that Christ has been transformed into wisdom, righteousness, holiness, and redemption for the believer. So holiness is used soteriologically to describe Christ Jesus as the source of the believer's life and holiness (1 Cor 6:11; see also 1 Thess 5:23). The two occurrences of the term in Romans 6 relate this theme to righteousness, for Paul advises his readers: "so now present your members as slaves to righteousness for sanctification [holiness]" (v. 19; see also v. 22). From the context it is clear that the term is to be understood in an ethical sense (as "the harvest of righteousness," Phil 1:11), not as producing righteousness but as issuing in ethical purity. Lastly, Paul's use of the verb *hagiazō* in 1 Thess 5:23 underscores the fact that "being made holy" is God's work.

The threefold occurrence of *hagiasmos* in 4:3-8 is clarified by these usages. The term's meaning in verse 3 is determined by its relation to 2:12, Paul's exhortation that the readers "conduct themselves or walk worthily of God." Thus, holiness is related to proper conduct, an interpretation confirmed by what Paul says immediately following in his paraenesis. Further, the passage does not imply process or the gaining of holiness but rather the ethical bearing witness in the body to the state of holiness which it was God's will to confer upon believers, or to which God called them (see Rom 6:19). Paul does not speak here of the achievement of purity but rather of a pure life as proof of one's having been made holy by God through Christ. The last point, the soteriological, is implicit both in verse 3 and verse 7 since "God's will" for humanity is Christologically conditioned (see 1 Thess 5:18; Gal 1:4) and since "God's summons of the believer" (2:12; 4:7; 5:24) is made in and through Christ (Gal 1:6).

In verse 4 *hagiasmos* takes on an adverbial function (*en* with the dative) and describes the manner in which believers master their God-given potential. A characteristic of the gift is now employed to describe the believer's manner of life, which is said to be a mirror of that gift. In verse 7 one encounters a similar usage to that of verse 3, namely, the state of holiness to which God calls those who believe. In this case the emphasis is less on manifestation of this holiness in a pure life than on description, by contrast with "impurity," of the state to which God calls. Verses 3a and 7 then form an inclusion within which Paul describes what the Christian life should be, namely, one of purity, mandated by the God who empowers believers by giving them the Spirit of holiness (v. 8) that they might walk worthily of God in view of the kingdom and glory (2:12).

(2) Holiness as a Divine Vocation (v. 7). Just as Paul began his advice to the community concerning holiness by insisting that God's will for them is a life of purity as ethical evidence of the gift they have received (4:3), so in verse 7 he returns to the subject under the heading of divine call. He insists further that as the whole of verses 3-6 is put under the Lord's judgment by the phrase "in all these things" (v. 6), so the whole paraenetic sentence, as part of an inclusion, is motivated once again as being the result of God's initiative. The verb Paul employs in verse 7 to express the theme of divine call (*kaleō*) appears also in 2:12 and 5:24 where the focus, indicated by the use of the present tense, seems to be on God's very nature or name: "the one who calls." In the present case Paul uses the past tense to indicate the effective work of God in the Christ-event, for "at the right time Christ died for the ungodly" (Rom 5:6) thereby effecting God's choice of a people (Rom 8:28-30). The basis of Paul's paraenetic statement, therefore, is God's definitive (past) action or choice.

Paul employs the curious phrase, *ou . . . epi akatharsia all' en hagiasmō*, a construction which requires some explanation. On the one hand, the contrast between the nouns is obvious but the use of different prepositions is curious and much debated. While some see the prepositions as interchangeable, others suggest specific usages for each: *epi* with the dative to indicate purpose ("for" or "with a view to") and *en* in place of *eis*, as abridgement for "to live in," or to express a "state or sphere" (see BDF 235.4; *IBNTG*, 50, 78). The last mentioned is usually called a "pregnant construction" and fits well into the Pauline context regarding holiness as a state of being (*GNTG*, 4:263; *BG*, 99).

On the other hand, the contrasting nouns require some attention. The first, *akatharsia* ("impurity") and its cognates which originally referred to cultic impurity, came to designate inward or moral lack of cleanliness. While it has often been claimed that the term refers generally in Paul to sexual issues (contrast 2:3) and in 4:7 specifically to sexual morality, closer examination of Pauline usage does not support such a conclusion. In effect, Paul in stating that "God gave [Gentiles] up in the desires of their hearts to impurity" does not list sexual aberrations in Rom 1:24 as he does in verses 26f. but, much as in 1 Thess 4:4-5, speaks of them "dishonoring their bodies" and "worshipping and serving the creature rather than the Creator." One reads too easily the whole of Romans 1 as a scene of sexual immorality rather than one of rebellion against God that involves all manner of wickedness (vv. 29-31). In 2 Cor 12:20-21 Paul laments the moral failure of the Corinthian community and lists three types of sin of which they have failed to repent: impurity, (sexual) immorality, and licentiousness (*akatharsia, porneia,* and *aselgeia,* respectively). Only the middle term etymologically and often designates sexual behavior; the other two refer in a more general way to lack of inward or moral purity and to unrestrained behavior or violence (LSJ 255). The same can be said of the vice list of Gal 5:19 where the same three terms appear at the head of a longer, diverse list of vices said to be "works of the flesh." Finally, Rom 6:19 lists two categories of vices as characterizing the believers' former allegiance: "their members were slaves to impurity and iniquity *(anomia).*" Again the categories imply general usage and suggest what one finds in 1 Thess 4:3-6: sins involving personal and social behavior. Thus, I conclude that *akatharsia* refers generally to uncleanness, functions as an antonym to holiness, and includes both the *porneia* of verse 3b (as immorality with focus on improper use of the body) and the transgression and robbery of verse 6a (as sin against brother and sister).

The second term *hagiasmos* is repeated from verse 3a and its meaning here is similar to that of the opening of the paraenetic section, "state of holiness." Thus, the first term ("impurity") designates the ungodly state of the readers before conversion and the second ("holiness") describes the state of purity in which believers have been placed and to which they are to be faithful in their behavior. Verse 7 then repeats verse 3a by restating its thesis and by summing up verses 3b-6 in a contrasting negative; *akatharsia* represents the negatively stated advice of verses 3b-6 and *hagiasmos* expresses in positive terms the new state to which believers are called.

First Injunction: Refrain from Immorality (4:3b-5). The whole of verses 3-6 consists of a series of infinitival constructions which modify Paul's initial statement about holiness. As explained earlier (see Notes) the infinitives of verses 3b and 6 introduce two injunctions, while that of verse 4 explains the first regarding immorality. Paul's first explanation of holiness is stated as "refraining from immorality." The term used is the problematic noun *porneia*. Though the object of debate, its present context indicates a general prohibition against sexual immorality, including its more restrictive sense of fornication or incest. Thus, the first infinitive introduces the first of two general areas of conduct which Paul discusses as relating to a life of holiness. By use of this term he initiates a discussion of pure behavior as it relates to sexual concerns and, as emerges from the following discussion, to mastery of one's body.

The second infinitive construction (v. 4) is here viewed as an epexegetical explanation of what the avoidance of *porneia* entails for a life of holiness. Paul's use of terminology, however, is problematic. Debate centers on his use of the noun *skeuos* which bears the meaning "thing or vessel" and, in a more figurative way, refers to "tool or instrument." It is in relation to the last mentioned that both the Church Fathers and modern scholars have been divided in their interpretation of the term's use in 4:4 as referring either to "wife" ("to take a wife for oneself"), to "body" ("to control one's body"), or to the "male sexual organ." Also, the verb *ktaomai* can mean "acquire, possess, control" (M-M 362-63). The literature discussing these three options is voluminous but the issues can be conveniently summarized and evaluated. The evidence adduced for the first option is both ambiguous (1 Pet 3:7 refers to men and women as "vessels") and questionable in linguistic terms (rabbinic usage might explain Pauline idiom, even the possible conflation as a result of bilingualism of two Jewish phrases, but not Gentile-Christian grasp of the text in question). Also, the view of women that would be ascribed to Paul is not.in keeping with what we know from 1 Corinthians 6-7 and, lastly, such an interpretation points logically not to an honorable marriage practice but to refraining from sexual relationships outside of marriage. Evidence for the second option (and the third in relation to it) is more favorable to Pauline usage (whether 2 Cor 4:7 where the body is described as an earthen vessel or Rom 9:21f. where humans are compared to vessels of clay), other NT (1 Pet 3:7), LXX (1 Sam 21:5), and early Christian (Barnabas 21:8) examples. I would conclude that the meaning of *skeuos* is that of sexual self-control, expressed especially as mastery of one's body, for such a reading agrees with attested Greek idiom.

Two final, related issues need to be raised: the reason for Paul's use of a term as vague as *skeuos* and explanation of the possessive pronoun *heautou* ("one's own"). Presumably, Paul employs a metaphorical term to underscore the human being's function as creature destined to reflect the holiness of the Creator. Indeed, the body is a vessel provided to the creature (*heautou*) to manifest the holiness which God has bestowed upon the believer. Such a conclusion is comparable to Paul's idea that the body is either a vessel destined for wrath or for mercy (Rom 9:22-23).

At the end of verse 4 and throughout verse 5 Paul dwells on the manner in which believers should master every aspect of their bodily existence. He employs two interesting phrases to convey this concept. The first, "in a holy and honorable way," characterizes a life of holiness as reflecting the gift of holiness (see discussion of *hagiasmos* in v. 3) and secondly as conferring dignity or honor on other human beings (see v. 4). Thus, believers, having been made holy by God (5:23) and established in a state of holiness, must now reflect that gift in the manner they deal with their own bodies and in the way they treat others. In the case of the body, the temple of the Spirit, they are to consider it a gift from God that is destined to show glory to the Creator (1 Cor 6:19-20) by means of a chaste life; see verse 8 below where God is described as giver of the Spirit. As regards honor, not only is it owed the neighbor, but believers are even to "outdo one another in showing honor" to those about them (Rom 12:10); see 4:9f. where Paul dwells on the theme of *philadelphia*. The believers' state of holiness demands a life that is characterized by personal, bodily purity and altruistic behavior; this is how believers are to live their lives: fully incarnated and respectful of self and others.

The second phrase of the contrast, "not in covetous passion," reflects on the life of holiness as being opposed not to sexual behavior or attitudes but to the human creature's rebellious tendency described as coveting divine lordship (see preceding Excursus). The believer's life is to reflect the divine glory and respect others but is also defined negatively as not coveting God's dominion or being under the sway of human motives. Further confirming this interpretation is Paul's qualification of the idiom by the statement "as do the pagans who do not know God." For him, human beings without Christ are those who do not know God or, as is said in Rom 1:21, 28, refuse to acknowledge God's existence and lordship and so act out of covetous or rebellious passion. In Rom 1:18f. Paul describes the consequences of pagan refusal to acknowledge the knowable God, while in 1 Thess 4:5 he simply assumes this ignorance. His advice to the Thessalonian community concerning what it should refrain from (4:3f.) has much in common first with traditional Jewish views of the immorality of the pagan world as owing to a turning away from God or idolatry (Wis 14:12-31; Rom 1:18-31; Philo, *Allegorical Laws* 3:8) and secondly that of Jewish believers as becoming slaves to impurity (T.Simeon 5:3; T.Reuben 4:6-7; in the former *porneia* is called "the mother of all evil acts since it separates from God and draws one near to Beliar"). Thus, by means of the phrase "pagans who do not know God" Paul makes even clearer the contrast begun in verse 4b, that there is to be a distinct difference between the way believers live their lives or "master the vessel provided them" and the way nonbelievers approach life. These verses set the boundaries between the converts and their former allegiances and beliefs; they have turned away from idols to serve God (1:9) in a new way, a way that will distinguish them further from their pagan neighbors.

A Second Injunction regarding Social Morality (v. 6). (1) Discussion of Issues. With the introduction of verse 6 we are led to another difficulty in determining the nature of the Pauline paraenesis: whether this verse continues a discussion of sexual morality or whether Paul introduces a new ethical issue regarding justice. While the former is the preference of many ("wronging one's brother in sexual matters"), an increased number of recent scholars seriously consider a second option ("defrauding one's brothers in their business"). Four basic kinds of evidence are considered in assessing these options. [1] A first issue concerns the grammar and style of verse 6. As noted earlier, while the single Greek sentence of verses 3-6 contains five infinitives, the first three of these are expressed positively but the last two are introduced by an article and a negative particle *(to mē).* These two features have been variously explained. The articular infinitive would signal a change of subject, whether commercial or sexual (in the case of the latter the shift would be from marital to extra-marital relations). Use of the negative particle would underscore Paul's love of negative-positive contrasts. Both features, however, are used to support the two options, either in arguing for a significant break between verses 3-5 and 6 or for a lesser shift involving the theme of sexual morality.

[2] Debate centers on the double infinitive used in verse 6: *hyperbainō* which denotes "go beyond or transgress" and *pleonekteō* whose meaning ranges from "taking advantage of," to "outwitting," and "defrauding." The former occurs only here in the NT and the latter only in Paul (five times, though its cognates appear in Paul a few times and elsewhere in the NT), so their particular nuances and semantic contexts are hard to determine with certainty. Those who champion the justice option insist that it is hard to imagine these verbs bearing anything but a commercial sense and certainly not a sexual connotation. While the first infinitive does not demand a commercial sense (but rather a general nuance of "offending or sinning against"), the second is usually employed by Paul in the context of "cheating, greed, extortion" (1 Thess 2:5; 1 Cor 5:10-11; 6:11; 2 Cor 9:5; Rom 1:29) and "taking advantage" in relation to the collection (2 Cor 12:17-18). However, Paul also uses it in the general sense of "outwitting or taking advantage of" (2 Cor 2:11; 7:2). To explain how a believer might "wrong or defraud" another believer, scholars either insist that the issue concerns violation of another's marital rights or, relying on a statement by Musonius Rufus (Fragment 12), point out more concretely that an adulterer wrongs the husband of a corrupted woman.

[3] Another area of discussion is the meaning of the phrase *en tọ pragmati*, whose noun has a wide, generic range of meaning which depends greatly on literary context. Though the phrase means literally "in the matter (at hand)," it could bear the interpretation of "affair" (euphemism for sexual matters), of "law suit" (relying on Paul's use of the term in 1 Cor 6:1), or business. Defenders of the sexual option usually choose the simplest meaning for the phrase ("in this matter") and insist that the matter at hand is sexual morality. Many assert that *pragma* means "business" only in the plural, though it would be more correct to say that when the term has a commercial sense it usually appears in the plural. Thus, it should be noted that LSJ (1457) lists a third major grouping of uses of the noun in the plural. Under this category are presented five subheadings, two of which are "fortunes, cause, circumstances" and "business, esp. law business"; four of these also list less frequent examples of these meanings in the singular. Interestingly, several of these uses in the singular refer to "profession," "activity or conduct," or dying as "a better lot" (Plato, *Hippias Major* 286e, *Crito* 53d, *Apology* 42a). Also significant is the judgment of BAGD (697.2) that *pragma* in 1 Thess 4:6 is classified under the category "that which is to be done, *undertaking, occupation, task*," along with other similar uses of the singular: Eccl 3:1; 1 Sam 11:3; and especially Rom 16:2. I will return below to this third issue.

[4] In the final analysis, the decision to favor the sexual over the justice option seems to depend on scholarly interpretation of the overall unit. Each of its ambiguous items is perceived as bearing sexual nuances, from *porneia* as "sexual" immorality, to the choice of *skeuos* as meaning "wife," to the viewing of *epithymia* as "lustful" passion, and of the interpretation of *akatharsia* in verse 7 as "sexual" immorality. In the context of such exegesis, the conclusion is often drawn that the precept about defrauding a brother most likely concerns marriage.

(2) Overall Conclusion. From the above analysis I am led to see the thrust of Paul's paraenesis in 4:3-7 not as sexual morality but as general advice concerning "holiness" (3a) which is further specified as two areas of human activity. The first is characterized by the term *porneia* which is itself explicated not as the dishonoring of one's own and the bodies of others (v. 4; also Rom 1:24, 26-27) but as the pure and honorable mastery and use of one's God-given humanity. The field of moral praxis is situated precisely in the body, that incarnated reality, which was given by God as a vessel destined for holiness. It is a life that is to be lived in a state of holiness, one that treats others with honor rather than a life that is motivated by service of creature (Rom 1:25) or led by covetous passion in the manner of rebellious creatures that do not recognize their Creator.

The second area of activity which defines a life of holiness is that described by the double infinitive of verse 6 and the phrase translated "in their activity." Paul employs a substantivized infinitive with a negative particle *(to mē)* to underscore the verb's resumptive function as it alludes back to *hagiasmos* of verse 3a and further explicates another characteristic of what a pure life must be. He uses first a general verb meaning "offense against" a neighbor and then epexegetically defines that activity with a more precise infinitive. The latter suggests an offense against justice, namely, stealing from the activity or livelihood of others. *Pragma* then is interpreted as "activity, profession, or circumstances" by or under which another lives. Such a conclusion is further supported by what follows in verse 6 (see discussion of *ekdikos* as "executor of justice"), by a closer analysis of Rom 1:18f., and by the focus of 1 Thess 4:9-12 on love and work.

Paul's description of Gentiles without Christ (Rom 1:18f.) or, in Thessalonian terms, of "the pagans who do not know God," is the antitype of the life of holiness expected of believers in the new age. As a result of their refusal to honor and give thanks to God, Gentiles, in four successive passages, are associated with the following characteristics; they are people [1] with darkened minds that turn to idolatry (choice of mortal creatures in place of the immortal God, 21-23), [2] with covetous or rebellious hearts that dishonor their bodies (service of creature rather than Creator, 24-25), [3] with dishonoring passions that practice all types of sexual immorality (26-27), and [4] with debased minds that are given to every type of evil, especially those that dishonor fellow creatures (28-31). Thus, we see here the themes Paul develops in his Thessalonian paraenesis. Pagans, those who do not acknowledge or know God, are those who practice all types of immorality by dishonoring their own and the bodies of others in their daily excesses and who turn against their fellow creatures in every type of deception and fraud. The believer is called to a different life, one of holiness and honor and one characterized by love of neighbor, a topic to which Paul returns in verses 9-10.

The four issues described earlier have a direct bearing on our interpretation of verse 6a. The two primary infinitive constructions, the first expressed in the positive but employing a negative prohibition ("to refrain from") and the second expressed resumptively and negatively by *to mē*, indicate not a change of subject but the two major areas of moral activity. Further, the double infinitives of verse 6a focus first on "offense against" the neighbor and secondly, epexegetically, on the characteristic areas of social justice. Also, the term *pragma* is interpreted in a manner which is basic to its etymology ("praxis") and frequent usage ("livelihood, profession, or commercial activity"). Finally, the overall interpretation of verses 3-7 is that of holiness in daily activity, including sexual and social morality as ethical manifestation of that state of holiness.

God's Judgment as Motive for Purity of Action. An issue that is raised in interpreting verse 6b is the identity of the judge, for Paul simply states "the Lord is a judge or executor of justice" *(ekdikos kyrios).* Scholars traditionally opt for a Christological interpretation, citing two basic reasons for their decision: *kyrios* normally refers to Christ in Pauline usage and the use of *theos* in the following verse would confirm such a reading. Some recent scholars, however, argue for a theological reading, relying primarily on the statement's OT and intertestamental background and the paraenetic text's theological focus. Indeed, the theme of God as judge, employing cognates of *ekdikos,* is frequent in the LXX, whether in the Torah (Exod 7:4; 12:12; Deut 32:35), the prophets (Amos 3:2, 14; Jer 11:20), or the Psalms (17:47; 93:1 offers a close linguistic parallel: "the Lord is a God of justice") as well as in the Testaments of the Twelve Patriarchs (T.Reuben 6:6; T.Gad 6:7; T.Joseph 20:1; T.Benjamin 10:8-10). Judgment certainly is God's domain in Jewish literature where God is called "an avenger or judge of the wicked" (Wis 12:12, as lone example, employs *ekdikos*). Further, citing 1 Thess 1:10, the latter insist that Jesus is savior or deliverer while God as lord remains the judge of Jewish tradition. Finally, it is pointed out that the paraenetic passage begins by dwelling on God's will for the believer (v. 3), contrasts the believer with pagans who do not know God (5), and insists that believers are called (7) and are thus commanded by God the giver of the Spirit (8).

The issue, however, is more complex since the term *ekdikos* occurs only twice in the NT, both in Paul (4:6 and Rom 13:4), since the other pertinent use of a cognate, paraphrasing Deut 32:35, refers to God as judge, and since Paul, in effect, refers both to God and to Christ as judge. In the first case *ekdikos* is used ambiguously of Lord in 1 Thess 4:6 and of a government authority in Rom 13:4. In the second case judgment seems, in Jewish terms, to be restricted to God (Rom 12:19). In the third case, the inconsistency of Pauline usage in later letters gives reason for pause. While in Rom 14:10 Paul speaks of believers "standing before the judgment seat of God" to whom one will be accountable, he also, in the only other place where he employs the term *bēma,* states "all of us must appear before the judgment seat of Christ so that each may receive recompense for what has been done in the body" (2 Cor 5:10). Thus, both God and Christ are said to exercise the role of end-time judge. Two other passages, among others, point to a better understanding of Paul's thought on this matter. In 1 Cor 4:4-5 Paul states: "it is the Lord who judges me. Therefore do not pronounce judgment before the time, before the Lord comes." While "Lord" might be ambiguous, the description of the Lord as "coming" clearly identifies the figure as the returning Christ. The verse, however, ends: "then each one will receive commendation from God." In this case the judgment is an activity of the returning Christ and the giving of reward, the role of God. In Rom 2:16, however, Paul is more clear in expressing himself, when he speaks of Gentiles being judged "on the day when God will judge the human secrets, which according to my gospel, will take place through Christ Jesus" (author's translation). Strictly speaking, judgment is the role of God and Jesus is God's agent in this activity.

At this point we might ask about Paul's meaning in 1 Thess 4:6. Scholars who see a reference to God's role as judge in verse 6 are probably correct since Paul is employing OT language and sees God the Father as ultimate judge (1:10—source of wrath) and the one to whom humanity and the rest of creation must turn in repentance, in honor and thanksgiving, and in subjection (1:9; Rom 1:21; 1 Cor 15:28). Paul, the Jewish-Christian missionary, is using traditional language to express the fundamental role of God as ultimate judge. Such a conclusion is further confirmed by Paul's insistence that it is God who chooses, calls, judges missionaries, and gives the Spirit (1:4; 2:4, 12; 4:8). That Paul's Gentile readers might have heard the statement in the manner most modern readers do is likely, a fact which might be supported by Paul's later non-reluctance (see 1 Cor 4:4-5; 2 Cor 5:10; Rom 13:4) to associate Christ in the activity of judgment itself, since for Paul Christ's judgment is God's judgment. We should see here a development in Paul's thought regarding judgment; see comments on 1:8 and 5:2 for other instances of double readings of the term *kyrios*, i.e., Pauline Jewish usage and Gentile reader's interpretation.

Of what then is God a judge? The expression *peri pantōn toutōn* ("in all these things") presumably refers immediately to the matter of defrauding fellow believers in verse 6a and to the immoral use of the body in verses 3-5. In Greek romance literature and in the prophets, particularly Hosea, God is said to be an "avenging judge" in sexual matters, though the latter is really concerned with adultery as an image for idolatry. More generally, God is said to be judge in all matters of human wickedness, namely, pride, injustice, affliction of God's people, murder (Ps 93:1-7). Also in the intertestamental literature cited earlier God is said to be an avenging judge for all manner of sexual impurity, lack of piety, injustice, and lack of love toward neighbor (T.Gad 6:1-9).

To emphasize the importance of the paraenesis and the source of its motivation Paul insists that the community was told of this during the foundation visit. Indeed, when the missionaries were at Thessalonica the paraenesis and especially the warning of eschatological judgment as motivation formed part of their message to the new converts. Thus, the teleological structure of ethical motivation permeates the Thessalonian correspondence (see 2:19-20; 1:10; 2:12) and one presumes it was a major and clearly enunciated factor in the formation of the community from the beginning. So in 4:6, Paul reminds his readers that they have been taught already about God's aversion for impurity, a subject to which he returns in verse 7. Not only does God examine and approve the hearts of missionaries (2:4) but that same Lord, on the one hand, as God of peace, is the one who makes believers holy and keeps them blameless for the Lord Jesus' coming (5:23) and on the other, as executor of justice, is the one who judges all human secrets and actions.

Further Paraenetic Motivation. Paul concludes his paraenetic discussion with an intriguing verse which offers added motivation to his readers (4:8). The traditional interpretation of this text supplies an object for the first occurrence of the verb *atheteō* and renders the text: "whoever rejects (this or these instructions) rejects not a human being but God." Implied in such an interpretation is that some within the community are rejecting the apostolic paraenesis and are being severely reprimanded. Regardless, the tone of the passage is thereby heightened and the whole suggests a direct challenge to apostolic authority.

In defense of the above position scholars point to the similarity of Paul's text to a saying of the Jesus tradition. This logion concerning the reception or rejection of Jesus' disciples, as implying both the rejection or reception of Jesus and in turn that of God, appears in various forms in the gospel tradition (Mark 9:37 par.; John 12:44f.). Since the Pauline text is expressed negatively, its closest parallel is the second half of the Lukan version, especially since it employs the same verb: "whoever rejects you rejects me, and whoever rejects me rejects the one who sent me" (10:16). The probability of Pauline use of some form of the Jesus or the OT *shaliah* ("emissary") tradition is postulated as the basis for interpreting 1 Thess 4:8 and the paraenesis as underscoring the authority of this ethical advice as deriving from God's human ambassadors. The rejection then of the advice becomes the rejection of God, the one who sends the ambassador. While the rejection of human agent and divine sender is implied later in the verse, one suspects that much of the *shaliah* theme is imported from the Lukan text, even to the extent of recalling the first half of the logion: "whoever listens to you listens to me." More importantly, in the Lukan version, while the word *atheteō* is employed twice (as participle and as present, finite verb), its usage in both cases is transitive and related each to a personal object. In the Lukan text rejection of the one sent implies the refusal of the sender, but, in a less than parallel reading of 1 Thess 4:8, it is disregard or rejection of the ambassador's teaching which suggests the rejection of ambassador and sender.

A more careful analysis then is needed. *Atheteō* appears five times in Paul, four of which are transitive uses. While the three non-Thessalonian occurrences of the verb make reference to things (1 Cor 1:19; Gal 2:21;

3:15), in its second occurrence in 1 Thess 4:8 it is employed with a double object of the person. The participle of verse 8, however, represents an absolute, intransitive use of the term. These grammatical uses also represent a semantic range, well attested in the LXX. The transitive use of the verb as related to objects of the thing offers the meaning "nullify or set aside" some agreement (true of the three non-Thessalonian occurrences; see also Isa 24:16; Pss 32:10; 88:34). When the verb is used with an object of the person or intransitively in relation to a person, it means "to act unfaithfully toward," "to reject," or, in more legal terms, "to break faith with" that person or "rebel against" (Isa 1:2; Jer 5:11; Ps 14:4). Lastly, the verb's absolute use suggests the meaning "to commit an offense or act wickedly" (Isa 21:2; 48:8; Jer 12:1; Jdt 14:1; see *TDNT* 8:158-59; BAGD 21; LSJ 31).

In light of the above data concerning the LXX usage of *atheteō*, an OT parallel casts considerable light on the Pauline text: "woe to those that act wickedly, they are the ones who violate the law *(ouai tois athetousin, hoi athetountes ton nomon)*" (Isa 24:16). The hermeneutical key of this LXX text as well as of 1 Thess 4:8 lies in the proper reading of the verb first as absolute statement regarding sinful activity (the LXX passage refers back to the ungodly, that of Paul to those who indulge in impurity) and the second either as relating to an object of the thing or of the person (the Law in one case and human/divine agent in the other).

In the case of 1 Thess 4:8 *ho athetōn* should not be supplied an object but be treated as an absolute, intransitive use of the verb and be translated "anyone who acts wickedly." In effect 4:3b-6 is about sinful activity as incompatible with the believer's state of holiness. Sinful action has its consequences, a point which is described in the rest of the verse. Also, the second use of *atheteō* represents a transitive use with a double object of the person and could be translated in a mild way as "disregard," more severely as "reject" or in a legal fashion as "break faith with." The reason for opting for the legal sense is the text's context, namely, the theme of election immediately preceding in verse 7.

What then are the hermeneutical ramifications? Paul's meaning is not that his paraenesis has a divine origin as new law or that he is God's representative whose task is the explanation of God's will concerning behavior but that impurity in the lives of the converts implies a break in faith not with the fellowship developed between the missionaries and their audience but with the God who called, chose, and empowers them to live lives of purity by the giving of the Spirit. The focus of 4:8 is not on the divine authority of the apostolic paraenesis but on the notion of sinful activity as being incompatible with the call to holiness.

A Final Note on God as Giver of the Spirit. By means of a contrastive construction, Paul insists that the implied rupturing of relations (v. 8a) will not be with those who did the preaching or treated the audience as a father, or nurse their own children but with the one who gives the Spirit. The Pauline text presents two anomalies. The first concerns his use here of the present tense (see Notes on textual problem) to describe the giving of the Spirit (see 1 Cor 12:7) whereas he usually speaks of this as a past event (see Gal 3:2 for the reception and 4:6 for the sending of the Spirit). The best explanation for this is Paul's aim here, as in 2:4 and 12, to focus not on the giving of the Spirit at conversion or baptism but on God as the giver. Paul insists that immoral behavior brings about a rupture with God precisely as giver of the Spirit.

A second anomaly needing attention is Paul's formulation of the pneumatological title. The generic expression "the Holy Spirit" is used 11 times by Paul, eight of which represent the standard formation *pneuma hagion* (1 Thess 1:5, 6), two the variant *to hagion pneuma*, and once the anomalous *to pneuma autou to hagion* of 4:8. The last mentioned resembles the classical construction of arthrous noun followed by arthrous adjective, *to pneuma to hagion*, used occasionally in Mark and Luke and found also in the LXX. However, two unusual features of the Pauline expression (use of the possessive pronoun and an unusual *eis hymas* in place of the usual dative of the indirect object as in Rom 5:5; 1 Cor 1:27) lead us to the OT for clarification.

(1) The title "Holy Spirit" occurs in the LXX in various formulations as it does in the NT, some of which bear a resemblance to the Pauline form using the possessive pronoun, whether *to hagion sou pneuma* (Wis 9:17), *to pneuma to hagion sou/autou* (Isa 63:10/Ps 50:11), or *to pneuma sou to hagion* (Ps 142 in MSS B S A). The last mentioned would provide the requisite word order for the Pauline construction and attest to such usage in the early Church's Greek Bible. (2) While most passages in the LXX which speak of "having" or "giving" the Spirit employ *en* with the dative to introduce the recipient, two identical texts from Ezekiel (37:6, 14) offer the curious combination and order of "giving the Spirit," possessive pronoun, and the preposition *eis* to introduce the recipients. Thus, it is probably correct to see 1 Thess 4:8b as a paraphrase of Ezek 37:6, 14 and to seek there the background of Paul's intended meaning, particularly concerning the role the Spirit is to play since, following the archaic text of Ezekiel, the Spirit is not simply given but placed within the believer.

Indeed Ezekiel 37 sheds light on many themes of Paul's second missive. According to Ezek 37:6, 14, those who receive the Spirit shall live (see 1 Thess 4:13; 5:10) and know God as Lord (4:5: "pagans do not know God"; note also that believers "are taught by God"—4:9). In verse 14 God is made to add: "I have spoken and will do this" (5:4: "the one who calls you is faithful and he will do this"). Later Ezekiel (v. 23) speaks

of those who have been given the Spirit as avoiding defilement with idols
and transgressions, of being cleansed, delivered, and belonging to God,
themes which Paul discusses in 1:9-10 (turning from idols, serving God,
being delivered by the Son—use of the rare verb *rhyomai*) and in 4:3-8
(immorality and impurity). Both Ezek 37:24 and Paul suggest that the
reception of the Spirit relates to behavior; for the former it must be according to God's ordinances and its aim is entry into the holy land, for
the latter it is a walk that is pleasing to God and that promises entrance
in God's kingdom and glory (2:12). Finally, as Ezekiel (37:26-28) points
out, the giving of the Spirit is for the establishment of a "covenant of
peace," whereby God gains a people and "sanctifies *(hagiazō)* them" via
a holy sanctuary. Paul insists that God is the God of peace, sanctifies
those who believe, establishes a breakable bond with them, preserves
them for Jesus' return and calls them to a life of holiness (5:23; 4:3f.).

Paul the Jewish Christian inherited much of his thought, not the least
regarding the Spirit, from such classic texts and from apocalyptic Judaism and the early Church. Already in this early correspondence we see
him referring often and in a variety of ways to the Spirit. In 1:5 one encounters the Jewish notion of the Spirit as signifying God's power as divine or extraordinary acts which accompanied the missionary preaching
and formation of communities, probably glossolalia, healings or other
miraculous events as listed in 1 Corinthians 12 and 14 (*TDNT* 6:423). For
Paul as for apocalyptic Judaism these signs of the Spirit's presence were
an indication that the new age was at hand. In 1:6, however, one must
probably perceive, in the "joy inspired by the Holy Spirit," a more
evolved, Hellenistic notion of the Spirit's role. No longer is the Spirit and
its activity primarily a sign of the approaching end-time but the Spirit
is giver of joy, that is, one of the "fruits of the Spirit" (Gal 5:22). This
gift is received and discerned only by those who have received the Spirit
(1 Cor 2:10-14). Indeed, the perseverance of the converts is characterized
as joy, in imitation of the apostles and the Lord, for the new existence
of the believer is able to overcome the difficulties of the world and express itself in a paradoxical happiness that anticipates the kingdom as
"righteousness, peace, and joy in the Holy Spirit" (Rom 14:17). Indeed,
the Spirit in 1:6 manifests joy as the divine sign of the community's commitment and behavior, a sign that the new age has begun in the lives
of the believers of Thessalonica as they live lives of holiness and mission.

In 4:8 Paul is more explicit yet as he focuses on the giving of the Spirit
as God's special prerogative. It is God's gift par excellence, a gift which
empowers the believer to live a pure, sanctifying life, and whose life in
turn becomes the barometer of commitment to the God who called to
a life of purity. Finally, Paul will return in 5:19 to the theme of the Spirit
(also see v. 9 below) as he advises his converts to live fully under the

spell of the Spirit whose gifts are directed to a holy life and to the good of the community in view of the Lord's return.

For Reference and Further Study

Baumert, N. "Brautwerbung—das einheitliche Thema von 1 Thess 4, 3-8." *TC*, 316-39.

Carras, G. P. "Jewish Ethics and Gentile Converts: Remarks on 1 Thes 4, 3-8." *TC*, 306-15.

Collins, R. F. " 'This is the will of God: your sanctification.' (1 Thess 4:3)." *SFLT*, 299-325.

_____. "The Unity of Paul's Paraenesis in 1 Thess 4, 3-8: 1 Cor 7, 1-9, a Significant Parallel." *SFLT*, 326-35.

Fee, G. D. "On Text and Commentary on 1 and 2 Thessalonians." *SBLSP* (1992), 165-83.

Jensen, J. "Does *Porneia* Mean Fornication? A Critique of Bruce Malina." *NovT* 20 (1978) 161-84.

Jewett, R. *Paul's Anthropological Terms: A Study of Their Use in Conflict Settings.* Leiden: Brill, 1971.

Laub, F. *Eschatologische Verkündigung und Lebensgestaltung nach Paulus: Eine Untersuchung zum Wirken des Apostels beim Aufbau der Gemeinde in Thessalonike.* Regensburg: Pustet, 1973.

Malherbe, A. J. "Exhortation in First Thessalonians." *NovT* 25 (1983) 238-56.

McGehee, M. "A Rejoinder to Two Recent Studies Dealing with 1 Thess 4:4." *CBQ* 51 (1989) 82-89.

Whitton, J. A. "A Neglected Meaning for *SKEUOS* in 1 Thessalonians 4,4." *NTS* 28 (1982) 142-43.

Yarbrough, O. L. *"Not Like the Gentiles": Marriage Rules in the Letters of Paul.* Atlanta: Scholars, 1985.

12. *On Love of Others* (4:9-12)

9. Now concerning love of brother and sister, you do not need us to write you; certainly, you are yourselves taught by God to love one another; 10. and besides, you are doing this for all the brothers and sisters throughout Macedonia. But we exhort you, brothers and sisters, to abound even more, 11. whether in aspiring to live quietly and attend to your affairs, or in working with your hands, just as we directed you, 12. so that you may conduct yourselves properly in the company of outsiders and may be lacking in nothing.

NOTES

9. *Now concerning love of brother and sister:* Paul turns his attention to specific issues raised by the community. Presumably by letter, indicated by *peri de tēs . . .* ("now concerning . . ."; see discussion below), he is asked to clarify a question members of the community have concerning the extent of love as it applies to fellow believers. He employs as introduction what seems to be the key term for the community's discussion, *philadelphia.* The word is rare in pre-Christian literature and there always refers to the love of one's siblings, e.g., in Josephus, *JA* 2:161 where Joseph tests his brothers' love for their brother Benjamin or in 4 Macc 13:23 which speaks of the mutual affection of the seven brothers. Presumably under the influence of early Christian usage of *adelphos* as meaning "fellow believer" (see 2:17), the term came to be used for mutual affection within the Christian community (Rom 12:10; Heb 13:1; 1 Pet 1:22; 2 Pet 1:7).

   you do not need us to write you: The MS evidence is divided regarding the reading of this text, though scholars agree with recent textual critics (*TCGNT*, 632) in following the more unusual reading "you do not need" (*echete*—S* A D^c K L *pc*) rather than the more regularized "we do/did not need" (*echomen/ eichomen*—S² D* F G *pc*/B I). Some commentators have taken this clause to mean that no further instruction is needed, but it seems more likely that here and in 5:1 Paul is employing a traditional figure of speech called a *paralipsis,* whereby an "orator pretends to pass over something which he in fact mentions" (BDF 495).

   certainly, you are yourselves taught by God to love one another: The reason Paul and cowriters need not write about *philadelphia* is explained by two *gar* clauses, usually translated as "for . . . and for" but here as "certainly and besides" (see discussion of v. 10 below). The text, however, presents several challenges. (1) Why does Paul employ the intensive construction "you yourselves"? While some have tried to envision some type of opposition ("you" as opposed to someone), we should see Paul as insisting that the community is as much a recipient of divine teaching on this score as are the missionaries. (2) The background and meaning of the term *theodidaktoi* ("taught by God") is debated and rendered more complex by Paul's use of the present tense. Since the issue is discussed below, it suffices to say that Paul's meaning is that the community, in its dealings with others, is guided by God's Spirit, whose first fruit is love (Gal 5:22). (3) The expression "to love one another," while couched in the familiar Pauline *eis* with articular infinitive to express purpose (see 3:10), is to be read in a Pauline rather than a Johannine sense (see below).

10. *and besides, you are doing this for all the brothers and sisters throughout Macedonia.* Verses 9b and 10a relate to one another much as 3:3b and 4a do (see above), for the double use of postpositive *gar* indicates successive arguments for a single assertion and the introduction of the second *gar* by the coordinating conjunction *kai* stresses the supplementary function of the second argument. The assertion concerns the community's knowledge about *philadelphia* (there is no need to write about it), while the first argument involves the evi-

dent statement that the Thessalonians like other Christians are taught to love by God's Spirit (*gar* is translated "certainly") and the second is drawn from the community's experience ("and besides"); see also Phil 2:26-27. Also, "you are doing this for . . ." is a literal rendering of the Greek to allow for Paul's intentional vagueness, for the term "this" points backward and forward to his discussion of love as an intra- and extra-community concern. Lastly, the seemingly exaggerated phrase "for all [believers] throughout Macedonia" refers as does 1:7-8 to the community's missionary endeavor on the Greek mainland.

But we exhort you, brothers and sisters, to abound even more: One can hardly fail to note the break which occurs at this point by the introduction of a *parakaleō* formula and the adversive conjunction *de*. While the latter marks a shift in Paul's approach to the issue of love, the former, with its traditional direct address and command expressed in an infinitive construction (see 4:1 for discussion of the formula), indicates his rhetorical sensitivity as he exhorts but does not command what follows. His direct approach is mollified by use of diplomatic language. Paul's exhortation concerns greater effort, or that the community "abound even more" in its activity. This expression is clarified by its use in the earlier missive to the community (3:12) and points in a similar manner to the theme of love as it extends to those in and those outside the community.

11. *whether in aspiring to live quietly and attend to your affairs:* Paul begins his concrete advice with a series of infinitives. The first of these, *philotimeomai*, as is the case for its two other NT occurrences (Rom 15:20; 2 Cor 5:9), is best explained as a verb that takes an infinitive complement (BDF 392.1) and therefore has the meaning of "aspire or have as one's ambition." This term introduces a double infinitive complement, whose first verb, *hēsychazō* and cognates have a range of meaning from "being silent, at rest, or living a quiet life" (BAGD 349). While in the Lukan writings the term represents the first two meanings, its only Pauline usage seems to require the third sense: "living quietly" (also 1 Tim 2:2; see discussion of 2 Thess 3:12). The second infinitive complement is stated as "attending to your affairs" (*prassō ta idia*) and presumably corresponds to the classic idiom *ta hautou prassō* ("to mind one's own affairs"—see Plato, *Republic* 6.496D and 4.433A), which later was combined with *ta idia*, meaning "one's own affairs" (BAGD 370.2b). The Pauline usage and meaning of each admonition are discussed below.

    or in working with your hands: This passage offers several challenges. (1) Some important MSS (S* A Dᶜ *pc*) add *idiais* ("own") before the noun, but such an addition seems unnecessary and explainable in terms of the occurrence of the term in the previous phrase (see 1 Cor 4:12 for a similar idiom and Eph 4:28 for an identical problem). (2) Formerly scholars explained Paul's positive advice and attitude toward work as owing to Jewish high esteem for manual labor and work generally (*TDNT* 2:249), an attitude opposed to what was perceived as Greco-Roman disdain for the trades. Recent scholarship shows, however, that, not only are the trades permitted the higher classes in extreme circumstances but are highly valued and recommended by moral philosophers to the masses in Roman cities (Dio, *Oration* 7:103-27). (3) The expression "working with one's hands," relates to the biblical idiom "work of one's hands" and refers not to manual labor but to trades deemed proper by outsiders (see below).

just as we directed you: The Greek text of 10b-12 and its translation suggest that verse 11 is a convenient list reiterating the boundaries of Christian life as formerly taught by the missionaries. By means of the term *kathōs* ("just as") Paul refers back to the apostolic preaching and its content (including issues of behavior) and by the use of the verb *parangellō* (use of cognate at 4:2) stresses the instruction's directive and educative rather than authoritative nature.

12. *so that you may conduct yourselves properly in the company of outsiders:* Paul concludes the pericope with a double purpose clause introduced by the conjunction *hina* ("so that"). The first of these speaks literally of "walking with decorum or elegance." The verb *peripateō* appears at the end of the first missive (see 4:1) and earlier in this document prior to the paraenetic section of the letter (2:12). Again, the term is used as in Jewish tradition to describe proper behavior, behavior in this case which is judged as to its suitability not before God but vis-à-vis outsiders (see also 1 Cor 5:12f.). The term *euschēmonōs* is frequently used by Paul to designate the suitability of conduct (Rom 1:27; 13:13; 1 Cor 7:36). This is its usual meaning in Greek literature (see also Prov 11:25), where it means "to behave with decorum" or "elegance" or even to display "an outward show of goodness" (LSJ 734). Interestingly Dio Chrysostom (*Oration* 7.110-25), in discussing various forms of work, insists on these not being "improper" or "unseemly" *(aschēmōn)*. Paul too appeals to the theme of public decorum as a way to motivate and judge not only work but the whole Christian life and behavior.

and may be lacking in nothing: This second purpose clause presents grammatical ambiguity since the initial word of the construction *(mēdenos)* can be neuter or personal in form and therefore translated "may be lacking in nothing" or "dependent on no one." While both are defended, the former is preferable in the present context and supports our interpretation of the letter's social and paraenetic setting (see below).

INTERPRETATION

Following the paraenetic section on holiness, Paul introduces a series of topics which are of concern to the community of Thessalonica. The first of these, on the topic of mutual love, offers interesting rhetorical and thematic insights into Paul's early activity and thought.

Epistolary Character and Function of 4:9-12. Scholars readily note the threefold structural indicator of 4:9, 13; and 5:1: "(now) concerning the

. . .," which introduces successive topics of discussion. While some insist instead on the relation of verses 9-12 to 3-8 (see discussion of 4:3-8), thereby minimizing the break between verses 8 and 9 and the importance of the *parakaleō* formula of 10b, it is generally recognized that the threefold formula introduces distinct subjects, first "love of brother and sister" (4:9-12), then "the faithful departed and the parousia" (4:13-18), and finally "being ready for the Lord's return" (5:1-11). On the basis of these as well as other epistolary features and the content of 1 Thessalonians, it has been suggested that Paul, in chapters 4-5, is responding either to an oral report or to a community letter brought back by Timothy on the occasion of his report to Paul regarding his trip (3:6).

Also, it is suggested that various "epistolographic conventions" used by Paul, particularly in 2:17-3:10, support epistolary communication from the community, whether the involuntary separation, loneliness, and joy and prayer for renewed contact or the longing for and the mutual remembrance of the parties. Such an argument is predicated on the unity of 1 Thessalonians and on the entire document being Paul's response to Timothy's report. Interestingly, these observations apply almost entirely to what we call the first missive. These themes play a significant part in Paul's strategy for the first letter (see earlier discussion). He recently left Thessalonica and misses his beloved converts; the feeling is mutual, as Timothy testifies (3:6). Thus, we conclude that the earlier missive is a brief letter written to absent friends.

The issue about whether 4:9f. represents answers to questions must be seen in a different setting. The issues raised in chapters 4-5 are those of a maturing community, at a later stage in its development. It is in this context that the formula *peri tou/tōn* takes on significance, especially in its relation to 1 Corinthians and its epistolary structure. As in 1 Corinthians 1-6 one finds Paul's reactions to oral reports brought by letter carrier and in 7-16, specific responses to written inquiries, so one should see 1 Thess 2:1-12 and 4:3-8 as addressing oral reports sent to Paul and the remainder as responding to written questions.

As one turns specifically to 4:9-12, one is led to inquire about Paul's purpose in treating the topic of mutual love at this point and in dispensing the advice of verses 11-12. If one disregards the possibility that he is responding to a question, then one might assume that verses 9f. constitute a positive statement, as a balance to the preceding negative treatment of holiness, concerning God's will. If, however, one grants that Paul is responding to an oral or written question, one might wish to inquire about the question behind 4:9-12. Is the question about the extent or manner of "love of brother and sister" or is Paul, in his use of *theodidaktoi* ("taught by God"), contrasting Christian love with Epicurean claims about "self-taught" concepts of friendship? Each of these claims presents problems, whether ignoring the clear break between verses 8 and 9, failing to explain the relationship between verses 9-10a and 10b-12 and the function of "we exhort" in verse 10b, or explaining the relationship of "taught by God" to the rest of the pericope. One may be right in pointing to the extensive use by Paul of traditional philosophical advice in formulating verses 11-12, but use and contrast of these *topoi* with the more focused "love of brother and sister," while having a possible bearing on popular notions of friendship, need to be explained in relation to the entire pericope.

There is a basic relationship between verses 9-10a and 10b-12 and yet an obvious difference. Also, the exhortation of 10b provides the necessary clue to the interpretation of the pericope. The movement of thought from verse 9 is love of fellow Thessalonian Christians and, in verse 10, of Christians throughout Macedonia. At this point one encounters the *parakaleō* formula with contrastive *de*, "but we exhort you," to urge more not only in terms of intensity but also in terms of extent. "Love of brother and sister" *(philadelphia)* is of prime concern for a fellowship that must foster inner unity and outer definition, but it also involves social behavior which of necessity concerns relations with outsiders. The question then will have been about *philadelphia* and its inner dynamic as a unifying force, while Paul's answer, after a calculated statement of praise for the community's devotion to one another, focuses on love's outer dynamic as it influences life, concerns, work, and the social milieu in which these are engaged.

Thessalonian Question Regarding Love of Brother and Sister. The question represented a discussion or conflict regarding the extent and manner of Christian love and Paul is asked to clarify this issue. Already in the thanksgiving (1:3 and 7-8), he signals his approval of the outward dynamic of the community's concern for believers beyond Thessalonica and for unbelievers as well. Furthermore, Paul's use of the limiting term *philadelphia*, as love of fellow Christians (see Notes), indicates one aspect of the discussion and borrows from its terminology. Thus, Paul quotes from the community's question, "now concerning *philadelphia*," and begins his discussion at that point. He knows that use of this expression, along with other family terminology, underscores the separation from familial and socioreligious bonds and reinforces the inner unity of the new spiritual community, but he is also cognizant of the fact that this term also contributes to the inner rather than the outer focus of the members' concerns and lives. Both the question and the problem are characterized by the term "love of brother and sister," as a limiting concept. His response intends to show that the dynamics of love, while particularly concerned with mutual affection among believers, generate outward concern beyond one's community in geographical as well as socioreligious terms. *Philadelphia*, as a community endeavor, is praised and encouraged, but as a concept and incarnated reality, is redefined and refocused.

Initial Pauline Response: 4:9-10a. (1) Rhetorical Approach. Paul begins his response by employing a traditional figure of speech (see Notes) to draw added attention to the first part of his discussion. Thus, by emphasizing its known character ("you do not need us to write you"), he is able to lend special attention to *philadelphia*, by reflection on the source of the community's knowledge and the genuineness of its practice, and to focus instead, in verses 10b-12, on what is less well understood despite prior instruction. Paul, in using this and other rhetorical devices, intends to stress continuity with prior instruction and prepare the readers for a broader application of what they know and are practicing.

(2) Love of One Another. In a first *gar* clause Paul explains why he need not write to the community about the matter. He insists that they are already being taught by God (see Note below on *theodidaktoi*) "to love one another." The expression which Paul employs seems, at first blush, to be a common Christian expression which he would readily use. In effect the expression "to love one another" or have "love for one another" is rare in Paul and in the NT generally, being relatively frequent only in Johannine tradition (John 13:34f.; 1 John 3:11f.). Where Paul uses this expression either it applies also to those beyond the community (Rom 13:8; even 12:10: "be devoted to one another as though to loving siblings"—own translation) or is so qualified as to include other neighbors (1 Thess 3:12: "abundance in your love for one another and for all"; 4:9 and its sequel in verses 11-12). In contrast to the Johannine tradition, Paul is concerned that love not have an exclusively inward direction, despite his great interest in community dynamics and boundaries. In the present case he defines love as mutual love, love for members of the fellowship, a concept which agrees with the spirit of Jewish teaching where the neighbor is a fellow Jew and with that inherited by early Christianity. Verse 9 begins with an inward concept of love, because that is the issue raised by the community's missive, and rhetorically ends on that same note. Paul wishes to establish the first step of his argument: love for one another is essential to fellowship; it is fostered by God's Spirit and provides the dynamism for the community's life of purity. In verse 10 Paul posits the second step of his argument: the community's "labor of love" already extends beyond the confines of Thessalonica and its fellowship.

(3) Note on "God-taught." Since the expression *theodidaktoi* is found nowhere else in the NT nor attested prior to Paul, it is correctly assumed to be a Pauline creation (see its later use in Barnabas 21:6), though the concept of being "taught by God" was hardly a new one; see Isa 54:13

which speaks of the Israelites as "being taught by God" (*didaktoi theou*—
text cited in John 6:45; see also Jer 31:33 and Ezek 37:6, 14). Additionally,
later Jewish tradition speaks of the messianic king being "taught by God"
(PssSol 17:32) and rabbinic tradition, employing the above Isaiah passage,
of God teaching the Torah in the future age. That Paul formulated this
expression on the basis of such tradition is probable; its import, however, is not thereby clarified.

The meaning of the term is variously interpreted as God teaching the
Thessalonians to love via OT, dominical, Pauline, or prophetic injunctions
or through some interior impulse, conscience, or teaching. Objection can
be raised against all of these. Paul speaks of being "taught by God" not
by the Lord Jesus, other envoys or the Jewish scriptures; this would not
correspond to his usage. He seems to suggest some type of internal force,
i.e., by the term *theodidaktoi* he insists that the Thessalonians and other
believers are in fact continually being taught by God's Spirit.

One might defend such an interpretation in several ways. In terms
of context, it must be noted that the previous pericope ended (4:8) by
stressing that God continually gives believers the Holy Spirit (note the
stress on God's Spirit: *autou*). Also the present character of the activity
is underscored for the Spirit is a continuous gift and believers are being
taught by God. Also, Paul's discussion of the Spirit as the believer's source
of knowledge, 1 Cor 2:9-16, provides light on this topic. Because believers
are "taught by the Spirit" (13), they grasp the things of God since they
are revealed through God's Spirit (10-11). Finally, they are spiritual and
spiritually discerning because they "receive the gifts of God's Spirit" (14).
This last passage leads us to another crucial Pauline text concerning the
things that belong to the Spirit, Gal 5:22f. After having listed the works
of the flesh, in a manner reminiscent of 1 Thess 4:3-8, and insisting that
such activity leads to disinheritance from the kingdom or breaking faith
with God, Paul gives in contrast "the fruit of the Spirit," the first of which
is love. Because they "are taught" or, in Galatian terms, "are guided
by the Spirit" they will "live by the Spirit" (5:25) a life which is characterized by love, joy (see 1 Thess 1:6: "joy inspired by the Holy Spirit"),
peace, etc. (Gal 5:26f. has much in common with 1 Thess 4:11-12 and
5:12f.). A last text should be cited to capture Paul's full meaning, namely,
Rom 5:5, to the effect that "God's love has been poured into our hearts
through the Holy Spirit that has been given to us." Being taught by God
how to love one's neighbor is to have one's heart inundated by a God-
given, Spirit-inspired love that is open to all.

From this discussion, therefore, I conclude that *theodidaktoi* is an early
formulation of Paul's concept of "being taught and guided by God's
Spirit," that same Spirit that allows the spiritual person to "understand

the gifts bestowed by God" (1 Cor 2:12). By insisting on the present tense, Paul is paying the Thessalonians the ultimate compliment by stating that they are spiritual beings whose lives are led by God's Spirit and whose love is enduring, dedicated, and hard-working (see 1:3).

(4) Love for Christians beyond Thessalonica. In a second *gar* clause Paul gives an added reason for the community's well-earned reputation for "love of brothers and sisters." Two issues may be addressed to appreciate more fully Paul's meaning: the vague expression, "you are doing this" and the seemingly exaggerated local phrase, "for all believers throughout Macedonia." In the first case some are wont to supplement the general expression ("you love all") or to explain Pauline language as a wish to avoid redundancy by not repeating the verb "love" in this new statement (see 4:1 where the verb is employed twice in a similar context). I suspect, however, that the statement is intentionally vague so as to draw attention to the content and focus of love. The term "this" (see v. 10) allows Paul to point to the following discussion concerning a life of love, to expand the recipient of loving action (from immediate community members, to more distant brothers and sisters, to the actors in one's social and economic milieu—including those outside the fellowship), and to plead gently for greater effort in this expanded vision of love.

Secondly, reference to "all" Macedonians has generated discussion concerning the community's activity in the province. Because of Paul's focus on fellow Christians in this verse, scholars propose that the community's love was manifested in financial support for missionaries (much as the apostles received help in Thessalonica from the community of Philippi: Phil 4:15-16) and especially in hospitality shown fellow believers traveling through this busy Roman political and commercial center. While commentators insist that Paul exaggerates when he speaks of "all" believers "throughout" the province of Macedonia as being the recipients of the community's good will, one should not dismiss too readily the statement's implications. In light of 1:7-8 one should see here a reference to the community as a missionary center. However one describes the concrete form their love took in relation to their fellow Macedonians, one can at least assume that they provided finances and personnel for the missionary endeavor on the Greek mainland and more intensely within their own province (see earlier discussion of missionary strategy). Beyond that, their reputation as committed, hospitable Christians became an example to believers elsewhere of what it means to be "guided by the Spirit." In this way Paul lends support to those within the community who insisted that Christian commitment and community activity have an outward direction as they confronted the world mission and Roman society as the social context of their lives of holiness.

Pauline Shift to a Broader Perspective (4:10b). (1) Exhortation to Greater and Broader Effort. While Paul's introduction in verse 10b of an exhortation formula along with an adversive conjunction ("but we exhort you") tempt some to suggest a new subject for the following verses, most recognize his encouragement to greater efforts as related to mutual love. I suggest that, with verse 10b and its exhortation formula, Paul is becoming less reticent in his advice to the community as he defines more concretely what a life of love entails as its members encounter not the temptation of going back to their pagan ways but the difficulties presented by the social, religious separation from their Roman neighbors (see earlier discussion of 3:2-5, 12). Paul in 4:11-12 encourages, in traditional Greco-Roman terms, engagement in the social context and quiet, self-sufficiency.

Thus, Paul exhorts the community "to abound even more" in its activity. Interestingly, he employs the verb *perisseuō* on two occasions in his previous missive, both texts of which shed light on his new instructions. In 3:12, as the letter draws to a close, Paul prays for "an increase and abundance" in the community's "love for one another and for all." While he is pleased to receive from Timothy a splendid report about the community's "faith and love" (3:6) he also expresses his wish to return and strengthen their faith (3:10). Thus, both their faith and their love require further attention. For our purpose it is important to note that the hoped-for abundance in love concerns both insiders and outsiders and that from the very beginning of the community's existence Paul's concern and the converts' challenge embrace the world in which they live, both fellow Christians and outsiders. In 4:1 Paul employs *perisseuō* a second time to encourage more intensive progress in proper conduct. Thus, the hearers are familiar with Paul's pleas for "greater effort" and would not fail to see that the object of this greater effort is love and its social character or behavior that is pleasing to God as it involves brothers and sisters in daily activity and proper conduct in the company of nonbelievers. The refrain then concerning greater effort as involving the inner and outer dimensions of love was a constant in Paul's dialogue with the community.

(2) Christian Context (4:11). Having exhorted the hearers to greater effort, Paul in verse 11 provides content, and motivation in verse 12, for this added instruction as well as a reminder that they are already instructed in these matters. The series of infinitives of verse 11, following "to abound even more" and connected by *kai,* are epexegetical for they give concrete examples (BDF 442.9) on how love of others applies to daily life. Further, the first two concerning the quiet life and minding one's own affairs form a pair and are complementary in addressing the sociopolitical sphere, while the third addresses a second area of life, earning one's living.

First, Paul advises the members of the community "to aspire to live quietly." The precise context and Pauline meaning are debated. From the outset some opt either for an inner community context, usually through the lenses of the apocalyptic fervor of 2 Thessalonians and its problem with idleness, or for a political setting and application. In the first case it is assumed that Paul wishes to calm apocalyptic fervor or spiritual enthusiasm (such motivation applies more readily to the exhortation of 2 Thess 3:6-12) or that he is countering the lack of work which resulted from the community's newly acquired belief in the imminence of Jesus' return. Others note that the idea of the quiet life, along with other themes of verses 11-12, is due to use of contemporary *topoi* of moralists concerning withdrawal from political involvement. Indeed, the term *hēsychazō* ("live a quiet life") refers to politically and philosophically motivated retirement from public life and the physical withdrawal to a more idyllic setting, advice which one finds in many philosophers of the NT period. Its use, however, extends beyond political quietism to the quiet life, rest, and peace (Job 3:26; Ezek 38:11) which is antithetical to the rule of the vicious tongue (Sir 28:16), of the noisy urban crowds (Josephus, *JA* 18:245; Diogenes Laertius, *Lives of Eminent Philosophers* 10.143), of the active civic life (Josephus, *JA* 13:407) or even of the demands of married life (POxyrhynchus 129.8). Also, in political terms it is defined as a state opposed to war and desired by the wise (Thucydides, *Peloponnesian War* 1.120; PSI 1.41.23); and, in religious terms, as having a pure heart before God and dwelling in peace and tranquility without opposition (Job 11:13-20; see M-M 281). From such evidence and from the context provided by verses 11-12, it seems that Paul intends to make a sociopolitical statement. But whether emphasis is to be placed on political withdrawal, on inner community tranquility, or on the Greek ideal of the quiet life as eschatological reality can be determined only in light of the entire context and Paul's sociopolitical thought.

Secondly, Paul speaks of "attending to one's affairs," an idiom and theme which relates to Platonic tradition. Indeed, Paul's use of this idiom could be interpreted in relation to two Platonic references. In the first, *Republic* 6.496D, Plato describes the philosopher who, in choosing the quiet life or retirement from public life, devotes his time to "his own affairs" (also Dio Cassius, *Roman History* 60.27). In light of this one would understand Paul as insisting on attention to community as opposed to public or state affairs. In the second, *Republic* 4.433A-B, Plato defines justice *(dikaiosynē)* as "attending to one's own affairs" or accomplishing the one service for the state for which one is best suited by nature. In such a context one would see Paul as defining the ideal Christian life as one of tranquility, peace, and activity among and for fellow believers and in the company of outsiders. The Christian believer then is "to aspire to" or have as goal, much as the wise Greek would wish, the quiet life which attends to the demands of a pure life of loving activity.

Thirdly, Paul exhorts the community: "to work with your hands." The question of meaning has recently been posed in terms of trades versus manual labor. The idiom has led some to conclude, employing Lukan data regarding Paul's trade, that he, like Dio Chrysostom and other classical writers, recommends manual labor or trades to his readers, much as those recommending retirement from political life also advocated political quiet-ism coupled with "working with one's hands." On the one hand, it is difficult to see where this leads the reader in trying to understand Paul's insistence, apparently, on manual labor. On the other hand, the idiom it-self and its origin require some attention. A reading of Dio's *Oration* 7 is instructive because it is so often invoked in the scholarly literature and be-cause of its advice and attitude toward work. Dio's discussion of work is to be situated within the context of Greco-Roman disdain for work and pov-erty. There follows his defense of "employments and trades" as befitting free persons and as providing them with what is necessary and seemly (7.103, 109, 113). While he speaks approvingly of "handcraftsmen" (124), he nonetheless speaks of "employments and trades *(peri ergasiōn kai tech-nōn)*" and "doing one's own work *(autourgeō)*" and not really of "working with one's hands," as though he were stressing manual labor. To my knowledge this expression is not of Greek but of Jewish origin. The idiom "to work with one's hands" is rare in the NT (here and 1 Cor 4:12; Eph 4:28) while the idiom "works of one's hands" is only slightly more fre-quent, and in each case is either a citation or paraphrase of an OT pas-sage: Acts 7:41; Heb 1:10; 2:7; Rev 9:20. Since the expression "works of one's hands" is a common OT phrase (Deut 2:7f.; Job 1:10; Ps 89:17; Isa 2:8f.; Jer 1:16f.; see also T.Judah 2) and means "work or deeds" (see Isa 5:12 where "works of the Lord" parallels "works of his hands"), it is logical to assume that Paul is using a scriptural idiom to express his in-junction to the community and that he is not stressing the manual aspect of work (no more than is Dio) but rather its function as providing per-sonal and community needs and as "proper in the eyes of outsiders."

From the above then I conclude that Paul's injunction about work fits well with those about the quiet and committed life since he is interested first in describing the ideal context of the community's life (what believers must aspire to) and secondly in listing those areas in which greater effort is urged, particularly as they concern the community and its relation to outsiders. In Jewish and popular moral terms Paul commends greater effort and stronger motivation (v. 12) for Christian involvement in the socioeconomic context not because of idleness caused by exaggerated apocalypticism but for the reason underlying the entire section, namely, an expanded, outer-directed concept of love of others.

A Redefined and Refocused Concept of Love. (1) Motives for Christian Behavior. In verse 12 Paul in a double purpose clause proposes two reasons why one should adopt the ideal Christian activity proposed in the previous verse. [1] He appeals to proper behavior in the company of outsiders as a first motive. Ultimately, why would Paul appeal to such a public forum or even suggest that appearance is so important, since God is the only judge and the one who knows the reality? Is Paul interested here in avoiding a bad reputation for the new Christian fellowship or in warding off further persecution of the community? That Paul is concerned about substance more than appearance is confirmed by Rom 13:13 where he exhorts his readers to "live honorably as in the day" and then provides a list of vices which derive from "the desires or covetousness" of the flesh (much as in 1 Thess 4:5); Christian behavior is not a show for outsiders. Why then does he appeal to pagans as judges of Christian behavior? Presumably, Paul is interested in helping his community survive and thrive in a potentially hostile pagan environment, but more basically, as indicated by the letter's profound missionary concern and advice concerning love as an outward movement, he sees the community's behavior toward outsiders as an outreach of the Christian mission. Just as he is able to say that the Thessalonians (in 4:10 and 1:7) extended their love to all in Macedonia by providing resources and example, so here he implies that behavior, judged proper according to Christian standards, will be proper also vis-à-vis those outside the community. Love then, in the thinking of the missionary, extends beyond the community and allows, even compels, all to participate in the missionary outreach (see also 1 Pet 2:11-17). With this clause Paul's thinking regarding love has come full circle; as he began his advice by discussing love of brother and sister, or those inside, so he brings his answer to their question to a climax by insisting that loving behavior also include those outside, ultimately that they too may "turn to God from idols to serve the living and true God" (1:9) and in their turn "conduct (them)selves worthily of the God who calls" (2:12).

[2] Paul adds another reason for proper Christian activity. This motive, however, is problematic owing to the ambiguity of its formulation (see Notes on *mēdenos*). Thus, scholars are divided on the matter, opting to see Paul's main concern as fearing that some will either go hungry ("lacking in nothing") or live as parasites ("dependent on no one"). Scholars cite the Stoic ideal of self-sufficiency or *autarkia* in defense of the second option and stress that Paul wants respect but not assistance from outsiders or that he is dealing with the problem of idleness. Nonetheless, it is preferable to opt for the former since *chreia* more often takes the genitive of the thing (BAGD 884-85), since the immediate context regarding work supports such a reading, and since Paul's ideal fellowship

predicates mutual dependence and sharing among members rather than Stoic self-sufficiency or economic and social isolation.

(2) Overall Paraenetic Conclusion. In light of the above analysis what then does Paul advise in verses 11-12? In his discussion of love and its boundaries, starting as it does with a focus on community, he consistently expands its horizon in verses 9-10a. Then in 10b he adopts a new tactic as he directs the community to an all-pervasive notion of activity and service, in effect exhorting to greater effort in what they have already been instructed. It is at this point that the series of infinitive constructions in verse 11 is situated, namely, to present the context for Christian activity and for the greater effort which he encourages. [1] Paul reminds the community of the ideal life to which the fellowship should aspire, namely, one that is at peace within and without (i.e., free of dissension within its ranks and open to those outside) and whose members are devoted to a pure life. While certain aspects of Paul's description have affinities to the life to which the wise Greek aspires, whether in civic life or in retirement, one should nonetheless view his stance in 1 Thessalonians in light of other texts where he does not so much shun sociopolitical realities as focus on the Christian's motivation and modus vivendi. In Rom 13:1-7, for example, Paul takes seriously the state's role in political and economic matters but advises the community against divisive participation in public debate over tax reform. In 1 Corinthians 7 Paul repeatedly advises moderation, inaction, or the status quo that believers might be more "devoted to prayer" (5), "save" others (16), or be more "anxious about the affairs of the Lord" (vv. 32, 34). Paul's goal is "to promote good order and unhindered devotion to the Lord" (35). Finally, we might note Paul's discussion of spiritual gifts in 1 Corinthians 12-14. Beyond his concern about the abuse of these, he insists on their social function ("building up the Church"—14:4f.), the community's need for intelligible speech (whether involving believer or outsider—vv. 3f., 11, 16), and the necessity for "decorum and order" (4). Paul's description of the "quiet life" then involves order, peace, and decorum within and without the community.

[2] His advice also stresses "attending to one's affairs." While some stress "one's *own* affairs" (i.e., Christian concerns, particularly the Lord's coming) as contrasted with civic or public issues, it seems more likely that "attending to your affairs" (*ta idia*) is to be explained as doing the things to which believers have been called, i.e., "being anxious about the affairs of the Lord (*ta tou kyriou*)," an expression which Paul defines as knowing "how to please the Lord" (1 Cor 7:32, 34). What Christians are to think about ("whatever is true . . . honorable . . . just . . . pure . . .") or do is beautifully expressed by Paul in Phil 4:9: "keep on doing the things that you have learned and received and heard and seen in me,

and the God of peace will be with you." Believers are to attend to their affairs or more particularly to the affairs of the Lord as they seek to conduct themselves worthily of the God who has called them (1 Thess 2:12).

[3] The concern with work could be related to a specific Thessalonian problem concerning idleness (5:14) or could address this perennial issue as it existed in Roman cities at the time (see Dio, *Oration* 17.4). Its function in the paragraph on mutual love, however, points to a more basic issue. Work along with a developed notion of the Christian life and ideal formed part of the apostolic missionary activity. Christians were to be productive members of the society in which they lived and their activity was to contribute to the well-being, unity, and outreach of the fellowship. Thus, Paul's concluding motivational statements (v. 12) focus on two important facets of loving activity. On the one hand, the conduct of the community's members could have a profound impact on the lives of outsiders. Thus, Paul insists that this influence be positive or proper. On the other hand, loving activity involves self-help, mutual dependence, and sharing among members so that all may have their needs met, whether in physical or spiritual terms. A discussion, therefore, that began in terms of the boundaries and responsibilities of mutual Christian love ends on the note that the whole of Christian activity and behavior must envision the inner and outer dynamics and concerns of love.

FOR REFERENCE AND FURTHER STUDY

Barclay, J. M. G. "Thessalonica and Corinth: Social Contrasts in Pauline Christianity." *JSNT* 47 (1992) 49–74.

Faw, C. E. "On the Writing of First Thessalonians." *JBL* 71 (1952) 217–32.

Hock, R. F. *The Social Context of Paul's Ministry: Tentmaking and Apostleship.* Philadelphia: Fortress, 1980.

Kloppenborg, J. S. "*Philadelphia, Theodidaktos* and the Dioscuri: Rhetorical Engagement in 1 Thessalonians 4.9-12." *NTS* 39 (1993) 265–89.

Malherbe, A. J. "Exhortation in First Thessalonians." *NovT* 25 (1983) 238–56.

_____. "Did the Thessalonians Write to Paul?" *The Conversation Continues: Studies in Paul and John in Honor of J. Louis Martyn.* Eds. R. T. Fortna and B. R. Gaventa. Nashville: Abingdon, 1990, 246–57.

Perkins, P. "1 Thessalonians and Hellenistic Religious Practices." *To Touch the Text: Biblical and Related Studies in Honor of Joseph A. Fitzmyer, S.J.* Eds. M. P. Horgan and P. J. Kobelski. New York: Crossroad, 1989, 325–34.

Spicq, C. "La charité fraternelle selon 1 Th 4, 9." *Mélanges bibliques rédigés en honneur de André Robert.* Paris: Bloud et Gay, 1957, 507–11.

13. *On the Faithful Departed and the Parousia* (4:13-18)

13. Now we do not want you to be in ignorance, brothers and sisters, concerning those who fall asleep, so that you may not grieve as others do who have no hope. 14. For if we believe that Jesus died and rose, so too should we believe that God will fetch with Jesus those who will have fallen asleep believing in him. 15. The above then we say to you as a message of the Lord, namely, that we who are alive—who survive until the coming of the Lord—will by no means precede those who will have fallen asleep, 16. because the Lord himself, with a cry of command, that is, with an archangel's shout and a blast of God's trumpet, will come down from heaven. And so the dead in Christ will have risen beforehand, 17. then we who are alive—who survive—will be caught up together with them in the clouds to meet the Lord in the air and so we will be with the Lord forever. 18. Therefore, console one another with these words.

NOTES

13. *Now we do not want you to be in ignorance, brothers and sisters:* Paul begins his second response with a rhetorical disclaimer (see also 4:9; 5:1 and 1 Cor 12:1) and addresses his audience directly, both elements which contribute to the interaction between writer and addressees. The disclaimer itself, whether expressed negatively or positively is variously employed by Paul in his correspondence and thus diverse conclusions are drawn in relation to the idiom's meaning and function in the present context. See discussion below for the conclusion that the idiom has the meaning: "we want you to be fully informed" or "not in ignorance."

concerning those who fall asleep: The topic of concern is stated simply: *peri tōn koimōmenōn*. The initial phrase ("concerning those . . .") operates in the same fashion as in 4:9 and 5:1 (see also 1 Cor 7f.); Paul is responding to a question sent to him. The verb *koimaomai* literally means "to sleep" and is so used in Matt 28:13; Luke 22:45; and Acts 12:6. In its most frequent NT and exclusive Pauline usage, however, it stands as a metaphor for death. Beginning from the time of Homer this term and synonyms were used for the sleep of death and continued to be so used in inscriptions, epitaphs, and Hellenistic literature; in the LXX it is particularly employed of "sleep with the ancestors" or the death of kings (LSJ 967; BAGD 437; TDNT 3:14). Such usage, therefore, was common in the NT period (Matt 27:52; Acts 7:60; 15:26; 2 Pet 3:4) and appealing to Paul (1 Cor 7:39; 11:30; 15:6, 18, 20, 51; three times in 1 Thessalonians: vv. 13, 14, 15). Since he employs other more concrete terms for death (e.g., *apothnęskō* and *nekroi* in vv. 14 and 16) and since he makes no use of the word's metaphorical possibilities (e.g., resurrection as awakening from sleep; see Dan 12:2 where the synonym *katheudō* is so used; also see Notes below on 5:10), one might wonder why he insists on its triple use in

this pericope (see below). Also, Paul in verse 13 employs the present participle of the verb whereas he uses the aorist in verses 14 and 15. In the first
case the present tense underscores the topic of discussion ("concerning the
[Christian] dead"); in the second Paul speaks of those who die before Jesus'
return. Such usage further indicates that he is responding to a problem formulated in a precise question communicated to him.

so that you may not grieve as others do who have no hope: This clause gives the
purpose for Paul's advice concerning "grief" *(lypeō)*. The term and its cognates are often employed by Paul to describe the pain one human causes
another (Rom 14:5; 2 Cor 2:1f.), a pain that can lead to repentance (1 Cor
7:9) or be qualified as excessive or obstructive (2 Cor 2:7; 9:7). Here the term
is employed without qualification; the concept is not condemned as though
grief of itself were a denial of the promise of resurrection. Paul is not saying
that the community should not grieve but that it should "not grieve as *(kathōs
kai*—"in the way that") others do. . . ." Grief at a friend's death (Phil 2:27)
is normal, but a grief of despair, one that sees only helplessness, is a denial
of hope itself. The term translated "others" *(hoi loipoi*, lit.: "the rest") could
designate the non-Christian world but probably refers to people who experience the kind of grief which is antithetical to belief in the Christ-event.
Those who lament as though there is no afterlife or resurrection are like so
many in the pagan world who are lacking in "hope" *(elpis)*. The concept of
hope, which appears earlier in the first (2:19) and second (1:3) missives, is
basic to the Pauline vision of life. His initial point is not a full-blown notion
of hope as waiting for the future, confidence, and patience, but, as in 1:3
(see discussion), a focus on confidence in a divinely assured future (even
beyond death) that translates in present belief and action.

14. *For if we believe that Jesus died and rose:* Paul appeals to the kerygma, expressed
in a succinct credal formula, to explain why *(gar)* Christians should have hope
and not act in a despondent way in the face of death. He begins with a conditional clause, but by employing the indicative following *ei* ("if") and a subsequent *houtōs kai* ("so too") he insists that the first clause of the sentence
is factual, "closely bordering on causal 'since' " (BDF 372.1). By employing
this type of conditional clause, he is saying: "if (since) we believe (for we
surely do) that Jesus died and rose, so too (should we believe that). . . ."—the
certitude of the protasis leads to assurance in the apodosis. The whole is introduced by the expression "we believe that" (see also Rom 10:9), a phrase
which appeals to the proclamation of the whole Church, a phrase too which
becomes, in later centuries, a feature of official creeds (see below).

so too should we believe that: The second part of Paul's sentence is somewhat
disjointed since he leaves out the actual contrast intended by "so too." While
some allow the disjointedness to stand, my rendition supplies what Paul
presupposes in his train of thought. Comment should be made here concerning a possible subjective interpretation of the two clauses of the conditional
sentence. Paul does not mean that if Christians believe in the Christ-event,
then God will act on their behalf at the parousia; instead, he insists, the second statement is as firmly grounded in fact as the first is. Most translators

avoid giving this impression by either omitting the conditional particle "if" or by converting it to "since."

God will fetch with Jesus those who will have fallen asleep believing in him: The translation of the lengthy Greek clause (*ho theos tous koimēthentas dia tou Iēsou axei syn autō,* lit.: "God will bring with him those who have fallen asleep through Jesus") depends on conclusions drawn regarding debated issues: that *axei syn autō* refers to God causing the dead to accompany Jesus and that *dia tou Iēsou* indicates those who die as faithful Christians; it also presupposes decisions concerning the goal or direction of the "processional" movement and concerning the relationship of verses 14b to 14a; see below. Also, it should be noted (a) that the name of Jesus is associated with the first preposition rather than the second for translation purposes—the Greek word order allows the opposite and (b) that the translation "who will have fallen asleep" relates the aorist not to the past of the letter writer but to that of the parousia.

15. *The above then we say to you as a message from the Lord:* The opening words of verse 15 have traditionally been interpreted as introducing a dominical saying ("for this we declare to you by the word of the Lord"—NRSV), a saying which is presumed to consist of verses 16-17. Instead, the above translation and the interpretation that follows argue for *touto* as referring back to what has been said in verse 14 and for the hapax legomenon, *en logō kyriou,* as designating prophetic speech on Paul's part, namely, Paul's claim in verse 14b serves "as a message from the Lord."

namely, that we who are alive—who survive until the coming of the Lord: Scholars who see verse 15a as introducing a dominical saying intriguingly qualify the remainder of verse 15 as Pauline introduction to the actual logion which is said to begin in verse 16. The language is indeed Pauline, but instead of introducing what follows, it explains the conclusion (the initial *hoti* is epexegetical and so translated "namely") drawn in verse 14b concerning God's call to those who have already fallen asleep. Additionally, verse 16 with its own *hoti* particle gives the reason why ("because") the living will not gain an advantage over the dead. The expression "we who are alive" stresses a change in address from "you" to "us" and underscores the term "alive" (*zaō*) as an unequivocal opposite to the euphemism "those who fall asleep," a term which in turn provides a clue to the problem being addressed. Being "alive" is an essential precondition to the welcoming back of the returning Lord and to the possibility of heavenly assumption. The living are said to be those "who remain" (*perileipō*), a term which occurs only here and in verse 17 in the entire NT. While cognates of this term are used by Paul to characterize the remnant of Israel (Rom 9:27), its infrequent appearance in the LXX (e.g., 2 Chr 34:21; 4 Macc 12:6) and its use in 1 Thessalonians 4 suggest that Paul is simply referring to those who have survived. Once again Paul employs the term *parousia* for Jesus' coming at the end-time (see 2:19 and 3:13). In this case the term commands more attention since he describes in some detail the pomp and circumstance which will accompany the Lord's coming down from heaven. The term is employed initially to establish the temporal setting (*eis*—"until") of the discussion.

will by no means precede those who will have fallen asleep: Paul's statement, introduced by an emphatic negative with the aorist subjunctive (*ou mē phthasōmen*—"will by no means precede"), is a deliberate challenge to a traditional apocalyptic view that the generation of the end-time will be more blessed than those who have already died. To express this idea Paul employs the verb *phthanō*, a verb which sometimes retains its classic sense of "precede" (here in v. 15; also true of the compound *prophthanō* in Matt 17:25) but which also tends to weaken in the Hellenistic period to mean "arrive at or reach" (*TDNT* 9:90). Since in its other Pauline occurrences (Rom 9:31; 2 Cor 10:14; Phil 3:6; see comments on 1 Thess 2:16) the verb provides the weaker sense, one might be tempted to see here a sign of Paul's use of a source. Indeed, owing to the term's frequent use in inscriptions and the papyri (BAGD 856.1) and to its context within the Pauline argument, I propose to see it as a key term employed by the Thessalonians in describing what they see as the problem concerning the dead. For the phrase "those who will have fallen asleep" see verse 14.

16. *Because the Lord himself . . . will come down from heaven:* By his use of the emphatic pronoun *(autos)* Paul contrasts the Christian view of the end-time with that of most Jewish scenarios where the Messiah has no role to play and reminds his readers that the Lord will take the initiative. Again, as in verse 15, Paul identifies the descending figure as "Lord" because, here as later in verse 17, he wishes to underscore Jesus' exalted role at the parousia and to emphasize that the basis for Christian hope is the promised return of the risen Lord. Additionally, at a given time and signal the Lord "will come down from heaven." Just as God can be said to come down *(katabainō)* to earth to inspect or judge (Gen 11:5; Mic 1:3) or as holy watchers, angels, Jerusalem, or Jesus as Son of Man or bread of life are said to come down from heaven (Theodotionic Dan 4:13, 20; Matt 28:2; Rev 3:12; 10:1f.; John 3:13; 6:33f.), so Paul, who envisions Jesus as having been raised and enthroned at God's right hand (Rom 8:34; 10:6), picture him as descending from heaven (or the heavens in 1:10).

    . . . with a cry of command, that is, with an archangel's shout and a blast of God's trumpet . . .: The Greek noun phrases underlying the above translation are presumed to refer to the same agent, the returning Lord, and best describe concurrent signs of the Lord's return. Their background, meaning, and function are discussed below in an Excursus on the end-time signs.

    And so, the dead in Christ will have risen beforehand: Paul's use of the term *prōton* ("first") to end his next clause and *epeita* ("then") to begin the following requires some clarification. While insisting that these terms signify temporal sequence, scholars either underscore the ironic reversal of the dead actually having precedence over the survivors or distinguish still another stage in the final drama of salvation. Others more correctly note that the time sequence is as simultaneous as the Pauline phrase "in the twinkling of an eye" indicates (1 Cor 15:52) and that Paul does not intend to establish a sequence of events but to assure the audience that the dead will be alive prior to and so making possible their heavenly assumption. Furthermore, an analysis of the

Pauline construction *kai . . . prōton* ("and so . . . beforehand") confirms the latter. The initial *kai* has a consecutive sense (BDF 442.2) and so describes the action of its clause as a consequence of the preceding apocalyptic drama. Also, the position of the adverb *prōton* is unusual for Paul, who places it in initial position, whether as related to clauses (Rom 1:8; 3:2; 1 Cor 11:18; 15:46) or to individual terms (Rom 2:9, 10; 1 Cor 12:28; 2 Cor 8:5). Its final position here focuses on the raising of the dead prior to their heavenly assumption. Further, the expression "the dead in Christ" is rightly seen as indicating the fidelity of those who have died; in this life they had belonged to, hoped in, and fallen asleep committed to Christ (1 Cor 15:18-19, 23).

17, *then we who are alive—who survive:* Paul resumes the argument of verse 15 at the point of contention: that the survivors are more blessed than those who die in fidelity to Christ. In verse 17 he repeats the beginning of the clause of verse 15, leaving out only the modifying phrase "until the coming of the Lord" for, in his telling of the events, the coming is in progress.

will be caught up together with them in the clouds: Paul begins his description of the terrestrial part of the meeting by emphasizing, in another way, the fact that neither group will be at a disadvantage when the day of the Lord arrives, since the survivors will participate "together with them," that is, the living together with the newly resurrected. By his use of *hama* ("together or at the same time"; also 5:10) along with the preposition *syn* ("with"—*IBNTG*, 81-82) Paul underscores both the unity and the simultaneity of the action. He is being faithful to apocalyptic tradition which insists that at the end both those who lived earlier and those who come later will come to judgment at one and the same time (4 Ezra 5:41-45; 6:20; 2 Bar 30:2; 51:13). For a discussion of "caught up together . . . in the clouds," see below.

to meet the Lord in the air: Both the expression "to meet" *(apantēsis)* and "in the air" *(eis aera)* have generated considerable discussion concerning, in the first case, the background and meaning of the idiom and, in the second, the goal of the heavenly journey; both are discussed below.

and so we will be with the Lord forever: Paul concludes his treatment of the apocalyptic scene, not so much by summarizing what precedes as by drawing a conclusion from his eschatological discussion ("and so"). Based on what he has told the audience concerning the parousia, Paul assures them that their fondest hope and the goal of their commitment to the Lord is precisely "being with the Lord forever" or "living with him" (4:17; 5:10).

18. *Therefore, console one another with these words:* Paul concludes his treatment of the issue by drawing an important conclusion (*hōste*—"therefore"; see *IBNTG*, 144); the entire response has as its goal mutual consolation, the consolation of those who grieve the loss of their friends. While the verb *parakaleō* has a range of meaning and is employed eight times in 1 Thessalonians (see 2:12 and 3:2), its use in the context of grief for the dead demands the sense of consolation or comfort. Finally, not only are they to receive consolation from Paul's words ("with these words"—use of instrumental *en*), but they

are to employ this authoritative message (v. 15) in helping one another to cope with the loss of loved ones.

Paul's use of apocalyptic imagery causes difficulty in relating the three terms to their proper antecedents and in determining their overall meaning. Each noun phrase is introduced by the preposition *en* ("in, with, by") and the last two are joined by the connective *kai* ("and"). Does God issue the directive and therefore Jesus acts at God's command accompanied by two other signs or does Jesus, marking the beginning of the parousia, give a loud command, which is put into effect by the angel and trumpet? The latter is preferable in grammatical and apocalyptic terms. Since the three phrases are introduced by identical prepositions they seem inextricably linked in function and meaning, i.e., they refer to the same agent and have a related purpose. Also, apocalyptic scenes with messianic figures usually present the Messiah as initiating and participating in the visitation, whether it is the Son of Man who sends out angels with the trumpet to gather the elect (Matt 24:31; also Mark 13:27), the Lord Messiah who warns, condemns, or gathers (PssSol 17:25-26), the lion-like Messiah's roaring voice and activity vis-à-vis the wicked and the remnant (4 Ezra 11:37; 12:31-34), or the Lamb who opens the scroll and the seals (Rev 5:1f.; 6:1f.).

What remains to be determined, however, is the relationship that exists between the three apocalyptic images. The function of these prepositional phrases is best described as attendant circumstance (*IBNTG*, 78), that is, the signs occur at the same time as the main action of the sentence. The first expression, lit.: "with a cry of command," presents further difficulty since this is the only occurrence of the noun *keleusma* in the NT and since Paul does not employ its cognate verb. Its meaning, however, is not in doubt since in classical usage (also represented by one, similar occurrence in the LXX: Prov 30:27) it expresses an "order or command" and becomes a technical military term (Thucydides, *Peloponnesian War* 2.92.1; Josephus, *JA* 17:140). But the word can also be employed for a divine command (Euripides, *Iphigenia in Tauris* 1483), for God's gathering of the elect (Philo, *On Rewards and Punishments* 117), or more generally for a simple "cry." Since the term's meaning can range from a command to an inarticulate sound (*TDNT* 3:657), in the present context it seems to represent a command from the celestial Lord that implies both a loud cry and a military apocalyptic scene.

The following two prepositional phrases are used epexegetically to explain "the cry of command" and so the connective is translated "that is." Such an interpretation is suggested by the joining of the last two by the conjunction *kai* (contrary to Paul's usage in 1 Cor 15:52 where three similar *en* phrases have no connecting conjunction) and by the absence in the first phrase of a genitive modifier. The first of these, "with an archangel's shout," introduces the reader to the first of two end-time signs, which is described as an angelic "voice" or "shout." The term *phōnē* is used of angelic speech which causes the divine temple to tremble (Isa 6:1-4) or which sounds like the roar of a crowd or a lion, like the sound of many waters, loud thunder, the music of harps, or even the blast of a trumpet (Dan 10:6; Rev 1:10; 14:2; 19:6). In this connection it should be recalled that of the messianic Man from the Sea it is said: "whenever his voice issued from his mouth, all who heard his voice melted as wax melts when it feels the fire" (4 Ezra 13:4). Further, this is the voice of an archangel, a term that appears elsewhere in the NT only in Jude 9, but a category of angels which is well documented in intertestamental literature (1 En 20:1-8) and whose members perform various functions for the Almighty (Dan 10:13; Tob 12:15f.; 1 En 9:1; SibOr 2:215; T.Isaac 2:1). The appearance and involvement of angels in apocalyptic contexts is well known, whether in Daniel (10:13; 12:1), intertestamental apocalypses (1 En 1:9; 4 Ezra 4:1f.; T.Levi 2:6f.; ApocZeph 2:1f.; T.Isaac 2:1f.), or Christian apocalyptic texts (Mark 8:38; 13:27; Matt 24:31; Jude 14; Rev passim; 1 Thess 3:13). What then is the function of the angelic voice or shout? Is it a sound that causes hearts to melt in fear at the coming of the heavenly visitor or is it as in Matt 24:31 a beacon announcing the arrival of the Messiah to gather the elect? The latter seems the more satisfactory since battle and judgment are conspicuously absent in Paul's statement. Whether the angelic shout is meant, along with the trumpet blast, primarily to awaken or call the dead to life seems less compelling when one considers that the scene, while attempting to allay the survivors' fears concerning the dead, intends to emphasize that the Lord comes to gather both those who have fallen asleep and those who are alive. The apocalyptic signs are precisely signs of the parousia for all believers not calls to those who have died.

The third prepositional phrase, "with a blast of God's trumpet," introduces a second apocalyptic sign. The *salpinx* was in antiquity first of all a war trumpet used to sound the battle cry (Xenophon, *Anabasis* 4.2.7f.; Job 39:24-25; Jer 4:5; 1 QM passim; 1 Cor 14:8) but in peacetime it acquired cultic use related to temple ceremonies and, particularly in Judaism, became a standard image to describe theophanies (Exod 19:13f.) and scenes of eschatological judgment. It is in OT and intertestamental apocalyptic traditions, that the trumpet becomes a frequent end-time sign. Thus, it is often situated in the context of the great apocalyptic battle (Joel 2:1-2; Zeph 1:15-16; in Zeph 9:14 God is said to blow the trumpet) or serves as an instrument to gather the elect (Isa 27:13; PssSol 11:1-3), to raise the dead (SibOr 4:173-82), or is simply presented as an end-time sign (4 Ezra 6:23; SibOr 8:239). The trumpet also appears as a traditional apocalyptic motif in Christian contexts (Matt 24:31; 1 Cor 15:52; Rev 8:2f.; see also ApocZeph 9:1f.). Additionally, the expression "God's trumpet" in 4:16 refers not to God as trumpeter but emphasizes the sound of the instrument (see SibOr 4:175) as well as its divine authority. Equally important, the apocalyptic signs do not seem to have the awakening of the dead in view (as in 1 Cor 15:52) but rather the signaling of the end and the concomitant approach of the Lord out of the heavenly sphere.

INTERPRETATION

This new pericope, like those that precede and follow, is clearly marked off by the formula "concerning those [who fall asleep]" and so introduces a new topic of discussion: "the faithful departed and the parousia." At this point Paul considers another, seemingly unrelated, question relayed to him from the community.

The Thessalonian Question. (1) A New Question from the Community. While the question forms part of a series (see 4:9 and 5:1) and is thus unrelated to the preceding discussion, it still expresses an important Pauline concern. He already announces in the thanksgiving his interest in such an issue, particularly in 1:10 when he speaks of the Son's return from heaven. Even prior to this he stresses the community's election by God (1:4), its exemplary acceptance of the word and its imitation of and fidelity to the Lord (5-6) as the basis for its hope in awaiting the risen Jesus' return at the end-time (10). So the question has a clear context in the apostolic preaching about eschatology. Paul addresses the community's question as it relates to the recent death of believers.

Paul's text has generated debate both about the question and Paul's response. Interestingly, the community asks him "about those who are asleep" (a euphemism for death), a topic which he notes in his introductory remarks and about which he insists that his response is designed to counter pagan-like grief. Thus, scholarly debate concerning the need for Paul's advice has generated five types of solutions. [1] It has been proposed that Paul is combating a Gnosticized interpretation of the resurrection by the community as the result of the arrival of new missionaries. Such a solution, however, is not convincing owing to the use of disputable data on Gnosticism and the equally questionable reading of the Corinthian situation into that of 1 Thessalonians. [2] Another proposal suggests that the community has lost hope in the parousia. Such a position also seems unlikely since Paul and community share a common belief in the Lord's imminent return (1:10; 2:19; 3:13; 4:15; 5:23).

[3] Some conclude that the community's problem relates to Paul's failure to instruct the converts concerning the resurrection of the dead. Either owing to the nearness of the parousia, the hurried situation of the Thessalonian mission (shortness of time as stated in Acts 17), or the undeveloped character of early Christian thinking, the community was not instructed in the matter and was greatly upset at the death of fellow believers—such a position is usually associated with studies on the development of Pauline thought or analyses of his chronology. Several factors argue against such a position. Careful reading of 4:13-18 suggests that it is not the resurrection of the dead which is at issue, but the status

of those who die before the Lord's return. Additionally, belief in the resurrection of Jesus and in the promise of future resurrection of believers is basic to Pauline thought already in this correspondence, whether the believer is rescued from the coming wrath (1:10), is called to be with God in the kingdom (2:12; 3:13), or is to be "with the Lord" at the parousia (4:14, 17; 5:10). Lastly, too much weight is put on a reading of verse 13 ("we do not want you to be in ignorance") as supporting Paul's introduction of new doctrine.

[4] Others have proposed that the community, though instructed in the matter, did not sufficiently understand the ramifications as regards the death of fellow believers. Objections can be leveled against this conclusion also. If one were to follow the standard chronology and view 1 Thessalonians as composed shortly before the other documents and at a considerable remove from the scenario of the "early death" of Christians, one hardly understands why such a problem does not occur often and in other communities. Again, the issue is not the resurrection but the parousia and the status of the Christian dead and living vis-à-vis the returning Lord. That there is misunderstanding at Thessalonica is obvious but the object of this misconception needs clarification and better focus.

[5] Taking an important clue from Paul's response (4:15b) it is suggested that the problem concerns the relative disadvantage of these dead who will be deprived of the joyful reunion with the returning Lord. The community's concern is that "those who have fallen asleep" should miss the great jubilation of the Lord's coming. Drawing on the theme of the assumption of the righteous, Paul assures the readers that the God who raised Jesus will likewise raise those who have died and so allow both, as living beings, to join the returning Lord (see discussion below).

(2) Rhetorical Disclaimer Rather than Deficiency of Message. Paul's opening statement, "we do not want you to be in ignorance," seems problematic. The idiom, employed only by Paul in the NT, appears in a number of contexts and has a positive as well as a negative form. Thus, for the modern reader two issues emerge: the phrase's function and meaning and its proper relation to its positive form. In the first case, in trying to defend the thesis that Paul did not preach the resurrection of the dead prior to writing the community, it is claimed that every use of this phrase in Paul concerns something new or previously unknown. On the contrary, a careful reading of each occurrence either does not allow one to speculate about the audience's prior knowledge (Rom 1:13; 2 Cor 1:8) or concerns the proper understanding of an issue being discussed (Rom 11:25; 1 Cor 10:1; 12:1). In the second case, assuming that the positive is the same as the negative form is to point the interpretation in the right direction and, in overlooking the rhetorical function of the litotes, to allow

the phrase to be read in too literal a sense. The idiom, along with its positive form, stresses positive knowledge, but in its negative form points to a misconception that needs to be clarified or dismissed (BAGD 11 gives numerous examples; see especially Josephus, *JA* 13:354: "I want you to have no doubt [not be in ignorance] that an injustice done to this man will make all us Jews your enemies"). Paul's text, therefore, might be paraphrased: "we want you to know very well about those who have died"; he then sets out to clear some misconception the community has about a topic he already discussed with them.

(3) About Those Who Fall Asleep. The topic requiring further clarification is stated simply: "concerning those who fall asleep." Since Paul employs the verb *kaimaomai* without any specifically Christian meaning (i.e., reference to the resurrection), it is assumed by most that the term functions simply as a euphemism for death (see Rom 7:2 and 1 Cor 7:39 where *apothnēskō* and *koimaomai* are used as synonyms). Still others observe that since the term is almost always used of dead believers in the NT, Paul's intention is to focus on the Christian dead and not the dead generally (see also 1 Cor 7:39; most reach this conclusion from a contextual reading). Recently, it has been suggested that Paul, in his attempt to provide consolation to the bereaved of Thessalonica, employs the language and themes used by moral philosophers to minimize death by comparing it to sleep (see Cicero, *Tusculan Disputations* 1.38.92 and Plutarch, *Letter of Consolation to Apollonius* 107DEF).

The last mentioned offers some interesting possibilities. First, however, the two sets of motivation for comfort seem contradictory, namely, the minimizing of death and the offering of hope in some type of afterlife, the first being antithetical to Pauline advice and the second offering a credible parallel to Christian teaching. I suggest that Paul's use of "falling asleep" is not an attempt to minimize the threat of death but rather his use of Thessalonian terminology (as is true in 4:9 and 5:1). Some in the community are appealing to traditional motifs (death as eternal sleep) for coping with the death of believing friends, motifs which Paul castigates and describes in the following clause as lacking in hope. Paul employs the terms used by members of the community in verses 13, 14, and 15 but argues against the motivation it implies, whether this be endless sleep or inevitable fate (see Seneca, *Epistle 99: On Consolation to the Bereaved* and Lucretius, *On the Nature of Things* 3). Paul's attack is not against non-Christian notions of death, whether Jewish, Stoic, or other, but against popular fatalistic concepts that were contrary to the meaning of the Christ-event, concepts that were not based on the promise of resurrection or afterlife. Thus, Paul cites a key term from the question and turns his attention, negatively and positively, to a discussion of the issue: how a Christian should confront the death of fellow believers.

Paraenetic Function of Paul's Response. (1) Grief, Consolation, and Hope (4:13b). Having stated the problem to be discussed, Paul states the purpose for his advice: "that you may not grieve as others do who have no hope." From the outset it is clear that the issue is not grief itself but the manner in which the community grieves. He insists that, while grief for the departed is permissible, lamentation born of fatalism is incompatible with the hope which undergirds Christian belief and commitment.

Paul's manner of comparison merits attention, for the manner of grieving which he condemns is described as that of "others who have no hope." The expression rendered "others" can be translated "the rest," that is, the term would designate the remainder of the whole (see Rom 11:7; 1 Cor 7:12; 2 Cor 13:2), and presumed to include all non-Christians. Scholars who follow this rendition find themselves in the position of defending Paul for having exaggerated the situation of the pagan world or insisting, on the basis of Eph 2:12, that Paul meant not some vague notion of immortality, as existed in the Jewish and pagan world, but Christian hope or life with Christ. It is unnecessary, however, to opt for so absolute a rendition, since the term can designate "others" beyond the group in question (Rom 1:13; 1 Cor 9:5; Phil 4:3; 1 Thess 5:6) and especially since the term is qualified by the articular substantive *hoi mē echontes* "(the) others, that is, the ones who have no. . . ." Paul's contrast is not with everyone else in the world but people whom he describes as "having no hope" in anything beyond death. Whether this is simply being kind to Paul must be judged on the basis of the overall exegesis of 4:13-18 and Paul's consistent judgment of the world beyond the Christian fellowship. Besides, it is hard to believe that Paul would so characterize either apocalyptic Judaism and its belief in the awakening "to everlasting life" or "to shame and everlasting contempt" (Dan 12:2) or the varying, widespread notions of afterlife, heavenly assumptions, and immortality of the soul in the Greco-Roman world of his time. Thus, Paul begins by opposing fatalistic notions of the future but also aligns the Christian position, at least initially, with similar optimistic notions of human fate.

Also, the issue is raised whether the question and the Pauline answer address only the fate of the Thessalonian believers who had died or also the converts' fear of death itself. First, Paul's use of the present tense for *koimaomai* in verse 13, "those who fall asleep," suggests that the topic is broader than the death of specific believers (use of aorist in vv. 14 and 15) and that the notion of death before the Lord's return is a concern for some among the living. Secondly, Paul's concluding statement in verse 18 suggests that the living should grieve in a different way for their dying friends and approach life more fully in the light of Christian hope which promises future life with the Lord for all believers, for those who have fallen asleep and for those who survive until the Lord's return.

(2) Teleological Thrust of Argument (4:17b). The discussion of 4:13-18 aims at the conclusion of verse 17: "and so we will be with the Lord forever." Both those who have died in Christ and those who survive until his coming will join him for eternity. Already in popular Greek piety after death one could expect communion with the gods or life with the great figures of the past (*TDNT* 7:781). Also in late Jewish literature the righteous could look forward to eternal fellowship with God (Pss 138:18; 139:14), to life with the great figures of Israel's past (ApocZeph 8:4-5; T.Isaac 6; see also Luke 16:22), and especially to a relationship with the Messiah (1 En 39:6-8; 45:4; 62:8, 14; 71:16; see also Rev 21:3; 22:4). Paul inherits such concepts from the culture of his time and envisions hope as union, whether after death (Phil 1:23) or at the parousia, with the risen Lord (Rom 6:8; 8:17; 1 Cor 1:9). What content "being with the Lord" should receive in this context is hard to determine though Paul on later occasions speaks of the believer being joint heirs with Christ and being glorified with him (Rom 8:17) or of being raised with Jesus and brought into God's presence (Rom 6:8; 2 Cor 4:14). One might suggest, on the basis of the triumphant imagery of verse 17, that Paul is speaking of participation in Jesus' victory, glory, and fellowship. All the same we insist that such questions are subsidiary to his purpose and that the details singled out for mention in his description of the parousia only serve to highlight his notion of hope.

(3) Return to Theme of Consolation (4:18). Paul ends his response much as he began by addressing the theme of consolation. What he formulates in verses 13-18 has as its goal to achieve the end stated in the final verse: "therefore, console one another with these words." His discussion is centered on one goal: providing the grieving community with a solid basis for hope. All, the missionaries included, will at the same time and together share eternal fellowship with the Lord regardless of who dies prematurely or survives until the parousia. Paul intends to console the survivors, exhorts them to console one another, and commands them, by repeating his advice, to motivate their lives and activity as the first stage in their lives with the Lord. Rather than lack of hope seen as fear for those who die before Christ's return, the Thessalonians are to view life and death not as futile threats of hardship or hopelessness but as the model and promise (in Christ) provided by God for holiness and eternal fellowship with the risen Lord. Present optimism and dynamism then are based on hope, itself the promise of a present and future relationship with the Lord.

Kerygmatic Basis for Eschatological Belief. (1) Paul's Use of a Kerygmatic Formula. Verse 14, with its "we believe that" formula, introduces a striking credal statement: "Jesus died and rose." The name of "Jesus" occurs frequently in both Thessalonian missives (see 2:19 and 1:1, respectively), though it appears only in 1:10 and twice in 4:14 without titles. For the two verbal expressions one finds very different data. The first, *apothnēskō*, is frequently employed by Paul to speak of Christ's death (Rom 5:6; 14:9; 1 Cor 8:11; Gal 2:21; see also 1 Thess 5:10), also of that of believers (Rom 5:15; 1 Cor 15:22), but the second, *anistēmi*, is rare in Paul, being used only in two OT citations (Rom 15:12 and 1 Cor 10:7) and in 1 Thess 4:14 and 16 (the last two concerning Jesus' and believers' resurrection, respectively). Paul prefers the verb *egeirō* (37 times) to speak of the resurrection. The Christological statement is of considerable interest and most scholars, on good grounds, assume it is a pre-Pauline credal formula, owing to its succinct formulation of the Christ-event but principally because it employs *anistēmi* rather than the usual Pauline *egeirō*. However, it is objected, employing standard typology, that 1 Thess 4:14 and Rom 14:9 resemble not credal statements but resurrection formulas and so suggest Pauline redaction. It is argued that in both cases the context has affected the formulation of the alleged credal text. In the case of Rom 14:9, "Christ died and *lived again*" would have been influenced by the traditional formula immediately following "Lord of both the dead and *the living*," while in that of 1 Thess 4:14, "Jesus died and *rose*," would have been formulated in relation to verse 16: "the dead in Christ *will rise*" (use also of *anistēmi*). Since, however, this last verb is also frequently employed in the Synoptic tradition in stereotyped passion summaries to describe the resurrection, since verse 14 likewise employs the name of "Jesus" in this kerygmatic statement, and since the saying adds to the disjointed character of Paul's argument, I am led to conclude with most scholars that Paul is here employing an early credal formula. Whether Paul modified the original formula for the occasion by omitting a phrase such as "for us" is possible in view of 5:10 but conjectural.

Paul's use of this early formula is of further interest in relation to his use of the name "Jesus" without titles on two occasions in verse 14. Since the name of Jesus appears in resurrection formulas whether alone (Rom 8:11) or in developed formulations (Gal 1:1; 2 Cor 4:14; Rom 10:9), it should offer no surprise that it does here and that the formulation itself comes from formulaic sayings of the early Church (see comments on 1:10). Paul's choice of this formula with its use of the name "Jesus" is consistent with his overall usage and sheds light on his meaning in 4:13-18 when examined in conjunction with *christos* and *kyrios*. Since his use of the name "Jesus" generally emphasizes death, that of "Christ" the resurrection, and that of "Lord" the believer's profession of faith (see comments on 1:1), it is hardly accidental that the name of Jesus appears first in a formula which emphasizes his death as corresponding to that of Thessalonian believers and then again in a parallel statement where believers are said to "have fallen asleep believing in (that same) Jesus." Both uses of the name of Jesus focus on death, the issue of grave and immediate concern. Interestingly, the title *christos* appears later in the pericope in a resurrection context, partly formulated on the basis of verse 14a (use of *anistēmi*): "the dead in Christ will rise." The third term "Lord" is surprisingly employed 5 times in verses 15, 16, 17.

From the above we can draw several conclusions. [1] The issue of death is of obvious importance (see repeated use of "fall asleep," "die," "dead," "survive") and is further emphasized by relating the issue to the death of Jesus even to the extent of stressing the name of the historical figure who died for all. [2] As already stated, the focus of this pericope is not the resurrection, whether one assumes that Paul neglected to preach that concept early on or that the believers have a distorted notion of the resurrection, but the status of the dead at the parousia. Paul's use of "Christ" in verse 16c demonstrates that the notion of resurrection is involved in the issue at hand but only secondarily since "being alive" at Jesus' return is a precondition for a heavenly assumption. [3] The preponderant use of the title *kyrios* or Lord focuses attention on verse 14 and its faith formula and parallel statement: "as we believe that Jesus died and rose, so should we believe that . . . we will (all) be with the Lord forever" (vv. 14-17). The focus is on profession of faith in the Lord's role vis-à-vis the dead and the living at the end-time and therefore an answer to the question of hope alluded to in verse 13. Thus, Paul's choice of the formula used in 14a is consistent with his general usage and treatment of the issue at hand.

(2) Initial Eschatological Conclusion. Paul's conclusion in verse 14 then is the following: just as we believe in Jesus' death and resurrection, so should we believe in the following: (lit.) "God will bring with him those who have fallen asleep through Jesus." His initial conclusion regarding the eschatological fate of those who have died, however, is far from clear. Indeed, the entire clause requires attention. [1] We begin with the sense of the final phrase, *axei syn autō*, which literally means "(God) will bring with him." While most accept such a translation and interpret the verbal phrase as anticipating what verses 16-17 state concerning the heavenly assumption of believers, others, stressing the importance of *syn*, view the phrase as referring to "the bringing together of the (dead) believers with Jesus" or, drawing contextually from the phrase "those who have fallen asleep" and claiming a parallel with the preceding death-resurrection formula, interpret the verbal phrase as God "bringing forth . . . from the dead" those who have died. In the case of the last mentioned, too much is read from the context and besides the text does not seem to imply a calling forth from the tomb or back from death. Also, the second reading does double duty with the preposition *syn;* besides,

the verbal expression does not read "bring together with" but "bring or fetch with." The first, literal translation correctly points to the notion of assumption which is more fully developed in the following verses; however, this particular rendition of the verb *agō* strangely has God coming down to earth "to bring" or even "lead" the dead back to heaven. It is better to translate as "cause to come or fetch" (see LSJ 17) since Jesus as Lord of the parousia will come down to get the faithful in God's name (v. 16; see also 2 Cor 4:14; 1 Pet 2:12).

[2] These issues bring us to consider the relation of verse 14b to 14a. It is readily acknowledged that following logically the death-resurrection formula one expects Paul, if his major concern were the resurrection of those who had fallen asleep, to speak not of them being assumed into heaven with Jesus but, by repeating the verb *anistēmi*, to insist on their rising with him (by rendering *axei* as "bring forth to life" some eliminate this difficulty). This anomaly is variously explained, whether as Paul adding the theme of resurrection secondarily to a parousia context, as Paul hinting at some inner connection related to his later "dying and rising with Christ" theme, or as indicating Paul's interest in the theme of heavenly assumption at the parousia. The last of these makes the best sense of Paul's text as he proceeds from the initial statement of the problem, all the while assuming belief in the resurrection, and works his way to the resolution of the difficulties which the community had sensed in the premature deaths of fellow believers. Between the two parts of the verse then Paul presupposes an unexpressed but assumed statement such as "and that having died with him we will also rise with him."

[3] There is debate whether the prepositional phrase *dia tou Iēsou* modifies the preceding participles ("those who have fallen asleep") or the following verb ("will fetch or bring"). In following the latter one would translate "through Jesus" (instrumental genitive), seeing the phrase as an early version of the Pauline "through Christ," and therefore interpreting the expression soteriologically (Jesus as intermediary of God's salvation). While scholars admit that this would be a normal translation of the idiom, they also note that the prepositional phrase "with him" following the verb precludes such an interpretation. The former is preferable. Interpreting the phrase as a parallel to "in Christ" (see v. 16b and 1 Cor 15:18) or as a genitive of attendant circumstance or manner (*IBNTG*, 57; *GNTG*, 4:267), scholars render *dia tou Iēsou* simply as those having fallen asleep "in him," "as Christians," or "as believing in (Christ)." Further, it is also noted that Paul's use of the aorist for the participle *koimaomai*, as opposed to the present tense in verse 13, marks the moment of death and so stresses the Christian's relationship to Jesus at the moment of death.

[4] Two issues should be noted briefly. (a) It has been noted that since

Paul does not in this instance indicate where believers are being led that one must assume that they are headed to the terrestrial millennial kingdom. But such is not a Pauline concept; Paul says simply in verse 17 that the destination is "in the clouds or in the air." It should be noted that Paul's statement in verse 15, that the living will certainly not go ahead of the dead, also precludes a millennial, earthly kingdom. At best, one can appeal to later statements to suggest that the destination Paul had in mind might be the divine judgment seat or presence (Rom 14:10; 2 Cor 4:14). (b) This point brings us to a related issue, namely, that "being raised by God" and assumed with Christ necessarily includes judgment by God. At best one can only conjecture whether Paul had judgment in mind since he says nothing explicitly concerning this issue in verses 13-18. The most explicit reference to judgment is to be found in his comment here in verse 14, if I am correct in my interpretation of the phrase *dia tou Iēsou*, that "God will fetch with Jesus those who will have fallen asleep believing in him"—a distinction is made then between the faithful and unfaithful followers.

Verse 14b then focuses on God's role in determining the destiny of all believers. It is a destiny that is determined by one's relationship to Jesus. Belief in what is stated in 14b then should be as well grounded as the foundational statement of 14a, that Jesus died and was raised by God.

(3) A Message from the Lord. Paul's discussion in verse 14 regarding the kerygmatic basis for eschatological belief, in the traditional view, comes to a halt since in verse 15 he introduces a dominical saying concerning the parousia and its scenario. The beginning of the verse, however, introduces a phrase which generates debate and conjecture concerning Paul's meaning and source for verses 15-17. Conversely, such debate pays little attention to the relationship between verses 14 and 15. The expression *en logō kyriou*, literally, "in/by a word of the Lord," is found nowhere else in the NT. Its closest parallel is the arthrous "the word of the Lord," which is never employed with the preposition *en* in the NT and which usually refers to the gospel message (1 Thess 1:8; often in Acts).

Discussion begins with the presupposition that the expression designates an apocalyptic statement, whose context is described in the following verses and which Paul relates to the risen Lord. This well-known discussion focuses on three areas. [1] Various sources for the alleged logion have been proposed: a gospel-like logion, a lost saying of Jesus, a revelatory utterance of an early Christian prophet or of Paul himself, or a Pauline construct based on traditional apocalyptic themes. Recent scholarship favors early Christian prophecy as the most credible source, a source which nonetheless would have undergone Pauline redaction. [2] Though most commentators limit the logion to verses 16-17, some point instead to 15b or 15b-17 and most insist on some type of Pauline adaptation of the logion to fit the Thessalonian situation. [3] Finally, employing redactional analysis some have attempted to recreate the original saying and to trace its pre-Pauline to Pauline evolution.

Two features of Paul's text, however, lead me in a direction differing from the present consensus. First, while scholars usually take the phrase *en logō kyriou* to mean a literal saying of the Lord, some suggest that this unusual Pauline expression is meant to describe Paul's way of speaking: "as a message from the Lord" (*IBNTG,* 79). The phrase's OT background confirms this. The idiom, "the word of the Lord" (anarthrous *logos kyriou*), is a common OT phrase to designate God's law or will and frequently to describe prophetic activity ("the word of the Lord came to . . ."—Hos 1:1 and often). The phrase *en logō kyriou* (also with *rhēma*), while less frequently used, also appears in prophetic contexts to describe the power of inspiration under which a holy person acts or speaks (six times in 2 Kings 13; also Sir 48:3 to speak of Elijah). Second, almost without exception and without discussion commentators state that the initial *touto* ("this or the above") of verse 15 refers not to what precedes but to what follows. In effect the examination of Pauline usage in the case of initial *touto* indicates that often, as in classical Greek, the term in Paul refers back to what has just been discussed (Rom 6:6; 12:20; 1 Cor 7:6; 13:9, among others). More precisely the expression *touto gar* (used also in 2 Cor 8:10 and 1 Thess 4:3, 15; 5:18) always refers back to what has been discussed (see comments above on 4:3). I therefore conclude that the beginning of verse 15 is not an introductory formula to a dominical saying but an attempt on Paul's part to underscore the authority of what has been said in verse 14. The Christ-event and its significance, as interpreted by messengers who have been divinely approved and commissioned (2:2-4), can certainly qualify "as a message from the Lord." Paul's claim then is one of prophetic authority.

Paul's prophetic stance here is not less striking than the claims he makes for himself and his colleagues in 2:2-4, that they "spoke openly as the agents of God" and that they were "examined and approved by God to be entrusted with the gospel." Also, his statement in 1:5, "our gospel came to you not only in word, but also in power, both with the Holy Spirit and with full conviction," appeals to prophetic categories of authority, divine power, and inspiration. In 4:15 Paul makes a claim to divine knowledge in the way the prophets of Israel saw themselves as conduits of a divine message. Here, as in 1 Corinthians 15, especially verses 50-52 regarding the "mystery," Paul draws from the community's basic kerygmatic tradition to convey the Lord's message concerning hope. What Paul is writing to the disconsolate readers is not human wisdom aimed at minimizing death and its terror but a message from the Lord Jesus who has died, has been raised, and promises to return to gather the faithful (both the newly raised and survivors) and lead them to the heavenly kingdom and glory.

The Faithful Dead and the Apocalyptic Scenario. After an initial response that the dead in Christ will ascend with him at the end-time, Paul in verses 15-17 shifts the discussion in a twofold way. In the first place he qualifies the addressees no longer as "you" ("who grieve for" the fallen) but as "we" ("who are alive"). Secondly, he employs the term "alive" *(zaō),* a univocal rather than euphemistic term, to speak to the community, and, in this connection pays greater attention to the parousia and its attendant circumstances for both the living and the dead.

(1) The Living Faithful or Survivors. Paul's statement in verse 15 addresses the basic problem: the advantage of the living over those who have died. He employs the term "alive," not only to describe the status of his addressees but also to concretize the problem envisioned by them: that certain believers are no longer alive and so will be at a disadvantage when the Lord returns. The term provides a clue to the discussion that follows, since being "alive" is a precondition for welcoming the Lord when he returns and for participating in the heavenly journey of the end-time. Paul further qualifies the addressees by the important expression "who survive until the coming of the Lord," a phrase which also indicates that the issue is not life versus death but being alive when the Lord returns.

Paul is speaking of two groups, those who died before and those who survive until the Lord's coming, and their relative situation vis-à-vis this event. In this connection several issues deserve attention. [1] In verse 15 Paul speaks of the coming "of the Lord," not "of the Lord Jesus" as he does in 2:19 and 3:13. He wishes to emphasize the believers' profession of faith in the future event which provides the hope mentioned in verse 13. [2] Paul includes himself within the group that will survive until the end. Reservations are often expressed regarding his possible error and the meaning of his statement. Did Paul expect to see the parousia firsthand? This is to be explained in light of later statements where he either envisions the possibility that he might die before the end (1 Cor 6:14; 2 Cor 4:14; Phil 1:20; 1 Thess 5:10) or implies that he would still be alive (1 Cor 15:51-52; Rom 13:11). Simply stated: Paul along with his contemporaries believed in an imminent parousia and his texts reflect the possibility that he might be alive when the Lord returns and that he might be called earlier to be "at home with the Lord" (2 Cor 5:8). [3] Paul's use of the term "survive" in verses 15 and 17 refers not to the travails of the end-time but already implies, at this early date in his career, that he envisions survival until the end as an exception rather than the rule for believers vis-à-vis the parousia (1 Cor 15:51).

(2) No Advantage or Precedence for the Survivors. Apocalyptic Judaism had stressed the importance of being part of the generation of the end-time and, by envisioning a period of time between the general resurrection and the messianic era and by focusing on prophetic visions of a happy future, had stressed the blessedness of being among the remnant (Dan 12:12-13; 4 Ezra 6:18-28; 7:27-28; 13:24; PssSol 17:44; SibOr 3:367-80; see 2 Bar 30:1-3 which, like Paul, stresses the joy of both the living and the dead). While some importance is attached in these Jewish texts to being alive at the end—survivors are on the whole more blessed than the dead (4 Ezra 13:16-20)—it should be noted that it is rather the notion of perseverance, righteousness, or deliverance from evil which is stressed as it is for Paul who describes the dead (and by implication the living) as those who believed in Jesus (vv. 14 and 17). Thus, Paul adopts in part "the answer of the apocalypses" to show that indeed the living had no real advantage over the dead. By his use of an emphatic negative with the aorist subjunctive ("will by no means precede") he wishes to emphasize this lack of advantage. Often in the apocalypses one hears that in the end all will arrive at judgment at the same time, together, or as one (4 Ezra 5:41-45; Barnabas 20:2; 51:13; Pseudo-Philo, *Biblical Antiquities* 19:20), much as we see in Paul's response that both the living and the dead "will be caught up together" in the final journey "to meet the Lord" (v. 17: also 5:10).

What, in Thessalonian terms, is this advantage about which some speak? In the context of the promise of a happy future, of a millennial period, or the anticipation of a joyous reunion with the returning Messiah, the members of the community feared that the dead would not be able to participate in the events of the triumphant welcome of the Lord Jesus since only the survivors would be able to do so. The advantage then consisted in the living being able to welcome the returning Lord, going on ahead, and being assumed bodily with him prior to the final, general resurrection. Paul insists in verse 15 that this will not happen and explains in verses 16-17 why this will be the case.

(3) The Apocalyptic Scenario and Its Heavenly Activity. Paul begins his explanation as to why the dead will not be at a disadvantage by describing in graphic detail the Lord's return to gather the elect. He directs his attention to the heavenly activity or downward movement which will take place (v. 16). In clearly delineated Christian terms Paul insists both that the Lord Jesus will take the initiative and will himself descend from the heavens where he is enthroned (1:10; Rom 8:34).

In a stark series of signs Paul describes the Lord's coming to gather the elect. Employing traditional apocalyptic imagery, he speaks of "a cry of command" uttered by the heavenly Lord to begin the apocalyptic scene of the gathering of the end-time harvest. There then follow two explanatory expressions, "an archangel's shout" and "a blast of God's trumpet," signs that the heavenly activity of ingathering is underway and that the Lord Jesus approaches. In this connection one interesting feature regarding the apocalyptic scenario should be noted. While each of the prepositional phrases could point to military, apocalyptic possibilities, whether the command, angelic shout, or trumpet blast, they do not in this context require such—only in 5:8 does Paul have recourse to explicit military imagery. In this context he is not interested in the darker side of the apocalyptic scenario but in its reassuring aspect.

(4) The Faithful and the Apocalyptic Scenario. At the end of verse 16, Paul continues his argument by introducing the dead and the survivors into the apocalyptic scenario to bring home the point of his response and to introduce the upward movement of the scenario. He insists that first, prior to the upward movement with the Lord, "the dead in Christ" will be raised. It is not his intention to stress the resurrection but the raising from the dead as a precondition of the believers' meeting and being with the Lord; it will happen before the upward movement of believers occurs.

Paul by use of the expression "the dead in Christ," focuses not on some intermediate Christ-like existence between death and resurrection but on the fact that those who have died as faithful followers of Jesus before his return can expect to be raised from the dead. It is their relationship to Christ which is of paramount importance, both in life and in death as the promise of future resurrection. Interestingly, Paul no longer employs the euphemism "fall asleep" but more directly speaks of death in stark contrast to resurrection, much in the same way as the kerygmatic formula of verse 14 speaks starkly of Jesus dying (not falling asleep) and rising. Also in relation to that same formula, one must see Paul's use of the traditional verb *anistēmi* rather than *egeirō* to speak of resurrection as consciously relating the resurrection of believers to that of their Lord. By his emphatic use of "then" to introduce the second, simultaneous phrase of the parousia ("then we who are alive—who survive"—v. 17), Paul negates all speculation concerning intermediate states of existence, millennial or terrestrial reigns with the Lord, or other possible advantages one group of believers might have over the other.

Finally, in a series of statements in verse 17 Paul emphasizes further the related points he wishes to impress on his readers. [1] The living and the newly risen will be taken together from this earth. [2] There will be an unforgettable meeting of all with the returning Lord. [3] All will remain forever with the Lord they have served faithfully in this life.

Note on Verse 16: Source and Tradition Analysis. Analysis of Paul's brief apocalypse can proceed methodologically in one of four ways, depending on one's conclusion regarding the nature and source of verses 16-17. (1) If one believes that Paul is employing an apocalyptic saying of Jesus related to a gospel text such as Matt 24:29-44, then one is most concerned with determining that relationship. Indeed, Matthew 24 and parallels provide an interesting apocalyptic scenario and context for understanding Paul's text, particularly the coming of the Son of Man on the clouds, the presence of angels, the Matthean detail of "the loud trumpet call," the gathering of the elect, concern with the people of the last generation, the Matthean comparison of the end with the coming of a thief (see 1 Thess 5:2, 4), and the Matthean midnight call to meet the bridegroom (25:6). Nonetheless, scholars are not convinced that Paul employed such a source or that such a conclusion assists in examining the composition of the Pauline passage. (2) If Paul borrowed an apocalyptic saying of an early Christian prophet, then one would attempt to distinguish redactionally between Pauline and non-Pauline terms and themes and then reconstruct the original logion on that basis. The lack of consensus regarding such reconstructions and the difficulty of distinguishing, in so short a passage with unique content and terms, between Pauline editing of a logion and borrowing of traditional apocalyptic language and content, make analysis a conjectural exercise. (3) Some have concluded that the parallels between 1 Thess 4:15-17 and 1 Cor 15:51-52 are so striking that one must assume a common origin for them. But careful comparison shows that beyond general similarities there is only one clear linguistic parallel (the trumpet) and much difference in *Sitz im Leben* and therefore the message between the two. (4) I therefore proceed with the assumption maximally that Paul composed verses 16-17 employing traditional apocalyptic imagery and presuming a standard end-time scenario or minimally that he employed early tradition which he moulded to fit the epistolary occasion.

What traditions then did Paul have at his disposal when he composed his answer to the community? While not attempting to be exhaustive, I would propose the following. From his own Thessalonian correspondence we know that Paul and contemporary Christians held firmly that Jesus, as God's Son, raised from the dead, is considered a Messiah figure who would come from heaven in a savior-like role (1:10; also 5:9). Also, since Paul speaks of Jesus' parousia in a somewhat casual way in 2:19; 3:13, we must assume that Jesus' return as Messiah (also 5:23) was a commonly accepted notion among colleagues and one readily preached to new communities. In relation to 1:10 and the Son's coming from heaven we conclude that Paul was acquainted with the Son of Man tradition represented by Dan 7:13-14 and embedded in the Jesus tradition (Mark

13:26; 14:62 and parallels). Matthew's apocalyptic editing of this material in 24:29-44 lends independent confirmation of the widespread application by early Christian thinkers of these traditions to Jesus' coming in the end-time. At least in passing I would refer to the development in the Book of Revelation of traditions similar to those found in 1 Thess 4:15-17: the apocalyptic function of trumpets and angels and the raising of two dead witnesses prior to their heavenly assumption (11:11-12). Lastly, we must take serious note of several Jewish intertestamental texts which explicitly speak of the coming of the Messiah. In the PssSol 17:26, 32 we read of the "Lord Messiah," who is taught by God and who gathers a holy or righteous people who are God's children (see 1 Thess 4:3f. and the Pauline references to God as Father). In 2 Bar 30:1-3 the Anointed One is said to "return in glory," at which time "all who sleep in hope of him . . . rise" and "appear together, in one mind," and share equally in joy.

Finally, in 4 Ezra 6, in a vision about the end-time when God "draws near to visit the inhabitants of the earth" (18), we hear of the signs of the end, among which is the loud sound of the trumpet (23) and the promise of salvation for those who survive (25). Of course, in 7:28, we are told of the revelation of God's Messiah Son along with his followers who enjoy a 400-year terrestrial reign and, in 12:31-34, of the lion-like Messiah who delivers judgment on the wicked and deliverance and joy on the holy remnant in lieu of the day of judgment. Also, in the vision of the Man from the Sea (chapter 13), one encounters an apocalyptic situation similar to that of 1 Thess 4:16-17. A Man, a messianic figure, comes out from the sea, flies with the clouds of heaven, and issues commands with the voice from his mouth (3-4). After having conquered the threatening multitudes, he comes down from his mountain perch and calls to himself a peaceful multitude (12), the blessed who remain until the end (13:24, 48). A final note is of interest in the following vision, for in 14:9 the Lord tells Ezra: "you shall be taken up from among men, and henceforth you shall live with my Son and with those who are like you until the times are ended."

It is with such traditions in mind that Paul tackles the issue of the living and the dead vis-à-vis the parousia. Expressing himself in the mythic terms of his time, Paul accepts the fact that Jesus has been raised by God from the dead, was enthroned in glory at God's right hand (Rom 8:34), and awaits a future time when he will come down from heaven to rescue (1 Thess 1:10) and gather the elect at the sound of the trumpet (4:16; 1 Cor 15:52; also Matt 24:31).

A Further Note on the Imagery of Verse 17: Rapture in the Clouds and Meeting the Lord in the Air. (1) "Caught up together . . . in the clouds." To describe what happens to the elect Paul employs the verb *harpazō*, a term which has a range of meaning from "steal," to "take by force," to "snatch away" in relation to visions and heavenly powers. It is the last mentioned which provides the context for its use in 4:17. The term was popular in apocalyptic literature to describe heavenly journeys either of the soul after death or of a visionary who is taken up to heaven. While the LXX prefers other words to describe Enoch's and Elijah's translation into heaven, Wis 4:11 employs this verb to speak about Enoch's disappearance into paradise. It is especially in intertestamental literature that one encounters the term to describe visionaries being taken up to the heavens (1 En 39:3; 52:1; 2 En 3:1; 7:1f.; 3 Bar 2:1; ApocZeph 2:1; see Philo, *Special Laws* 3.1; Plato, *Republic* 10.614-21), to dwell in the heavenly sphere or to learn its eschatological secrets. Paul employs this term in 2 Cor 12:2, 4 to describe a heavenly journey he experienced to the third heaven or paradise (see also Rev 12:5 and Acts 8:39). The term's use in 1 Thess 4:17 represents Paul's attempt, by means of apocalyptic imagery, to describe the indescribable fate of the elect, their sudden translation into the heavenly sphere on that great and terrible day of the Lord. While his choice of a term, which implies the violent, immediate separation of the elect from their terrestrial context and conflict, might suggest, in light of 1:10, a separation of the righteous from the ungodly and a subsequent apocalyptic battle, such a scenario reads too much into Paul's short, pointed response. Paul is interested in what the term suggests concerning God's power in "fetching" (v. 14b) and "snatching away" those whose lives and deaths reflect their relationship to the risen Lord.

The heavenly journey is effected by means of clouds, a popular means of transportation in mythological and religious literature. While clouds were a frequent motif in OT theophanies (Exod 16:10; 19:16f.) they were also a divine and heavenly vehicle (Isa 19:1; Dan 7:13) suggesting divine power and presence. Just as the Jesus tradition is never sure whether Jesus comes on or with *(en, epi, meta)* the clouds (Mark 13:26; 14:62 and parallels), so is the Pauline text unclear as to whether the elect are borne heavenward on the clouds as vehicle or are enveloped in the clouds as symbols of divine power and the heavenly sphere.

(2) "Meet the Lord in the air." The goal of the heavenly journey is described simply "to meet the Lord." It is generally admitted that the term for the meeting, *apantēsis*, became in the Hellenistic world a technical expression for the public, civic welcome accorded important visitors (*TDNT* 1:380-81). Such processions of leading citizens going out of the city walls to welcome and accompany an approaching visitor would have been common in Hellenistic times (BGU 2.362.7.17; Polybius, *History* 5.26.8; Josephus, *JA* 11:8:4; Cicero, *Letters to Atticus* 8.16.2; 16.11.6; Chrysostom, *Thessalonians: Homily* 8.62.440) and would have been used

by Paul to describe the triumphal meeting of believers and their Lord at the end-time. A second avenue of research points to Jewish background for this term, for in the LXX it is used for meetings with Abraham and David (Gen 14:17; 2 Sam 19:16) and for the Israelites' encounter with God at Sinai (Exod 19:17). So it has been suggested that Paul was influenced by such usage, especially theophanic imagery, in formulating his thought. It is thus possible that a double influence is at work here. Regardless, whether Paul thinks of LXX language or Hellenistic custom, the readers, whose acquaintance with Jewish scriptural background would have been weak, would certainly have understood Paul's suggestive imagery.

The assembly of believers is to encounter the returning Lord "in the air," which, according to ancient Jewish cosmology, is the ethereal region between heaven and earth (*TDNT* 1:165-66). Clearly Paul states that the Lord "descends from heaven" and the assembly leaves the earth ("in the clouds" and "in the air"), but what such imagery suggests beyond this is unclear. If one follows the logic of the *parousia* and *apantēsis* imagery, one might expect the aerial meeting to represent the assembly's going out of the city walls (earth) first to welcome the distinguished visitor and then to accompany the dignitary back to the city, to set up the millennial kingdom according to some. While one might envision the assembled groups as remaining "in the air," one must assume that Paul does not intend this since the region between heaven and earth, especially the lower air, had demonic association and since verse 14 by its use of "fetch with Jesus" suggests further movement. Lastly, one could assume that Paul intends a heavenly entrance following the aerial meeting, though one might ask why it is necessary for the Lord to descend partly from heaven.

Several considerations point to a heavenly entrance as Paul's intention. [1] The cloud and rapture imagery suggests an assumption of the elect into heaven after an aerial meeting. [2] The aerial or halfway meeting of the parties is suggested by the aerial setting of the classic Christian texts where the Son of Man comes in clouds and sends out angelic helpers to gather the elect from the ends of earth and heaven (Mark 13:26-27 par.) as well as Jesus' statement, citing Dan 7:13, concerning the Son of Man coming with the clouds of heaven (14:62 par.). In the latter it is unclear whether the Son of Man's destination is earth for judgment or the heavenly throne as in Dan 7:13. [3] While 1:10 suggests that Jesus, at his coming, will rescue the elect from wrath, it is possible to see the rapture itself as a protection of the elect from the trials of the end-days. [4] It has been suggested that the procession imagery implies both a movement to meet and welcome the dignitary and a return to the city in accompaniment. Interestingly, in 2 Cor 5:8, in speaking of "being home with the Lord," Paul suggests that the ultimate goal of the believer is a heavenly domicile (Phil 3:20) and one might presume that the goal of the triumphant procession is the heavenly throne where the Son will subject himself and all things to God (1 Cor 15:28). Paul's intention, however, is not a discourse on the end-time but an attempt to reassure his readers that all faithful followers will be united with their risen Lord.

For Reference and Further Study

Chapa, J. "Consolatory Patterns? 1 Thes 4, 13, 18; 5, 11." *TC*, 220–28.

Collins, R. F. "Tradition, Redaction and Exhortation in 1 Thess 4, 13–5, 11." *SFLT* 154–72.

Delobel, J. "The Fate of the Dead according to 1 Thessalonians 4 and 1 Corinthians 15." *TC*, 340–47.

Gillman, J. "Signals of Transformation in 1 Thessalonians 4:13-18." *CBQ* 47 (1985) 263–81.

Harnisch, W. *Eschatologische Existenz: Ein exegetischer Beitrag zum Sachenliegen vor 1 Thessalonicher 4, 13–5, 11.* Göttingen: Vandenhoeck & Ruprecht, 1973.

Havener, I. "The Pre-Pauline Christological Credal Formulae of 1 Thessalonians." *SBLSP* (1981), 105–28.

Hyldahl, N. "Auferstehung Christi, Auferstehung der Toten (1 Thess 4, 13-18)." *Die paulinische Literatur und Theologie: The Pauline Literature and Theology.* Aarhus: Forlaget Aros, 1980, 119–35.

Klijn, A. F. J. "1 Thessalonians 4, 13-18 and Its Background in Apocalyptic Literature." *Paul and Paulinism: Essays in Honour of C. K. Barrett.* Eds. M. D. Hooker and S. G. Wilson. London: SPCK, 1982, 67–73.

Lüdemann, G. *Paul, Apostle to the Gentiles: Studies in Chronology.* Philadelphia: Fortress, 1984.

Marxsen, W. "Auslegung von 1 Thess. 4, 13-18." *ZTK* 66 (1969) 22–37.

Plevnik, J. "The Parousia as Implication of Christ's Resurrection: An Exegesis of 1 Thess 4, 13-18." *Word and Spirit: Essays in Honor of David Martin Stanley.* Ed. J. Plevnik. Willowdale: Regis College, 1975, 199–277.

_____. "The Taking Up of the Faithful and the Resurrection of the Dead in 1 Thessalonians 4:13-18." *CBQ* 46 (1984) 274–83.

Schmithals, W. *Paul and the Gnostics.* Nashville: Abingdon, 1972.

14. On Being Ready for the Lord's Return (5:1-11)

1. Now concerning times and seasons, brothers and sisters, you do not need to have anything written to you. 2. For you yourselves know perfectly well that the day of the Lord, like a thief at night, comes in the same way. 3. Indeed, just when people say "Peace and security," without fail sudden ruin descends upon them, like the onset of birth-pains on one who is pregnant; in no way then will they escape. 4. But you, brothers and sisters, are not in darkness, for that day to overtake you like a thief. 5. No, you are all children of light and children of the day—we belong neither to the night nor to darkness. 6. So then, let us not sleep as others do, but let us be alert and self-controlled, 7. for sleepers sleep by night; drunkards drink by night. 8. But we for our part, since we belong to the day, let us be self-controlled, armed as we are with faith and love as a breastplate and the hope of salvation as a helmet, 9. for God did not destine us for wrath but for the attainment of salvation through our Lord Jesus Christ, 10. who died for us so that, whether we be alert or asleep, together we might live with him. 11. Therefore, encourage one another and build each one up, as you are indeed doing.

NOTES

1. *Now concerning times and seasons, brothers and sisters:* Both the formula "now concerning . . ." (see 4:9, 13) and direct address indicate a change of topic (see 2:1; 4:10, 13; also 5:12). The community's new question concerns "times and seasons," an expression which is stereotypical and evidently parallel to "the day of the Lord" in verse 2. While these two temporal nouns (*chronos* and *kairos*) have distinguishable meanings (length of time versus period of time) their tandem usage in the LXX (Dan 2:21; 7:12; Wis 8:8) and Acts (1:7; 3:20-21) suggests a standard phrase for characterizing the temporal schema of the end-time (*TDNT* 9:592). This suggestion is further indicated by the usage of Acts 1:7 regarding the divine timetable, by the frequent use of *kairos* to introduce the time of judgment (Jer 6:15; 27:31; Dan 8:17; Mark 13:13; 1 Cor 4:5; Rev 1:3), and by the interest of apocalypticists in determining the end-time schema (Dan 12:6-7; Mark 13:32; 4 Ezra 4:33; 6:7; 2 Bar 21:19; 25:1-4). We are probably right in seeing a connection between the discussion of 4:13-18 regarding the faithful dead and the fear of some that further delay of the Lord's return would place them in a similar position.

you do not need to have anything written to you: Again employing *paralipsis* as he does in 4:9 but with a more felicitous turn of phrase, Paul draws added attention to what the missionaries already preached regarding the subject. As the succeeding text underscores, Paul cites the community's proverbial thief-in-the-night motif to defuse the highly charged apocalyptic expectation of his addressees by redirecting their attention to the apostolic preaching.

2. *For you yourselves know perfectly well:* As in 4:9 the grammatical and logical connection between what was just said and the new clause is clearly expressed by a *gar* clause. By employing the emphatic pronoun and the verb *oida* ("you yourselves know"; see 1:4) Paul notes that the community has a personal acquaintance with the facts. Rhetorically, he compliments them on their knowledge of the subject but at the same time, by employing the term *akribōs*, stresses ironically the accuracy of the teaching they have received as opposed to the inaccuracy of temporal speculation regarding the Lord's day. Thus, it seems most likely that Paul has been asked for precision regarding the time of the Lord's day.

that the day of the Lord, like a thief at night, comes in the same way: What the audience knows with accuracy is introduced by a *hoti* clause, whose content is reminiscent of a Q saying from the Jesus tradition (Matt 24:43-44; Luke 12:39-40). Though it has been proposed that Paul's source could have been early Christian prophetic or apocalyptic tradition (see Rev 3:3; 16:15; 2 Pet 3:10), it is readily conceded that he had access to Q-like Jesus tradition (also GTh 21) for the use of the thief motif. Dependence of Paul on similar Jesus tradition in the following verses adds credence to this conclusion and is best explained by oral borrowing. The formulaic expression, "the day of the Lord," is frequently employed by the prophets, beginning with Amos, to speak of the day of judgment (5:18-20) and deliverance (Joel 2:32). Thus, while early Christian tradition borrowed this eschatological phrase to refer to Jesus' return in glory (Phil 1:6; 1 Cor 1:8; even 1 Cor 5:5), it is probable, in the present eschatological context and in view of this early formulation of his thought, that Paul is employing an OT formula for the end-time rather than making an explicit reference to Jesus' coming. Such a conclusion is confirmed by the comparison of the thief not to the Lord's coming (so Rev 3:3; 16:15; Luke 12:39-40 par.) but to the arrival of the Lord's day (also 2 Pet 3:10). Paul's text is usually translated "the Lord's day comes like a thief at night," but since in this statement he employs two terms of comparison, *hōs* and *houtōs*, one should recognize two comparative elements: the day of the Lord is both *like* a thief at night and comes *in the same manner*.

3. *Indeed, just when people say, "Peace and security":* While it is granted that much of the vocabulary of the verse is non-Pauline ("security," "sudden," "descend," "birth-pains," "womb/pregnant," or "in no way"), not employed in a Pauline fashion ("peace" and "people say") or rare in his letters ("ruin" and "escape"), it is also noted that the overall structure is due to Paul (*hotan . . . tote . . . hōsper . . . kai . . .*) and bears an unmistakable proverbial character. Literally, the text reads "when people say . . . then sudden ruin . . .," but to convey its proverbial character and to avoid giving the impression of a "harsh threat" (which some think they detect in the text) it is rendered "indeed, just when people say . . ., without fail sudden ruin descends upon them." Again one is led to a Synoptic parallel (Luke 21:34-36) to account for Pauline themes, vocabulary, and sequence of ideas, namely, false security, the sudden coming of the end, comparison to a snare, and the theme of escape. However, while the Lukan passage warns in moralistic terms

against dissipation and drunkenness, Paul's text appeals in a more general way to the well-known false cry of peace and deceptive sense of security preached by false prophets (Jer 6:14-15; Ezek 13:10-16) or experienced by the unthinking and callous in the face of divine judgment (Matt 24:37-39; Luke 17:26-27).

without fail sudden ruin descends upon them: "Without fail" renders *tote* and captures the text's proverbial character. Again linguistic similarity to the Lukan tradition is evident: "that the day descend upon you suddenly" (21:34), and again there is a difference in usage. The Lukan text stresses the need for moral readiness; Paul describes the unexpected, logical, and sudden reversal of a false sense of security. Not only does he stress the suddenness of the outcome, as does Luke, but develops further the original image by dwelling on the antithesis of the householder's imagined security. Rather than peace, quiet, and mastery of possessions (following the thief imagery), the misguided householder encounters "ruin" *(olethros)*, a term which implies destruction of property, death, or even eschatological destruction (Jer 48:3-6; see *TDNT* 5:168; LSJ 1213-14). Finally, Paul's use, here only, of *ephistēmi* ("descend, come upon") stresses the proverbial source and meaning of the imagery since the term is often employed to describe the sudden arrival of misfortune (BAGD 330.1).

like the onset of birth-pains on one who is pregnant: Paul compares the arrival of disaster (the thief or the Lord's day) to the inescapable "birth pangs of a woman in labor" (lit.: "the birth-pangs of a woman [with a child] in her belly"). The expression *ōdin* ("birth-pains" in the plural) appears often in the Greek OT where it stresses the pain, anxiety, or distress associated with a situation, particularly in view of divine judgment (Ps 47:7; Isa 13:8; Jer 6:24; also Gal 4:19). In apocalyptic and Qumran texts the term is used in a similar fashion to speak of the woes of the end-days (1 En 62:4; Mark 13:17 par.; Rev 12:2; also SibOr 5:514; 4 Ezra 4:40 and 1 QH 3.7-10). In 5:3 however the term is used in the singular and seems to refer to the beginning of birth-pains. Thus, it is not an indication of destruction or a sign of the end-time but a statement concerning the ineluctable character of the ruin that will descend on all who live in false security and self-deception (*TDNT* 9:672). Paul's use of such terminology allows his text to appeal to the proverbial lack of readiness and sudden downfall of the overconfident and to hint eschatologically at the suddenness of the end and inevitability of judgment.

in no way then will they escape: With this clause Paul brings to an end the proverbial, prophetic imagery of the complacent and self-confident person. Having stated that ruin is sudden and almost mockingly elicited, Paul emphasizes its inescapable reality. By use of the expression *kai ou mē* ("in no way then," a double negative which most decisively negates a future activity; see BAGD 517D) he stresses the absolute character of what follows. The falsely confident have no way of fleeing their merited fate, a fate that is described as the antithesis of their expectations: ruin rather than security and peace. Again, the structural and thematic similarities between the Lukan (21:34-36) and Pauline text as well as the divergent manner in which each author employs the themes argue for independent use of popular, proverbial material taken from the Jesus tradition. Thus, verse 3 describes how the thief comes, suddenly and inescapably, and so warns that the Lord's day will come in the same way.

4. *But you, brothers and sisters, are not in darkness:* There is a shift here in Paul's train of thought, indicated both by the expression "but you, brothers and sisters" (see also 4:10b) and by a shift in imagery from considering night as cover for the thief's evil activity to viewing night and darkness as images for the sphere of evil. For this purpose he employs traditional Jewish light-darkness terminology, dualistic imagery with a complex moral and eschatological background and function. In the first instance, he would have known OT usage of characterizing behavior which is pleasing or not to God as deriving from the domains of light or darkness (Job 22:9-11; 29:3; Ps 74:20; Isa 2:5). This is also true of later Jewish literature's frequent expressions of moral dualism (e.g., T.Levi 19:1—"choose for yourselves light or darkness, the Law of the Lord or the works of Beliar"). In the second instance, he would have known the frequent mingling of moral and eschatological dualism in current apocalyptic literature, whether of the intertestamental period or of Qumran (T.Naphtali 2:7-10; T.Benjamin 5:3; 1 QS 3:13–4:26; 1 QM passim). The remainder of Paul's pericope develops the behavioral character of the light-darkness imagery and its eschatological potential. The readers therefore are told: "you are not in darkness," for you belong to the sphere of light, a statement which will be made positively and repeated negatively in verse 5.

for that day to overtake you like a thief: Since the audience does not belong to the realm of darkness, the result (use of *hina:* BDF 391.5) is that the Lord's day will still come upon them unexpectedly but will not overtake them menacingly in the way a thief does an unprepared victim. Leaving aside the suddenness motif Paul focuses now on the unwelcome aspect of the Lord's day, for part of the picture of that day, one aspect of its coming, is its negative inescapable character—he employs the verb *katalambanō* ("to seize with hostile intent"; BAGD 413) to stress its menancing quality—for those who are unprepared. Also, the Greek text reads literally "the day" but since Paul's obvious referent for this passage is verse 2 where he speaks of "the Lord's day" and "its coming in the manner of a thief," the translation tries to make clear such a back-reference by using the expression "that day." Lastly, one should note that the variant "the thieves" (*kleptas* in B A) is suspect for several reasons (see *TCGNT*, 633), not the least being weak textual authority for such a reading and the probable misunderstanding of the light-darkness imagery by a scribe intent on comparing not the coming of the Lord's day to that of a thief but the readers to thieves surprised by the coming of dawn.

5. *No, you are all children of light and children of the day:* The affirmation is introduced by a postpositive *gar* but, since it affirms a negative statement, it is translated by an emphatic "no" (BAGD 152.4). The imagery employed, "sons of light," comes from a Hebraic construction which describes a quality of a person or the sphere to which that person belongs. The actual phrase is often employed at Qumran (1 QS 1:9f. and 1 QM 1:1f.—both "children of light" and "of darkness") and occurs elsewhere in the NT (Luke 16:8; John

12:36; see Eph 5:8). Paul states in positive terms that the readers belong to the sphere of light, both of revelation and consequent moral activity, as opposed to that of darkness. The second phrase, "sons of day," is a NT hapax and probably a Pauline creation. Its meaning is more problematic—is it a synonym of the preceding phrase or does it refer instead to the Lord's day? The translation indicates that the second option is preferred. Further, Paul's use of the term "all" indicates not apologetic intent (attempt to soften earlier harshness by insisting that "all of you" are ready for the Lord's day) but an insistence on his part that the state of Christian existence makes the initiate a "child of light"—light in this case indicates not simply a state of moral activity but existence in Christ, which is focused on the coming day of the Lord. Thus, the readers by their baptismal commitment are children of the sphere of light and are conditioned by the coming of the Lord's day.

—we belong neither to the night nor to darkness: A new phrase, which follows starkly without a coordinating conjunction, restates in positive terms, employing a chiastic form of light/day and night/darkness, what has been stated in negative imagery. Again one might ask whether night and darkness are synonymous terms to be interpreted as a contrast between light and darkness (see Eph 5:8-14) or whether darkness and light form one pair while night and day constitute another, each with their nuanced meaning. The second is preferable and discussed below. Thus, night and day refer more particularly to the end-time while darkness and light focus on the present struggle within Christian lives of commitment. Paul thereby dwells on eschatological motivation and paraenesis.

6. *So then, let us not sleep as others do:* The sentence is introduced by an emphatic inferential coordinating conjunction *ara oun* ("so then") to stress the following paraenetic statement (see also Rom 5:18; 7:3; Gal 6:10), which in turn is expressed as a hortatory subjunctive "let us not sleep" (also vv. 7, 10). Christians as opposed to "others" (see discussion of 4:13) are not to be found sleeping or living in indifference to the coming day of the Lord, which they have been told comes unexpectedly and menacingly like a thief during the night time. Being "asleep," whether as lack of awareness or as lack of spiritual focus, is to be foolhardy or deceived and to miss an important aspect of Christian awareness, for believers are those who know that the Lord's day comes in the same way as does a thief. The only protection in view of such an eventuality is vigilance.

but let us be alert and self-controlled: Paul expresses the opposite of unpreparedness as being awake or alert on the one hand and sober or self-controlled on the other. Both verbs are rare in Paul. *Grēgoreō*, "being awake, alert, or watchful," is commonly employed in general paraenesis and eschatological warnings (v. 10; 1 Cor 16:13; Mark 14:34 par.; 13:34 par.; also Rev 3:2f.). The term signifies the opposite of sleep both physically and metaphorically. The second verb, *nēphō*, means to "be sober" or, in more figurative language, "self-controlled or balanced" and occurs in Paul only in 1 Thess 5:6, 8. It too, though less frequent, occurs in general paraenesis and in eschatological contexts (see 1 Pet 5:8 and 4:7; note that both verbs occur in 1 Pet 5:8).

Interestingly, the first verb occurs here and in verse 10 as the opposite of sleep, while the second introduces a synonymous clause in the following verse (regarding drunkenness) and is repeated in verse 8. Thus, both verbs refer in a figurative way to vigilance and mental balance, while still suggesting the original images of being awake from sleep and unaffected by wine. Again, for distant echoes of the Jesus tradition see Luke 21:34-36 and Matt 24:42-44.

7. *for sleepers sleep by night; drunkards drink by night:* To drive home the point just made that Christians belong to the sphere of light and so daytime, Paul employs a double proverbial observation taken from daily experience. Just as it is true in daily living that night is the time for sleeping and also the time for revelry and drunkenness, so too on the metaphorical level is night or darkness the sphere of reprehensible activity (also Rom 13:11-14) and, in the present case, the antithesis of Christian living in anticipation of the Lord's return. It should be noted that daytime drunkenness is seen as even more reprehensible than that at night (see Isa 5:11; Acts 2:15; and 2 Pet 2:13).

8. *But we for our part, since we belong to the day, let us be self-controlled:* It has been suggested that verses 7-8a constitute a Pauline parenthesis or a later gloss on the text, since one could omit the material between the identical verbal forms *nephōmen* ("let us be self-controlled") at the end of verse 6 and the beginning of verse 8. However, the content and style of the contested material is seemingly Pauline. Also, the resumptive technique of verse 8a fits well into Paul's train of thought. Indeed, verse 8 introduces a new section of Paul's developing thought by use of the contrastive "we for our part" (see also 2:17). The participial construction, "belonging to the day," is best seen as having a causal relation to the main verb (*IBNTG*, 103), but its function is more than resumptive. On the one hand it reiterates ideas previously stated negatively ("not in darkness" in v. 4 and "belong neither to the night nor the darkness" in v. 5) and positively ("you are all children of light and children of the day" in v. 5), but the thought shifts from light-darkness imagery to a focus on that of "the day." Paul directs his attention more particularly to the eschatological motivation of the believer's behavior. It is not the theme of belonging to the sphere of light which is of concern to him but of being motivated by the Lord's day. He then repeats his earlier exhortation concerning self-control and what this entails.

armed as we are with faith and love as a breastplate and the hope of salvation as a helmet: Paul's extended participial construction raises a number of problems. The verb *endyō* ("dress" or "put on" clothing or armor—BAGD 264) appears in the aorist and is traditionally interpreted as a present tense whose action is identical to that of the main verb ("let us be self-controlled and put on . . ."). Such a conclusion relates directly to the function of the armor mentioned since Christians are told to arm themselves as would a sentry on guard and thus to be "vigilant" for the Lord's return. Instead, one must see the participle as insisting on a past action, namely, the time of baptism when converts became children of light and were armed with the armor of light (see Rom 13:12—with aorist also). Additionally, the relation of the participle to the main verb is not one of means or concurrent action but of consequence:

"since we are armed or armed as we are . . . let us be self-controlled." There is an exhortation to make better use of one's gifts or armor. As regards the origin of the imagery, scholars point to Isa 59:17 which speaks of God who *"put on* righteousness like a *breastplate,* and a *helmet* of *salvation* on his head" (the italicized terms appear also in 1 Thess 5:8). There is evidence that this text and its imagery influenced later generations: Wis 5:17-20; Eph 6:10-17; and rabbinic text *Baba Bathra* 9b. In 1 Thess 5:8, along with the last two mentioned texts, human beings possess the divine armor (see also Rom 13:12). Paul's use of this imagery owes probably less to direct contact with Isa 59:17 than to current paraenetic tradition which made use of armor imagery precisely because life itself and particularly the end-time struggle were seen as a contest between the spheres of light and darkness or good and evil. Many would see here the influence of Qumran literature (*TDNT* 5:298-300). The believer's weapons are "faith and love" (commitment to God and Christ and concern for others, respectively; see 3:2, 6) functioning as a breastplate (*thō-rax;* see Eph 6:14) and "the hope of salvation" (for the first term see 1:3 and 2:19; for the second see v. 9 below) which is said to act as a "helmet" (*perikephalaia;* see Eph 6:17).

9. *for God did not destine us for wrath:* This clause provides the basis for the exhortation which Paul has just enunciated; hope is based on God's choice and promise, while self-control or a balanced life is related to the attainment of salvation. Paul introduces his explanation in two parts, first a negative and then a positive eschatological statement which is further qualified by a soteriological justification. The concept of election, "God destined us" (use of *tithēmi*), is a frequent Pauline theme—see 1:4; 2:12; 4:7; and 5:24. This Pauline concept is one of "invitation" on the one hand and one of "being made for" on the other, not of predisposition to condemnation or reward. The unusual expressions of both parts of the verse, "destine us for" and "for the attainment of salvation," have led some to postulate a credal formula encompassing verses 9 and 10 or verse 9 alone to account for Pauline use of an election tradition. While there is much to discourage acceptance of the former, there is some basis for viewing verse 9 as making use of Jewish and early Christian tradition regarding divine election. In the present case the unusual though Septuagintal expression *tithēmi tina eis* ("to destine someone for"— Ps 65:9; Mic 4:7; Jer 25:12) is found nowhere else in Paul but has a parallel in 1 Pet 2:8 ("for which they were also destined"). On the expression "for wrath," see 1:10.

but for the attainment of salvation: The second part of the "not . . . but" structure focuses also on an eschatological reality that should have a bearing on present behavior. The expression "for the attainment of salvation" also raises questions of origin and meaning. It is particularly the first term (*peripoiēsis*) and its occurrence in other NT passages in the context of election and light-darkness imagery (1 Pet 2:8-9; Heb 10:39; Eph 1:11-14; also 2 Thess 2:14 without light/darkness imagery) which suggest use of an early election tradition by Paul. There is debate also whether the term has a passive ("possession") or active ("preservation" or "attainment") meaning. Since the reality is one that is yet to come the second meaning is eliminated. Either of the other two fit the context. The first emphasizes the concept of gift while the last implies human activity. Owing to Paul's focus on exhortation and proper behavior in view of salvation, the latter ("attainment") is preferable. Additionally, the believer is destined for "salvation" *(sōtēria)*, an eschatological reality dear to Paul's heart. The concept of salvation is a future reality for Paul and concerns the relation between God and humanity. The believer lives with participation in God's glory in mind or with the threat of divine wrath. In verse 8 Paul's use of the term focuses both on its future aspect and on its present ramifications—this future concept is nonetheless a present reality which has its basis on a promised future reality. In verse 9, as well as 1:10, the thrust of Paul's statement is on the contrast between the negative judgment (or disaster) awaiting those who are asleep and the positive actualization of salvation (attained with the armor of light) which in this missive means "living with the Lord" (4:17; 5:10) and in others, being endowed with God's glory, sharing in a heavenly citizenship, attaining bodily redemption, or being conformed to the image of God's son (Rom 8:23, 29-30; Phil 3:20-21).

through our Lord Jesus Christ: Paul employs what will become for him a standard formula, "through *(dia)* our Lord Jesus Christ" and variations thereof, to express the Christological grounding of God's plan for the attainment of salvation (on the titles and their function see 1:1). See 4:2 and 14 for indications of the formula's development.

10. *who died for us that . . . together we might live with him:* It is generally admitted that Paul uses an early Christological formula concerning Jesus' death, a formula which consists of an aorist participle (use of *apothnēskō* as in 4:14) modifying the Lord Jesus Christ, followed by a prepositional phrase ("for us"; there is MS confusion between *hyper* and the synonymous *peri*) which gives an explicit soteriological interpretation to Jesus' death. Similar idioms are used by Paul in his later correspondence (Rom 5:6, 8; 14:15; 1 Cor 15:3; 2 Cor 5:15). The soteriological motif is undeveloped here though its placement in this paraenetic context underscores the connection salvation has with present behavior and its motivation. Christians belong to the Lord's day because they are committed to the Lord's death which has set in motion the dynamics which are defined as a firm hope that governs the present daily struggle. The ultimate purpose of Jesus' death is that his followers "might live together with him." The verb *zaō* is in the aorist and suggests an inceptive meaning, namely, "may enter into or begin to live" *(BG, 250)*. From this one might underscore the beginning of a life with Christ in the present, as in 2 Cor 5:14-15, or more probably, owing to the text's eschatological focus and this passage's parallel function with 4:17, opt for life with the Lord, (i.e., resurrection and assumption) as defining one aspect of the attainment of salvation. Once again the expression "together . . . with" (see 4:17) stresses unity and simultaneity, i.e., all believers will live with the risen, glorified Lord.

. . . whether we be alert or asleep . . .: This short phrase is obviously intended by Paul to be read as a parenthesis, a fact that is emphasized by the double

eite ("whether . . . or"; on *ei* in place of *ean*, see *BG*, 332). The two verbs, *grēgoreō* and *katheudō*, occur earlier in the pericope, verse 6 for the first and verses 6, 7 for the second, where they have the meanings "be alert" and "sleep," respectively. Scholars routinely assume that in verse 10 these change meaning and should be rendered "whether we are awake or asleep" or more explicitly "alive or dead." It is amply demonstrated that the first, even following LXX usage, does not mean being "alive," though it presumes that state, but "awake from sleep and alert" (only 1 Thess 5:10 would offer such a meaning: BAGD 167.2). The second also offers interesting data. Both in secular and religious usage it has the physical sense of sleep (5:7) and the metaphorical meaning of spiritual indifference. It does not usually have the euphemistic sense of being "dead" as does *koimaō* (see 4:13f.). Two exceptions are found, however, in the LXX: Ps 87:6 ("sleep in the grave") and Dan 12:2 ("sleep in the dust of the earth"). It is the latter, with its promise of resurrection, which seems to have suggested Paul's abbreviated expression: "whether we are alert (and waiting for the Lord's day) or whether we are asleep (in the dust of the earth) we will live together with him." The passage emphasizes the vigilance theme of the pericope and the all-inclusive nature of assumption, involving both those who have survived and those who have already gone to the grave.

11. *Therefore, encourage one another:* Paul's conclusion, in part identical with that of the previous pericope, "encourage one another," is repeated from 4:18 (see discussion). One presumes that the remainder of the previous instruction ("with these words") also applies—his letter continues to have a ministerial as well as a paraenetic function.

   and build each one up: Paul adds a new element to his exhortation, a theme that will play an important role in his developing ecclesiology, namely, the readers are told to "build up or strengthen each one" *(oikodomeō)*. The concept probably derives from Jewish consideration of itself as God's house. Thus, passages such as Jer 40:7 which speaks of God rebuilding exiled Israel or of Ps 27:5 which appeals to God, because of Israel's disobedience, to pull down and not build up Israel (see also T.Benjamin 8:3), contribute to Paul's notion that members, as constituting one unified building, have the duty to assist one another in the growth process. Christians have received gifts (see 1 Cor 8:1; 14:3f.) which are to be used for each others' benefit (some of these will be developed in the concluding exhortation of 5:12f.). In the present context Paul's words of warning and exhortation must be shared and their advice put into practice with vigilance, self-control, and the aid of divine weapons. These words of exhortation have communal edification as their goal. Later in his correspondence Paul will employ the term to apply particularly to apostolic missionary activity (2 Cor 10:4; see *TDNT* 5:140-42). Finally, the unique expression *heis ton hena* is usually viewed as a Semitic parallel for the preceding *allēlous* (BDF 247.4) and also translated "one another." But Paul's individualistic note in 2:11 that the missionaries "treat each one of [them] like a father his own children" (see also 1 Cor 4:6) points to a similar nuance here (so the translation: "each one"). The focus nonetheless would be less on the individual than on the totality.

as you are indeed doing: The final phrase of Paul's exhortation recalls the conclusion of the first missive (4:1) and plays a similar role. The seeming harshness either of indirect warning or the more direct advice to live not as
sleepwalkers but alert warriors is softened by his acknowledgment that what
he is requesting is not new since they are already doing just that. In this way
he prepares his readers for further application.

INTERPRETATION

This new chapter introduces a second pericope devoted to apocalyptic concerns. It too is delineated by the introductory formula "now concerning . . ." and directs the reader to a new topic of discussion: "on
being ready for the Lord's return." Several characteristics of the passage
(the seeming repetition of what 4:13-18 explains, its extensive use of non-
Pauline vocabulary and themes, and its apparent nonresponse to the question raised in v. 1) generate discussion: (1) concerning the text's Pauline
character (its authenticity, the role played by tradition and redaction in
its composition, and its relation to 4:13-18), (2) concerning the inner logic
of the passage (the train of Paul's thought and the pericope's structure),
(3) concerning the text's overall message (about the when and how of
the parousia, about Christian behavior as eschatological or daily struggle,
and about its Christological motivation), and (4) concerning the purpose
of the pericope (whether about Thessalonian questions or Pauline answers
and their motivation).

(1) *Concerning the Text's Pauline Character.* The question of the pericope's
authenticity has been raised. Based on its large number of borrowed or
non-Pauline literary and apocalyptic features, it is proposed that the passage is an interpolation into Paul's letter by a member of the Lukan school.
Additionally, the few terms, expressions, and stylistic features which are
noted as Pauline are seen as being different in tone and purpose from
4:13-18. Thus, these occasional Pauline stylistic features are explained as
the result of the interpolator's imitation of Paul's text to situate it in its
present context (e.g., use of *peri* as in 4:9,13, "sleep" as in 4:13; or the
verb *parakaleō* as in 4:18). The alleged difference in tone between the two
texts concerns calm and confidence as Paul's goal in 4:13-18 and warning and exhortation as that of the interpolator who wishes to combat the
false security engendered by the delay of the parousia. Scholars have
reacted negatively to this proposal, though admitting that Paul makes
considerable use of traditional apocalyptic and paraenetic materials and
insisting that the apparent relation of the passage to Lukan texts owes
to Paul's use of Synoptic-like tradition, that the difference in tone and
purpose between the two apocalyptic passages is more apparent than real

(and certainly misunderstood), and that the pericope is both Pauline in construction and intentionally related structurally and thematically to its surrounding narrative, particularly 4:13-18.

Various sources are proposed by scholars for the traditions found in 5:1-11, but since the preceding Notes discuss the particulars for each passage, it suffices to state overall conclusions regarding these and the extent of Pauline redaction. It is generally conceded that Paul creatively employs various resources for the composition of the pericope: themes from a Synoptic-like tradition most closely related to the Q-material found in Luke 12:39-40 par. and to the special material used in Luke 21:34-36, proverbial motifs from general and possibly baptismal paraenesis, images from Isa 59:17 or related Qumran tradition, and traces of a credal formula. Paul borrows then from early Christian eschatological, paraenetic, and liturgical traditions to formulate his response to a pressing question of the community.

As regards the relationship between 5:1-11 and 4:13-18, it has been noted, in defending the Pauline character of the former, that the two passages not only treat related topics but also begin and end with formal similarity (opening *peri tōn* and concluding *parakaleō*), that both end by focusing on the eschatological goal of "being with the Lord" (4:17; 5:10), and that 5:10, about being "alert or asleep," connects the two apocalyptic sections. Further, one should see the two passages as answering interrelated questions, first regarding those who have died (4:13f.) and then, from a heightened sense of the imminence of the Lord's day, about the living and their eschatologically conditioned lives.

(2) *Concerning the Inner Logic of the Passage.* It is important to examine fully the train of Paul's thought. Scholars readily point to a shift in Paul's treatment of the topic from a severe nonanswer of a question concerning "times and seasons" to a congenial discussion of Christian existence, vigilance, and action in light of the Lord's imminent parousia. One should consider the pericope as a response to a misleading question concerning the date of Jesus' parousia. Verses 1-2 introduce the implied question along with Paul's response employing the traditional and well-known ("you know perfectly well") theme of the "thief at night." It is usually noted that verse 3 conveys a harsh threat particularly when one considers the consoling ending of the preceding discussion (4:18) and the disclaimer immediately following this statement (vv. 4-5). Such an impression, however, is more apparent than real—the above translation attempts to avoid giving such an impression. Verse 3 describes in a graphic way what is said in the previous verse regarding the manner of a thief's coming. The household is lulled to complacency and the unfortunate arrival of the thief is compounded by a lack of preparedness which spells disaster. Paul, in

verse 3, describes the proverbial state of the unprepared person (the expression "peace and security" underscore the text's traditional character), a state which goes beyond lack of readiness to a denatured sense of the future. Also, Paul's statement in verse 3 prepares for his admonition in verse 5, "let us not sleep as others do," and gives an important clue to the problem being discussed. In a manner reminiscent of 4:13 ("you may not grieve as others do who have no hope"), Paul compares the believer's vision of the future to that of the unbelieving neighbor whose focus is on the present. The issue once again, as earlier, is one of hope, i.e., living in the present in view of the future, sudden return of the Lord. In verse 3 then Paul is confronting directly the pagan adage: "eat, drink, and be merry (in the present), for tomorrow we die." The "peace and security" of the Pauline text indicates more than unpreparedness; the expression typifies for Paul the deceptiveness of a vision of life which is not grounded in the concept of hope (see vv. 8-9).

It is at verse 4 that there occurs a shift in Paul's argument. Having been asked about the date of the end-time and having addressed their concern, Paul as in 4:10 announces a shift in his argument. The community should be concerned not about the calendar but about the impact of the end-time on daily behavior. By addressing the community directly and contrasting its members to the complacent mentioned in the previous verse, Paul is able gently to redirect the concerns of his addressees; he reminds them of their status as converts who have chosen light in place of darkness.

We have in 5:1-11, therefore, a Pauline response with great similarity to his earlier discussion of *philadelphia* in 4:9-12. In both cases Paul begins by citing the issue and terminology of the question and, by means of *paralipsis* or *praeteritio* ("no need to write"—4:9; 5:1), emphasizes that the issue is well known to the addressees and that the discussion of the topic is about to undergo a shift in direction. As in 4:10 the direction is from the inner to the outer dynamics of love of fellow believers and "others," so here the discussion changes from the date and manner of the Lord's coming to the way believers or "children of light" are to act since they are already "children of the (Lord's) day."

In light of the above discussion what then can be said regarding the variety of suggestions made concerning the pericope's structure? A standard proposal is to divide the passage according to its contents: verses 1-3 concerning the Lord's day, 4-8a consisting of paraenesis, 8b-10 devoted to exhortation, and 11 offering a conclusion for the whole apocalyptic section. But since such an outline does not correspond to the text's grammatical structure, others offer a tripartite division: 1-3 as the announcement of the topic, 4-10 consisting of the Pauline paraenesis, and 11 as the final exhortation. By far the most convincing approach is to consider the passage's rhetorical and stylistic features to discern its major divisions: verses 1-3, introduced by *peri de . . .* about "the when and how" of the Lord's day, 4-7, introduced by *hymeis de,* concerning who the believer is, and 8-11, introduced by *hēmeis de,* about what the believer is to do. Such an overall division is convincing since it respects the stylistic and rhetorical features of Paul's text. One might be tempted to isolate verses 1 and 11 as introduction and conclusion respectively, but since each of the proposed sections begins with clear stylistic indicators and since each ends with an explicit conclusion to be drawn, verse 3: "in no way then *(kai ou mē)* will they escape," verse 6: "so then *(ara oun),* let us not sleep . . .," and verse 11: "therefore *(dio),* encourage one another," this tripartite division is best suited to Paul's meaning and serves as outline for our discussion of the passage's overall message.

(3) *The Text's Overall Message.* In the first part of the pericope, verses 1-3, Paul introduces the topic of concern to the audience. He is asked about the "when" of the parousia but prefers to discuss the "how" of that event. Despite the formulaic character of 1b ("you do not need to have anything written to you") and of 2a ("you yourselves know perfectly well"), one is correct in assuming that the topic had been the object of earlier apostolic instruction. The precise problem concerning the end-time, however, seems unclear to the modern reader apart from the implication derived, from Paul's statement, that the audience is interested in his teaching about the time of the Lord's return. True to the approach taken in the Jesus tradition generally, Paul responds that the Christian does not know when it will come ("only the Father knows," Mark 13:32), only that it will come "suddenly" (Mark 13:36) "like a thief in the night."

There is a shift in response from concern about the date of the Lord's day to the manner of its coming, a point which needs attention. Paul's statement about the thief is invariably translated: "the day of the Lord will come like a thief in the night" even though his text employs two terms of comparison. The first adverb draws a general comparison, whose imagery furnishes further motifs for the subsequent discussion, between the Lord's day and the thief ("the Lord's day is like *[hōs]* a thief at night"); the second comparative adverb, between the coming of the thief and that of the Lord's day ("the Lord's day comes in the same way *[houtōs]*"). One might be tempted to translate the Pauline clause as "comes just as unexpectedly," but Paul insists that a burglar's coming bears elements of surprise and unwelcomeness, themes borne out in subsequent discussion, especially in verse 3 where he characterizes the coming of the Lord's day as sudden and unavoidable. Such an interpretation bears out the proverbial nature of the image, especially as it is used in the OT (Jer 30:3; Job 24:14; Obad 5), namely, that thieves, unexpectedly and menacingly, are wont to come by night to despoil unsuspecting victims of their possessions.

The day of the Lord then comes suddenly for all (''like birth-pains''), but for outsiders, who are lulled by a deceptive sense of security, the Lord's day comes as utter disaster. In place of the imagined peace and security of the misguided household, nonbelievers will encounter an inescapable, sudden, and menacing judgment. There is then a logical and sudden reversal of the false sense of security engendered by a life focused on what is perceived to be present reality. Rather than a peaceful night's sleep with undisturbed control of one's possessions, following the images of the thief at night, careless, misguided believers encounter sudden ''ruin,'' whether destruction of property, life or eschatological promise. It should be noted finally that, behind this stark description of the Lord's day vis-à-vis outsiders, is a stern reminder to the Christian audience that being prepared for that day also means being children of the Lord's day (v. 5) whose behavior is conditioned by the promise of salvation (v. 10).

Verses 4-7 introduce a clear shift in Paul's discussion, for he turns from a description of outsiders to that of believers and focuses first on who they are and then on how they are to act. Already Paul has redirected the topic of concern about when and how the Lord's day comes to a consideration of the nature of Christian existence and its consequent behavior in relation to the imagery provided by the thief-at-night motif. There is a shift now in imagery, however, from considering night as the opportune time offering a shield for (the thief's) evil activity to viewing night and darkness as images for the sphere of evil as opposed to that of good as represented by light and day.

This section of Paul's text focuses on the images of light and darkness. Verse 4, if one follows the thief-at-night image of the timing of the unwelcomed visitor, should focus on alertness on the part of the Christian. Instead Paul assures his readers that they do not belong to the realm of darkness and so will not encounter the Lord's day as a thief (i.e., being overtaken as in verse 4b or being inescapably ruined as in verse 3) but rather as a welcomed bearer of salvation (v. 9). The Lord's day is like a thief at night for those who belong to the darkness. Paul repeats the content of this verse in the chiastic arrangement that follows:

> no, you are all children of light
> and *children of the day*
> —we belong neither *to the night*
> nor to darkness.

The italicized terms seem to be Pauline creations; the other images are traditional (see Notes). Paul here reiterates the Christian's identity on the one hand as belonging to the reestablished domain of God, that of light and as being in opposition to that of darkness and then adds to this, on the other, a parallel but extended characterization of the believer as belonging also to the day of the Lord's return when deeds are judged according to their source (2 Cor 5:10). Verses 4-7 focus on light/darkness imagery but verses 8f. pick up the new feature and address the shift from light to day (note they "are not in darkness" in verse 4 and "belong to the day" in verse 8) and dwell on hope as the outcome of being "children of the Lord's day."

Light and darkness imagery addresses the Pauline belief in two mutually exclusive spheres of power. Humans are under the sway of the power of light or darkness and produce its works (see Rom 13:12-13 for the works of darkness and how to combat them with the armor of light). One is even described as belonging to the darkness or of being illuminated "like the stars in this world" (Phil 2:15). Thus, for Paul and contemporary Jewish writers (1 QS 3.2-3, 13-21; T.Levi 14:4; 19:1) there is a choice to be made between the warring sides, each with its loyalties and weapons. If one belongs to the light, the Lord's day will not be like an unwelcomed burglar but a welcome, expected judge. "Children of the light" already share in the luminous quality of the Lord's day by choosing the path of light and so are not asleep like those who belong to the darkness but watchful for the Lord's return and confident warriors in the battle being waged against the agents and works of darkness. Darkness, as typified by nighttime, is characterized by works of false security, arrogant disregard of the approaching end, and lack of preparedness characterized by drunken revelry (v. 7). Just as "others" are physically and mentally unaware of the eschatological reality so believers, as partisans of the domain of light, must be vigilant for the approaching end and devoted to the works of light.

After dwelling on the contrasting spheres of light and darkness which characterize the context of the believer, Paul returns more directly in verses 8-11 to the original subject of discussion, the Lord's day. With a final sharp contrast ("but we for our part") Paul addresses exclusively Christian believers who are now described as "belonging to the day." The concept of self-control or vigilant commitment to the works of light is resumed and situated less in an ethical, dualistic context of human activity but more in the Christian context of commitment to God and Lord, of edification of neighbor (believers and others), and of absolute confidence in the promise of salvation: faith, love, and hope (respectively) as the weapons of those who await the Lord's return.

Verse 8 then provides the key to Paul's exhortation. Belonging to the day means having one's whole life under the influence of the parousia. The present of the Christian is conditioned by that future reality which in turn depends on the armor provided for the ensuing battle involving the "sons of light" and the "sons of darkness." By their turning to the living God (1:9-10) and with their commitment to the realm of light, believers are armed with weapons by the God of light, whether breastplate or helmet. To describe the believer's ethical challenge Paul draws on traditional weapons imagery. Originally these, in Near Eastern contexts, are in the hands of the deity as they wage cosmic combat and in the case of Israel, are in the hands of Yahweh who, as warrior and judge comes as deliverer on Zion's behalf: armed in righteousness as a breastplate, head covered with the helmet of salvation, and clothed with a garment of vengeance (Isa 59:17-20). In a much later period these divine weapons (see Wis 5:17-20) are either in the hands of the Messiah whom God has adorned with crown and helmet (of salvation) or at the disposal of the righteous, as at Qumran (see 1 QM) and in the NT, either to do battle in the eschatological conflict or as weapons of preparedness.

The function these weapons play in the imagery of 5:1-11 may be sought in several directions. If one approaches this in terms of weapons, one would see the breastplate and helmet as providing protective covering for the believers' daily struggle against the evil powers which oppose salvation. These would therefore act as defense weapons for Christian behavior. One could, however, consider other Pauline passages, e.g., Rom 13:11-14, as suggestive for examining the function of this imagery. One could stress the apocalyptic features of the text and insist that Paul sees the present as a siege wherein believers are continually exposed to attack and urges the "laying aside of the works of darkness and putting on the armor of light" (13:12). More probably, however, the conclusion of this same passage gives a key both to its meaning and to our own passage. Paul advises: "put on the Lord Jesus Christ, and make no provision for the flesh, to gratify its desires" (v. 14). The battle, therefore, is more readily applicable to daily living and the believer's battle against the flesh as referring to the earthly sphere and its power. Such an observation brings us to a final approach to the Pauline imagery of 1 Thess 5:8, namely, the contextual use Paul makes of the weaponry. More particularly, the breastplate and the helmet function for Paul in the way faith, love and hope operate in believers' lives. After all, Paul has already spoken, earlier in his missive, about "the dynamism of [their] faith, the dedication of [their] love, and the constancy of [their] hope" (1:3). These weapons of war are hardly limited to defensive action in a siege context or to an apocalyptic struggle or defense. Instead, they describe the community's vibrant faith which has had far-reaching results in the lives of the converts and tangible consequences far beyond their city (1:6-10); they refer to the never-weary, constantly dedicated commitment of members to others whether inside or outside the community; and they underscore steadfastness (based on the promise of salvation) in the face of the challenges of daily Christian living (see 1:3). These weapons serve the believers as protection against the forces of darkness but they also serve the dynamic inner and outward thrust of Christian living and mission.

In verses 9f. Paul returns to the topic of concern, readiness for the Lord's return. The basis for Christian vigilance and focused activity is the promise of salvation, that to which God destined humanity. Thus, after an indirect, but clear warning ("not wrath") Paul dwells, in typical fashion on the motivation for Christian behavior, the Christ-event in God's plan. The salvific death of the Lord Jesus had as its goal the union of believers with their Lord. Christian existence therefore is conditioned by its basic orientation toward the Lord's return and presence. Readers are reminded in verse 10 that all believers, whether they are watchful "in the flesh or in the grave," will meet the Lord upon his return. It is with such exhortation that Paul ends his response to the community's query "concerning the times and seasons," exhorting ever-more mutual encouragement and help.

(4) *Thessalonian Questions, Pauline Answers, and Their Motivation.* Discussions of Paul's early thought usually focus on the eschatological character of the Thessalonian correspondence. Not only is the Paulinist 2 Thessalonians often brought into the discussion but the conversation is often limited to the two apocalyptic sections: 1 Thess 4:13-18 and 5:1-11. Even for a review of Paul's advice to the Thessalonian community, such a purview is misleading. Paul's advice to the community and therefore his concerns at this early stage in his career must be seen in light also of the two more generally paraenetic sections which precede and follow the three responses given in 4:9-12; 4:13-18; and 5:1-11.

Paul's thought in 1 Thessalonians is hardly limited to apocalyptic concerns and not more focused on the parousia than his other letters. Paul's discussion of holiness in 4:3-8, his concerns about love of fellow Christians and others beyond the fellowship (4:9-10), and his discussion of the ideal Christian milieu (4:11-12) already point to a Paul who is dedicated to discussion of Christian living in a non-Christian world. Thus, his responses in the two apocalyptic sections should be seen in that light, despite the fact that some among his audience are unduly worried about the faithful departed and their union with the returning Christ or that others have a misplaced interest in the time of the parousia. Additionally, while the first of these apocalyptic sections concludes by focusing on the fate of those who have died and those who have survived and therefore on the Lord's day, the second emphasizes not the arrival of the Lord's day but the Christian behavior which is to precede and prepare for that day. The focus of the latter therefore is on Christian behavior in the present. Finally, these two sections must be seen in light of the concluding exhortation which Paul gives about community life in 5:12-22.

In each of the responses he sends the community, Paul addresses a misplaced, or partially misplaced, concern of the audience. In each case he addresses their question by quoting some of its terminology and then gradually changing the focus of the discussion. In the first response (4:9-12) a concern about love of brothers and sisters changes into a reminder concerning behavior toward outsiders as well. In the second, complex answer to the community's hopeless feeling in the face of the death of loved ones (4:13-18), Paul rehearses for the audience his teaching concerning the nature and basis of hope which provides an optimism and dynamism in the present as believers, both departed and survivors, await full participation in their future relationship with the Lord. The third response (5:1-11), beginning as it does by considering when and how the Lord's day will come, addresses the vigilance and behavior required of those who are both children of light and of the Lord's day.

Paul's texts are responses to issues of concern to the people of Thessalonica. The concerns are theirs; the responses are Paul's. But they are conditioned first by what is asked, secondly by Paul's corrective resituating of the issue, and thirdly by the focus of his new insights or emphases, whether they concern love also of outsiders, the nature of hope and the promise of union with the Lord, or the character of Christian behavior as conditioned by the promise of salvation. It is in such a context that believers must continue to foster mutual encouragement and assistance to each and every member of the community.

For Reference and Further Study

Collins, R. F. "Tradition, Redaction, and Exhortation in 1 Thess 4, 13–5, 11." *SFLT*, 154–72.

Edgar, T. R. "The Meaning of 'Sleep' in 1 Thessalonians 5:10." *JETS* 22 (1979) 345–49.

Focant, C. "Les Fils du Jour (1 Thes 5, 5)." *TC*, 348–55."

Friedrich, G. "1. Thessalonicher 5, 1-11, der apologetische Einschub eines Späteren." *ZTK* 70 (1973) 288–315.

Harnisch, W. *Eschatologische Existenz. Ein exegetischer Beitrag zum Sachanliegen von 1. Thessalonicher 4.13–5.11.* Göttingen: Vandenhoeck & Ruprecht, 1973.

Kuhn, H. W. "The Impact of the Qumran Scrolls on the Understanding of Paul." *The Dead Sea Scrolls: Forty Years of Research.* Eds. D. Dimant and U. Rappaport. Leiden: Brill, 1992, 327–39.

Lautenschlager, M. "*Eite grēgorōmen eite katheudomen*: Zum Verhältnis von Heiligung und Heil in 1 Thess 5, 10." *ZNW* 81 (1990) 39–59.

Lövestam, E. *Spiritual Wakefulness in the New Testament.* Lund: Gleerup, 1963.
Hartman, L. *Prophecy Interpreted.* Lund: Gleerup, 1966.
Malherbe, A. J. "Exhortation in First Thessalonians." *NovT* 25 (1983) 238–56.
Plevnik, J. "1 Thess 5, 1-11: Its Authenticity, Intention and Message." *Bib* 60 (1979) 71–90.
Rigaux, B. "Tradition et rédaction dans 1 Th. V.1-10." *NTS* 21 (1974–75) 318–40.
Tuckett, C. M. "Synoptic Tradition in 1 Thessalonians?" *TC,* 160–82.

15. *Final Exhortation on Community Life* (5:12-22)

12. So we urge you, brothers and sisters, to acknowledge those who labor among you, both those who are your benefactors in the Lord and those who admonish you, 13. and to regard them most highly out of love on account of their work. Be at peace among yourselves. 14. Again we exhort you, brothers and sisters: admonish the disorderly; encourage the faint-hearted; assist the weak—be patient toward all. 15. See that none of you repays anyone evil for evil; rather, always aspire to what is good both for one another and for all. 16. Rejoice always; 17. pray continually; 18. give thanks in all circumstances, for this is God's will for you in Christ Jesus. 19. Do not quench the Spirit; 20. do not despise prophetic utterances; 21. instead, examine everything: that is, hold fast to what is good; 22. abstain from every kind of evil.

NOTES

12. *So we urge you, brothers and sisters:* Paul's final exhortation is introduced by formal paraenetic language and characterized by a long series of commands. The new section is marked by *de,* as are the other paraenetic divisions, by direct address, and the verb *erōtaō* ("to urge or ask"). The last mentioned appears in the conclusion of the first missive in tandem with *parakaleō* and serves a similar function (4:1; see also 5:11 and 14).

to acknowledge those who labor among you: The verb of exhortation introduces a double infinitive phrase, the first of which bears three participial substantives as objects. While the verb *oida* usually means "to know," it is here employed in a peculiar way. While some propose the translation "respect or honor" (following BAGD 556.5; see a parallel phrase in 1 Cor 16:18 with the verb *epiginōskō*), it is preferable to retain the term's more basic meaning of "recognize or acknowledge," a meaning which would fit for the texts usually cited. This meaning will be discussed in relation to the overall sense of verses 12-13 (see below). The first of three objects "those who labor" is modified by the prepositional phrase "among you" and introduces a general statement (only it bears an article) which is then described by a twofold participial construction. Though there is discussion concerning this and the following statements in regard to the types of offices that existed in the Pauline churches, the participle in this case refers in a generic way to people who "work or labor" within the Thessalonian community (see discussion of *kopos* at 3:5).

both those who are your benefactors in the Lord: The second and third participles joined by *kai . . . kai* ("both . . . and") are subordinate to the first and so describe what type of "labor" Paul has in mind. The first of these, *proïstamenous*, is variously interpreted. Literally the term means "to be at the head of" and so translated "lead or rule" but it also has the well-attested meaning of "care for or be concerned about" (BAGD 707; LSJ 1482-83). The first meaning is preferred by many and serves as an important factor in discussions of early ecclesial structures. The term appears elsewhere in Paul only in Rom 12:8 where it represents one of a series of gifts; it also occurs six other times in the NT, all in the Pastorals. One suspects that scholars are reading later usage into the two Pauline passages. In favor of the second usage is Paul's use of the feminine form of the cognate noun *prostatēs* in Rom 16:2 where Phoebe, a deacon, is said to have assisted many, Paul included. The term in secular Greek has the meaning of "leader, presider, guardian, patron, benefactor" (LSJ 1526). Its sense in Rom 16:2 is not that she was Paul's leader but that she performed tasks for or was a benefactor to many in the community. This meaning fits Rom 12:8 also as it renders more logically the series of gifts: exhorter, giver, *benefactor* (rather than leader), and compassionate person (see below). The participle is further qualified by "your" and "in the Lord." The first as in the case of Phoebe focuses on the recipients of the care. The second expression, *en kyriǫ*, represents a familiar Pauline phrase. Related to it are 1:1; 3:8; and 4:1 where similar constructions with the preposition *en* are employed. The first two have a different function and meaning, while that of 4:1 and the present case relate to the classic Pauline usage: "rejoice in the Lord" (Phil 3:1), "boast in the Lord" (1 Cor 1:31), or "welcome her in the Lord" (Rom 16:2). Paul here refers to the sphere of Christian existence whereby activity on the part of believers is directed toward other believers as though they were Christ himself. At issue is the acknowledgment of Jesus' lordship, which impinges on Christian behavior. The preposition *en* here means "belonging to" and one detects here an incipient "being in" (see 4:1; also 5:18).

and those who admonish you: The verb, *noutheteō*, is less controversial since its sense of "admonition or instruction" fits well into its context. One could focus on its more positive aspect as happens in Rom 15:14 ("filled with all knowledge and able to instruct one another") or on its more negative meaning as in 1 Cor 4:14 ("to admonish you" in the context of shame) or in 1 Thess 5:14 (see below). Its general usage focuses on the will and moral disposition rather than on the intellect (*TDNT* 4:1019) and its paraenetic function is predominant in the Greco-Roman world of Paul's time (Dio Chrysostom, *Orations* 51.5.7; 56.10; Plutarch, *On Moral Virtue* 12). See discussion below of community workers and activity.

13. *and to regard them most highly out of love on account of their work:* The second part of the exhortation involves the verb *hēgeomai* meaning "to think or consider" but contextually suggests "to regard highly," especially since the term is modified by the adverbial expression "most highly or beyond all measure" (see 3:10). This respect is to be expressed *en agapē* (see 1:3), an expression which, in light of 1 Cor 16:14, must be interpreted "out of or through acts of love," whereby *en* is either adverbial or instrumental. Lastly, these people have a special claim on their fellow believers "on account of their work." The simple term *ergon* acts as a synonym of and resumes *kopiaō* of verse 12. The exhortation of verses 12-13a then is about proper recognition and regard of those who assist the members of the community in their work and life as Christians, an example then of "encouraging one another and building each one up."

Be at peace among yourselves: With this phrase Paul introduces the first of a series of traditional paraenetic imperatives. The community is exhorted to "live at peace with one another." Parallel phrases urging mutual peace occur also in Rom 12:18 (also 14:19) and 2 Cor 13:11 (see also Mark 9:50) in contexts and with phraseology which underscore mutual, community exhortation and so reassure us that in the present case also one should follow the majority of MSS in reading the reflective form (*en heautois*—"among yourselves") rather than the less well-attested *autois* ("be at peace with them"—the alleged leaders of vv. 12-13). The peace to which believers are exhorted is that state of well-being to which they are admitted by the God of peace (see 5:23; see also 1:1) who bestows this gift as a fruit of the Spirit (Gal 5:22). This godly life is to be one of quiet and mutual understanding devoted to a productive life and deeds of love toward one another and all (4:10-12). So Paul exhorts the community to a quiet life of holiness, because it is God's means of sanctifying the believer in view of the Lord's return (5:23), for God's kingdom "consists of righteousness, peace, and joy in the Holy Spirit" (Rom 14:17).

14. *Again we exhort you, brothers and sisters:* The end of verse 13, with its seemingly unrelated exhortation to mutual peace, gives the impression that Paul intended to present a general list of paraenetic statements as found in verses 15 or 16f. Instead, he returns directly to the Thessalonian context in verse 14 by means of a complex resumptive construction, repetition of a traditional paraenetic structure ("we exhort you"; see 4:1, 10b; 5:1), direct address, and a resumptive *de* ("again"—BAGD 171.3).

admonish the disorderly: Three groups are singled out for attention and care. The verb *noutheteō*, directed to this first group, already appears at 5:12 and its nuance here is seemingly negative. Paul wishes to correct a problem that exists in the community and commands its members (not addressed to leaders;

see *adelphoi* in verses 12 and 14) to "admonish" the people involved. These last mentioned are called *hoi ataktoi,* a term which means "to be disorderly or insubordinate" but which, it is claimed, also has the attested, contemporary meaning of "idleness or laziness" (M-M 89). While the latter meaning has tended to predominate in discussions, one suspects that, even for scholars who no longer defend Pauline authorship of 2 Thessalonians, this tendency derives from interpreting 1 Thess 5:14 in light of the term's threefold usage in 2 Thess 3:6, 7, 11. There it is employed in the context of idleness or irresponsibility vis-à-vis social obligations. The term in this instance, however, alludes to problems of order and behavior within the community, problems that fly in the face of mutual peace and tranquility. See discussion of 2 Thess 3:6-12.

encourage the faint-hearted: The second group, to which Paul exhorts the community to extend cheer or encouragement (*paramytheomai:* see 2:12), is classified as *hoi oligopsychoi,* i.e., as "faint-hearted or discouraged." This relatively rare word (LSJ 1215) is also vague in meaning and as one can deduce from its LXX usage usually signifies religious despondency (Exod 6:9; Isa 35:4; Sir 7:10; see *TDNT* 9:666). The reference here is probably to those who grieve over the loss of loved ones (4:13f.), not to past issues of temptation and social difficulties (see 3:3, 5).

assist the weak: To a final group, the "weak," Paul commands that they give assistance. The verb *antechomai* means "to hold on to" or even "defend the rights of" (M-M 46). Scholars tend to interpret the phrase in a general way as referring to assistance given those characterized as "the weak." For discussion of the three groups, see below.

—be patient toward all: There follows a general reminder that no matter what problem or what group is addressed, the attitude of believers toward their brothers and sisters ("toward all" refers to the whole community; verse 15 expands beyond; see below) must be that of forbearance or patience (*makrothymeō*), presumably because of the demands of love (1 Cor 13:4; see v. 12 above). Whether positive or negative, conciliatory or admonishing, the community's activity toward its members must be aimed at mutual encouragement and upbuilding (5:11), a goal which requires a slow temper, another divine gift or fruit of the Spirit (Gal 5:22).

15. *See that none of you repays anyone evil for evil:* Employing a classical imperative to introduce a prohibitive aorist subjunctive (BDF 364.3), verse 15 presents first a negative and then a positive statement concerning the *lex talionis.* The construction itself, a second-person imperative *(horate)* followed by an impersonal singular command *(mē tis . . . tini apodǭ)*, suggests Paul's use of a traditional formulation of the principle. Relying on Ancient Near Eastern legal and thus proverbial limitation of vengeance, Paul, following the late OT and contemporary tendency of forbidding retaliation altogether (from the classical formulation of Exod 21:23-25 to the gradual denials of the principle's validity in Sir 28:1-7; JosAs 23:9; 1 QS 10:17-20), rejects in absolute terms (focus on "none of . . . you repays anyone") the returning of evil for evil.

Paul will return to this theme (Rom 12:17) as he and other Christian writers will focus on love of enemies, the ramifications of the golden rule, and, more generally, the relation of Christians to one another and to those outside and even inimical to the community (Matt 7:12; 5:38f., 43f.; 7:12; Luke 6:27f.; 1 Pet 3:9).

rather, always aspire to what is good both for one another and for all: The overall construction is clearly Pauline for he employs a "but . . . not" construction to contrast his agreement with contemporary Jews and Christians concerning the rejection of retaliation with the consequences which flow from acceptance of the golden rule. The term rendered "aspire to" *(diōkō)* also means "actively pursue or strive for" ("hospitality" in Rom 12:13 or "what makes for peace and mutual upbuilding" in 14:19) and is interpreted as emphasizing continued action (use of present tense). Also, this is to be a state of mind, something to be done at all times and to be directed to the well-being ("the good" or love actively seeking mutual upbuilding) both of insiders and outsiders. What Paul seeks here is not "the good" (or "the noble" as in Rom 12:17) in a philosophical sense but "the good" as determined by God's will for fellow Christians and others.

16–18. *Rejoice always; pray continuously; give thanks in all circumstances, for this is God's will for you in Christ Jesus:* As in verse 14 there follow three paraenetic imperatives in rapid succession; unlike those of the previous verse, however, the focus is on the adverbial constructions (implying attitude) rather than on the verbs. The first of these (v. 16) enjoins the community: "rejoice always." The concept of joy is not new in this document for it occurs in the first missive at 2:19, 20 and 3:9, where it relates primarily to the missionaries and in the second missive at 1:6 and 5:16 where the concept concerns the believing community. In the first instance they "accept the word with joy inspired by the Spirit," a passage which shows that Paul is reintroducing the concept in his paraenesis and a passage which also sheds light on the injunctions to "rejoice always" and later in verses 19f. to welcome the activity of the Spirit in their midst. The term "always" underscores Paul's notion that joy is to be an attitude of Christian living, whether in good times or in bad. The second imperative (v. 17) addresses the concept of prayer, also as constituent of ecclesial inner life and attitudes: "pray continuously." The audience is exhorted to adopt prayer as a conscious, continuous state of mind (see 1:2 and 2:13 for prayer and thanksgiving). Again, the adverb underscores the concept of attitude; in 5:25 Paul returns specifically to the concept of intercessory prayer. The final imperative (v. 18) reintroduces in a paraenetic context the concept of thanksgiving, "give thanks in all circumstances." While in 1:2 the object of thanksgiving is God's gift of faith to the residents of Thessalonica, in 5:18 it refers generally ("in all things or circumstances") to the Pauline concept that the human being's principal duty is that of giving honor and thanks to God (Rom 1:21). On the concept of "will of God" see 4:3 above. The *en Christō (Iēsou)* formula indicates means and implies context within which (see 1:1; 4:1-2; and 5:12).

19-20. *Do not quench the Spirit; do not despise prophetic utterances:* The final verses also consist of a rapid series of paraenetic imperatives whose function is characterized by its relation to spiritual gifts. The first two are joined by their negative expression and the last three as positive contrasts. The first negative command, "do not quench the Spirit," employing a Pauline hapax *(sbegnymi)*, emphasizes the fire-like imagery of the Spirit, for the community is encouraged not "to put out the Spirit's fire" or in more metaphorical terms not to suppress its activity (see discussion of the Spirit's activity in 1:5-6). The second negative imperative speaks specifically about one aspect of the Spirit's activity within the community, the work of prophecy *(prophēteia)* or its concrete manifestation "prophetic utterances." Further and surprisingly, the hearers are warned not about rejecting but about "despising" *(exoutheneō)* the work of prophets. The term itself implies "rejection with contempt" (BAGD 277.2) and points to a concrete problem within the community.

21-22. *instead, examine everything, and so, hold fast to what is good and abstain from every kind of evil:* Responding to the two negative commands is a single contrast "examine everything" (21a), introduced by contrastive *de* ("but or instead"). Paul employs the term "to test or examine" (see 2:4) and reinforces his command with the term "all," thereby encouraging those who are reluctant to accept prophetic activity to be more open to authenticated pneumatic phenomena; on discernment see 1 Cor 12:10. Paul's command in verse 21a is followed, without transitional particle ("and so . . . and" is added to the translation), by two rapid injunctions which offer believers the criteria for true discernment. First, believers are advised to "hold fast or guard" what they judge from prophetic activity to be for the good of the community and in the second, negative command advises all to "abstain or refrain" (see 4:3) from all manner of evil. The final phrase ("from every kind of evil") is likely a traditional one, drawn from passages such as Job 1:1, 8; 2:13 to characterize evil in general. In this particular context it would refer to questionable charismatic activity.

INTERPRETATION

Having responded to the audience's questions, Paul returns more generally to his role as pastor as he addresses less specific issues of community life. His exhortation is marked by characteristic paraenetic language, direct address, and a mixture of pointed commands and brief imperative statements of advice.

Structure and Character of 5:12-22. In light of early form-critical study of epistolary exhortation debate continues concerning the nature of Pauline paraenesis, whether it is of a general, formulaic nature or whether it has a particular relation to the community being addressed. On the one hand, the traditional character of exhortation, whether its content or its formulaic, impersonal style, has led scholars to seek parallels to Pauline epistolary closings and to see little connection between his advice and the community's situation. On the other hand, better knowledge of community issues has led many to relate Paul's advice to issues discussed elsewhere or presupposed by a given letter. The situation is interesting for 1 Thessalonians and for 5:12-22 in particular, whether one refers to theories of Gnostic pneumatics or millenarian radicals at Thessalonica as providing the letter's background, or whether one accepts the pericope as general or situation-directed paraenesis.

An issue of concern is the relation of 5:12-22 to Rom 12:9-18, where there exist similarities of a linguistic and thematic nature.

1 Thess 5		Rom 12	
13b	*peace* among yourselves	18	*peace* with all
15	*do not repay evil for evil*	17a	*do not repay evil for evil*
	good: one another and all		*noble:* sight of all
16	*rejoice* always	12a	*rejoice* in hope
17	*pray* continually	12c	persevere in *prayer*
19	don't quench the *Spirit*	11b	be fervent in *spirit*
21b	hold fast to *noble*	9b	hold to *good*
22	abstain from *evil*	9b	hate *evil*

In general terms the parallels are striking and the differences are revealing. Structurally there is a reverse correspondence in order; linguistically the wording is considerably free (verbal parallels are italicized); but thematically the similarities are more ambiguous, since context (not terms) determines their specific function. The use in both of the exhortations to choose the good and to reject the evil may seem striking but appears less so since in Romans the saying addresses general behavior while in 1 Thessalonians it relates to the discernment of prophetic activity. There are other differences, differences which provide insight concerning the nature of Paul's advice to the community of Thessalonica. Verses 12-13 really offer no parallels to the Roman exhortation nor does verse 14. Verses 15-17 consisting of general advice correspond more closely to the text of Romans. Finally, while verses 19-22 offer linguistic and formulaic similarities there is no thematic correspondence—the Thessalonian passage addresses pneumatic activity within the community; that of Romans focuses on community love.

The above observations alert us to the fact that verses 12-13a, 14, and 19-22, which correspond least to Paul's later paraenetic text, address particular Thessalonian issues (more on that below). The other verses offer advice which Paul deemed appropriate for most converts. In some cases a general statement (see 2 Cor 13:11; Rom 12:18; 1 Cor 13:4) serves as a conclusion to specific issues ("be at peace among yourselves" in v. 13b and "be patient toward all" in 14c) or in others they remind the audience of basic Christian beliefs (vv. 15-18; see also 4:3).

In structural and compositional terms, therefore, 5:12-22 consists of alternating sections of situation-inspired paraenesis and general exhortation from an interested and concerned pastor. Verses 12-13a address an issue of concern to Paul and his readers, the proper treatment of those who work within the community. The style is balanced and the issues addressed in pointed fashion—the initial and important term "labor" is underscored by the repetition of "work" at the end of the statement. Paul then draws from his paraenetic repertoire an appropriate statement which concludes on unity and concord.

The general conclusion of verse 13b might have led him to make several other general paraenetic statements (as he does in Rom 12:9f. or 2 Cor 13:11f.) before drawing the letter to a close, but he begins again with a similar paraenetic introduction in verse 14 to address other pressing issues for the community's benefit. Verse 14 consists of terse statements about three groups in the Church, each of which requires the members' attention. Since these activities range from admonition to assistance, Paul is led in conclusion to advise that one of love's main characteristics ("patience") be applied to these activities vis-à-vis needy fellow believers.

As the end of verse 14 leads him to general considerations, Paul in verses 15f. begins a series of exhortations which are basic to apostolic moral teaching and a commonplace for Pauline preaching and epistolary communication. This part has the closest similarity to Rom 12:12-17, whether dealing with retaliation and love of others in verse 15 or with the community's life and attitudes in 16-18. Interestingly, by its reference to the will of God, verse 18 brings the paraenetic section to an end much as it began at 4:3. Significantly, the first paragraph of this exhortation (4:3-8) concludes with a statement about the giving of the Spirit (v. 8) while 5:18 leads to a focused treatment of the Spirit's activity in the community.

The final verses are devoted to pneumatic concerns, first by addressing negative attitudes vis-à-vis the Spirit's activity and then, in a conciliatory manner, by advocating caution on the part of all. The good of the community has priority in the discernment of pneumatic activity.

Focused and General Exhortation. Paul's paraenesis, in this case, consists of a combination of general statements of advice and concern as well as pointed discussions of community issues. The pericope serves, as Paul brings his letter to a close, as a recapitulation of the problems discussed earlier in his missive.

(1) 5:12-13. Having responded in 5:1-11 to the final question addressed to him, Paul begins his final paraenetic section by returning to the issue of laborers in the community. He urges the members *(adelphoi)* of the community to do two things. First, they are "to acknowledge" and secondly "to regard highly" a certain group of people. The two infinitives are crucial to Paul's meaning. While some wish to interpret the verb *oida* in an unusual, presumably contextual way as meaning "respect," it is best to retain its basic sense of "knowing or recognizing," especially since the second infinitive along with its adverb has roughly that very meaning, namely "to regard highly or honor." Paul's focus is the recognition of the individuals and their proper regard.

Who then are these laborers of whom Paul speaks? Interestingly, he employs the general verb *kopiaō* which, besides having the sense of physical labor, usually refers to the work done by Christian missionaries and others within the community. The term as employed in verse 12 seems intentionally vague, an impression which is confirmed by the closing phrase of the sentence: "on account of their work," another general but synonymous term. Paul further qualifies this group by giving two examples of Thessalonian workers, either those who render assistance to the members of the community or else those who counsel them. Once again the terms and their interpretation are crucial. If *proïstēmi* means "leader" or "presbyter" the sense of verses 12-13 is considerably different than if the term, as a parallel to *prostatēs* in Rom 16:2, is taken to refer to people like Phoebe and others who minister either as missionaries and teachers or in a more general way as deacons or generous patrons. Further, the fact that this activity is done "in the Lord" underscores its general nature, i.e., all types of activities done for the building up of the community and the encouragement of its members. The second type of service Paul alludes to is that of "admonition" or possibly "instruction"— the term's use two verses later would seem to favor the former. Thus, he seems to have in mind a spectrum of ecclesial activity which might be illustrated by the text which best parallels this paraenetic section of 1 Thessalonians, namely, Rom 12:6-7. Paul seems to be referring to the gifts and functions which exist among members and which vary according to the grace given each: prophecy, ministry, teaching, exhortation, giving, service, and showing compassion. It is not Paul's purpose to establish respect and honor for the incipient leadership of the community but to present a basic exhortation within a charismatic group to foster proper functioning of the gifts operating among the members.

The first item within Paul's final exhortation is a reminder of what he has said in 2:1-12 about the apostolic ministry and its motivation. While he does not seem to defend his ministry in the earlier pericope, he still takes pains to describe what proper ministry is by distinguishing the apostolic activity from that of contemporary charlatans. Paul's text in 2:1-12 is paraenetic, not only in his claim that the Thessalonians are his imitators, but also in his describing at length how and why ministers do their ministering. He and his colleagues in view of their devotion to the gospel and to their converts encountered difficulties but were received with affection. Paul's reminder then in 5:12-13 is that fellow believers who labor, whether through their generosity or by their exhortation and admonition, are to be acknowledged as ministers in the Lord and thereby deserve the affection and reciprocal assistance of other believers. As the missionaries had ministered and shared with their converts (2:2f.) and had admonished them with gentleness (2:7, 11-12), so were others ministering within and beyond the community (1:6-8; 5:12). To the community Paul gives the reminder that just as the builders were well received and loved, so must those who continue the process of community-building and development. What problems lay behind such exhortation, one can only guess. The stress on the apostolic mission serves Paul both in showing how one should minister and how great the affection should be between those who give and those who receive. Without this sense of thanksgiving and affection there can only be the beginning of trouble. Thus, Paul concludes that such affection should lead to community peace. Once the members of the one body appreciate and cultivate their various gifts (Rom 12:3-8), peace becomes a communal reality.

(2) Verse 14. The concept of peace, a wish Paul always makes to his communities as he begins his letters, immediately brings to his mind the series of issues which are causing some disruption within the community or at least impeding its growth. Employing a paraenetic formula Paul addresses once more community issues treated earlier and singles out three groups for special attention. Each group apparently relates in a general way to the issues raised in chapters 4 and 5.

[1] The first group is characterized by the term *ataktoi* and refers not to idleness (see 2 Thess 3:6-12) but, in more general terms and according to its basic meaning, to problems of disorder and discord within the community. The believers are told "to admonish" these disorderly members. It is likely that Paul is reiterating in a paraenetic context the advice given in 4:3-8 and 9-12. While discoursing on the believer's call to a state of holiness (4:7) and answering the community's query concerning the nature and boundaries of *philadelphia* (4:9, 12), he is led to discuss problems of immorality in daily activity (including sexual and social morality) and issues of social conduct (vis-à-vis fellow believers and outsiders) and responsibility. The issues raised in these earlier sections of the letter relate to order and proper conduct—note the vocabulary: "refrain," "mastery," "holy and honorable way," "transgress," etc. Paul, as he concludes his letter, reminds the community in paraenetic terms regarding their re-

sponsibility to warn and challenge its members to live "in a holy and honorable way" (4:4) and to "conduct themselves properly" (4:12) because they have been chosen by the God who gives the Holy Spirit (4:8). The warning against disorderliness is one against "breaking faith with God" and violating the state of peace which should exist between brothers and sisters and even toward those outside (4:12). So important is peace and orderliness that Paul insists that Christian living aspire to "a quiet life" of purposeful activity.

[2] The second group singled out are called *hoi oligopsychoi,* i.e., the "faint-hearted or discouraged." This injunction probably has in mind those who grieve over the loss of loved ones (4:13f.). It is the statement about "lack of hope" which leads to this conclusion. As Paul's goal was to console those who grieve, so now he reminds the readers that they have a responsibility to encourage those who are despondent. They have received consolation, but they must continue to be encouraged by one another to cope with the loss of loved ones and, by repeating Paul's advice and giving their own, to motivate their lives on the basis of hope. Faint-heartedness is a weakness based on hopelessness and must be overcome by mutual encouragement in view of a present and future relationship with the Lord.

[3] The third injunction addresses people labeled *hoi astheneis* or "the weak," to whom the Thessalonians are told to render assistance. Who are these "weak" individuals and what does Paul mean by such a phrase? Does the term refer to the physically or morally weak, to people who refuse to eat certain foods, especially that offered to idols (as in 1 Corinthians 8; 10; Romans 14), or to those who are tempted to return to polytheism? This is perhaps the least clear of the references. Since there seems no real reason to read later problems, like those of the Corinthian or Roman Churches, into the situation, one must assume that Paul means those who find the Christian way of life a hard one. That is why 5:1-11 comes to mind as one remembers that Paul advocates not idle discussion of the "times and seasons" of the Lord's coming but wakefulness, self-control, and use of divine weapons (5:6-8). Thus, it is at the end of this passage that he reiterates mutual encouragement and the continued upbuilding of each, weak and strong alike.

Having readdressed a representative sampling of community problems, Paul reminds the community that positive and negative, conciliatory and admonishing assistance must be done with patience or gentleness and always have the community's good in view.

(3) Verses 15-18. It is debated whether verse 15 is a negative and positive commentary on verse 14 regarding forbearance or whether it is a general exhortation concerning behavior within the community. Structural and source considerations lead me to choose the second option. As noted

earlier verse 14 acts as a conclusion to the threefold injunctions to the community regarding internal problems. Verse 15 seems less directed to specific community problems than to general moral attitudes, especially as it, along with verses 16-18, corresponds so closely to the advice Paul gives to the Roman community (Rom 12:12-17). Verse 15 addresses the issue of love in the form of nonretaliation. Rejecting the classic formulation of the *lex talionis* as does contemporary Judaism, Paul insists both that no member of the community repay evil in kind (the negative formulation of the golden rule) and that there be a focus of Christian perspective on the good for all, insiders and outsiders. Presumably for Paul and for other early Christian preachers, such teaching derived from Jesus' command to refrain from retaliation, to espouse the golden rule, and to love one another, even one's enemy (Matt 5:38-48; Luke 6:27-36). For Paul the believer has only one responsibility toward others: to work for their good or to be indebted to them through love (Rom 13:8-10).

As in verse 14 there follows in 16-18 a succession of short imperatives which address a series of paraenetic concerns. As those of verse 14 address the community's responsibility to its members' mutual encouragement and upbuilding as these involve activities of daily life (focus is on initial verbal position), so in verses 16-18 the exhortations are directed to its life and attitudes (focus is on initial adverbial constructions: "always, continually, in all circumstances") which make communal life possible and productive. Paul's paraenesis resembles that of Rom 12:9f. (also 2 Cor 13:11-12), where behavior toward insiders and outsiders is related to the hearers' response to God. The first imperative addresses the community's response to the Christ-event and its present effect. Essentially, as in Rom 12:12, joy is rooted in hope and underscores the deep joy that believers manifest in the daily actualization of their commitment; thus, they are exhorted to have joy ("rejoice always") as their demeanor and normal attitude. The second imperative focuses on believers and their need to address God in prayer. This general term applies to all types of prayer, including set times of prayer, and here (as contrasted to the following injunction) it refers to intercession on one's behalf and that of others (see also 5:25). The Thessalonians are exhorted to prayer as a conscious, continuous state of mind. The final imperative, commanding "thanks in all things," points to an important Pauline theme that what God desires most of human creatures are honor and thanks (Rom 1:21). Finally, this attitude, characterized by joy, intercession, and thanks, is mandated as encompassing God's salvific will through the Christ-event (see 4:3). All three imperatives are characterized as based on God's purpose for humanity but in this instance Paul focuses on the Christological means chosen by God to bring about this state of holiness ("in Christ Jesus"); also implied is the Pauline notion that Christ is the domain and power of Christian holiness (see also 5:12). The general paraenetic commands of verses 15-18 end, therefore, on a suggestive Christological note. Their function, though clearly seen as general exhortation, fits well in Paul's concern for community life at Thessalonica.

(4) 19-22. Interestingly, as 4:3 introduces the notion of "God's will" and discussion of the call to holiness leads to a statement that this holiness is related to being faithful to the God who bestows the Spirit (4:8), so a restatement of the concept of God's will in 5:18b leads to a paraenetic injunction to welcome the activity of the Spirit.

First, Paul warns in successive, negative commands against the rejection of the Spirit and its activity, whether "quenching" its fire-like activity or having disdain for the utterances of people who claim prophetic inspiration. Since the Spirit's activity is already described to the community earlier in the letter as characterized by power and its result as inspiring joy (1:5-6), we can presume that the community saw its members as having received the Spirit (4:8) and that Paul was here concerned with the charismata associated with the Spirit (such as prophecy). Additionally, one assumes that Paul is alluding to the fruits of the Spirit which are manifest in the community life of Thessalonica, whether love, joy, peace, or patience (see Gal 5:22-23). Paul goes one step further and mentions a more concrete, and presumably actual example of pneumatic activity within the community. Some members are sceptical of or even have disdain for the powerful, ecstatic activity around them and Paul, mindful of the role of prophecy in the community's upbuilding, encouragement and consolation (1 Cor 14:3; see also 1 Thess 2:12; 5:11), suggests, in negative terms, that the community be open to the Spirit's activity through the prophets in their midst.

Secondly, by means of a third, positive imperative, Paul follows up on the advice just given and, diplomatically, encourages the reluctant members to shift from a disdainful attitude to a more open yet cautious testing of the prophetic activity. They are told to "examine everything." Paul's advice finds its parallel in what we may presume was a similar ecclesial situation at Corinth, namely, Paul's comment in 1 Cor 14:29: "let two or three prophets speak, then let others [or "the others"] discern what is said." The goal in Corinth, as in Thessalonica, is that "all may learn and all be encouraged" (v. 31). Discernment, finally, has very distinct Pauline criteria: what is good (for the community) must be held fast and taken to heart, but what has any resemblance to evil must be avoided (5:21b-22).

Community Life and Work. Much can be deduced about the Church of Thessalonica and community life generally from Paul's second missive.

Already he speaks in the thanksgiving section about the dynamism of the community's faith, the dedication of its love, as well as the constancy of its hope. While reflecting on its Spirit-filled reception of the gospel and of its ministers, he is led to extol its members as imitators of the missionaries and of the Lord, and to suggest that they have become an example to believers, and some of the members envoys to nonbelievers throughout the Greek mainland. With this auspicious introduction in mind, what more can be said about the community's life and work?

(1) Ideals and Goals. The framework for the community's life and work is spelled out by means of an early formula: the Thessalonians have turned to God from their pagan past to serve God in the present as they await the Son's return (1:9-10). Relying on their commitment to God through the Christ-event (1:9; 4:14; 5:10) and being firm in their hope that Jesus will return for them (1:10; 2:12; 4:14; 5:10, 23), they have as their ideal a conduct worthy of God in view of the kingdom and glory (2:12), a life of holiness to which they have been called. This holiness to which they are exhorted (in rejoicing, prayer, and thanksgiving as being God's will for them in Christ Jesus: 5:16-18) and which is said also to be God's will (4:3) and work (5:23) calls for commensurate behavior, for the call is one not "to impurity but to a state of holiness" (4:7). Already in 4:8 there is a hint about this goal: the community is reminded that the Spirit is given for its well-being, upbuilding, and preparation for the Lord's return.

Its ideal therefore is a life of love for the good of fellow believers and all (5:12-15). In a negative sense they are to abstain from immorality whether involving sexual, social, or economic realities (4:4-6), and in a positive sense they are to continue their God-taught (Spirit-directed) activity of love toward all (4:9-10). Interestingly, Paul describes this activity in social terms as living a quiet life of purposeful work which has both a community-sustaining function ("lacking in nothing") and an outward exemplary goal ("proper conduct toward outsiders"—4:11-12).

A life of such exemplary behavior is proposed as God's will for the present as believers look to the Lord's return. God sanctifies and keeps them "sound and blameless" in view of eternal life with the Lord (4:17; 5:10, 23). This goal has its present effects in a life of hope and in a state of wakefulness and concerted activity in view of salvation (5:8-9).

(2) Actuality. Beyond these ideals and goals of community life what then is the actuality? There is no doubt for Paul that despite difficulties the community began in joyful acceptance of the gospel (1:6) and that its present can be described in terms of vibrant faith, love, and hope (1:3; 5:8). Further, they are expressly praised for the exemplary nature of their community life and generosity (1:7-8). They are said to love their brothers and sisters and are encouraged to broaden the scope of their commitment (4:9-12). Their faith is firm; their love is active. Some within the commu-

nity need encouragement and so are instructed in proper eschatological concerns, but they are praised for the constancy of their hope (1:3) and said to be armed with hope as the helmet of salvation (5:8). They are exhorted to continue not only their loving activity toward others but also their mutual upbuilding (4:10; 5:11). Paul leaves no doubt that the Thessalonian foundation was a success since he insists that the missionaries' visit there "was not ineffective" (2:1) as he had feared in the earlier missive (3:5). Finally, in stating that the Thessalonians had become the imitators of the missionaries he implies that their behavior is also "devout, upright, and blameless" (2:10).

There is, however, a darker side to this reality. In 5:14 we learn about "the disorderly" who need admonition, the "faint-hearted" that require encouragement, and "the weak" who also need assistance. These amorphous groups and their problems are variously identified but nonetheless point to difficulties within the community's daily activity, whether these reveal problems of discipline, lack of proper behavior, social disruption, or theological concerns. Certain aspects of the community's eschatological understanding were lacking; Paul's responses in 4:13-18 and 5:1-11 were meant both to console and to explain further what the early credal formula expressed: "to await the Son from heaven whom God raised from the dead" (1:10). What other problems existed beyond these general issues is hard to say, since it is risky to argue from paraenesis to problem unless something in the text suggests otherwise.

(3) Community's Work. From the outset one must presume that the inner life and outer work of the community are vigorous and exemplary. Not only are the Thessalonians assumed to have contributed personnel to the missionary effort (1:8) but are said to have people who labor among them. It is to this latter issue that we now turn our attention. In discussions of ecclesial structures, particularly those of the Pauline Churches, 1 Thess 5:12 figures prominently since it is assumed, in relation to various other passages, to offer evidence of early developments. Though many scholars insist on rendering the participle *proïstamenos*, both in Rom 12:8 and 1 Thess 5:12, as "leader" it is preferable to view the term as referring, according to Greek idiom, to the concept of benefactor, patron, or guardian; see also Rom 16:2. While it is customary to view the usage in 1 Thessalonians 5 as parallel or complementary to 1 Cor 16:15-18, it is questionable that the later Corinthian situation, text, and terminology should be read back in the Thessalonian passage. The Corinthian community is urged to submit itself to the household of Stephanas which has devoted itself to the service of the saints. Further, they are told to give recognition to their envoys. There is no doubt that the concept of "service" and "recognition," though employing different terms, are reminiscent of those found in 1 Thess 5:12; the other concepts, however,

whether the issue of "submission" or the role played by Stephanas and his household, point to a different situation. The Corinthian context is that of internal ecclesial problems and organization; that of the Thessalonian passage of the proper use of pneumatic gifts.

In 1 Thess 4:18; 5:11; and 5:12-14, the exhortations, despite the claim of some past commentators concerning the last mentioned, are addressed not to Church leaders but to the *adelphoi*, whether one speaks of consolation, encouragement, upbuilding or the series of paraenetic imperatives at the end of the letter. Further, all are expected to test the validity of prophetic oracles (5:21) much as Paul advises in 1 Cor 14:29 (it is debated, for the latter, whether such activity is incumbent on other prophets or the community generally). Thus, in 1 Thessalonians Paul gives advice to the community and is not seemingly concerned about leadership. His paraenesis is addressed to all members for he stresses mutual encouragement, upbuilding, and admonition.

The concept of admonition is particularly interesting in this context. The verb *noutheteō* which means "to admonish, warn, or instruct" is employed for mental or moral discipline and frequently of a father who admonishes his children (Wis 11:10; PssSol 13:19; Josephus, *JW* 1.481; 1 Cor 4:14). The community is to "admonish the disorderly"; some laborers within the community assist other members through admonition as well. Thus, while Paul does not employ this term in speaking of gifts in Rom 12:8 but rather the noun *paraklēsis* to designate exhortation more generally, he nonetheless describes the missionaries in 1 Thess 2:7, 11-12 as acting like a father who encourages, consoles, and implores his children, or like a nurse who cares fondly for her own children. Paul speaks in his final paraenesis not of the functions of leaders, though he does not exclude this, but of the work of the whole community or that of individuals who possess the gift of exhortation.

The laborers of 1 Thess 5:12 as well as the work performed refer not to the work of leaders but address the proper use of the charismata which operate for the community's development. Further, just as the whole community is said to have become imitators of the apostles, who assisted their converts with the gentleness of a nurse or the discipline of a father, who showed great love and affection for their children in Thessalonica, and who conducted themselves worthily of God, so the members of the community, with their respective gifts, are urged to admonish, encourage, and help—with patience (5:14), to show love and affection to those who labor among them—in the quest of peace (12-13), and to strive always for holiness of life and behavior—according to God's will (16-18). The concept of imitation which is introduced in 1:6 prepares for the autobiographical exposition of 2:1-12, and finds its motivation and development in the paraenetic conclusion of the letter.

(4) Community's Situation and Pauline Purpose. A constant thread connects the various parts of Paul's letter. The final topic of his paraenesis alerts the reader that it is the Spirit and the function of pneumatic gifts which motivate Paul from start to finish in writing to the Thessalonians about their community's situation. A key to the themes of order, peace, and holiness is a proper attitude toward, recognition of, and the proper functioning of these divine gifts within the community. The members are warned "not to quench the Spirit" (5:19) and so are reminded that the process began with "joy inspired by the Spirit" (1:6) and that God gives them the Spirit (4:8) and its accompanying gifts or weapons for the good of all and for the building up of the community. Lastly, Paul advises that all pneumatic activity must be examined—the criteria are very simple: choose what is good for the community and reject what is not. Throughout the letter they have been reminded that what is good for the community might best be described as fruits of the Spirit, whether love, joy, peace, patience, etc., and what is not as the works of the flesh, whether immorality, impurity, idolatry, etc. (Gal 5:19-23). The paraenesis is about love of brothers and sisters and others, is about rejoicing always, is especially about peace and the proper treatment of those in need; but it is also about refraining from immorality, wicked acts, and causes of dissension. Paul's advice to the Galatians, after speaking of the above, could have been given to the Thessalonians as well: "if we live by the Spirit, let us also be guided by the Spirit" (5:25).

What then was Paul's purpose for writing the letter? The immediate purpose is the arrival of questions from the community whether oral or written or both. Paul is apprised of its problems, particularly its uneasy charismatic dynamism and development. From the start he addresses the issue as he, twice in the thanksgiving period, addresses the activity of the Spirit as being proof of their election on the one hand and evidence of their Christian maturity on the other as they are said to be imitators both of the missionaries and of the Lord (1:5-6). But he is quick to underscore the community's knowledge of the missionaries, their imitation, and their role as God's fearless agents (2:2), agents of a God who chooses, calls to a life of holiness, and gives the Spirit as the dynamism of the quest for salvation. Paul therefore writes to answer some specific questions, to address underlying problems of growth and concord, and to encourage those who have misgivings about pneumatic activity to be bold in their examination of that activity but also to be wise in their choice for it is in this way that the God who bestows the Spirit chooses to sanctify and to prepare those "called to his own kingdom and glory" (2:12).

FOR REFERENCE AND FURTHER STUDY

Black, D. A. "The Weak in Thessalonica: A Study in Pauline Lexicography." *JETS* 25 (1982) 307–21.

Holmberg, B. *Paul and Power: The Structure of Authority in the Primitive Church as Reflected in the Pauline Epistles.* Philadelphia: Fortress, 1978.

Laub, F. *Eschatologische Verkündigung und Lebensgestaltung nach Paulus: Eine Untersuchung zum Wirken des Apostels beim Aufbau der Gemeinde in Thessalonike.* Regensburg: Pustet, 1973.

Malherbe, A. J. *Paul and the Thessalonians: The Philosophic Tradition of Pastoral Care.* Philadelphia: Fortress, 1987.

Roetzel, C. J. "1 Thessalonians 5:12-28: A Case Study." *SBL Proceedings* (1972), 367–83.

Schade, H.-H. *Apokalyptische Christologie bei Paulus: Studien zum Zusammenhang von Christologie und Eschatologie in den Paulusbriefen.* Göttingen: Vandenhoeck & Ruprecht, 1981.

Van Unnik, W. C. " 'Den Geist löschet nicht aus' (1 Thessalonicher V 19)." *NovT* 10 (1968) 255–69.

16. *Final Prayer and Epistolary Closing* (5:23-28)

23. Now may the God of peace himself make you perfectly holy and may your whole being—spirit, soul, and body—be kept blameless for the coming of our Lord Jesus Christ. 24. The one who calls you is trustworthy and so will accomplish this. 25. Brothers and sisters, pray also for us. 26. Greet all the brothers and sisters with a holy kiss. 27. I adjure you by the Lord to have this letter read to all the brothers and sisters. 28. The grace of our Lord Jesus Christ be with you.

NOTES

23. *Now may the God of peace himself:* The final section of Paul's second missive begins in the same way as does the final prayer of the first (3:11): with the unique idiom *autos de ho theos* followed by an archaic optative mood to express a formal prayer. For a similar idiom employing *kyrios* in place of *theos,* see 2 Thess 2:16 and 3:16. The expression "the God of peace" occurs elsewhere in Paul in situations similar to this one, namely, in concluding prayers and letter closings (Rom 15:33; 16:20; 2 Cor 13:11; Phil 4:9). "Peace" (see 1:1) in this case refers to the state of eschatological well-being which God bestows upon those who commit themselves to the redemptive Christ-event

(Rom 5:1). Though this peace should affect human and divine relations (see 1 Thess 5:13), in the present context the term refers to human, wholistic salvation (as the rest of the verse makes clear) and to God as the source of this well-being.

make you perfectly holy: The prayer formula employs an aorist optative active to express God's direct action (23a) and an aorist optative passive to speak of the result of that activity (23b). God is called upon to "make holy" the Thessalonian readers. The verb *hagiazō* is used only here in 1 Thessalonians though its cognates also appear: *hagiōsynē* in 3:13; *hagiasmos* in 4:3, 4, 7; and *hagios* in the idiom "the Holy Spirit" (1:5, 6; 4:8; see also 3:13; 5:26). Its meaning and nuance in the present context must be sought in relation to Pauline usage and from its context within the final prayer. (1) The other uses of the verb indicate that the activity is divine in origin ("made holy by the Holy Spirit"—Rom 15:16 and other uses of the divine passive), owes to the Christ-event (1 Cor 1:2; 6:11—conversion generally), and places the convert in a state of holiness (1 Cor 7:14, 14; see *TDNT* 1:114). Additionally, its use here relates not to *hagiasmos* but to *hagiōsynē* (see 4:3 and 3:13) as the context indicates. (2) The punctiliar aorist and the following adjectival modifier ("perfectly") indicate that Paul is not here speaking of holiness as an ethical process or as social community activity (for this he employs *hagiasmos* as in 4:3f.). Instead, he is referring to that soteriological activity which was begun by God in the Christ-event (the believers' new state) and which God is beseeched to make complete (one action) at the end-time when Jesus returns. The prayer is eschatological, not ethical, in focus (see below).

and may your whole being—spirit, soul, and body—be kept blameless: The second part of the prayer is readily acknowledged to be a synonymous parallel to the first part; its meaning is to be sought in relation to it. As in the first part, Paul wishes that believers will be blameless or completely holy at Jesus' coming; he adds, however, the notions of completeness and preservation and offers a baffling tripartite anthropology consisting of "spirit, soul, and body." The anthropology and grammar of this verse are much debated. (1) As regards the anthropology, scholars readily admit that, apart from this passage, Paul thinks of the human being in Jewish terms as consisting of body and soul or as body and spirit. Thus, some attempt to read the present text as offering such a bipartite view (e.g.: "may your spirit, both the soul and body, be kept blameless"), while others explain Paul's adoption of the tripartite terminology as owing to Gnostic polemics, Christian pneumatology (the spirit is identified with the divine Spirit), or to his desire to underscore the unity of the human being. It is the last mentioned, however one explains the origin of the formula, which offers the most satisfactory explanation. Whether Paul sees these three terms (the usage of the three is quite complex both in biblical and classical literature) as referring anthropologically (as in popular Hellenistic thought) to various parts of the believer's personality (the spiritual, the affective or mental, and corporeal components) one can see how a text with a tripartite view such as Deut 6:5, as known in the Jewish Christian tradition (Matt 22:37: "you shall love the Lord your God with all your heart, and with all your soul, and with all your mind"), might have influenced him or the prayer tradition he was using. (2) The grammar also presents problems. Since the initial term is an adjective it could be construed as a predicate adjective modifying the three anthropological terms (either: "may your whole spirit, body, etc. be kept" or "may your spirit, etc. be kept whole"). The most appealing solution, however, sees the expression *holokleron hymon* as a substantive phrase ("your whole being") which acts as the subject and considers the anthropological terms as an appositional subject; see translation above. The focus is on the unity of the person in all aspects. Further, the activity is described by means of an aorist and so emphasizes not the process or duration of the divine protection but its overall or complexive sense (BDF 318, 332). On the expression "blameless," see 2:10 and 3:13.

for the coming of our Lord Jesus Christ: Just as the prayer of the first missive ends by appealing to the Lord Jesus' return (3:13) so does the second, though Paul employs a fuller title "our Lord Jesus Christ." His full use of the formula in this eschatological prayer serves to underscore not just the parousia but also the death, resurrection, and profession of faith and therefore the Christological foundation of the believer's hope. In both prayers Paul's wish is that his converts be judged blameless by God in view of the Lord's coming.

24. *The one who calls you is trustworthy and so will accomplish this:* On God as the "one who calls," see discussion of 1:4. Note also Paul's striking use of the present tense, thereby giving God the name "the one who calls"; see also 2:12. The concept of election leads to that of "trustworthiness"; God is the one par excellence who is reliable, whose promises can be trusted. Because of this (use of a relative construction with an iterative conjunction: *hos kai*—"and so"), one can be sure that God will accomplish what has been promised. Interestingly, this text sounds like a concatenation of themes from Deutero-Isaiah who designates God as the one who calls Israel in righteousness (42:6; also 48:12), the one who is trustworthy (49:7), and the one who plans and accomplishes what is planned (46:10). For Paul these characteristics define who God is and what God is able to do; hope is based on promise and trust in the one who promises. See 1 Cor 1:8-9 where Paul reiterates the same themes: God's call and faithfulness and the believer's blamelessness in view of the day of the Lord Jesus Christ.

25. *Brothers and sisters, pray also for us:* As Paul began his letter by noting that the missionaries have invoked God in their behalf (1:2), so now he closes his missive by requesting that they do the same in their turn (use of *proseucho*). *Kai* ("also") is read though the MS evidence is evenly divided—omission seems more probable. Paul's request follows the missionaries' prayer for them (v. 23). His letters, as do many Hellenistic letters, sometimes end with prayer and the request for prayers: Rom 15:30; Phil 4:6; Phlm 22 (see also 2 Cor 1:11 and Phil 1:19).

26. *Greet all the brothers and sisters with a holy kiss:* Paul regularly ends his letters by greeting various individuals or by commanding that the audience greet their fellow believers. In this case he emphatically (repeated use of *adelphos*

in vv. 25, 26, and 27 and "all" in vv. 26 and 27) notes that they are to greet all the members of the community, presumably to underscore the unity and concord which has figured so prominently in the paraenesis. As he will do in later missives (Rom 15:16; 1 Cor 16:20; and 2 Cor 13:12) he specifies that they express this greeting "with a holy kiss." It is agreed that the kiss was a common custom in Greco-Roman and Jewish cultures to show affection toward family members and friends and honor toward people of superior rank. Kisses, which were given on the cheeks, forehead, eyes, shoulders, and hands and feet, served many purposes and in various contexts (*TDNT* 9:119-23). In Paul's case the kiss is characterized as being "holy" and so serving as a Christian greeting, i.e., the greeting of those who have been called by God and made "holy" (see also 1 Pet 5:14). It has been argued from the custom's contexts in 1 Cor 16:20 (followed by the anathema and maranatha formulas) that it might have served as introduction to the Lord's Supper. Indeed, the command, expressed in the aorist (also the following injunction about reading the letter), suggests a specific occasion for the holy kiss, i.e., during the community gathering when the Lord's Supper was celebrated and Paul's letter would have been read. Presumably such a custom in the early Church gave rise to the well-known liturgical "kiss of peace." Its function, if it preceded the Eucharistic celebration, would have been to serve as a seal of reconciliation or, more generally, as a sign of ecclesial unity and mutual affection. The latter is preferable since Paul is asking that the members, as a sign of mutual life, greet everyone in the community with a special sign of affection.

27. *I adjure you by the Lord to have this letter read to all the brothers and sisters:* Paul's last injunction is strange on several counts. It is the only letter where he makes such a demand (see the Paulinist Col 4:16); the strong verb *enorkizō* ("to adjure or swear"), a NT hapax, unexplainably introduces a solemn adjuration; the demand is made suddenly in the first-person singular; and, again, there is the insistence that all the members of the community be apprised in public reading of the letter's contents.

28. *The grace of the Lord Jesus Christ be with you:* Paul ends his letter with the customary benediction, a form which occurs, with a certain variety, in his other letters. He replaces the secular greeting of "farewell" and creates a parallel with the opening greeting: "grace and peace to you." This is especially striking as we note the reference in 5:23 to "the God of peace" and in 5:28 to "the grace of our Lord Jesus Christ." On the concept of grace and peace and Paul's use of the full address "Lord Jesus Christ" both at the beginning and end of the letter (1:1, 3 and 5:23, 28), see comments on 1:1.

INTERPRETATION

After an extended exhortation Paul brings his letter to a close with traditional epistolary features: a formal prayer (5:23; see 3:11f., the ending of the first missive), a statement about God's trustworthiness in lieu of a doxology (5:24), a request for prayer (25), greetings with a holy kiss

(26), an unusual command that his letter be read in public assembly (27), and a traditional benediction (28). Survey of Paul's remaining correspondence reveals the use of these same features and others, but rarely in the same sequence. Clearly, Paul's letters varied in style and were influenced by the occasion for writing. Several features of this epistolary closing, therefore, will shed light on the concerns of the letter writer and addressees and on the reason for writing.

Paul's Eschatological Prayer. The closing begins with a formal prayer whose opening, content, and climax approximate those of the closing of the first missive (3:11-13). Equally important is the form of these prayers which employ aorist optatives. In the present case, Paul's prayer, whether one labels it a "wish prayer" or a "homiletic benediction" in origin or function, is addressed indirectly to "the God of peace himself," a phrase which is interesting on two counts. In the first place the intensive pronoun *autos* focuses attention not on God simply but on God as "the God of peace." In the second place, this last phrase, which seems to be a Pauline creation, draws a connection between peace and the conferral of holiness. Thus, 5:23 has often been interpreted, in relation to 4:3f., as underscoring the gaining of holiness, whether emphasizing divine assistance as in 5:23 or human activity as in 4:3-8. More particularly, 5:23 is seen as providing a clue to the reading of the letter as focused on the interconnection between sanctification and peace and thus insisting that peace has a temporal, social function. Chapters 4 and 5 are then read as a quest for *hagiasmos* or "holiness" which also brings about peace, order, and freedom from anxiety. Such an approach provides some insight on Paul's concerns regarding the community's behavior, concord, and social peace; however, one wonders how carefully the meaning of 5:23 has been discerned and how easily the eschatological "peace" of the verse has been reduced to inner calm and social concord. One may argue, correctly, that 5:13b ("be at peace among yourselves") refers to just such a social, religious reality but the same cannot be said for the verse in question.

We return therefore to further consideration of 5:23. The prayer reads: "may the God of peace himself make you perfectly holy." The verse by its use of the term "perfectly" states clearly that believers are already "holy" (Paul later calls them "saints" or *hagioi*) and that God is asked to make them "perfect in holiness." The precise meaning of the verb "to make holy or sanctify" is critical at this point. Its usage here conforms to Paul's other verbal uses; it indicates, in relation to the adjective modifier, the completion or perfection at the parousia of the soteriological activity which God brought about through Christ Jesus. Believers were sanctified by God (or by the Holy Spirit: Rom 15:16) at the time of conversion and so are placed in a state of holiness, a state for which Paul employs the term *hagiasmos* and which requires appropriate behavior (see 4:3-8). Paul is not speaking of the latter in 5:23 but of the former; in other words, the prayer is not ethical but eschatological in focus. Such a conclusion is further confirmed by his use of the aorist rather than the present optative. The activity is not that of bringing the believer's moral behavior to a perfect conclusion but of establishing the believer in the sphere of holiness (see 3:13 and its use of *hagiōsynē*).

We turn to the Pauline expression "the God of peace." What in Paul does the God of peace do? In Rom 16:20 God, in the eschatological future, "will soon crush Satan under your feet." Lives of social concord are explicitly related in 2 Cor 13:11 and Phil 4:9 to the presence of the God of peace among believers. A similar usage can be discerned at 1 Cor 14:33 where Paul insists that if one is devoted to the God of peace it should follow that there be no discord among those devoted to that God. The wish at Rom 15:33 as well as the meaning in 1 Thess 5:23 is that the God of peace be the guarantor of perfect holiness and eternal communion with the returning messianic Son. The expression "the God of peace" then is an eschatological one, even when Paul points to ethical ramifications.

The prayer, however, does not end with verse 23a but provides a synonymous parallel to the first part. Paul prays: (and as a result) "may your whole being—spirit, soul, and body—be kept blameless for the coming of our Lord Jesus Christ." Paul insists that perfect holiness means wholeness of the human person and blamelessness before the God of peace, activities which are God's domain (see also 3:13). The whole human being, not just the spirit or soul, but the composite and its corporeal involvement are addressed in the verse. There are ethical ramifications, and Paul is well aware of those, but at this point he is interested in the eschatological goal of Christian living. Even the aorist reinforces such a conclusion for Paul is not concerned here with preservation of the believer during the interim period (a present tense would have been used). Instead he is interested in the completion of the activity.

Focus on Hope. As if to underscore the point further Paul insists that the "God who calls" is by definition the "trustworthy one," the God of promise whose ability to accomplish what is promised is beyond doubt. The issue of verse 24 is one of hope, of eschatological promise. The Thessalonian problem then was the opposite of that of the Philippians who imagined themselves already in a state of perfection (Phil 3:12-16).

Paul's prayer of hope and his affirmation of God's dependability are not unique elements of the ending of the letter, for the concerns of this prayer permeate the document. Just as faith focuses on the initial aspect of holiness, the time when God chose, gave the Spirit and thus sanctified believers (1:4; 4:8) and just as love stresses, in the body in the present, the ethical manifestation of that state of holiness, so hope and its motivation looks to the end-time when the "Almighty" will complete the process that leads to salvation. As the letter begins by focusing on the concepts of faith, love, and stresses hope (1:3), so it ends by reiterating faith and love as weapons of self-control and hope, once again underscored contextually, as related to the attainment of salvation (5:8). The role of faith Paul repeatedly notes in speaking of the community's reception of the gospel (1:4-6, 9-10) and of the apostles' ministry during the original visit (2:1-12). That of love is often illustrated in his references to their ministry to others (1:7-8), their need to live lives of holiness in their relation to others (4:3-8), and their concern for one another and for outsiders (4:9-12). That of hope is more focused since some grieve as though they "have no hope" (4:13) and others act without the alertness which the Lord's day and the attainment of salvation require (5:4-9).

If Paul treats at length the community's initial commitment and therefore faith in his treatment of the opening mission in the city, he nonetheless concludes on the note of love as conduct worthy of God and of hope as being called to God's kingdom and glory (2:12). If Paul deals at even greater length in his paraenesis with the duties of love or the believer's state of holiness, he nonetheless often refers back to the giving of the Spirit (4:8), to being God-taught (4:9), or to common beliefs (4:6, 11, 14; 5:2) and to future judgment (4:6) and the eschatological concerns of the community (4:13–5:11). At the same time while the final exhortation is on community life in the present and its concerns about love of fellow workers, patient assistance and admonition to those in need, and attention to the community's inner life and relation to the activity of the Spirit, the exhortation is nonetheless said to be God's will in Christ Jesus and is followed by the letter's eschatological prayer that God the faithful and almighty one will make the believers perfect in holiness that they might be with the Lord forever (5:23; see 4:17 and 5:10). The final note on hope (whether eschatological prayer or statement on God's reliability) is hardly fortuitous when one considers that Paul is writing to a community that has a strongly motivated mission toward others (1:6-8), a concern for the love of one another and all (4:10; 5:15), and yet a community that has members who can act like "pagans who do not know God" (4:5), who "grieve as others do who have no hope" (4:13), who fail to appreciate what it means to be "children of light and children of the day" (5:5), and who show disdain for the Spirit's activity within the community. For those in doubt or in grief, for those who found the going rough, and for those who considered the present reassuring but the future disheartening, Paul expresses the reminder that the one who calls is trustworthy and able to deliver on the promise of salvation.

The Letter Closing. The remainder of Paul's letter, traditional though it may seem, shows appropriateness to the Thessalonian situation. A call for prayer at the end of letters has become so common that one might be tempted to overlook the role this plays in Paul's early correspondence. The call for prayer reiterates the letter's repeated insistence on mutual affection, underscores the concepts of reciprocal and continuous prayer, and further stresses the fact that the addressees have become imitators of the apostles and the Lord.

The "greeting with a holy kiss" underscores the need for greater peace and concord (5:13). Its function is intended to stress familial relationship between members of the community as they strive to live as children of the one Father and as brothers and sisters. It is not accidental that Paul employs the term *adelphoi* three times in verses 25-27 (twice with the added term "all"). Indeed, "the holy kiss," at home in a family context, is meant to emphasize the community's new family relationships.

Finally, the benediction (regarding "the grace of our Lord Jesus Christ"), which has also become formalized in epistolary and liturgical contexts, has a peculiar Thessalonian emphasis. Along with 5:23 ("the God of peace") it forms an inclusio with the letter's greeting as both refer to the dual concepts of divine peace and grace. Nonetheless, as his prayer in 5:23 focuses on and ends with a Christological, eschatological wish (so important to the community's motivation), so his benediction emphasizes a Christological but actual blessing, namely, that the grace, which comes from God through the one whom believers acknowledge as Lord, be active in their lives and everyday activity.

Public Reading or the Function of Paul's Second Missive. Of the various items composing the epistolary closing only that of 5:27 will not become a standard feature of Paul's future correspondence. Thus, its uniqueness and special features call for closer attention, particularly the injunction's relation to the community's situation. Indeed, the switch from the plural to the singular first person, the solemn, forceful tone of the adjuration, the insistence that "all the brothers and sisters" be addressed, and lastly that the letter be "read publicly," all require some explanation. Various suggestions are made to explain Paul's use of such strong terminology, ranging from the need to impose his authority in absentia, to overcome internal divisions, to reach the illiterate, or to make sure that both leaders and others became acquainted with the letter's contents. It is also suggested that Paul, since he is writing his first letter as a community letter, sees himself as instituting a new practice and so one requiring strong language. Or else the demanding terminology is seen as being required by

Paul who wanted to introduce his letter into the community's synagogue-like list of public readings.

The unusual features as well as suggestions noted above lead me to a number of considerations. (1) Why the change from "we" to "I"? Most suggest that Paul is probably taking over the letter from his amanuensis or secretary to whom he was dictating and writes the finale in the first-person singular. Such a reason may indeed be true and may explain Paul's need in some cases to make an authenticating statement at the end of the letter (e.g., 1 Cor 16:21: "the greeting is from my own hand, that is, Paul's"; see also Gal 6:11). Also, Paul sometimes brings his letters to a conclusion by expressing what is described as a statement of "motivation for writing." Such statements are made in Rom 15:14-15; 2 Cor 13:10; Gal 5:2f.; and Phlm 21. Each passage mentions the reason for writing, is usually expressed forcefully (linguistically or contextually) in the first-person singular, and, in two cases, brings about a shift from "we" to "I" (2 Cor 13:10 and Gal 5:2f.). Paul's use of the strong legal term "I adjure" and his change to the first-person singular fit such a pattern.

(2) One might add further that the other unusual aspects of 5:27 are related to Paul's reason for writing. If we are correct in seeing the second missive as a letter generated by questions sent to Paul from Thessalonica, then we would likewise be right in viewing his text as responses to the problems of some members within the community. Indeed, his responses are focused on the issues which some have formulated into questions, presumably those of other members, but, as demonstrated repeatedly, these responses expand and redirect the subjects at issue. In other words, questions raised by some regarding problems others were having, give rise to a complex of discussions and exhortations on Paul's part. Even the admonitions are addressed in part to the underlying problems of the community and to general issues of Christian faith, love, and hope. There is in Paul's second missive something for everyone, something which troubled, doubtful, working, and attentive members need to hear and to repeat to one another as exhortation (4:18). The apostles have been gentle as nurses and now through their paraenesis treat everyone like their own children as they "encourage, console, and implore" (2:7, 11-12). Public reading of the letter in the presence of every brother and sister assures that each member of the community is either admonished, encouraged, or assisted with patience, love, and concord (5:12-14). In this way the Spirit is allowed to work freely for the good of the community as all are allowed to work, admonish, help, or prophesy—each in relation to the Spirit's gifts.

Paul then is writing this paraenetic letter as a concerned missionary. He and his cosenders could have insisted on their authority as apostles (2:7); instead Paul commands, on the authority of the Lord, that the letter serve to continue their pastoral work among the members of the Thessalonian community who will variously perceive the gentle hand of the nurse and the discipline of the father, both urging renewed effort in mutual exhortation and community building.

FOR REFERENCE AND FURTHER STUDY

Bassler, J. M. "Peace in All Ways: Theology in the Thessalonian Letters: A Response to R. Jewett, E. Krentz, and E. Richard." *PT*, 71–85.
Collins, R. F. " '. . . that this letter be read to all the brethren.' " *SFLT*, 356–70.
Langevin, P.-E. "L'intervention de Dieu selon 1 Thes 5, 23-24." *TC* 236–56.
White, J. L. *The Body of the Greek Letter*. Missoula: Scholars, 1972.
Wiles, G. P. *Paul's Intercessory Prayers: The Significance of the Intercessory Prayer Passages in the Letters of St. Paul*. Cambridge: Cambridge University, 1974.

SECOND THESSALONIANS

17. *Epistolary Opening* (1:1-2)

1. Paul, Silvanus, and Timothy; to the Church of the Thessalonians in God our Father and the Lord Jesus Christ; 2. grace to you and peace from God our Father and the Lord Jesus Christ.

NOTES

1. *Paul, Silvanus, and Timothy:* The series of missionaries mentioned in 1 Thess 1:1, Paul, Silvanus, and Timothy, is repeated verbatim. The author chooses close imitation of a well-known Pauline letter as strategy to counter the charismatic and epistolary claims of apocalyptic preachers (2:2). Thus, all participants in the debate could compare the new composition to the Pauline letter they all knew and to which the author refers in 2:15.

   to the church of the Thessalonians in God our Father and the Lord Jesus Christ: Again, the author takes the text over verbatim from 1 Thess 1:1, save for the addition of the formulaic pronoun "our" following "father." The above translation reflects the interpretation of extended readers who would view the term *ekklēsia* ("church") in a less local sense than it had for Paul, and would not distinguish between the gentilic and place names.

2. *grace to you and peace:* The salutation is taken over verbatim from 1 Thess 1:1 and corresponds to Pauline and Paulinist epistolary tradition. While in 1 Thessalonians the concept of grace relates to divine election and initiative and to blessings bestowed in the present through Christ (1:1, 4; 5:28) and that of peace focuses on eschatological well-being and demands concord within the community (1:1; 5:13, 23), in 2 Thessalonians these two concepts take on a new meaning and function. If the usage of the term grace in the salutation and final blessing (1:2; 3:18) resembles that of 1 Thess 1:1 and 5:28, its use at 1:12 following the apocalyptic development of 1:5-10 and at 2:16 in relation to "eternal comfort and good hope" points to its anti-apocalyptic function. Grace for this author is intimately related to the letter's attempt to counteract the community's apocalyptic perspective. The concept of peace

also is thus focused. It is no longer the "God of peace" who acts to make the believer completely holy in view of the kingdom (1 Thess 5:23), but the Lord Jesus as the "Lord of peace" who is beseeched to grant not the peace which the addressees perceive they need as a persecuted holy community but the peace which a Christian community needs "at all times in all ways" (2 Thess 3:16).

from God our Father and the Lord Jesus Christ: The author adds, from other Pauline letters, a standard theological and Christological modifier to the salutation. Grace and peace, seemingly as in Paul, have a divine origin and a Christological medium. Two further points should be made. (1) The use of virtually identical theological-Christological formulas following both the statements of address and salutation results from the imitation of 1 Thessalonians and the attempt to standardize the salutation. (2) While the majority of MSS read "God our Father," a few omit the pronoun *hēmōn* (B D 33 *pc*). In textual and redactional terms, either option could be defended: addition of pronoun owing to assimilation to other Pauline prescripts or omission to a desire to avoid repetition of verse 1. Two considerations point to "our" as original. [1] The author favors the formulaic expression "God our Father" (see 1:1; 2:16) and [2] the textual weight of Vaticanus is lessened owing to the tendency of its scribe to omit seemingly minor textual features; among others see 1 Thess 1:4 (omission of *tou*); 1:5 (*en*); 1:8 (*en tē*); 2:5 (*en*); 4:1 (*oun*); 4:8 (*kai*); 2 Thess 2:1 (*hēmōn*); 2:8 (*Iēsous*), 2:14 (*kai*); 2:16 (*ho*); 3:6 (*hēmōn*).

INTERPRETATION

A reading of 2 Thessalonians must keep an eye on 1 Thessalonians because of the similarities between the two in terms of structure, style, and content, and must focus repeatedly on the document's unique character and on its integrity as a work written for a specific purpose and with an identifiable strategy. While attention to the first will be an overall preoccupation, whether in dealing with comparative linguistic usage, theological considerations, or interpretive perspectives, the focus of the interpretation will be on the second in an effort to discern the document's occasional nature and unique perspective.

Reading and Translation of the Letter Opening. There is in 2 Thess 1:1-2, as in other letters of the Pauline corpus, a tripartite prescript which mentions the sender and addressees and ends with a greeting. This epistolary opening, however, is virtually identical with that of 1 Thessalonians. On the one hand, the introductory verses reproduce the form and content, even the peculiarities of the tripartite Thessalonian opening: the names of the three missionaries (with repetitive *kai*), that of the addressees (with gentilic noun rather than the usual reference to the people of the city and with the equally unusual addition of a binary reference to

God and Jesus), and the customary blessing. On the other hand, the author expands the blessing to make it conform to other Pauline letters. There results an anomalous, ponderous double reference to God the Father and the Lord Jesus Christ. Thus, the author's strategy involved both the close imitation of Paul's letter to the Thessalonians and the use of other Pauline epistolary features, thereby standardizing the new document, in view of its broader Pauline appeal.

The translation given above is intentionally less interpretive than that of 1 Thess 1:1. For example, *ekklēsia Thessalonikeōn* is rendered "to the church of the Thessalonians" rather than "to the community of Thessalonians," since the author, at a further remove from Paul, would read *ekklēsia* in a less local sense and would see no reason to distinguish between the partitive genitive of the gentilic noun and the name of the city. A first conclusion one may draw is that the author's verbatim use of phraseology points to the functional use of Paul's text to add authority to the new composition and indicates a traditional, extended reading of some of its contents. The author, as a later reader of Paul, is interested not in the nuances shared by the original author and reader but in the effect which traditional Pauline language has on the reader of the new document.

There is, however, another important consideration in reading a pseudonymous document. It is often assumed that the liberal use of structures and text by a later writer implies lifeless repetition of these. This is a danger of comparative studies, especially when they involve an unflattering comparison between Paul and later writers. In effect, the use of Pauline terms may serve two purposes. The first has been noted above as serving the strategy of pseudonymity: the text sounds like Paul and so the writer must be Paul. The second purpose is more germane to the reason for writing. The author usually contributes new content to the themes being used and applies them to a different situation. For example, the terms "grace and peace" have a distinct Pauline meaning and function in 1 Thessalonians (1:1 and 5:23, 28) but both are put at the service of the new author's anti-apocalyptic strategy. Grace and peace as themes serve to extend the Pauline meaning of grace as gift and election to that of grace as present glorification and comfort in contrast to the community's overly apocalyptic concerns (2 Thess 1:12; 2:16) and of peace as participation in God's well-being to that of peace as protection from what the community sees as apocalyptic woes (3:16). Pauline terms and their meaning, in a pseudonymous document, must be sought in that writing's overall perspective and other uses of these terms and related idioms.

Companions and Apostolic Authority as Issues of Authorship. The following two issues are raised in discussions of authorship. (1) Why does the author of 2 Thessalonians, if not Paul, mention the Pauline companions in the greeting since they play no role in the letter or the communication of its message and (2) if 2 Thessalonians is interested in establishing apostolic authority for a later generation, why does its author not give Paul his apostolic title as one would expect? The first is seen as a possible argument for and the second a potential objection to pseudonymity. On the one hand, that neither Silvanus nor Timothy reappear in 2 Thessalonians need not support non-Pauline authorship since neither Sosthenes (mentioned as cosender in 1 Cor 1:1) nor Silvanus (listed as cosender along with Timothy in 1 Thess 1:1) reappear in the remainder of the respective letter. The same is true of Timothy in Paul's letter to Philemon; a similar situation obtains for the Paulinist letter to the Colossians. Only in 1 Thessalonians, Philippians, and 2 Corinthians does Timothy as Paul's envoy, reappear in the body of the letter.

As regards the second issue, it is well known that Paul does not employ the title of apostle for himself in the openings of 1 Thessalonians, Philippians, and Philemon and that Paulinist writers, though all interested in claiming apostolic authority, do not emphasize this title. While Ephesians, Colossians, and the Pastorals employ the title in their opening only the Pastor makes a point of stressing this claim (1 Tim 2:7; 2 Tim 1:11). Thus, Paul's rare and nontechnical use of the term apostle in his Macedonian correspondence (1 Thess 2:6 and Phil 2:25), the relative non-use of this theme among the Paulinists, including Luke in Acts, and the author's close imitation of 1 Thessalonians, suffice to explain its absence in 2 Thessalonians.

The first issue, however, has a further bearing on the question of authorship. As noted earlier, the writer of 2 Thessalonians opts for close imitation of 1 Thessalonians as strategy to establish credibility. Thus, the appeal to the three letter senders of 1 Thess 1:1 is in keeping with this strategy and well-known Pauline usage, where the focus is on Paul himself. With the exception of two references to Timothy as emissary in 3:2, 6, the focus in 1 Thessalonians is on Paul, whether as part of a group ("we") or individually ("I"—2:18; 3:5; 5:27). The author of 2 Thessalonians, as an extended reader, reads 1 Thessalonians as exclusively the work of Paul and attempts to create a document that operates in the same fashion. Reference to Paul's companions serves the same function in the new document as it does in a reading of the older one. Beyond that, the author imitates Pauline usage of "we-discourse" and on two occasions, much as Paul does, focuses the addressees' attention on Paul first by reminding them of his teaching while he was with them (2:5: "*I* told you these things while *I* was still with you"—contrast with 1 Thess 3:4: "when *we* were with you, *we* told you") and secondly, again in Pauline fashion, ends the letter by directing attention specifically to Paul (3:17). In the latter, rather than employing "I-discourse" to bring the letter to a close as Paul does in 1 Thess 5:27 and usually in his letters, the author combines "I-discourse" with a statement found in 1 Cor 16:21 to construct a postscript to bolster further the claim of authenticity. Thus, 2 Thessalonians, in its close, intentional imitation of Paul's text, was not written to refute 1 Thessalonians and its eschatology or to clarify misunderstandings of earlier eschatological preaching, but to discredit the claims, made in Paul's name, of apocalyptic preachers which were causing alarm within the community (2:2) and social unrest within its ranks (3:6-12).

Early Clues to the Author's Theology and Christology. One is struck by the author's double use of a theological and Christological formula: "God our Father and the Lord Jesus Christ." The first repeats verbatim that of 1 Thess 1:1 and the second seeks to standardize the greeting to agree with Pauline practice (1:2). In both cases the formulas qualify God as "our Father" and Jesus as "Lord Jesus Christ."

(1) In examining the presentation of God's role one detects a new emphasis as well as some modification of Pauline usage. On all three occasions where God is called "Father" (1:1, 2; 2:16), the term is modified by "our." In this way the author emphasizes the theme of God as Father of all believers. This is confirmed by the omission of the reference to Jesus' sonship in 1 Thess 1:10 and the author's further imitation of Paul (1 Thess 2:2; 3:9) in calling God "our God" (1:11, 12). In the development of God's role in the believers' lives, the Paulinist writer appeals to Pauline, as well as traditional Christian, motifs: one gives thanks to the God (1:3, 11; 2:13), who chooses and calls (1:11; 2:13-14), the God who likewise sanctifies, makes worthy, and brings human activity to fruition (1:5, 11; 2:13). There are, however, in this theological perspective two important emphases which need examination throughout the commentary. The first, the author's concern for God's role in the apocalyptic drama, is occasioned by the community's belief that the end-days have indeed arrived. Thus, one hears of God's righteous judgment, equitable treatment of oppressor and oppressed (1:5-7), satanic opposition to divine power (2:4f., 9f.), and God's aversion to the unrighteous (2:1). Secondly, and as a consequence of the first issue, there is a Christological focus, particularly with attention being taken from divine activity and being given to Jesus' lordship.

(2) In Christological terms there is a marked preference for the title *kyrios*, for it appears 22 times in this short epistle, 9 times with "Jesus Christ," 4 times with the name of "Jesus," and 9 times alone. With these data in mind and considering what is usually perceived as the document's consistent apocalyptic perspective, one might be tempted to view Jesus

uniformally as eschatological lord and judge. Indeed, there is limited interest in the earthly Jesus, for his name is never used without *kyrios* and references to his earthly activity are indirect at best—see 2:14 ("our gospel"), 16b ("through grace"), and 3:5 ("constancy of Christ"). Instead, the author seems concerned about the Lord Jesus' return as avenging warrior "with his mighty angels" (1:7-8), the same Lord Jesus who "will destroy [the lawless one] with the breath of his mouth" (2:8). There is much interest in his coming, glory (1:9-10; 2:14), and lordship. God's role from this apocalyptic perspective is to see that judgment is done when Jesus is revealed (1:8); in fact believers have been called "for the attainment of the glory of our Lord Jesus Christ" (2:14).

An important distinction, however, should be made between the author's strategic interest in Jesus as eschatological lord (in response to the community's apocalyptic fervor) and that same author's focus on Jesus' lordship in the present. Thus, present glorification of the Lord Jesus' name is the object of one's prayer to God (1:11-12). Also, the author insists that the joint role of the Lord and of the Father is that of granting comfort and strength (2:16-17). Also, following apocalyptic passages the author addresses Jesus' present lordship as the basis of pertinent paraenetic considerations (1:11-12; 2:10f., 13f.). One discerns in these the author's concern about the community's present welfare as being related to acknowledgment of Jesus' lordship in the present. Thus, the use of *kyrios* relates not only to Jesus' return, vengeance, and judgment but also, and more traditionally, to his influence in the lives of believers, since he is to be glorified in them and they in him, not according to the glory promised at Jesus' return, but "according to the grace of our God and of the Lord Jesus Christ" (1:12). This dual emphasis helps to explain the author's constant references to Jesus as "Lord Jesus," "our/the Lord Jesus Christ," or simply as "Lord," for Jesus is the faithful Lord who guards his followers from the evil one (3:3) and also the Lord who directs human hearts to God's love and Christ's constancy (3:5). The author's theology and Christology are presented in view of the community's perceived situation and its received tradition (2:15).

For Reference and Further Study

Collins, R. F. "The Second Epistle to the Thessalonians." *Letters That Paul Did Not Write: The Epistle to the Hebrews and the Pauline Pseudepigrapha.* Wilmington: Glazier, 1988, 209–41.

Doty, W. G. *Letters in Primitive Christianity.* Philadelphia: Fortress, 1973.

Fitzmyer, J. A. "Introduction to the New Testament Epistles." *NJBC*, 768–71.

Giblin, C. H. "The Second Letter to the Thessalonians." *NJBC*, 871–75.

Krodel, G. "2 Thessalonians." *The Deutero-Pauline Letters: Ephesians, Colossians, 2 Thessalonians, 1-2 Timothy, Titus.* G. Krodel, et al. Minneapolis: Fortress, 1993, 39–58.

Trilling, W. *Untersuchungen zum zweiten Thessalonicherbrief.* Leipzig: St. Benno-Verlag, 1972.

18. First Thanksgiving (1:3-12)

3. We ought to give thanks to God always for you, brothers and sisters, as it is fitting, because your faith is growing abundantly and the love each and every one of you has for one another is increasing, 4. so much so that we ourselves boast about you in the Churches of God concerning your endurance and faith in all your persecutions and in the afflictions which you endure 5. —this is evidence of the just judgment of God that you might be made worthy of the kingdom of God for which you also suffer. 6. Since it is indeed just on God's part to repay with affliction those who afflict you 7. and to you who are afflicted to grant rest with us at the revelation of the Lord Jesus from heaven, who, with his mighty angels 8. in a flaming fire, inflicts punishment on those who do not know God and on those who do not obey the gospel of our Lord Jesus, 9. then such people will pay the penalty of eternal ruin apart from the Lord's presence and apart from the glory of his power, 10. when, on that day, he comes to be glorified by his holy ones and to be marveled at by all who have believed—including you because our testimony to you was believed. 11. That is why then we pray always for you that our God may make you worthy of his calling and by his power bring to fruition every good intention and work of faith, 12. so that the name of our Lord Jesus may be glorified by you and you by him according to the grace of our God and of the Lord Jesus Christ.

NOTES

3. *We ought to give thanks to God always for you:* In place of the standard "we or I give thanks" of the Pauline letters (1 Thess 1:2; 1 Cor 1:4), the author employs a non-Pauline variation: "we ought or are bound to give thanks" (see also 2:13). The phrase expresses a profound sense of indebtedness to God as is confirmed by the following "as it is fitting," rather than a dispassionate imitation of Pauline language. Indeed, both thanksgiving statements are followed by exuberant expressions of the reason why such an attitude toward God is the only proper one. The obligation terminology derives from contemporary Jewish and Christian liturgical usage where its contextual relation to the positive value of suffering is well attested (as in Shepherd of Hermas, *Similitudes* 9:28:5). Beyond the initial wording of the clause, the text

follows closely that of 1 Thess 1:3 (true also of 2:13). The themes as well as the form and language are a genuine appropriation of the Pauline model, since the text not only establishes the writer's authority but expresses deeply felt emotion in regard to the community's reaction to affliction (1:4). As in Paul, the term "always" modifies "give thanks" and so indicates a prayerful attitude rather than reinforcing the concept of obligation.

brothers and sisters, as it is fitting: Another unusual feature of this thanksgiving, as well as that of 2:13, is use of direct address, before in fact giving the reason for the thanksgiving; only 1 Thess 1:3-4 employs direct address relatively early, i.e., toward the end of the thanksgiving structure (see 1:4). One senses here, in contrast to Pauline practice, an eagerness on the author's part to establish an authoritative relationship with the addressees. This is underscored by the use of direct address to begin all major sections of the ensuing letter: 2:1, 13; 3:1, 6. The author returns to obligation terminology, "as it is fitting," to underscore the appropriateness not only of God's just judgment (1:5) but especially of the human sufferer's reaction to affliction. The author draws on a theology of suffering and from its terminology to address the positive purpose of suffering and to insist on the appropriateness of divine judgment.

because your faith is growing abundantly: Following traditional epistolary practice (1 Thess 2:13; Rom 1:8) the author offers immediately the reason for the thanksgiving, expressed in a double *hoti* ("because") clause. The first of these focuses on the growth of the community's faith. The concept of a growing faith (employing the unaugmented verb *auxanō*) is found in Paul (2 Cor 10:15) but the focus of the usage here is different. The hapax *hyperauxanō* ("to grow abundantly or beyond measure") and the repetition of "faith" in verse 4, in the context of commitment tested by affliction, indicate a dual meaning for faith as intimately related either to the author's message or the community's apocalyptic perspective. The term in verse 3 points to a faith that is growing abundantly toward a mature grasp of spiritual realities and in verse 4 refers to fidelity under pressure, i.e., increase in one's fidelity or loyalty to God (BAGD 662.1a). Further, the use of the strong verb in the present tense underscores the community's perseverance in confronting the ultimate test of suffering for its beliefs. The author's use of *hyper* terminology then indicates not a superabundant faith but the writer's great pleasure at witnessing the community's every act of resistance to "wicked and evil people" (3:2).

and the love each and every one of you has for one another is increasing: The extended subject, "the love each and every one of you has for one another" *(hē agapē henos hekastou pantōn hymōn eis allēlous)* is unique. The closest parallel is from 1 Thess 3:12 which reads: "the love for one another." The expression "for one another" *(eis allēlous)* is found only 6 times in Paul (4x in Romans and 2x in 1 Thessalonians), while "each one of you/them" *(heis hekastou +* genitive plural) occurs twice in Paul (once each in 1 Corinthians and 1 Thessalonians). The entire expression, especially with the overemphatic "of all," is unique and suggests non-Pauline authorship. This extended phrase provides the second reason for thanksgiving, namely, the concept of mutual love. Again as in the reason given previously the concept seems straightforward enough. Nonetheless, the language and epistolary context suggest the reader look more closely. The pleonastic phraseology stands out starkly and contrasts sharply with 3:11 where "some in the community" are described as less than laudable in their love for others. Instead of explaining this anomaly as owing to the author's less-than-exact use of complimentary language, one should view the whole clause as alluding to the community's solidarity in opposing the forces of evil and oppression. The use of such emphatic terminology is paraenetic and probably actual. Love (see 3:5) in this context seems to imply mutual help in adversity as the community increasingly and more successfully (*pleonazō*—"is increasing") protects all its members from outside threats—note the omission from 1 Thess 3:12 of the phrase "and for all" in Paul's statement about love. Contrast the usage of 1 Tim 1:14.

4. *so much so that we ourselves boast about you:* The conjunction *hōste* ("so that") indicating an actual result is here translated "so much so that" to indicate the force of the two previous verbs underscoring growth. The accusative and infinitive result clause introduces the theme of "boasting" (use of hapax *egkauchaomai*) in the sense of praising someone, much as is done in 2 Cor 7:15; 9:1-5, and seems to echo 1 Thess 1:7-8 and 2:19. Two problems, however, are raised in regard to this text which reflect on meaning and authorship. The first concerns use of the intensive pronoun "we ourselves." It is unclear what contrast is meant or why it is employed. The same is true of the second thanksgiving clause (2:13); the solution is to be found in the author's repeated insistence on Pauline authority, especially by use of the first-person plural pronoun (e.g., "our testimony," "as though from us," "through our gospel," etc.; see 1:10; 2:2, 14, respectively). The second problem is usually summarized as follows: Paul seemingly begins to boast about the community's growth in faith and love but ends up praising the addressees' endurance in affliction. The issue is thus formulated in Pauline terms, but, if viewed from the perspective of a later writer, one must interpret verse 4 as clarifying what is said in verse 3; the community's "endurance and faith" in the face of affliction (4) are a test in adversity and so a proof of its faith and love as present, growing realities (3).

in the Churches of God: This vague expression is found once in Paul (1 Cor 11:16) who frequently uses the plural of "church" (see 1 Cor 7:17; Gal 1:2) to speak of widespread communities or of the whole Church. In the present situation the author employs this phrase to refer to Churches beyond that of the addressees (see also 1 Thess 2:14—the letter's only contact with the interpolated passage). Further, the author's reference to Christian communities as "Churches of God" corresponds to the God-centered character of the letter and points to a developed sense of Church.

concerning your endurance and faith: The two terms about which the author boasts are given as *hypomonē* and *pistis*, both governed by a single preposition, united by a single article, and modified by one possessive pronoun. They are intended as parallel concepts with related meanings. The first underscores not confidence as in 1 Thess 1:3 but perseverance in the face of affliction (see also T.Joseph 2:7). The second, contrary to its earlier use in 1:3, suggests the concept of faithfulness in difficulty. Thus, the two terms have related meanings and are conditioned by the remainder of the statement.

in all your persecutions and in the afflictions which you endure: The community is described as persevering (present tense of the following verb) in its persecutions *(diōgos)* and afflictions *(thlipsis).* Once again the two terms are interconnected by a unifying construction consisting of a single preposition, numerical adjective, and possessive pronoun and extended by a relative clause whose pronoun subsumes both nouns as antecedents. In this case too the terms are closely related in meaning. The first occurs in Paul only in lists of hardships (Rom 8:35; 2 Cor 12:10) but is employed by the Synoptics and Acts (Mark 4:17; 10:30; Acts 8:1; 13:50) to describe active persecution of believers. The second is used in Paul and in the NT generally with a range of meaning (see 1 Thess 3:3) but usually with the sense of suffering or affliction. Scholars are agreed that the tandem use of these parallel terms is intentional and seeks to include all external pressure applied against the believing community. The biblical author is speaking not of virtue acquired through the endurance of suffering (Rom 5:3-4) but of believers' patient endurance in the face of what they consider ungodly opposition (1:8—see *TDNT* 4:587).

5. *—this is evidence of the just judgment of God:* The text introduces the neuter hapax noun *endeigma* ("proof or evidence"; Paul prefers *endeixis,* 4x; see Phil 1:28) without indication of its relation to what precedes. With most scholars it is best to see it as a nominative or accusative and as having a resumptive function: "the above or this is clear evidence of. . . ." The author is referring back to the community's endurance and fidelity in suffering (v. 4) and to the fact that these are bringing about a growth in that community's faith and love (v. 3; see below). The expression "God's just judgment" is unique in the NT and has its closest analogue in the Pauline expression: "God's righteous judgment" (Rom 2:5) though in the case of the latter that judgment is to be revealed on "the day of wrath." For this author, just as evil is said already to be working in anticipation of the lawless one's parousia (2:7), so is God's judgment already at work in the present. Related to the author's unique use of *krisis* ("judgment"—never in Paul) is the appearance of the verb *krinō* in the passive in 2:12 where the persecutors are again said to be repaid by God for the delight they take in wickedness. The concept of righteousness (see 1:5, 6) refers to God's merciful treatment of believers and to the divine affliction of those who persecute the holy ones. In both cases, nonetheless, the concept focuses on the future rather than the present. Also, it is unclear to whom the evidence is given. Scholars point to Phil 1:28 where the community's resistance vis-à-vis its opponents is said to be evidence to oppressors of their destruction and to believers of their salvation. So they conclude from the present context that the author intends this as reassurance to the readers that present evil does not go unnoticed by a just Judge. However, the context is different. The author's focus is on growth in faith and love (in the context of suffering) as evidence of God's judgment, not on

the oppressors' treatment. The issue is the evidence of God's just treatment of the elect as seen in their abundant growth (1:3).

that you might be made worthy of the kingdom of God: The concept of worthiness relates to Pauline usage in 1 Thess 2:12 (use of simple adverb *axiōs;* see 2 Thess 1:11 where the unaugmented verb is employed). The function of the theme in each writing is instructive. In the Pauline context it relates to Christian conduct and Paul's paraenesis, while in the Paulinist passage it addresses eschatological judgment linked to the endurance of present suffering. In the first there is a focus on pleasing the God who calls to the kingdom, in the second on inheriting or suffering for God's kingdom. Further, the author in verse 5 stresses the eschatological aspect of worthiness, but in verse 11 returns to this theme in terms of election and Christian living (see below on author's strategy and thought). On the concept of kingdom in the Pauline tradition, see 1 Thess 2:12.

for which you also suffer: With this short relative clause the author brings back the discussion to the addressees' situation, the afflictions which have led them to conclude that the end-times are upon them. Three points need attention. (1) The author's use of the expression "on account of or for which" may raise the issue of earning entrance into the kingdom. One should probably point to the author's Paulinist background and insist on the concept of being worthy to suffer for the kingdom (see Phil 1:29); such a view is confirmed by the interpretation of verse 11 below. (2) Use of the verb *paschō* would seem to underscore the physical and external suffering of the community (perceived and real) rather than the socio-religious conflicts indicated in 1 Thess 3:3-4 (see earlier—note that only in the interpolated passage of 2:14 is the verb *paschō* employed). (3) The term *kai* in the present context can be interpreted as meaning "even now" or "also." As regards the former, the sense is that the community suffers as the letter is being written. Focus on the present agrees with the author's acknowledgment that suffering is a present but not-yet apocalyptic sign (2:7). Such a view fits in the author's discussion of future punishment for those who are now afflicting the members of the community. Nonetheless, the latter is preferable since the "with us" of verse 7 and insistence on "all who have believed" in verse 10 support such a reading, i.e., other Christians suffer as well. Focus on the common nature of these afflictions is part of the author's strategy.

6. *Since it is indeed just on God's part:* For a discussion of verses 6-10 as forming a distinct unit, see discussion below of the pericope's structure. The conditional particle *eiper* is employed not to introduce a questionable belief but a new fact (BDF 454.2) and should be rendered "if it is just, as indeed it is" or "since it is indeed just." Verses 6-8 consist of the protasis and present the fact, while verses 9-10 as apodosis offer an unassailable conclusion. The author employs a construction which states the obvious; God by nature is just and acts justly toward good and evil (Pss 7:10-13; 118:137). To this end the author employs traditional legal terminology *(dikaion)* which is then given a theological focus *(TDNT* 2:188).

to repay with affliction those who afflict you: God's activity is described in parallel, antithetical statements, the first of which describes the negative character of God's judgment. The emphatic verb *antapodidōmi* ("to give back or repay") can, and is thus used by Paul, in a positive (1 Thess 3:9; Rom 11:35) and negative (Rom 12:19) sense. In the case of the latter, Paul paraphrases Deut 32:35 to the effect that God is an avenger (on the day of judgment) who repays in kind. This clue, as well as other textual and thematic parallels in 2 Thessalonians 1 to OT passages, lead me to the Jewish Scriptures for treatment of this theme, particularly the apocalyptic conclusion of Isaiah (chapter 66) which presents a cluster of themes employed by this author for the composition of 1:6f. (see below). Having described the addressees' situation as consisting of persecutions and afflictions, the author expands the latter (*thlipsis*—noun and verb) owing to its frequent use in late Judaism to describe the Lord's day and its tribulations (Dan 12:1; Nah 1:7; Hab 3:16; Zeph 1:15; Obad 12-14; see *TDNT* 3:142) and because it is the community's term to describe its difficulties interpreted as apocalyptic turmoil. Both the sufferings of the elect and of their oppressors are qualified by this term (see Rev 1:9f.).

7. *and to you who are afflicted to grant rest with us:* The parallel, positive statement focuses on the oppressed and their reward. The latter is described as "rest or peace" *(anesis)*, a term employed by Paul to describe relaxation (2 Cor 2:13; 7:5; 8:13) but never in an eschatological sense as eternal peace or entry into the kingdom (1:5). By use of the expression "with us" the author underscores the common lot of Christians whether in suffering (v. 5: "you *also* suffer") or in obtaining eternal rest. In this way the audience is prepared for the message that its present sufferings, though real, are not a sign of the end-time but an indication that "the mystery of lawlessness is already at work" (2:7) in the lives of all believers. The sufferings of the end-days like the eschatological rest promised to the righteous are yet to come, contrary to the preaching of some in the community (2:2).

at the revelation of the Lord Jesus from heaven: In the expression "at the revelation" the preposition *en* could be interpreted in a temporal or in an instrumental sense, thereby indicating the means by which God's judgment is exercised. Since the author is following Pauline usage (as in 1 Thess 2:19; 3:13; 5:24) and since verse 8b describes how the Lord Jesus will inflict punishment, the former is preferable: all of the above will occur when the Lord returns. Interestingly, the author employs the noun *apokalypsis* rather than the Pauline *parousia* (see passages noted above). The former, which focuses on the hidden or mysterious character of the event, is thus used by Paul who speaks both of the Lord Jesus and of God's righteous judgment being revealed (1 Cor 1:7; Rom 2:5; see also 1 Pet 1:7). For this author it is the term's mysteriousness and eschatological potential which is paramount. The Lord Jesus will be revealed from heaven where he is now hidden with God. In a similar way, the author employs the verb *apokalyptō* three times (2:3, 6, 8) to speak of the coming of the lawless one. According to the standard Christian apocalyptic scenario, Jesus is in heaven with God (1 Thess 1:10; 4:16; Mark 13:26) and the satanic powers imprisoned in the deepest darkness or bottomless pit prior to the final battle (Jud 6; Rev 17:8). But choice of the term "revelation," a traditional term for the appearance of the Messiah in current apocalyptic literature (2 Bar 27:3; 39:7; 4 Ezra 7:28; 13:32), also indicates the author's intention to stress that the Lord, who is now graciously present (1:12; 3:18), as also the lawless one who even now works mysteriously (2:7), will be fully revealed only at the parousia, when their claims to lordship, in the first case, will be vindicated and, in the second, will be denied.

who, with his mighty angels 8. *in a flaming fire:* The scenario is further developed by means of two descriptive prepositional phrases, which relate to traditional apocalyptic imagery and betray OT influence, particularly Isa 66:15. The first of these (lit.: "with the angels or agents of his power") reflects the Jewish and Christian concept of God or a messianic figure being accompanied at the end-time by "holy ones," angels, or a heavenly host (Zech 14:5; Isa 13:3-5; 1 En 1:9 [= Jude 14]; 1 Thess 3:13; 4:16; Mark 8:38; 13:26; Rev 19:14). The unusual terminology has led to a variety of identifications: a host of angels who exercise the Messiah's might or a specific angelic class. What seems to be the author's meaning, in view of the text's dependence on Isa 66:15 (and 1 Thess 3:13) and the tradition of Mark 13:26, is that the Lord Jesus is accompanied by heavenly messengers who do his bidding. The second phrase ("in or by means of a flaming fire") focuses on one particular aspect of the apocalyptic scene. Employing a phrase once used for theophanies (Exod 3:2) but later applied to the scenario of the Lord's visitation (Isa 29:6; 66:15) or descriptions of the heavenly throne (Dan 7:9), the author likens the end-time judgment to a consuming fire. Also, though *pyri phlogos* is preferred by the majority of MSS and agrees with the textual tradition of some OT passages, there is solid support in the MS tradition (B D G *al*) for the reading adopted here: *phlogi pyros*. Rather than argue that the latter reading was assimilated to the Exodus LXX tradition by scribes, one should note that manuscripts B and D are notorious for not assimilating to the LXX and so probably represent the original as borrowed from Isa 66:15. The meaning, however, is not affected by the reading chosen. Finally, it is preferable, again following the lead of the OT passage cited, to connect the two prepositional phrases to the following participle ("inflicting punishment").

inflicts punishment: For this verbal statement, a common LXX phrase (Ezek 25:14, 17; Ps 17:48), the author continues to draw from Isa 66:15. If in verse 6 it is God who is the righteous Judge, in verse 8 Jesus, in connection with his manifestation at the end-time, is mentioned as the agent of the punishment considered repayment for persecution of the elect.

on those who do not know God and on those who do not obey the gospel of our Lord Jesus: There follows the mention of two groups on whom Jesus will inflict punishment (1) "those who do not know God," a phrase borrowed from 1 Thess 4:5 and classically employed in the OT to describe Gentiles (Jer 10:25; Ps 78:6) and (2) "those who do not obey the gospel of our Lord Jesus," a phrase which seemingly would refer to non-Christian Jews who, by Paul,

are described as "those who have not obeyed the gospel" (Rom 10:16). Instead, the two dative phrases form a parallel construction typical of the author and serve as a description of the totality of those who will receive
punishment at Jesus' hand. The first group refers to non-Christians (among
them the audience's persecutors) and the second points to Christians who
are less than faithful to the gospel message. The verb for "obey" is *hypakouō*,
a term employed again in 3:11 where it refers not to adherence to the Christian message but to performing what is commanded. This latter group would
therefore refer to the apostates of 2:3 and to Christians who "delight in
wickedness" (2:12—see also 2:10: "accept the love of truth"). Thus, the author addresses both the apocalyptic concerns of the readers and insists that
Jesus will return as judge of all evildoers. Interestingly, the people to be
punished by the returning Lord are described in theological and Christological, not in apocalyptic terms. Also, the expression "the gospel of our Lord
Jesus," though non-Pauline (Paul uses "the gospel of God or of Christ"—
1 Thess 2:2; 3:2), is traditional and relates to the author's anti-apocalyptic
stance; the community will undergo its suffering far better if it "holds fast
to [its] traditions" (2:15), that is, the gospel that was instrumental in its conversion (2:14).

9. *then such people will pay the penalty of eternal ruin:* Verse 9 introduces the second part of the conditional clause which began at verse 6. The construction
begins with the indefinite pronoun *hoitines* (BAGD 587.2), rendered "such
people" and is introduced in the translation by "then" to indicate the grammatical relationship between the apodosis and the distant protasis. Employing a classical, nonbiblical idiom "to pay the penalty" (BAGD 818), the author
is able to play on the term *dikē* (see Jud 7 for similar usage) and insist that
persecutors will receive "justice" and so attest to God's just judgment. Further confirming the reading of verses 6-10 as a well-formed conditional clause
is the author's use of the future tense in the apodosis to support the latter's
message that the end and its just reward are still in the future. Finally, the
author describes the persecutors' penalty as "eternal ruin." *Olethros* can mean
"annihilation or death" but in the present case, owing to the following double
apo phrase ("separated from") and the term's origin in 1 Thess 5:3, it is best
to view its meaning as "ruin" or reversal from a previous enviable situation.
In the first case separation from the Lord demands continued existence (not
annihilation) and in the second the condition of peace in Paul or situation
of the persecutor here are transformed into ruin, namely disaster on the one
hand and eternal powerlessness on the other. Eschatological finality is underscored by the qualifying adjective "eternal."

apart from the Lord's presence and apart from the glory of his power: The concept
of eternal ruin is qualified by another parallel construction, both parts of which
are introduced by *apo* and derived from Isa 2:10 which states that idolators
are to flee from the Lord and the glory of his might. The first of these, presuming as background Paul's statement that the faithful will be with the Lord
forever (1 Thess 4:17; 5:10), insists that the persecutors will be deprived of
his face or presence for eternity; the second, referring back to the statement

that the Lord Jesus will come with power (1:7), ironically contrasts the persecutors' position of power to the Lord Jesus' coming with power and assures the audience that these oppressors will be deprived of the Lord's glorious and majestic presence.

10. *when, on that day, he comes:* The second part of the long conditional sentence terminates with mention of the Lord's coming. The author employs *hotan* with the aorist subjunctive to suggest a precise event at an indefinite future time but borrows the structure of the *hotan* clause from Isa 2:10, which provided the two preceding *apo* clauses. The expression "on that day" (verbally from Isa 2:11) comes climactically at the end of the verse in Greek but is placed here to facilitate comprehension of the author's meaning. For explicit reference to "the Lord's Day," see 2:2.

to be glorified by his holy ones and to be marveled at by all who have believed: The purpose of the Lord's coming is expressed by parallel infinitive constructions. It is generally admitted that their terminology and content derive from OT passages. The first, "to be glorified by his holy ones," is connected to Ps 88:8 (God is said to "be glorified in the council of the holy ones") owing to the rarity of the verb *endoxazomai* both in the LXX and NT (only in Psalm 88 and 2 Thess 1:12) and its prepositional modifier. The second infinitive construction "to be marveled at by all who have believed," is hesitatingly related to Ps 67:3 (God is declared "marvelous among or by his holy ones"), since the similarities are less obvious. Rather than an adjective, the NT author employs, as a parallel to the previous infinitive construction, the aorist passive of the verb *thaumazō*. One can conclude that from this verse the author also took the exact wording of the prepositional compliment of the first infinitive construction: "by his holy ones." The meanings of these constructions require more attention. The concept of glory (use of *doxa*), appearing at 1:9, 10, 12; 2:14; and 3:1, is important for the author who invariably uses the theme in a Christological context. The idea of wonderment occurs only here and serves as a synonym of the parallel *doxa*. Discussion centers on the interpretation of the two *en* phrases and the identity of the people involved. The preposition *en* is interpreted as indicating glorification: (1) among or in the presence of (locutive), (2) because of or in the person of (causal), or (3) by (instrumental). While the first seems to be supported by the LXX passage being used, and the second is the more popular owing to its alleged parallel with verse 12, the third option is chosen since it fits into and further develops the author's Lord Christology. On the identity of the "holy ones" as the accompanying angelic host and of "all who have believed" as the members of the universal Church, see discussion below.

including you because our testimony to you was believed: Traditionally this clause has been viewed as a loosely formulated parenthesis. Further, since its surface meaning seems to contradict the universal sense of the previous "all who have believed," it seems best to consider the clause as presuming the unstated assumption that the audience will form part of the eschatological retinue owing to its faith commitment. The author's use of the aorist for both occurrences of the verb "believe" stresses the definitiveness of the commitment at conversion and the perseverance of those believers. Lastly the expression "our testimony to you," though employed in a non-Pauline fashion for preaching the gospel, has as its purpose to underscore the author's Pauline authority.

11. *That is why then we pray always for you:* The new movement of thought is introduced by *eis ho kai* ("that is why then"—see also 2:14), an expression which indicates a loose connection with what precedes and serves a resumptive purpose as it picks up what is stated in 5b about being worthy of the kingdom, just prior to the long conditional sentence concerning God's just judgment (vv. 6-10). The expression "we pray always for you" is superficially Pauline; the idiom *proseuchomai peri* occurs in Paul only at 1 Thess 5:25 and not with *pantote*, which is employed instead with "give thanks" (as in 1 Thess 1:2). Further, the author uses this same idiom again at 3:1, where the community, as in 1 Thess 5:25, is asked to pray for the writer.

that our God may make you worthy of his calling: The reason for the prayer is stated in an aorist subjunctive clause introduced by *hina* (see also 3:1-2). Again the author's wish, as in verse 5, is that God make the readers worthy of their divine "calling"—the context seems to favor "make" rather than "deem" worthy. For discussion of the concept of "election" see 2:13-14 and 1 Thess 1:4. There is a shift from emphasis on the eschatological kingdom of verse 5 to the theme of election and the concerns of daily life in verses 11-12. In the first the audience's concerns are addressed directly (persecution and treatment of oppressors), while in the concluding prayer the author's own modified eschatology comes to the fore. The expression "our God" is Pauline (see 1 Thess 2:2; 3:9) and is chosen to allow the author, in speaking of their common God, to broaden the scope of the discussion beyond the audience's narrow perspective.

and by his power bring to fruition every desire for goodness and work of faith: The petition continues by asking that God "bring to fruition" the believers' projects and activities. The author uses the aorist subjunctive, as often in prayer, to underscore the eschatological finality of divine activity. In Pauline terms the author insists that human desires and acts can only receive their completeness at the conclusion of the process and, equally in Pauline terms, that it is God who gives this growth. The object of this growth is expressed as a double object, literally: "every desire of goodness" and "work of faith." There is debate concerning the meaning and interpretation of the first expression. While the noun "desire" is usually employed in biblical literature to refer to divine will or pleasure, it is also used for living creatures (Ps 144:16; Sir 39:18; Rom 10:1) and so fits the present context where the "desire" is that of the believer. The real difficulty arises in interpreting the following, modifying noun as a subjective or an objective genitive, either "goodness' desire" ("good intention") or "desire for goodness" (as translated above). One could argue for the former by insisting on the parallel function of the constructions and therefore conclude that the first is a subjective genitive as is "work of faith" (see 1 Thess 1:3 for the source of this idiom). However, the idiom should be compared with 2:12 and seen as its counterpart; here in 1:11 true believers "desire or take pleasure in goodness" while in 2:12 the unrighteous "take delight in wickedness." God therefore is called upon to bring to completion every yearning for goodness which believers have and every deed which faith leads them to undertake. In this way the author is moving away from Pauline anthropology by insisting on human activity though still within a Paulinist perspective (see 2:17). The desires and the works belong to the human agent but their strengthening and completion belong to God for this will be done "by his power"; the expression in Greek occurs at the end of the verse to underscore a Paulinist perspective.

12. *so that the name of the Lord Jesus may be glorified by you and you by him:* The result of this divinely enhanced human activity is expressed by the idiom employed earlier in 10a: "to be glorified by." There is a parallel between these. In the first the Lord Jesus returns to be glorified by the assembled holy ones and believers at the parousia; in the second, while the concept of glorification is again central, there are several important modifications: invocation of the Lord Jesus' name, mutual glorification, and a switch to the present. The un-Pauline invocation of the "name" (see also 3:6), in a context of glorification, owes to the author's use of Isa 66:5 ("that the name of the Lord be glorified") and relates further to the development of a *kyrios* Christology. Also un-Pauline is the concept of mutual glorification (see John 13:31; 17:4-5, 22) as well as the exclusive association of glory with Christology. Finally, verse 12 deals not with the end-time acknowledgment and praise given the returning Lord by his retinue but with the honor which believers bestow on their Lord in their daily lives and the honor which accrues to them in return. The author's strategy is one of acknowledging the importance of eschatology but of focusing on the present as a time of doing good (3:13) despite the opposition of "wicked and evil people" (3:2) and the apparent activity of the lawless one (2:7). Thus, honor will be given to Christ and to believers as they express their yearning for goodness and work of faith among their neighbors (see 3:1 for further discussion of "glory").

according to the grace of our God and of the Lord Jesus Christ: The honor which believers bestow on their Lord and which he confers on them takes place "according to grace," a well-known Pauline concept which focuses on divine election and Christological mediatorship (see 1 Thess 1:1) and underscores the concept of divine gift which makes a Christian life possible (see 2:16 below). Thus, the author recalls the theme of election mentioned earlier in verse 11 and, following Pauline usage (see Notes on 1:2), relates grace both to "our God and the Lord Jesus Christ." The unusual character of the Greek (one article in the genitive governing two objects) has led some to translate the phrase as though Jesus is both "God and Lord." Such usage is neither Pauline nor Paulinist and one should view the expression as translated above and consider it as related to the author's conflated use of Pauline idiom (see discussion of 1:2; also 1 Thess 5:28).

INTERPRETATION

Following standard epistolary convention, the author introduces a lengthy, well-developed thanksgiving period immediately after the opening. The thanksgiving employs unusual terminology and distinctive meanings for familiar themes and it also provides a relentless focus on divine judgment and Jesus' apocalyptic role. Clearly, one of the major functions of this long section is to introduce the reader to the letter's major concern: discussion of the Lord's day. The author's concerns in this regard are evident as one examines the passage's structure and themes.

Style, Structure, and Epistolary Character of 1:3-12. The pericope consists of a loosely constructed thanksgiving period whose dependent consecutive clause about boasting (v. 4) and conclusion concerning God's judgment and plan for the community (v. 5) lack a defined relation to the reason for thanksgiving. The passage is extended by the addition of a long conditional construction (vv. 6-10) and a summarizing prayer (vv. 11-12). It is much lamented that verses 3-10 consist of a long, poorly constructed Greek sentence. So attempts are made to ease the loose connection between verses 4 and 5 by relating the term "evidence" with what precedes in verse 4. Such suggestions, however, fail to convince owing to the obvious binary rhythm of the construction of verse 4. With most scholars it is best to view verse 5 as a loosely connected nominative or accusative construction in apposition with what precedes. Thus, the verse acts as a resumptive conclusion to the previous statement about the community's endurance and fidelity and the author's widespread boasting about these.

Rather than seeing the thanksgiving period as extending to verse 10, it is best to envision a new structure as beginning at verse 6. This long complex conditional clause introduces a further fact, namely, the principle of God's just treatment of the wicked (and righteous: vv. 6-8), as the basis for confidence that the Lord's day will be one of doom for the oppressor (and glory for believers: vv. 9-10). In effect, the author is telling the audience: "if it is just on God's part to avenge oppression, then will not such people undergo eternal ruin on the Lord's day?" Verses 6-8 dwell on the common belief in divine justice and verses 9-10 apply this theme to the Lord's day, which is yet to come (note the use of the future tense in v. 9). Verses 6-10 then form a distinct independent structure that develops further the theme of divine judgment introduced in verse 5. Finally, this pericope, as do most sections (2:16; 3:5 and 16), ends with a formal prayer, which itself acts as its summarizing conclusion as it repeats its themes: prayer always (in place of thanksgiving), worthiness of calling (for worthiness of kingdom), fruition and work of faith (for perseverance and faithfulness), and Jesus' glorification.

The style of the thanksgiving period offers many unique features such as the expression "we ought to give thanks" (also 2:13), direct address of audience at the beginning of the thanksgiving period, and the idiom "as it is fitting." Further, the thanksgiving focuses immediately and repeatedly on the document's primary concern, the apocalypticism of the community. While it is customary for Pauline letters to express thanks to God for the community's faith and well-being, to pray for a continued commitment in faith and love, and to announce themes that are developed later in the letter, this document treats some of these in a decidedly apocalyptic fashion. Faith in verse 3 is not commitment to God through Christ but fidelity (to one's commitment) in adversity, while love is mutual assistance in view of perseverance. The themes of the pericope are those of a pastor concerned about the afflictions being endured and the hearers' need to live in the present. Also, these themes allow the author to speak in 2:1-12 of the present evils as not yet announcing the Lord's day (2:7) and in 3:6-16 of the need to live responsible lives of peace, work, and doing good (3:12-13, 16). From the start one sees in this letter an effort to communicate in apocalyptic terms with the community about its false claims regarding the Lord's day and yet one also perceives the author's own focus on the present not only as a time of lawlessness but also as one of mission (3:1), Christian harmony (3:12f.), and responsible behavior.

Pauline and Non-Pauline Character of Terms and Themes. The relation of the author's text to that of Paul varies from one passage to another. The two letter openings are virtually identical, a fact which is noted earlier. The relationship of the thanksgiving passages is more complex, since the documents have double thanksgivings and since the respective pericopes address different communities and situations.

The following table will facilitate our comparative study:

2 Thess 1:3-12	1 Thess
3. we ought to *give thanks to God always for you,* brothers	1:2
and sisters, as it is fitting because *your faith* is growing	1:3
abundantly and the *love* each and every one of you has *for*	3:12
one another is *increasing,* 4 so much so that we ourselves	
boast about you in *the Churches of God* concerning your	2:19, 14
endurance and faith *in all* your *persecutions* and in the	1:3; 2:15
afflictions which you endure 5—this is evidence of the	1:6
just judgment of God so that you might be considered	
worthy of the kingdom of God for which *you* also *suffer.*	2:12, 14
6. Since it is indeed just on God's part to repay with	
affliction those who afflict you 7 and to you who are	
afflicted to grant rest with us *at the revelation of* the	3:13
Lord Jesus from heaven 8 who, *with his mighty angels* in	4:16

2 Thess 1:3-12	1 Thess
a flaming fire, inflicts *punishment* on *those who do not*	4:6, 5
know God and on those who do not obey *the gospel of our*	3:2
Lord Jesus, 9 then such people will pay the penalty of	
eternal *ruin* apart from the Lord's presence and apart from	5:3
the *glory* of his power, 10 when, *on that day,* he comes to	2:12; 5:2
be glorified by *his holy ones* and to be marveled at by *all*	3:13
who have believed—including you because our testimony	1:7
to you was believed. 11 That is why then *we pray always*	1:2
for you, that *our God may make you worthy* of *his calling*	2:2; 3:9; 2:12
and *by* his *power* bring to fruition every desire for goodness	1:5
and *work of faith,* 12 so that the name of our Lord Jesus	1:3
may *be glorified* in you, and you in him, according to the	2:12
grace of our God and *of the Lord Jesus Christ.*	5:28

Similar but less extensive comparison was done in the past but different conclusions were drawn from such analysis. What is striking to the modern scholar, far less reluctant to deny Pauline authorship than previously, is the obvious borrowing of terms and themes by the author of 2 Thessalonians from Paul's letter. The italicized terms and expressions mark linguistic connections between the two. Clearly the thanksgiving begins as a reworking of 1 Thess 1:2-3; thus, one notes the similarity of themes: thanks to God always, focus on love (embellished with terms from 3:12), faith, and endurance. It is the last mentioned, *hypomonē,* expressed by Paul as "constancy of hope," which becomes the focus of the remainder of the thanksgiving section and the theme around which the others (whether love, faith, or divine justice) are developed. From verse 4 on, once the theme of endurance is introduced, the new text takes a life of its own as the author addresses the community's situation, the perception that its "persecutions and afflictions" are signs of the end-days. To this end the author appropriates various themes from Paul's letter to give authority to the composition and to express a new message for a new situation.

The contacts with Paul's text, beginning with verse 4, are of three types. (1) One notes repeated use in 1:5, 7, 9, 10, 11, 12 of convenient eschatological and call terminology from 1 Thess 2:12 ("to conduct yourselves worthily of the God who calls you to his own kingdom and glory") and 3:13 ("blameless . . . in the presence of God our Father at the coming of our Lord Jesus with all his holy ones"). (2) The author borrows *thlipsis* terminology from Paul (1:6; 3:3), which is then extended and developed in verses 4-7 in terms of persecution and affliction. (3) The author employs a variety of terms which either indicate the borrowing of Pauline terminology or fortuitous contact with 1 Thessalonians: e.g., "our God" in 1:11 (see 1 Thess 2:2; 3:9), "those who do not know God" in 1:8 (see 4:5) or "ruin" in 1:9 (see 5:30). The terms in this last category are employed with no concern for the original Pauline context or usage. The impression one has in surveying the above text is that of conscious, habitual imitation of a text known to author and audience, much as does a pastor who borrows and imitates a biblical translation when formulating a prayer or in preaching to a congregation. Seeing the author as a Paulinist and the addressees as belonging to a community that was founded in the Pauline tradition best explains the unique character of the composition and its setting.

Author's Use of the OT: *Study of Verses 6f.* Just as verses 3-5 follow closely the beginning of Paul's thanksgiving concerning faith, love, and endurance (1 Thess 1:2-3), so verses 4-5 develop the last mentioned of the triad and set the stage in verses 6f. for a development of God's just treatment of oppressors and oppressed. Verses 6-10 constitute a long conditional sentence concerning God's just judgment, a sentence whose terminology and themes are in great part inspired by Isaiah 66, the book's apocalyptic conclusion. It is particularly the elements of the fiery description of Jesus' return in verses 7-8 that are drawn from Isa 66:15, whose various features are accommodated to the traditional apocalyptic scenario:

> For behold the Lord will come like a fire, and his chariots like a storm, to repay his punishment (*apodounai . . . ekdikēsin autou*) with anger, and his rebuke with a flaming fire (*en phlogi pyros*).

The scene of the Lord Jesus coming out of heaven (where the Lord is enthroned—Isa 66:1) is drawn from the Isaian description, for in place of the war imagery of chariots Jesus is given a traditional retinue of angels to do his bidding (Mark 13:26-27). Thus, he comes "to inflict punishment" (*didōmi ekdikēsin*) in a scene "of flaming fire."

In addition to the above, one wonders whether other terms and themes were not suggested to the author by a more extensive reading of the Isaian chapter. The theme of divine retribution is enunciated in 66:3-4 (*antapodidōmi*—see also Deut 32:35; Obad 15) in a context of pleasure in wickedness (see 2:12), where the offenders are called but refuse to obey (see the themes of election in 1:11 and of disobedience in 1:8). Further, one encounters the theme of glorification of the Lord's name in 66:5, a theme that is put to use in 1:12. In 66:11-13 there is a description of eschatological peace and rest, a theme found in 1:7. Finally, in 66:16-18 one finds themes germane to a description of the fate of the oppressors and the oppressed. The fiery destruction of the wicked in verses 16-17 would lead in 1:9 to a description of their eternal ruin and, with the assistance of Isa 2:10, banishment from the Lord's presence and glorious power. The statement in 66:18 about the gathering of all the nations to see the Lord's glory suggests the theme of 1:10 where the holy one and the multitude of believers glorify and marvel at the returning Lord, a description which is further embellished with the aid of Pss 67:3 and 88:8.

The impression one gets is that of an author's use of and meditation on the text of Isaiah to formulate a credible end-time scenario first in preaching and then in the composition of a pseudonymous letter to counter the claims of apocalyptic preachers. The basic description is taken from Isa 66:15 and is supplemented by other OT passages offering pertinent details and terminology. The method employed is similar to the author's use of 1 Thessalonians in structural and linguistic terms.

Thanksgiving and Evidence of God's Just Judgment. Two important features of the thanksgiving lead to debate concerning its function and meaning. On the one hand, the author states that the reason for giving thanks is the audience's exemplary faith and love and yet boasts not of these but of the community's perseverance in persecution and affliction (see v. 4). On the other hand, the difficult and enigmatic introduction to verse 5 adds to the confusion since it points back ambiguously to what is previously said as "evidence of God's just judgment." Authors express uncertainty in identifying the term's antecedent: whether the immediately preceding "persecutions and afflictions" being endured, the author's boast about this, or, in a more ambiguous way, the community's courage under persecution or even its members' rigorous faith and love.

In defense of the traditional view, it is proposed that, once one recognizes the undue influence exercised on the interpretation of the passage by Phil 1:28, one is led to see not the community's endurance of suffering as the referent but the sufferings themselves, the topic immediately preceding verse 5. Such a view is defended by appealing to a contemporary, emerging "theology of suffering" attested in works such as 2 Baruch and early rabbinic literature. The thesis runs as follows: God demands recompense for all evil deeds and gives reward for all good actions. Thus, while the wicked and the elect will receive their just reward in the age to come, both are the object of justice in the present life; the wicked enjoy their few merits now and the elect receive punishment for their few sins in the present. It is then concluded (1) that 2 Thessalonians was composed to counter confidence lost in God's justice as the result of the Church's present afflictions, afflictions that were to cease with the arrival of the Lord's day and (2) that the community's present sufferings are evidence of God's justice which requires that the few sins of the righteous be addressed in the present (so the community's suffering) and guarantees the salvation of the righteous (so its comfort).

Such focus on the positive value of suffering offers insights for the interpretation of the chapter but the above thesis and conclusions fail to convince. These reflect a questionable reading of chapter 1 and a faulty understanding of the issue being addressed by the document. [1] It is not the persistence of suffering in the end-times which is at issue but the problem of deception ("being easily shaken in mind . . . disturbed . . . deceived"—2:2-3). The audience is misreading its sufferings as though they are part of the messianic woes when in effect they are an anticipation of "the mystery of lawlessness" (2:7). [2] There is, in my reading, no evidence of a "suffering theology" focusing on the just, temporary punishment of the elect. There is instead a stress on the just, final reward of the oppressor and oppressed (1:6-10). At best, one might assume that informed readers could see their present sufferings as payment for their few sins. Such an assumption seems gratuitous, at least judging from the clues one finds in the text. [3] It is the reading of verses 3-4 which is the most questionable. If there seems to be some incongruence between the author's stated reason for giving thanks (faith and love) and for boasting (endurance in suffering), what is perceived as disjointedness between verses 3 and 4 owes to a Pauline reading of the two verses rather than a reading of what the author of 2 Thessalonians says. Proper interpretation of verses 3-4 affects fundamentally the conclusions one draws about the antecedent for verse 5 and about the author's meaning and strategy.

Form and Function of the Thanksgiving Pericope. The thanksgiving consists of three parts, each of which plays a role in the development of the document. Rather than seeing chapter 1 as a preface to the following description of the Lord's day, my discussion views the various parts of the thanksgiving section as focusing on issues of concern to the audience, the purpose for writing, and the author's message and strategy.

(1) Reason for Thanks (vv. 3-5). In traditional fashion the letter opens with a twofold expression of thanks to God: "your faith is growing abundantly and the love each and every one of you has for one another is increasing." The Pauline origin of the terms faith and love (1 Thess 1:3) and even the notion of a growing faith as deriving from Paul (2 Cor 10:15) should not obscure the fact that faith, especially as used again in verse 4, means fidelity under persecution. The author's use of the augmented verb *(hyperauxanō)* further stresses what is expressed in verse 4 as the community's continued success in confronting its afflictions. Additionally, the author's use of love, in what can only be described as pleonastic phraseology ("each and every one of you . . . for one another"), points also to an apocalyptic sense of increased mutual assistance among believers in warding off communal adversity—the pleonastic language underscores the community's inward, defensive posture. Verse 3 then must be viewed against the community's apocalyptic perspective.

Another important element in the discussion is the author's fondness for parallel statements and phrases. Thus, verses 3 and 4 should be considered parallel constructions:

> 3. the author gives thanks   (about them—as is fitting)
>   re. faith and love
> 4. the author boasts   (about them—in the Churches)
>   re. endurance and faith/fidelity
>   + in all the persecutions and affliction being endured.

This diagram suggests that the statement in verse 3 about growth in faith and love is synonymous with that about endurance and fidelity in verse 4. The faith and love of the community are described in terms of its success and perseverance in affliction. The conclusion of verse 4 stresses even further that it is the faithful endurance of these difficulties which forms the antecedent of verse 5 and thereby provides the evidence of God's just judgment. There is no disjointedness between verses 3 and 4, when these are read in a Paulinist way. There is instead a parallel whereby verse 4 explicates, in terms of the community's suffering, the meaning of tested faith and mutual assistance that fosters endurance.

Verse 5 then resumes the author's statement of thanksgiving and the repetition of this sentiment through ecclesial boasting by insisting not only that the community has persevered against opposition but that its commitment and devotion have increased abundantly. Proof of God's just judgment is the reversal of human expectations, whereby unsought affliction not only is preparing them for the kingdom but has increased their commitment to God and to each other. The theological answer to the community's suffering is God's mysterious plan for inclusion in the kingdom. In the community's situation, however, there is evidence of that plan in the community's growth in the midst of suffering. The author's reason for thanks then is expressed by the *hoti* clause and its two verbs of growth. Before turning in verses 6-10 to the oppressors' treatment, the author concludes the discussion of the community's suffering by insisting not only that the suffering is related to God's plan for entry into the kingdom but also that the community's exemplary reaction to it is clear proof that God, in allowing persecutions and afflictions, is indeed a just judge. The suffering of the righteous is a perennial theme of apocalyptic literature and its mention in the thanksgiving section prepares for its treatment later as part of the time frame for the end-time scenario.

(2) God's Just Judgment (6-10). The lengthy conditional sentence which follows focuses on another theme dear to the apocalypticist: revenge against the satanic persecutor. This theme is the reverse side of the coin. Verses 6-8 state what the believer accepts as axiomatic: God treats both good and evil in a just way. From Isaiah 66 the author borrows the theme of divine recompense, first the repayment of affliction to the oppressor and secondly the granting of eternal rest to the elect—a process which

will be put into effect when the Lord Jesus returns with his angelic reti- nue to deal with believers and nonbelievers according to their just des- serts. The author's focus is on the treatment of the persecutor. In verses 9-10 the conclusion is then drawn for the reader that "such people will pay the penalty" they deserve. The author carefully underscores the rela- tionship of the principle (God is just) and the conclusion to be drawn (punishment) about its future consequences.

The repeated treatment of themes has a bearing on the concept of God's just judgment. On three occasions the author treats the punish- ment of the wicked: first in verse 6 they are characterized as persecutors, secondly in verse 8 they are identified as the unbelievers in final judg- ment, and thirdly in a concluding statement in verse 9 they are given their just sentence, particularly the deprivation of coveted power. With less emphasis but with subtle stress the author twice alludes to the re- ward of the elect, first in verse 7 as the reception of eternal rest and sec- ondly in verse 10 as part of the group acknowledging and welcoming the returning Lord. Thus, the powerful oppressor is deprived of power and banished from its source while the afflicted form part of the glorious retinue of the Lord Jesus.

Treatment of God's just judgment is related to the presentation of the end-time scenario. There may be some evidence in the present of God's just judgment (amazing growth in the midst of adversity) but basically God's judgment is a mysterious and future reality. Having treated the community's present suffering as evidence already of God's judgment, the author returns to the theme in verse 6 but in terms of final judgment. To lay stress on the future and mysterious nature of this reality a num- ber of indicators are employed. In place of the Thessalonian parousia or coming of the Lord, the author speaks of the Lord being "revealed from heaven." Also, there is stress on the future character of the event and its apocalyptic details. For the apocalypticist the end-time scenario is the ultimate means for God's just judgment to be realized. The Lord Jesus will return with his angels to gather and reward the oppressed elect and "to inflict punishment" on the oppressors. This part of the thanksgiving pericope then prepares explicitly for the author's discussion of the Lord's day and its proper understanding. But already in verse 8 there is a hint concerning the author's concern not only with oppression by outsiders and their just punishment but also full commitment or obedience to the gospel. The end-time judgment will involve all unrighteous, both oppres- sors and lovers of evil (for the latter see 2:11-12).

(3) Author's Prayer (11-12). The third part of the thanksgiving section changes in tone and topic. Nonetheless, by its introductory particles ("that is why then") it is suggested that a conclusion is to be drawn from what has just been said. The concluding verses are couched in the form of a

prayer and express more directly the author's thinking; the passage functions in two ways. In epistolary terms, as part of the thanksgiving pericope, it announces a number of themes and concerns: repeated prayer (2:16; 3:1, etc.), theme of election (2:13-14, 16, etc.), focus on work (2:17; 3:4, 6f.), and glory (2:14; 3:1). Its second function, related in part to the first, is to allow the author to express more directly the letter's message and for the reader to discern the document's strategy.

Author's Strategy and Thought. Analysis of the thanksgiving pericope reveals decided interest in apocalyptic matters on the one hand and much sympathy for the community's suffering on the other. Both topics relate to the community's perception that the end-time has arrived (2:1-2). In the first case, the end-time scenario of the returning Lord is developed to treat the just eschatological treatment by God of the oppressor and oppressed as applied to the community's situation. It is within verses 6-10 that one encounters overt apocalyptic detail and concerns. As regards the second issue, the author finds the community's patient endurance and mutual support inspiring and employs this fact, along with the assurance of just recompense at the parousia, to establish a rapport with the beleaguered readers. Having addressed these issues in verses 3-10, the author shifts the discussion to deal with nonapocalyptic themes.

Before dealing with verses 11-12, however, it should be noted that there are several prior indications of the author's anti-apocalyptic message. In other words, verses 3-10, while devoted primarily to strategy (rendering the audience susceptible to the new message), still provide hints about the author's purpose and thinking. In verses 5 the author's use of *kai* in the expression "for which you *also* suffer" already suggests to the audience that they are not the only ones who suffer for the kingdom. By stressing the common suffering of Christians the author begins to dispel the myopic notion of apocalypticists that their sufferings necessarily announce the messianic woes. The phrase in verse 7 "to grant rest *with us*" serves a similar purpose by noting that Christians outside their own community form part of the elect now and will share in the promised eschatological rest. In like manner, in verse 10 the author in describing the end-time scenario notes that the returning Lord will be welcomed "by all who have believed," including the audience. Finally, the author's choice in verse 7 of the traditional term "revelation" to speak of Jesus' coming should be considered a means of counteracting the audience's overly apocalyptic view of the Christ-event. Just as the lawless one, who at present is secretly at work (2:7b), is yet to be revealed, so Jesus, who is expected to come from heaven is in 1:7 said to be revealed from heaven. Though he is to come with angels at the end-time he is nonetheless secretly present.

It is the shift in verses 11-12, however, which makes clearest the author's message. The prayer is that God will, in a final act (use of the aorist), make the readers worthy of their calling. The remainder of verses 11-12 make clear both the present and Christological character of this calling. On the one hand, God is asked, again by means of an aorist, to make completely fruitful the believer's "desire for goodness and work of faith." The goal of this Christian praxis is the "glorification" of both the Lord Jesus and the believer. On the other hand, the worthiness and productivity of the believer is to have as goal the glorification of the Lord Jesus' name and to be done "according to or by means of the grace of our God and of the Lord Jesus Christ." The shift is from a focus on the eschaton (as the community would have it) to a Christian life of activity consistent with one's call through Christ.

In light of the shift described above several points of interpretation need consideration. The author's statement in verse 5 that the community's suffering is evidence of God's just judgment takes on a new meaning, for the author insists that the community's suffering has a moral rather than an apocalyptic significance. There is then a positive and teleological sense to its suffering. See also the discussion in Notes (v. 8) of the author's description of people to be punished not in eschatological (the unrighteous) but in more traditional theological and Christological terms. Additionally, the author's double use of themes, whether worthiness in verses 5 and 11, glory in verses 10 and 12, and *kyrios* Christology in verses 10 and 12, emphasizes the dual aspect of these as future and present realities. The worthiness of the believer and the glorification of the Lord Jesus are future, eschatological realities, as the community insists, but, as the author in verses 11-12 stresses, these have a bearing on the present as well. The author's strategy then focuses on eschatology but the document's message concerns Christian living in the present despite terrible times.

Finally, there is a stress in this document on Jesus' lordship both as an eschatological and present reality. In verse 10 it is said that he returns to be acknowledged as cosmic Lord by all creatures (holy ones and believers). But it is also requested in verse 12 that he ("the name of our Lord Jesus") may be acknowledged as Lord by the community of believers. Interestingly, the author, with a sympathetic glance to the readers' beleaguered mentality, prays that the Lord Jesus might in turn empower them ("glorified by him") "according to the grace of our God and of the Lord Jesus Christ" (see discussions of 3:1 on "glory" and 3:6 on "name").

FOR REFERENCE AND FURTHER STUDY

Aus, R. D. "The Liturgical Background of the Necessity and Propriety of Giving Thanks according to 2 Thess 1:3." *JBL* 92 (1973) 432–38.

_____. "The Relevance of Isa. 66:7 to Revelation 12 and 2 Thessalonians." *ZNW* 67 (1976) 252–68.

Bassler, J. M. "The Enigmatic Sign: 2 Thessalonians 1:5." *CBQ* 46 (1984) 496–510.

Hartman, L. "The Eschatology of 2 Thessalonians as Included in a Communication." *TC*, 470–85.

Holland, G. S. *The Tradition That You Received from Us: 2 Thessalonians in the Pauline Tradition.* Tübingen: Mohr-Siebeck, 1988.

Krentz, E. "Through a Lens: Theology and Fidelity in 2 Thessalonians." *PT*, 52–62.

O'Brien, P. T. *Introductory Thanksgiving in the Letters of Paul.* Leiden: Brill, 1977.

Schubert, P. *Form and Function of the Pauline Thanksgiving.* Berlin: Töpelmann, 1939.

Trilling, W. "Literarische Paulusimitation im 2. Thessalonicherbrief." *Paulus in den neutestamentlichen Spätschriften: Zur Paulusrezeption im Neuen Testament.* Freiburg: Herder, 1981.

19. *Concerning the Lord's Day* (2:1-12)

1. So we urge you, brothers and sisters, with regard to the coming of our Lord Jesus Christ and our assembling before him, 2. not to be so easily and radically shaken in mind nor repeatedly disturbed whether by spirit, by word, or by letter allegedly by us, to the effect that the Lord's day has come. 3. Let no one deceive you in any way, for, until the apostasy comes and the lawless one is revealed, that is, the one destined for destruction, 4. the one who opposes and exalts himself over every so-called god or object of worship, to the point of taking his seat in God's temple, proclaiming that he himself is God— 5. Do you not recall that while I was still with you I often told you these things? 6. And so you know what is now restraining him that he might be revealed at his appointed time. 7. Certainly, the mystery of lawlessness is already at work, but only until the restrainer is gone. 8. And then the lawless one will be revealed whom the Lord Jesus will destroy with the breath of his mouth and render powerless by the manifestation of his coming, 9. the one whose coming is characterized by the activity of Satan, whether by every show of power, both deceptive signs and wonders, 10. or by every kind of enticement to wickedness for those on the road to ruin because they did not accept the love of truth so as to be saved. 11. So for this reason God is sending on them a deluding influence to make them believe the deception, 12. so that all who have not believed the truth but have taken delight in wickedness may be condemned.

NOTES

1. *So we urge you, brothers and sisters:* Turning to the most pressing issue at hand, the Lord's day and its timetable, the author, borrowing the entire clause from 1 Thess 5:12, addresses the community again and urges them to reconsider their hasty conclusions about the Lord's coming. The verb *erōtaō* appears only here in the letter and represents the author's diplomatic attempt to sway the readers into accepting what follows.

with regard to the coming of our Lord Jesus Christ: Before introducing the exhortation that follows the verb, the author states the subject of concern for the whole passage, the Lord's coming, a theme described at the end of verse 2 as "the Lord's day." The subject, in contrast to 1 Thess 4:9, 13; and 5:1, is introduced by *hyper* rather than *peri* with the genitive. The author speaks of "the coming" *(parousia)* of Jesus, a term employed again in verses 8 and 9. It is used as in 1 Thess 2:19; 3:13; 4:15; 5:23 but with important differences. Whereas in Paul the term deals with Jesus' coming at the end-time as judge of believers (see 1 Thess 2:19), in 2 Thess 2:8-9 (cf. 1:7) the focus is on the apocalyptic battle or in 2:1 on the arrival and public manifestation of Jesus. Again, the author employs an extended Christological formula but with the usual, formulaic possessive pronoun "*our* Lord Jesus Christ." Since this pronoun is regularly employed in a non-apocalyptic way to speak of Jesus' present lordship (see 1:8, 12; 2:14, 16; 3:6, 18 and note omission of "our" in 1:7; 2:8), the use of "our" in 2:1 hints at the author's cautious treatment of the community's false concerns. Finally, some MSS (B *pc* sy^h) omit the possessive pronoun *hēmōn*. Though one should usually follow a cardinal rule of textual criticism and follow the shorter text, the tendency of Vaticanus to omit seemingly unimportant textual elements reinforces our judgment that the major MSS represent the original text (see further discussion in Notes for 2 Thess 1:2).

and our assembling before him: The underlying Greek expression offers difficulties both as regard the noun and its modifying prepositional phrase. (1) The term *episynagōgē* appears elsewhere in the NT only in Heb 10:25 where it refers to the Christian assembly. This noun is rare in all literature, including the LXX, though the verb is relatively frequent. Its general meaning is "to collect or gather," particularly the gathering of crowds, a meaning found in Mark 1:33; Luke 12:1. Important for our analysis is its Jewish usage first to speak of the gathering of Israel from exile or dispersion (Isa 52:12; 2 Mac 2:18) and then in the late OT and intertestamental periods to speak in eschatological contexts of the gathering of the nations against Israel (Zech 12:3) or of God assembling the righteous from among the nations (T.Naphtali 8:3; also T.Asher 7:7). It is in this sense that the verb is used in Mark's eschatological discourse (13:27; also Matt 24:31; Luke 13:34) and the noun in 2 Thess 2:1. The term apparently was traditionally employed for the gathering of the elect or the unrighteous at the end-time. Determining the nuance the author intended the term to bear in its relation to *parousia* will require further discussion. (2) The prepositional phrase which modifies the noun is more problematic. The idiom *episynagō epi* which appears in the LXX some 14 times (with some variants) means "gathering against" (Ps 30:13; Zech 12:3) or "before" someone to accuse them or seek redress (Jdt 7:23; 2 Macc 4:39). The only reason given for not adopting a negative meaning for the phrase is the suggestion that *pros* has replaced *epi* (see LXX MSS of Hab 2:5) owing to the influence of the augmented noun (as in Gal 4:9). Even conceding such a grammatical shift it is hard to see how *episynagō epi* (or *pros*) *auton* supports its traditional rendering ("to assemble to meet him"), a translation which relies more on the meaning of the noun and its end-time context than on the idiomatic sense of the prepositional phrase. A more appealing suggestion is to view *epi auton* as indicating motion toward someone and, borrowing especially from the terminology of the law-courts, as meaning "appear or come before" a magistrate or official (as in Matt 10:18; Luke 12:11, 58). Thus, believers are said to appear or gather "before" Jesus as the returning judge (see BAGD 288.III.1a).

2. *not to be so easily and radically shaken in mind nor repeatedly disturbed:* The object of exhortation is introduced by the articular construction *eis to* and consists of an accusative subject with two infinitives and their modifiers. The first verb, *saleutheuō*, an aorist passive infinitive, has the literal meaning of being physically "shaken" or moved to its foundation, usually by wind or storm. In the present context, modified both by the adverb "so easily or quickly" and the prepositional phrase "in mind," the term has a figurative meaning and describes the change of the audience's "mind" or balanced way of thinking as a shaking of its foundation rather than a loss of calmness (BAGD 544.3 not 544.1). Such a conclusion is further indicated by the author's use of the aorist (addition of "radically" to the translation) to indicate a one-time basic change and of the adverb "so easily" to contrast the seriousness of the issue with the audience's recent, seemingly facile change of perspective. The second verb, *throeō*, a present passive infinitive, addresses the volatile situation of the community. Employing a verb which since classical times dealt with a heightened sense of speech and emotion and one employed in the Jesus tradition to describe the agitation accompanying apocalyptic fervor (Mark 13:7; Matt 24:6), the author focuses on the state of mind (use of present tense, rendered "repeatedly") which results from stirred-up apocalyptic activity.

whether by spirit, by word, or by letter allegedly by us: There follows a series of sources, each introduced by *mēte* ("whether/or"). Many view these as sources of the addressees' misunderstanding of Pauline teaching; they are better seen, however, as a variety of sources contributing to the mental agitation noted earlier—each term is said to be a cause of disturbance. In effect the author later counteracts these present sources of apocalyptic fervor by appealing to the preaching of the foundation visit and Paul's balanced letter to the community (2:15). The first source is stated simply: "by spirit." One could appeal to earlier Pauline statements about prophetic activity and the discernment of these (1 Thess 5:19-20), but owing to the author's wish to establish true doctrine as related to tradition and the gospel received from apostolic times (2 Thess 1:8; 2:13-15), it is best to interpret the phrase as referring to spirit-inspired utterances similar to those of apocalypticists who claim to be "in the spirit" (Rev 1:10; 4:2) when receiving or uttering their apocalyptic visions. The second source of agitation is described as coming "by word." Coming immediately after "by spirit" one presumes this new source represents the nonecstatic, oral preaching of apocalyptic teachers. The third source is said to be "by letter." From this sequence it is clear that the author designates first the missionary utterances of seers in the community, then the extended discourses of the doomsday prophets, and finally a written document, which the author qualifies as "allegedly by us" (lit: "as though by or from us"). It is debated whether the phrase, which follows the third item qualifies all three, the last two (see 2:15 where "word and letter" are again mentioned), or only the third. It is in the context of explaining the situation as owing to a misunderstanding of Pauline statements and in the defense of authenticity that scholars are wont to insist that the phrase concerning forgery applies to all three items. In view of the situation presumed in this commentary, "allegedly by us" is best understood as referring to the third item; it is a letter which the apocalyptic group has written in Paul's name, a letter which defends their view that "the Lord's day has come." The author refers in more positive terms to Paul's letter in 2:15.

to the effect that the Lord's day has come: The final clause of the verse, introduced by the nonclassical *hōs hoti* ("to the effect that"; only in 2 Cor 5:19; 11:21 and in later Greek writers; see BDF 396), presents, in a climactic fashion, the crucial information about the situation of the addressees; as a result of apocalyptic fervor within the community some have concluded that the Lord's day has arrived. The clause is explicit, "the Lord's day has come." The verb *enistēmi* in the perfect form can only mean "is present" or "has come"— other expressions or forms of this verb would be used to indicate the imminence rather than the actual arrival of the end-time (see 1 Cor 3:22; 7:26; Rom 8:38; Heb 9:9). What the addressees believed or what the writer understood by such a statement is another matter and is addressed below. On the classical prophetic and later apocalyptic expression "the Lord's day," see 1:10 and 1 Thess 5:2.

Verses 3-8a. Beginning in verse 3 the author sets out to counteract the teachings of those in the community who are expounding overt apocalypticism. In verse 3a there is an attempt rhetorically to include all possible deviant sources of such teaching by stating the basic conditions for the end-time scenario, namely the coming of apostasy and of the lawless one. Thus, two possible solutions are offered: either verse 3a introduces what will develop into an incomplete conditional sentence, a construction that one could interpret as having an "implied apodosis" ("it cannot happen"—see *IBNTG*, 151), or else it could be viewed as an incomplete conditional sentence whose apodosis is never stated because the author becomes entangled in the description of the lawless one (vv. 3c-4). The translation here adopted chooses the second option to remain closer to the author's treatment of the topic. In this way one sees more clearly the resumptive function of verse 5 as it recaptures the train of thought, lost as the author sought to describe the lawless one, and the function of verse 8, which reiterates the theme of the coming of the law-less one after a digression concerning the restrainer (see discussion of 1:5).

3. *Let no one deceive you in any way:* The author employs an aorist subjunctive to express a firm prohibition *(IBNTG,* 22). Use of the term *exapataō* (see also Rom 16:18; 2 Cor 11:3; and 1 Tim 2:14) points to intentional deception by some within the community rather than inadvertent misrepresentation of Pauline or traditional teaching. Further, the author's use of the third-person singular and rhetorical emphasis ("in any way") confirms the interpretation that various people in the community are stirring up apocalyptic expectations and employing every means at their disposal to convince other members of the community that the end has come. Possibly the author employs the apocalyptic theme of end-time deception (see Mark 13:5, 22—use of *planaō*) as a rhetorical means to undermine the apocalyptic fervor of the community and to prepare for the teaching of 2:3f., which, the author claims, is a reminder of apostolic preaching (2:5). Verse 3a then serves as culmination of the list of ways that are being used to "disturb" (author's polemical term) or sensi-tize (preachers' perspective) the community in regard to the end-time signs.

for, until the apostasy comes: The term "until" represents an attempt to com-bine the conditional particle *(ean mē*—"unless") with the final word of the clause *prōton* ("first or before [this]") since the latter signifies the priority not of the apostasy over the revelation of the lawlessness but of the following as a group of signs before the Lord's return. The first sign concerns "the apostasy," a term whose simple article indicates a subject known to the au-dience. Its meaning in this vague context, however, is difficult to discern. The term *apostasia* is a Hellenistic formation replacing the earlier *apostasis* and bearing both a political ("rebellion" as in Polybius, *History* 5.46.6 and Josephus, *Life* 43) and a religious sense (Josh 22:22; Jer 2:19; Acts 21:21). Thus, three types of interpretation are advanced. (1) The term would represent a worldwide political revolt against divinely instituted structures of government and so would require the translation "the rebellion." While such a view interestingly relates to a political interpretation of the chapter (including the figures of the lawless one and the restrainer), it does less than justice to the community's situation and its temptation to turn away from the Christian message (see 2:9-10). (2) Some explain the term as representing Jewish rejec-tion of its monotheistic tradition and of the Christian Messiah. Again, one wonders how a Jewish figure could ever claim to be God (2:4) or how refus-ing the Christian message can be portrayed as apostasy. Such a theory leaves many features of chapter 2 unexplained. (3) With more credibility it is sug-gested that, following intertestamental Jewish tradition about a general apostasy or lack of moral integrity before the end-time (1 En 91:3-10; Jub 23:14-23; 4 Ezra 5:1-2; 2 Bar 41:3; 42:4), the author, along with other NT writers (Mark 13:5; Matt 24:10-12; Luke 8:13; 2 Tim 3:1-9; Jude 18; Rev 3:8), envi-sions the end-time as signaled by a period of wrongdoing (see 2:7) and en-ticement to apostasy (2:10). Such a conclusion is further indicated by the nuance which the *aphistēmi* word-group has of "seduction or winning away," a role which is explicitly attributed to the lawless one in 2:10 (see *TDNT* 1:512-14).

and the lawless one is revealed: The second sign involves a figure who on three occasions (2:3, 6, 8) is said "to be revealed." Presumably, as in 1:7 where the author speaks of Jesus' return not by employing the term "coming" or *parousia* (contrast 2:1, 8) but "revelation" *(apokalypsis)* to emphasize his present lordship and its relation to his final manifestation, so here the term is used of this evil figure rather than "coming" (contrast 2:9) to show its role and activity in relation to present evil and the community's affliction (see 2:7). This end-time evil figure is introduced simply as was the apostasy but is described subsequently by a series of statements in verses 3-4 and 8-10. The introductory title reads literally, "a person of lawlessness," an expression viewed as Semitic in origin. Indeed, the following descriptive title (lit: "son of destruction") is a parallel construction consisting of a generic personal noun (son, person, daughter, master, etc.) followed by an adjectival genitive ("of lawlessness" or "destruction") designating the person's condition or quality *(IBNTG, 174-75; GNTG, 4:207-8).* The evil one is said to be a person characterized by *anomia*, a term describing willful opposition to the law or a sinful person. Both in the LXX and in the NT a person is said to participate in a state of *anomia* (Ps 31:5; Rom 6:19—see *TDNT* 4:1085); so here in 2 Thess 2:3 (also vv. 7 and 8) one can envision "the lawless one" as being in the service of "lawlessness" or even (as in 2:9) acting through the power of evil personified. Thus, one should envision this figure as an individual who is at the service of the power of lawlessness that is opposed to God and divinely established order. On the use of the adjective to describe this figure, see Notes on verse 8 and references to PssSol 17:11, 18. Finally, the variant, "the sinful one" (read by the majority of MSS but not by the two oldest and more trustworthy: Vaticanus and Sinaiticus), should probably be seen as an attempt, *ad sensum*, to interpret the author's meaning by substituting the more frequent equivalent *hamartia* (*TCGNT*, 635).

that is, the one destined for destruction: The author provides a parallel title, in apposition ("that is"), to describe the evil figure of the end-times. In this case the adjectival genitive "of destruction" indicates not its place of origin but the lawless one's relationship to destruction ("destined for or doomed to"). *Apōleia* has a range of meaning from "the *destruction* that one experiences, *annihilation* both complete and in process, *ruin*" (BAGD 103). Its meaning in this apocalyptic context is probably more that of "destruction" in the sense of "ruin" than "annihilation," for the verb is also employed of the unrighteous who are said to be on the "road to ruin" (2:10; see Matt 7:13) or to "pay the penalty of eternal ruin *(olethros)* apart from the Lord's presence" (1:9). In both cases the author presumes punishment during continued existence. So also the apocalyptic schema assumes not the extinction of the evil one but final imprisonment in the bottomless pit (Rev 20:10, 14-15). Thus, the author of 2 Thessalonians is interested in demonstrating the eventual powerlessness of the evil one and God's ultimate victory. See also discussion in verse 8 of *anaireō* and *katargeō* ("destroy and render powerless" respectively) as describing the lawless one's ultimate fate or doom.

4. *the one who opposes and exalts himself:* The appositive construction begun in verse 3 continues as the author adds a more complex title to the description

by characterizing this figure by a double participial phrase introduced by a unique article and complemented by a prepositional phrase. The first participle, *antikeimenos*, meaning "the one who opposes or the opponent," is a common term for opposition (Luke 13:17; 1 Cor 16:9) but one that suggests a satanic ally (see v. 9 where the lawless one performs satanic activity), one who like Satan is God's adversary (see 3:3 and Zech 3:1). The second verbal form *hyperairomenos*, having the meaning "rise up over or exalt oneself over" (so used in 2 Cor 12:7), paraphrases an idea borrowed from Daniel's description of Antiochus Epiphanes (11:36). The image is further developed by what follows.

over every so-called god or object of worship: Borrowing from the classic example of the Syrian king's divine pretensions, described as "exalting and magnifying himself over every god" (Dan 11:36), the author, employing the double verbs discussed above, cites and edits the remainder of the OT phrase: "over every [so-called] god [or object of worship]." The first part of the phrase emphasizes the lawless one's total opposition to the divine world, much in the tradition of past apocalyptic figures, who like Antiochus, opposed not only the Jewish high God but the gods of the nations as well as his ancestral gods. By adding "every so-called god" or "every being given the name of god" (see 1 Cor 8:5), the author underscores the universal character of the end-time rebellion as opposing all semblance of order and goodness. The second, added part, of the phrase "object of worship" (Acts 17:23; Josephus, *JA* 18:344) serves further to underscore the absolute enmity as extending even to objects used in worship.

to the point of taking his seat in God's temple: The result and climax ("to the point of") of this opposition is the attempt to usurp the power of the one and true God. The imagery chosen provokes discussion as regards the referent of *naos* ("temple") and so the author's intention and meaning. Use of this imagery is variously related to the Jerusalem edifice, to an alleged temple of the end-days, to the Church as temple, to a heavenly reality, or to an image portraying divine power. Each has its defenders, particularly in relation to the issues of authorship and identity of the lawless one. The first two presume too literal a reading of the text, as though the entire chapter were referring to historical events, places, or the reconstruction of the temple before the end. The third option is too limited, for the author envisions not an ecclesial but a universal context for the events described. The expression "taking his seat in the temple of God" should be viewed in apocalyptic terms, no matter how vivid or dramatic the imagery. (1) There is much background in apocalyptic literature for the desecration of the Jerusalem Temple, whether the activity of the king of Tyre, who haughtily claimed to be a god (Ezek 28:2), of the provocative Antiochus Epiphanes (Dan 9:27; 11:31; 12:11; also Mark 13:14), of Pompey the Roman general who entered the holy of holies (PssSol 2; 17:11-14), or of Gaius Caligula, who tried "to erect an image of himself in the temple of God" (Josephus, *JA* 18:261). Such lore served as model for end-day conduct of the apocalyptic evil one. (2) Also, the temple and the divine throne often figure in apocalyptic scenarios as heavenly realities representing the site of God's power and presence (Ps 11:4; 2 Bar 4; T.Levi 5; Rev passim: both heavenly throne and temple). The author therefore employs temple imagery as symbol for the site of God's power and the phrase "taking his seat" to represent the ancient theme of human aspirations to divinity, whether Adam and Eve (Gen 3:5) or Herod Agrippa I (Acts 12:21-23; Josephus, *JA* 19:343-47), in addition to the examples given above. Finally, the addition in some late mss of the phrase "as God" is both unnecessary in the context and poorly attested textually (*TCGNT*, 635-36).

proclaiming that he himself is God: The passage explicates the meaning of the previous symbolic action (verb of proclamation introducing indirect discourse); the activity of sitting on God's throne signifies not only the declaration of one's divinity but also the attempt to usurp God's position and power (use of reflexive "himself"; see BAGD 89.1). Additionally, while it is possible grammatically to translate *estin theos* as "he is a god" or "he is God," the latter is preferable as representing not what a pagan or apostate might say ("I am a god or am divine") but rather the claim of a Christian writer (a usurper declares: "I am God"). For an interesting parallel to the declaration, see the case of the king of Tyre in Ezek 28:2.

5. *Do you not recall that while I was still with you I often told you these things?* The involved sentence which began in verse 3 is interrupted by an abrupt rhetorical question. The terminology is reminiscent of 1 Thess 2:9 ("you recall") combined with 3:4 ("when we were with you, we often warned you"). Here also the imperfect is employed (and translated "often told") to underscore the repeated nature of the process of instruction. There is, however, a switch ("we" to "I") from apostolic instruction to a focus on Paul alone. This question stresses the author's appeal to tradition or past instruction as a device to counteract apocalyptic teaching (see 2:15) and appeals to passages in 1 Thessalonians where Paul refers to past instruction (3:4; 4:2, 6, 9; 5:1-2). Rather than a reprimand by Paul (claiming authenticity), the passage represents the author's strategy of appealing to apostolic teaching about the Lord's day to insist that the community is "too easily and radically being shaken in mind" (2:2).

6. *and so you know what is now restraining him:* Verse 6 is introduced by the expression *kai nyn* ("and now") and is variously interpreted as indicating some temporal sequence between the several time indicators of verses 5-8. If "now" modifies the verb "you know," the author would be contrasting the readers' present knowledge of the mysterious figure as opposed to their past instruction ("while I was still with you"—v. 5) and to the future revelation of the lawless one ("and then"—v. 8). It is preferable, however, to view *kai* as having an explicative meaning "and so" (BAGD 393.3) and *nyn* as modifying the following participle ("what is now restraining him"). In this way one explains more easily the relation between verses 5 and 6 (past teaching as explaining present knowledge), the author's use of *oida* ("you know") to underscore present experiential awareness, and the connection between the two parts of verse 6 (contrast between current restraint and revelation "at

his appointed time"). Finally, explanation of the participle *katechon*, meaning "hold back, retain, hold fast, or possess" and here translated "restrain," is treated in an Excursus and discussed below.

that he might be revealed at his appointed time: The clause expresses the purpose (use of *eis to*—also 1:5; 2:2) for present restraint of the lawless one as owing to the divine plan for the end-time scenario. The expression "at his appointed time" suggests several important points. (1) The variant *heautou* (the reflexive "his own" rather than "his"), offered by a number of important MSS (B K D G *al*), is probably a later attempt to underscore the identity of the figure to be revealed as the lawless one. (2) The expression employed to designate time *kairos* is chosen for its apocalyptic overtones, in terms of usage (Mark 13:33; 1 Thess 5:1; 1 Pet 1:5; Rev 1:3; Acts 1:7) and of implied meaning ("appointed or proper time"—BAGD 394.2-3; see 1 Tim 6:15). (3) The terminology employed contrasts the unknown time of this event (see Mark 13:32-33) with the present distress (see following verse) and underscores the divinely established scenario of the end-time.

7. *Certainly, the mystery of lawlessness is already at work:* In explaining the relationship of verse 7 to what precedes, scholars routinely speak of the former, introduced by *gar* ("for"), as providing an explanation either of the *katechon* or its activity in restraining evil. In fact, verse 7 brings up a disquieting fact, the actual appearance of evil when it has just been stated that the evil one has been restrained from the human scene. *Gar* then would seem to introduce an inferential statement which the author readily concedes, "certainly . . . [evil] is already at work" (BAGD 152.3). The expression employed to describe this state of affairs; "the mystery of lawlessness" is a unique phrase and its meaning unclear. While the word *mystērion* is employed in classical literature as a technical term for secret rites and teaching, in Daniel for the communication of divine knowledge (2:18f.; also 1 En 63:3; 71:33; passim), and in the NT for God's eternal plan in Christ or as a revelation of Jesus Christ (see Gal 1:12; 1 Pet 1:7; also 2 Thess 1:7), there do exist parallels for the negative usage of this verse. Among the Dead Sea Scrolls one finds the idiom "the mystery of iniquity" (in the plural always: 1 QH 5:36), a usage which seems to confer "hidden" eschatological significance to human wrongdoing. In fact, these "mysteries" are clearly identified in 1 QM 14:9 as owing to Satan's malevolence. Also, a passage from Josephus (*JW* 1:470) describing the life of Antipater as "a mystery of evil or iniquity," implies that the term mystery refers to the hidden character of the evil activity. Finally, the usage of Rev 17:5, 7 also confirms the hidden character of the harlot's evil activity (*TDNT* 4:823-24). In light of these parallels, I am led to see the new expression "the mystery of lawlessness" (on *anomia*, see 2:3) as referring not to the apostasy or tribulations of the end-days but rather to the evils and persecutions which the community is undergoing (1:4-6) and is misreading as signs of the Lord's day. By employing the term "mystery" the author is agreeing with the community's estimate that these evils have eschatological significance, but by calling them activities of lawlessness, the author further cautions that they are the hidden and limited activity of the lawless one who

is to be revealed at a later date. Lastly, this evil activity is said "already to be at work." Clearly, by use of the term "already," the author intends to stress the apparent contradiction between the statement that the satanic power is being kept at bay (vv. 6-7) and the realism that the community is encountering affliction. Further, the author's use of the term *energeō* calls for comment. While one could insist that the form is a passive and see God as the ultimate source of the power at work, it is best, in light of an examination of the use of this verb in Paul and in the NT generally (see Excursus on 1 Thess 2:13), to see this occurrence also as a middle to stress the clandestine, limited but nonetheless satanic character of the activity. This conclusion is confirmed by two other considerations. (1) Use of the *energeō* word-family in the NT invariably relates to the activity of supernatural, whether divine or demonic, beings. This is particularly the case for occurrences of this verb in the middle voice. (2) The further use in 2 Thessalonians of the noun *energeia* in 2:9, 11 to describe satanic activity suggests that in the present passage it is also the lawless one or Satan directly who is the secret, energizing force behind the community's problems.

but only until the restrainer is gone: The translation presumes that the word order (the subject preceding the conjunction *arti heōs*) owes to the author's desire to lay emphasis on the restrainer once more (BDF 475.1—one should also note the initial position of the term earlier in v. 6). Thus, it is unnecessary to conclude that 7b is an elliptical construction requiring that the reader supply an object or verb for the participial form *katechōn*. Instead, the text reads as a temporal clause dependent on the first part of verse 7. Two further points should be noted. (1) While discussion of the concept of the restrainer is deferred, it should be noted that the concept in verse 7 takes on a personal quality, since it is no longer the neuter but the masculine form of the participle that is employed. (2) The expression "is gone" represents the Greek phrase *ek mesou genētai*, an idiom that is unattested in biblical but found in a few contemporary nonbiblical texts (e.g., Plutarch, *Timoleon* 5.3; see BAGD 159.4c). Such references indicate the sense of "being removed or out of the way" and suggest a neutral rather than a negative connotation, a point that bears noting when interpreting the role played by and the identity of the *katechōn*.

8. *And then the lawless one will be revealed:* The beginning of the verse serves a resumptive function. Just as in verse 5, by means of a rhetorical question, the author was able to resume the train of thought begun earlier regarding the nonarrival of the Lord's day, so now in verse 8 again the question of the delay of the lawless one is addressed after a brief discussion of the one that restrains the onslaught of evil. Interestingly, the resumptive technique employed is that of near-repetition of an earlier clause regarding the lawless one. Three minor modifications are made: the addition of *tote* ("then"), the modification of the verbal form, and a slight change in the title given the apocalyptic figure. The first modification indicates temporal sequence: after the restrainer is out of the way, "then" the lawless one will appear. The second

change involves the use of the future indicative for the aorist subjunctive required by the conditional clause. Again, the focus is on the future appearance of the apocalyptic figure in contrast to the community's belief that the Lord's day has arrived. The third modification, involving the title "the lawless one" for "the person of lawlessness" (see v. 3), indicates no more than a stylistic variation. Nonetheless, it should be noted that the latter is distinctly Semitic in form while the former reflects a Hellenistic use of an adjective to describe a person. Whether one postulates the use of a Semitic tradition for the composition of chapter two (see also "the one destined for destruction" in v. 3), one still must underscore the author's ability to employ Hellenized forms as is here the case. Also, it should be noted that the term *anomos* is employed in PssSol 17:11, 18 to speak first of the Roman general Pompey and then of his army. It is unclear whether in this apocalyptic context the term refers to these people as Gentiles (see 17:8: "a man alien to our race") or as evildoers. The context and general usage of the term, nonetheless, favors the latter, even in the Psalms of Solomon 2 and 17 where Pompey is described as an apocalyptic lawless or evil figure (see Paul's interesting usage in 1 Cor 9:21).

whom the Lord Jesus will destroy with the breath of his mouth: Rather than pursue the description of the lawless one's activity, the author instead addresses its fate, already announced by the title "the one destined for destruction." The relative clause introduces "the Lord Jesus" as the warrior of the end-days and employs imagery borrowed from Isa 11:4. It is uncertain whether one should read "Lord Jesus" with major MSS and verions (S A D* G al lat sy Ir) or simply "Lord" with Vaticanus and a less impressive list of witnesses. While the text-critical rule of following the shorter text supports the latter, the author's tendency to repeatedly employ the title "Lord Jesus," the possibility of accidental omission of IC ("Jesus") in transcribing OKCIC ("Lord Jesus"), and the propensity of Vaticanus for parsimonious transcription (see Notes on 2:1), I am inclined to follow the stronger textual evidence for the longer text (*TCGNT*, 636). Strangely, the verb also offers textual difficulties, but scholars are generally agreed that an original *anelei* (future of *anaireō:* "to destroy or kill" and borrowed from Isa 11:4), supported by the best and majority of MSS, was modified by a few MSS to the unusual optative *aneloi,* and, more radically, by others to *analōsei,* a new verb patterned on the verb from the following clause, one deemed more compatible with the context: "will consume" (*TCGNT*, 636). Apparently, the author derived the imagery and grammatical forms by editing two clauses from Isa 11:4 into one: "he will strike the earth *with the* word *of his* mouth and with *the breath* of his lips *he will destroy* the ungodly." This would have been done under the influence of other biblical or intertestamental passages employing identical (Ps 32:6; also 134:17; 1 En 14:2; 84:1) or similar idioms dealing with the force of the mouth or breath, particularly in apocalyptic literature, to destroy or consume the unrighteous (Job 4:9; Isa 30:27-28; 1 En 62:2; 4 Ezra 13:10-11; PssSol 17:24, 35; Rev 19:15). Interestingly, in the last three texts noted it is the messianic figure, as in 2 Thess 2:8, not God directly who punishes the ungodly. Finally, the verb *anaireō* can mean "do away with, destroy, or slay" (BAGD 54-55) and its particular nuance depends on identification of the lawless one and its fate. One might speak of the lawless one as being "done away with or destroyed," or, in focusing on the figure as a human being, as being "killed," or, more generally as a cosmic figure or power, as being "destroyed, defeated or done away with" (see BAGD 54-55; LSJ 106). It is probably the hint of military imagery ("killing or defeating") that one detects here. The following clause also has a bearing on this issue.

and render powerless by the manifestation of his coming: This passage offers a close stylistic and thematic complement to the text immediately preceding, for the word order and grammatical structure (articles, instrumental dative, possessive pronoun) form a striking parallel. The verb *katargeō* has the meaning of "making ineffective, powerless, or useless," its meaning both in classical and NT literature (LSJ 908; BAGD 417). It also means "abolish or nullify" in a legal sense (Rom 3:3; 1 Cor 1:28) but hardly "annihilate" in the sense of "complete destruction" (*TDNT* 1:454). Instead, the verb is employed by Paul and other NT writers (1 Cor 2:6; 15:24, 26; 2 Tim 1:10; Heb 2:14) to describe the Christ-event's robbing of power from the demonic powers and their allies. There is then a disarming or a "rendering powerless" of the evil one (on *ergon* see also vv. 7, 9, 11). The following dative phrase presents a challenge since its two nouns have similar meanings. The first term, *epiphaneia*, is a technical religious and political term from the Hellenistic period to describe the public appearance of a hidden deity or the visitation of a benefactor and would here be applied to the risen Jesus' coming in judgment (BAGD 304.1). Thus, the term's meaning in this context, in relation to the second word *(parousia)*, might be sought in two directions. On the one hand, it is suggested that the phrase be read as "the splendor of his presence or coming," a meaning which looks to the term's adjectival use (see Acts 2:20 [= Joel 3:4]: "the Lord's great and glorious day"). On the other, it is interpreted as stressing the Lord's public manifestation as opposed to his present hiddenness. Either sense fits the context; the first underscores the text's military overtones (see 1:8) and the second its apocalyptic theme of hiddenness and revelation. The above translation suggests the second as preference. See Note on 2:1 for discussion of *parousia*.

9. *the one whose coming is characterized by the activity of Satan:* The reintroduction of the lawless one at the beginning of verse 8 should have led to a description of its activity, but immediately the author introduces the theme of Jesus' coming and defeat of this figure. Verse 9 then represents a resumption of the initial theme by means of a relative construction. Surprisingly, the author employs the term *parousia* for the lawless one's arrival, a term which is reserved for Jesus in early literature. So the immediately preceding mention of Jesus' public and powerful coming calls for a contrast with the lawless one's arrival manifested through a rival, evil power and inducements. Since the new clause contains no explicit predicate, it is presumed that the following prepositional phrase qualifies the subject. Thus, the text should read: his "coming is characterized by (*kata*—BAGD 407.II.5) the activity of Satan." In this way the author insists that the lawless one is an agent of Satan (see Rev 13:2), that its coming will result from satanic power *(energeia)*

and that its works will betray, at every turn, the characteristics of its evil master. What Satan is now doing in a hidden way (use of the verb *energeō* in 2:7) is a foretaste of satanic activity in the end-day as accomplished through the auspices of the lawless one. For a discussion of Satan, see 1 Thess 2:18.

whether by every show of power, both deceptive signs and wonders: This qualifying phrase along with the following one form a carefully structured parallel to introduce first works of power and then the theme of deception. The passage is a long prepositional phrase which consists of three successive nouns in the dative and a final genitive noun. While one could treat these as parallels ("power, signs, and wonders"), it is preferable to view the first, which is singular in form, as a generic term for "works of power" and the following two, both in the plural, as specific types. Thus, "by every show or deed of power" (*dynamis*—BAGD 208.4) underscores the public, outward show of activity which is meant to impress and entice. The following nouns, *sēmeion* and *teras*, joined by double *kai* ("both . . . and"), consist of an OT word pair to denote miracles or supernatural acts (Exod 7:3; Rom 15:19; Acts 2:43; 7:36). The same pair is used (Mark 13:22; Matt 24:24) to describe the activity of the evil figures of the end-time. Also, the long prepositional phrase ends with a noun in the genitive: "of falsehood" (use of *pseudos*). This construction is called a "Hebrew genitive" and can be interpreted as indicating a quality ("spurious or false"—*BG*, 40) or intention ("deceptive"—BAGD 892). The latter is preferable for several reasons. Neither the Synoptic tradition (Mark 13:22) nor Revelation (13:13-14; 19:20) questions the existence of these by qualifying them as "false." Also, these texts speak of their purpose as being the deception of the elect. Lastly, a similar note is sounded in Rev 13:14 and 2 Thess 2:11. In the former it is said of the second beast "that it is allowed [by God] to perform" the signs; in the latter "God sends . . . a deluding influence to make them believe the deception."

10. *or by every kind of enticement to wickedness:* The second theme, already hinted at by the term "deceptive," is presented in a parallel phrase consisting of two nouns. The first (*apatē*) can mean "deception or enticement" and the second (*adikia*), having the sense of "wrongdoing or wickedness" and relating to the first as a Hebrew genitive, can either describe it ("wicked deception") or state its purpose ("enticement to wickedness"—*BG*, 40). While either meaning fits the context, one can object against the first that all "deception" is evil (note the use of *exapataō* in 2:3 to mean "deceive"), and in favor of the second that verse 12b ("those who have taken delight in wickedness") favors such a reading.

for those on the road to ruin: The phrase *tois apollymenois* represents the present (indicated by "on the road" or "in the process") middle participle of the verb *apollymi* which has a range of meaning from "perishing," "dying," to "being ruined." The cognate noun appears in 2:3 to describe the lawless one ("one destined for destruction"). The meaning of the term can be sought in relation to Pauline usage (1 Cor 1:18; 2 Cor 2:15; 4:3) where there exists a contrast between "those who are in the process of being saved" and those described by the term *apollymi*. For Paul and for this author such people, even the lawless one, are not destined for annihilation but for a fate described as "ruin" or eternal separation from the Lord's presence (see 1:9 and 2:3).

because they did not accept the love of truth: The reason for considering someone as "on the road to ruin" is given in non-Pauline terms, for in place of "receive the word" (1 Thess 1:6; 2:13), the author employs the unusual and unique expression "the love of truth" (see v. 12 for "believe the truth"). This phrase parallels the earlier "enticement to wickedness" and probably is a creation of the author as well. In this case the expression refers to believers' welcoming of the gospel as contrasted to nonbelievers and their delight in wickedness (2:12). It is one's relation to the gospel, here characterized as "the truth," which determines one's status as headed either to ruin or salvation (see v. 13: "chosen for salvation"). The author's insistence that it is acceptance of "the love of the truth" that leads to salvation stresses fidelity to the gospel message (see Matt 24:12). That is why those who lack "love for the truth" are able to be enticed. For discussion of the themes of "truth" and love of the truth," see below.

so as to be saved: The sense of the text is not that they did not want to be saved but that they did not accept and "so as a result are not saved." Also, while one could insist that use of the aorist points to salvation, in non-Pauline terms, as a past event, one already achieved by acceptance of the gospel, other factors argue against this. The earlier idiom "being on the road to ruin" (use of the present participle) indicates that perdition is a present process. Likewise, the expression in 2:13, "being chosen from the beginning for salvation," makes clear that salvation is a process whose achievement, as for Paul, is in the future. For a somewhat different construction with a similar meaning, see 1 Thess 2:16 and 1 Cor 10:33.

11. *So for this reason God is sending on them a deluding influence:* The author draws a connection with what precedes by means of a common phrase *dia touto* (an uncharacteristic *kai* is added—see discussion of 1 Thess 2:13). Not only is the evil one, under the influence of Satan, responsible for enticing sinners but even God has a role in this matter. God is said to send upon them (use of the present tense) "a deluding influence" *(energeian planēs)*. The first term, *energeia*, appears in 2:9 and its cognate verb in 2:7 (see also *katargeō* in 2:8). Since this term is used to describe divine or supernatural activity frequently in Greek literature, including the NT (LSJ 564; BAGD 265), it is no surprise that two uses of the term concern Satan or the power of evil (2:7, 9) and the third describes God's intervention in human lives. The term is combined with the noun *planē*, meaning "delusion or error"; the latter relates to the former as a "Hebrew genitive." Thus, the second might describe the first and be translated "an active or powerful delusion" or might indicate its purpose and be rendered "a deluding influence" or "power of error." The latter is preferred since it corresponds better to the influence which the lawless one has over the unrighteous. God is said here, as in other biblical texts (1 Kgs 22:23; Ps 81:12; Ezek 14:9; Rom 1:14f.; 11:25; see also Mark 4:11-12), to cooperate

actively in making situations of sin and disobedience worse. For further discussion of this theme, its relation to other biblical passages, and its function in the author's strategy, see below.

to make them believe the deception: The purpose (use of articular infinitive with accusative subject) is stated as making possible further commitment to falsehood and as cooperation with the lawless one in enticing those already "on the road to ruin." So, the infinitive, *pisteusai*, is rendered "to make them believe" (use of aorist) to describe the definitive acceptance of the commitment to evil as a parallel to believers' firm commitment to truth (v. 10; use of aorist). *Pseudos* as in verse 9 means "the deception" (use of article) rather than "error" more generally.

12. *so that all who have not believed the truth:* Verse 12 consists of a final clause (use of *hina* followed by the subjunctive) to express the ultimate goal of God's intervention; the verb occurs immediately in Greek but is moved to the end of the clause in the translation. The clause consists, in typical fashion, of parallel statements which serve as subject of the dependent verb. The double subject is introduced by a single numerical adjective and article and contrasting particles "not . . . but." The first part of the construction employs another unusual, non-Pauline idiom, "have not believed the truth"; both the grammatical form (aorist of *pisteuō* with the dative for the usual Pauline present tense with a preposition and object—true also v. 11 above) and theme are unique. Again, the term "truth" is employed with an article (see v. 10) and refers to "the gospel" but its context suggests that the meaning is more precise. The reference to "all" at the beginning of the clause suggests the totality referred to in 1:8-10 and so broadens the perspective of the verse. This is especially true if one examines what follows.

but have taken delight in wickedness: The author's designation of those to be condemned is further clarified by the second, parallel part of the subject construction. The aorist participial phrase reveals another non-Pauline trait, for where Paul employs an object with the verb *eudokeō*, he also inserts the preposition *en* rather than the dative as is here the case (see 1 Cor 10:5; 2 Cor 12:10). As for the meaning of the verb ("consider good or take pleasure") one must refer to 1:11 where the noun is used in a similar but antithetical fashion. In contrast to believers, who are on the road to salvation and are being assisted by God's power to develop their every desire for goodness and to increase their works of faith (1:11), the unrighteous, whether unbelievers or less-than-faithful brothers and sisters, are "on the road to ruin" since they have refused to commit themselves to the gospel ("believe the truth") or its practice ("love of the truth") and instead are perversely finding pleasure in wickedness. The complete subject of verse 12 then encompasses all whom the author classifies as "on the road to ruin." On the term "wickedness," see verse 10 above.

may be condemned: The outcome of evil human activity and God's intervention in the lives of the ungodly is the negative aspect of judgment. The author once again (see 1:5-6) uses technical legal terminology (*krinō*—frequent in Paul) to express the ultimate outcome of "God's just judgment" for it is applied both to those who afflict the righteous (1:6) and to those who turn away from the truth and prefer the pleasure of evil (2:12).

EXCURSUS
on the Restrainer (2:6-7)

One should begin a discussion of this debated issue with the basic data of the Greek text. The term appears twice only in the NT: in 2 Thess 2:6 as a neuter participle suggesting a force of restraint or possession and in verse 7 as a masculine participle identifying this source of power as a living being; in both cases the participles have no complementary object. The term itself suggests a range of meaning from "holding fast or back" to "possessing or occupying" to "having mastery or self-control" (LSJ 926; BAGD 422-23). Presumably, the concept was easily understood by the addressees who are said to be instructed in the matter (2:5-6). Beyond these data there is not much agreement since interpretation depends on how one translates the participles and what identification one offers for this force or being. Scholars are not even agreed on whether this power is evil or benign or what its relation is to the lawless one and the mystery of lawlessness.

The traditional identification of the *katechon* (*-ōn*), beginning at least ca. A.D. 200 with Tertullian, has been to see in this enigmatic figure the role of the Roman Empire and its emperor. This interpretation which opts for the meaning "restrain" and posits both a power and a person as the restrainer (neuter and masculine respectively), has met, however, with increasing disfavor. While still opting for the translation "restrain" for the term *katechon*, scholars propose a number of new identifications for this figure, whether the preaching of the gospel as a restraining principle and Paul particularly as providing the personal element or God as the one who restrains while the community experiences its suffering as a sure sign of divine retributive justice. Others identify the *katechon* as a satanic agent (even the lawless one) and opt for the meaning "having mastery or control." Another option is to interpret the term as referring to prophetic activity (prophetic seizure) to characterize this figure as hostile to God, and to identify it as a false prophet whose removal is a precondition for the coming of the Lord's day. Finally, others claim to perceive in some Semitic or LXX passage (whether Isa 66:9 or Hab 2:3) the clue to postulate God in some way as the cause for delay of the end. Each of these proposals encounters extensive criticism and invites the present interpreter to reexamine the issue in view of the traditional identification proposed at least as early as the time of Tertullian.

The translation given above of verses 6-7 assumes that the term means "hold back or restrain," a meaning read by the early Church Fathers (see Tertullian, *On the Resurrection of the Body* 24 and Chrysostom, *2 Thessalonians: Homily* 4) and by the majority of modern scholars (BAGD 422.1a); it is important to note that a Greek writer such as Chrysostom understood the term to mean "restrain." What immediately comes to mind in considering this view is that, by appealing to the Roman Empire and its personal agent the emperor, one accounts for the use of both the neuter and masculine participial forms. Crucial to such a theory, however, is the perception scholars have of the author's attitude toward the Roman Empire and its culture. Thus, appeal is made, while presuming Pauline authorship, to Paul's concern for the preaching of the good news throughout the Roman Empire. For him, it is claimed, the greatest benefaction to be derived from such an established governmental system is the potential for evangelization. Besides, the Empire was a welcome curb to rampant evil and unjust persecution. Others object, however, that Paul was not an enthusiast for civil law and religion but, Rom 13:1-7 notwithstanding, a severe critic of the powers of this world. Also, Paul would see Rome not as benefactor but enemy of the Christian community. Also, it is objected that Paul employs not political and legal but apocalyptic imagery.

Initially, it must be stated that the issue is not Paul and his alleged historical context but the accepted theory of statecraft. Often discussion focuses on whether Paul had a positive view of government as protector of the Christian community or a negative perception of the Empire as cohort of the lawless one. Whether Paul or a Paulinist is author of this letter, the issue revolves around the role the author of the document sees the government or restrainer playing in the scenario of chapter 2.

(1) Statecraft or the Role of Government. As heirs to the Hasmonean traditions and those of Hebrew wisdom, the Jews of the Diaspora and their Christian heirs looked on governing authorities with respect, for they subscribed to Prov 24:21: "my son, fear the Lord and the king, and do not disobey either of them." In fact, Wisdom 6:1-4, would serve as a charter, for judgment is threatened and wisdom is counseled:

> Hear therefore, O kings, and understand; learn, you that judge the ends of the earth; be attentive, you that rule the people and glory in the multitude of nations, for power is given to you by the Lord and sovereignty by the Most High, who shall examine your works and search out your counsels, because, being ministers of his kingdom, you have not judged properly, nor kept the Law, nor walked according to the counsel of God.

Many such statements are forthcoming from writers of the period, whether Josephus, Philo, Aristeas, or other intertestamental works. Such a theory of government is presupposed both by Paul in Rom 13:1-7 and by the author of 1 Pet 2:13-17. These texts fit well in this tradition, for they presume that there is no authority except that which comes from God, that these rulers are subject to God's judgment, and that these are servants of the kingdom and work for its good. In no way are they possessors of the kingdom and it is presumed that they are responsible for wise and just government.

On the one hand, government provides a harmonious structure. Thus, submission to government institutions means living within divinely established world order ("instituted by God") and resistance to these structures implies rebellion against "what God appointed" (Rom 13:1-2). Order or chaos, these were the alternatives for people of the Greco-Roman world. Indeed, Vergil when describing Aeneas in life-threatening storms at sea, employs terms that evoke chaos; also the *pax romana* of Augustus is said to be a divinely established victory over chaos. Thus, even Greek Jews and Christians could easily relate to such a concept of state since in their minds the king or authorities were servants of God who had to do God's bidding or suffer the consequences. On the other hand, a major function of governmental authority, in the words of First Peter, was "to punish those who do wrong and to praise those who do right" (2:14; see also Rom 13:3-4). This function of authority was both negative and positive. Thus, only the evil person had reason to fear; the good was to expect approval and freedom of action. So government acted as a curb on the forces of evil and chaos.

(2) Roman Empire and Emperor as "Restrainer." While Paul and First Peter employ a topos about governing powers to provide rationale for their exhortations (for the former, the payment of taxes and for the latter, the doing of good despite maltreatment), the present author, presuming a similar, beneficent role for government, appeals to this role to modify the end-time scenario in addressing the community's apocalyptic fervor. In assuming that the end-day scenario was speeding toward the cataclysmic battle between the forces of good and evil, the addressees had to presume that primordial chaos was exerting itself. To counter this notion the author formulates the concept of the restrainer, a force powerful and personal which keeps the lawless, satanic power of evil at bay. Like Mark 13:7-8, the author insists that the time of apocalyptic turmoil is yet to come. But unlike Mark who posits mission as delaying factor (13:10; but see 3:1), this author notes that the institutions of government are playing their role in imposing order over the forces of chaos, but only until the appointed time of their manifestation. In this way the exaggerated apocalyptic notions of the addressees are countered by use of traditional political theory. The end will come when the forces of chaos overcome the forces of order or, as stated in 2:7b, "when the restrainer is gone." Then the lawless one will indulge in satanic activity to entice those who believe. Order, the author insists, reigns supreme, not chaos; thus the lawless one is being kept at bay by divinely established institutions.

Furthermore, the forces of order continue to be a curb on evil, even the satanic forces of lawlessness, and provide respite for those who do good. To account for the community's afflictions the author formulates what appears to be a neologism: "the mystery of lawlessness." This expression and its context might be paraphrased: "certainly, evil or lawlessness in a secretive or surreptitious way is already at work among you." Thus, the evils of everyday life or even those of particularly trying times, which the community mistakes for the end-time woes, are not signs of the end-time, though they participate in a surreptitious way in satanic activity. These serious (for the addressees) afflictions and persecutions are nonetheless temporary and a pale comparison of the events accompanying the apocalypse of the lawless one.

The restrainer then can hardly be God, since it must "be removed or taken out of the way" nor does it represent a grandiose concept of the Pauline mission to the Gentile world. Instead, the restrainer, both as an impersonal and a personal entity, is related to the forces of order and antithetic to everything that the lawless one represents. It is, moreover, a beneficent force that keeps evil at bay. Like other NT writers, that of 2 Thessalonians looks on governmental institutions as divinely ordained and having a cosmic function. Among these is the restraining of the forces of chaos which were to emerge as part of the end-time scenario. Even in the minds of the apocalypticist addressees it could appear as a beneficent force whose activity lessened the afflictions of the present by keeping the lawless one away.

INTERPRETATION

Following upon the long thanksgiving period about the community's success and the additional reassurance regarding divine vengeance on those who afflict the addressees (1:3-12), the author introduces more directly the major issue of concern, the alleged arrival of the Lord's day. After introducing this theme the author offers several considerations to convince the readers that the end is not yet, especially the nonarrival of the evil figure of the end-days. When that figure, called the lawless one, is revealed there will be clear signs of satanic activity and apostasy; what is now discernible, expressed as "the mystery of lawlessness," is far less ominous. This section, nonetheless, offers a challenge to the reader who is obliged to grapple with the text's style and structure, the community's situation, and the author's strategy in dealing with that situation.

Style, Structure, and Paulinist Character of Body-Opening. Chapter 2 begins on a paraenetic note: "we urge you, brothers and sisters . . . not to . . ." (v. 1) and the author pursues this objective later in verse 3: "let no one deceive you. . . ." This, however, is the extent of its paraenetic character and tone. While it is the author's goal to dissuade the audience from believing that "the Lord's day has come," it is nonetheless not exhortation which is paramount but a logical restatement of the community's eschatological tradition. Thus, the pericope consists of a long introductory sentence which states the topic of discussion and the source of the problem within the community. In attempting to convince them not to be led astray, the author begins a demonstration of why the Lord's day has not arrived, namely, several events must precede the coming of the Lord Jesus from heaven. The author, intent on describing the lawless one and its activity, fails to complete the sentence and is led to resume the train of thought by means of a rhetorical question in verse 5, "do you not remember. . . ." After introducing the concept of "the restrainer" as the reason for the delay of the lawless one's coming, the author resumes discussion of that figure's activity in verse 8. The passage ends with a concluding statement (see also 1:5f.) regarding the certainty of divine condemnation of unbelievers and evildoers (vv. 11-12). In less-than-elegant style then, the author focuses on the crucial evidence for the conclusion that the Lord Jesus' return is yet to come, namely, the antecedent arrival and show of satanic power by the lawless one.

This new section of the letter, serving as a transition from the involved thanksgiving of 1:3-12, functions as body-opening, a fact which is borne out by the focus on the topic of discussion and by the direct address of the audience. Further, the tone of the passage is set by the author's use of exhortation to underscore the urgency of the situation and of eschatological imagery to combat apocalyptic fervor. Thus, the letter shifts from a focus in chapter one on the community's suffering and desire for divine judgment to an extended discussion of the author's principal concerns: the community's apocalyptic stance and its consequences. There is also in this opening a reference to the causes for this disinformation and a reassurance that all will be well since the readers already know the traditional eschatological doctrine (v. 5) concerning "the restrainer" and "the mystery of lawlessness" (vv. 6-7) and how these fit into the Christian scenario for the end-days.

This pericope offers a number of Paulinist features, even though the borrowing from 1 Thessalonians is minimal. The author begins the body of the letter with the term "we urge or beg" (the introductory formula is borrowed verbatim from 1 Thess 5:12), a term which in 1 Thess 4:1; 5:12 (see also Phil 4:3) comes at the end of Paul's missives and introduces concluding paraenesis, not the body of the letter as here. Also, topics of discussion, especially in response to questions (1 Thess 4:9, 13; 5:1; also 1 Cor 7:1ff.) are introduced in Paul by *peri*, not *hyper*, with the genitive. Also, verse 5 ("do you not remember that while I was still with you, I often told you these things?") has a striking resemblance to 1 Thess 3:4 ("when we were with you, we often warned you"—see also 2:9 where the verbal expression "you remember" is used). One should note, however, the Paulinist writer's switch, in pseudepigraphic fashion, from "we" to "I." While the term *parousia* is borrowed from 1 Thessalonians (2:19; 3:13; 4:15; 5:23), where it relates to Jesus' role as judge of believers, its use by this author is focused on Jesus' military role vis-à-vis the lawless one (2:1, 8), the coming of that figure (2:9), and complemented by the term "revelation" for both figures (1:7; 2:3, 6, 8). Further, Paul's treatment of "the Lord's day" in 1 Thess 5:2 concerns its sudden coming and the readiness required of believers; while for this author the interest is in the end-time scenario and the conflict between Jesus and the lawless one. Beyond these similarities there are few contacts between this passage and Paul's treatment of eschatological themes in 1 Thess 4:13–5:11. In general terms, one might say that Paul is concerned about helping his readers confront the problems encountered in view of the Lord's imminent coming and that the Paulinist author is dedicated to showing an apocalypticist readership that the end is not yet and that it is misreading the signs of the times.

Situation of Community. From a careful reading of the letter one is able to discern the general contours of the community's situation. (1) Persecutions and afflictions. In 1:4 the author refers to "the persecutions and afflictions" which the community is enduring and so praises its endurance and fidelity in times of hardship. While it is impossible to reconstruct the social context which brought this about, it is nonetheless possible to get some idea about these afflictions and how they contributed to the addressees' impression that the end-time was at hand or that the process had begun. The terms used, *diōgos* and *thlipsis*, both in non-Pauline usage and employed in tandem, suggest external pressure on or maltreatment of the community's members by outsiders (see 1:4). While in the Pauline context the latter term requires the meaning "present difficulties" (see discussion of 1 Thess 3:3) and refers to the converts' adoption of a new value system with consequent socioreligious ostracization (the Christians' "appointed lot"), in the present context the meaning is not as easily discerned.

One is obliged to deduce the meaning of these two terms from their context and other data within the letter testifying to the community's situation. The addressees are said to have successfully resisted these difficulties to the extent of being an exemplary community (vv. 3-4) and to the point that their endurance contributes to God making them worthy (v. 5); indeed, they suffer for God's kingdom. The author insists, however, that this affliction will have some resemblance to the divine affliction which the oppressors will receive (6) as they pay the penalty of eternal ruin (8-9). Also adding to the seriousness of the situation is the fact that these difficulties have been interpreted as the turmoil of the end-days (see also 3:2-3). The author's insistence, nonetheless, in 2:7 and 9 that these difficulties represent the hidden, pre-apocalyptic activity of lawlessness points to a situation wherein the addressees are undergoing the prosecutorial effects of being a foreign, outlawed religion much as one sees in Heb 10:32-39. On the one hand, one must sense the seriousness of the situation, whether the public humiliation and prosecution which led some to perceive the messianic woes or which led others to apostasy. On the other, one sees how stark a picture the author draws of the real messianic difficulties and how the community's "persecutions and afflictions" are portrayed as less-than-ominous end-time signs.

(2) Apocalyptic Speculation and Fervor. It is difficult to say which came first: whether some within the community saw their hardships in light of traditional Christian eschatological teaching and the early sense of an imminent return of the Lord Jesus or whether the community was in-

fluenced by apocalyptic preachers. But it is clear from the beginning of chapter two that the author considers the problem as issuing from a variety of sources within the community, whether from spirit-inspired utterances of visionaries, the more extensive preaching or interpretations of apocalyptic preachers, and even a supporting apocalyptic document alleged to be from Paul (2:2). The community is put on its guard against these influences for it is warned, in apocalyptic language, against being "so easily shaken in mind" or "repeatedly disturbed." The impression one gets is that the community itself or some of its members would be more balanced were it not for these nefarious influences. The author's goal, in combating apocalyptic preaching and fervor, is to convince the community's members that the Lord's day has not yet arrived.

Community's Apocalyptic Beliefs (2:1-2). Beyond the author's insistence that the community is well acquainted with the concept of the restrainer, one is led to seek the addressees' apocalyptic conclusions in the opening verses of the chapter. The introductory sentence lends some intriguing insights to the issue of the community's beliefs. The author suggests that in discussions of Jesus' coming and the reception to be accorded him the community is to avoid the conclusion "that the Lord's day has come." Indeed, the author insists, it is owing to apocalyptic fervor that the addressees have abandoned their balanced views regarding the end-time. What therefore are the concepts which the hearers have abandoned and those which they have adopted in so facile a fashion?

(1) The Lord's Day. It is stated at the end of verse 2 that members of the community, as a result of apocalyptic preaching and interpretation of its severe afflictions, have concluded that the Lord's day has arrived. The author employs the traditional formula for the time when divine judgment is supposed to occur (see 1 Thess 5:2). Scholars have expressed some hesitation regarding the interpretation of that clause, arguing either that *enestēken* means "about to occur or take place" or that the community postulated a spiritualized resurrection in a Gnostic sense. Both views are rejected, the first on linguistic grounds since the verb cannot bear such a meaning and the second on the logical premise that the episode would not have been an issue since not only the Lord's day but the Lord's return as well would have been spiritualized. Clearly, a solution to the obvious objection that the Lord had not yet returned depends on the relationship one sees between the Lord's day and Jesus' return and also on the understanding the community had of the former.

One notes from verses 1-2 that the author draws a distinction between the Lord Jesus' coming and the Lord's day. The latter is the general concept, the term that encompasses the entire apocalyptic scenario; the Lord Jesus' *parousia* is the final major event of the process. Presumably, the community believes that the initial stage of the process, the coming of the evil one, has begun, that its afflictions are evidence of that process, and that the next stage, Jesus' arrival, is about to occur.

(2) The Traditional Apocalyptic Scenario. The community and author presume a standard schema for the end-time, a schema which can be viewed from two angles, either that of reading the signs of the times or that of the process' principal stages. In the first case, a variety of natural and cosmic signs such as wars, earthquakes, and famines, along with the activity of false prophets and messiahs and the ominous participation of the celestial bodies (Mark 13:5-8, 21-22, 24-25; 4 Ezra 5:1-13; 6:11-28; 9:1-12) will announce the coming of the Son of Man or Messiah as warrior and judge. In the second case, it is assumed that the end-time scenario has two principal stages, first that of the reign of evil and chaos (the time of temptation, apostasy, and rampant immorality) and then the time of the parousia when the Lord or some otherworldly figure comes with a band of holy ones to do battle with the forces of evil and to act as judge of the righteous and unrighteous. The latter is presumed by the authors of 2 Thessalonians, Revelation, and Daniel.

In light of such a scenario one understands the author's presentation of the community's beliefs. Owing to the severity of its difficulties and to the apocalyptic fervor resulting from the preaching there, the addressees have come to the conclusion that they are witnessing the first stage of the scenario—the Lord's day has come or is in process.

(3) Culmination of Process (2:1b). The careful examination of this document allows the reader to perceive the importance of crucial points. In chapter one the addressees' sufferings and desire for divine judgment are an obvious concern as the author speaks of Jesus' return. A second important consideration is the conclusion the community has drawn from its apocalyptic interpretation of its own experience with evil, namely, that the Lord's day has dawned. These points, however, only serve to underscore an even more basic concern of the community. Presumably, the community spends much of its time discussing the Lord's coming and it is in this context that the apocalyptic fervor of some has led the addressees, far too readily, to conclude that the first stage of the Lord's day has begun. The author does not oppose this concern about the Lord Jesus' coming, only the conclusion that the twofold process has begun.

Author's Strategy. The letter is not about the community's beliefs but about the author's attempt to disabuse it of the conclusion that the Lord's day is rapidly unfolding. To that effect the author employs several approaches. (1) Initially there is an appeal to avoid apocalyptic enthusiasm and a warning against succumbing to various disturbing influences. In the first case, the author employs the apocalyptic theme of end-time disturbances (Mark 13:5-6, 22) to characterize the emotional tone of the community's deliberations. The terminology reflects on the author's strategy. The expression "shaken in mind" suggests a change in the community's formerly balanced approach to eschatological matters, while the adverbial modifier "so easily" suggests that this change in perspective came about in a less-than-considered fashion. The second verb "disturbed" points to a continued process (translation of the present tense by "repeatedly") and one which is highly emotional and unstable.

In the second case, the author warns against a variety of unsettling influences. Clearly there is opposition between the writer and the sources of apocalyptic influence. First, they are listed as spirit-inspired utterances, apocalyptic preaching, and an alleged Pauline document, and then in a more global way as people who "deceive you in any way." The objective of this warning is to counteract the conclusion drawn and to prepare the readers to listen to a logically presented denial that the process they call the Lord's day has begun to unfold.

A final note is in order here concerning the "letter allegedly by us." There is discussion concerning the provenance and content of such a letter. Some, in the context of Pauline authorship, either conclude or object that such a document might be pseudonymous. Others, while insisting on pseudonymity, consider the letter as either an attack against the Pauline 1 Thessalonians and its eschatology or a document produced by the apocalyptic teachers to bolster their argument that the Lord's day has arrived. Other references in 2 Thessalonians, particularly 2:15 and 3:17, and the overall tone and interpretation of the document suggest to me that the last mentioned is the more acceptable. Also, the author's reverential use of Paul's letter as a model and source of themes argues against considering the "letter allegedly by us" as being an attack against it.

(2) Another means used to counteract the community's apocalyptic conclusion is an appeal, in Paulinist fashion (see 1 Thess 3:4), to past teaching: "do you not remember that while I was still with you I often told you these things" (v. 5). This is a rhetorical convention; in appealing to past, traditional teaching one bolsters one's present argument. While verse 5 is directly employed to defend the theme of the restrainer in verses 6-7, the technique, following directly on the author's insistence that the lawless one has not yet been revealed, refers the community back to its balanced perspective prior to its being "shaken in mind." Further, the author in other parts of the letter underscores traditional teaching as the basis for present conclusions; see 1:10; 2:14-15; 3:1, 4, 6.

(3) Proposal of a Modified Scenario. Beyond situating the audience within the letter's perspective, the author sets out to reinterpret the traditional apocalyptic schema. The community agrees that first the age of evil will be in full force and secondly that this era will be followed and brought

to an end by the arrival of the Lord Jesus from heaven. Thus, the author sets up the following modified scenario to address the issue of the Lord's day and its relation to the community's situation.

[1] time of the "mystery of lawlessness"
   and of the restrainer
[2] revelation and activity of the lawless one
   and the apostasy
[3] revelation or coming of the Lord Jesus.

The community readily accepts the last two stages but interprets its afflictions as indicating that the age of evil is in full force. Instead the author argues that the community and its contemporaries should, in more balanced fashion, situate their difficulties in stage one and as representing God's testing of their endurance and faith (1:4-5).

Description of the Lord's Coming (3). The final stage of the scenario involves the Lord Jesus' *parousia* or *apocalypsis* (2:1 and 1:7). The community agrees on the basics for this discussion for it is the subject of its deliberations. As noted earlier, the community has not concluded that the Lord Jesus has returned but that the scenario of the Lord's day is in progress and that the Lord's return, as part of this process, is imminent. There is also speculation about "gathering" for his coming. While many presume, following 1 Thess 4:17, that the goal of this assembly is the joining in procession with the Lord to a heavenly abode, the Greek text does not support such a conclusion. Instead, one should view *ep' auton,* as related to the law-courts and as meaning "before him," and thus paraphrase the whole as "gathering together to appear before the Lord Jesus who returns as judge of good and evil." Such a conclusion supports the author's constant attempt to lead the community away from exclusively apocalyptic concerns to a more traditional view of the Christ-event; in this case not just vengeance toward oppressors but also punishment of evildoers as further motivation for Christian commitment.

How then does the author present Jesus' coming? Several passages offer the reader some interesting details: 1:7-8, 10; and 2:8. In a discussion of "God's just judgment" of the community's oppressors, the author insists that their punishment ("repayment with affliction"—1:6) will occur "when the Lord Jesus is revealed from heaven" (v. 7). One notes the unambiguous appeal to and development of the Christian story that Jesus will be coming from his heavenly abode (see 1 Thess 1:10; 4:16; Mark 13:16; 14:62) to assume his end-time messianic role. In a passage designed for apocalypticist readers, the author employs the military imagery of Isa 66:15 to describe Jesus' descent: "with the angels of his power in a fire of flame." Undoubtedly, the author intends a fully apocalyptic description of Jesus' return as warrior accompanied by a heavenly host that does his bidding. Even the fire imagery suggests the nondescribed battle of the end-days, in the way Isa 66:15 had imagined the Lord's fiery coming with chariots to do vengeance "in a fire of flame," the divine instrument of both war and judgment. The Lord's coming will be a time of affliction for all evildoers, both nonbelievers (especially the persecutors) and other lovers of evil (see Notes on vv. 8, 11; and 2:12).

The author gives further detail for this end-time scenario by referring to the Lord Jesus' battle against the lawless one. Less interested in the conflict than in its resolution, the author simply describes the evil one of the end-days as the one "whom the Lord Jesus will destroy with the breath of his mouth and render powerless by the manifestation of his coming" (2:8). The first part of the statement contains imagery borrowed ostensibly from Isa 11:4 and consistent with the messianic imagery employed in 4 Ezra 13 for the vision of "the Man from the Sea" who comes "with the clouds of heaven" not with the standard weapons of war but "a flaming breath" to do battle against the multitudes gathered for war (13:3, 8, 10-11; see also PssSol 17:23-24, 34). In this case it is the evil leader who is the focus of the author's attention, for in this figure is personalized the evils being endured by the community at present and those represented by the turmoil of the end-days (see 2 Bar 39:7–40:4). The Lord Jesus comes to put an end to the reign of evil. While some focus on the term *anaireō* to insist on a personal battle whereby the Lord Jesus "slays" an anti-Christ figure and on the following, but parallel verb *katargeō*, to underscore the annihilation of that figure, it is best to envision a development of the traditional apocalyptic scenario. The Lord Jesus defeats, renders powerless, and punishes the lawless one (see Rev 20:1f.). The author's objective is to insist on the ultimate victory of the forces of good, the punishment of evil, and the reward of the righteous, a victorious outcome further stressed by the use of graphic images: "breath of his mouth" and "epiphany or manifestation of his coming."

Two additional passages relate to the final stage of the scenario, 1:10 which describes the reaction to the Lord's arrival and 1:9 which pertains to the reward of the righteous. In the first case the Lord Jesus, presumably following the final conflict, is awarded glory by the accompanying angelic host and is received in wonderment by all believers (1:10a and b). The theme of end-time glory and wonderment (the second employed only here and as a synonym of glory) is of interest for the apocalyptic scenario and for the author's strategy. Glory is, first of all, an eschatological reality since the ultimate goal of divine choice is the believer's reception of "our Lord Jesus Christ's glory" (2:14; see 1:9 for the reverse situation for the unrighteous). Thus, when he comes, the assembled heavenly and earthly host will reciprocate by glorifying and standing in awe of the returning Lord of glory. There is no mention of the presence of the unrighteous either for final recognition (as in Mark 13:26; Matt 24:30; Luke 21:27) or for judgment (as in Rev 20:11-15), because their fate is mentioned in the previous verse. On the present aspect of "glory" see discussion below of the first stage of the modified scenario.

In the second case (1:9) the author focuses attention on the fate of the unrighteous. What begins in verse 6 as an indictment of the community's oppressors becomes an eschatological judgment of all unbelievers and wrongdoers (v. 8), who will pay the divinely determined penalty, described as "eternal ruin." The author explains this punishment by means of a parallel *apo* construction; the unrighteous will be separated, on the one hand, "from the Lord's presence" and, on the other, "from the glory of his power." In the first instance, being in the Lord's presence, much as in Paul (1 Thess 4:17; 5:10), is the equivalent of receiving his glory; the unrighteous will be eternally deprived of this ultimate blessing. In the second instance, a new theme is proposed, one which addresses the community's situation. Employing the theme of glory the author suggests that evil people, particularly the persecutors, who seemingly have the upper hand, will experience a reversal of roles in the final judgment when they will be deprived of the Lord's glorious and mighty presence.

The description then of the Lord's coming corresponds to the traditional scenario found in Jewish works of the intertestamental period (Psalms of Solomon, 2 Baruch, and 4 Ezra) and early Christian tradition (Mark 13 par.; 1 Thessalonians 4-5; Revelation) of the messianic figure of the end-days who comes to bestow divine justice on good and evil and to reestablish God's rule. His functions are consistent with those ascribed to the warrior-judge who comes on the clouds with an angelic host, engages the evil one whom he defeats, renders powerless, and punishes along with the other participants in the final battle. More importantly, he acts as judge who inflicts punishment on evildoers and rewards the righteous by bestowing his glory, power, and presence on them. In this case nothing is said about a paradisiac existence; but life after death, whether of eternal ruin or glorious presence, is presumed.

Apocalypse, Description, and Activity of the Lawless One (2). Prior to the Lord Jesus' coming is a stage marked by the flowering of evil, itself initiated by the coming of a false-messiah figure who is an ally of Satan. To prove that this period has not begun or that the Lord's day is not yet dawning, the author in verse 3 presents two unrealized signs: the arrival of a figure called "the lawless one" and a phenomenon labeled "the apostasy." The author insists: the Lord's day will not come until these two events occur. As one reads further, there is the realization that these two occurrences form part of a stage prior to the Lord's coming and that the second sign initiates this period of evil while the first, the apostasy, is a result of the lawless one's activity.

(1) The Coming or Revelation of the Lawless One. While the term *parousia* or "coming" is employed to describe the evil one's arrival (2:9), as a parallel to the usage for Jesus' arrival, it is nonetheless the verb "to reveal" *(apokalyptō)* which is used to introduce this figure (2:3) and repeatedly in the following discussion (vv. 6, 8; see also use of the noun to express Jesus' coming in 1:7). Several reasons may be given for this choice. [1] The term "revelation" is traditional for expressing the arrival of the Messiah (see Notes on 1:7), so its use also for the evil figure of the end-days, like that of *parousia* in 2:9, signals its anti-Christ function. [2] The choice relates to the author's diplomatic use of language since such usage allows for an explanation of the audience's misreading of the signs of the time. The recognition of the lawless one is a matter of recognition of a figure whose identity will not be immediately discernible. Their error is understandable since they are forgetting some of what they have been taught (2:3, 5-6, 15). [3] There is in verse 6 a clear indication that the term "revelation" reflects its more traditional use in referring to the divine plan and its eschatological disclosure and interpretation. [4] More importantly, the choice indicates the author's attempt to convince the addressees that their afflictions, though serious, are not a sign of the messianic woes, but a foretaste and mysterious indication of the work of that evil figure that is yet to come.

Finally, it should be noted that the coming of the evil one is not a matter of human doing but will happen according to the divine timetable or at "the appointed time." This is what the community has learned from its apostolic tradition (2:5; see Mark 13:32). It is only at the appointed time that the scenario for the Lord's day will begin to play itself out.

(2) Description of the Lawless One. The series of descriptive statements about the end-time figure is an interesting one. First, in verses 3 and 8 the author characterizes it by the terms *anomia* or *anomos*. The first involves the Semitic construction "the person of lawlessness" and the second simply calls it "the lawless one." Presumably, the author is referring to the individual not as a Gentile (see 1 Cor 9:21) but as one who opposes all semblance of law, order, and goodness (see Psalms of Solomon 17 where Pompey is thus characterized). Verse 4 then presents a series of activities which provide content for the title "the lawless one": one who rebels against divinely established order, who aspires to divine status and even attempts to usurp God's position and power. These activities are treated as they reflect on the figure's principal title, the lawless one.

Additionally, in verse 4 the lawless one is characterized, in Semitic idiom once more (lit.: "the person or son of destruction"), as "the one destined for destruction." From the outset, the author insists on the terrible figure's ultimate destiny. In a similar way, after reintroducing the lawless one in verse 8, following a parenthetical discourse on the role of the restrainer, the author again dwells on the fate of that hapless end-time figure by describing its defeat by the returning Lord Jesus. The lawless one is assured a fate of destruction and powerlessness after a graphic encounter with the warlike Jesus who destroys its satanic power by his fiery breath and resplendent appearance.

(3) End-time Satanic Activity. Starkly expressed, the lawless one's activity is said to be characterized by Satan's energy or power. See verses 7, 8, 9, and 11 where various aspects of evil activity (whether work, power, activity, or powerlessness) are described by the root *ergon* ("work"). The end-days will witness the full brunt of evil as the forces of wickedness are allowed to exercise their power. Evil, as personified in the lawless one, will employ all manner of deceit to entice believers and nonbelievers to the love of wickedness. It will, in anti-Christ fashion, perform miraculous deeds to gain followers or, in the author's words, to deceive "those on the road to ruin." Thus, verses 9-10 describe the activity which relates to the human realm.

Earlier in verse 4, the reader is given a description of the lawless one's activity as it relates to the otherworldly realm. Like other end-time figures of apocalyptic literature, it declares its opposition to the entire divine realm. It opposes the true God and, like Antiochus (Dan 11:36-39), all semblance of otherworldly power and reverence to the divine order. So perverse is its nature that it claims divine status and, by seizing the heavenly throne, desires to usurp divine power and take God's place.

(4) Background of Lawless One in Apocalyptic Literature and Its Identity. There are in Jewish and early Christian literature a number of figures which serve as models for an understanding of the lawless one of 2 Thess 2:3. The list of evil apocalyptic figures is lengthy: the Hellenistic kings of the Ptolemaic period as models for the evil watchers (1 Enoch 6–16), Antiochus Epiphanes as the personification of evil and chaos (Daniel 6–11), Pompey as the lawless destroyer of Palestine (Psalms of Solomon 2 and 17), and Rome, its empire and emperor either as the evil destroyer of Jerusalem and its Temple (4 Ezra; 2 Baruch) or as demonic persecutor and murderer of the Christian saints (Revelation). In each case an identifiable political situation led to the identification of a specific figure as the end-time personification of evil and provoked an apocalyptic response on the part of a religious community and its author. Attempts therefore to identify the lawless one of 2 Thess 2:3 often focus on such a solution even to the extent of lending to the figure of the restrainer a negative role in the apocalyptic scenario.

Several factors require a reevaluation of the data concerning the identity of the lawless one. [1] Its relation to the Restrainer. It is clear that the lawless one is different from the restrainer of verses 6-7. Further, it seems certain enough that the latter is both neutral as regards the present activity of evil ("the mystery of lawlessness" of v. 7) and independent of the lawless one, acting as an obstacle, not an aid, to its coming. [2] Point of View. Regardless of what the community may have perceived as the satanic or politically connected cause of its difficulties, what one finds in chapter 2 is not the community's but the author's presentation of the traditional apocalyptic scenario. Thus, one should deduce the clues to that figure's identity from what is given in the description. [3] Typological Presentation of Character. One must insist that the figure as presented has no distinct human features; we are dealing with a stylized evil figure drawn from apocalyptic lore, whether from the anti-divine behavior of Antiochus, the lawless description of Pompey, or the early Christian claim that such figures would "produce signs and omens, to lead astray, if possible, the elect" (Mark 13:22). Thus, there is no attempt to provide any characteristic details for identifying this figure as in the various examples given above. The lawless one simply acts like the worst godless figures of apocalyptic tradition.

[4] Apocalyptic Agent of Satanic Power. From the opening verses of chapter two one gets a hint concerning the activity and identity of the lawless one. Just as the focus of the pericope is said to be the Lord's day and the arrival of Jesus as judge ("assembling before him"), so the activity of the lawless one encompasses two areas: opposition to the divine world and power (v. 4) and to all concepts of morality and loyalty (9-10). The anti-God forces will oppose all semblance of divine authority and order through the agency of a godless figure which receives its authority or energy from Satan, the master of evil. As in Revelation 13 (also true of Antiochus as the representative of the forces of chaos: Dan 7:2-3) the human personification of satanic power will attempt to usurp the place and power of God and will try to entice the righteous away from the truth or from adherence to God's ways. Further, the author chooses the term *anomos* ("lawless one") to describe the role of this figure, a role which is characterized as opposition to divine order and law. The lawless one then is a satanic agent which opposes God and the divine plan for human salvation; it is the personification of the forces that oppose God.

(5) Note on the First Sign: the Apostasy (v. 3). It is not only the revelation of the lawless one that is to precede the coming of Jesus but also what the author terms "the apostasy." Scholars debate the meaning of this phenomenon, suggesting that it refers to a worldwide rebellion against divine order, to Jewish rejection of the Christian message, or to the great moral falling away of the end-days. While admitting that the

last mentioned fits best in this apocalyptic context, many still find it puzzling that the apostasy is mentioned before the revelation of the lawless one who is clearly active in enticing believers away from "the love of the truth" (2:10); the apostasy should follow the arrival of its cause.

The order of the two signs offers a clue to the understanding of an issue which permeates the letter. From beginning to end one notices a heightened tone and urgency to the document's exhortation, whether its stress on the growth of the community and inclusion of its members in the end-time reception of Jesus (1:3-4 and 10), the author's exhortation to greater effort (1:11-12; 2:15; 3:4, 6f.), repeated appeals for comfort and strength (1:11; 2:16-17; 3:1-3, 5, 16), and, especially in chapter two, the focus on deception, enticement, road to ruin, nonacceptance of the love of the truth, and even delight in wickedness. One senses that a major issue confronting the community is apostasy or a general lack of moral integrity. The urgency of this moral concern then is underscored by placing the issue of apostasy first and then by devoting the last part of the pericope to immorality as an end-time sign and as a present danger (2:10-12; see Note below on author's strategy).

Time of the Mystery of Lawlessness and of the Restrainer (1). Prior to the arrival of the lawless one and so the beginning of the end-time process, there exists an amorphous period in which the community and its activities are more correctly situated. It is in this time period that the community finds itself. Admitting readily that the afflictions are of concern the author nonetheless insists that they cannot be a sign that the end-time scenario has begun to unfold. Instead, they are a foretaste of satanic activity in the present; they are evidence of lawlessness working in a mysterious but limited way in the lives of believers (see 2:7). It is the same lawlessness, which is now working and enticing, that will erupt on the human scene once its forces are unencumbered.

This period is also characterized by a divinely instituted principle of order, the organs of statecraft which keep the forces of chaos at bay. It is proposed that the Roman Empire and its emperor represent the (neuter and personal) entity that restrains the forces of chaos, personified in the lawless one, from asserting their power over divine order and goodness (see Excursus). As long as the organs of government function properly, i.e., "punishing those who do wrong and praising those who do right" (1 Pet 2:14; also Rom 13:3-4), there is for the Christian a context within which a life of work and of the pursuit of the good is possible (chapter 3). The author of 2 Thessalonians, in fact, manifests a relatively positive attitude toward contemporary culture and the milieu it offers believers, for the addressees are admonished, in the present, to imitate "the constancy of Christ" (3:5—the community's situation) and to "work quietly," "eat their own bread," and "not grow tired of doing what is right" (3:12-13—the readers' ethical concerns).

A Final Note on the Author's Strategy: Those on the Road to Ruin. Much has been said above concerning strategy, particularly the author's desire to convince the community that the Lord's day has not yet arrived. Thus, one finds warnings against disturbing influences (2:1-3), appeal to traditional teaching (5), and proposal of a modified scenario (3-4, 6-10) to counter that false conclusion. As one approaches the end of the pericope, one senses a change in focus from a future, apocalyptic setting to a universal appeal that includes the addressees; see also 1:10 where the addressees are included in the end-time scene of messianic reception.

In verse 9 one encounters the decidedly future activity of the lawless one in its attempt to entice believers and nonbelievers to wickedness. In verse 10, however, one finds the phrase "those on the road to ruin," an idiom which implies that these people are already, prior to satanic inducement, on the path to doom. The origin of this unhappy situation owes to activity or choice that extends to the period prior to the lawless one's coming. The reason given for being "on the road to ruin" ("because they did not accept the love of the truth so as to be saved") though puzzling, confirms this conclusion. The unrighteous are the ones enticed by the evil one; they are the apostates and evildoers of the present, those who accepted the truth but did not possess "the love of the truth." This puzzling phrase might be clarified by Matthean usage that in the end-days there will be an "increase of lawlessness [and] the love of many will grow cold. But the one who endures to the end will be saved" (24:12-13). In both texts the meaning is that a prior commitment has disappeared or weakened so as to make these people susceptible to the activity of the lawless one.

In fact verse 11 leads further in this direction for it is stated that "God sends on them a deceiving power," a passage which stresses the present, continuous, and punishing initiative of God in the lives of the unrighteous (*TDNT* 6:249). The concept of a "deceiving power" or divine inducement to further error is not uncommon, whether the hardening of Israel (Rom 11:7, 25), the darkening of the mind (Mark 4:11-12), the refusal to repent (Rev 9:20-21; 16:9, 11), or God's giving up unbelievers to further depravity (Rom 1:24, 26, 28)—interestingly, these examples concern divine activity in the present. This "deceiving power" is sent "to make them [those who do not "love the truth"] believe the deception" or lawlessness, a deception that affects believers and all who "delight in wickedness" (2 Thess 2:12).

Thus, the author's strategy is to stress that those on "the road to ruin," whether nonbelievers, apostates or Christian doers of evil, will be most susceptible to the satanic (deceptive and enticing) activity of the lawless one. Additionally, since the present period is subject, at least minimally, to "the mystery of lawlessness," humans are even now exposed to the deception of lawlessness. Beyond that, God already sends on the ungodly "a deceiving power" that punishes sin with further sin.

The author's strategy then in combating apocalyptic fervor and the lack of moral integrity in the community involves a complex list of means. A final and effective one should be noted in guise of a conclusion. As the community has been insistently warned about being "so easily shaken in mind" or moved to its foundation (2:2), so it is starkly advised that "those on the road to ruin" are already experiencing condemnation since their refusal of the truth or of the love of the truth makes them blind to the truth itself as God sends a force of delusion over their minds.

For Reference and Further Study

Aus, R. D. "God's Plan and God's Power: Isaiah 66 and the Restraining Factors of 2 Thess 2:6-7." *JBL* 96 (1977) 537–53.

Barnouin, M. "Les problèmes de traduction concernant II Thess ii.6-7." *NTS* 23 (1976–1977) 482–98.

Betz, O. "Das Katechon." *NTS* 9 (1962–1963) 276–91.

Giblin, C. H. *The Threat to Faith: An Exegetical and Theological Re-examination of 2 Thessalonians 2*. Rome: Pontifical Biblical Institute, 1967.

_____. "2 Thessalonians 2 Re-read as Pseudepigraphal: A Revised Re-affirmation of *The Threat of Faith*." *TC*, 459–69.

Hartman, L. "The Eschatology of 2 Thessalonians as Included in a Communication." *TC*, 470–85.

Holland, G. S. "Let No One Deceive You in Any Way: 2 Thessalonians as a Reformulation of the Apocalyptic Tradition." *SBLSP* (1985), 329–41.

Koester, H. "From Paul's Eschatology to the Apocalyptic Schemata of 2 Thessalonians." *TC*, 441–58.

20. *Second Thanksgiving* (2:13-17)

13. We for our part ought to give thanks to God always for you, brothers and sisters, loved by the Lord, because God chose you from the beginning for salvation through sanctification by the Spirit and belief in the truth. 14. That is why then he called you through our gospel, that is, for the attainment of the glory of our Lord Jesus Christ. 15. So then, brothers and sisters, stand firm and hold fast to the traditions which you were taught by us either by word or by letter. 16. Now may our Lord Jesus Christ himself, as also God our Father, who has loved us and through grace given us unfailing comfort and good hope, 17. comfort your hearts and strengthen them in every good work and word.

NOTES

13. *We for our part:* The new section is introduced by *hēmeis de* ("we for our part") and draws a contrast between groups (see 1 Thess 2:17), in this case, signaling a change of focus from the first to the second group. The shift is from those "on the road to ruin" in the previous discussion to the author's appeal in verses 13f. to the community's tradition as the basis for a proper eschatological and moral perspective (vv. 14, 17). Just as 2:1f. appeals to the community to remember its apostolic instruction and not to be shaken in its fundamental convictions, so the author, after describing the fate of those so deceived, now dwells on the basic Christian themes which some have abandoned in their newly found apocalyptic fervor.

ought to give thanks to God always for you, brothers and sisters loved by the Lord: 2 Thessalonians follows the pattern once more of the composite 1 Thessalonians by adding a second thanksgiving, but, contrary to the Pauline document which employs two types of thanksgiving periods (1 Thess 1:2 and 2:13), forms the new structure by borrowing verbatim from its own first thanksgiving (see 1:3). Two changes have been made. (1) The order of the principal verb and infinitive has been changed, owing to the addition of the transitional phrase discussed above. (2) The expression of direct address has been modified by the addition of "loved by the Lord," a phrase borrowed from 1 Thess 1:4: "brothers and sisters loved by God." One should note the change from "God" to "Lord," in 3:3, 16; note 2:16; 3:5.

because God chose you from the beginning for salvation: The reason for thanksgiving, following standard epistolary practice (see 1 Thess 2:13), is expressed by a *hoti* ("because") clause. The reason, as often in Paul though usually employing *kaleō* or related vocabulary (see 1 Thess 1:4), is that of divine election, for which the author uses the rare NT verb *haireomai*. Only here in NT Greek does it refer to election though it is so used in the LXX (see Deut 26:17-18 for God's choice of Israel and Israel's choice of God). The author's insistence on the choice of "you" is in keeping with "giving thanks to God always for you" and with the repeated focus on the audience in verses 14 ("called you"), 15 (imperatives and "you were taught"), and 17 ("your hearts"). The author's concern is less that of the Christian call as it is this particular community and its fidelity to the apostolic teaching; only verse 16 stands outside this perspective. There follows a difficult textual choice, either *ap' archēs* with S D PS *pm* and early versions meaning "from the beginning" or *aparchēn* with B G 33 *al* and early versions having the sense "as first fruits." The reasons given for choosing the second (*TCGNT*, 636-37) are linked to the presumption of authenticity: the first occurs nowhere else in the Pauline corpus, the term *archē* almost always means "power" in Paul, and the term "first fruits" occurs in six other Pauline passages. Also, it is claimed that some MSS alter the second by writing the former. One might object; it is no surprise to find a non-Pauline phrase in a Paulinist writer and it is to be assumed that some copyists would replace the unusual term by the better-known Pauline term and theme of "first fruits." Lastly, as most scholars concede it is difficult if not impossible to find a satisfactory interpretation for the concept in its present context since the Thessalonians, for Paul or for a Paulinist writer, would not be considered the first fruits or converts of Macedonia (see 1 Thess 2:2; Phil 4:15-16). The first expression "from the beginning" fits well into the author's train of thought and will receive further attention below. Finally, the expression translated "for salvation" is a common NT construction (Rom 1:16; 10:1; 2 Tim 3:15; Heb 9:28; 1 Pet 1:5) and a virtual equivalent of "so as to be saved" (2:10) or "for the attainment of salvation" (an expression used by Paul in 1 Thess 5:9 and serving as a model for 2 Thess 2:4: "for the attainment of the glory"). On the concept of "salvation," see 1 Thess 5:9 and comments below.

through sanctification by the Spirit and belief in the truth: To express the means by which salvation is attained the author employs a complex prepositional phrase introduced by *en* with instrumental force ("through or by means of") and governing parallel phrases, each consisting of nouns followed by a second noun in a genitival relation. The first can mean either "sanctification by the Spirit" or "of one's spirit," subjective or objective genitive respectively. The second, functioning as an objective genitive, indicates "faith or belief in the truth" (see 1:12) though it could ostensibly mean "trust in the truth." One could insist on the parallel nature of the construction and treat both as objective genitives, pointing out further that the absence of the article before "spirit" supports the reading "sanctification of spirit." Several factors favor the option taken here, namely, viewing the first as a subjective and the second as an objective genitive. (1) In anthropological terms, the author shows concern for the heart (2:17; 3:5) and mind (2:2) rather than the spirit, soul, and body as in 1 Thess 5:23. (2) In stylistic terms one should point to the analogous situation of 1:11 where genitival constructions also require not parallel but different readings, an objective followed by a subjective genitive. (3) Choice of the reading "sanctification by the Spirit" points to a traditional phrase and theme; the identical idiom occurs in 1 Pet 1:2 in an obvious pneumatological context. Also one expects the author of 2 Thessalonians to appeal to traditional themes which are being ignored. Besides, the two phrases focus first on divine action (see also 1:5, 11 for being "made worthy") and then on the human response to that action.

14. *That is why then:* Interpretation of the verse can go in two different directions depending on how one views the transitional phrase *eis ho kai.* In the first case, one would focus on the preposition *eis* as indicating a resumptive connection between the preceding ("for salvation") and the following ("for the attainment of the glory") *eis* phrases. In this way one would stress the eschatological meaning and goal of salvation in the author's thought. In the second case, one would view the phrase in question as identical to that of 1:11 and similar in meaning and function to it and another phrase in 2:11. The expression would mean "that is why then" and provide a confirmatory or additional reason why the previous statement is true. Such a reading is preferable and affects one's understanding of the author's twofold purpose, that is, stressing present activity and eschatological motivation as addressing and counteracting lax moral behavior and apocalyptic fervor. On the omission of *kai* by some MSS (especially Vaticanus) see notes on 1:2. Also since the identical phrase with *kai* occurs at 1:11 one could argue for scribal conflation but owing to the author's tendency for formulaic repetition, it is better to view the entire idiom as owing to stylistic preference.

he called you through our gospel: In parallel fashion the author in verses 13-14 addresses two facets of the theme of divine election, first employing the non-Pauline term *haereomai* to focus on present activity as it relates to salvation and, in connection with 1 Thess 1:4 ("your election"), the Pauline term *kaleō* to speak of end-time glory as the goal of election. It is debated whether the statement "God called you through our gospel" could have been written by Paul who prefers to treat the theme of election as an exclusively divine activity. There undoubtedly exist passages where Paul presumes a connection between the themes of election and preaching of the good news, but one must admit that he is reluctant to draw a close connection between these owing to the propensity of his communities to allow the fame of the messenger to overshadow the importance of the message. What one finds in 2:14 is a Paulinist reading of 1 Thess 1:4-5: "we . . . are sure of your election, since our gospel came to you . . . in word and . . . in power." It is especially important to view the addition of "through our gospel" (see 1 Thess 1:5 and 3:2) as having an anti-apocalyptic function as it prepares for the author's great insistence on apostolic tradition. The community owes its call to the medium of apostolic preaching and it is now involved in an apocalyptic nightmare because it has forgotten (2:5) or not taken seriously (2:2) that tradition.

that is, for the attainment of the glory of our Lord Jesus Christ: The expression "that is," is added to the translation to facilitate the discernment of the full verbal idiom: "to be called for the purpose of attaining. . . ." The new phrase is patterned on 1 Thess 5:9 "destined . . . for the attainment of salvation through the Lord Jesus Christ." Two changes have occurred. Rather than focus on salvation the author treats salvation (in the community's present context) and adds glory (as future reality) to address the concerns of the addressees. Beyond this, it is not Jesus as means of salvation which is of concern as it was for Paul but his eschatological role and its proper understanding.

15. *So then, brothers and sisters:* The new sentence is introduced by an emphatic inferential coordinating conjunction *ara oun* ("so then"—see 1 Thess 5:6) to stress the connection between the statements about "our gospel" and about traditions received "from us" and to draw an important inference. The latter is expressed by means of two present imperatives, while Paul employs a hortatory subjunctive in 1 Thess 5:6. This pericope is one of two major sections of the letter which not only begin with direct address but also contain a second such feature (see 3:13).

stand firm and hold fast to the traditions: The inference to be drawn is expressed as a double present imperative. The first employs a Pauline term *(stēkō)* whose meaning must usually be determined by its modifying prepositional phrase ("in the Lord," "in one Spirit," "in faith"—1 Thess 3:8; Phil 4:1; 1:27; 1 Cor 16:13) or context (Rom 14:4; Gal 5:1) and in the case of its usage in 1 Thess 3:8 refers to the Lord as the source of the community's strength and fidelity. In the present instance the context is twofold: the following imperative dealing with tradition and the author's earlier comment that the community "has been . . . radically shaken in mind." Thus, "standing firm" relates to the community's situation, that is, resistance to the apocalyptic fervor that has undermined its balanced approach to Christian living (2:2) and return to apostolic teaching (2:5, 15). The second verb, *krateō*, appears elsewhere in the Pauline corpus only in Col 2:19 but is much used in other parts of the NT, either to indicate "taking possession or custody" or "holding back or holding fast to" someone or something. It is in the latter sense that one finds the usage of "observing or being faithful to traditions" (Mark 7:3, 4, 8) or God's will (T.Naphtali 3:1). For this author the issue is that of fidelity to apostolic tradition. The author employs the term *paradosis* ("tradition or teaching"), a term which has both a negative and a positive use in early Christian texts. While in Paul there is a limited but positive use of the term both as related to Jewish (Gal 1:14) and Christian usage (1 Cor 11:2; also frequent use of the verb *paradidōmi*), the concept often receives a negative, polemical nuance and is labeled "human tradition" (Mark 7:3f.; Col 2:8). For this Paulinist writer the term is employed in an entirely positive sense (see also 3:6) and so a synonym for apostolic teaching. In both instances of the term's usage there is a connection made to the alleged apostolic authors who either taught or transmitted the doctrine in question.

which you were taught by us either by word or by letter: A relative clause specifies the source of the teachings being discussed; they are the result of apostolic teaching. The concept of teaching itself (use of *didaskō*) presumes a certain development. While both the verb and noun are employed in Paul to indicate the particular task some within the community had of communicating the tradition (Rom 12:7; 1 Cor 14:6), one often gets a sense of a changing terminology wherein the preaching and general communication of Christian ideas is characterized as teaching (Rom 6:17; 1 Cor 4:17; Gal 1:12). In the present instance the whole process of pastoral care is characterized as a teaching activity, beginning with the oral preaching of the foundation visit and extending to pastoral care given at a distance through correspondence. For these activities the author employs the phrases "by word" and "by letter" (the possessive pronoun modifies the two nouns but for translation's sake is connected to the verbal expression: "taught by us"). While some see here a later development wherein oral and written (or scriptural) traditions are being underscored, it is best to view verse 15 as a direct response to the activity referred to in 2:2. The author proposes that the apostolic tradition in its oral and written form (the letters of Paul) be placed in opposition to the apocalyptic activity of the preachers mentioned earlier. Significantly, all thought of "apocalyptic, ecstatic pronouncements" has been omitted and the community's traditional doctrine called on to invalidate premature conclusions regarding the Lord's day and to prepare for the forthcoming paraenesis regarding work, community life, and "doing what is right."

16. *Now may our Lord Jesus Christ as also God our Father:* The pericope ends with a formal and unusual prayer which borrows its opening and terminology from 1 Thess 3:11. The opening *autos de* ("now . . . himself") functions in the same way as it does in the source but is now applied to the "Lord Jesus Christ" as opposed to "God our Father" in Paul. On the full title "our Lord Jesus Christ" see 1:1-2.

who has loved us: Introduction of "God our Father" leads to an immediate participial qualification, "the one who has loved us . . ."; a second participial phrase, also governed by the initial article, follows. Such a stylistic feature is relatively common in Jewish and Christian prayer, e.g., "Blessed is the Lord, the God of Israel, who alone performs wonders" (Ps 71:18; also 2 Chron 2:12; Eph 1:3-4; 1 Pet 1:3), and allows the author to reintroduce, on a theological level, the theme of election (love) and its benefactions (gift). The theme of love occurs frequently in this document whether for one another (1:3), for the truth (2:10), of the Lord for believers (2:13), or of God for humanity (2:16; 3:5). The author's use of the aorist participle along with the following reference to grace points to God's part in the Christ-event. Love would then refer to election from the beginning and the following development to the way God chose to exhibit that love.

and through grace given us: The expression "through grace" comes at the end of the clause in Greek but is here placed at the beginning to clarify more clearly its function. The term *charis* ("grace") occurs four times, twice in the epistolary opening and closing (1:2; 3:18), as is true of 1 Thess (1:1; 5:28), and at the ends of chapters 1 and 2. Use of the term here recalls its function in 1:12 where it encompasses divine benefaction which makes Christian life possible. Here the term, related as it is to the two participles ("loved" and "given"), suggests "God loved us and so through grace has given us. . . ." Further, use of the aorist participle indicates that the author has the Christ-event in mind and is emphasizing its temporal character and present effect through God's gifts.

unfailing comfort and good hope: The divine benefaction is expressed by means of unusual parallel phrases, whose nouns are nowhere else in the NT employed with the verb "to give" and whose respective adjectives are also peculiar modifiers. The first represents a phrase whose meaning and overall context are hard to determine. The noun *paraklēsis* could mean "encouragement or comfort" and its adjective *aiōnios*, "eternal or unfailing." While it is hard to see what "eternal encouragement" might mean, it is logical, in relation to the cognate verb's usage in the following verse, to opt for "unfailing comfort." Christ's example is an unfailing model of comfort (and encouragement) which the community needs in its afflictions. The second phrase, "good hope," raises some difficulties. Some propose an eschatological context for the idiom and see it as a virtual synonym of the parallel phrase; others, also insisting on this presumed apocalyptic context, point to the expression's use in the mystery cults to designate "life after death." But a number of factors lead the interpreter in a different direction. The author's focus in this short pericope is not on eschatological realities but on a proper approach to Christian life in the present. Thus, the hope that the author speaks of is related to proper behavior which allows an optimistic approach to the future. Such a concept is related to classical Greek usage where idioms such as "good or sweet hope" (use of *agathos, kalos, glykeios,* or *eu-*) underscore the relation between good moral behavior and the optimism which then accompanies a person in life. Perhaps the *textus classicus* for this concept is Plato, *Republic* 1.331a where the righteous person ("one conscious of no wrong") is said to have "sweet and good hope as an attendant, like a nurse in old age"; Plato then proceeds to cite Pindar (Fragment 214) to the effect that such hope "cheers the heart . . . (and) rules the ever-changing human mind" (Pindar, *Isthmian Odes* 8.15; Plato, *Laws* 4.718a; Aelius Aristides, *Oration* 48.28; see *TDNT* 2:518). The expression "good hope" then is a contemporary idiom which stresses the relationship of good, responsible behavior to its optimistic effect on one's perception of the future. For this author it is God who, through the grace which is the Christ-event, has given believers the basis for a firm and sure hope, a good hope that spells optimism in the world rather than the pessimism of an apocalyptic vision and inspires "good work and word."

17. *comfort your hearts and strengthen them in every good work and word:* After the parenthetical description of God's loving benefactions, the author completes the prayer begun in the previous verse by following closely the model of 1 Thess 3:11, even to the extent of employing a singular aorist optative verbal complement. Like its model this text focuses on the role played by the initial subject who, like and along with the Father, is called upon to "comfort your hearts." Again the root *parakaleō* is used and, in its present context as relating to "hearts" (on "heart" as meaning inner being, see 1 Thess 2:17) and "good works and words," means "comfort" rather than "encourage." As God through grace has given believers a source of "unfailing comfort," so now the author prays that the Lord Jesus himself may actualize this consolation in the addressees' daily lives. Also, there is a further request that the Lord "strengthen (these hearts) in every good work and word." The author

employs a term from the Pauline model (1 Thess 3:2, 13) but gives the term *stērizō* a slightly different nuance, no longer that of "establishing" but of "strengthening" or "bringing to fruition their every desire for goodness" (1:11); see similar usage of *stērizō* in 3:3. Finally, the form of the expression "in every good work and word" emphasizes its generic sense of total human behavior (see also 1:11; 2:12; 3:13).

INTERPRETATION

The author makes a new appeal to the addressees that they reconsider their loyalty to the apostolic tradition in contrast to their hasty capitulation to questionable apocalyptic fervor. Still employing 1 Thessalonians as model, the author uses its second thanksgiving structure to appeal to the basic Pauline concept of divine election as a means of bolstering apostolic tradition and providing an anti-apocalyptic interpretation of the addressees' situation. In this way the community's overly realized eschatology and less-than-laudable behavior are addressed in the framework of traditional Christian eschatology and moral teaching.

Source and Structure of 2:13-17. While some insist that all of chapter two (owing to a seeming inclusio involving 2:2 and 15 regarding "word and letter") or 2:1–3:5 (as devoted from beginning to end to the community's situation) belong to a single movement of thought, it is advisable to postulate in 2:13-17 a new but related movement in the letter's development. From the outset one is obliged to acknowledge a number of rhetorical features. This pericope, as is true throughout the document, is marked by a formula of direct address (see 1:3; 2:1; 2:13; 3:1; 3:6—only the epistolary opening and closing lack this). Additionally, any serious consideration of the structure of the document must acknowledge the presence of the second thanksgiving formula as more than an incidental feature; such a characteristic is due to the author's use and purpose for use of the source. Beyond this, there is a shift in thought at the end of 2:1-12, where the author focuses on those "on the road to ruin" as the result of the abandonment of apostolic teaching and in 2:13f., where the emphatic formula "we for our part" is employed to direct discussion to the source, content, and fidelity to apostolic tradition. Clearly, the tone between these two pericopes varies greatly.

These are also related in topic, for the new passage does not abandon the two major themes of 2:1-12, i.e., eschatological and moral concerns. At the outset the author relates these to the basic Christian belief in divine election. These are presented as salvation at work in the present (v. 13) and glory as the goal of human activity (14). Thus, there is a shift not in subject matter but in strategy, from a discussion and modification of the standard apocalyptic scenario to that of tradition as the basis of balanced Christian thinking and practice.

Crucial for this interpretation is the consideration of the author's use of 1 Thessalonians as source. The relationship between the new text and the model is particularly close for this pericope. In general terms, the model has provided the structural blocks for this section:

2:13-15   thanksgiving   1 Thess 2:13
   16-17   unusual prayer   1 Thess 3:11
   3:1   finally, brothers & sisters   1 Thess 4:1 (see next section).

Thus, in compositional terms, the present passage falls into two parts: 2:13-15 (thanks, purpose, exhortation) and 2:16-17 (prayer), each of which bears a specific relationship to the text of Paul.

In the case of 2:13-15, the wording and type of the thanksgiving clause are derived not from Paul but from the author's own formulation earlier in 1:3. The remainder of the development, however, is inspired, as is much of the document, from the first chapter of Paul's letter (see Introduction). The textual and thematic relationship is as follows:

2 Thess 2	1 Thess 1	
13 We for our part		
ought to give thanks to God	2 *we give thanks to God*	1 Thess 2:13
always for you,	*always for* all *of you . . .*	2 Thess 1:3
brothers and sisters	4 for we, *brothers and sisters*	
loved by the Lord,	*loved by God,*	
because *God chose you*	are sure *of your election*	
from the beginning		
for salvation		
through sanctification by the Spirit	5 since *our gospel came to you*	
and belief in the truth.	not only *in word,*	
14 That is why then	but also in power,	
he called you through our gospel,	both *with the Holy Spirit*	
that is, for the attainment of the	*and with full conviction.*	
glory of our Lord Jesus Christ.		
15 So then, brothers and sisters,		
stand firm		
and hold fast to the traditions		
which you were taught by us		
either *by word* or by letter.		

The author employs Paul's text as a quarry for terms and themes. (1) The idiom "brothers and sisters loved by God," by a simple modification, becomes "brothers and sisters loved by the Lord." A similar change occurs in 3:16 where Paul's title "the God of peace himself" (1 Thess 5:23) has become "the Lord of peace himself." (2) Paul's reference to divine election is typically transformed by the author into parallel statements on the same theme, the first employing a non-Pauline term *(haireomai)* and the second a well-known Pauline expression *(kaleō;* see 1 Thess 2:12; 4:7; 5:24). (3) The frequent Pauline expression "our gospel" occurs once only in each of the Thessalonian documents. (4) The dual expression "through sanctification by the Spirit and belief in the truth" is the thematic and stylistic equivalent of "with *(en)* the Holy Spirit and with full conviction." (5) The author's nonuse of the term "power" is explained by its appearance in apocalyptic contexts (1:7; 2:9), by its earlier use for God's present activity (1:11), and by the choice of a synonym ("strengthen") later in 2:17. (6) These Pauline terms and themes are employed to construct a new argument against the apocalyptic preachers' end-time solution to current problems. These Pauline features are also employed to bolster the writer's appeal to apostolic tradition.

In the case of 2:16-17, the author returns more directly to the Pauline prayer of the model:

2 Thess 2	1 Thess 3
16 *Now may our Lord Jesus Christ himself and God our Father* who has *loved* us and through grace given us unfailing comfort and good hope,	11 *Now may God our Father himself and our Lord Jesus* direct our path to you. (see 2 Thess 3:5) 12 . . . may the Lord bring about an increase and abundance in your *love* for one another . . .
17 comfort *your hearts* and *strengthen* them in every good work and word.	13 so as *to establish/strengthen your hearts* as blameless (see 2 Thess 3:5) in the sphere of holiness. . . .

The Pauline form of the prayer is adopted; among the elements borrowed are the initial *autos de* ("now . . . himself"), the double subject (though in reverse order to focus on Jesus' lordship), and the (double) singular aorist optative verb. Also taken from this source are a few terms and themes. [1] The singular use of *autos de,* followed by *ho theos,* occurs only twice in Paul, both in 1 Thessalonians where they function as concluding prayers (3:11 and 5:23) to the two missives. Significantly, that usage also occurs only twice in 2 Thessalonians, in roughly the same overall position as they do in the model, but in both cases *ho kyrios* not *ho theos* is used (2:16; 3:16). Thus, the focus, indicated by use of *autos,* is on God for Paul and on the Lord for the Paulinist writer. [2] The reversal of the order of the subjects also supports this change of emphasis. In Paul the prayer is addressed to God initially "and also" to the Lord Jesus, who is in the following verse again addressed in prayer. In the case of 2 Thess 2:16-17 it is the Lord who is addressed initially "and also God." The author refers to God's past gifts, especially "comfort," before asking for the Lord Jesus' "comfort and strength." The change involves not the replacing of theological by Christological themes but continued emphasis on Jesus' present lordship. [3] Use of a singular verb can be justified by insisting that the author follows the Pauline model and by noting that the emphasis is on Christological activity. [4] Again, Pauline structures, terms, and themes are employed to address the document's particular concerns. The author insists that just as through God's love and grace all believers have been granted comfort in the midst of present difficulties and hope which motivates daily behavior, so the author's prayer is that the Lord, who is present though hidden, may grant the addressees comfort in their sufferings and courage in their speech and work.

Function of the Second Thanksgiving. While showing evidence of dependence on the Pauline model, the new text nonetheless has a different function, one that relates to the community's situation. Having responded to the addressees' premature conclusion regarding the Lord's day and having focused on the theme of divine judgment for all evildoers, the author constructs a new thanksgiving period as a vehicle for further anti-apocalyptic strategy. Having hinted at the importance of adherence to solid apostolic teaching (see 2:2 on abandoning balanced thinking and 2:5 on recall to foundational instruction), the author focuses on fidelity to that tradition as the basis for proper Christian thinking and praxis.

The thanksgiving period introduces the theme of divine election as the reason for giving thanks. But the reason is adapted to the addressees' situation; they were chosen for a life of holiness in the present and one committed to the gospel (2:13). From this the author draws, in parallel structures, an added inference that they were called to an eschatological goal, the sharing of Jesus' glory. With this unassailable purpose in mind, the community is exhorted to a calm adherence to the tradition received from the apostolic missionaries (2:15). The author then concludes the passage by reformulating the Pauline prayer into a community appeal to the Lord Jesus to counter its troubled hearts with balanced tradition and to strengthen its every desire for goodness in speech and deed.

The function of the second thanksgiving with its concluding prayer is, on the one hand, a close imitation of the Pauline model to underscore the authority of apostolic tradition. On the other hand, the text functions as an appeal to the theme of divine election as the basis for balanced moral and eschatological doctrine, a doctrine which is contained in early apostolic oral preaching and written instruction. The community's problems then are subsumed under the rubric of divine election and the proper understanding of the divine purpose for the believer's choice, an understanding which is to be found in the traditions received from the community's founders, not its latter-day preachers' ecstatic activity.

Election as Choice and Call (2:13b-14). The author employs two different terms within varying contexts to describe the theme of divine election. (1) God's Choice. The first, non-Pauline term focuses on the traditional theme of the eternal plan and God's salvific purpose for humanity. This concept of salvation appears earlier in the letter when the author describes "those on the road to ruin" (2:10). They are the ones who refuse to accept not only the truth or gospel but "the love of the truth." Presumably, their refusal can be defined in the terms of what the remainder of 2:13 expresses, "salvation through sanctification by the Spirit and belief in the truth." "Those on the road to ruin" refuse this and so will be condemned (2:12), for believers were chosen for this purpose.

Salvation, within the context of the letter's purpose, consists of divine action (see Notes on "sanctification by the Spirit") and human reaction. God's Spirit makes believers holy and believers in turn are to adhere to the truth. In this way the author hints again at the ethical issues which are discussed more fully in the following chapter and addressed in the prayer of verse 17. God then has chosen humans for holiness.

(2) God's Call. Employing a Pauline term, the author addresses a second facet of divine election as it relates to the community's situation. Drawing an inference from the first statement about election the author proceeds to state: God "called you through our gospel for the attainment of our Lord Jesus Christ's glory." This divine call was made through the apostolic mission, for its means and time relate to the foundation visit and not to recent misguided preaching. In partial agreement, nonetheless, with the apocalyptic preachers, the author insists that its goal is that of obtaining the glory which the Lord Jesus will confer when he returns— eschatology was and is part of the gospel message, but that doctrine must be properly understood. In fact, employing a Pauline term *klēsis* (Rom 11:29; Phil 3:14) for "calling," the author (1:11) stresses the present reality of this vocation: the believers being made worthy and productive by God for the glorification of Jesus' name prior to his return.

Early Christian Tradition (2:15). Following the extended discussion of divine election in 2:13-14 as the reason for giving thanks, the author introduces the crucial concept of tradition. While the term "tradition" is employed in a negative sense in the context of Jewish polemics in the Gospels (Mark 7:3f.; par.) and heretical controversy (Col 2:8), it is nonetheless used, along with its cognate verb and other transmission terminology, in a positive way and in agreement with Jewish usage (see Gal 1:14; 1 Cor 11:2). Thus, this Paulinist writer would have found in Paul an extensive and positive sense of the process of preaching, teaching, and communication of the Christian community's beliefs and practices. In fact, 1 Thessalonians often speaks of various facets of this process whether in relation to the foundation visit and its activity (1:5; 2:2f., 13; 4:1f.) or the task of writing (1:2f.; 2:1f., 9; 4:13f.).

The use of the theme of tradition in this instance has a focused purpose. From the outset it is clear that by the term *paradosis* the author means apostolic teaching as the basis of Christian belief and practice. Its content involves all that the apostolic missionaries have preached and taught and all they have sent them in correspondence. By means of the convention of pseudonymity the author is able to appeal to Pauline and standard Christian teaching, more generally, to counteract the recent, volatile activity of the community's apocalypticists. In structural terms the appeal to tradition follows immediately the statements about divine election and from this the conclusion is drawn and stated as a command: "so then, brothers and sisters, stand firm and hold fast to the traditions." These traditions are ultimately of divine origin and were taught by God's appointed ministers. At the same time, the appeal to the addressees as *adelphoi* underscores the unity of thought, belief, and practice which should exist among the community and others elsewhere.

The appeal to and delineation of the concept of "traditions" as used here relates to the author's strategy. The community is to reconsider its apocalyptic concerns in light of what it has learned from tradition, whether its original evangelization, formation into a community, or the pastoral assistance it has received. In fact, the whole of chapter two qualifies as "traditions taught by us"; they are to "stand firm" in the knowledge they originally received as opposed to "being radically shaken" to their foundations. This foundation is precisely the Church's tradition as received through the apostolic gospel. Also, the author employs the plural "traditions" and appeals broadly to the variety of teachings and practices which characterized early Christianity as a means of addressing the community's concerns. See discussion later of the relationship between "tradition" and "command" (3:4, 6, 10); as well as the community's duty to imitate apostolic behavior as constituting received teaching (3:7).

Prayer for Eschatological and Moral Balance (2:16-17). The pericope ends with a formal, unusual prayer (see also 1:11-12; 3:5, 16), whose unusual character derives in part from its being patterned on 1 Thess 3:11-13. Whereas the Pauline model focuses first on "God the Father" and, immediately following, addresses the Lord Jesus in prayer, so the new prayer addresses Jesus in the first place and conjoins the Father in the petition. On mentioning the Father, however, the author, by means of a developed parenthesis, presents an interesting statement of God's past gifts as parallels to the community's present needs. As God out of love has given believers, in Christ or through grace, a source of comfort and a basis for optimism, so the Lord, who loves the community ("brothers and sisters loved by the Lord''—2:13), is asked for assistance in actualizing these divine gifts by comforting them and energizing their every word and work in the pursuit of goodness.

The author's call in prayer is for a correction of the imbalance which has occurred in the minds of the addressees. They are asked to reconsider their hasty conclusions and wrong-headed activity and to return to the traditions of the beginnings. God loved them from the beginning and gave them, through the gospel, what they needed to face life's difficulties, whether consolation or optimism. The prayer then asks the Lord Jesus' help (''as also'' that of the Father) to calm their apocalyptic fears and give them courage to desire what is good (see 3:6f.). The community then needs eschatological and moral balance.

Author's Traditional Perspective. If it has been more difficult in previous passages to perceive the author's perspective as opposed to that of the community and as distinct from the strategy employed, the task is simpler in this instance. This is so since the pericope is less focused on eschatology and more concerned with the traditional beliefs of the community as a means to counteract its problems. (1) The reason given by the author for thanksgiving is traditional: divine gift and human response. Though there is a stress on God's choice and call, the whole is applied to the community's situation and needs. (2) The author insists on the original, apostolic teaching or tradition rather than the new, emotional activity of recent preachers. (3) Also there is an attempt to present a more balanced view of the Christ-event, one that is theologically and Christologically engaged and less eschatologically centered. The Christ-event presupposes the reality of divine election, is based on divine love, works itself out through the gospel, and is defined as divine grace which bestows the gifts necessary for daily living. (4) The role of the Lord Jesus, while still involving the granting of end-time glory, is more traditionally presented for the community's benefit; the Lord Jesus loves the believer, is called on to grant consolation and strength to all who strive for sanctification, and is the believer's source of comfort and optimism. (5) The author focuses on the present, not as a stage of the apocalyptic scenario, but as a time of sanctification through response to the gospel and the activity of the Spirit, and as a time to live a life of holiness in word and act.

The author's thought then is decidedly traditional. The community is called upon to return to and hold fast the traditions received from the past and to call on the Lord Jesus as present lord to actualize the divine gifts received that its members might resist ''the mystery of evil'' and be guarded against the activity of the evil one (3:3). The community's

"false hope" and despairing view of its own afflictions are to be counterbalanced by knowledge of God's gifts (in the Christ-event or grace) of
"good hope and unfailing comfort" and by prayerful request that the
hidden Lord activate these gifts in their everyday lives.

FOR REFERENCE AND FURTHER STUDY

Collins, R. F. " 'The Gospel of Our Lord Jesus' (2 Thes 1, 8): A Symbolic Shift
    of Paradigm." *TC*, 426–40.
Fee, G. D. "On Text and Commentary on 1 and 2 Thessalonians." *SBLSP* (1992),
    165–83.
Holland, G. S. *The Tradition That You Received from Us: 2 Thessalonians in the Paul-
    ine Tradition.* Tübingen: Mohr-Siebeck, 1988.
Jewett, R. "A Matrix of Grace: The Theology of 2 Thessalonians as a Pauline
    Letter." *PT*, 63–70.
Laub, R. "Paulinische Autorität in nach paulinischer Zeit (2 Thes)." *TC*, 403–17.
O'Brien, P. T. *Introductory Thanksgivings in the Letters of Paul.* Leiden: Brill, 1977.
Van Aarde, A. "The Struggle against Heresy in the Thessalonian Correspondence
    and the Origin of the Apostolic Tradition." *TC*, 418–25.
Wiles, G. P. *Paul's Intercessory Prayers.* Cambridge: Cambridge University, 1974.

21. *Mutual Prayer* (3:1-5)

1. Finally, brothers and sisters, pray for us, that the word of the Lord
may advance rapidly and be glorified, just as it is happening in regard
to you, 2. and that we may be delivered from wicked and evil people;
certainly, all do not have faith. 3. Now the Lord, who will strengthen
and guard you from the evil one, is faithful. 4. Also, we are confident
in the Lord concerning you that what we command you are doing and
will continue to do. 5. Now may the Lord direct your hearts to the love
of God and the constancy of Christ.

NOTES

1. *Finally, brothers and sisters, pray for us:* A new section begins though the subject continues to be that of prayer. The pericope is marked off by the con-
spicuous use of "finally" (in imitation of the Pauline model; see 1 Thess 4:1),
the use of direct address, and a change of focus from prayer for the addressees to a request of prayer for the writers. While in Paul the expression
"finally" introduces exhortation or farewell (2 Cor 13:11; Phil 3:1; 4:8; 1 Thess

4:1), in 2 Thess 3:1 it introduces a complex section on mutual prayer. On the expression "pray for us," see Notes on 1:11. Also, the petition for prayer is placed in significantly different contexts in the Pauline and Paulinist texts. In Paul it forms part of a traditional letter ending whereby the writer prays for and requests prayers of the addressees; the stress then is on reciprocal prayer (see 1 Thess 5:25). In the case of 2 Thess 3:1 and following there is again a concern for mutual prayer but the focus is on the Christian mission and community practice.

that the word of the Lord may advance rapidly and be glorified: The reason for the prayer is stated in double clauses, each with subjunctive verb, introduced by *hina* (see 1:11), and concerned with some facet of the missionary endeavor. The first addresses the theme of the spread of the gospel but borrows from 1 Thess 1:8 the unique case of Paul's use of the expression "the word of the Lord" to describe the good news. In place of the Pauline expression "sound forth" an equally creative "run or advance rapidly" *(trechō)* is used. This verb which appears in Paul as part of the athletic imagery of the stadium is here used, under the influence of Ps 147:4 ("his word will run swiftly"), to describe the spread of the Christian message. The clause, however, contains a second verb which describes this missionary process, the well-known verb *doxazō* in the passive which can mean "be glorified, receive with honor, or triumph." While one could focus on the theme of a "triumphant" gospel, a meaning which fits the context, it is preferable, in light of a similar idiom in Acts 13:48, to view the verbal phrase as describing the otherworldly honor which in the first place God bestows and in the second place which believers acknowledge when they receive the word and, in light of the reciprocal character of "glorification" expressed in 1:12, to consider the term as implying acceptance and proclamation of the word in a missionary sense.

as it is happening in regard to you: This diplomatically expressed, parenthetical clause calls for some comment. The Greek expression, *kathōs kai pros hymas* (lit.: "as also among or in regard to you"—see BAGD 710:5 or 7 and *IBNTG*, 53), clearly intends to draw a comparison, but the point of comparison is unclear. Some appeal to the foundation visit as described in 1 Thess 1–2 as providing its background; others, however, see a reference to the immediately expressed "be glorified" as the concept intended and view the statement as a rhetorical device to appeal to the community's faith commitment and praxis. The translation therefore underscores not the immediate success of the mission among the addressees ("as it happened"—past event) but its present effects within the community (use of the present). The passage also refers to missionary work; thus, "in regard to you." Also the themes of present glory and mission reflect further on that of Jesus' present lordship.

2. *and that we may be delivered from wicked and evil people:* The second reason for the request of prayer is presented as a structural, antithetical parallel to the first, for it addresses a major obstacle to the mission's success. The terminology employed and the interpretation of the clause call for some attention. Again Pauline terminology is borrowed (use of *rhyomai:* "to deliver") but the thought is expressed by means of an OT passage: "you will deliver them from

evil people" (Isa 25:4). The author's liking for doublets leads to the expansion of the OT phrase by the addition of the non-Pauline term "wicked" *(atopōn)*, a term which means "unusual" but whose Hellenistic use points rather to moral perversity (BAGD 120.2). Also, two other considerations render interpretation more complex, the author's use of the aorist passive of the verb and the addition of an article to introduce the object of the preposition. Both suggest a specific context and seem to contrast with the present and general nature of the first reason for prayer; see discussion below.

certainly, all do not have faith: Many presume that the concluding clause of verse 2, introduced by *gar*, provides an explanation for the second *hina* clause, namely, the reason why there exist "wicked and evil people" or why nonbelievers act in a hostile way toward the Christian mission. Instead, the clause comes at the end of the long prayer (as do other unusual statements at the end of clauses or sentences in 1:4, 10, 11; 2:16) and, by means of an inferential *gar*, introduces an obvious statement (as in 2:7) which all would concede: "certainly, all do not have faith" (see BAGD 152.3). In this way the author provides a rationale for the urgent prayer for a successful missionary endeavor. Further, the understated idiom "all do not have faith" finds a Pauline parallel in Rom 10:16.

3. *Now the Lord . . . is faithful:* There follows, as in 3:12-14 a series of three statements interconnected by *de* ("but or and"); the function of these particles is that of connecting, yet distinguishing successive statements: "now . . . also . . . now" (see BAGD 171.1c). The first of these, seemingly suggested by the use of "faith" in the previous verse, addresses the theme of fidelity *(pistos)*. In place of the Pauline "the one who calls you is trustworthy or faithful" (1 Thess 5:24), the author speaks of the Lord's trustworthiness (on the substitution of "Lord" for "God," see 2:13).

. . . who will strengthen and guard you from the evil one . . .: The statement regarding the Lord's faithfulness is qualified by a relative clause containing two verbal complements in the future, indicating actions that are occurring and will continue into the future. The first verb *stērizō* has the meaning of "making firm," as in 2:17, rather than "establishing" (see 1 Thess 3:13). In this case the strength provided is that required in resisting the enticement to wickedness. The second verb *phylassō*, employed twice by Paul with the sense of "keeping the Law" (Rom 2:26; Gal 6:13), is here used with the OT meaning of "preservation or protection" from evil or evildoer (see especially Pss 11:8; 40:1-2; 120:5-8; 139:5; in the last example the Lord God is guardian and strength of the righteous; see v. 8). Lastly, the expression *apo tou ponērou* can be neuter or masculine and therefore refer to "evil" or "the evil one." Both options are vigorously defended. (1) In favor of the neuter option one could perhaps insist that the original Jesus tradition (the Lord's Prayer) appeals for protection from "the evil tendency" found in the human heart, that such a designation for Satan was not customary in contemporary Jewish literature, and that the context of its usage suggests an impersonal confrontation with wickedness. (2) The personal option, however, is better grounded since early Christian tradition does refer to the devil by such a designation

(Eph 6:16; Matt 13:19, 39; 1 John 2:13, 14), since the context is obviously apocalyptic, and since, on the contrary, evil is seen in 2:3-10 as both eschatologically and presently under the influence of Satan, God's rival and the Lord Jesus' personal opponent in the battle for lordship.

4. *Also, we are confident in the Lord concerning you:* A new, but slightly related statement is made concerning the author's confidence in the addressees (second successive use of *de:* "also"). The main clause, "we are confident in the Lord concerning you," though often characterized as typically Pauline is only superficially so, for this idiom with its three components (*peithō, en kyriō, epi* + *hymas*) appears nowhere in Paul. On the one hand, the verb occurs three times with "in the Lord": twice to express certitude or trust but not confidence in someone (Rom 14:14; Phil 2:24) and once with the preposition *eis* rather than *epi* and presenting a different word order ("confident about you in the Lord"—Gal 5:10; this is the closest parallel to our text). On the other hand, the verb is employed without "in the Lord" but followed by *epi pantas hymas* ("concerning all of you") only in 2 Cor 2:3 (see Rom 15:15 where the preposition *peri* is used). The idiom then is a construct of the author and its meaning, owing to its unique occurrence and epistolary context, must be sought without too readily assuming a Pauline connotation of confidence which relies on the Lord (see Gal 5:10). Instead, this unique *en kyriō* statement should be related to the author's repetition of the verb *parangellō* ("command") in verses 4, 6, 10, 12 and to the *en* phrases employed in three of these: "in the Lord" (v. 4), "in the name of our Lord Jesus Christ" (6), and "in the Lord Jesus Christ" (12). Finally, expressions of confidence are frequently used rhetorical conventions in epistolary contexts.

that what we command you are doing and will continue to do: After assuring the readers that the Lord does his part, the author addresses the community's part in terms of fidelity to tradition and its dictates. The verb *parangellō*, which recurs in verses 6, 10, 12, underscores the document's authoritative character. Its usage here and following suggests not the nuance of "directive or instruction" as in 1 Thess 4:2, 11 but that of authoritative command expressed in the present and addressing all facets of apostolic preaching, teaching, and moral exhortation, including the forthcoming commands of 3:6-15. Before broaching the specific topics of the following paraenetic section the author rhetorically expresses confidence in the community's commitment: "you are doing and will continue to do" what has been commanded. The phraseology is reminiscent of 1 Thess 4:1, in that it praises present efforts as a means of fostering future activity. While a few MSS place an additional *kai* before the first verb and others attempt to clarify the author's thought by stressing past, present, and future activity on the part of the community, it is best to follow the short and simpler text of S* A (D*) *pc.*

5. *Now may the Lord direct your hearts:* A formal prayer, acting as a third consecutive statement introduced by postpositive *de* ("now"), brings the pericope to a close. As in earlier instances (see 3:1, 2) the form and some of the terminology is borrowed from Paul (see 1 Thess 3:11-13: "the Lord," "direct,"

"hearts," "love") but the formulation is more closely that of the OT. The prayer as in 2:16, following the Pauline model, is expressed in the optative and the verbal form itself *(kateuthynai)* borrowed from 1 Thess 3:11. The idiom "direct your hearts," however, finds its closest parallel in 1 Chr 29:18 (see also 2 Chr 20:33; Prov 21:2; Sir 49:3) and has the meaning of orienting one's heart or entire being, that is, the source and center of affection, will, and thought (see 1 Thess 2:4).

to the love of God and the constancy of Christ: The heart is said to be oriented in a twofold direction, use of double *eis* to introduce parallel articular noun objects with modifying articular genitives. (1) The first phrase could be interpreted as an objective or subjective genitive: "love for God" or "God's love," respectively. While it is difficult to choose between the two owing to a paucity of data, it is nonetheless the second that is preferable. The author's usage, limited as it is, concerns human's love for one another (1:3) and for "the truth" (2:10) and the Lord's love (2:13) and God's love for humans (2:16); there is no mention of love for God ("argument from silence"). Thus, the author, as a Paulinist, is following Pauline usage. Also, interpretation of 2:10 and 16-17 supports such a conclusion (see below). (2) The other phrase could also bear such a dual interpretation, either "waiting for Christ" or "Christ's constancy or endurance" (objective and subjective genitives). But such an argument, based on parallelism, i.e., that the two represent the same type of genitive, does not bear great weight since other examples from this author do not measure up to this expectation (see 1:11 and 2:13). Again, it is difficult to make a confident choice since there are few data and since a case could be made for either option. While one could defend the phrase as meaning "patient waiting for Christ" as germane to the community's peculiar eschatology, it is preferable to choose the second as consistent with the term's use in 1:4 (see Notes), with Pauline usage generally, and with the author's anti-apocalyptic perspective. Appeal to "the constancy or endurance of Christ" then would be consistent with the author's strategy of employing traditional concepts to counteract apocalyptic fervor. The concept, interpreted as endurance (see 1:4) or preferably in a Paulinist way as constancy (see 1 Thess 1:3), refers to Jesus' death and resurrection as exemplary for Christians who are undergoing difficult times and provides the basis for present commitment and action.

INTERPRETATION

The letter continues to follow the pattern of its Pauline model, whether by offering a second thanksgiving (2:13f.) or by reproducing its characteristic closing formula: "finally, brothers and sisters." These literary features, however, are put at the service of the author's continuing strategy and prepare for a more extended paraenetic section. The focus of the new pericope is that of mission as a community duty while awaiting the Lord Jesus' return.

Form and Function of 3:1-5. Not only does the author follow the overall structure of 1 Thessalonians but borrows from the model several other themes and structures. Both the opening and closing prayers of the section (3:1-2 and 5) employ themes and structural features from the prayer immediately preceding Paul's "closing" structure (1 Thess 3:11-13), while the intermediate statements of confidence (vv. 3-4) borrow other concepts from the Pauline model. Clearly, themes and terms such as "word of the Lord," "be glorified," "deliver," "strengthen," "faithful," "command," "heart," and "love," are taken from 1 Thessalonians and incorporated into a new statement about the community's situation. Further, the concluding prayer (3:5), constructed on the model of 1 Thess 3:11f., adds to the number of prayer constructs since the two Pauline examples are retained and revised (see 2:16-17 and 3:16).

The passage nonetheless does not receive its shape from its Pauline source. Much is said about the passage's seeming lack of unity and focus. The request for prayer does not as in 1 Thess 5:25 focus on the missionaries but on the theme of mission and, in a seemingly disjointed way, on protection from eschatological woes. There is then a switch back to the addressees in a series of apparently disconnected statements, and a final prayer for the readers. In effect, the pericope consists of a major prayer structure (3:1-2) which introduces the major theme of the passage (mission), two slightly related statements (vv. 3-4), which apply the theme to the community's situation, and a concluding prayer (5), which brings the major issues of the letter into play with the new theme. The author therefore employs a prayer and related structures to present a new element of strategy, the role of the community and its members in causing the gospel to advance while awaiting the Lord's day. The passage seeks to relate the theme of mission to eschatological and moral concerns.

Prayer, Mission, and Strategy (vv. 1-2). The author's use of prayer to address the community's concerns and to refocus the discussion was noted in relation to 1:11-12 and 2:16, where the prayers function as conclusions to situate the discussion on a traditional basis. In the present case prayer introduces the major theme for consideration, though the author returns to the same pattern by composing a concluding prayer. Employing the structure used in 1:11 ("we pray for you that") the author offers extended clauses which present the reason for the request for prayer.

In general terms one might characterize this reason as a concern for mission. This is particularly clear in the first clause "that the word of the Lord may advance rapidly and be glorified." The second clause, in a distinctly eschatological tone, addresses the obstacle in the way of the spreading of the good news. This obstacle is characterized as "wicked and evil people," a group whose identity is the object of much speculation. Regardless, the theme of mission is clearly the focus of verses 1-2 and one might wonder why the author, at this point, introduces this new theme.

Initially, it is tempting to seek here a clue to the author's own background, which might be sought in the area of missionary work wherein a preacher undertakes to address a given community's erroneous conclusions regarding the Lord's day. The major problem, however, is that there are no other indications of such a context, save perhaps 3:14-15 and its ecclesial ramifications. The concept of mission, whether personal or thematic, is limited to the epistolary context (appealing to Pauline authorship raises an entirely different set of questions and problems).

A better approach to the problem is to view the issue as related to anti-apocalyptic strategy. As another way to focus on the present rather than the future, the author addresses the Christian community's present responsibilities: in general terms upright behavior (vv. 4-5) and in more specific terms the world mission (1-2). It was a well-established concept that prior to the end certain events were to occur, among them the urgent spread of the good news; the *textus classicus* is Mark 13:10: "the good news must first be proclaimed to all nations." Also related to this concept is "the entry of the full number of Gentiles" (Rom 11:25; Luke 21:24) and the apocalypticist concern that the gospel be proclaimed before the hour of judgment (Rev 14:6-7). In light of such a consideration several features of the text make more sense.

The world mission is presented here in its ultimate finality. Thus, the author asks that the good news be acknowledged with faith and thanksgiving in the present ("glorified") and also that it "advance rapidly" or "run." Also, the author prays that missionaries, and believers generally, be "delivered finally" (use of aorist) from lovers of evil. There is here a hint that the world mission is likewise a precondition for the unfolding of the final process. In this regard it might be noted that the verb *rhyomai* ("deliver") which is usually employed for present security is nonetheless used eschatologically in 1 Thess 1:10 and in the Matthean form of the Lord's Prayer (6:13) of final deliverance from evil or the evil one.

In structural terms two elements of the prayer highlight the perspective under discussion. (1) The first clause, which addresses the positive aspect of the mission, ends with the nonverbal clause: *kathōs kai pros hymas* (lit.: "as also in regard to or among you"). While most scholars opt to see the text as referring to the mission's success "among" the addressees, it seems that the author is complimenting the community, following the lead of 1 Thess 1:7-8, on its successful missionary work and present commitment ("as is happening in regard to you"—BAGD 710.5). (2) The two verbs of the clause refer to mission and its present effects, respectively, and the nonverbal clause rhetorically asks for the same success for the letter writer as is evident in the readers' lives.

Additionally, the second *hina* construction (v. 2) also ends with a cumbersome clause which generates discussion. The *gar* clause is regularly related to the immediately given reason for prayer, namely, the deliverance from unrighteous people. Discussion therefore is usually limited to identifying these people in light of the *gar* clause ("for not all have faith"), as Jewish or Gentile nonbelievers. Instead, it is best to view *gar* as an inferential particle that introduces an obvious statement, one that explains the reason for the urgency of the mission: "certainly, all do not have faith." Again, the focus is on mission as a Christian duty in view of the future arrival of the Lord's day.

A final reason for opting for this perspective is that one appreciates even more the author's focus on the hearers' apocalyptic problems. The present time, though one when "the mystery of lawlessness" is active and one which offers enticement to evil and opposition to the spreading of the gospel, is nonetheless one which bears responsibilities for the righteous.

The Lord's Part and the Community's Part (vv. 3-4). Few fail to express surprise at the train of thought within the verses following the opening prayer, even describing the whole as abrupt jumps from one topic to another. Two clues, however, lead to a different assessment of the passage. The first concerns the connection of verses 3, 4, and 5 by the simple postpositive *de.* The function of these is the listing of successive, complementary statements (BAGD 171.1c), whose connections are perceived as loose but nonetheless related. The second clue relates to the focus of the pericope on world mission; each of the following statements provides added considerations regarding that central theme and, by the change from "we" to "you," focuses the discussion on the community rather than on believers generally.

Verse 3 focuses on the Lord and his fidelity; it is a truism to state that the Lord Jesus is faithful. The author uses this accepted concept to insist that believers need not fear for they will continue to receive from the Lord the strength needed for their missionary and everyday duties, even to the extent of being protected from the hidden power and enticements of the evil one who is now secretly at work. The Lord will continually do his part in bringing about an advance of the good news everywhere. As noted in 2:17 he will strengthen their resolve in daily word and work and will protect them now against "the mystery of lawlessness" (2:7) and later against the threats of the satanic, lawless one (2:3-4, 9-10).

The transition to verse 4 is also indicated by postpositive *de* and translated "also" to underscore its complementary character. As the previous verse had employed a truism to stress the unassailable verity of its claim, so the present verse makes use of the stock rhetorical device of the confidence statement to elicit compliance with the author's demand. The new verse focuses on the community's part, a topic which is described in authoritative language ("in the Lord" and "command"), which prepares for the following discussion (3:6-15), and which is further solicited by diplomatic language ("you are doing and will continue to do"). The appeal to "command" or "what we command" is an obvious reference back to the author's insistence on "holding fast to the traditions" (2:15) and to the need for a balanced mind and a love for the truth (2:2, 10).

Verses 3 and 4 then, far from being a less-than-felicitous series of disconnected statements, are related to the author's theme of mission as a pre-apocalyptic duty of the community. By means of successive, complementary statements, the passage deals with a variety of issues related to that theme. In an effort to convince the community that the end-time process has not yet begun to dawn, the author returns repeatedly to a proper perspective on the present and its responsibilities.

Love and Constancy as Basic Orientation (V. 5). Once again the author brings a general discussion to an end with a formal prayer, whose relation to the overall meaning of the pericope needs attention. The prayer asks that the Lord determine the believer's basic orientation or, in Semitic Greek, that he "direct their hearts or inner beings." There is a reference here to the lack of balanced orientation (2:2) or the facile abandonment of apostolic tradition which they received in speech and writing. The request is that the one who is lord now, not the whimsical, ecstatic activity of recent preachers, determines the fundamental orientation of the community in its beliefs and practice.

Interestingly, the direction given for this Christian vision is a traditional theological and Christological one. In the first case the Lord is asked to direct believers' hearts "to God's love," a phrase which should be taken as a subjective genitive (see Notes). The sure point of entry for an interpretation of this theme is 2:16, a previous prayer where the author describes "God our Father" as "the one who has loved us and through grace given us unfailing comfort and good hope." God's love, it would seem, defines the choice for salvation and the call through the gospel (2:13) which God exercised through grace. God's love is one directed to human salvation through present sanctification. The expression "God's love" is the author's way of formulating the traditional basis for Christian belief and behavior, a belief that is grounded on divine election and love and a praxis that has as its goal sanctification by the Spirit and love of the truth. The expression "God's love" then points to the orientation of the believer's life as it relates to God's loving choice of believers for a life of holiness that seeks to do what is right, to glorify the Lord, and to spread his word rather than waiting idly for the end to arrive.

The second facet of the believer's basic orientation is described as focused on "Christ's constancy" (see Notes on v. 5 for discussion of subjective genitive). The theme of endurance or *hypomonē* has already surfaced in 1:4 in a laudatory discussion of the community's exposure to severe afflictions. While one might be tempted here to view Jesus' exemplary confrontation of his sufferings as a model for a beleaguered community, one might note the anomalous use of the title "Christ." This is the only use in 2 Thessalonians of the title by itself and oddly one hears of the Lord Jesus directing hearts to "Christ's constancy." It is to the Christ-event that the author appeals as the basis for Christian preaching (3:1), for endurance in the face of affliction (1:4), and for confidence in the present in terms of belief and action. By appealing to the risen Lord's constancy as the model for Christian action the author addresses again, in a Paulinist fashion (see 1 Thess 1:3), the present responsibilities of believers in advancing the good news and exhibiting its demands in a life of righteous behavior. "Christ's constancy" is a model for those who suffer and the basis for a balanced eschatology and righteous behavior with a more proper focus on ecclesial and missionary activity (3:1).

Verse 5 then returns to the community's traditional concepts whereby believers live in the present with a proper regard for past benefactions and the future coming of the Lord's day. The Lord is asked to orient the believer's whole being toward divine election as directed to present holiness and future glory (2:13-14), a sanctification made possible by the preaching of the constancy of Christ to all who would be saved.

FOR REFERENCE AND FURTHER STUDY

Dewailly, L. M. "Course et gloire de la parole (II Thess., III, 1)." *RB* 71 (1964) 25–41.
Jewett, R. "A Matrix of Grace: The Theology of 2 Thessalonians as a Pauline Letter." *PT*, 63–70.
Wiles, G. P. *Paul's Intercessory Prayers*. Cambridge: Cambridge University, 1974.

22. *Command and Exhortation* (3:6-16)

6. So, brothers and sisters, we command you in the name of our Lord Jesus Christ to remove yourselves from the presence of brothers or sisters who conduct themselves in an irresponsible way and not according to the tradition which they received from us. 7. For you yourselves know that you ought to imitate us, since we did not neglect our responsibilities while among you 8. nor ate someone else's bread without paying; instead, in labor and toil, night and day we worked so as not to burden any of you 9. —not that we do not have the right—instead, this was done that we might present ourselves to you as an example that you might imitate us. 10. Besides, when we were with you, we often commanded the following: "If anyone is unwilling to work, let that person not eat." 11. Indeed, we hear that some among you are conducting themselves in an irresponsible way, not doing any work except the work of busybodies. 12. So we command such persons and exhort them in the Lord Jesus Christ that, working quietly, they might eat their own bread. 13. You for your part, brothers and sisters, never grow tired of doing what is right. 14. Also, should some not obey what we say in our letter, take note of these, by not associating with them that they might be put to shame; 15. still do not regard them as enemies but rather admonish them as brothers and sisters. 16. Now may the Lord of peace himself give you peace at all times, in every way. The Lord be with you all.

Notes

6. *So, brothers and sisters, we command you:* A new section of the letter begins with the introduction of a new topic and bearing an authoritative tone. This beginning also is indicated by the use of direct address and postpositive *de* ("so"; see 2:1, 13). The new topic is clearly related to what precedes since the author repeats a theme mentioned two verses earlier, places the relevant term in initial, stress position, and employs that word and related terminology throughout the pericope. The pertinent verb ("command") already appears at 3:4 and is used again in verses 10 and 12.

in the name of our Lord Jesus Christ: Though the theme of Jesus' name appears already in 1:12 and in a significantly different context, both occurrences testify to a development of Jesus' lordship. The first addresses Christian behavior as it relates to the honor Christ shares with believers in their daily acts and words; the second focuses on the authority which appeal to Jesus' name confers (see 1 Cor 5:3-4). On the author's preference for the full title "Lord Jesus Christ," see discussion of 1:1-2. It should be noted that two major MSS (B D*) omit the possessive pronoun "our." The evidence is considerably weakened when one considers again Vaticanus' tendency to omit seemingly unimportant terms during the copying process (see Notes on 1:2).

to remove yourselves from the presence of brothers or sisters: The rare verb *stellō* occurs only in the middle in the LXX and NT and attempts to support the meaning "keep away or avoid" (BAGD 766.1-2) by appealing to LXX passages (Mal 2:5; Prov 31:25; Wis 14:1) cannot be called successful (*TDNT* 7:589) either for 2 Cor 8:20 or 2 Thess 3:6, the sole occurrences in the NT. The Pauline example is best viewed as "send out or dispatch" (2 Cor 8:20) and the present text is best interpreted as representing the standard meaning of the verb ("send or set out"—LSJ 1637) with its middle or reflexive nuance followed by the preposition *apo* and translated: "to send or remove oneself from the presence of." Such an interpretation approximates what has until the present been a translation *ad sensum*, since the command in verse 14 not to associate with such believers has always provided the basis for the interpretation of this usage. Further, this verse offers a synonym for the verb and the two passages form an inclusio around the paraenetic section. The author returns in verses 12f. to a more formal procedure for the treatment of such people and their relation to other believers. The expression in the singular, "from any brother," is rendered by the plural, gender-free expression "from the presence of brothers or sisters" since the meaning is clearly all-inclusive; see also verses 14-15 for a similar translation strategy.

who conduct themselves in an irresponsible way: The expression "conduct oneself" represents the standard Pauline usage of *peripateō* (see also v. 11) to indicate moral conduct (see 1 Thess 4:1). The following term *ataktōs*, here translated "in an irresponsible way" (also v. 11), and its cognate (*atakteō* and *ataktos*, used in verse 7 and 1 Thess 5:14 respectively) continue to be the subject of debate. For the term's use in 1 Thess 5:14, see earlier Notes. It is particularly in the context of the ecclesial discussion of 2 Thess 3:6-15 that the term has received attention. On the one hand, many insist that the word, owing to its context involving the refusal to work, takes on the particular nuance of "idleness, laziness, or loafing" (BAGD 119). Also, appeal is made to two contemporary texts, POxyrhynchus 275.24-25 and 725.39-40 (A.D. 66 and 183, respectively) which speak of individuals missing work owing to truancy or idleness (M-M 89), as supporting evidence. One suspects that the meaning is drawn more from the alleged context of idleness than from actual usage. Even the two papyri noted support the following option. On the other hand, the *ataktos* word group means to be "undisciplined or disorderly" and implies "neglect of one's duty or responsibilities" (LSJ 267; *TDNT* 8:47-48) or more generally the violation of military order or social and moral norms and laws (Plato, *Laws* 2.660B; 7.806C; *Timaeus* 30A; Isocrates, *Oration 9: Evagoras* 197E; Xenophon, *Oeconomicus* 5.15). One could opt for the meaning "in a disorderly fashion" and stress problems of discipline and unity as in 1 Thess 5:14 or for a general moral sense "in an irresponsible way" (see also vv. 7 and 11) and include the overall concerns of the paraenetic section of 2 Thess 3:6-15, as is done here (see below). Note that the themes of idleness and of work appear throughout the pericope and are subsumed under the general heading of "irresponsible" behavior.

and not according to the tradition which they received from us: This passage provides a parallel to the adverb *ataktōs* and counters the negative statement with a norm for Christian behavior. The concept of tradition is already introduced

at 2:15 to support the author's traditional apocalyptic scenario and to prepare for the important strand of tradition which is evoked in the following
paraenesis. The expression "which they received from us" derives from 1
Thess 2:13; 4:1 ("you received or learned from us"; also Gal 1:9, 12) but,
combined with the term "tradition," results in a tautologous phrase whose
closest analogy is Rom 16:17: "the teaching which you have learned." Lastly,
one should note a textual problem regarding the verb, whether one should
read "they" (S* A [D*] 33 *pc*) or "you (B G *pc*) received." The situation is
further complicated by the use of a dialectical third-person plural ending. With
others (*TCGNT*, 637) it is best to view the former as the reading that best
explains the correction in some MSS to a standard third-person ending and
the modification by others who sensed that a second-person form was required.

7. *For you yourselves know that you ought to imitate us:* What follows is not a statement of the tradition but a lesson drawn from apostolic example (vv. 7-9)
and only later from past (10) and present (11-12) apostolic teaching. One understands this seeming lack of logic by observing that a Paulinist perspective
would consider Pauline behavior and practice as part of the apostolic tradition inherited by the community. Thus, the author recalls Pauline language
("for you yourselves know": 1 Thess 2:1; 3:3; also 4:2 and 5:2) and theme
of imitation (1:6), and borrows extensively in verse 8 from 1 Thess 2:9. Use
of Pauline language reinforces the authoritative tone of the text. The tradition and all it implies is known and the duty of imitation is inescapable. The
idiom *pōs dei* (lit.: "how [you] ought"), borrowed from 1 Thess 4:1, takes
on a different focus. While in the Pauline text the emphasis is on "how" one
pleases God, the stress here is on obligation; *pōs* stands for *hoti* and introduces
a statement of obligation (BAGD 732.2). The theme of imitation is reiterated
at the end of verse 9.

since we did not neglect our responsibilities while among you: What begins as a
reason for imitating the apostolic example becomes a description of that behavior. In the name of Paul and associates the author wishes to draw a contrast between *atakteō* (with a focus on moral disorder; see v. 6) and behavior
according to apostolic tradition. Examples of behavior therefore are chosen
for their bearing on norms and responsibility. "While among you" (see also
v. 11 and 1 Thess 1:5) refers to the foundation visit and the apostles' activity
during that period.

8. *nor ate someone else's bread without paying:* The author's statements here and
in verse 12 presuppose the Semitic idiom (and its literal LXX rendering) "to
eat bread" (Gen 3:19; 2 Kgs 9:7; see also Amos 7:12) as meaning "to earn
a living" or "support oneself." It is conceded that if the apostles, in the spirit
of 1 Thess 2:9 (cited later), receive support ("eat someone else's bread" or
enjoy the fruits of someone else's labor), it is done with payment. The ideal
not only of apostolic behavior but also of community living is to "eat one's
own bread" (v. 12; see also 1 Thess 4:12).

instead, in labor and toil, night and day we worked so as not to burden any of you:
In contrast to a possible dependence on the hospitality of the converts, the

apostles "instead" devoted themselves to long hours of hard labor to pay for their keep. The author borrows literally from 1 Thess 2:9 the whole passage given above, modifying only the initial phrase to fit the new grammatical structure. The model focuses on work done alongside missionary activity to stress purity of motive by avoiding conflicts of interest, while here the writer's concern is in presenting the apostles as a model of responsible living and diligent attention given to duty.

9. *—not that we do not have the right—:* The writer reaffirms a Pauline and early traditional principle of the right of laborers to be paid or supported (see 1 Thess 2:7; Matt 10:10). For use of the same terminology ("to have the right") in Paul's discussion of apostolic right to recompense for labor yet his own nonuse of this right, see 1 Cor 9:3-18.

   instead, this was done that we might present ourselves to you as an example that you might imitate us: This part of verse 9 resumes the train of thought interrupted in verse 8 during the course of citing the Pauline text (repetition of *alla*—"instead"). Nonetheless one would have expected a parallel *hoti* ("since") as in verse 7. Instead, verse 9b reiterates in elliptical (addition of "this was done") and ponderous terms ("ourselves . . . us") the imitation themes expressed earlier (contrast Phil 3:17). Seemingly, the expression "we presented or gave ourselves to you" represents a rewriting of 1 Thess 2:8, "to share or give our very selves to you." Finally, the ending of the clause restates what the term *typos* ("example") already expresses, "that you might imitate us."

10. *Besides, when we were with you, we often commanded the following:* Verses 10 and 11, both introduced by postpositive *gar*, present successive reasons to bolster what was just said (see also 3:3b-4; BAGD 152.1c) and so are introduced in the translation by "besides . . . indeed." The clause "when we were with you" reiterates the earlier "while among you" of verse 7 (see 2:5) and recalls the foundation visit, the time when the directive was given. The author employs the imperfect to underscore repeated instruction, again uses the authoritative term "command" (followed by *hoti* it introduces direct discourse: BDF 397.3), and the pronoun *touto* to indicate what follows.

    "If anyone is unwilling to work, let that person not eat": The author's command, said to be a common apostolic injunction, is proverbial in character and draws from ancient wisdom the insight that one must support oneself through work or, as stated in Gen 3:19, "by the sweat of your face you shall eat bread" and its rabbinic commentary, "If I do not work, I do not eat" (Genesis Rabbah 2:2). Its Paulinist imperative form with a focus on unwillingness to work probably owes to its epistolary context. It is not a wisdom saying on work that the author wishes to communicate but a command against recklessness and irresponsibility designed to counteract the breakdown of order. The author returns in the following verses to the theme of earning one's way (v. 12), but in this context it is the apostolic authority of the principle which is of greatest concern, whether it be from repeated teaching or lived example.

11. *Indeed, we hear that some among you are conducting themselves in an irresponsible way:* By its use of postpositive *de*, verse 11 adds another reason (indicated by "indeed" in the translation) why the readers should follow the missionaries' example. By means of an authoritative "we have heard" (see 1 Cor 11:18 where the closest parallel is "I hear"), the author claims personal knowledge of the community's situation. The remark that "some among you" are at fault, picks up the hint already given in 3:6 concerning a hypothetical "fellow believer," where the same idiom is employed: "conducting themselves in an irresponsible way."

    not doing any work except the work of busybodies: The double participial phrase gives content to the general statement immediately preceding that these people are shirking their responsibilities. The first expresses a fact which, in light of the previous verse, is assumed to be refusal to work. The author's concern is not the role of work in the community but the breakdown of order which leads to further disorder. The second participle, by a play on the word "to work" (the translation attempts to capture that feature), suggests that the refusal to work leads the idle to do the "work of busybodies." The verb *periergazomai* means literally "to work beyond measure or to overwork" but acquired the sense of "being meddlesome," of "interfering with," or simply of "being a busybody" (LSJ 1373). In this particular context one could stress the intended play on words and suggest needless work ("never working but always busy"; though contrast Demosthenes, *Philippics* 4.150). One could be more specific and point to the topos of the "busybody" as indicating "meddling with other people's affairs." The latter is preferable in the present context.

12. *So we command such persons and exhort them in the Lord Jesus Christ:* Verse 12 begins a series of loosely connected statements (use of postpositive *de* in verses 12, 13, 14, and 16; see BAGD 171.1c), authoritative statements that have a bearing on the community's behavior. The first assertion, related in structural terms to 1 Thess 4:1, adopts a demanding and urgent tone. In the case of the first verb the author replaces the paraenetic "we urge" of Paul (see 2:1) by the insistent term "we command," used already at 3:4, 6 and 10. The second verb is retained from the Pauline formula but one senses a change in nuance. While one could appeal to its common Pauline meaning of "exhort" as used in a *parakaleō* formula (see 1 Thess 4:1) or insist on the starker sense of "demand or require" (as a synonym of its parallel verb), it seems better, in relation to what follows concerning treatment of wayward believers (see also 3:6), to opt for the meaning "exhort." The author is not interested in condemning such people but in their returning to a balanced state of mind and responsible living. Also, the appeal is made in the Lord Jesus Christ's name and carries coercive force since command and urgent appeal are made in the name of the Lord of the community (see v. 6 for similar stress on the Lord's authority).

    that, working quietly: The author continues to employ the Pauline text and borrows both terms from 1 Thess 4:11; thus, *hēsychazō* ("to live quietly") becomes *meta hēsychias* ("with silence or quietly") and the verb *ergazomai* ("to work") is employed once more (see also 3:8, 10, 11) to characterize a pressing problem within the community. Such textual contact would have been facilitated by the appearance together in 1 Thess 4:10 of the two verbs used earlier in the verse: *parakaleō* and *parangellō*.

they might eat their own bread: This idiom is a restatement of what was said earlier in verse 8 in a negative way concerning the missionaries' behavior. What was presented there as a model of good behavior is now stated as the ideal goal of quiet labor. The contrast is insistently made between "bread belonging to others" and "working for one's own bread." Also, one should see this idiom as a restatement of the Pauline injunction: "that you may be lacking in nothing" (1 Thess 4:12).

13. *You for your part, brothers and sisters:* Again the author employs an emphatic personal pronoun with a postpositive particle, "you for your part" (see 2:13), to contrast two groups ("such persons" of v. 12 and the remainder of the community) and to indicate a change to the second of these. The author now focuses on the duties of the upright members of the audience. The use of direct address a second time within the pericope (see also 2:15) stresses the positive exhortation given its members.

never grow tired of doing what is right: The rare verb *egkakeō* appears primarily in the Pauline corpus, always in a negative construction, and means "to be weary of or to lose heart." Its use with a supplementary participle to underscore the continuation of the activity marks a vestige of Attic usage (BDF 214.2). Its closest parallel, both linguistically and thematically, is Gal 6:9 ("so let us not grow weary in doing what is right"), where the present subjunctive is employed to encourage continued good behavior in view of the end-time. In the present case the aorist subjunctive is used to discourage the cessation of the activity. The participle of *kalopoieō*, which appears only here in the NT (though the expressions *poieō to kalon* or *agathon* are frequent), could be understood in two ways, either as insisting on the "good treatment" of the irresponsible or as exhorting the community to good moral behavior. The second option is preferable in view of the meaning of the expression, of the development of thought throughout the passage, and since verse 14 introduces, as an additional topic, the issue of the treatment of wayward believers.

14. *Also, should some not obey:* The construction is introduced by another postpositive *de* and indicates an additional, related topic; the author repeats the structure of a previous admonition (lit.: "if anyone should not" but rendered in the plural throughout; see v. 10b). The casuistic language ("a brother or sister who" in v. 6; "someone else's" in v. 8; "if anyone" in vv. 10, 14; "some among you" in v. 11; "such persons . . . their own" in v. 12; and "that one . . . that one . . . as an enemy . . . as brother or sister" in vv. 14-15) should not be interpreted as indicating the author's relation to the community but rather as part of the legal and authoritative treatment of the topic. The verb *hypakouō* already appears in 1:8 to indicate the nonacceptance of the gospel by nonbelievers. In the present situation the term underscores again not the exhortatory but the authoritative character of the pericope.

what we say in our letter: The Greek for this expression, *tǭ logǭ hēmōn dia tēs epistolēs* (lit.: "our word by letter") is not easily rendered to express the author's meaning. While one could interpret *logos* as indicating a specific "command or order," it probably should be related to 2:2: "by word or by letter allegedly by us" and 2:15: "taught by us either by word or by letter." The author is counteracting the apocalyptic preaching and writing of the community's preachers and equating the message of this letter (use of the article before *epistolē*) to apostolic tradition.

take note of these, by not associating with them: A lengthy, complex apodosis completes the conditional sentence. Its first verb *sēmeioō* is a NT hapax whose meaning could be "to note or write down" or more generally "to take or make special note of" (BAGD 748). Rather than assume a complex, advanced ecclesial system of roll-taking, one should probably choose the second option and appeal to the Pauline usage in Rom 16:17 where, in a similar context, the verb "watch or keep an eye on" *(skopeō)* is employed for this purpose: "keep an eye on those who cause dissensions and offenses, in opposition to the teachings that you have learned; avoid them." The means for signaling out such a person is by avoiding association with them. The verb employed is *synanamignymi,* whose only other occurrence in the NT provides an interesting but complicated context, for there Paul counsels nonassociation with immoral community members, a procedure which is said to include not eating with such a person (1 Cor 5:9-13); see discussion below.

that they might be put to shame: The purpose of the process, "putting to shame" (see Titus 2:8 for a similar usage), is that of winning back a fellow believer (Paul employs *entrepō* in the active in 1 Cor 4:14). Use of the aorist passive points not to a process but to the fundamental change sought for the wayward individual, the regaining of family honor by employing its opposite: shame or loss of honor.

15. *still do not regard them as enemies, but rather admonish them as brothers or sisters:* A double caution is noted in view of possible exaggeration; the community is commanded (imperative of *hēgeomai:* "consider or regard") to continue treating such a person as a fellow member. The term used is "enemy" *(echthros),* not one who hates or persecutes but one who receives hate and disdain from others. Instead, believers are to pursue the process described, namely, "to admonish or counsel" them *(noutheteō; see 1 Thess 5:12, 14 and Notes). God's choice and Christian commitment require restoration of wayward believers (in Pauline terms see Gal 6:1) and the means for this is limited association in the context of fellowship and admonition.

16. *Now may the Lord of peace himself give you peace at all times, in every way:* The opening of the prayer is borrowed from 1 Thess 5:23; only "Lord" has replaced "God" (see comments on 2:16 and 3:5). Additionally, the author employs an aorist optative as does the model to request ultimate peace. In place of the sanctification which Paul stresses in his letter, the author requests the peace that is sorely needed in the community. Further, while the Pauline letter focuses on the eschatological state of holiness which only the God of peace can give, that of the Paulinist views peace as a present reality. Though

requesting the ultimate actualization of peace by the Lord of peace (aorist), the author clearly states that the request is for peace "at all times, in every way," just as another prayer requests "strength in every good work and word" (2:17). It should be noted that, despite the obvious contact of this prayer with the opening of the Pauline model, its language in every respect is non-Pauline. "To give peace" is found in the NT only in Luke 12:51; John 14:27; and 2 Thess 3:16; "the Lord of peace" is a NT hapax legomenon; *dia pantos* is found in Paul only once, in a citation of Ps 68:24 and with a different sense (Rom 11:10); and *en panti tropǭ* is unique though the term *tropos* occurs in two slightly different Pauline constructions (Rom 3:2; Phil 1:18).

The Lord be with you all: The second benediction, also invoking the Lord rather than God, involves a traditional Jewish greeting (Jud 6:12; Ruth 2:4; Luke 1:28). It is found nowhere in Paul who favors a final benediction like the one used at the end of the letter (3:18; see 1 Thess 5:28); note, however, the double benedictions of 1 Cor 16:23, 24 and 2 Cor 13:11, 13. The author's use of this particular benediction underscores again the theme of Jesus' present lordship. Also, the addition of "all" here and in 3:18 makes it clear that the entire community, not its leaders or groups within it, is being addressed.

INTERPRETATION

Before bringing the letter to a close the author addresses an issue hinted at throughout the document, an issue which concerns community behavior. Seemingly, the problem is limited in scope for in 3:6 the author speaks of an individual acting irresponsibly or even in verse 12 of a number of such persons. Additionally, the pericope ends by positing a hypothetical "if someone should not obey what is commanded." Such language has led some scholars to speculate concerning the possible identities of such persons and their role within the community. Further, much has been said concerning the possible relationship between the *ataktoi* (whether the "irresponsible, disorderly, or idle persons") of 1 Thess 5:14 and of 2 Thess 3:6-15. It is obviously the community's behavior which is of concern to the author and it is the goal of this analysis to discern more clearly how that theme is presented in the pericope and how this particular issue relates to the overall purpose of the document.

Source and Structure of 3:6-16. It has been suggested in the past that the passage between the prayers of 3:5 and 16 sounds out of place. Indeed, its tone is different and it is, at first blush, relatively autonomous. Nonetheless, few fail to identify verse 6 as the beginning of a lengthy problem-oriented section. Its use of paraenetic terminology and of an opening formula of direct address confirm this conclusion. As to the tone and relation of the passage to what precedes and in fact to the whole document, we will have to address those issues below.

Comparison of the pericope with the ending of 1 Thessalonians reveals a number of important contacts. In fact, the whole passage corresponds to the paraenetic section of the Pauline model wherein community problems are addressed. 3:6 ("so we command you, brothers and sisters, in the name of the Lord Jesus Christ") begins much as do 4:1 ("brothers and sisters, we urge and exhort you in the Lord Jesus") or 5:12 ("so we urge you, brothers and sisters"). The verse, as do the corresponding texts of the Pauline model, goes on to introduce a substantial paraenetic section of immediate concern to the addressees. For this lengthy text the author borrows numerous terms and themes from 1 Thess 4:11-12: "conduct oneself," "quiet work," "earning one's bread" (as "working with one's hands" or "lacking in nothing"), or "busybodies" (as "attending to one's affairs") or from 5:12: "the irresponsible or disorderly," "admonish," patient treatment, "doing what is right or aspiring to what is good." From other passages the author draws the themes of "imitation and example" (1:6, 7), that of tradition or word received from the missionaries (2:13), or the theme of presence (3:4). Also strikingly similar to 1 Thess 1:5b ("what sort of persons we were among you for your sake") is 3:9 ("we presented ourselves to you as an example").

Several passages, however, show a closer textual relation. It is clear for example that "now may the Lord of peace himself give you . . ." (3:16) derives from 1 Thess 5:23: "now may the God of peace himself make you. . . ." The principal change is that of "Lord" for "God" (see also 2:13). Also, the author's reference to burdensome work and the statement that the missionaries had the right to claim support derive from Paul's text:

2 Thess 3:8	1 Thess 2:9
instead in *labor and toil*	you will recall . . . our *labor and toil*
(how) day and night we worked	*how day and night we worked*
so as not to burden any of you	*so as not to burden any of you.*

In this case, the only modification is of a grammatical character in order to situate the citation in a new sentence structure. A final example is drawn from Paul's paraenetic language:

2 Thess 3:12	1 Thess 4:1
. . . we *command such persons*	. . . we urge you
and *entreat* them	and exhort you [parakaleō]
in the Lord Jesus *Christ*	in the Lord Jesus
that . . .	that. . . .

Changes in the new text are italicized. The tone of the text is changed by the use of the verb *parangellō* ("command") and the second verb *parakaleō* seems to acquire a note of urgency. Also, the command is directed to the wayward rather than the community and finally from the addition of "Christ" one notes the author's preference for full Christological titles.

While the pericope shows many traces of borrowing from Paul's paraenetic discussion, its overall structure has no relation to its model and depends instead on the development of the themes of community behavior and the treatment of irresponsible members. Following a general command concerning persons of irresponsible behavior (6a), the author recalls the tradition taught the community (6b) either by command (10) or by example (7-9). Again, the author underscores the seriousness of the disorder within the community, insisting that it even affects outsiders (11). There then follows a series of related statements about the problem (successive use of *de* in verses 12, 13, and 14), statements which address the author's solution to this issue. Finally, the discussion is brought to an end, as are other passages of the letter, by a formal prayer addressed to "the Lord of peace" (v. 16).

Character and Function: Command and Exhortation. Noting the authoritative tone of the passage, especially as compared to Pauline paraenesis, some scholars have been reluctant to accept the routine characterization of this section as exhortation on idleness. There is no doubt, especially if one compares the two Thessalonian documents, that there is a decided shift from exhortatory to authoritative language. One of the most evident signs of this is the author's preference for the term *parangellō* three times in this pericope and once a few verses earlier (3:4, 6, 10, 12). Whereas the term, both verb and noun, is rare in Paul and its meaning is probably "direct or instruct" (1 Thess 4:2, 11; 1 Cor 11:17; though see 1 Cor 7:10), its usage in the present context, particularly 3:10 where an actual command is given, seeks to underscore authority. Also, its use with *en* phrases adds to this perception. The command is given "in the name of the Lord Jesus Christ," thereby stressing the authority and present lordship of the *kyrios* (see 1:12). Another *en* phrase is employed at 3:12 in relation to *parangellō* but in a more complex structure. After issuing a command to the irresponsible, the author adds "and we exhort them in the Lord Jesus Christ," a clause that causes some puzzlement. Some ignore the clause and focus solely on the command terminology; others insist that the author softens the authoritative language by turning to a more diplomatic approach. In reality the new verb of "exhortation" by the addition of the *en* phrase directs attention to the response desired; it is the Lord Jesus who will provide the strength needed (see 2:16-17; 3:3) to provide the proper response. A similar point is made earlier in 3:4 where the author expresses "confidence in the Lord," an expression that again stresses the outcome or obedience to the things commanded.

Also adding to the tone of command are the connotations deduced from *parangellō* passages, particularly 3:4. The author expresses confidence in the response in terms of doing continually precisely what has been commanded "by us," the apostles. Relating to and emphasizing this source of authority are: "the tradition received from us" (3:6) and "the traditions taught by us" (2:15). Further, the content of these commands ranges from the process for treating the problem of the irresponsible (3:6) to past and repeated imperatives concerning work ethics and conduct generally (vv. 10, 12). Finally, we might add that the author favors imperatives and hortatory statements, as well as *dei* in verse 7, and an undisguised presumption of authority in proposing a specific process for treating the disobedient and irresponsible.

There is no doubt then that the pericope bears a clearer tone of command than of exhortation. But it is within this context that one must situate the goal and function of the author's authoritative language. It is with the view of "shaming" the recalcitrant into submission (14) or of imposing a traditional type of behavior either by invoking the authority and assistance of the Lord Jesus or by appealing to apostolic tradition. Thus, while the passage's tone is that of command in order to make clear that acceptable behavior is based on apostolic tradition, its function is that of expecting and encouraging adherence to traditional values.

Problem within the Community. Clearly the author is concerned about the community's behavior, but what exactly is the issue of contention? What is the problem that exists among the addressees; how does it relate to the earlier eschatological discussion; and what precisely does the author command and exhort the hearers to do? Until recently most scholars viewed the community's situation as owing to the idleness of some members who refused to work so as to earn their living. Further, some insist on an apocalyptic cause for such inactivity while others, noting that such is not explicitly stated, propose other possible causes, such as an attempt to combat the problem of laziness or spiritualization within the early Church, whether on the part of Paul or that of a later Paulinist writer or redactor. Such analyses rely on the interpretation of the term *ataktōs* and its cognate verb (3:6, 7, 11) as indicating idleness or loafing. Also a factor in the analysis of many, who insist on Pauline authorship, is the conclusion that the problem represents a deterioration of the situation mentioned in 1 Thess 5:14. Others, however, object to such a reading of the term *ataktōs* and cognates and underscore instead its etymological sense of "disorderliness." Thus, various scenarios involving the challenge of authority are proposed, whether disorderliness which violates ecclesial harmony and discipline or charismatic or apocalyptic figures that demand support from the community.

What is the situation being addressed? It is usually presumed that the passage deals with a single issue in the community's life, especially idleness or violation of the ecclesial code as regard self-support. Careful analysis of the passage and its relation to the letter's overall message suggests a different situation. From the outset one can agree that whatever the problem, it involves self-support or earning one's way. This theme is explicitly treated in verses 8, 10, 12 and relates to the text's general preoccupation with work (vv. 8, 11, 12) and having the right to impose a "burden" (8-9) but choosing to teach industry by example (7-9).

It is less than accurate, however, to insist that the passage deals with a single issue. (1) Two Important Passages: 7b-8a and 11. Apostolic behavior, in the first case, is said to involve two issues: "we did not neglect our responsibilities while among you nor ate someone else's bread without paying." Minimally, there exist two issues, one described by the *ataktōs* word group and the other by the image of "eating one's bread," however one relates these themes or interprets the terms. Also verse 11 offers added data for such a conclusion. The errant members of the community are described as "conducting themselves in an irresponsible way" by "not doing any work except doing the work of busybodies." Again, some important, recurrent terms are employed, but regardless of their precise interpretation their usage points to a variety of issues. In this case the behavior that is described by the adverb *ataktōs* is qualified both as refusal (v. 10) to work and participation in the activity of busybodies. While the implication is that the first leads to the second, it is also clear that more than idleness or not earning one's keep is at stake.

(2) Focus on Three Important Expressions or Terms. [1] "Eat one's bread." While the expression "eat bread" is often employed to mean "take a meal," "eat one's bread" seems to recall Gen 3:19 where it is said that the human punishment and therefore condition involves the law of "earning one's keep" or "eating one's own bread" (2 Thess 3:8, 10, 12). Thus, the expression means to "earn one's living" and to do anything less is one way of "avoiding one's responsibility." [2] *Ataktōs* and *atakteō*. Since both uses of the adverb (3:6 and 11) involve the verb *peripateō* ("to conduct oneself"), one finds consistent usage with reference to behavior, as in verse 7 where the verb is employed. It is obvious that a moral sense is intended for the word group and that what is implied is the failure to live according to one's duty, whether it is the violation of contract, failure to perform one's expressed duty or the leading of a life that is contrary to one's accepted norms or tradition (see PElephantine 2.13; POxyrhynchus 275.25; other references in LSJ 276). The general sense

of the usage in 2 Thess 3:6f. then is that of violation of set order or failure to act according to tradition (see v. 6). [3] "Acting as busybodies" *(periergazomai)*. While the play on the word "work" (see Notes on 3:11) suggests superfluous or inane activity (see Plato, *Apology* 19B), several considerations lead us to suggest further the meaning "work of busybodies." Typologically, busybodies are described as those who ignore their own work and faults to search out everyone's business (Demosthenes, *Orations* 32.28; Polybius, *History* 18.51.2; Theophrastus, *Characters* 13; also Plutarch, *On Being a Busybody* 516-18) but also who annoy everyone and pretend to be superior (Demosthenes, *Orations* 26.15). Such typology suggests that the author is condemning not just the idle waste of other people's time but, in agreement with 1 Thess 4:11 (see also 1 Pet 4:15), calls for community members to mind their own affairs rather than seek boisterously to impose their misguided apocalyptic thinking and behavior.

(3) Rereading of Verses 6-12. [1] Neglect of Responsibilities. In verse 6 Christians are described as behaving irresponsibly because they fail to follow apostolic tradition. The author then proceeds to describe apostolic behavior as the discharge of duties and the earning of one's keep (vv. 7-8). Even the long hours of work were in support of their missionary charge (see 1 Thess 2:9), prevented them from forcing others to violate their own responsibilities, and set a pattern for Christian behavior. The repeated command to work and so to earn one's keep either recalls the community to its traditional responsibilities or attempts to resolve other problems which ensued. [2] Relation to Apocalyptic Issue. It is doubtful that the cessation of work by some within the community meant the annulment of the curse of Gen 3:19 regarding work as human punishment. Instead, the author, by the reference to "quiet work" urges the cessation of boisterous apocalyptic speculation (2:2) and idle, misguided chatter of those people who do nothing but discuss the end-time events (3:11). Those who are most prone to apocalyptic missionizing ("work of busybodies") are recalled to the duty of quiet self-sustaining work, a task that would bring an end to such disreputable activity. It is perhaps even suggested, following the apostolic model, that missionary work will succeed only through the earning of one's bread and certainly not through the chatter of busybodies who disdain the activity of traditional Christian morality.

Approach to Problem. A variety of means are taken to counteract the community's problems. (1) The author chooses as the principal approach to the community's behavioral problems a recall of the wayward to the Church's traditional moral teaching. Even the author's description of the wayward is in terms of adherence to or behavior in accord with "the tradition received" (3:6). Also constituting part of the apostolic tradition ("received from us") is the oft-repeated command of verse 10 concerning self-sustaining work. Interestingly, apostolic behavior becomes not just a good example to follow but the required (*dei:* "ought"—v. 7) and planned pattern (*taktōs* or *typos*) for Christian behavior (7-9). It too constitutes apostolic tradition for it was "taught" by word and now by letter (2:15).

(2) The role of verse 13 in the author's discussion is debated. Some wish to interpret the final participle (*kalopoiountes*) as referring to the treatment of the wayward ("treat these well"). Such an option seems ill-advised since the treatment of these people would be awkwardly reintroduced in the following verse. Besides, the introductory "you for your part" calls for a stronger change of direction in the argument. Instead, the author appeals to the whole audience and addresses overall behavior. The basic approach which the author advises is to continue "doing what is right," that is, doing the opposite of irresponsible activity in violation of accepted Christian norms. A reading of the entire passage indicates that the author wishes to minimize the number of the wayward (use of the hypothetical singular in vv. 6, 10, 14-15 and an indefinite plural in vv. 11-12), all the while addressing the entire community with commands, general remarks, and, as in the present case, with an expression of confidence. Verse 13 then implies that most of the members of the community are faithful in their good works and words (see also 2:17).

(3) Finally, the author addresses overtly the treatment of the wayward as a means of resolving the community's problems. In the very first verse it is already suggested that faithful members shun or remove themselves from any irresponsible believers (v. 6). The subject is resumed in detail at the end as an added way for all to respond to the problem of community behavior. Having appealed to tradition and apostolic teaching and example, the author turns to the purpose for writing, the counteracting of apocalyptic fervor which is destroying community unity, purpose, and general behavior. The tone of the letter is decidedly authoritative since it calls for obedience to the letter's dictates and provides for the proper treatment of the recalcitrant. Again, intentional shunning is recommended, not simply as a means of ending such behavior but in order to bring back the wayward (14). In fact, the author, in a conciliatory way, cautions that such treatment is to be done in fellowship not in enmity (15; see Marcus Aurelius, *Meditations*, 6.20, on similar treatment of deviant behavior in the gymnasium). How such a procedure relates to other NT data on community discipline (1 Cor 5:3-5; 2 Cor 2:5-11; Matt 18:15-18; 1 Tim 5:20; among others) is hard to determine in general and as related to the present situation. It is not said to what extent such advice concerns community life, association with other believers, or sharing in

the Eucharistic meal. Instead, the text provides the community with advice and motivation rather than with detailed disciplinary procedures. Thus, the letter contains exhortation against immoral behavior and balanced eschatological teaching to which the members are recalled. Thus, the author is more interested in providing sound teaching about eschatology and morality as a counterbalance to ecstatic preachers than a disciplinary procedure for dealing with people considered to have lost their orientation in doctrinal and moral terms. So the basic way of handling the community's problems consists of being aware of deviant thinking and behavior, of noting the people involved, and of admonishing them in the spirit of Christian fellowship (see 1 Thess 5:12-15). The author's method involves persuasion more than discipline.

Concluding Prayer for Peace. The author concludes the pericope with a prayer for peace, a prayer which brings together some of the letter's principal concerns. Focusing again on Jesus' present lordship the author addresses Jesus as Lord of peace—Jesus as one who shares God's peace (Paulinist reading of 1 Thess 5:23) is called upon to grant earthly calm in anticipation of the end-time. The author insists that this peace is for "all time" and to be given "in every way." It is a call for ecclesial and eschatological peace rather than apocalyptic turmoil; it is a request for community well-being, unity, and mutuality. Use of the aorist points to the author's wish, in deference to the members' apocalyptic interests and the tradition's eschatology, for the ultimate peace which only the Lord of peace can give when he returns to grant rest to the afflicted (1:7). Lastly, addition of the blessing "the Lord be with you all" stresses Jesus' present lordship and assistance and appeals to the entire community (use of "all") to submit to his lordship as he directs the hearts of all to a fellowship that has divine love as model and to a constancy in the face of affliction that reflects the endurance of the risen Lord (3:5).

The prayer for peace then brings together the author's dual concerns regarding balanced eschatology and traditional moral teaching. Peace in the present, whether the avoidance of apocalyptic agitation or the quiet work of the committed believer, is the author's wish for the community as it awaits and suffers for God's kingdom. The present age is not dominated by "the mystery of lawlessness" (2:7) for God through the Christ-event has given "unfailing comfort and good hope" (2:16) and since acknowledgment of Jesus' lordship provides comfort and strength in life's daily challenge (2:17; 3:5) as believers look forward to the continued advance of the gospel (3:1). The prayer for peace, along with the closing appeal to "the grace of the Lord Jesus Christ," reiterates the author's wish that the hearers' desire for eschatological relief be not an escape into apocalyptic speculation and idle agitation but a "bringing to fruition every desire for goodness and work of faith'' (1:11) as they receive the Lord's peace.

For Reference and Further Study

Bjerkelund, C. J. *Parakalō: Form, Funktion und Sinn der Parakalō-Sätze in den paulinischen Briefen.* Oslo: Universitetsforlaget, 1967.

Jewett, R. *The Thessalonian Correspondence: Pauline Rhetoric and Millenarian Piety.* Philadelphia: Fortress, 1986.

Laub, F. "Paulinische Autorität in nachpaulinischer Zeit (2 Thes)." *TC,* 403–17.

Menken, M. J. J. "Paradise Regained or Still Lost? Eschatology and Disorderly Behaviour in 2 Thessalonians." *NTS* 38 (1992) 271–89.

Russell, R. "The Idle in 2 Thess 3:6-12: An Eschatological or a Social Problem?" *NTS* 34 (1988) 105–19.

Spicq, C. "Les Thessaloniciens 'inquiets' étainent-ils des parasseux?" *ST* 10 (1957) 1–13.

23. *Epistolary Closing* (3:17-18)

17. This greeting is in my own hand, Paul's; this is the identifying mark in every letter—it is how I write. 18. The grace of our Lord Jesus Christ be with you all.

Notes

17. *This greeting is in my own hand, Paul's:* Interestingly, two Paulinist writers (2 Thess 3:17; Col 4:18) borrow verbatim from the conclusion of 1 Corinthians and reflect as well the custom of ancient letter writers in adding in their own hand an authenticating mark or sign (see Gal 6:11) at the end of a dictated letter, usually the composition of a greeting or postscript. The translation attempts to make clear that the final verses, not the previous prayer of peace, constitutes the final greeting.

this is the identifying mark in every letter—it is how I write: Several factors call for the translation given here. The passage represents a relative clause whose pronoun, a neuter singular *(ho)* agrees with neither preceding nouns which are either masculine or feminine. One can best explain the grammatical anomaly as an attempt to include the entire clause as antecedent. The term *sēmeion,* which has the general meaning "sign or mark" and the specialized sense of "miracle or wonder" (see 2:9), here indicates a distinguishing or identifying mark to indicate genuineness (BAGD 747.1). In fact, it has been suggested that the term replaces a more frequent *symbolon* "which indicates additions to the letters of antiquity in the writers' own hands" (*TDNT* 7:259). The following, absolute phrase ("in every letter") as well as the parenthetical clause ("it is how I write") point further to the writer's efforts to claim authenticity against the apocalyptic preachers of 2:2.

18. *The grace of our Lord Jesus Christ be with you all:* The closing benediction is borrowed verbatim from 1 Thess 5:28; only the term "all" has been added to stress rhetorically, as in 3:16b, the all-inclusive nature of the command and exhortation. The retention of the benediction owes both to epistolary and thematic considerations.

INTERPRETATION

The letter is brought to a rapid conclusion, one as brief as its opening. The first issue involves the letter's claim to authenticity. This is followed by a standard epistolary benediction.

Focus on Authenticity. 3:17 is ponderous in its insistence on authenticity. It is true that on several occasions Paul himself alludes to his handwriting, Phlm 19; Gal 6:11; and 1 Cor 16:21, to provide a sign of authentication to a dictated letter. In fact, the phrase of 2 Thess 3:17 is identical to that employed in the last mentioned: "this greeting is in my own hand, Paul's." Only in the Paulinist letter, however, does one find an explicit note that the handwriting serves as an authenticating mark. Besides this explicitness one cannot miss its insistence that all Pauline letters are thus marked. The final clause repeats, in a tautologous way, that the letter ends in customary Pauline fashion ("this is how I write").

The pseudonymous character of verse 17 is further confirmed by consideration of other references in the document to letter writing: 2:2, 15 and 3:14. The first of these ("by letter allegedly by us") provides a glimpse into the complex world of the post-Pauline years. Someone has composed a letter in Paul's name to authenticate the community's apocalyptic thinking. This perspective is described as deriving from the ecstatic and preaching activity of community members. The author thus urges the community to avoid such radical doctrine and so writes a letter, in Paul's name, to combat apocalyptic fervor and misguided interpretation of the signs of the times. The author's explicit discussion of authenticity then relates to the community's situation. Also, its use of a mark for authenticating purposes would thereby challenge the authority of the letter produced by the apocalyptic preachers.

The reference in 2:15 to writing as well as to preaching relates further to the author's strategy in appealing to apostolic, specifically Pauline, tradition to bring the community back to a realistic focus on the present and its demands. The author appeals to tradition as exemplified in the Pauline writings to combat the teachers' exclusive focus on the future and its apocalyptic nearness. Appeal to the Pauline tradition, including letters said to be by Paul, is an appeal to the past and its firm foundation— the addressees as readers will receive the author's letter as a message from the past, i.e., the traditions received from Paul and colleagues. Thus, the author's own letter, with its confirming mark of authenticity, would become part of the tradition to which the readers are called to adhere.

The final reference to letter writing comes at the end of the author's discussion of community activity (3:14). In the course of extended discussion of proper and improper behavior, the author makes repeated references to the sources which provide the norms for such behavior: "the traditions received from us" (6), and "the example" and "commands" provided "while among you" (7-9 and 10, respectively). The list ends with a daring reference to the present letter as the final source of authority and with a plea for compliance (14). Interestingly, the discussions of the two major topics, eschatology in 2:1-12 and behavior in 3:6-15, are both brought to an end by references to the authority of apostolic or Pauline writing (2:15 and 3:14). It is no accident then that the letter itself should close on that theme and with that preoccupation.

Final Benediction: Epistolary and Thematic Functions. As the letter began with near-verbatim borrowing, so it ends. The effect is the same; the author writes in Paul's name and wishes to sound like him. Repetition of the model's concluding benediction serves an epistolary function, for all of Paul's and Christian letters generally end in this way, particularly by the repetition of the themes of grace and peace (see 1:2 and 3:16, 18). Overall analysis shows that the author has done more than reproduce the structure of the composite 1 Thessalonians but has in turn composed a document that has the features and functions as a genuine letter.

There is another reason for the author's near-verbatim reproduction of the concluding benediction. It has already been noted that this letter begins and ends with references to the dual themes of peace and grace. Thus, 3:16 focuses on peace as a present reality ("may the Lord of peace give you peace at all times, in every way") and brings to a conclusion discussion of community behavior and problems. In a similar way 3:18 brings the letter to a close on grace as God's means (2:16-17) of "granting comfort and good hope" in the present through appeal to "our Lord Jesus Christ." Thus, it is no accident that the author repeats the Pauline "our" and adds "all" in stating the final benediction. Indeed, the addition in verse 16b of the unique, extra benediction ("the Lord be with you all") stresses the author's repeated concern about the present lordship of Jesus as ultimate antidote, through the exercise of grace, for combating "shaken minds" (2:2) and "irresponsible conduct" (3:6).

FOR REFERENCE AND FURTHER STUDY

Bassler, J. "Peace in all Ways: Theology in the Thessalonian Letters: A Response to R. Jewett, E. Krentz, and E. Richard." *PT,* 71–85.

Holland, G. " 'A Letter Supposedly from Us': A Contribution to the Discussion about the Authorship of 2 Thessalonians." *TC,* 394–402.

Krodel, G. "2 Thessalonians." *The Deutero-Pauline Letters: Ephesians, Colossians, 2 Thessalonians, 1–2 Timothy, Titus.* G. Krodel, et al. Minneapolis: Fortress, 1993, 39–58.

Trilling, W. "Literarische Paulusimitation im 2. Thessalonicherbrief." *Paulus in den neutestamentlichen Spätschriften: Zur Paulusrezeption im Neuen Testament.* Ed. K. Kertelge. Freiburg: Herder, 1981, 146–56.

INDEXES

1. *PRINCIPAL ANCIENT PARALLELS*

c. Early Jewish Writings

d. Early Christian Writings

2. SUBJECTS

a. 1 Thessalonians

b. 2 Thessalonians

c. Excurses

3. AUTHORS